Windows Server 2019 Automation with PowerShell Cookbook

Third Edition

Powerful ways to automate and manage Windows administrative tasks

Thomas Lee

BIRMINGHAM - MUMBAI

Windows Server 2019 Automation with PowerShell Cookbook
Third Edition

Commissioning Editor: Vijin Boricha
Acquisition Editor: Meeta Rajani
Content Development Editors: Abhishek Jadhav
Technical Editor: Mohd Riyan Khan
Copy Editor: Safis Editing
Project Coordinator: Jagdish Prabhu
Proofreader: Safis Editing
Indexers: Pratik Shirodkar
Graphics: Tom Scaria
Production Coordinator: Arvindkumar Gupta

First published: March 2013

Second edition: September 2017

Third edition: February 2019

Production reference: 1280219

Published by Packt Publishing Ltd.
Livery Place
35 Livery Street
Birmingham B3 2PB, UK.

ISBN 978-1-78980-853-7

www.packtpub.com

`mapt.io`

Mapt is an online digital library that gives you full access to over 5,000 books and videos, as well as industry leading tools to help you plan your personal development and advance your career. For more information, please visit our website.

Why subscribe?

- ▶ Spend less time learning and more time coding with practical eBooks and Videos from over 4,000 industry professionals

- ▶ Learn better with Skill Plans built especially for you

- ▶ Get a free eBook or video every month

- ▶ Mapt is fully searchable

- ▶ Copy and paste, print, and bookmark content

Packt.com

Did you know that Packt offers eBook versions of every book published, with PDF and ePub files available? You can upgrade to the eBook version at `www.packt.com` and as a print book customer, you are entitled to a discount on the eBook copy. Get in touch with us at `customercare@packtpub.com` for more details.

At `www.PacktPub.com`, you can also read a collection of free technical articles, sign up for a range of free newsletters, and receive exclusive discounts and offers on Packt books and eBooks.

Foreword

"Take my money!"

"I'll buy it now!"

I was confused.

I was in front of a couple of hundred people presenting Monad (what later became PowerShell) and some guy in the back of the room shouting, "Take my money!". That is how I met Thomas Lee. After the talk, Thomas comes up to me and gave me a $20 bill with his name on it and said that Monad was exactly what Windows administrators needed and it was going to revolutionize the world and that he wanted to be the first person in line to buy it. When I explained that it was going to be included as a free feature of Windows, Thomas said that he didn't care, he wanted to be the first to buy it anyway.

I just double checked and I still have that $20 bill in my wallet. I've kept it with me for the last 17 years to remind myself what Thomas saw so clearly that day – PowerShell is a critically important tool for every professional Windows administrator. I use the adjective "professional" because there really are two different types of Windows administrators: professional and non-professional. One of the reasons why Windows is so wildly successful is because non-professional administrators could successfully set up and run it to for simple scenarios. If you can click the Next button, then chances are that you can set up Windows successfully. What Thomas correctly saw was that the world of "click-next" administration was limited and that there was an increasing need for professional administrators that could understand the specific needs of their scenario and could craft Windows to meet those needs. That task needed a new tool. That task needed PowerShell.

If you are a professional administrator (or just a passionate power user), then you need to be skilled in PowerShell and you need to know how the specific version of the operating system you are working with is managed by PowerShell. Every version of Windows has added new capabilities that can be managed by PowerShell. In this book, Thomas shows you how to get the most of out your investment in Windows Server 2019 by explaining how to manage and automate it using PowerShell. Automation means that you can figure out how to manage one server and then use that script to manage 10s, 100s, 100,000s of other servers. It means consistency, repeatability, and productivity. It is all about professional administration.

Over the years, I have had so many administrators thank me for PowerShell and tell me their success stories. They were able to do things that saved the day, that their companies only dreamed was possible and that their click-next co-workers could not. They were rewarded with bonuses, raises, promotions, new jobs. I've had quite a few people tell me that they have tripled their salaries because of learning PowerShell.

PowerShell makes YOU powerful.

Thomas was the first one to understand this with absolute clarity and has been with the team from the beginning actively providing us feedback on what professional administrators needed from PowerShell. Thomas's views of administration are very much reflected in PowerShell you see today so I can think of few people better equipped to help you understand how to use this wonderful tool to manage Windows Server 2019 so that you can deliver great value to your company and get rewarded because of it.

Jeffrey Snover

Microsoft Technical Fellow

Contributors

About the author

Thomas Lee is a consultant/trainer/writer from England and has been in the IT business since the late 1960's. After graduating from Carnegie Mellon University, Thomas joined ComShare where he was a systems programmer building the Commander II time-sharing operating system, a forerunner of today's Cloud computing paradigm. In the mid 1970's he moved to ICL to work on the VME/K operating system. After a sabbatical in 1980/81, he joined what is today known as Accenture, leaving in 1988 to run his own consulting and training business, which is still active today.

Thomas holds numerous Microsoft certifications, including MCSE (one of the first in the world) and later versions, MCT (25 years), and was awarded Microsoft's MVP award 17 times. He lives today in a cottage in the English countryside with his family, a nice wine cellar, and a huge collection of live recordings by The Grateful Dead and The Jerry Garcia band.

I'd first like to thank Jeffrey Snover of Microsoft for the invention of PowerShell. I was lucky enough to be in the room the very first time he presented what was then called Monad. His enthusiasm was infectious, and over 15 years later I am still excited.

A huge thank you has to go to the Packt team: Meeta Rajani, Abhishek Jadhav, Mohd Riyan Khan, and Danish Shaikh. You guys did a great job getting this book out of the door and dealing with the issues that arose during the writing. And thanks too to our most excellent tech reviewer Alexander Wittig. Your reviews were always commendable.

As each recipe evolved, I would sometimes hit problems. I got a lot of help from the Spiceworks community. Their PowerShell forum is a great source of information and encouragement. If you have problems with PowerShell, this is a great place to get a solution.

And finally, I have to thank my wonderful wife, Susan. She has been patient as things progressed, she put up with my bad moods when progress was not as smooth as desirable, and kept me sane when all around me was craziness.

About the reviewer

Alex Wittig is a U.S. based Systems Engineer from Germany. He is a Spiceworks Hero Award winner and Moderator at PowerShell. He holds a BSc in IT Security and about half a pound worth of professional IT certifications. Coffee maven, cat stroker, internet fanatic and lifelong learner.

He can be found on Twitter @alexvvittig.

Packt is Searching for Authors Like You

If you're interested in becoming an author for Packt, please visit authors.packtpub.com and apply today. We have worked with thousands of developers and tech professionals, just like you, to help them share their insight with the global tech community. You can make a general application, apply for a specific hot topic that we are recruiting an author for, or submit your own idea.

Table of Contents

Preface

PowerShell was first introduced to the world at the Professional Developer's conference in Los Angeles in 2003 by Jeffrey Snover. Code-named Monad, it represented a complete revolution in management. A white paper written around that time, The Monad Manifesto (refer to `http://www.jsnover.com/blog/2011/10/01/monad-manifesto/`) remains an amazing analysis of the problem at the time – that of managing large numbers of Windows systems. A key takeaway is that the GUI does not scale, whereas PowerShell does.

PowerShell has transformed the management of complex, network-based Windows infrastructure, and, increasingly, non-Windows infrastructure. Knowledge of PowerShell and how to get the most from PowerShell is now obligatory for any professional IT Pro. The popular adage continues to be true: Learn PowerShell or learn golf.

This book takes you through the use of PowerShell in a variety of scenarios using many of the rich set of features included in Windows Server 2019. This preface provides you with an introduction to what is in the book, along with some tips on how to get the most out of it.

What this book covers

Chapter 1, Establishing a PowerShell Administrative Environment, looks at setting up your work station and your environment to make use of PowerShell.

Chapter 2, Managing Windows Networking, shows you how to manage Windows networking with PowerShell. Networks are today central to almost every organization and this chapter looks at a variety of network-related tasks, including looking at new ways (with PowerShell) to do old things, setting up DNS, DHCP, and Active directory.

Chapter 3, Managing Windows Active Directory, examines how to install, manage and leverage Active Directory, including managing AD objects and Group Policy.

Chapter 4, Managing Windows Storage, looks at managing storage in Windows Server 2019.

Chapter 5, Managing Shared Data, examines different ways to share data with Windows Server and PowerShell including SMB shares, iSCSI and Distributed File System.

Chapter 6, Managing Windows Update, helps you get to grips with managing updates via Windows Update. With the importance of keeping all your Windows clients and servers fully patched.

Chapter 7, Managing Printers, shows you how to manage printers, printer queues, and printer drivers, including deploying printers via Group Policy.

Chapter 8, Leveraging Containers, introduces Docker Containers in Windows Server 2019. You download and use container images as well as build your own.

Chapter 9, Managing Windows Internet Information Server, shows you how to conduct a variety of IIS-related tasks, including IIS installation and configuration, setting up SSL and managing cipher suites, as well as configuring Network Load Balancing.

Chapter 10. Managing Desired State Configuration, shows how to use this important feature to ensure a server is setup correctly and continues to remain so. This covers setting up a pull server and configuring partial configurations.

Chapter 11, Managing Hyper-V, demonstrates the use of Hyper-V. This chapter shows you how to build and deploy VMs with Hyper-V. This includes nested Hyper-V running a Hyper-V VM inside another Hyper-V VM which is useful for a number of scenarios.

Chapter 12, Managing Azure, looks at managing IAAS and PAAS resources in Azure using PowerShell. To test the recipes in this chapter, you need access to Azure. This chapter describes how to setup a Virtual Machine, an Azure website and an SMB3 file share.

Chapter 13, Managing Performance and Usage, how to measure, monitor, and report on the performance of your Windows 2019 servers. There are several recipes that demonstrate how to get specific performance measurements and how to create graphs of performance for further analysis.

Chapter 14, Troubleshooting Windows Server, looks at a number of aspects of both reactive and proactive troubleshooting. This includes getting events from the event log and using the Best Practice Analyzer contained in Windows Server 2019.

What you need for this book

To get the most out of this book, you need to experiment with the code contained in the recipes. To avoid errors impacting live production servers, you should instead use either test hardware, or adopt virtualization to create a test lab, where mistakes do not cause any serious damage.

This book uses a variety of servers within a single Reskit.Org domain containing multiple servers, and using an IP address block of 10.10.10/24 described in the *Getting the most from this book* section.

You should have a Windows 10 or Windows Server 2019 host with hardware virtualization capabilities enabled and use a virtualization solution. If you have access to a cloud computing platform, then you could perform most of the recipes on cloud-hosted virtual machines, although that has not been tested by us. You can use any virtualization.

The book was developed using Hyper-V and nested Hyper-V on Windows 10 and Windows Server 2019.

Who this book is for

This book is aimed at IT professionals, including system administrators, system engineers, architects, and consultants who need to leverage Windows PowerShell to simplify and automate their daily tasks.

Getting the most from this book

This book was written based on some assumptions and with some constraints. You should read this section to understand how I intended the book to be used and what I have assumed about you. This should help you to get the most from this book.

The first assumption I made in writing this book is that you know the basics of PowerShell. This is not a PowerShell tutorial. The recipes do make use of a wide range of PowerShell features, including WMI, Remoting, AD and so on, but you need to know the basics of PowerShell. The book uses PowerShell language, syntax, and cmdlets that come with Windows Server 2019 and Windows 10.

The second, related, assumption is that you have a reasonable background in Windows infrastructure including AD, networking and storage. The recipes provide an overview of the various technologies and links for more information. And I provide links to more information on the topics in this book.

The recipes provide the basics—you adopt, adapt, and extend. The recipes are designed to show you the basics of how to manage aspects of Windows Server. In many cases, a recipe suggests method for improving it for your environment. A recipe is meant to show you how features work, enabling you to leverage and extend it for your environment.

Start by running the recipes step-by-step using either the PowerShell ISE or VS Code. An exception is the recipes in *Chapter 8* (*Introducing Containers*). The main tool you use in that chapter, `docker.exe`, runs differently in a GUI (ISE or VS Code), so run these recipes from the PowerShell console.

I built and tested the recipes in this book step-by-step (i.e. not running the entire recipe as a single script file. If you run a recipe as a single step, some of the output may not be what you see here, due to how PowerShell formats objects.

Once you have any recipe working, try to re-factor the recipe's code into your own reusable functions. In some cases, we build simple functions as a guide to richer scripts you could build. Once you have working and useful functions, incorporate them in to organizational or personal modules and reuse the code.

As any author knows, writing PowerShell scripts for publication in a book is a layout and production nightmare. To reduce the issues specifically with line width and line wrapping, I have made extensive use of methods that ensure the command line width fits in the chapters in this book without wrapping. Many recipes use hash tables and property spatting and other devices to ensure that every line of every recipe is both 65 characters or less and that there are no unintended line breaks. I hope there are not too many issues with layout!

Many of the cmdlets, commands, and object methods used in this book produce output that may not be all that helpful or useful, particularly in production. Some cmdlets generate output which would fill many pages of this book but with little added value. For this reason, many recipes pipe cmdlet output to `Out-Null`. Feel free to remove this where you want to see more details. I have also adjusted the output in many cases to avoid wasted white space. Thus, if you test a recipe, you may see the output that is laid out a bit differently, but it should contain the same information. Finally, remember that the specific output you see may be different based on your environment and the specific values you use in each step.

To write this book, I have used a large VM farm consisting of over 20 Windows 2019 servers and Windows 10 clients. My main development host was a well configured Windows 10 system (96 GB RAM, 2 x 6 core Xeon processors and fast SSDs). All the hosts used in this book are a combination of some physical hardware (running almost entirely on Windows 10 and a large set of VMs) as described in the recipe.

To assist in writing this book, I created a set of scripts that built the Hyper-V VMs which I used to develop this book. These scripts are published at: `https://github.com/doctordns/ReskitBuildScripts`. I have also published some details of the network of VMs created by using these scripts, complete with host names and IP addresses, is at: `https://github.com/doctordns/ReskitBuildScripts`. The full set of VMs, at the end of this writing, took up around 600 GB of storage. Fortunately, storage is cheap!

PowerShell provides great feature coverage—you can manage most of the functions and features of Windows Server 2019 using PowerShell, but by no means all. In some cases, you can dip down into WMI using the CIM cmdlets to get to object properties and methods not exposed by any cmdlet. The advent of CDXML-based cmdlets has increased the number of networking and other cmdlets that are WMI-based. But even then, there are still a number of places where you need to use a Windows console application or invoke an unmanaged DLL. The bottom line is that to manage some aspects of Windows, such as event forwarding or performance logging, you need to use older tools. We try to avoid these, but in many cases the recipe demonstrates how to use the console applications within PowerShell.

In many cases, there are no official Microsoft authored cmdlets included in Windows Server 2019 that might help you manage aspects of your infrastructure. The advent of the PS Gallery, and great third-party add-ins, has meant that you can find a wealth of functionality, download it and install it.

All the code provided in this book has been tested; it worked and did what it says (at least during the writing stage). The production process is complex and it's possible that errors in code creep in during the production stages. Some of the more complex steps may have errors introduced during production. If any step fails for you, please contact Packt and we can help. Feel free to post issues to the Spiceworks PowerShell forum for quick resolution.

In writing the recipes, I use full cmdlet names with no aliases and with all parameter names spelled out in full. Thus, no abbreviated parameter names or positional parameters). This makes the text a bit longer, but hopefully easier to read and understand.

In writing this book, I set out to create content around a number of features of Windows Server 2019. As the book progressed, we quickly hit (and broke) several content limits. In order to publish the book, it was necessary to remove some content, which we did most reluctantly. Just about every chapter could easily have become a small book. To paraphrase Jeffrey Snover, *To ship is to choose*. **I hope I chose well**.

Some recipes in this book rely on other recipes being completed. These related recipes worked well when we wrote them and hopefully work for you as well.

There is a fine line between PowerShell and a Windows feature. To use PowerShell to manage a Windows feature, you need to understand the feature itself. The chapters describe each feature although in the space limited, thus I can't provide complete details of every feature. I have provided links to help you get more information. And as ever, Bing and Google are your best friends.

Conventions used

There are a number of text conventions used throughout this book.

`CodeInText`: Indicates code words in text, database table names, folder names, filenames, file extensions, pathnames, dummy URLs, user input, and Twitter handles. Here is an example: "Create a `PSSession` with both HV servers."

A block of code is set as follows:

```
$Sb = {
    Install-WindowsFeature -Name Hyper-V -IncludeManagementTools
}
Invoke-Command -ComputerName HV1, HV2 -ScriptBlock $Sb
```

Bold: Indicates a new term, an important word, or words that you see on the screen, for example, in menus or dialog boxes, also appear in the text like this. Here is an example: "Select **System info** from the **Administration** panel."

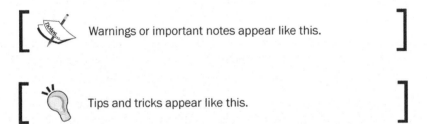

Warnings or important notes appear like this.

Tips and tricks appear like this.

Sections

In this book, you find several headings that appear frequently (Getting ready, How to do it, How it works, There's more, and See also).

To give clear instructions on how to complete a recipe, we use these sections as follows.

Chapter and recipe headings

Every chapter and every recipe introduces some part of Windows which the recipes help you to manage. I've attempted to summarize the key points about each feature - but as ever there is more detail you can discover using your favorite search engine.

Getting ready

This section tells you what to expect in the recipe, and describes how to set up any software or any preliminary settings required for the recipe. It also indicates the hosts (VMs) you need for the recipe and any files, folders, or other resources you need to complete the recipe successfully.

How to do it...

This section contains the steps required to follow the recipe. We show the PowerShell code you use to perform each step. With the exception of the Containers' chapter, all the recipes can be used and run in the PowerShell ISE. In the container's chapter, you should use the PowerShell console to run the recipe steps.

How it works...

This section contains a detailed explanation of what happened in the previous section along with screen shots to show you the results of the recipe.

There's more...

This section consists of additional information about the recipe in order to make the reader more knowledgeable about the recipe.

See also

In some recipes, this section provides some pointers to further information you may find useful.

Get in touch

Feedback from our readers is always welcome.

General feedback: If you have questions about any aspect of this book, mention the book title in the subject of your message and email us at customercare@packtpub.com.

Errata: Although we have taken every care to ensure the accuracy of our content, mistakes do happen. If you have found a mistake in this book we would be grateful if you would report this to us. Please visit, http://www.packt.com/submit-errata, selecting your book, clicking on the Errata Submission Form link, and entering the details.

Piracy: If you come across any illegal copies of our works in any form on the Internet, we would be grateful if you would provide us with the location address or website name. Please contact us at copyright@packt.com with a link to the material.

If you are interested in becoming an author: If there is a topic that you have expertise in and you are interested in either writing or contributing to a book, please visit http://authors.packtpub.com.

Reviews

Please leave a review. Once you have read and used this book, why not leave a review on the site that you purchased it from? Potential readers can then see and use your unbiased opinion to make purchase decisions, we at Packt can understand what you think about our products, and our authors can see your feedback on their book. Thank you!

For more information about Packt, please visit packt.com.

1
Establishing a PowerShell Administrative Environment

In this chapter, we cover the following recipes:

- ▸ Installing RSAT tools on Windows 10 and Windows Server 2019
- ▸ Exploring package management
- ▸ Exploring PowerShellGet and PSGallery
- ▸ Creating an internal PowerShell repository
- ▸ Establishing a code-signing environment
- ▸ Implementing Just Enough Administration

Introduction

Before you can begin to administer your Windows Server 2019 infrastructure, you need to create an environment in which you can use PowerShell to carry out the administration.

The recipes in this chapter focus on setting up a PowerShell administrative environment, which includes getting the tools you need, setting up an internal PowerShell repository, and (for organizations that require a high level of security) creating a code-signing environment. The chapter finishes with setting up JEA to enable users to perform administrative tasks (but only those assigned to the user).

Installing RSAT tools on Window 10 and Windows Server 2019

In order to manage many of the feature of Windows Server 2019, you need to install and use the **Windows Remote Server Administration** (**RSAT**) tools. These tools include PowerShell modules, cmdlets, and other objects that enable you to manage the various features as described in this book.

This recipe configures several hosts: a domain controller (DC1), two domain-joined servers (SRV1, SRV2), and a Windows 10 domain-joined client (CL1).

This recipe enables you to use a Windows 10 computer to manage your Windows 2019 servers remotely. As needed, you can also log in to a server using remote desktop tools to carry out any needed administration locally.

Getting ready

This recipe assumes you have set up the VM farm for this book as described in the *Preface* to the book. In particular, this recipe uses a Windows Server 2019 host running as a domain controller (DC1), a Windows 10 client computer (CL1), plus two domain-joined servers (SRV1, SRV2).

Your client system should be Windows 10 Enterprise or Professional. Once you have installed the operating system, you should customize it with some artifacts used throughout this book, as follows:

```
#    Set execution Policy
Set-ExecutionPolicy -ExecutionPolicy Unrestricted -Force
#    Create Local Foo folder
New-Item C:\Foo -ItemType Directory -Force
```

```
#    Create basic profile and populate
New-Item $profile -Force -ErrorAction SilentlyContinue
'# Profile file created by recipe' | OUT-File $profile
'# Profile for $(hostname)'        | OUT-File $profile -Append
' '                                | OUT-File $profile -Append
'#   Set location'                 | OUT-File $profile -Append
'Set-Location -Path C:\Foo'        | OUT-File $profile -Append
' '                                | OUT-File $profile -Append
'# Set an alias'                   | Out-File $Profile -Append
'Set-Alias gh get-help'            | Out-File $Profile -Append
'###   End of profile'             | Out-File $Profile -Append
# Now view profile in Notepad
Notepad $Profile
# And update Help
Update-Help -Force
```

These steps create the C:\Foo folder, create a profile, and update the PowerShell help information. You can add other customizations to these steps, such as adding VS Code or other third-party modules.

How to do it...

1. From CL1, get all available PowerShell commands:

```
$CommandsBeforeRSAT = Get-Command -Module *
$CountBeforeRSAT    = $CommandsBeforeRSAT.Count
"On Host: [$Env:COMPUTERNAME]"
"Commands available before RSAT installed: [$CountBeforeRSAT]"
```

2. Examine the types of command returned by Get-Command:

```
$CommandsBeforeRSAT | Get-Member |
  Select-Object -ExpandProperty TypeName -Unique
```

3. Get the collection of PowerShell modules and a count of modules before adding the RSAT tools:

```
$ModulesBeforeRSAT = Get-Module -ListAvailable
$CountOfModulesBeforeRSAT = $ModulesBeforeRSAT.Count
"$CountOfModulesBeforeRSAT modules installed prior to adding RSAT"
```

4. Get the `Windows Client Version` and `Hardware Platform`:

```
$Key      = 'HKLM:\SOFTWARE\Microsoft\Windows NT\CurrentVersion'
$CliVer   = (Get-ItemProperty -Path $Key).ReleaseId
$Platform = $ENV:PROCESSOR_ARCHITECTURE
"Windows Client Version : $CliVer"
"Hardware Platform      : $Platform"
```

5. Create a URL for the download file—note this recipe only works for `1709` and `1803`:

```
$LP1 = 'https://download.microsoft.com/download/1/D/8/' +
       '1D8B5022-5477-4B9A-8104-6A71FF9D98AB/'
$Lp180364 = 'WindowsTH-RSAT_WS_1803-x64.msu'
$Lp170964 = 'WindowsTH-RSAT_WS_1709-x64.msu'
$Lp180332 = 'WindowsTH-RSAT_WS_1803-x86.msu'
$Lp170932 = 'WindowsTH-RSAT_WS_1709-x86.msu'
If     ($CliVer -eq 1803 -and $Platform -eq 'AMD64') {
  $DLPath = $Lp1 + $lp180364}
ELSEIf ($CliVer -eq 1709 -and $Platform -eq 'AMD64') {
  $DLPath = $Lp1 + $lp170964}
ElseIf ($CliVer -eq 1803 -and $Platform -eq 'X86')   {
  $DLPath = $Lp1 + $lp180332}
ElseIf ($CliVer -eq 1709 -and $platform -eq 'x86')   {
  $DLPath = $Lp1 + $lp170932}
Else {"Version $Cliver - unknown"; return}
```

6. Display what is to be downloaded:

```
"RSAT MSU file to be downloaded:"
$DLPath
```

7. Use BITS to download the file:

```
$DLFile = 'C:\foo\Rsat.msu'
Start-BitsTransfer -Source $DLPath -Destination $DLFile
```

8. Check the download's Authenticode signature:

```
$Authenticatefile = Get-AuthenticodeSignature $DLFile
If ($Authenticatefile.status -NE "Valid")
  {'File downloaded fails Authenticode check'}
Else
  {'Downloaded file passes Authenticode check'}
```

9. Install the RSAT tools:

```
$WsusArguments = $DLFile + " /quiet"
'Installing RSAT for Windows 10 - Please Wait...'
$Path = 'C:\Windows\System32\wusa.exe'
Start-Process -FilePath $Path -ArgumentList $WsusArguments -Wait
```

10. Now that RSAT features are installed, see what commands are available on the client:

```
$CommandsAfterRSAT = Get-Command -Module *
$COHT1 = @{
  ReferenceObject  = $CommandsBeforeRSAT
  DifferenceObject = $CommandsAfterRSAT
}
# NB: This is quite slow
$DiffC = Compare-Object @COHT1
"$($DiffC.Count) Commands added with RSAT"
```

11. Check how many modules are now available on CL1:

```
$ModulesAfterRSAT        = Get-Module -ListAvailable
$CountOfModulesAfterRsat = $ModulesAfterRSAT.Count
$COHT2 = @{
  ReferenceObject  = $ModulesBeforeRSAT
  DifferenceObject = $ModulesAfterRSAT
}
$DiffM = Compare-Object @COHT2
"$($DiffM.Count) Modules added with RSAT to CL1"
"$CountOfModulesAfterRsat modules now available on CL1"
```

12. Display modules added to CL1:

```
"$($DiffM.Count) modules added With RSAT tools to CL1"
$DiffM | Format-Table InputObject -HideTableHeaders
```

That completes adding the RSAT tools to the client; now we add the tools to SRV1 and look at comparisons with tools on other servers via CL1.

13. Get details of the features and tools loaded on DC1, SRV1, and SRV2:

```
$FSB1 = {Get-WindowsFeature}
$FSRV1B = Invoke-Command -ComputerName SRV1 -ScriptBlock $FSB1
$FSRV2B = Invoke-Command -ComputerName SRV2 -ScriptBlock $FSB1
$FDC1B  = Invoke-Command -ComputerName DC1  -ScriptBlock $FSB1
$IFSrv1B = $FSRV1B | Where-object installed
$IFSrv2B = $SRV2B  | Where-Object installed
$IFDC1B  = $FDC1B  | Where-Object installed
$RFSrv1B = $FeaturesSRV1B |
              Where-Object Installed |
                Where-Object Name -Match 'RSAT'
$RFSSrv2B = $FeaturesSRV2B |
              Where-Object Installed |
                Where-Object Name -Match 'RSAT'
$RFSDC1B = $FeaturesDC1B |
              Where-Object Installed |
                Where-Object Name -Match 'RSAT'
```

14. Display details of the tools installed on each server:

```
'Before Installation of RSAT tools on DC1, SRV1'
"$($IFDC1B.Count) features installed on DC1"
"$($RFSDC1B.Count) RSAT features installed on DC1"
"$($IFSrv1B.Count) features installed on SRV1"
"$($RFSrv1B.Count) RSAT features installed on SRV1"
"$($IFSrv2B.Count) features installed on SRV2"
"$($RFSSRV2B.Count) RSAT features installed on SRV2"
```

15. Add the RSAT tools to the SRV2 server.

```
$InstallSB = {
  Get-WindowsFeature -Name *RSAT* | Install-WindowsFeature
}
$I = Invoke-Command -ComputerName SRV1 -ScriptBlock $InstallSB
$I
If ($I.RestartNeeded -eq 'Yes') {
  'Restarting SRV1'
  Restart-Computer -ComputerName SRV1 -Force -Wait -For PowerShell
}
```

16. Get details of RSAT tools on `SRV1` vs `SRV2`:

```
$FSB2 = {Get-WindowsFeature}
$FSRV1A = Invoke-Command -ComputerName SRV1 -ScriptBlock $FSB2
$FSRV2A = Invoke-Command -ComputerName SRV2 -ScriptBlock $FSB2
$IFSrv1A = $FSRV1A | Where-Object Installed
$IFSrv2A = $FSRV2A | Where-Object Installed
$RSFSrv1A = $FSRV1A | Where-Object Installed |
              Where-Object Name -Match 'RSAT'
$RFSSrv2A = $FSRV2A | Where-Object Installed |
              Where-Object Name -Match 'RSAT'
```

17. Display after results:

```
"After Installation of RSAT tools on SRV1"
"$($IFSRV1A.Count) features installed on SRV1"
"$($RSFSrv1A.Count) RSAT features installed on SRV1"
"$($IFSRV2A.Count) features installed on SRV2"
"$($RFSSRV2A.Count) RSAT features installed on SRV2"
```

How it works...

This recipe installs the RSAT tools on both a Windows 10 domain-joined computer (`CL1`) and on several Windows 2019 servers. The recipe also displays the results of the installation. You begin, in *step 1*, by getting all the commands available on the Windows 10 host and display a count.

Depending on the specific version of Windows 10 you use and what tools you may have already added to the client, the counts may be different. Here is what the output of this step looks like:

```
PS C:\foo> $CommandsBeforeRSAT = Get-Command -Module *
PS C:\foo> $CountBeforeRSAT    = $CommandsBeforeRSAT.Count
PS C:\foo> "On Host: [$(hostname)]"
"Commands available before RSAT installed: [$CountBeforeRSAT]"

On Host: [CL1]
Commands available before RSAT installed: [1528]   ⬅
```

As you can see, `1528` total commands existed prior to adding the RSAT tools. In *step 2*, you examine the different types of command that make up that total, as shown here:

```
PS C:\foo> $CommandsBeforeRSAT |
            Get-Member |
               Select-Object -ExpandProperty TypeName -Unique
System.Management.Automation.AliasInfo
System.Management.Automation.FunctionInfo
System.Management.Automation.FilterInfo
System.Management.Automation.CmdletInfo
```

PowerShell includes aliases, functions, filters, and cmdlets as commands. Adding the RSAT tools increases the number of commands available. In *step 3*, you display a count of the modules installed currently, which looks like the following:

```
PS C:\foo> $ModulesBeforeRSAT = Get-Module -ListAvailable
PS C:\foo> $CountOfModulesBeforeRSAT = $ModulesBeforeRSAT.Count
PS C:\foo> "$CountOfModulesBeforeRSAT modules installed prior to adding RSAT"

77 modules installed prior to adding RSAT       ←
```

In *step 4*, you obtain the hardware platform and the Windows 10 version, which looks like this:

```
PS C:\foo> $Key      = 'HKLM:\SOFTWARE\Microsoft\Windows NT\CurrentVersion'
PS C:\foo> $CliVer   = (Get-ItemProperty -Path $Key).ReleaseId
PS C:\foo> $Platform = $ENV:PROCESSOR_ARCHITECTURE
PS C:\foo> "Windows Client Version : $CliVer"
PS C:\foo> "Hardware Platform      : $Platform"

Windows Client Version : 1803       ←
Hardware Platform      : AMD64       ←
```

In *step 5*, you create a URL for downloading the RSAT tools. Different versions exist for different hardware platforms (for example, `x86` and `amd64`) and for major Windows 10 versions (`1709` and `1803`). In *step 6*, you display the URL, which looks like this:

```
PS C:\foo> "RSAT MSU file to be downloaded:"
PS C:\foo> $DLPath                                              ⟋

RSAT MSU file to be downloaded:
https://download.microsoft.com/download/1/D/8/1D8B5022-5477-4B9A-8104-6A71FF9D98AB/WindowsTH-RSAT_WS_1803-x64.msu
```

In *step 7*, you use the **Background Intelligent Transfer Service** (**BITS**) to retrieve the URL and store it as `C:\Foo\Rsat.msu`. The transfer produces no output.

In *step 8*, you check the Authenticode digital signature of the downloaded file to ensure the file was transferred correctly and has not been tampered with, which looks like this:

```
PS C:\foo> $Authenticatefile = Get-AuthenticodeSignature $DLFile
PS C:\foo> If ($Authenticatefile.status -NE "Valid")
PS C:\foo>    {'File downloaded fails authenticode check'}
PS C:\foo> Else
PS C:\foo>    {'Downloaded file passes authenticode check'}
Downloaded file passes authenticode check
```

In *step 9*, you run the downloaded file that installs the RSAT tools. Aside from the message that the script is installing the RSAT tools, PowerShell runs this silently and there is no additional output from this step.

In *Step 10*, you determine that `CL1` now has a total of `1270` commands, as shown:

```
PS C:\foo> $CommandsAfterRSAT = Get-Command -Module *
PS C:\foo> $COHT1 = @{
              ReferenceObject  = $CommandsBeforeRSAT
              DifferenceObject = $CommandsAfterRSAT
            }
PS C:\foo> # NB: This is quite slow
PS C:\foo> $DiffC = Compare-Object @COHT1
PS C:\foo> "$($DiffC.count) Commands added with RSAT"

1270 Commands added with RSAT
```

In *step 11*, you discover the number of RSAT tools and the total of modules now available on `CL1`, as shown:

```
PS C:\foo> $ModulesAfterRSAT          = Get-Module -ListAvailable
PS C:\foo> $CountOfModulesAfterRsat = $ModulesAfterRSAT.count
PS C:\foo> $COHT2 = @{
              ReferenceObject  = $ModulesBeforeRSAT
              DifferenceObject = $ModulesAfterRSAT
            }
PS C:\foo> $DiffM = Compare-Object @COHT2
PS C:\foo> "$($DiffM.count) Modules added with RSAT to CL1"
PS C:\foo> "$CountOfModulesAfterRsat modules now available on CL1"

26 Modules added with RSAT to CL1
103 modules now available on CL1
```

In *step 12*, you display the modules that were added to CL1, which looks like this:

```
PS C:\foo> "$($DiffM.count) modules added With RSAT tools to CL1"
26 modules added With RSAT tools to CL1    ⬅
PS C:\foo> $DiffM | Format-Table InputObject -HideTableHeaders
ActiveDirectory
BestPractices
ClusterAwareUpdating
DFSN
DFSR
DhcpServer
DnsServer
FailoverClusters
GroupPolicy
HgsClient
IpamServer
IscsiTarget
NetLldpAgent                                    ⬅
NetworkController
NetworkControllerDiagnostics
NetworkLoadBalancingClusters
NFS
RemoteAccess
RemoteDesktop
ServerManager
ServerManagerTasks
ShieldedVMDataFile
ShieldedVMTemplate
StorageQoS
StorageReplica
UpdateServices
```

The preceding steps complete the task of installing the RSAT tools on a Windows 10 client. In some cases, you may also want to install the relevant tools on some or all of your servers.

In this part of the recipe, you are installing the RSAT tools onto server SRV1. You then compare the tools added to SRV1 with what is available on other servers (for example, DC1 and SRV2). In this case, DC1 is a domain controller with other features added during creation of the DC1 server. SRV2, on the other hand, starts as just a domain-joined server with no additional tools.

In *step 13*, you determine the features available on the three servers—this produces no output. In *step 14*, you display a count of the features and RSAT features available on each server, which looks like this:

```
PS C:\foo> "Before Installation of RSAT tools on DC1, SRV1"
PS C:\foo> "$($IFDC1B.count) features installed on DC1"
PS C:\foo> "$($RFSDC1B.count) RSAT features installed on DC1`n"
PS C:\foo> "$($IFSrv1B.count) features installed on SRV1"
PS C:\foo> "$($RFSrv1B.count) RSAT features installed on SRV1`n"
PS C:\foo> "$($IFSrv2B.count) features installed on SRV2"
PS C:\foo> "$($RFSSRV2B.count) RSAT features installed on SRV2"


Before Installation of RSAT tools on DC1, SRV1
26 features installed on DC1
0 RSAT features installed on DC1              ◀——————

0 features installed on SRV1                  ◀——————
0 RSAT features installed on SRV1

0 features installed on SRV2                  ◀——————
0 RSAT features installed on SRV2
```

In *step 15*, you install the RSAT tools remotely on SRV1. To complete the installation, you also reboot the server if the installation requires a reboot. The output looks like the following:

```
PS C:\foo> $InstallSB = {
            Get-WindowsFeature -Name *RSAT* | Install-WindowsFeature
          }
PS C:\foo> $I = Invoke-Command -ComputerName SRV1 -ScriptBlock $InstallSB
PS C:\foo> $I
PS C:\foo> If ($I.RestartNeeded -eq 'Yes') {
            "Restarting SRV1"
            Restart-Computer -ComputerName SRV1 -Force -Wait -For PowerShell
          }
WARNING: You must restart this server to finish the installation process.   ◀——————

PSComputerName : SRV1
RunspaceId     : 98e45193-d170-4079-b21c-36fff5c9207e
Success        : True                                              ◀——————
RestartNeeded  : Yes
FeatureResult  : {BitLocker Drive Encryption, RAS Connection Manager Administration Kit (CMAK), Enhanced Storage, Group Policy Management...}
ExitCode       : SuccessRestartRequired

Restarting SRV1   ◀——————
```

In *step 16*, you determine the features now available on the three servers, producing no output, and finally, in *step 17*, you display the results, as follows:

```
PS C:\foo> After Installation of RSAT tools on SRV1"
PS C:\foo> "$($IFSRV1A.count) features installed on SRV1"
PS C:\foo> "$($RSFSrv1A.count) RSAT features installed on SRV1"
PS C:\foo> "$($IFSRV2A.count) features installed on SRV2"
PS C:\foo> "$($RFSSRV2A.count) RSAT features installed on SRV2"
PS C:\foo> After Installation of RSAT tools on SRV1
90 features installed on SRV1
50 RSAT features installed on SRV1   ◀——————
13 features installed on SRV2
0 RSAT features installed on SRV2
```

There's more...

In *step 1*, you saw that there were `1528` commands loaded on `CL1` while in *step 4* you saw that you had 77 modules on your system. PowerShell gets commands primarily from modules, although older PowerShell snap-ins also contain cmdlets. If you wish to use a command contained in a snap-in, you have to load the snap-in explicitly by using `Add-PSSnapin`. PowerShell can only auto-load commands found in modules.

In *step 4* and *step 5*, you calculate and display a URL to download the RSAT tools. These recipe steps work for two versions of Windows 10 and for two hardware platforms. The URLs and versions of Windows 10 available may have changed by the time you read this. Also, the recipe caters just for Windows 10 versions 1709 and 1803. Download files for earlier versions are not available in the same way as for later versions. And for versions later than 1893, the mechanism may change again.

In *step 15*, when you displayed the results of adding features to `SRV1`, the output looked different if the formatting had been done on the server. On the server, PowerShell is able to display XML that states how to format output from `WindowsFeature` cmdlets. Windows 10 does not display XML, hence the list output in this step.

Exploring package management

The `PackageMangement` PowerShell module implements a provider interface that software package management systems use to manage software packages. You can use the cmdlets in the `PackageMangement` module to work with a variety of package management systems. You can think of this module as providing an API to package management providers such as `PowerShellGet`, discussed in the *Exploring PowerShellGet and PowerShell Gallery* recipe.

The key function of the `PackageMangement` module is to manage the set of software repositories in which package management tools can search, obtain, install, and remove packages. The module enables you to discover and utilize software packages from a variety of sources (and potentially varying in quality).

This recipe explores the `PackageManagement` module from `SRV1`.

Getting ready

This recipe uses `SRV1`—a domain-joined server that you partially configured in the *Installing RSAT Tools on Windows 10 and Windows Server 2019* recipe.

How to do it...

1. Review the cmdlets in the `PackageManagement` module:

```
Get-Command -Module PackageManagement
```

2. Review the installed providers with `Get-PackageProvider`:

```
Get-PackageProvider |
   Format-Table -Property Name,
                         Version,
                         SupportedFileExtensions,
                         FromtrustedSource
```

3. Get details of a packages loaded on SRV1 of the MSU type (representing Microsoft Updates downloaded by Windows Update):

```
Get-Package -ProviderName 'msu' |
   Select-Object -ExpandProperty Name
```

4. Get details of the NuGet provider, which provides access to developer library packages. This step also loads the NuGet provider if it is not already installed:

```
Get-PackageProvider -Name NuGet -ForceBootstrap
```

5. Display the other package providers available on SRV1:

```
Find-PackageProvider |
   Select-Object -Property Name,Summary |
     Format-Table -Wrap -AutoSize
```

6. Chocolatey is a popular repository for Windows administrators and power users. You have to install the provider before you can use it, as follows:

```
Install-PackageProvider -Name Chocolatey -Force
```

7. Verify that the Chocolatey provider is now available:

```
Get-PackageProvider | Select-Object -Property Name,Version
```

8. Display the packages now available in Chocolatey:

```
$Packages = Find-Package -ProviderName Chocolatey
"$($Packages.Count) packages available from Chocolatey"
```

How it works...

In *step 1*, you review the cmdlets contained in the `PackageManagement` module, which looks like this:

```
PS C:\foo> Get-Command -Module PackageManagement

CommandType     Name                          Version   Source
-----------     ----                          -------   ------
Cmdlet          Find-Package                  1.0.0.1   PackageManagement
Cmdlet          Find-PackageProvider          1.0.0.1   PackageManagement
Cmdlet          Get-Package                   1.0.0.1   PackageManagement
Cmdlet          Get-PackageProvider           1.0.0.1   PackageManagement
Cmdlet          Get-PackageSource             1.0.0.1   PackageManagement
Cmdlet          Import-PackageProvider        1.0.0.1   PackageManagement
Cmdlet          Install-Package               1.0.0.1   PackageManagement
Cmdlet          Install-PackageProvider       1.0.0.1   PackageManagement
Cmdlet          Register-PackageSource        1.0.0.1   PackageManagement
Cmdlet          Save-Package                  1.0.0.1   PackageManagement
Cmdlet          Set-PackageSource             1.0.0.1   PackageManagement
Cmdlet          Uninstall-Package             1.0.0.1   PackageManagement
Cmdlet          Unregister-PackageSource      1.0.0.1   PackageManagement
```

In *step 2*, you review the package providers installed by default in Windows Server 2019, which looks like this:

```
C:\foo> Get-PackageProvider |
           Format-Table -Property Name,
                                  Version,
                                  SupportedFileExtensions,
                                  FromtrustedSource

Name          Version SupportedFileExtensions FromTrustedSource
----          ------- ----------------------- -----------------
msi           3.0.0.0 {msi, msp}                          False
msu           3.0.0.0 {msu}                               False
PowerShellGet 1.0.0.1 {}                                  False
Programs      3.0.0.0 {}
```

In *step 3*, you examined the packages downloaded by the `msu` provider. In this case, you only see one update, but you may see more, and it looks like this:

```
PS C:\Foo> Get-Package -ProviderName msu |
           Select-Object -ExpandProperty Name

Definition Update for Windows Defender Antivirus - KB2267602 (Definition 1.275.727.0)
```

In *step 4,* you examine details of the `NuGet` provider. If the provider doesn't exist, then using the `-ForceBootstrap` parameter installs the provider without asking for confirmation, like this:

```
PS:C:\Foo> Get-PackageProvider -Name NuGet -ForceBootstrap

Name     Version     DynamicOptions
----     -------     --------------
NuGet    2.8.5.208   Destination, ExcludeVersion, Scope, SkipDependencies, Headers, Fil...
```

In *step 5,* you search for additional package providers, like this:

```
PS:C:\Foo> Find-PackageProvider |
           Select-Object -Property Name,Summary |
           Format-Table -Wrap -AutoSize


Name                        Summary
----                        -------
nuget                       NuGet provider for the OneGet meta-package manager
ps1                         ps1 provider for the OneGet meta-package manager
chocolatey                  ChocolateyPrototype provider for the OneGet meta-package manager
PowerShellGet               PowerShell module with commands for discovering, installing, upd...
ChocolateyGet               An PowerShell OneGet provider that discovers packages from https...
DockerProvider              PowerShell module with commands for discovering, installing, and...
ContainerImage              This is a PackageManagement provider module which helps in disco...
                            For more details and examples refer to our project site at https...
DockerMsftProvider          PowerShell module with commands for discovering, installing, and...
NanoServerPackage           A PackageManagement provider to  Discover, Save and Install Nano...
DockerMsftProviderInsider   PowerShell module with commands for discovering, installing, and...
GistProvider                Gist-as-a-Package - PackageManagement  PowerShell Provider to in...
GitHubProvider              GitHub-as-a-Package - PackageManagement PowerShell Provider to i...
GitLabProvider              GitLab PackageManagement provider
TSDProvider                 PowerShell PackageManager provider to search & install TypeScrip...
OfficeProvider              OfficeProvider allows users to install Microsoft Office365 ProPl...
MyAlbum                     MyAlbum provider discovers the photos in your remote file reposi...
0install                    Zero Install is a decentralized cross-platform software-installa...
WSAProvider                 Provider to Discover, Install and inventory windows server apps
AppxGet                     Powershell Package Management (OneGet) Provider for AppX package...
```

In *step 6,* you install the `Chocolatey` package provider, which looks like this:

```
PS C:\foo> Install-PackageProvider -Name Chocolatey -Force

Name         Version     Source           Summary
----         -------     ------           -------
chocolatey   2.8.5.130   https://onege... ChocolateyPrototype provider...
```

In *step 7*, you examine the list of package providers now available to confirm that the `Chocolatey` provider is available, which looks like this:

```
PS C:\Foo> Get-PackageProvider | Select-Object -Property Name,Version

Name         Version
----         -------
Chocolatey   2.8.5.130     ◄──────────
msi          3.0.0.0
msu          3.0.0.0
NuGet        2.8.5.208
PowerShellGet 1.0.0.1
Programs     3.0.0.0
```

In *step 8*, you check to see how many packages are available to download from `Chocolatey`, as follows:

```
PS C:\Foo> $AvailableChocolateyPackages = Find-Package -ProviderName Chocolatey
PS C:\Foo> "$($AvailableChocolateyPackages.Count) available from Chocolatey"

5987 packages available from Chocolatey     ◄──────────
```

There's more...

In *step 6*, you installed the `Chocolatey` package provider. To see more details about what `Install-PackageProvider` is doing, run this step with the `-Verbose` flag.

Exploring PowerShellGet and the PSGallery

`PowerShellGet` is a module that enables you to work with external repositories. A repository is a site, either on the internet or internally, that hosts software packages. You use the cmdlets in this module to access one or more repositories that enable you to find, download, and use third-party packages from a package repository.

`PowerShellGet` leverages mainly the `PSGallery` repository. This repository, often referred to as a **repo**, is sponsored by Microsoft and contains a wealth of PowerShell functionalities, including PowerShell modules, DSC resources, PowerShell scripts, and so on. Many of the recipes in this book utilize `PSGallery` resources.

To some extent, the `PowerShellGet` module is similar to tools in the Linux world such as **apt-get** in Ubuntu or **RPM** in Red Hat Linux.

The `PowerShellGet` module implements a number of additional `*-Module` cmdlets that extend the module management cmdlets provided in the `Microsoft.PowerShell.Core` module.

It's simple and easy to find and install modules from the PSGallery. In some cases, you may wish to download the module to a separate folder. This would allow you to inspect the module, loading it manually before putting it into a folder in $env:PSModulePath (where commands might be auto-loaded).

Getting ready

This recipe runs on the SRV1 server. The recipe also assumes you have performed the previous recipes in this chapter. In particular, you should have added the latest version of the NuGet package provider to your system. If you have not already done so, ensure the provider is installed by performing the following:

```
Install-PackageProvider -Name NuGet -ForceBootstrap
```

How to do it...

1. Review the commands available in the PowerShellGet module:

    ```
    Get-Command -Module PowerShellGet
    ```

2. View the NuGet package provider version:

    ```
    Get-PackageProvider -Name NuGet |
        Select-Object -Property Version
    ```

3. View the current version of PowerShellGet:

    ```
    Get-Module -Name PowerShellGet -ListAvailable
    ```

4. Install the PowerShellGet module from PSGallery:

    ```
    Install-Module -Name PowerShellGet -Force
    ```

5. Check the version of PowerShellGet:

    ```
    Get-Module -Name PowerShellGet -ListAvailable
    ```

6. View the default PSGallery repositories currently available to PowerShell:

    ```
    Get-PSRepository
    ```

7. Review the package providers in the `PSGallery` repository:

```
Find-PackageProvider -Source PSGallery |
  Select-Object -Property Name, Summary |
    Format-Table -Wrap -autosize
```

8. Use the `Get-Command` cmdlet to find `Find-*` cmdlets in the `PowerShellGet` module:

```
Get-Command -Module PowerShellGet -Verb Find
```

9. Get the commands in the `PowerShellGet` module:

```
$Commands     = Find-Command -Module PowerShellGet
$CommandCount = $Commands.Count
```

10. Get the modules included:

```
$Modules     = Find-Module -Name *
$ModuleCount = $Modules.Count
```

11. Get the DSC resources available in the `PSGallery` repository:

```
$DSCResources      = Find-DSCResource
$DSCResourcesCount = $DSCResources.Count
```

12. Display the counts:

```
"$CommandCount commands available in PowerShellGet"
"$DSCResourcesCount DSCResources available in PowerShell Gallery"
"$ModuleCount Modules available in the PowerShell Gallery"
```

13. Install the `TreeSize` module. As this is a public repository, Windows does not trust it by default, so you must approve installation or use `-Force`:

```
Install-Module -Name TreeSize -Force
```

14. Review and test the commands in the module:

```
Get-Command -Module TreeSize
Get-Help Get-TreeSize
Get-TreeSize -Path C:\Windows\System32\Drivers -Depth 1

Uninstall the module:
Uninstall-Module -Name TreeSize
```

15. To inspect prior to installing, first create a download folder:

```
$NIHT = @{
  ItemType = 'Directory'
  Path     = "$env:HOMEDRIVE\DownloadedModules"
}
New-Item @NIHT
```

16. Save the module to the folder:

```
$Path = "$env:HOMEDRIVE\DownloadedModules"
Save-Module -Name TreeSize -Path $Path
Get-ChildItem -Path $Path -Recurse | format-Table Fullname
```

17. To test the downloaded `TreeSize` module, import it:

```
$ModuleFolder = "$env:HOMEDRIVE\downloadedModules\TreeSize"
  Get-ChildItem -Path $ModuleFolder -Filter *.psm1 -Recurse |
    Select-Object -ExpandProperty FullName -First 1 |
      Import-Module -Verbose
```

How it works...

This recipe uses the cmdlets in the `PowerShellGet` module to demonstrate how you can obtain and leverage modules and other PowerShell resources from the public `PSGallery` site (`https://www.powershellgallery.com/`).

In *step 1*, you review the commands contained in the `PowerShellGet` module, which looks like this:

```
PS C:\Foo> Get-Command -Module PowerShellGet

CommandType     Name                             Version     Source
-----------     ----                             -------     ------
Function        Find-Command                     1.0.0.1     PowerShellGet
Function        Find-DscResource                 1.0.0.1     PowerShellGet
Function        Find-Module                      1.0.0.1     PowerShellGet
Function        Find-RoleCapability              1.0.0.1     PowerShellGet
Function        Find-Script                      1.0.0.1     PowerShellGet
Function        Get-InstalledModule              1.0.0.1     PowerShellGet
Function        Get-InstalledScript              1.0.0.1     PowerShellGet
Function        Get-PSRepository                 1.0.0.1     PowerShellGet
Function        Install-Module                   1.0.0.1     PowerShellGet
Function        Install-Script                   1.0.0.1     PowerShellGet
Function        New-ScriptFileInfo               1.0.0.1     PowerShellGet
Function        Publish-Module                   1.0.0.1     PowerShellGet
Function        Publish-Script                   1.0.0.1     PowerShellGet
Function        Register-PSRepository            1.0.0.1     PowerShellGet
Function        Save-Module                      1.0.0.1     PowerShellGet
Function        Save-Script                      1.0.0.1     PowerShellGet
Function        Set-PSRepository                 1.0.0.1     PowerShellGet
Function        Test-ScriptFileInfo              1.0.0.1     PowerShellGet
Function        Uninstall-Module                 1.0.0.1     PowerShellGet
Function        Uninstall-Script                 1.0.0.1     PowerShellGet
Function        Unregister-PSRepository          1.0.0.1     PowerShellGet
Function        Update-Module                    1.0.0.1     PowerShellGet
Function        Update-ModuleManifest            1.0.0.1     PowerShellGet
Function        Update-Script                    1.0.0.1     PowerShellGet
Function        Update-ScriptFileInfo            1.0.0.1     PowerShellGet
```

Because the `NuGet` package provider is required to use the PowerShell Gallery, you need to have this provider loaded. In *step 2*, you check the version of the provider, which looks like this:

```
PS C:\foo> Get-PackageProvider -Name NuGet |
                Select-Object -Property Version

Version
-------
2.8.5.208
```

PowerShellGet requires `NuGet` provider version 2.8.5.201 or newer to interact with NuGet-based repositories, including `PSGallery`. In this case, you have a later version of the `NuGet` provider.

In *step 3*, you check what version of `PowerShellGet` is currently installed on `SRV1`, which looks like this:

```
PS C:\foo> Get-Module -Name PowerShellGet -ListAvailable

    Directory: C:\Program Files\WindowsPowerShell\Modules

ModuleType Version  Name          ExportedCommands
---------- -------  ----          ----------------
Script     1.0.0.1  PowerShellGet {Install-Module, Find-Module, Save-Module, Update-Module...}
```

In *step 4*, you install the latest version of the `PowerShellGet` module from `PSGallery`, which produces no output. In *step 5*, you view the versions of `PowerShellGet` that are now available on `SRV1`, like this:

```
C:\foo> Get-Module -Name PowerShellGet -ListAvailable

    Directory: C:\Program Files\WindowsPowerShell\Modules
ModuleType Version  Name          ExportedCommands
---------- -------  ----          ----------------

Script     1.6.7    PowerShellGet {Find-Command, Find-DSCResource, Find-Module, Find-Role...}
Script     1.0.0.1  PowerShellGet {Install-Module, Find-Module, Save-Module, Update-Modul...}
```

In *step 6*, you examine the repositories PowerShell knows about (thus far), like this:

```
PS C:\foo> Get-PSRepository

Name      InstallationPolicy   SourceLocation
----      ------------------   --------------
PSGallery Untrusted            https://www.powershellgallery.com/api/v2/
```

In *step 7*, you examine other providers contained in the PSGallery, which you can download and use as needed:

```
PS C:\foo> Find-PackageProvider -Source PSGallery |
    Select-Object -Property Name, Summary |
        Format-Table -Wrap -autosize

Name                       Summary

----                       -------

PowerShellGet              PowerShell module with commands for discovering, installing, updating and publishing
                           the PowerShell artifacts like Modules, DSC Resources, Role Capabilities and Scripts.
NanoServerPackage          A PackageManagement provider to  Discover, Save and Install Nano Server Packages on-demand
ChocolateyGet              An PowerShell OneGet provider that discovers packages from https://www.chocolatey.org.
DockerProvider             PowerShell module with commands for discovering, installing, and updating Docker images.
ContainerImage             This is a PackageManagement provider module which helps in discovering, downloading and
                           installing Windows Container OS images.
                           For more details and examples refer to our project site at
                           https://github.com/PowerShell/ContainerProvider.
DockerMsftProvider         PowerShell module with commands for discovering, installing, and updating Docker images.
DockerMsftProviderInsider  PowerShell module with commands for discovering, installing, and updating Docker images.
GistProvider               Gist-as-a-Package - PackageManagement  PowerShell Provider to interop with Github Gists
GitHubProvider             GitHub-as-a-Package - PackageManagement PowerShell Provider to interop with Github
GitLabProvider             GitLab PackageManagement provider
TSDProvider                PowerShell PackageManager provider to search & install TypeScript definition files from the
                           community DefinitelyTyped repo
MyAlbum                    MyAlbum provider discovers the photos in your remote file repository and installs them to
                           your local folder.
0install                   Zero Install is a decentralized cross-platform software-installation system
OfficeProvider             OfficeProvider allows users to install Microsoft Office365 ProPlus from Powershell.
WSAProvider                Provider to Discover, Install and inventory windows server apps
AppxGet                    Powershell Package Management (OneGet) Provider for AppX packages.
```

To discover some of the things you can find using PowerShellGet, in *step 8* you get the commands in the module that use the Find verb, like this:

```
PS C:\foo> Get-Command -Module PowerShellGet -Verb Find

CommandType     Name                 Version     Source

-----------     ----                 -------     ------

Function        Find-Command         1.6.7       powershellget
Function        Find-DscResource     1.6.7       powershellget
Function        Find-Module          1.6.7       powershellget
Function        Find-RoleCapability  1.6.7       powershellget
Function        Find-Script          1.6.7       powershellget
```

There are a variety of resources you can obtain from the PSGallery. In *step 9*, *step 10*, and *step 11*, you get the command, modules, and DSC resources respectively that are in the PSGallery. This generates no output. In *step 12*, you display those counts, which looks like this:

```
PS C:\foo> "$CommandCount commands available in PowerShellGet"
PS C:\foo> "$ModuleCount Modules available in the PowerShell Gallery"
PS C:\foo> "$DSCResourcesCount DSCResources available in PowerShell Gallery"

25 commands available in PowerShellGet
3201 Modules available in the PowerShell Gallery
1320 DSCResources available in PowerShell Gallery              ⬅
```

In *step 13*, you install the `TreeSize` module from the `PSGallery`, which generates no output. In *step 14*, you look at the commands contained in the module (there is only one), then you run the command, which looks like this:

```
PS C:\foo> Get-Command -Module TreeSize

CommandType     Name              Version     Source
-----------     ----              -------     ------
Function        Get-TreeSize      2.0         TreeSize

PS C:\foo> Get-TreeSize -Path C:\Windows\System32\Drivers -Depth 1

      ├ Drivers\       95462517
        ├ UMDF\        2043848
          ├ en-US\     66560
        ├ en-US\       1464320
        ├ wd\          448584
        ├ etc\         23907
        ├ DriverData\  0
```

In *step 15*, you remove the module—this generates no output.

In some cases, you may wish to download the module to a separate folder to enable you to test the module before formally installing it. In *step 16*, you create a folder in your home drive, generating no output. Next, in *step 17*, you save the module into that folder and look at what's in the downloaded files folder, which looks like this:

```
PS C:\foo> $Path = "$env:HOMEDRIVE\DownloadedModules"
PS C:\foo> Save-Module -Name TreeSize -Path $Path
PS C:\foo> Get-ChildItem -Path $Path -Recurse | format-Table Fullname

FullName
--------
C:\DownloadedModules\TreeSize
C:\DownloadedModules\TreeSize\2.0
C:\DownloadedModules\TreeSize\2.0\ReadMe.md
C:\DownloadedModules\TreeSize\2.0\TreeSize.Format.ps1xml
C:\DownloadedModules\TreeSize\2.0\TreeSize.psd1
C:\DownloadedModules\TreeSize\2.0\TreeSize.psm1
```

In *step 18*, you load the module from the download folder. Using the `-Verbose` switch enables you to see what `Import-Module` is actually doing. The output is as follows:

```
PS C:\foo> $ModuleFolder = "$env:HOMEDRIVE\downloadedModules\TreeSize"
Get-ChildItem -Path $ModuleFolder -Filter *.psm1 -Recurse |
    Select-Object -ExpandProperty FullName -First 1 |
        Import-Module -Verbose
VERBOSE: Loading module from path 'C:\downloadedModules\TreeSize\2.0\TreeSize.psm1'.
VERBOSE: Exporting function 'Get-TreeSize'.
VERBOSE: Exporting alias 'TreeSize'.
VERBOSE: Importing function 'Get-TreeSize'.
VERBOSE: Importing alias 'TreeSize'.
```

Once you have imported the module you can then use either the `Get-Treesize` function or its alias, `TreeSize`.

There's more...

In *step 3*, you discover that the version of the `PowerShellGet` module on the host is version 1.0.0.1 which ships with Windows 10. Since the initial release of Windows 10, `PowerShellGet` has become a community-developed project, based at GitHub. The latest version of the module is available both from GitHub or via `PSGallery`, with the latter being easier to work with for most IT pros. Visit the GitHub site to get more information: `https://github.com/PowerShell/PowerShellGet`.

In *step 4*, you added the latest version of the `PowerShellGet` module onto your system and in *step 5*, you saw you now had two versions. PowerShell, by default, uses the later version, unless you explicitly load an earlier version prior to using the commands in the module.

In this recipe, you downloaded, used, and removed the `TreeSize` module—one of thousands of modules you can freely download and use. Other popular modules in the `PSGallery` include:

- Azure modules (including `MSOnline`): Azure provides a large number of smaller modules and most of these are frequently downloaded
- `PowerShellGet` and `PackageManagement`
- `PSWindowsUpdate`
- `PSSlack`
- `IISAdministration`
- `SQLServer`
- `CredentialManager`
- `Posh-SSH`

For most IT pros, `PSGallery` is the go-to location for obtaining useful modules that avoid you having to re-invent the wheel. In some cases, you may develop a particularly useful module (or script or DSC resource), which you can publish to the `PSGallery` to share with others.

See `https://docs.microsoft.com/en-us/powershell/gallery/concepts/ publishing-guidelines` for guidelines regarding publishing to the `PSGallery`. And, while you are looking at that page, consider implementing best practices in any production script you develop.

Creating an internal PowerShell repository

Public galleries such as `PSGallery` are great sources of interesting and useful modules. You can also create your own PowerShell repository for either personal or corporate use.

There are several ways to set up an internal repository, for example using a third-party tool such as ProGet from Inedo (see `https://inedo.com/` for details on ProGet). The simplest way is to set up an SMB file share and use the `Register-PSRepository` command to set up the repository. Once set up, you can use the `Publish-Module` command to upload modules to your new repository and then use the repository to distribute organizational modules.

Getting ready

This recipe runs on the SRV1 server.

How to do it...

1. Create the repository folder:

```
$LPATH = 'C:\RKRepo'
New-Item -Path $LPATH -ItemType Directory
```

2. Share the folder:

```
$SMBHT = @{
  Name        = 'RKRepo'
  Path        = $LPATH
  Description = 'Reskit Repository'
  FullAccess  = 'Everyone'
}
New-SmbShare @SMBHT
```

3. Create the repository and configure it as trusted:

```
$Path = '\\SRV1\RKRepo'
$REPOHT = @{
  Name               = 'RKRepo'
  SourceLocation     = $Path
  PublishLocation    = $Path
  InstallationPolicy = 'Trusted'
}
Register-PSRepository @REPOHT
```

4. View the configured repositories:

```
Get-PSRepository
```

5. Create a Hello World module folder:

```
New-Item C:\HW -ItemType Directory | Out-Null
```

6. Create a very simple module:

```
$HS = @"
Function Get-HelloWorld {'Hello World'}
Set-Alias GHW Get-HelloWorld
"@
$HS | Out-File C:\HW\HW.psm1
```

7. Load and test the module:

```
Import-Module -Name c:\hw -verbose
GHW
```

8. Create a module manifest for the new module:

```
$NMHT = @{
  Path               = 'C:\HW\HW.psd1'
  RootModule         = 'HW.psm1'
  Description        = 'Hello World module'
  Author             = 'DoctorDNS@Gmail.com'
  FunctionsToExport = 'Get-HelloWorld'
}
```

9. Publish the module to the RKRepo:

```
Publish-Module -Path C:\HW -Repository RKRepo
```

10. View the results of publishing the module:

```
Find-Module -Repository RKRepo
```

11. Look at what is in the C:\RKRepo folder:

```
Get-ChildItem -Path C:\RKRepo
```

How it works...

You begin this recipe, in *step 1,* by creating the folder you are going to use to hold your repository, in this case C:\RKRepo, as follows:

```
PS C:\Foo> New-Item -Path $LPATH -ItemType Directory

    Directory: C:\

Mode              LastWriteTime     Length Name
----              -------------     ------ ----

d-----     06/09/2018     12:19            RKRepo
```

In *step 2*, you share this folder, like so:

```
PS C:\Foo> $SMBHT = @{
            Name        = 'RKRepo'
            Path        = $LPATH
            Description = 'Reskit Repository'
            FullAccess  = 'Everyone'
}
New-SmbShare @SMBHT

Name    ScopeName Path       Description
----    --------- ----       -----------
RKRepo  *         C:\RKRepo  RK Repo
```

In *step 3*, you create the repository in the shared folder, which produces no output. In *step 4*, you view the repositories configured on the system, like this:

```
PS C:\Foo> Get-PSRepository

Name       InstallationPolicy   SourceLocation

----       ------------------   --------------

PSGallery  Untrusted            https://www.powershellgallery.com/api/v2/
RKRepo     Trusted              \\SRV1\RKRepo
```

You next create a simple module to be published into your repository. You begin, in *step 5*, by creating a working folder for your module, then in *step 6* you create a very simple script module with a single function. Neither step produces any output.

In *step 7*, you test the module by importing it from the working module folder. By using the -Verbose switch, you can observe how PowerShell imports the module, then you invoke the Get-HelloWorld function via its alias GHW, as follows:

```
PS C:\Foo> Import-Module -Name c:\hw -verbose
VERBOSE: Loading module from path 'C:\hw\hw.psm1'.
VERBOSE: Exporting function 'Get-HelloWorld'.
VERBOSE: Exporting alias 'GHW'.
VERBOSE: Importing function 'Get-HelloWorld'.
VERBOSE: Importing alias 'GHW'.

PS C:\Foo> GHW
Hello World
```

Although the module `works` as-is, you need a manifest in order to publish the module. In *step 8*, you create a very simple module manifest and store it in the module folder. In *step 9*, you publish the module. None of these three steps produce any output.

With the module published, in *step 10* you can use `Find-Module` to discover what is in the repository, like this:

```
PS C:\foo> Find-Module -Repository RKRepo

Version     Name     Repository     Description

-------     ----     ----------     -----------

1.0.0       hw       RKRepo         Hello World module
```

The repository is just a file share holding a set of one or more `NuGet` packages. As you can see in *step 11*, our repository has just one item published, as shown here:

```
PS C:\RKRepo> Get-ChildItem -Path C:\RKRepo

    Directory: C:\RKRepo

Mode            LastWriteTime       Length Name

----            -------------       ------ ----

-a----     06/09/2018     13:26       3696 hw.1.0.0.nupkg
```

There's more...

In *step 2*, you create a share that allows everyone full access to the repository. In a corporate environment, you should review the access to the repository. Perhaps you should give authenticated users read access, and grant write access to a smaller group of administrators.

As you can see in *step 11*, a `PowerShellGet` repository is just a file share that holds `NuGet` packages. One approach might be to keep your module source in your source code repository and publish it to the internal `PowerShellGet` repository as needed.

Establishing a code-signing environment

In some environments, it can be important to know that a program or PowerShell script has not been modified since it was released. You can achieve this with PowerShell scripts by digitally signing the script and by enforcing an execution policy of `AllSigned` or `RemoteSigned`.

After you digitally sign your script, you can detect whether any changes were made in the script since it was signed. Using PowerShell's execution policy, you can force PowerShell to test the script to ensure the digital signature is still valid and to only run scripts that succeed. You can set PowerShell to do this either for all scripts (you set the execution policy to `AllSigned`) or only for scripts you downloaded from a remote site (you set the execution policy to `RemoteSigned`).

One thing to remember—even if you have the execution policy set to `AllSigned`, it's trivial to run any non-signed script. Simply bring the script into PowerShell's ISE, select all the text in the script, then run that selected script. And using the `Unblock-File` cmdlet allows you to, in effect, turn a **remote** script into a **local** one.

Signing a script is simple once you have a digital certificate issued by a Certificate Authority. You have three options for getting an appropriate certificate:

- ▸ Use a well-known public Certificate Authority such as Digicert (see `https://www.digicert.com/code-signing`) for details of their code-signing certificates).
- ▸ Use an internal CA and obtain the certificate from your organization's CA.
- ▸ Use a self-signed certificate.

Public certificates are useful but are generally not free. You can easily set up your own CA, or used self-signed certificates. Self-signed certificates are great for testing out signing scripts and then using them. All three of these methods can give you a certificate that you can use to sign PowerShell scripts.

Getting ready

Run this recipe on the Windows 10 client (`CL1`) you used in the earlier *Installing RSAT Tools on Windows 10 and Server 2019* recipe.

How to do it...

1. Create a code-signing, self-signed certificate:

```
$CHT = @{
  Subject           = 'Reskit Code Signing'
  Type              = 'CodeSigning'
  CertStoreLocation = 'Cert:\CurrentUser\My'
}
$Cert = New-SelfSignedCertificate @CHT
```

2. View the newly created certificate:

```
Get-ChildItem -Path Cert:\CurrentUser\my -CodeSigningCert |
  Where-Object {$_.Subjectname.Name -match $CHT.Subject}
```

3. Create a simple script:

```
$Script = @"
  # Sample Script
  'Hello World!'
  Hostname
"@
$Script | Out-File -FilePath C:\Foo\signed.ps1
Get-ChildItem -Path C:\Foo\signed.ps1
```

4. Sign the script:

```
$SHT = @{
  Certificate = $Cert
  FilePath    = 'C:\Foo\signed.ps1'
}
Set-AuthenticodeSignature @SHT -Verbose
```

5. Look at the script after signing:

```
Get-ChildItem -Path C:\Foo\signed.ps1
```

6. Test the signature:

```
Get-AuthenticodeSignature -FilePath C:\Foo\signed.ps1 |
  Format-List
```

7. Ensure the certificate is trusted:

```
$DestStoreName  = 'Root'
$DestStoreScope = 'CurrentUser'
$Type = 'System.Security.Cryptography.X509Certificates.X509Store'
$MHT = @{
  TypeName = $Type
  ArgumentList  = ($DestStoreName, $DestStoreScope)
}
$DestStore = New-Object  @MHT
$DestStore.Open(
  [System.Security.Cryptography.X509Certificates.OpenFlags]::
    ReadWrite)
$DestStore.Add($cert)
$DestStore.Close()
```

8. Re-sign with a trusted certificate:

```
Set-AuthenticodeSignature @SHT | Out-Null
```

9. Check the script's signature:

```
Get-AuthenticodeSignature -FilePath C:\Foo\signed.ps1 |
  Format-List
```

How it works...

In *step 1*, you create a self-signed code-signing certificate which you store in the current user's personal certificate store (also known as `Cert:\CurrentUser\My`). Since you store the certificate in `$Cert`, there is no output from this step. In *step 2*, you examine the code-signing certificates in the current user's personal certificate store, like this:

```
PS C:\foo> Get-ChildItem -Path Cert:\CurrentUser\my -CodeSigningCert |
            Where-Object {$_.Subjectname.Name -match $CHT.Subject}

   PSParentPath: Microsoft.PowerShell.Security\Certificate::CurrentUser\my

Thumbprint                                Subject

----------                                -------

20411849607AAA9D93B0960C1ECF57E9DD837A83  CN=Reskit Code Signing
```

In *step 3*, you create a very simple PowerShell script, which you store in `C:\Foo\Signed.ps1`. Then you display the file's details, like this:

```
PS C:\foo> $Script = @"
                    # Sample Script
                    'Hello World!'
                    Hostname
"@
$Script | Out-File -FilePath c:\foo\signed.ps1
Get-ChildItem -Path C:\foo\signed.ps1


    Directory: C:\foo

Mode                 LastWriteTime         Length Name
----                 -------------         ------ ----
-a----       07/09/2018     21:00              94 signed.ps1
```

Now that you have a script, in *step 4* you sign it. Note that this generates a status error of `UnknownError` (which means the signing certificate is not trusted). The output of this step looks like this:

```
PS C:\foo> $SHT = @{
          Certificate = $cert
          FilePath    = 'C:\foo\signed.ps1'
          }
PS C:\foo> Set-AuthenticodeSignature @SHT


    Directory: C:\foo

SignerCertificate                         Status        Path
-----------------                         ------        ----
20411849607AAA9D93B0960C1ECF57E9DD837A83  UnknownError  signed.ps1
```

In *step 5*, you view the script file and note the file is considerably larger (due to the length of the digital signature), which looks like this:

```
PS C:\foo> Get-ChildItem -Path C:\foo\signed.ps1

    Directory: C:\foo

Mode                 LastWriteTime         Length Name
----                 -------------         ------ ----
-a----       07/09/2018     21:05            4210 signed.ps1
```

In *step 6*, you test the script to validate the signature, like this:

```
PS C:\foo> Get-AuthenticodeSignature -FilePath C:\foo\signed.ps1 |
           Format-List

SignerCertificate        : [Subject]
                             CN=Reskit Code Signing
                           [Issuer]
                             CN=Reskit Code Signing
                           [Serial Number]
                             514B5D33CA8385A441E913E5FBD9706C
                           [Not Before]
                             07/09/2018 20:49:47
                           [Not After]
                             07/09/2019 21:09:47
                           [Thumbprint]
                             20411849607AAA9D93B0960C1ECF57E9DD837A83
TimeStamperCertificate   :
Status                   : UnknownError
StatusMessage            : A certificate chain processed, but terminated in a
                           root certificate which is not trusted by the trust provider
Path                     : C:\foo\signed.ps1
SignatureType            : Authenticode
IsOSBinary               : False
```

As you can see, the underlying reason for the `UnknownError` status is that the signing certificate is not trusted. You can configure Windows to trust your signed certificate by copying your self-signed certificate into the Root CA store (either for the current user or for the computer).

In *step 7*, you copy your self-signed certificate into the current user's Root CA store, using the .NET Framework. Copying a certificate into the root store produces no console output, but does generate a pop-up message, which looks like this:

Now that the signing certificate is trusted, in *step 8* you re-sign the script, which produces no
output. In *step 9,* you test the re-signed script, as shown here:

```
PS C:\foo> Get-AuthenticodeSignature -FilePath C:\foo\signed.ps1 |
            Format-List


SignerCertificate        : [Subject]
                             CN=Reskit Code Signing
                           [Issuer]
                             CN=Reskit Code Signing
                           [Serial Number]
                             514B5D33CA8385A441E913E5FBD9706C
                           [Not Before]
                             07/09/2018 20:49:47
                           [Not After]
                             07/09/2019 21:09:47
                           [Thumbprint]
                             20411849607AAA9D93B0960C1ECF57E9DD837A83

TimeStamperCertificate :
Status                 : Valid          ◄─────────────
StatusMessage          : Signature verified.   ◄────────
Path                   : C:\foo\signed.ps1
SignatureType          : Authenticode
IsOSBinary             : False
```

There's more...

PowerShell's certificate provider does not support copying a certificate into the root CA store.
You can overcome this limitation by dipping down into the .NET framework as shown in *step 7,*
although this does generate a pop-up dialog box as shown previously.

Once you complete the steps in this recipe, you can experiment with an execution policy and
make changes and observe the results. After signing the script, for example, as you did in
step 8, try updating the script and running it with an execution policy set to `AllSigned`.

Establishing a secure code-signing environment can be a lot of work. Once you have the
code-signing certificate, you need to keep it secure (for example on a smart card that is locked
in a safe with highly limited access). Then you need procedures to enable the organization's
scripts to be signed. Creating the infrastructure to manage the whole process, including
dealing with the smart cards and the safe, is possibly overkill for many.

If you release PowerShell scripts commercially or publicly (for example via GitHub or
PSGallery), signing what you publish is probably a good thing to do, preferably with a public
CA-issued certificate.

See `https://www.globalsign.com/en/blog/the-importance-of-code-signing-`
`redux` for some thoughts on the importance of code signing in general.

Whether or not you deploy code signing, it's useful to know how to do it.

Implementing Just Enough Administration

Just Enough Administration, also known as JEA, is a security framework providing you with the ability to implement fine-grained administrative delegation. With JEA, you enable a user to have just enough administrative power to do their job, and no more. JEA is a more secure alternative to just adding users to the Domain Administrator or Enterprise Administrator groups.

With JEA, you could enable a domain user to access your domain controllers for the purposes of administering the DNS Service on the server. With JEA, you constrain what the user can do on the protected server. For example, you could allow the user to stop and start the DNS Service (using `Stop-Service` and `Start-Service`) but no other services.

JEA makes use of a number of objects:

- JEA role capabilities file (`.psrc`): This file defines a role in terms of its capabilities. The JEA role `RKDnsAdmins` is allowed access to a limited set of cmdlets on the Domain Controller (those related to the role of administering DNS).

- JEA Role module: This is a simple module that holds the JEA role capabilities file within the module's `RoleCapabilities` folder. The module could be called `RKDnsAdmins`.

- JEA session configuration file (`.pssc`): This file defines a JEA session in terms of who is allowed access to the session and what they can do in the session. You could allow anyone in the `RKDnsAdmins` domain security group to access the server using the JEA endpoint. The session configuration file defines the actions allowed within the JEA session by reference to the role capabilities file. The JEA protected session can only be used by certain people who can do whatever the role capabilities file dictates.

Once you have these files and the module in place, you register the JEA endpoint to the server (and test the configuration).

Once the JEA endpoint is registered, a user who is a member of the domain security group called `RKDnsAdmins` can use `Invoke-Command` or `Enter-PssSession`, specifying the remote server and the JEA-protected endpoint to access the protected server. Once inside the session, the user can only do what the role capabilities file allows.

The following diagram shows the key components of JEA:

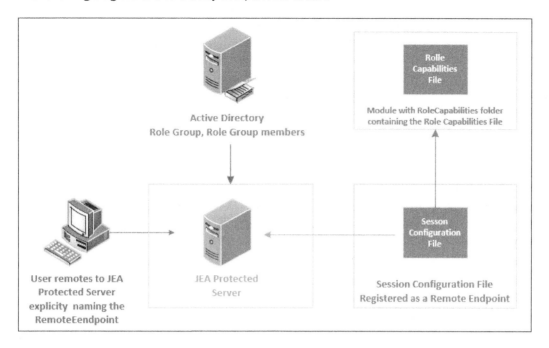

Getting ready

Before you use the recipe, you need to create the domain accounts and groups that you use in this recipe. This includes a user (JerryG) and a security group (RKDnsAdmins) which contains the user, with both of these under an Organizational Unit (IT). You installed the RSAT tools in the *Installing RSAT Tools on Windows 10* recipe on CL1—so you can run this step on either CL1 or on DC1. Creating these AD objects looks like this:

```
# Create an IT OU
$DomainRoot = 'DC=Reskit,DC=Org'
New-ADOrganizationalUnit -Name IT -Path $DomainRoot
# Create a user - JerryG in the OU
$OURoot  = "OU=IT,$DomainRoot"
$PW      = 'Pa$$w0rd'
$PWSS    = ConvertTo-SecureString   -String $PW -AsPlainText -Force
$NUHT    = @{Name                   = 'Jerry Garcia'
             SamAccountName         = 'JerryG'
             AccountPassword        = $PWSS
             Enabled                = $true
             PasswordNeverExpires   = $true
```

```
                    ChangePasswordAtLogon = $false
                    Path                  = $OURoot
}
New-ADUser @NUHT
# Create ReskitDNSAdmins security universal group in the OU
$NGHT  = @{
   Name         = 'RKDnsAdmins '
   Path         = $OURoot
   GroupScope   = 'Universal'
   Description  = 'RKnsAdmins group for JEA'
}
New-ADGroup -Name RKDnsAdmins -Path $OURoot -GroupScope Universal
# Add JerryG to the ReskitAdmin's group
Add-ADGroupMember -Identity 'RKDNSADMINS' -Members 'JerryG'
# Create JEA Transcripts folder
New-Item -Path C:\foo\JEATranscripts -ItemType Directory
```

How to do it...

1. On DC1, create a new folder for the RKDnsAdmins JEA module:

    ```
    $PF = $env:Programfiles
    $CP = 'WindowsPowerShell\Modules\RKDnsAdmins'
    $ModPath = Join-Path -Path $PF -ChildPath $CP
    New-Item -Path $ModPath -ItemType Directory | Out-Null
    ```

2. Define and create a JEA role capabilities file:

    ```
    $RCHT = @{
       Path              = 'C:\Foo\RKDnsAdmins.psrc'
       Author            = 'Reskit Administration'
       CompanyName       = 'Reskit.Org'
       Description       = 'Defines RKDnsAdmins role capabilities'
       AliasDefinition   = @{name='gh';value='Get-Help'}
       ModulesToImport   = 'Microsoft.PowerShell.Core','DnsServer'
       VisibleCmdlets    = ("Restart-Service",
                           @{ Name = "Restart-Computer";
                               Parameters = @{Name = "ComputerName"}
                               ValidateSet = 'DC1, DC2'},
                           'DNSSERVER\*')
       VisibleExternalCommands = ('C:\Windows\System32\whoami.exe')
       VisibleFunctions = 'Get-HW'
       FunctionDefinitions = @{
    ```

```
    Name = 'Get-HW'
    Scriptblock = {'Hello JEA World'}}
} # End of Hash Table
New-PSRoleCapabilityFile @RCHT
```

3. Create the module manifest in the module folder:

```
$P = Join-Path -Path $ModPath -ChildPath 'RKDnsAdmins.psd1'
New-ModuleManifest -Path $P -RootModule 'RKDNSAdmins.psm1'
```

4. Create the role capabilities folder and copy the role configuration file into the module folder:

```
$RCF = Join-Path -Path $ModPath -ChildPath 'RoleCapabilities'
New-Item -ItemType Directory $RCF
Copy-Item -Path $RCHT.Path -Destination $RCF -Force
```

5. Create a JEA session configuration file:

```
$P = 'C:\Foo\RKDnsAdmins.pssc'
$RDHT = @{
   'Reskit\RKDnsAdmins' = @{RoleCapabilities = 'RKDnsAdmins'}
}
$PSCHT= @{
   Author              = 'DoctorDNS@Gmail.Com'
   Description         = 'Session Definition for RKDnsAdmins'
   SessionType         = 'RestrictedRemoteServer'
   Path                = $P
   RunAsVirtualAccount = $true
   TranscriptDirectory = 'C:\Foo\JEATranscripts'
   RoleDefinitions     = $RDHT
}
New-PSSessionConfigurationFile @PSCHT
```

6. Test the JEA session configuration file:

```
Test-PSSessionConfigurationFile -Path C:\foo\RKDnsAdmins.pssc
```

7. Register the JEA session definition:

```
Register-PSSessionConfiguration -Path C:\foo\RKDnsAdmins.pssc
-Name 'RKDnsAdmins' -Force
```

8. Check what the user can do with configurations like this:

```
Get-PSSessionCapability -ConfigurationName rkdnsadmins -Username
'reskit\jerryg'
```

9. Create credentials for the user `JerryG`:

```
$U = 'Reskit\JerryG'
$P = ConvertTo-SecureString 'Pa$$w0rd' -AsPlainText -Force
$Cred = New-Object System.Management.Automation.PSCredential $U,$P
```

10. Define two script blocks and an invocation hash table:

```
$SB1   = {Get-HW}
$SB2   = {Get-Command -Name '*-DNSSERVER*'}
$ICMHT = @{
  ComputerName      = 'LocalHost'
  Credential        = $Cred
  ConfigurationName = 'RKDnsAdmins'
}
```

11. Invoke the JEA defined function (`Get-HW`) in a JEA session and do it as `JerryG`:

```
Invoke-Command -ScriptBlock $SB1 @ICMHT
```

12. Get the `DNSServer` commands in the JEA session that are available to `JerryG`:

```
$C = Invoke-command -ScriptBlock $SB2 @ICMHT | Measure-Object
"$($C.Count) DNS commands available"
```

13. Examine the contents of the JEA transcripts folder:

```
Get-ChildItem -Path $PSCHT.TranscriptDirectory
```

14. Examine a transcript:

```
Get-ChildItem -Path $PSCHT.TranscriptDirectory |
  Select -First 1 |
    Get-Content
```

How it works...

This recipe sets up a JEA endpoint on `DC1` and then uses that to demonstrate how JEA works. The recipe relies on a user (`JerryG`), who is a member of a group (`RKDnsAdmins`) in the IT organizational unit within the `Reskit.Org` domain. The recipe provides the user with the commands necessary to do the job of a DNS administrator, and no more.

In *step 1*, you create a temporary folder on DC1 that is to hold the role capabilities file, which you define in *step 2*. In *step 3*, you create a module manifest in the module folder. Then, in *step 4*, you create a folder for the Role Capacities folder inside the module and copy the previously created .PSRC file into this new folder. In *step 5*, you create the JEA session configuration file. There is no output from these five steps.

In *step 6*, you test the session configuration file, as shown here:

```
PS C:\foo> Test-PSSessionConfigurationFile -Path C:\foo\RKDnsAdmins.pssc
True
```

This step returns a value of True, which means the session configuration file can be used to create a JEA session.

With all the prerequisites in place, in *step 7* you register the JEA endpoint, like this:

```
PS C:\foo> Register-PSSessionConfiguration -Path C:\foo\RKDnsAdmins.pssc -Name 'RKDnsAdmins' -Force

    WSManConfig: Microsoft.WSMan.Management\WSMan::localhost\Plugin

Type            Keys                        Name
----            ----                        ----
Container       {Name=RKDnsAdmins}          RKDnsAdmin
```

In *step 8*, you check to see what commands (including aliases, functions, cmdlets, and applications) a user would have if they used this JEA endpoint. Because the role capabilities folder was set up to enable the user to have access to all the DNS server commands, there are a large number of DNS cmdlets available which are not shown simply to conserve space, like this:

```
PS C:\foo> Get-PSSessionCapability -ConfigurationName rkdnsadmins -Username 'reskit\jerryg'

CommandType   Name                                      Version    Source
-----------   ----                                      -------    ------
Alias         clear -> Clear-Host
Alias         cls -> Clear-Host
Alias         exsn -> Exit-PSSession
Alias         gcm -> Get-Command
Alias         gh -> Get-Help
Alias         measure -> Measure-Object
Alias         select -> Select-Object
Function      Add-DnsServerClientSubnet                 2.0.0.0    DnsServer
Function      Add-DnsServerConditionalForwarderZone     2.0.0.0    DnsServer
Function      Add-DnsServerDirectoryPartition           2.0.0.0    DnsServer
Function      Add-DnsServerForwarder                    2.0.0.0    DnsServer
...
Cmdlet        Restart-Service                           3.0.0.0    Microsoft.PowerShell.Management
Application   ipconfig.exe                              10.0.17... C:\Windows\system32\ipconfig.exe
Application   nslookup.exe                              10.0.17... C:\Windows\system32\nslookup.exe
Application   whoami.exe                                10.0.17... C:\Windows\system32\whoami.exe
```

The final task is to discover what a user can do in a JEA session. In *step 9*, you create a credential object for the `JerryG` user and in *step 10* you define hash tables for later use. These two steps produce no output.

In *step 11*, you invoke a script block that invokes the JEA-defined function `Get-HW`, which looks like this:

```
PS C:\foo> Invoke-Command -ScriptBlock $SB1 @ICMHT
Hello JEA World
```

In *step 12*, you calculate how many DNS commands are available within an `RKDNSAdmins` JEA session, like this:

```
PS C:\foo> $C = Invoke-command -ScriptBlock $SB2 @ICMHT |
                Measure-Object
PS C:\foo> "$($C.Count) DNS commands available"

131 DNS commands available
```

In *step 13*, you examine the contents of the JEA transcripts folder, which you defined as part of the session configuration file (for example in *step 5*). You can see the two transcripts created in response to the two calls to `Invoke-Command` (in *step 11* and *step 12*), like this:

```
PS C:\foo> Get-ChildItem -Path $PSCHT.TranscriptDirectory

    Directory: C:\foo\jeatranscripts

Mode            LastWriteTime    Length Name
----            -------------    ------ ----
-a----   10/09/2018      15:05      789 PowerShell_transcript.DC1.Ghn9VlHr.20180910150536.txt
-a----   10/09/2018      15:06    12831 PowerShell_transcript.DC1.Gp5N+WJN.20180910150539.txt
```

In *step 14*, you examine the contents of the first transcript (a result of *step 11*). In the transcript header, you can see that user `RESKIT\JerryG` remoted in as a virtual `RunAs` user using the `RKDnsAdmins` JEA endpoint on `DC1`. In the body of the transcript, you can see the call to the `Get-HW` function and the response. This transcript looks like this:

```
PS C:\foo> Get-ChildItem -Path $PSCHT.TranscriptDirectory |
    Select -First 1 |
        Get-Content
*************************
Windows PowerShell transcript start
Start time: 20180910150536
Username: RESKIT\JerryG
RunAs User: WinRM Virtual Users\WinRM VA_6_RESKIT_JerryG
Configuration Name: RKDnsAdmins
Machine: DC1 (Microsoft Windows NT 10.0.17733.0)
Host Application: C:\Windows\system32\wsmprovhost.exe -Embedding
Process ID: 5772
PSVersion: 5.1.17733.1000
PSEdition: Desktop
PSCompatibleVersions: 1.0, 2.0, 3.0, 4.0, 5.0, 5.1.17733.1000
BuildVersion: 10.0.17733.1000
CLRVersion: 4.0.30319.42000
WSManStackVersion: 3.0
PSRemotingProtocolVersion: 2.3
SerializationVersion: 1.1.0.1
*************************
PS>CommandInvocation(Get-HW): "Get-HW"
Hello JEA World
*************************
Windows PowerShell transcript end
End time: 20180910150536
*************************
```

If you compare this output with the output of *step 11*, you can see that the transcript is a more detailed examination of precisely what happened in the remote JEA session.

There's more...

The DNSServer module, which the recipe gives the RDDnsAdmins JEA endpoint access to, includes three aliases. Since these aliases are not explicitly allowed in the role capabilities file, they are not available in the JEA session.

In this recipe, you used Invoke-Command to run two simple script blocks in a JEA session. Once you have JEA set up on DC1 (or any other server for that matter), you can enter a JEA session like this:

```
#  Enter a JEA session and see what you can do
$ICMHT = @{
  ComputerName     = 'Localhost'
  Credential       = $Cred     # Reskit\JerryG
  ConfigurationName = 'RKDnsAdmins'
}
Enter-PSSession @ICMHT
```

Once in the remoting session, you can explore what commands are available to the JerryG user.

See also

In this recipe, you examined the transcripts generated by each remoting session. In addition to transcripts, PowerShell also logs the use of a JEA endpoint in the event log. For more information on event log entries and the general topic of auditing and reporting on JEA, see: `https://docs.microsoft.com/en-us/powershell/jea/audit-and-report`.

In this recipe, you used some of the key lock-down features provided by JEA. But there is more! For a fuller look at the things you can do with JEA and how to go about them, look at the JEA documentation beginning at: `https://docs.microsoft.com/en-us/powershell/jea/overview`.

2
Managing Windows Networking

In this chapter, we cover the following recipes:

- ► New ways to do old things
- ► Configuring IP addressing
- ► Installing and authorizing a DHCP server
- ► Configuring DHCP scopes
- ► Configuring an IP address from static to DHCP
- ► Configuring DHCP failover and load balancing
- ► Configuring DNS servers, zones, and resource records

Introduction

At the heart of every organization is the network—the infrastructure that enables client and server systems to interoperate. Windows has included networking features since the early days of Windows for Workgroups 3.1 (and earlier with Microsoft LAN Manager).

Many of the tools that IT pros use today have been around for a long time, but have more recently been replaced by PowerShell cmdlets. In the *New ways to do old things* recipe, we look at some of the old commands and their replacement cmdlets.

Every server or workstation in your environment needs to have a correct IP configuration. In the *Configuring IP addressing* recipe, we look at how to set a network interface's IP configuration, including DNS settings.

As an alternative to creating static IP addresses, you can set up a DHCP server to issue IP address configuration to clients by using the *Installing and authorizing a DHCP* server recipe. Once your DHCP server is set up, you can use the *Configuring DHCP scopes* recipe to set up the details that your DHCP server is to hand out to clients. In the *Configuring IP address from static to DHCP* recipe, we set a network interface to get IP configuration from DHCP.

In the *Configuring DHCP failover and load balancing* recipe, we deploy a second DHCP server and configure it to act as a failover/load balancing DHCP service.

In the final recipe of this chapter, *Configuring DNS zones and resource records*, we will configure the DNS server on DC1 with zones and additional resource records.

New ways to do old things

Networking IT pros in the Windows Server space have been using a number of console applications to perform basic diagnostics for decades. Tools such as Ipconfig, Tracert, and NSlookup are used by IT pros all over the world. The network shell (netsh) is another veritable Swiss Army Knife set of tools to configure and manage Windows networking components.

PowerShell implements a number of cmdlets that do some of the tasks that older Win32 console applications provided. Cmdlets, such as Get-NetIPConfiguration and Resolve-DnsName, are newer alternatives to ipconfig.exe and nslookup.exe.

These cmdlets also add useful functionality. For example, using Test-NetConnection enables you to check whether a host that might block ICMP is supporting inbound traffic on a particular port. ping.exe only uses ICMP, which may be blocked somewhere in the path to the server.

One administrative benefit of using cmdlets rather than older console applications relates to remoting security. With JEA, as discussed in the *Implementing Just Enough Administration* recipe in *Chapter 1, Establishing a PowerShell Administrative Environment*, you can constrain a user to only be able to use certain cmdlets and parameter values. In general, cmdlets make it easier for you to secure servers that are open for remoting.

This recipe shows you some of the new cmdlets that are available with PowerShell and Windows Server 2019.

Getting ready

This recipe uses two servers: DC1.Reskit.Org and SRV1.Reskit.Org. DC1 is a domain controller in the Reskit.Org domain and SRV1 is a member server. See the recipe *Installing Active Directory with DNS* for details on how to set up DC1 as a domain controller. You must run this recipe on SRV1.

How to do it...

1. Examine two ways to retrieve the IP address configuration (ipconfig versus a new cmdlet):

    ```
    # Two variations on the old way
    ipconfig.exe
    ipconfig.exe /all

    # The new Way
    Get-NetIPConfiguration
    ```

2. Ping a computer:

    ```
    # The old way
    Ping DC1.Reskit.Org -4

    # The New way
    Test-NetConnection -ComputerName DC1.Reskit.Org

    # And some new things Ping does not do!
    Test-NetConnection -ComputerName DC1.Reskit.Org -CommonTCPPort SMB
    $ILHT = @{InformationLevel = 'Detailed'}
    Test-NetConnection -ComputerName DC1.Reskit.Org -port 389 @ILHT
    ```

3. Use the sharing folder from DC1:

    ```
    # The old way to use a shared folder
    net use X:  \\DC1.Reskit.Org\C$

    # The new way using an SMB cmdlet
    New-SMBMapping -LocalPath 'Y:' -RemotePath '\\DC1.Reskit.Org\C$'

    # See what is shared the old way:
    ```

```
net use

# And the new way
Get-SMBMapping
```

4. Share a folder from SRV1:

```
# Now share the old way
net share Windows=C:\windows
# and the new way
New-SmbShare -Path C:\Windows -Name Windows2
# And see what has been shared the old way
net share
# and the new way
Get-SmbShare
```

5. Display the contents of the DNS client cache:

```
# The old way to see the DNS Client Cache
ipconfig /displaydns
# Vs
Get-DnsClientCache
```

6. Clear the DNS client cache using old and new methods:

```
ipconfig /flushdns
# Vs the new way
Clear-DnsClientCache
```

7. Perform DNS lookups:

```
nslookup DC1.Reskit.Org
Resolve-DnsName -Name DC1.Reskit.Org  -Type ALL
```

How it works...

In *step 1*, you examined the old/new way to view the IP configuration of a Windows host using ipconfig.exe and the Get-NetIPConfiguration cmdlet. First, you looked at two variations of using ipconfig.exe, which looks like this:

```
PS C:\Foo> ipconfig.exe

Windows IP Configuration
Ethernet adapter Ethernet:
   Connection-specific DNS Suffix  . :
   Link-local IPv6 Address . . . . . : fe80::295c:a764:6ffe:4ec7%7
   IPv4 Address. . . . . . . . . . . : 10.10.10.50
   Subnet Mask . . . . . . . . . . . : 255.255.255.0
   Default Gateway . . . . . . . . . : 10.0.0.10

PS C:\Foo> ipconfig.exe /all

Windows IP Configuration
   Host Name . . . . . . . . . . . . : SRV1
   Primary Dns Suffix  . . . . . . . : Reskit.Org
   Node Type . . . . . . . . . . . . : Hybrid
   IP Routing Enabled. . . . . . . . : No
   WINS Proxy Enabled. . . . . . . . : No
   DNS Suffix Search List. . . . . . : Reskit.Org
Ethernet adapter Ethernet:
   Connection-specific DNS Suffix  . :
   Description . . . . . . . . . . . : Microsoft Hyper-V Network Adapter
   Physical Address. . . . . . . . . : 00-15-5D-01-2A-68
   DHCP Enabled. . . . . . . . . . . : No
   Autoconfiguration Enabled . . . . : Yes
   Link-local IPv6 Address . . . . . : fe80::295c:a764:6ffe:4ec7%7(Preferred)
   IPv4 Address. . . . . . . . . . . : 10.10.10.50(Preferred)
   Subnet Mask . . . . . . . . . . . : 255.255.255.0
   Default Gateway . . . . . . . . . : 10.0.0.10
   DHCPv6 IAID . . . . . . . . . . . : 100668765
   DHCPv6 Client DUID. . . . . . . . : 00-01-00-01-23-20-49-92-00-15-5D-01-2A-68
   DNS Servers . . . . . . . . . . . : 10.10.10.10
   NetBIOS over Tcpip. . . . . . . . : Enabled
```

The Get-NetIPConfiguration cmdlet returns similar information, as follows:

```
PS C:\Foo> Get-NetIPConfiguration

InterfaceAlias       : Ethernet
InterfaceIndex       : 7
InterfaceDescription : Microsoft Hyper-V Network Adapter
NetProfile.Name      : Reskit.Org
IPv4Address          : 10.10.10.50
IPv6DefaultGateway   :
IPv4DefaultGateway   : 10.0.0.10
DNSServer            : 10.10.10.10
```

In *step 2*, you examined the `ping.exe` command and the newer `Test-NetConnection` cmdlet. Using these two commands to ping `DC1` (from `SRV1`) looks like this:

```
PS C:\Foo> Ping DC1.Reskit.Org -4

Pinging DC1.Reskit.Org [10.10.10.10] with 32 bytes of data:
Reply from 10.10.10.10: bytes=32 time<1ms TTL=128
Reply from 10.10.10.10: bytes=32 time<1ms TTL=128
Reply from 10.10.10.10: bytes=32 time<1ms TTL=128
Reply from 10.10.10.10: bytes=32 time<1ms TTL=128

Ping statistics for 10.10.10.10:
    Packets: Sent = 4, Received = 4, Lost = 0 (0% loss),
Approximate round trip times in milli-seconds:
    Minimum = 0ms, Maximum = 0ms, Average = 0ms




PS C:\Foo> Test-NetConnection DC1.Reskit.Org


ComputerName          : DC1.Reskit.Org
RemoteAddress         : 10.10.10.10
InterfaceAlias        : Ethernet
SourceAddress         : 10.10.10.50
PingSucceeded         : True
PingReplyDetails (RTT) : 0 ms
```

The `Test-NetConnection` cmdlet is also able to do some things that `ping.exe` cannot do, including testing access to a specific port (as opposed to just using ICMP) on the target host and providing more detailed information about connecting to that remote port, as you can see here:

```
PS C:\Foo> Test-NetConnection DC1.Reskit.Org -CommonTCPPort SMB

ComputerName     : DC1.Reskit.Org
RemoteAddress    : 10.10.10.10
RemotePort       : 445
InterfaceAlias   : Ethernet
SourceAddress    : 10.10.10.50
TcpTestSucceeded : True

PS C:\Foo> $ILHT = @{InformationLevel = 'Detailed'}
PS C:\Foo> Test-NetConnection DC1.Reskit.Org -port 389 @ILHT


ComputerName           : DC1.Reskit.Org
RemoteAddress          : 10.10.10.10
RemotePort             : 389
NameResolutionResults  : 10.10.10.10
                         10.10.1.30
MatchingIPsecRules     :
NetworkIsolationContext : Private Network
InterfaceAlias         : Ethernet
SourceAddress          : 10.10.10.50
NetRoute (NextHop)     : 0.0.0.0
TcpTestSucceeded       : True
```

In *step 3*, you examined new and old ways to create a drive mapping on the local host (that points to a remotely shared folder). The net.exe command, which has been around since the days of Microsoft LAN Manager, enables you to create and view drive mappings. The SMB cmdlets perform similar functions, as you can see here:

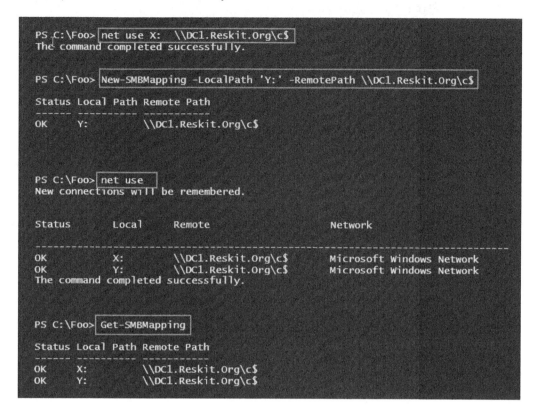

In *step 4*, you created and viewed an SMB share on `SRV1`, using both `net.exe` and the SMB cmdlets. This step looks like this:

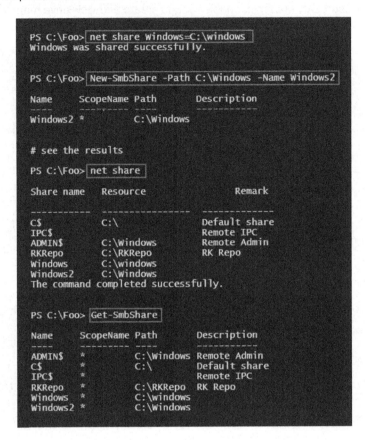

DNS is all too often the focus of network troubleshooting activity. The Windows DNS client holds a cache of previously resolved network names and their IP addresses. This avoids Windows systems from having to perform DNS lookups every time a network host name is used. In *step 5*, you looked at the old and new ways to view the local DNS cache, which looks like this:

```
PS C:\Foo> ipconfig /displaydns

Windows IP Configuration

    dc1.reskit.org
    ----------------------------------------
    Record Name . . . . . : dc1.reskit.org
    Record Type . . . . . : 1
    Time To Live  . . . . : 3494
    Data Length . . . . . : 4
    Section . . . . . . . : Answer
    A (Host) Record . . . : 10.10.10.10

    dc1
    ----------------------------------------
    Record Name . . . . . : dc1.Reskit.Org
    Record Type . . . . . : 1
    Time To Live  . . . . : 3568
    Data Length . . . . . : 4
    Section . . . . . . . : Answer
    A (Host) Record . . . : 10.10.10.10


PS C:\Foo> Get-DnsClientCache

Entry            RecordName      Record Status   Section TimeTo Data   Data
                                 Type                    Live   Length
-----            ----------      ------ ------   ------- ------ ------ ----
dc1.reskit.org   dc1.reskit.org  A      Success  Answer  3490   4 10.10.10.10
dc1              dc1.Reskit.Org  A      Success  Answer  3564   4 10.10.10.10
```

One often-used network troubleshooting technique involves clearing the DNS client cache. You can use `ipconfig.exe` or the `Clear-DNSClientCache` cmdlet, as shown in *step 6*. Neither the `ipconfig.exe` command or the `Clear-DNSClientCache` cmdlet produce any output.

Another troubleshooting technique involves asking the DNS server to resolve a DNS name. Traditionally, you would have used `nslookup.exe`. This is replaced with the `Resolve-DNSName` cmdlet. The two methods that you used in *step 7* look like this:

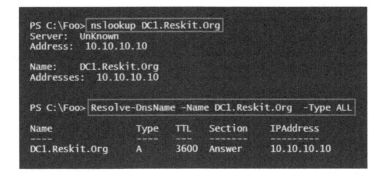

```
PS C:\Foo> nslookup DC1.Reskit.Org
Server:  UnKnown
Address: 10.10.10.10

Name:    DC1.Reskit.Org
Addresses: 10.10.10.10

PS C:\Foo> Resolve-DnsName -Name DC1.Reskit.Org  -Type ALL

Name            Type  TTL   Section  IPAddress
----            ----  ---   -------  ---------
DC1.Reskit.Org  A     3600  Answer   10.10.10.10
```

There's more...

In *step 1*, you looked at two ways of discovering a host's IP configuration. Get-NetIPconfiguration, by default, returns the host's DNS server IP address, whereas ipconfig.exe doesn't. On the other hand, ipconfig.exe is considerably quicker.

Ping is meant to stand for **Packet InterNetwork Groper** and has been an important tool to determine whether a remote system is online. ping.exe uses ICMP echo request/reply, but many firewalls block ICMP (it has been an attack vector in the past). The Test-NetConnection cmdlet has the significant benefit that it can test whether the remote host has a particular port open. On the other hand, the host might block ICMP, if the host is to provide a service, for example, SMB shares, then the relevant port has to be open. Thus, Test-NetConnection is a lot more useful for network troubleshooting.

In *step 2*, you pinged a server. In addition to ping.exe, there are numerous third-party tools that can help you determine whether a server is online. The TCPing application, for example, pings a server on a specific port using TCP/IP by opening and closing a connection on the specified port. You can download this free utility from https://www.elifulkerson.com/projects/tcping.php.

Configuring IP addressing

By default, Windows uses DHCP to configure any NICs that are found during the installation process. Once you complete the installation of Windows, you can use the settings application netsh.exe, or, of course, PowerShell to set IP configuration manually.

Getting ready

This recipe runs on SRV2.Reskit.Org. This host is a domain-joined system with an NIC that is initially set up to be configured from DHCP.

How to do it...

1. Get existing IP address information for SRV2:

```
$IPType = 'IPv4'
$Adapter = Get-NetAdapter |
  Where-Object Status -eq 'Up'
$Interface = $Adapter |
  Get-NetIPInterface -AddressFamily $IPType
$IfIndex = $Interface.ifIndex
$IfAlias = $Interface.Interfacealias
Get-NetIPAddress -InterfaceIndex $Ifindex -AddressFamily $IPType
```

2. Set the IP address for SRV2:

```
$IPHT = @{
  InterfaceAlias = $IfAlias
  PrefixLength   = 24
  IPAddress      = '10.10.10.51'
  DefaultGateway = '10.10.10.254'
  AddressFamily  = $IPType
}
New-NetIPAddress @IPHT | Out-Null
```

3. Set the DNS server details:

```
$CAHT = @{
  InterfaceIndex  = $IfIndex
  ServerAddresses = '10.10.10.10'
}
Set-DnsClientServerAddress @CAHT
```

4. Test the new configuration:

```
Get-NetIPAddress -InterfaceIndex $IfIndex -AddressFamily IPv4
Test-NetConnection -ComputerName DC1.Reskit.Org
Resolve-DnsName -Name SRV2.Reskit.Org -Server DC1.Reskit.Org |
  Where-Object Type -eq 'A'
```

How it works...

In *step 1*, you examined the current IP configuration for SRV2, which looks like this:

```
PS C:\foo> $IPType = 'IPv4'
PS C:\foo> $Adapter = Get-NetAdapter |
             Where-Object Status -eq 'Up'       |Select -First 1
PS C:\foo> $Interface = $Adapter |
             Get-NetIPInterface -AddressFamily $IPType
PS C:\foo> $IfIndex = $Interface.ifIndex
PS C:\foo> $IfAlias = $Interface.Interfacealias
PS C:\foo> Get-NetIPAddress -InterfaceIndex $Ifindex -AddressFamily $IPType

IPAddress              : 10.10.10.150
InterfaceIndex         : 4
InterfaceAlias         : Ethernet
AddressFamily          : IPv4
Type                   : Unicast
PrefixLength           : 24
PrefixOrigin           : Dhcp
SuffixOrigin           : Dhcp
AddressState           : Preferred
ValidLifetime          : 7.23:54:40
PreferredLifetime      : 7.23:54:40
SkipAsSource           : False
PolicyStore            : ActiveStore
```

In *step 2*, you set a static IP address for the NIC in SRV2, which produces no output. In *step 3*, you set the DNS server IP address, which also produces no output.

In *step 4*, you tested the new IP configuration, which looks like this:

```
PS C:\Foo> Get-NetIPAddress -InterfaceIndex $IfIndex -AddressFamily $IPType

IPAddress              : 10.10.10.51
InterfaceIndex         : 4
InterfaceAlias         : Ethernet
AddressFamily          : IPv4
Type                   : Unicast
PrefixLength           : 24
PrefixOrigin           : Manual
SuffixOrigin           : Manual
AddressState           : Preferred
ValidLifetime          : Infinite ([TimeSpan]::MaxValue)
PreferredLifetime      : Infinite ([TimeSpan]::MaxValue)
SkipAsSource           : False
PolicyStore            : ActiveStore

PS C:\Foo> Test-NetConnection -ComputerName DC1.Reskit.Org

ComputerName            : DC1.Reskit.Org
RemoteAddress           : 10.10.10.10
InterfaceAlias          : Ethernet
SourceAddress           : 10.10.10.51
PingSucceeded           : True
PingReplyDetails (RTT)  : 1 ms

PS C:\Foo> Resolve-DnsName -Name SRV2.Reskit.Org -Server DC1.Reskit.Org |
             Where-Object Type -eq 'A'

Name                Type   TTL   Section    IPAddress
----                ----   ---   -------    ---------
SRV2.Reskit.Org     A      1200  Question   10.10.10.51
```

There's more...

In *step 1,* you used the `Get-NetIPConfiguration` cmdlet. Two other closely related cmdlets that were not shown in the recipe are `Get-NetIPInterface` and `Get-NetAdapter`. Both provide additional information about the network adapter/network interface.

In *step 4,* you checked the IP configuration by using `Get-NetIPAddress` to show the IP address and subnet mask. You could have used the `Get-NetIPConfiguration` cmdlet to return the IP address and subnet mask, plus details of the default gateway and your DNS server IP address.

Installing and authorizing a DHCP server

In most organizations, your servers are configured with a static IP address configuration, but client computers can get IP addresses from a DHCP server. In Windows (and with most Linux, Macintosh, and mobile phones), the operating system contains a DHCP client that communicates with a DHCP server to obtain an IP address configuration (including the IP address, subnet mask, default gateway, and DNS server IP address).

Installing and authorizing a DHCP server is easy and straightforward. You can use Server Manager to achieve this. Server Manager, though, is a GUI that's layered on top of PowerShell. Alternatively, as you see in this recipe, you can use PowerShell to automate the installation and configuration of DHCP.

Getting ready

This recipe installs the DHCP service and the related management tools on the `DC1.` `Reskit.Org` computer. `DC1` is a domain controller in the `Reskit.Org` domain and is also a DNS server.

How to do it...

1. Install the DHCP server feature on `DC1`:

    ```
    Install-WindowsFeature -Name DHCP -IncludeManagementTools
    ```

2. Add the DHCP server's security groups:

    ```
    Add-DHCPServerSecurityGroup -Verbose
    ```

3. Let DHCP know that it's all configured:

```
$RegHT = @{
   Path  = 'HKLM:\SOFTWARE\Microsoft\ServerManager\Roles\12'
   Name  = 'ConfigurationState'
   Value = 2
}
Set-ItemProperty @RegHT
```

4. Authorize the DHCP server in AD:

```
Add-DhcpServerInDC -DnsName DC1.Reskit.Org
```

5. Restart DHCP:

```
Restart-Service -Name DHCPServer -Force
```

How it works...

In *step 1,* you used the `Install-WindowsFeature` cmdlet to add the DHCP server and the DHCP management tools, which looks like this:

```
PS C:\Foo> Install-WindowsFeature -Name DHCP -IncludeManagementTools

Success Restart Needed Exit Code     Feature Result
------- -------------- ---------     --------------
True    No             Success       {DHCP Server, DHCP Server Tools}
```

In *step 2,* you added the necessary DHCP security groups. By default, this cmdlet does not produce any output. If you want to see some additional output, you can use the `-Verbose` switch. If you do, the cmdlet produces a bit of output, as follows:

```
PS C:\Foo> Add-DHCPServerSecurityGroup -Verbose
VERBOSE: Adds DHCP users and DHCP administrators security groups on the DHCP server DC1
```

In *step 3,* you told Windows that the configuration of DHCP is complete. This step produces no output, but is needed to let DHCP know that the necessary security groups are complete.

Before a DHCP server is able to provide IP address information to DHCP client hosts, you need to authorize it in AD. You performed this in *step 4,* which produces no output.

With the last step, *step 5,* you restarted the service. Since you authorized the DHCP server in the AD, the DHCP service can now start. After restarting, you can configure the DHCP server with address details and DHCP option values to distribute to DHCP clients.

There's more...

In *step 1,* you installed the DHCP server service on your system using the `Install-WindowsFeature` cmdlet. In earlier versions of the Server Manager PowerShell module, the cmdlet was named `Add-WindowsFeature`. In Windows Server 2019, `Add-WindowsFeature` is an alias for `Install-WindowsFeature`.

In *step 2,* you used the `-Verbose` switch. When you use the `-Verbose` switch with a cmdlet, you can get some additional output that shows you what the cmdlet (or function) is doing. The amount of extra information returned when using the `-Verbose` switch depends on the cmdlet. Some cmdlets are remarkably terse and provide little or no extra verbose output. Other cmdlets provide more detailed verbose output.

In *step 4,* you authorized the DHCP server explicitly in the Active Directory. Authorization helps your organization avoid the potential for a rogue user setting up a DHCP server and handing out inappropriate IP address details. If you have multiple domain controllers, you may wish to force AD replication so that all DCs show this server as authorized. While the replication should occur pretty quickly, it never hurts to check the replication status before enabling the DHCP service (as you do in *step 5*).

Configuring DHCP scopes

In the previous recipe, *Installing and authorizing a DHCP server,* you installed and authorized a DHCP server on `DC1.Reskit.Org`. Before that server can begin to provide IP address configuration information to DHCP clients, you need to create a DHCP scope and DHCP options. A DHCP scope is a range of DHCP addresses that your DHCP server can give out (for a given IP subnet). DHCP options are specific configuration options your DHCP server provides, such as the IP address of the DNS server. DHCP options can be set at a scope level or at a server level, depending on the needs of your organization.

Getting ready

This recipe adds and configures a DHCP scope for your DHCP service on `DC1`. You installed the DHCP service and authorized it by completing the *Installing and authorizing a DHCP server* recipe.

How to do it...

1. Create a new DHCP scope:

```
$SHT = @{
  Name         = 'Reskit'
  StartRange   = '10.10.10.150'
  EndRange     = '10.10.10.199'
  SubnetMask   = '255.255.255.0'
  ComputerName = 'DC1.Reskit.Org'
}
Add-DhcpServerV4Scope @SHT
```

2. Get scopes from the DHCP server:

```
Get-DhcpServerv4Scope -ComputerName DC1.Reskit.Org
```

3. Set DHCP option values for the DHCP server:

```
$OHT = @{
  ComputerName = 'DC1.Reskit.Org'
  DnsDomain = 'Reskit.Org'
  DnsServer = '10.10.10.10'
}
Set-DhcpServerV4OptionValue @OHT
```

4. Get the options set:

```
Get-DhcpServerv4OptionValue -ComputerName DC1.Reskit.Org
```

How it works...

In this recipe, which uses the DHCP server module, you did some basic DHCP scope management. In particular, you created and updated a DHCP scope. In *step 1*, you created a new scope for the `10.10.10.0/24` subnet. There is no output from this step.

In *step 2*, you used the `Get-DHCPServerV4Scope` cmdlet to retrieve details of the scopes defined on `DC1`, which includes the scope that was set up in *step 1*. The output looks like this:

```
PS C:\Foo> Get-DhcpServerv4Scope  -ComputerName DC1.Reskit.Org

ScopeId       SubnetMask       Name      State     StartRange       EndRange         LeaseDuration
-------       ----------       ----      -----     ----------       --------         -------------

10.10.10.0   255.255.255.0   Reskit   Active    10.10.10.150   10.10.10.199   8.00:00:00
```

To enable a DHCP server to provide all the necessary IP configuration details to DHCP clients, you specified DHCP options. A DHCP option is a particular setting that the server can provide a client, for example, the IP address of a DNS server. You can set an option at the server level of a scope level, depending on your needs.

In *step 3,* you set two server-wide DHCP options, the DNS domain name (used in client DNS registrations), and the DNS server IP address. There is no output from this step.

In *step 4,* you used the Get-DHCPServerV4OptionValue cmdlet to see the server-wide DHCP options set on DC1, which looks like this:

```
PS C:\Foo> Get-DhcpServerv4OptionValue  -ComputerName DC1.Reskit.Org

OptionId   Name               Type        Value            VendorClass    UserClass     PolicyName
--------   ----               ----        -----            -----------    ---------     ----------
15         DNS Domain Name   String      {Reskit.Org}
6          DNS Servers       IPv4Add...  {10.10.10.10}
```

There's more...

In *step 1,* you created the scope using the New-DHCPServerV4Scope cmdlet. This creates a DHCP scope for the 10.10.10.0/24 subnet, which contains a range of IP addresses that the server can provide to DHCP clients coming from this subnet (that is, 10.10.10.150 – 10.10.10.199).

In *step 3,* you set an option and option value for the DNS server using the Set-DhcpServerV4OptionValue cmdlet. If you set a DNS server IP address, this cmdlet helpfully checks to see whether the IP address that's provided really is a DNS server (and returns an error message if so).

In this recipe, you created a simple scope for just one subnet that contained only two options. There is more complexity that you may encounter when scaling DHCP, including scope versus server options and client classes, which are outside the scope of this chapter. Nevertheless, the cmdlets used in this recipe form the core of what you might use in practice.

Configuring IP addresses from static to DHCP

In some cases, you may need to switch the IP address of a server from static back to DHCP. The server may have had a static IP address based on the role it used to perform a role, but you plan to repurpose this server and want to reconfigure the server to obtain IP configuration from DHCP.

Getting ready

This recipe uses SRV1 which, at the start of the recipe, has manual IP configuration, such as what you created in the *Configure IP addressing* recipe. In this recipe, you changed from static to DHCP configuration. Also, this recipe assumes that you have DHCP running based on the *Installing and authorizing a DHCP server* and the *Configuring DHCP scopes* recipes.

How to do it...

1. Get the existing IP address' information:

   ```
   $IPType = 'IPv4'
   $Adapter = Get-NetAdapter |
               Where-Object Status -eq 'up'
   $Interface = $Adapter |
                   Get-NetIPInterface -AddressFamily $IPType
   $IfIndex = $Interface.ifIndex
   $IfAlias = $Interface.Interfacealias
   Get-NetIPAddress -InterfaceIndex $Ifindex -AddressFamily $IPType
   ```

2. Set the interface to get its address from DHCP:

   ```
   Set-NetIPInterface -InterfaceIndex $IfIndex -DHCP Enabled
   ```

3. Test the results:

   ```
   Get-NetIPAddress -InterfaceIndex $Ifindex -AddressFamily $IPType
   ```

How it works...

In *step 1*, you checked the IP address assigned to SRV1, which is manually configured. The output of this step looks like this:

```
PS C:\Foo> $IPType = 'IPv4'
PS C:\Foo> $Adapter = Get-NetAdapter |
             Where-Object Status -eq 'up'
PS C:\Foo> $Interface = $Adapter |
             Get-NetIPInterface -AddressFamily $IPType
PS C:\Foo> $IfIndex = $Interface.ifIndex
PS C:\Foo> $IfAlias = $Interface.Interfacealias
PS C:\Foo> Get-NetIPAddress -InterfaceIndex $Ifindex -AddressFamily $IPType

IPAddress          : 10.10.10.50    ◀━━━━━━━
InterfaceIndex     : 7
InterfaceAlias     : Ethernet
AddressFamily      : IPv4
Type               : Unicast
PrefixLength       : 24
PrefixOrigin       : Manual    ◀━━━━━━━
SuffixOrigin       : Manual
AddressState       : Preferred
ValidLifetime      : Infinite ([TimeSpan]::MaxValue)
PreferredLifetime  : Infinite ([TimeSpan]::MaxValue)
SkipAsSource       : False
PolicyStore        : ActiveStore
```

In *step 2*, you set the NIC to get its IP configuration via DHCP. This step produces no output.

In *step 3*, you checked the results of changing back to DHCP, which look like this:

```
PS C:\Foo> Get-NetIPAddress -InterfaceIndex $Ifindex -AddressFamily $IPType

IPAddress          : 10.10.10.150    ◀━━━━━━━━━━━━━
InterfaceIndex     : 7
InterfaceAlias     : Ethernet
AddressFamily      : IPv4
Type               : Unicast
PrefixLength       : 24
PrefixOrigin       : Dhcp
SuffixOrigin       : Dhcp    ◀━━━━━━━
AddressState       : Preferred
ValidLifetime      : 7.23:59:03
PreferredLifetime  : 7.23:59:03
SkipAsSource       : False
PolicyStore        : ActiveStore
```

There's more...

In *step 3*, you obtained the IP address for SRV1 using Get-NetIPAddress. As noted in the *New ways to do old things* recipe, you could have used ipconfig.exe for a faster result.

Configuring DHCP failover and load balancing

The basic installation and configuration of a single DHCP server, as shown in the two previous recipes, is straightforward. However, a single DHCP server represents a single point of failure. A standard solution to this shortcoming is to implement DHCP Failover and Load Balancing. Microsoft added this to DHCP with Windows 2012. This feature, and indeed DHCP, is still provided with Server 2019.

Getting ready

This recipe requires two servers, with one server (DC1) set up with a working and configured DHCP scope. You achieved this by using the *Configuring and authorizing a DHCP server* and *Configure DHCP scopes* recipes. This recipe needs a second server (in this case, DC2. Reskit.Org).

How to do it...

1. Install the DHCP server feature on DC2:

```
$FHT = @{
  Name         = 'DHCP','RSAT-DHCP'
  ComputerName = 'DC2.Reskit.Org'
}
Install-WindowsFeature @FHT
```

2. Let DHCP know it's all configured on DC2:

```
$IPHT = @{
  Path  = 'HKLM:\SOFTWARE\Microsoft\ServerManager\Roles\12'
  Name  = 'ConfigurationState'
  Value = 2
}
Set-ItemProperty @IPHT
```

3. Authorize the DHCP server in AD and view the results:

```
Add-DhcpServerInDC -DnsName DC2.Reskit.Org
```

4. View the DHCP servers that are authorized in the domain:

```
Get-DhcpServerInDC
```

5. Configure DHCP failover and load balancing between DC1 and DC2:

```
$FHT= @{
  ComputerName       = 'DC1.Reskit.Org'
  PartnerServer      = 'DC2.Reskit.Org'
  Name               = 'DC1-DC2'
  ScopeID            = '10.10.10.0'
  LoadBalancePercent = 60
  SharedSecret       = 'j3RryIsG0d!'
  Force              = $true
}
Add-DhcpServerv4Failover @FHT
```

6. Get active leases in the scope (from both servers):

```
'DC1', 'DC2' |
    ForEach-Object {Get-DhcpServerv4Scope -ComputerName $_}
```

7. Now, get server statistics from both servers:

```
'DC1', 'DC2' |
ForEach-Object {
    Get-DhcpServerv4ScopeStatistics -ComputerName $_}
```

How it works...

In *step 1*, you added the DHCP server feature to DC2.Reskit.org, which looks like this:

```
PS C:\Foo> $FHT = @{
             Name         = 'DHCP','RSAT-DHCP'
             ComputerName = 'DC2.Reskit.Org'}
PS C:\Foo> Install-WindowsFeature @FHT

Success Restart Needed Exit Code     Feature Result
------- -------------- ---------     --------------
True    No             Success       {DHCP Server}
```

In *step 2*, you set a registry key to indicate to Windows that DHCP is fully configured. In *step 3*, you authorized this DHCP server in the AD. There is no output from either of these two steps.

In *step 4*, you viewed details about the authorized DHCP servers in the `Reskit.Org` domain, which looks like this:

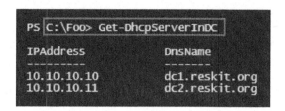

```
PS C:\Foo> Get-DhcpServerInDC

IPAddress                    DnsName
---------                    -------
10.10.10.10                  dc1.reskit.org
10.10.10.11                  dc2.reskit.org
```

In *step 5*, you configured DC1 and DC2 to be in a failover and load-balancing state. This step produces no output.

In *step 6*, you viewed the active leases on each DHCP server, which looks like this:

```
PS C:\Foo> 'DC1', 'DC2' |
             ForEach-Object {
               Get-DhcpServerv4ScopeStatistics -ComputerName $_}

ScopeId       Free   InUse   PercentageInUse   Reserved   Pending   SuperscopeName
-------       ----   -----   ---------------   --------   -------   --------------
10.10.10.0    47     3       6                 0          0
10.10.10.0    47     3       6                 0          0
```

There's more

In *step 2*, you set a registry key on the DHCP server that indicates that the DHCP server service is fully installed. If you install DHCP using the Server Manager (GUI), this step is performed automatically.

With *step 3*, you authorized this DHCP server in Active Directory. Without this step, the DHCP service on DC2 would never start up fully. This is intended to ensure that only authorized DHCP servers can hand out DHCP addresses. In *step 4*, you viewed the authorized servers in the domain.

In *step 5*, you set up DC2 as a failover and load-balancing DHCP server (with DC1 as the other partner in the relationship). As you can see in *step 6*, both DHCP servers are synchronized (with 3 addresses used and 47 free).

Configuring DNS servers, zones, and resource records

In *Chapter 3, Managing Windows Active Directory,* in the *Installing Active Directory with DNS* recipe, you installed a DNS server as part of the installation of AD. This enabled DC1 to be an initial DNS server that provided a home for the various DNS records that were created by AD for the Reskit.Org domain. Adding a DHCP scope with DHCP options that specify 10.10.10.10 (the IP address of DC1.Reskit.Org) means that DHCP clients use DC1 as their DNS server (and register their IP addresses with DC1).

After you perform these two recipes, DHCP clients receive IP address configuration, which includes a DNS server. Thus, DHCP clients can easily resolve IP address for each other and for the domain forest infrastructure (DNS resolution provides AD clients with IP address details for the domain controller and global catalog servers).

The DC installation process, combined with DNS auto registration, means that basic DNS operations just work for DHCP configured clients (and DCs). Each Windows client and Windows server registers its details with the DNS servers on DC1 for others to resolve. This provides a good, basic DNS infrastructure. If you have statically configured servers, you need to ensure that each host has properly configured DNS settings that are pointing to both DNS servers. The IP addresses you assign statically must not interfere with the IP address range(s) provided by DHCP.

Once you have your first DNS server up and running (and AD installed), you should add both a second DC to the domain (outside the scope of this chapter) and add a second DNS server (and update DHCP to ensure that clients are configured with the IP addresses of both DNS servers). Adding a second DNS server (and a second DC) provides resilience and continuity, should a DC/DNS server fail.

In this recipe, you add a second DNS server, update DHCP, and then add a new DNS zone and new resource records.

Getting ready

This recipe uses three systems: DC1 and DC2, and a client computer, CL1. DC1 is a domain controller with DNS installed, DC2 is a second domain controller, but without DNS installed, and CL1 is a Windows 10 system configured to be a DHCP client.

How to do it...

1. Add the DNS server service to DC2:

    ```
    Add-WindowsFeature -Name DNS -ComputerName DC2.Reskit.Org
    ```

2. Check that DC1 has replicated Reskit.Org to DC2 after installing DNS:

    ```
    $DnsSrv = 'DC2.Reskit.Org'
    Resolve-DnsName -Name DC1.Reskit.Org -Type A -Server $DnsSrv
    ```

3. Add the new DNS server to the DHCP scope:

    ```
    $OHT = @{
      ComputerName = 'DC1.Reskit.Org'
      DnsDomain    = 'Reskit.Org'
      DnsServer    = '10.10.10.10','10.10.10.11'
    }
    Set-DhcpServerV4OptionValue @OHT
    ```

4. Check the options on DC1:

    ```
    Get-DhcpServerv4OptionValue | Format-Table -AutoSize
    ```

5. On CL1, check the IP configuration:

    ```
    Get-DhcpServerv4OptionValue | Format-Table -AutoSize
    ```

6. Create a new primary forward DNS zone:

    ```
    $ZHT = @{
      Name              = 'Cookham.Reskit.Org'
      ReplicationScope  = 'Forest'
      DynamicUpdate     = 'Secure'
      ResponsiblePerson = 'DNSADMIN.Reskit.Org'
    }
    Add-DnsServerPrimaryZone @ZHT
    ```

7. Create a new IPv4 primary reverse lookup domain:

```
$PSHT = @{
  Name               = '10.in-addr.arpa'
  ReplicationScope   = 'Forest'
  DynamicUpdate      = 'Secure'
  ResponsiblePerson  = 'DNSADMIN.Reskit.Org'
}
Add-DnsServerPrimaryZone @PSHT
```

8. Check that both zones are available:

```
Get-DNSServerZone -Name 'Cookham.Reskit.Org', '10.in-addr.arpa'
```

9. Add an A resource record to the Cookham.Reskit.Org zone:

```
$RRHT1 = @{
  ZoneName        =  'Cookham.Reskit.Org'
  A               =  $true
  Name            =  'Home'
  AllowUpdateAny  =  $true
  IPv4Address     =  '10.42.42.42'
  TimeToLive      =  (30 * (24 * 60 * 60))  # 30 days in seconds
}
Add-DnsServerResourceRecord @RRHT1
```

10. Check the results of the resource records in the Cookham.Reskit.Org zone:

```
$Zname = 'Cookham.Reskit.Org'
Get-DnsServerResourceRecord -ZoneName $Zname -Name 'Home'
```

11. Check the reverse lookup information for DC2:

```
$RRH = @{
  ZoneName     = '10.in-addr.arpa'
  RRType       = 'Ptr'
  ComputerName = 'DC2'
}
Get-DnsServerResourceRecord @RRH
```

12. Add the resource records to the Reskit.Org zone:

```
$RRHT2 = @{
  ZoneName        = 'Reskit.Org'
  A               = $true
  Name            = 'Mail'
```

```
      CreatePtr      = $True
      AllowUpdateAny = $True
      IPv4Address    = '10.10.10.42'
      TimeToLive     = '21:00:00'
}
Add-DnsServerResourceRecord @RRHT2

$MXHT = @{
   Preference    = 10
   Name          = '.'
   TimeToLive    = '1:00:00'
   MailExchange  = 'Mail.Reskit.Org'
   ZoneName      = 'Reskit.Org'
}
Add-DnsServerResourceRecordMX @MXHT
$GHT = @{
   ZoneName = 'Reskit.Org'
   Name     = '@'
   RRType   = 'Mx'
}
Get-DnsServerResourceRecord @GHT
```

13. Test the DNS service on DC1:

```
Test-DnsServer -IPAddress 10.10.10.10 -Context DnsServer
Test-DnsServer -IPAddress 10.10.10.10 -Context RootHints
Test-DnsServer -IPAddress 10.10.10.10 -ZoneName 'Reskit.Org'
```

How it works...

In *step 1*, we started by adding the DNS server feature to DC2. The output from this step looks like this:

```
PS C:\Foo> Add-WindowsFeature -Name DNS -ComputerName DC2.Reskit.Org

Success Restart Needed Exit Code    Feature Result
------- -------------- ---------    --------------
True    No             Success      {DNS Server}
```

In *step 2*, you checked the DNS server on DC2 to ensure that it has replicated zone details from DC1 by checking to see whether DC2 can resolve DC1's IP address, which looks like this:

```
PS C:\Foo> $DnsSrv = 'DC2.Reskit.Org'
PS C:\Foo> Resolve-DnsName -Name DC1.Reskit.Org -Type A -Server $DnsSrv

Name                   Type   TTL   Section    IPAddress
----                   ----   ---   -------    ---------
DC1.Reskit.Org         A      1200  Question   10.10.10.10   <----
```

In *step 3*, which produces no output, you add DC2's IP address to the DHCP scope you created earlier. This enables DHCP clients to obtain the IP address of both DC1 and DC2.

With *step 4*, you checked on the DHCP options to ensure that the second DNS server address is configured as part of DHCP, which looks like this:

```
PS C:\Foo> Get-DhcpServerv4OptionValue | Format-Table -AutoSize

OptionId Name            Type        Value                         VendorClass UserClass PolicyName
-------- ----            ----        -----                         ----------- --------- ----------
15       DNS Domain Name String      {Reskit.Org}
6        DNS Servers     IPv4Address {10.10.10.10, 10.10.10.11}   <----
```

After configuring DHCP to issue both DNS server IP addresses with any leases from the DHCP service, you can validate this by running *step 5* on CL1 (a domain joined Windows 10 host set up for DHCP). The output looks like this:

```
PS C:\Foo> ipconfig /all

Windows IP Configuration

   Host Name . . . . . . . . . . . . : CL1   <----
   Primary Dns Suffix  . . . . . . . : Reskit.Org
   Node Type . . . . . . . . . . . . : Hybrid
   IP Routing Enabled. . . . . . . . : No
   WINS Proxy Enabled. . . . . . . . : No
   DNS Suffix Search List. . . . . . : Reskit.Org

Ethernet adapter Ethernet

   Connection-specific DNS Suffix  . :
   Description . . . . . . . . . . . : Microsoft Hyper-V Network Adapter #3
   Physical Address. . . . . . . . . : 00-15-5D-01-2A-71
   DHCP Enabled. . . . . . . . . . . : Yes
   Autoconfiguration Enabled . . . . : Yes
   Link-local IPv6 Address . . . . . : fe80::340b:dd6d:1a00:e5bd%11(Preferred)
   IPv4 Address. . . . . . . . . . . : 10.10.10.181(Preferred)   <----
   Subnet Mask . . . . . . . . . . . : 255.255.255.0
   Lease Obtained. . . . . . . . . . : 31 October 2018 14:18:53
   Lease Expires . . . . . . . . . . : 08 November 2018 14:25:47
   Default Gateway . . . . . . . . . :
   DHCP Server . . . . . . . . . . . : 10.10.10.11   <----
   DHCPv6 IAID . . . . . . . . . . . : 184554845
   DHCPv6 Client DUID. . . . . . . . : 00-01-00-01-23-07-54-79-00-15-5D-01-2A-2E
   DNS Servers . . . . . . . . . . . : 10.10.10.10   <----
                                       10.10.10.11   <----
   NetBIOS over Tcpip. . . . . . . . : Enabledbled
```

In *step 6*, you carried out some additional DNS maintenance by creating a forward lookup zone for `Cookham.Reskit.Org`. Then, in *step 7*, you created a new IPV4 reverse lookup domain. Neither step produces any output.

In *step 8*, you checked that these two zones are available, which looks like this:

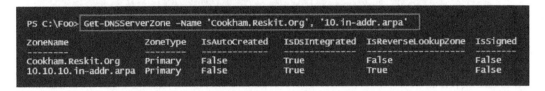

In *step 9*, you added a resource record for `Home.Cookham.Reskit.Org`. This produces no output. In *step 10*, you checked that the resource record(s) are available, which looks like this:

In *step 11*, you looked at the contents of the reverse lookup zone. Depending on how many hosts have registered with DNS, the output of this step may vary, but should look like this:

In *step 12*, you added an A resource record (for `Mail.Reskit.Org` and a mail exchanger (MX) resource record (pointing to `Mail.Reskit.Org`). Adding these two resource records to DNS creates no output.

In *step 13*, you tested the DNS service on DC1 by using the `Test-DNSServer` cmdlet. You used this cmdlet to test that the overall DNS service is up and running, is properly configured with root hints, and that the server is resolving addresses within the `Reskit.Org` domain. The output of this step appears as follows:

```
PS C:\Foo> Test-DnsServer -IPAddress 10.10.10.10 -Context DnsServer

IPAddress      Result   RoundTripTime TcpTried UdpTried
---------      ------   ------------- -------- --------
10.10.10.10    Success  00:00:00      False    True

PS C:\Foo> Test-DnsServer -IPAddress 10.10.10.10 -Context RootHints

IPAddress      Result   RoundTripTime TcpTried UdpTried
---------      ------   ------------- -------- --------
10.10.10.10    Success  00:00:00      False    True

PS C:\Foo> Test-DnsServer -IPAddress 10.10.10.10 -ZoneName 'Reskit.Org'

IPAddress      Result   RoundTripTime TcpTried UdpTried
---------      ------   ------------- -------- --------
10.10.10.10    Success  00:00:00      False    True
```

There's more...

In *step 1*, you installed the DNS service on DC2, which is a domain controller. When you installed Active Directory on DC1 in the *Installing Active Directory with DNS* recipe in *Chapter 3, Managing Windows Active Directory*, the installation process created a DNS zone for Reskit.Org, and set the replication to replicate to all DCs in the forest. Thus, when you install DNS on DC2, it should be able to immediately resolve the resource records for the Reskit.Org domain. As you can see, DC2 is able to resolve the addresses in the Reskit.Org zone on DC1.

In *step 3*, you adjusted the DHCP scope that was created in the *Configuring DHCP Scopes* recipe, which you then tested by first ensuring that the DHCP scope was configured with the IP addresses of both DNS servers and that a DHCP client was configured via DHCP with those addresses.

In *step 6*, you created a forward lookup DNS zone and, in *step 7*, you created a reverse lookup zone for the 10.0.0.0/8 set of IP addresses. In *step 8*, you checked that those two zones were up and running.

In *step 9*, you create an A resource record for Home.Cookham.Reskit.Org host and, as you can see in *step 10*, this resource record was successfully resolved.

In *step 11*, you examined the resource records in the 10.in-addr.arpa zone (that is, hosts with a 10.0.0.0/8 IP address).

In *step 12*, you added an A resource record for a mail server (Mail.Reskit.Org) and a MX resource record to point to the mail host. Hosts wishing to send mail to any user in the Reskit.Org domain (for example, ThomasLee@Reskit.Org) would be sent to Mail. Reskit.Org. Note that this DNS server (and the mail-related RRs) exist only inside the Reskit.Org network. If Reskit.Org is to receive mail from the internet, then you need to configure your external DNS zones with the appropriate mail server addresses.

These days, many organizations are moving to cloud mail, for example, Google's Gmail. In such cases, you should check with your cloud mail provider as to what resource records are to be set up and what they should contain. You also need to set up the **Sender Protected Framework** (**SPF**) to minimize spam coming from your domain. Setting up a mail server and configuring SPF records is outside the scope of this chapter. Look at https://support. google.com/domains/answer/6304562?hl=en-GB for an example of how you can set up mail security for G Suite (Google's cloud mail product).

3
Managing Windows Active Directory

In this chapter, we cover the following recipes:

- ▶ Installing Active Directory with DNS
- ▶ Creating and managing AD users, groups, and computers
- ▶ Adding users to AD via a CSV file
- ▶ Creating a group policy object
- ▶ Reporting on AD users
- ▶ Finding expired computers and disabled users in AD

Introduction

A core component of almost all organizations' IT infrastructure is **Active Directory** (**AD**). Active Directory provides access control, user and system customization, and a wealth of directory and other services.

Using AD Domain Services, you can deploy a series of domain controllers throughout your organization. Use the *Installing Active Directory and DNS* recipe to install a pair of domain controllers that also provides a DNS service for your newly created AD forest. In the *Creating and managing AD users* recipe, you create, move, and remove user objects, as well as creating OUs and groups and establishing membership of these AD objects. In the *Adding users to AD via a CSV* recipe, you use a comma-separated value file containing details of users you wish to add to the AD.

The group policy is another important feature of Active Directory. With the group policy, you can define policies for users and computers that are applied automatically to the user and/or computer. In the *Creating a group policy object* recipe, you create a simple GPO and observe applying that policy.

In the penultimate recipe, *Reporting on AD users*, you examine the AD to find details on users who haven't logged on for a while, computers that have not been used for a while, and users who are members of special security groups (such as *enterprise administrators*). The final recipe, *Finding expired computers and disabled users*, finds computer and user objects that have not been used in a while. This can help you to keep your AD free of stale objects.

Installing Active Directory with DNS

Installing Active Directory and DNS has always been fairly straightforward. You can always use Server Manager, but using PowerShell is really quite simple.

Getting ready

This recipe starts with two non-domain joined hosts, DC1 and DC2. Each host is running Windows Server 2019 with no tools loaded. After creating the initial forest and forest root server (DC1), you convert DC2 to be another domain controller that also runs DNS.

How to do it...

1. On DC1, install the AD Domain Services feature and the associated management tools:

    ```
    Install-WindowsFeature AD-Domain-Services -IncludeManagementTools
    ```

2. Install DC1 as the forest root domain controller in the DC1.Reskit.Org forest:

    ```
    $PSSHT = @{
      String      = 'Pa$$w0rd'
      AsPlainText = $true
      Force       = $true
    }
    $PSS = ConvertTo-SecureString @PSSHT
    $ADHT = @{
      DomainName                    = 'Reskit.Org'
      SafeModeAdministratorPassword = $PSS
      InstallDNS                    = $true
    ```

```
    DomainMode                    = 'WinThreshold'
    ForestMode                    = 'WinThreshold'
    Force                         = $true
    NoRebootOnCompletion          = $true
}
Install-ADDSForest @ADHT
```

3. Restart the DC1 computer:

```
Restart-Computer -Force
```

4. After rebooting, log back in to DC1 as Reskit\Administrator, then view the RootDSE entry on DC1:

```
Get-ADRootDSE |
  Format-Table -Property DNS*, *Functionality
```

The next part of this recipe runs on DC2. Based on the previous steps, DC1 is now a domain controller. DC2 begins as a workgroup server with no additional roles/features added:

1. Log on to DC2 and check that DC1 can be resolved and can be reached over 445 and 389 from DC2:

```
Resolve-DnsName -Name DC1.Reskit.Org -Server DC1 -Type A
Test-NetConnection -ComputerName DC1.Reskit.Org -Port 445
Test-NetConnection -ComputerName DC1.Reskit.Org -Port 389
```

2. Add the AD DS features to DC2:

```
$Features = 'AD-Domain-Services', 'DNS','RSAT-DHCP',
            'Web-Mgmt-Tools'
Install-WindowsFeature -Name $Features
```

3. Promote DC2 to be an additional domain controller in the Reskit.Org domain:

```
$URK = "Administrator@Reskit.Org"
$PSSHT = @{
  String      = 'Pa$$w0rd'
  AsPlainText = $true
  Force       = $true
}
$PSS = ConvertTo-SecureString @pssht
$CREDHT = @{
  Typename = 'System.Management.Automation.PSCredential'
  ArgumentList = "$URK,$PSS"
}
```

```
$CredRK = New-Object @CREDHT
$IHT =@{
  DomainName                      = 'Reskit.org'
  SafeModeAdministratorPassword = $PSS
  SiteName                        = 'Default-First-Site-Name'
  NoRebootOnCompletion            = $true
  Force                           = $true
}
Install-ADDSDomainController @IHT -Credential $CredRK
```

4. Reboot the DC2 host:

```
Restart-Computer -Force
```

5. After rebooting, log on to DC1 and view the forest:

```
Get-AdForest |
   Format-Table -Property *master*,global*,Domains
```

6. View the details of the Reskit.Org domain:

```
Get-ADDomain |
   Format-Table -Property DNS*,PDC*,*Master,Replica*
```

How it works...

In *step 1*, you install the AD Domain Services feature and the management tools (the PowerShell module and AD-related MMC consoles), which looks like this:

```
PS C:\> Install-WindowsFeature AD-Domain-Services -IncludeManagementTools

Success Restart Needed Exit Code     Feature Result
------- -------------- ---------     --------------
True    No             Success       {Active Directory Domain Services, Group P...
```

In *step 2*, you install DC1 as the forest root domain controller, which looks like this:

```
PS C:\Foo> $PSSHT = @{
   String       = 'Pa$$w0rd'
   AsPlainText = $true
   Force        = $true
}
$PSS = ConvertTo-SecureString @PSSHT
$ADHT = @{
   DomainName                      = 'Reskit.Org'
   SafeModeAdministratorPassword = $PSS
   InstallDNS                      = $true
   DomainMode                      = 'WinThreshold'
   ForestMode                      = 'WinThreshold'
   Force                           = $true
   NoRebootOnCompletion            = $true
}
Install-ADDSForest @ADHT


WARNING: Windows Server 2019 domain controllers have a default
for the security setting named "Allow cryptography algorithms
compatible with Windows NT 4.0" that prevents weaker cryptography
algorithms when establishing security channel sessions.

For more information about this setting, see Knowledge Base article
942564 (http://go.microsoft.com/fwlink/?LinkId=104751).

WARNING: A delegation for this DNS server cannot be created because
the authoritative parent zone cannot be found or it does not run Windows
DNS server. If you are integrating with an existing DNS infrastructure,
you should manually create a delegation to this DNS server in the parent
zone to ensure reliable name resol
ution from outside the domain "Reskit.Org". Otherwise, no action is
 required.

Message                      Context              RebootRequired Status
-------                      -------              -------------- ------
You must restart this compute... DCPromo.General.4               True Success
```

This step generates several warning messages. In this case, these warnings are benign and you can ignore them. After the DC promotion has completed, in *step 3*, you reboot the host. This generates no console output. Once you have rebooted DC1, in *step 4,* after you log on to DC1, you examine the RootDSE, which looks like this:

```
PS C:\Foo> Get-ADRootDSE |
           Format-Table -Property dns*, *functionality

dnsHostName    domainControllerFunctionality domainFunctionality forestFunctionality
-----------    ----------------------------- ------------------- -------------------
DC1.Reskit.Org                 Windows2016    Windows2016Domain   Windows2016Forest
```

In *step 5*, after logging in to DC2, you check to ensure that you can resolve the IP address for DC1 from DC2 and that you can reach the other DC over ports 445 and 389. If these checks fail, promoting DC2 to be a domain controller is also going to fail. The output of this step looks like this:

```
PS C:\foo> Resolve-DnsName -Name DC1.Reskit.Org -Server DC1.Reskit.Org -Type A

Name                                          Type  TTL   Section    IPAddress
----                                          ----  ---   -------    ---------
DC1.Reskit.Org                                A     3600  Answer     10.10.10.10
DC1.Reskit.Org                                A     3600  Answer     10.10.1.30

PS C:\foo> Test-NetConnection -ComputerName DC1.Reskit.Org -Port 445

ComputerName     : DC1.Reskit.Org
RemoteAddress    : 10.10.10.10
RemotePort       : 445
InterfaceAlias   : Ethernet
SourceAddress    : 10.10.10.11
TcpTestSucceeded : True

PS C:\foo> Test-NetConnection -ComputerName DC1.Reskit.Org -Port 389

ComputerName     : DC1.Reskit.Org
RemoteAddress    : 10.10.10.10
RemotePort       : 389
InterfaceAlias   : Ethernet
SourceAddress    : 10.10.10.11
TcpTestSucceeded : True
```

These tests show that DC2 can contact DC1 over key ports, so should be capable of being promoted to be a domain controller. In *step 6*, you add the ADDS features to DC2, as you did earlier for DC1. The output of this step looks like this:

```
PS C:\Foo> $Features = 'AD-Domain-Services', 'DNS','RSAT-DHCP', 'Web-Mgmt-Tools'
PS C:\Foo> Install-WindowsFeature -Name $Features

Success Restart Needed Exit Code     Feature Result
------- -------------- ---------     --------------
True    No             Success       {Active Directory Domain Services, DNS Ser...
```

In this step, you add some additional tools, including the RSAT DHCP tools. You have options as to how much you add at each point. In this case, you need the AD-Domain-Services and DNS Services features, whilst the others are optional.

With connectivity tests succeeding and the pre-requisites installed, in *step 7*, you promote DC2 to be another domain controller in the Reskit.Org domain, like this:

```
PS C:\foo> $URK = "administrator@reskit.org"
PS C:\foo> $PSS = ConvertTo-SecureString -String 'Pa$$w0rd' -AsPlainText -Force
PS C:\foo> $CredRK = New-Object system.management.automation.PSCredential $URK,$PSS
PS C:\foo> $IHT =@{
            DomainName                   = 'Reskit.org'
            SafeModeAdministratorPassword = $PSS
            SiteName                     = 'Default-First-Site-Name'
            NoRebootOnCompletion         = $true
            Force                        = $true
          }
PS C:\foo> Install-ADDSDomainController @IHT -Credential $CredRK
WARNING: Windows Server 2019 domain controllers have a default for the security setting named "Allow cryptography algorithms compatible with Windows NT 4.0" that prevents weaker cryp
tography algorithms when establishing security channel sessions.

For more information about this setting, see Knowledge Base article 942564 (http://go.microsoft.com/fwlink/?LinkId=104751).

WARNING: A delegation for this DNS server cannot be created because the authoritative parent zone cannot be found or it does not run Windows DNS server. If you are integrating with a
n existing DNS infrastructure, you should manually create a delegation to this DNS server in the parent zone to ensure reliable name resolution from outside the domain "Reskit.Org".
Otherwise, no action is required.

WARNING: Windows Server 2019 domain controllers have a default for the security setting named "Allow cryptography algorithms compatible with Windows NT 4.0" that prevents weaker cryp
tography algorithms when establishing security channel sessions.

For more information about this setting, see Knowledge Base article 942564 (http://go.microsoft.com/fwlink/?LinkId=104751).

WARNING: This computer has at least one physical network adapter that does not have static IP address(es) assigned to its IP Properties. If both IPv4 and IPv6 are enabled for a netwo
rk adapter, both IPv4 and IPv6 static IP addresses should be assigned to both IPv4 and IPv6 Properties of the physical network adapter. Such static IP address(es) assignment should b
e done to all the physical network adapters for reliable Domain Name System (DNS) operation.

WARNING: A delegation for this DNS server cannot be created because the authoritative parent zone cannot be found or it does not run Windows DNS server. If you are integrating with a
n existing DNS infrastructure, you should manually create a delegation to this DNS server in the parent zone to ensure reliable name resolution from outside the domain "Reskit.Org".
Otherwise, no action is required.


Message                                         Context           RebootRequired  Status
-------                                         -------           --------------  ------
You must restart this computer to complete the operation... DCPromo.General.4       True  Success
```

After completing the installation of DC2 as a domain controller, in *step 8,* you reboot the host which produces no output.

After DC2 has completed rebooting in *step 9*, log in and examine aspects of the Reskit.Org forest, like this:

```
PS C:\foo> Get-AdForest |
  Format-Table -Property *master*,globaL*,Domains


DomainNamingMaster SchemaMaster   GlobalCatalogs                          Domains
------------------ ------------   --------------                          -------
DC1.Reskit.Org     DC1.Reskit.Org {DC1.Reskit.Org, DC2.Reskit.Org} {Reskit.Org}
```

In the final step, *step 10*, you examine details about the Reskit.Org domain, like this:

```
PS C:\foo> Get-ADDomain |
           Format-Table -Property DNS*,PDC*,*master,Replica*


DNSRoot    PDCEmulator    InfrastructureMaster RIDMaster      ReplicaDirectoryServers
-------    -----------    -------------------- ---------      -----------------------
Reskit.Org DC1.Reskit.Org DC1.Reskit.Org       DC1.Reskit.Org {DC1.Reskit.Org, DC2.Reskit.Org}
```

There's more...

In *step 2*, you create DC1 as the first domain controller in the Reskit.Org forest. After the installation process completes, you must reboot DC1 before it can function as a DC, which you do in *step 3*.

In *step 4*, you examine the Root Directory Server Agent Service Entry or RootDSE in your domain. This entry, which is part of the LDAP standard as defined in RFC 2251 Section 3.4, enables an LDAP server to provide information about the capabilities of that server and the data that it contains to other LDAP servers and clients. This information is available without requiring any authentication. For more details on the RootDSE object and its attributes, see: https://docs.microsoft.com/en-us/windows/desktop/adschema/rootdse.

In *step 5*, you checked for connectivity on ports 445 and 389. With Windows Server 2019, port 445 is used for SMB file sharing, while port 389 is the port for LDAP. Domain-joined systems need access to these ports to access the domain controller for group policy details.

After completing the installation of AD on DC2, you need to reboot DC2, after which DC2 is a second domain controller in the Reskit.Org domain and is also a DNS server.

Creating and managing AD users, groups, and computers

Once you have created your forest/domain and your domain controllers, you can begin to manage the core objects in AD, namely, users, groups, and computers and **organizational units (OUs)**.

User and computer accounts identify a specific user or computer. These objects are used to enable the computer and the user to log on securely. Groups enable you to collect users into a single (group) account that simplifies the setting up of access controls on resources such as files or file shares. OUs enable you to partition users, computers, and groups into separate containers.

OUs serve two important roles in your AD. The first is role delegation. You can delegate the management of any OU (and child OUs) to be carried out by different groups. For example, you could create a top-level OU called UK in the Reskit.Org domain. You could then delegate permissions to the objects in this OU to a group, such as UKAdmins, enabling a member of that group to manage AD objects in and below the UK OU. Another OU, for example NA, could be delegated to a separate group, such as the North America Admins group (for example, NAAdmins). This enables you to delegate management.

The second role played by OUs is to act as a target for group policy objects. You could create a group policy object for the IT team and apply it to the IT OU. You could create a separate OU and create GPOs that apply to only the computer and user objects in that OU. Thus, each user and computer in a given OU are configured based on the GPO.

In this recipe, you create, update, and remove AD user objects as well as creating an OU and a security group, which you also populate. This recipe only creates and manages the AD objects. You assign a group policy in a later recipe, *Creating a group policy object*.

This recipe creates objects that are used in other recipes in this book.

Getting ready

This recipe assumes you have the Reskit.Org domain created, as performed in the *Install Active Directory with DNS* recipe, and you have two working domain controllers (DC1 and DC2).

Run this recipe to create and manage OUs, users, computers, and groups on DC1. Once you have created the various objects in this recipe on one DC, AD replication replicates those updates to the other DC, DC2.

How to do it...

1. Create a hash table for general user attributes:

```
$PW = 'Pa$$w0rd'
$PSS = ConvertTo-SecureString -String $PW -AsPlainText -Force
$NewUserHT = @{}
$NewUserHT.AccountPassword        = $PSS
$NewUserHT.Enabled                = $true
$NewUserHT.PasswordNeverExpires   = $true
$NewUserHT.ChangePasswordAtLogon  = $false
```

2. Create two new users, utilizing the hash table created in the previous step:

```
# Create the first user ThomasL
$NewUserHT.SamAccountName    = 'ThomasL'
$NewUserHT.UserPrincipalName = 'thomasL@reskit.org'
$NewUserHT.Name              = 'ThomasL'
$NewUserHT.DisplayName       = 'Thomas Lee (IT)'
New-ADUser @NewUserHT

# Create a second user RLT
```

```
$NewUserHT.SamAccountName     = 'RLT'
$NewUserHT.UserPrincipalName = 'rlt@reskit.org'
$NewUserHT.Name               = 'Rebecca Tanner'
$NewUserHT.DisplayName        = 'Rebecca Tanner (IT)'
New-ADUser @NewUserHT
```

3. Create an OU and move users into it:

```
$OUHT = @{
    Name        = 'IT'
    DisplayName = 'Reskit IT Team'
    Path        = 'DC=Reskit,DC=Org'
}
New-ADOrganizationalUnit @OUHT     # create the eOUI
$MHT1 = @{
    Identity   = 'CN=ThomasL,CN=Users,DC=Reskit,DC=ORG'
    TargetPath = 'OU=IT,DC=Reskit,DC=Org'
}
Move-ADObject @MHT1                 # move ThomasL into OU
$MHT2 = @{
    Identity = 'CN=Rebecca Tanner,CN=Users,DC=Reskit,DC=ORG'
    TargetPath = 'OU=IT,DC=Reskit,DC=Org'
}
Move-ADObject @MHT2                # Move Rebecca into OU
```

4. Create a third user directly in the IT OU:

```
$NewUserHT.SamAccountName     = 'JerryG'
$NewUserHT.UserPrincipalName = 'jerryg@reskit.org'
$NewUserHT.Description         = 'Virtualization Team'
$NewUserHT.Name               = 'Jerry Garcia'
$NewUserHT.DisplayName        = 'Jerry Garcia (IT)'
$NewUserHT.Path               = 'OU=IT,DC=Reskit,DC=Org'
New-ADUser @NewUserHT
```

5. Add two users who then are to be removed:

```
#   First user to be removed
$NewUserHT.SamAccountName     = 'TBR1'
$NewUserHT.UserPrincipalName = 'tbr@reskit.org'
$NewUserHT.Name               = 'TBR1'
$NewUserHT.DisplayName        = 'User to be removed'
$NewUserHT.Path               = 'OU=IT,DC=Reskit,DC=Org'
```

```
New-ADUser @NewUserHT


#    Second user to be removed
$NewUserHT.SamAccountName      = 'TBR2'
$NewUserHT.UserPrincipalName   = 'tbr2@reskit.org'
$NewUserHT.Name                = 'TBR2'
New-ADUser @NewUserHT
```

6. View the users that exist so far:

```
Get-ADUser -Filter * -Property *|
   Format-Table -Property Name, Displayname, SamAccountName
```

7. Remove via a Get | Remove pattern:

```
Get-ADUser -Identity 'CN=TBR1,OU=IT,DC=Reskit,DC=Org' |
   Remove-ADUser -Confirm:$false
```

8. Remove directly from the distinguished name:

```
$RUHT = @{
   Identity = 'CN=TBR2,OU=IT,DC=Reskit,DC=Org'
   Confirm  = $false
}
Remove-ADUser @RUHT
```

9. Update then display the user details:

```
$TLHT =@{
   Identity     = 'ThomasL'
   OfficePhone  = '4416835420'
   Office       = 'Cookham HQ'
   EmailAddress = 'ThomasL@Reskit.Org'
   GivenName    = 'Thomas'
   Surname      = 'Lee'
   HomePage     = 'Https://tfl09.blogspot.com'
}
Set-ADUser @TLHT
Get-ADUser -Identity ThomasL -Properties * |
   Format-Table -Property DisplayName,Name,Office,
                          OfficePhone,EmailAddress
```

10. Create a new group:

```
$NGHT = @{
  Name        = 'IT Team'
  Path        = 'OU=IT,DC=Reskit,DC=org'
  Description = 'All members of the IT Team'
  GroupScope  = 'DomainLocal'
}
New-ADGroup @NGHT
```

11. Move all the users in the IT OU into this group:

```
$SB = 'OU=IT,DC=Reskit,DC=Org'
$ItUsers = Get-ADUser -Filter * -SearchBase $SB
Add-ADGroupMember -Identity 'IT Team' -Members $ItUsers
```

12. Display the members:

```
Get-ADGroupMember -Identity 'IT Team' |
  Format-Table SamAccountName, DistinguishedName
```

13. Add a computer to the AD:

```
$NCHT = @{
  Name                   = 'Wolf'
  DNSHostName            = 'Wolf.Reskit.Org'
  Description            = 'One for Jerry'
  Path                   = 'OU=IT,DC=Reskit,DC=Org'
  OperatingSystemVersion = 'Windows Server 2019 Data Center'
}
New-ADComputer @NCHT
```

14. View the computers in the `Reskit.Org` domain:

```
Get-ADComputer -Filter * -Properties * |
  Format-Table Name, DNSHost*,LastLogonDate
```

How it works...

In *step 1*, you create a hash table of user properties to be set for the new user. You use this hash table in *step 2* to create two users. In *step 3*, you create a new OU and move users into the new OU. In *step 4*, you add a third user directly into the OU. In *step 5*, you add two further users to the AD. These steps produce no output.

In *step 6*, you retrieve and display all the users in the `Reskit.Org` AD, like this:

```
PS C:\foo> Get-ADUser -Filter *  -Property *|
            Format-Table -Property Name, Displayname, SamAccountName

Name            Displayname          SamAccountName
----            -----------          --------------
Administrator                        Administrator
Guest                                Guest
krbtgt                               krbtgt
ThomasL         Thomas Lee (IT)      ThomasL
Rebecca Tanner  Rebecca Tanner (IT)  RLT
Jerry Garcia    Jerry Garcia (IT)    JerryG
TBR1            User to be removed   TBR1
TBR2            User to be removed   TBR2
```

In *step 7* and *step 8*, you remove two users using different removal patterns. The first user is removed via a `Get | Remove` pattern in which you get an object with a `Get-ADUser` cmdlet and then pipe it to the `Remove-ADUser` cmdlet. The second is the direct use of `Remove-ADUser`. Neither step produces any output.

In *step 9*, you update a user then display the updated user, which looks like this:

```
PS C:\foo> Get-ADUser -Identity ThomasL -Properties * |
    Format-Table -Property DisplayName,Name,Office,
                      OfficePhone,EmailAddress

DisplayName     Name    Office      OfficePhone EmailAddress
-----------     ----    ------      ----------- ------------
Thomas Lee (IT) ThomasL Cookham HQ  4416835420  ThomasL@Reskit.Org
```

In *step 10*, you create a new domain local security group, `IT Team`, and in *step 11*, you populate the group membership with the users in the IT OU. Neither of these steps produces output.

In *step 12*, you display the users in the `IT Team` group, which looks like this:

```
PS C:\foo> Get-ADGroupMember -Identity 'IT Team' |
            Format-Table SamAccountName, DistinguishedName

SamAccountName DistinguishedName
-------------- -----------------
JerryG         CN=Jerry Garcia,OU=IT,DC=Reskit,DC=Org
RLT            CN=Rebecca Tanner,OU=IT,DC=Reskit,DC=Org
ThomasL        CN=ThomasL,OU=IT,DC=Reskit,DC=Org
```

In *step 13*, you pre-stage a computer account for a new host (`Wolf.Reskit.Org`), which produces no output. In *step 14*, you display all the computer accounts in the `Reskit.Org` domain, which looks like this:

```
PS C:\foo> Get-ADComputer -Filter * -Properties * |
                Format-Table Name, DNSHost*,LastLogonDate

Name DNSHostName       LastLogonDate
---- -----------       -------------
DC1  DC1.Reskit.Org    01/09/2018 13:39:08
DC2  DC2.Reskit.Org    01/09/2018 14:24:11
CH1  CH1.Reskit.Org    01/09/2018 20:07:12
CL1  CL1.Reskit.Org    03/09/2018 19:23:57
SRV1 SRV1.Reskit.Org   04/09/2018 13:10:23
SRV2 SRV2.Reskit.Org   04/09/2018 13:10:30
Wolf Wolf.Reskit.Org
```

There's more...

In this recipe, we use two different approaches to creating a user. In the first, you use `New-ADUser` to create a new user which, by default, AD places in the `User` container in the domain. Since AD containers are not subject to a group policy, you need to move the created user objects into the appropriate OU in order to enable group policy and management delegation.

The second method used in this recipe to create a user involves using the `PATH` parameter to create the new user directly in an OU. When you create a new user, placing the user into the correct OU is better than leaving it in the `Users` container, especially if you want to apply GPOs to apply GPOs to the user.

The same logic applies to computer objects. By default, new computer objects are placed in the `Computer` container. As with users, objects in the `Computer` container are not subject to GPOs.

If you install Windows 2019 on a computer and promote it to be a domain controller, the domain installation process moves the computer account into the `Domain Controllers` OU. Computers in this OU are subject to a default GPO, the *Default Domain Controllers policy*.

You are also, in due course, likely to need to move users or computers between OUs. For example, the user *Rebecca*, created in *step 2*, might have initially been in the IT organization, but due to a job change, she moves to a new organization. To support that job move, you move her user and computer accounts to a different OU and change her group membership. After she reboots her computer and logs in, she acquires permissions needed for her new job and her user/computer accounts are then subject to any relevant GPOs.

In *step 7* and *step 8*, you use two different methods for removing an object from the Active Directory (in this case, an AD user object). The first method is useful from the command line, where you first find the object(s) (using `Get-ADUser`) to be deleted, then pipe the results into `Remove-ADUser`.

The second way to remove an object is to use `Remove-ADObject` (or `Remove-ADUser` or `Remove-ADComputer`). Assuming you have the full distinguished name for the object to be removed, this is a bit faster. One risk of this approach is that you could accidentally type an incorrect DN into the command, resulting in the wrong user/computer being removed. To minimize this risk, consider configuring the AD recycle bin.

Joining a computer to the domain involves two specific steps: creating an account for the computer in the AD, then configuring the computer to be a member of the domain. If you build a new computer, you can log on as an administrator and join the computer to the domain, which achieves both of these steps. Alternatively, you could pre-stage a computer account (the first of the two necessary steps) then complete the domain-join process later.

In *step 13*, you pre-stage a computer account. This involves creating the AD account for a computer but without it actually joining the domain. This needs to be done using an account that has the necessary permissions. By default, this means a member of either the domain admins or the enterprise admins groups. After the computer account is created, you can complete the process of joining the computer to the domain (for example, by using the `Add-Computer` cmdlet). By pre-staging the account, a less privileged user can do the final step without the need for privileged domain credentials.

Adding users to AD via a CSV file

As mentioned several times in this book, `https://www.spiceworks.com/` has a busy PowerShell support forum (accessible at `https://community.spiceworks.com/programming/powershell`). A frequently asked (and answered) question is: How do I add multiple users using an input file? This recipe does just that.

Start with a CSV file containing details of the users you are going to add. This recipe uses a CSV file and adds the users into the AD.

Getting ready

This recipe assumes you have a domain setup and that you have created the IT OU. You did this in earlier recipes in this chapter. This recipe also requires a CSV file of users to add. You can create a CSV file like so:

```
$CSVDATA = @'
Firstname, Initials, LastName, UserPrincipalName, Alias, Description,
Password
S,K,Masterly, skm, Sylvester, Data Team, Christmas42
C,B Smith, CBS, Claire, Claire, Receptionist, Christmas42
Billy-Bob, Joe-Bob, Bob, BBJB, BBJB, One of the Bob's, Christmas42
Malcolm, DoWrite, Duelittle, Malcolm, Malcolm, Mr Danger, Christmas42
'@
$CSVDATA | Out-File -FilePath C:\Foo\Users.Csv
```

How to do it...

1. Import a CSV file containing the details of the users you wish to add to AD:

```
$Users = Import-CSV -Path C:\Foo\Users.Csv |
   Sort-Object -Property Alias
$Users | Sort-Object -Property alias |FT
```

2. Add the users using the CSV:

```
ForEach ($User in $Users) {
#    Create a hash table of properties to set on created user
$Prop = @{}
#    Fill in values
$Prop.GivenName          = $User.Firstname
$Prop.Initials           = $User.Initials
$Prop.Surname            = $User.Lastname
$Prop.UserPrincipalName  = $User.UserPrincipalName+"@reskit.org"
$Prop.Displayname        = $User.FirstName.trim() + " " +
$user.LastName.Trim()
$Prop.Description        = $User.Description
$Prop.Name               = $User.Alias
$PW = ConvertTo-SecureString -AsPlainText $user.password -Force
$Prop.AccountPassword    = $PW
#    To be safe!
$Prop.ChangePasswordAtLogon = $true
#    Now create the user
```

```
New-ADUser @Prop -Path 'OU=IT,DC=Reskit,DC=ORG' -Enabled:$true
#   Finally, display user created
"Created $($Prop.Displayname)"
}
```

How it works...

In *step 1*, you import the CSV file from `C:\Foo\Users.Csv`, which was noted in the *Getting ready* section of this recipe. Importing the CSV file generates no output.

In *step 2*, you iterate through the users in the CSV. For each user in the file, you first generate a hash table (`$Prop`) which you pass to the `New-ADUser` cmdlet to add the user to AD.

After you add each user, the recipe displays a message noting that the new user is now added to the AD. If you run the entire recipe as a single script, saved as `Add-UsersToAD.ps1`, and use the `C:\foo\Users.Csv` file created at the start of this recipe, then the output looks like this:

```
PS C:\Foo> Add-UsersToAD.ps1
Created Billy JoeBob
Created C Smith
Created Malcolm Duelittle
Created S Masterly
```

There's more...

The basic approach of adding a user based on data in a CSV is straightforward. There are many variations on this approach that you can take depending on your circumstances.

You can expand the data included in the CSV file to populate more user properties for each AD user. For example, you could include a cell phone number, office address, and much more. Another variation is extending the CSV file and including one or more security groups that should have the user added.

Creating a group policy object

Group policy allows you to define computer and user configuration settings that ensure a system is configured per policy.

With group policy, you first create a group policy object within the Active Directory. You then configure the GPO, for example, enabling computers in the IT organizational unit to be able to use PowerShell scripts on those systems. There are literally thousands of settings you can configure for a user or computer through group policy.

Once you configure your GPO object, you link the policy object to the OU you want to configure. You can also apply a GPO to the domain as a whole, to a specific AD site, or to any OU. A given GPO can be assigned in multiple places which can simplify your OU design.

The configuration of a GPO typically results in some data being generated that a host's group policy agent (the code that applies the GPO objects) can access. This information tells the agent how to work. Settings made through administrative templates use registry settings inside `Registry.POL` files. The group policy agent obtains the policy details from the `SYSVOL` share on a domain controller and applies them whenever a user logs on or off or when a computer starts up or shuts down.

The group policy module also provides the ability to create nice-looking reports describing the group policy object.

Getting ready

This recipe runs on the `DC1` domain controller that has been set up and configured in the three prior recipes in this chapter.

How to do it...

1. Create a group policy object:

   ```
   $Pol =
     New-GPO -Name ITPolicy -Comment 'IT GPO' -Domain Reskit.Org
   ```

2. Ensure that only computer settings are enabled:

   ```
   $Pol.GpoStatus = 'UserSettingsDisabled'
   ```

3. Configure the policy with two settings:

```
$EPHT1= @{
  Name      = 'ITPolicy'
  Key       = 'HKLM\Software\Policies\Microsoft\Windows\PowerShell'
  ValueName = 'ExecutionPolicy'
  Value     = 'Unrestricted'
  Type      = 'String'
}
Set-GPRegistryValue @EPHT1 | Out-Null
$EPHT2= @{
  Name      = 'ITPolicy'
  Key       = 'HKLM\Software\Policies\Microsoft\Windows\PowerShell'
  ValueName = 'EnableScripts'
  Type      = 'DWord'
  Value     = 1
}
Set-GPRegistryValue @EPHT2 | Out-Null
```

4. Create another GPO to disable the screen server, set the status, and add a description:

```
$Pol2              = New-GPO -Name 'Screen Saver Time Out'
$Pol2.GpoStatus    = 'ComputerSettingsDisabled'
$Pol2.Description = '15 minute timeout'
```

5. Set a registry value:

```
$EPHT3= @{
  Name      = 'Screen Saver Time Out'
  Key       = 'HKCU\Software\Policies\Microsoft\Windows\'+
              'Control Panel\Desktop'
  ValueName = 'ScreenSaveTimeOut'
  Value     = 900
  Type      = 'DWord'
}
Set-GPRegistryValue @EPHT3 | Out-Null
```

6. Assign the GPOs to the IT OU:

```
$GPLHT1 = @{
  Name      = 'ITPolicy'
  Target    = 'OU=IT,DC=Reskit,DC=org'
}
New-GPLink @GPLHT1 | Out-Null
$GPLHT2 = @{
```

```
    Name     = 'Screen Saver Time Out'
    Target   = 'OU=IT,DC=Reskit,DC=org'
}
New-GPLink @GPLHT2 | Out-Null
```

7. Display the GPOs in the domain:

```
Get-GPO -All -Domain Reskit.Org |
  Sort-Object -Property DisplayName |
    Format-Table -Property Displayname, Description, GpoStatus
```

8. Create and view a GPO report:

```
$RPath = 'C:\Foo\GPOReport1.HTML'
Get-GPOReport -Name 'ITPolicy' -ReportType Html -Path $RPath
Invoke-Item -Path $RPath
```

How it works...

In *step 1*, you begin by creating a group policy object. In *step 2*, you update the GPO to indicate the GPO object has computer settings only. Next, in *step 3*, you configure the policy with two settings. In *step 4* and *step 5,* you create a user GPO that sets values for the screen saver, which you apply in *step 6*. These steps produce no output.

In *step 7*, you display all the GPO objects in the Reskit.Org domain, which looks like this:

```
PS C:\foo> Get-GPO -All -Domain Reskit.Org |
            Sort -Property DisplayName |
              Format-Table -Property Displayname, Description, GpoStatus

DisplayName                        Description            GpoStatus
-----------                        -----------            ---------
Default Domain Controllers Policy                         AllSettingsEnabled
Default Domain Policy                                     AllSettingsEnabled
ITPolicy                           IT GPO                 UserSettingsDisabled
Screen Saver Time Out              15 minute timeout ComputerSettingsDisabled
```

In *step 8*, you create and view a GPO report. This report shows the details of the GPO object, including the settings configured by the GPO, which looks like this:

There's more...

Group policy is a rich topic—possibly one worthy of a book all of its own. In this recipe, you have seen the basics of creating, assigning, updating, and reporting on GPO objects. There is much more to group policy, including inheritance, backup/restore, export/import, and more.

See also

With the group policy administrative templates, there are literally thousands of settings that are available—each with a registry setting for you to use, as shown in this recipe. Finding the specific settings and their respective registry values can be hard work. To assist you, Microsoft publishes an Excel spreadsheet that lists the settings. You can find this at `https://www.microsoft.com/en-us/download/details.aspx?displaylang=en&id=25250`.

Reporting on AD users

Managing the Active Directory is an important albeit time-consuming task. Discovering a user account that has not been used for a reasonable period or a user that has membership in a privileged account (for example, enterprise administrators) could represent security risks to the organization. Regular reporting can help to place a focus on accounts that could be usefully de-activated. That could mean the account being removed from a security group or removed altogether.

This recipe creates a report of users, computers, and privileged group membership and displays this report on the console.

Getting ready

This recipe, which you run on `DC1`, reports on users with possible issues: a user hasn't logged on for a while, has made a lot of bad password attempts, or a user is in a privileged group inappropriately.

How to do it...

1. Define the `Get-ReskitUser` function:

```
Function Get-ReskitUser {
# Get PDC Emulator DC
$PrimaryDC = Get-ADDomainController -Discover -Service PrimaryDC
# Get Users
$ADUsers = Get-ADUser -Filter * -Properties * -Server $PrimaryDC
# Iterate through them and create $Userinfo hash table:
Foreach ($ADUser in $ADUsers) {
  # Create a userinfo HT
  $UserInfo = [Ordered] @{}
  $UserInfo.SamAccountname = $ADUser.SamAccountName
```

```
$Userinfo.DisplayName      = $ADUser.DisplayName
$UserInfo.Office           = $ADUser.Office
$Userinfo.Enabled          = $ADUser.Enabled
$userinfo.LastLogonDate    = $ADUser.LastLogonDate
$UserInfo.ProfilePath      = $ADUser.ProfilePath
$Userinfo.ScriptPath       = $ADUser.ScriptPath
$UserInfo.BadPWDCount      = $ADUser.badPwdCount
New-Object -TypeName PSObject -Property $UserInfo
}
} # end of function
```

2. Get the users in the `Reskit.Org` domain:

```
$RKUsers = Get-ReskitUser
# Build the report header:
$RKReport = ''
$RkReport += "*** Reskit.Org AD Report`n"
$RKReport += "*** Generated [$(Get-Date)]`n"
$RKReport += "******************************`n`n"
```

3. Report on the disabled users:

```
$RkReport += "*** Disabled Users`n"
$RKReport += $RKUsers |
  Where-Object {$_.Enabled -NE $true} |
    Format-Table -Property SamAccountName, Displayname |
      Out-String
```

4. Report on the users who have not recently logged on:

```
$OneWeekAgo = (Get-Date).AddDays(-7)
$RKReport += "`n*** Users Not logged in since $OneWeekAgo`n"
$RkReport += $RKUsers |
  Where-Object {$_.Enabled -and $_.LastLogonDate -le $OneWeekAgo} |
    Sort-Object -Property LastlogonDate |
      Format-Table -Property SamAccountName,lastlogondate |
        Out-String
```

5. Users with high invalid password attempts:

```
$RKReport += "`n*** High Number of Bad Password Attempts`n"
$RKReport += $RKUsers | Where-Object BadPwdCount -ge 5 |
  Format-Table -Property SamAccountName, BadPwdCount |
    Out-String
```

6. Add another report header line for this part of the report and create an empty array of privileged users:

```
$RKReport += "`n*** Privileged  User Report`n"
$PUsers = @()
```

7. Query the enterprise admins/domain admins/schema admins groups for members and add to the `$Pusers` array:

```
# Get Enterprise Admins group members
$Members =
  Get-ADGroupMember -Identity 'Enterprise Admins' -Recursive |
    Sort-Object -Property Name
$PUsers += foreach ($Member in $Members) {
  Get-ADUser -Identity $Member.SID -Properties * |
    Select-Object -Property Name,
      @{Name='Group';expression={'Enterprise Admins'}},
        whenCreated,LastlogonDate
}
# Get Domain Admins group members
$Members =
  Get-ADGroupMember -Identity 'Domain Admins' -Recursive |
    Sort-Object -Property Name
$PUsers += Foreach ($Member in $Members)
  {Get-ADUser -Identity $member.SID -Properties * |
    Select-Object -Property Name,
      @{Name='Group';expression={'Domain Admins'}},
        WhenCreated, Lastlogondate,SamAccountName
}
# Get Schema Admins members
$Members =
  Get-ADGroupMember -Identity 'Schema Admins' -Recursive |
    Sort-Object Name
$PUsers += Foreach ($Member in $Members) {
  Get-ADUser -Identity $member.SID -Properties * |
    Select-Object -Property Name,
      @{Name='Group';expression={'Schema Admins'}},
        WhenCreated, Lastlogondate,SamAccountName
}
```

8. Add the special users to the report:

```
$RKReport += $PUsers | Out-String
```

9. Display the report to the console:

```
$RKReport
```

How it works...

This report writing recipe begins with *step 1* defining a function that returns some of the key properties of users in the `Reskit.Org` domain. In *step 2*, you invoke the function to return an array of all the users defined in the domain. These two steps produce no output.

In *step 2* through *step 9,* you build parts of the overall report and add it to the `$RKReport` variable. These steps also produce no output.

In *step 10,* you display the report to the console, which looks like this:

```
PS C:\foo> $RKReport

*** Reskit.Org AD Report
*** Generated [09/13/2018 06:45:59]
********************************

*** Disabled Users

SamAccountname      DisplayName
--------------      -----------
Guest
krbtgt
SueBob              SueBob JoeBob

*** Users Not logged in since 09/13/2018 12:45:59

SamAccountname LastLogonDate
-------------- -------------
RLT            23/08/2018 16:10:06
Claire         14/06/2018 11:14:51   <---
Sylvester      28/08/2018 02:26:09
JaneBob        20/04/2017 15:23:42   <---

*** High Number of Bad Password Attempts

SamAccountname BadPwDCount
-------------- -----------
ThomasL              6
Claire             218   <---

*** Privileged Group Members

Name           Group             whenCreated           LastlogonDate
----           -----             -----------           -------------
Administrator  Enterprise Admins 01/03/2016 13:04:04   12/09/2018 23:32:45
BillyBob       Enterprise Admins 01/08/2017 08:32:21   12/09.2018 04:00:20
Administrator  Domain Admins     01/09/2018 13:04:04   12/09/2018 23:32:45
BillyBob       Domain Admins     01/08/2017 08:32:21   12/09/2018 04:00:20
Administrator  Schema Admins     01/09/2018 13:04:04   12/09/2018 23:32:45
```

There's more...

In this recipe, you create the report and display it to the console. There are some things you could do that might increase the value of this recipe:

- Save the recipe as a script, then set up a scheduled task to invoke it every day
- Create an SMB share on the DC and save each report to that folder or email it to a mail-enabled group
- Automatically disable any account that has not been in use for, say, 30 days, sending mail to the user's manager letting them know
- Create a list of users authorized to be in the high-privilege groups and ensure the group contains only those members
- Adjust the recipe to output HTML to improve the readability and usability of the report

This recipe calls `Get-ADUser` several times in *step 7*, returning all properties. You might consider some optimization including restricting the properties to only those needed to generate the report.

Finding expired computers and disabled users in AD

The objects in your AD database—the users, computers, groups, OUs, policies, and so on, are constantly changing in almost all organizations. Users leave, computers die, OUs and policies are added/removed/renamed, and so on. Change is constant!

A side effect of this change is having orphaned objects: users who are no longer part of your organization, or computers that no longer actually exist physically. You can also find you have objects that may be valid but have not been used for a long time.

Those accounts represent a potential security risk. An unused user account, for example, due to a user leaving and their account not being removed, can represent a threat vector. Suppose Ruth in the accounting department (who has access to the firm's accounting data) has left. If her account is active, then someone guessing her password could attempt to use her credentials to access such information. The risk is magnified if Ruth could access that information from the internet.

Any expired computers (that is, ones that have not logged in for a long time) may no longer have a machine password synced with AD). This means the computer is probably not getting WSUS updates or GPO-based policies.

This recipe finds computers that have not been used and users that have not logged in for a month. The recipe then generates a nice report and saves that report to a file in a corporate file share for you and others to look at.

Getting ready

Run this recipe on DC1. Ideally, your domain should have enough users and computers created and configured.

How to do it...

1. Build the report header:

```
$RKReport = ''
$RkReport += "*** Reskit.Org AD Daily AD report`n"
$RKReport += "*** Generated [$(Get-Date)]`n"
$RKReport += "**********************************`n`n"
```

2. Report on the computer accounts that have not logged in the past month:

```
$RkReport += "*** Machines not logged on in past month`n"
$AMonthAgo = (Get-Date).AddMonths(-1)
$ADCHT2 = @{
  Properties = 'lastLogonDate'
  Filter     = 'lastLogonDate -lt $AMonthAgo'
}
$RkReport += Get-ADComputer @ADCHT2 |
  Sort-Object -Property lastLogonDate |
    Format-Table -Property Name, LastLogonDate |
      Out-String
```

3. Get the users who have not logged on in the past month:

```
$RKReport += "*** Users not logged on in past month`n"
$RkReport += Get-AdUser @ADCHT2 |
  Sort-Object -Property lastLogonDate |
    Format-Table -Property Name, LastLogonDate |
      Out-String
```

4. Find any user accounts that are disabled:

```
$ADCHT3 = @{
  Properties = 'Enabled'
}
$RKReport += "*** Disabled Users`n"
$RkReport += Get-ADUser @Adcht3 -Filter {Enabled -ne $true}|
            Sort-Object -Property lastLogonDate |
              Format-Table -Property Name, LastLogonDate |
                Out-String
```

5. Display the report:

```
$RKReport
```

How it works...

In *step 1*, you build a header for your report. In *step 2*, you add a list of computer accounts that have not signed on recently, and in *step 3*, you list the users who have not logged in for a while. In *step 4*, you add to the report details of disabled accounts. These first four steps produce no output.

In *step 5*, you display the report, which looks like this:

There's more...

In *step 5*, you can see some things to consider in the report. One user has not logged on for a very long time (and her system hasn't either). You can also see users who are disabled. The first two (Guest and krbtgt) are normal and are to be expected. The final entry shows a user who is disabled and has not logged on for a very long time. Both user accounts should be reviewed to see if they are still needed by the business.

4

Managing Windows Storage

In this chapter, we cover the following recipes:

- ▶ Managing physical disks and disk volumes
- ▶ Managing NTFS permissions
- ▶ Managing Storage Replica
- ▶ Managing Filestore quotas
- ▶ Using filesystem reporting

Introduction

Windows Server 2019 provides a range of features that allows access to a wide variety of storage and storage devices. Windows supports spinning disks, USB memory sticks, and SSD devices (including MVMe SSD devices).

Before a disk can be used, you need to create partitions or volumes on the device, then format the volume. When you first initialize a disk, you need to define which partitioning method to use. You have two choices: **Master Boot Record** (**MBR**) or **GUID Partition Table** (**GPT**). For a good discussion of the differences between these two mechanisms, see: https://www.howtogeek.com/193669/whats-the-difference-between-gpt-and-mbr-when-partitioning-a-drive/.

With a volume created, you can then format the disk volume. Windows supports five key filesystems you can use: ReFS, NTFS, exFAT, UDF, and FAT32. For details of the latter four, see: `https://docs.microsoft.com/en-us/windows/desktop/fileio/filesystem-functionality-comparison`. The ReFS filesystem is newer and is based on NFTS, but lacks some features a file server might need (it has no encrypted files). For a comparison between the ReFS and NTFS filesystems, see: `https://www.iperiusbackup.net/en/refs-vs-ntfs-differences-and-performance-comparison-when-to-use/`. You examine partitioning and formatting volumes in the *Managing physical disks and disk volumes* recipe.

NTFS (and ReFS) volumes allow you to create **access control lists** (**ACLs**) that control access to files and folders stored in Windows volumes. Managing ACLs is somewhat difficult and lacks rich PowerShell support. To manage ACLs on NTFS volumes, as you will see in the *Managing NTFS permissions* recipe, you can download and use a third-party module, `NTFSecurity`.

The **Windows File Server Resource Manager** (**FSRM**) feature in Windows Server 2019 helps you to manage filestore resources. With FSRM, you can set Filestore quotas. With soft quotas, users can exceed their Filestore quota and administrators are notified when this occurs. With hard quotas, users are prohibited from storing more than their allocated quotas. You'll work with quotas in the *Managing Filestore quotas* recipe.

FSRM also supports detailed file server reporting, which you examine in the *Using filesystem reporting* recipe. These reports, and the supporting XML files, can provide assistance in managing and controlling file servers.

This chapter, specifically the *Managing Filestore quotas* recipe, makes use of a free email account from `Sendgrid.com`. This enables you to set up the Windows SMTP server to forward mail to SendGrid for onward transmission. This could be a great way to test reporting or to avoid issues with internal SMTP servers.

Managing physical disks and disk volumes

Windows Server 2019 requires a computer with at least one disk drive (that is, the C:\ drive). A disk drive can be connected via different bus types, such as IDE, SATA, SAS, or USB. Before you can utilize a disk in Windows, you need to initialize it and create volumes or partitions.

There are two partitioning schemes you can use: the older format of MBR, and the newer GPT. The MBR scheme, first introduced with the PC DOS 2 in 1983, had a number of restrictions. For example, the largest partition supported with MBR is just 2 TB. And creating more than four partitions required you to create an extended partition and create additional partitions inside the extended partition. The GPT scheme provides much larger drives (partition limits are OS-imposed), as well as up to 128 partitions per drive.

In this recipe, you add two new disk devices to a server, SRV1, and then create new volumes/partitions on those disks.

Getting ready

You run this recipe on SRV1. To perform this recipe, SRV1 needs two additional disks. If you're using a Hyper-V VM to test this recipe, you can use the following script to add the necessary disks. Run this on your Hyper-V Host that runs the SRV1 VM:

```
# Create Virtual Disks to add to SRV1
New-VHD  -Path D:\v6\SRV1\SRV1-F.vhdx -SizeBytes 20gb -Dynamic
New-VHD  -Path D:\v6\SRV1\SRV1-G.vhdx -SizeBytes 20gb -Dynamic
# Add them to the VM
$HDHT1 = @{
  VMName           = 'SRV1'
  Path             = 'D:\v6\SRV1\SRV1-F.vhdx'
  ControllerType   = 'SCSI'
  ControllerNumber = 0
}
Add-VMHardDiskDrive @HDHT1
$HDHT2 = @{
  VMName           = 'SRV1'
  Path             = 'D:\v6\SRV1\SRV1-G.vhdx'
  ControllerType   = 'SCSI'
  ControllerNumber = 0
}
Add-VMHardDiskDrive @HDHT2
```

The GitHub repository for this book contains a script, `Add-DiskstoSrv1+2.ps1`, which creates the disks used in this and other recipes in this chapter. Once you've added the (virtual) disks to the `SRV1` server, you can use **Disk Management**, a **Control Panel** applet, to view the starting disk configuration for this recipe, like this:

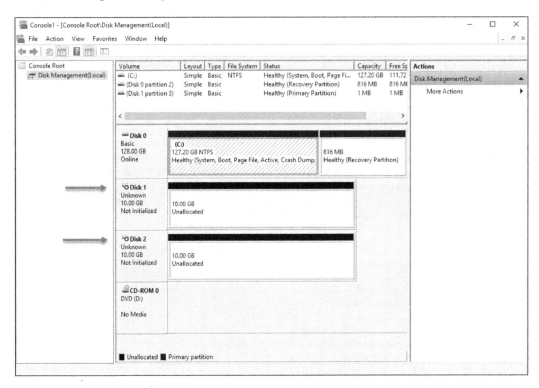

How to do it...

1. Get physical disks on this system:

```
Get-Disk |
   Format-Table -AutoSize
```

2. Initialize the disks:

```
Get-Disk |
  Where PartitionStyle -eq Raw |
    Initialize-Disk -PartitionStyle GPT
```

3. Redisplay the disks on SRV1:

```
Get-Disk |
   Format-Table -AutoSize
```

4. Create a volume in Disk 1:

```
$NVHT1 = @{
   DiskNumber   =  1
   FriendlyName = 'Storage(F)'
   FileSystem   = 'NTFS'
   DriveLetter  = 'F'
}
New-Volume @NVHT1
```

5. Create two volumes in disk 2—first, create G:

```
New-Partition -DiskNumber 2  -DriveLetter G -Size 4gb
```

6. Create a second partition, H:

```
New-Partition -DiskNumber 2  -DriveLetter H -UseMaximumSize
```

7. Format the G: and H: drives:

```
$NVHT1 = @{
   DriveLetter        = 'G'
   FileSystem         = 'NTFS'
   NewFileSystemLabel = 'Log'}
Format-Volume @NVHT1
$NVHT2 = @{
   DriveLetter        = 'H'
   FileSystem         = 'NTFS'
   NewFileSystemLabel = 'GDShow'}
Format-Volume @NVHT2
```

8. Get partitions on this system:

```
Get-Partition  |
   Sort-Object -Property DriveLetter |
      Format-Table -Property DriveLetter, Size, Type
```

9. Get volumes on SRV1:

```
Get-Volume |
   Sort-Object -Property riveLetter
```

How it works...

In *step 1*, you look at the disks available on SRV1, noting the two new disks:

```
PS C:\Foo> Get-Disk |
              Format-Table -AutoSize

Number Friendly Name      Serial Number HealthStatus OperationalStatus Total Size Partition Style
------ -------------      ------------- ------------ ----------------- ---------- ---------------
0      Virtual HD                       Healthy      Online            128 GB     MBR
1      Msft Virtual Disk                Healthy      Online            10 GB      RAW
2      Msft Virtual Disk                Healthy      Online            10 GB      RAW
```

In *step 2*, you initialize the two new drives—this produces no output. In *step 3*, you redisplay the disks, which looks like this:

```
PS C:\Foo> Get-Disk |
              Format-Table -AutoSize

Number Friendly Name      Serial Number HealthStatus OperationalStatus Total Size Partition Style
------ -------------      ------------- ------------ ----------------- ---------- ---------------
0      Virtual HD                       Healthy      Online            128 GB     MBR
1      Msft Virtual Disk                Healthy      Online            10 GB      GPT
2      Msft Virtual Disk                Healthy      Online            10 GB      GPT
```

In *step 4*, you use the New-Volume cmdlet to partition and format a disk volume (F:) in the first added disk, which looks like this:

```
PS C:\Foo> $NVHT1 = @{
             DiskNumber   = 1
             FriendlyName = 'Storage(F)'
             FileSystem   = 'NTFS'
             DriveLetter  = 'F'
           }
PS C:\Foo> New-Volume @NVHT1

DriveLetter FriendlyName FileSystemType DriveType HealthStatus OperationalStatus SizeRemaining    Size
----------- ------------ -------------- --------- ------------ ----------------- -------------    ----
F           Storage(F)   NTFS           Fixed     Healthy      OK                9.94 GB  9.98 GB
```

With *step 5*, you create the first of two new partitions on the second drive added to SRV1, which looks like this:

```
PS C:\Foo> New-Partition -DiskNumber 2  -DriveLetter G -Size 4gb

   DiskPath: \\?\scsi#disk&ven_msft&prod_virtual_disk#000001#{53f56307-b6bf-11d0-94f2-00a0c91efb8b}

PartitionNumber DriveLetter Offset   Size Type
--------------- ----------- ------   ---- ----
2               G           16777216 4 GB Basic
```

In *step 6*, you create a second partition on the second disk, the `G:` drive. That looks like this:

```
PS C:\Foo> New-Partition -DiskNumber 2  -DriveLetter H -UseMaximumSize

   DiskPath: \\?\scsi#disk&ven_msft&prod_virtual_disk#000001#{53f56307-b6bf-11d0-94f2-00a0c91efb8b}

PartitionNumber DriveLetter Offset          Size Type
--------------- ----------- ------          ---- ----
3               H           4311744512   5.98 GB Basic
```

In *step 7*, you format the two partitions you just created, which looks like this:

```
PS C:\Foo> $NVHT1 = @{
              DriveLetter        = 'G'
              FileSystem         = 'NTFS'
              NewFileSystemLabel = 'Log'}
PS C:\Foo> Format-Volume @NVHT1
PS C:\Foo> $NVHT2 = @{
              DriveLetter        = 'H'
              FileSystem         = 'NTFS'
              NewFileSystemLabel = 'GDShow'}
PS C:\Foo> Format-Volume @NVHT2

DriveLetter FriendlyName FileSystemType DriveType HealthStatus OperationalStatus SizeRemaining    Size
----------- ------------ -------------- --------- ------------ ----------------- -------------    ----
G           Log          NTFS           Fixed     Healthy      OK                3.97 GB          4 GB
H           GDShow       NTFS           Fixed     Healthy      OK                5.95 GB       5.98 GB
```

In *step 8*, you use the `Get-Partition` cmdlet to return the partitions on the `SRV1` server, which looks like this:

```
PS C:\Foo> Get-Partition  |
             Sort-Object -Property DriveLetter |
             Format-Table -Property DriveLetter, Size, Type

DriveLetter        Size Type
-----------        ---- ----
              855638016 Unknown
               16759808 Reserved
               16759808 Reserved
C          136579393024 IFS
F           10719592448 Basic
G            4294967296 Basic
H            6424625152 Basic
```

In *step 9*, you use the `Get-Volume` cmdlet to return the volumes (also known as the partitions) on the `SRV1` server, which looks like this:

```
PS C:\Foo> Get-Volume |
            Sort-Object -Property DriveLetter

DriveLetter FriendlyName FileSystemType DriveType HealthStatus OperationalStatus SizeRemaining      Size
----------- ------------ -------------- --------- ------------ ----------------- -------------      ----
                         NTFS           Fixed     Healthy      OK                   348.11 MB     816 MB
A                        Unknown        Removable Healthy      Unknown                    0 B        0 B
C                        NTFS           Fixed     Healthy      OK                   111.72 GB   127.2 GB
D                        Unknown        CD-ROM    Healthy      Unknown                    0 B        0 B
F           Storage(F)   NTFS           Fixed     Healthy      OK                     9.44 GB    9.98 GB
G           Log          NTFS           Fixed     Healthy      OK                     3.47 GB       4 GB
H           GDShow       NTFS           Fixed     Healthy      OK                     5.45 GB    5.98 GB
```

There's more...

In the *Getting ready* section of this recipe, you add two new disks to `SRV1`. These new disks are uninitialized, thus the first thing to do, in *step 1*, is to initialize the disks.

In *step 4*, you create a new volume on `Disk 1`. This creates the partition and then formats the drive. In *step 5* and *step 6*, you create two new partitions on disk 2 which, in *step 7*, you format. This shows two ways of creating drives within a disk.

In *step 8* and *step 9*, you use different cmdlets to return what's essentially the same set of objects—the volumes/partitions on `SRV1`.

Managing NTFS permissions

Every file and folder in an NTFS filesystem has an **Access Control List** (**ACL**). The ACL contains a set of **Access Control Entries** (**ACEs**). Each ACE defines a permission to a file or folder for an account. For example, the `Sales` AD global group could be given full control of a file.

Permissions can also be inherited from parent folders. If you create a new folder and then create a file within that folder, the new file inherits permissions from the parent folder and from any further parent folder(s) by default. You can manage the ACL list to add or remove permissions and you can modify inheritance.

There's limited PowerShell support for managing NTFS permissions. PowerShell does have the `Get-ACL` and `Set-ACL` cmdlets, but creating the individual ACEs and managing inheritance requires the use of the .NET Framework (by default). A simpler approach is to use a third-party module, `NTFSSecurity`, which makes managing ACEs and ACLs, including dealing with inheritance, much simpler.

Getting ready

This recipe uses SRV1, a general-purpose domain-joined server that runs Windows Server 2019. You also need to have a domain controller (such as DC1) up and running. The Sales group should exist in Active Directory (AD), but if not, this recipe creates the group. You should use an account that's a member of the Domain Admins group and run this recipe from an elevated console. Additionally, you should have the AD RSAT tools loaded onto SRV1.

How to do it...

1. Download and install the NTFSSecurity module from the PowerShell Gallery:

    ```
    Install-Module NTFSSecurity -Force
    ```

2. Use the following Get commands in the module:

    ```
    Get-Command -Module NTFSSecurity
    ```

3. Create a new folder and a new file in the following folder:

    ```
    New-Item -Path C:\Secure1 -ItemType Directory
    "Secure" | Out-File -FilePath C:\Secure1\Secure.Txt
    ```

4. View the ACL of the folder:

    ```
    Get-NTFSAccess -Path C:\Secure1 |
      Format-Table -AutoSize
    ```

5. View the ACL of the file:

    ```
    Get-NTFSAccess C:\Secure1\Secure.Txt |
      Format-Table -AutoSize
    ```

6. Create the Sales group, if it doesn't already exist:

    ```
    try {
      Get-ADGroup -Identity 'Sales' -ErrorAction Stop
    }
    catch {
      New-ADGroup -Name Sales -GroupScope Global
    }
    ```

7. Display the group:

```
Get-ADGroup -Identity Sales
```

8. Give the domain administrators full control of the folder:

```
$AHT1 = @{
  Path         = 'C:\Secure1'
  Account      = 'Reskit\Domain Admins'
  AccessRights = 'FullControl'
}
Add-NTFSAccess @AHT1
```

9. Remove the `Builtin\Users` access from the `Secure.Txt` file:

```
$AHT2 = @{
  Path         = 'C:\Secure1\Secure.Txt'
  Account      = 'Builtin\Users'
  AccessRights = 'FullControl'
}
Remove-NTFSAccess @AHT2
```

10. Remove the inherited rights for the folder:

```
$IRHT1 = @{
  Path                       = 'C:\Secure1'
  RemoveInheritedAccessRules = $True
}
Disable-NTFSAccessInheritance @IRHT1
```

11. Add `Sales` group access to the folder:

```
$AHT3 = @{
  Path         = 'C:\Secure1\'
  Account      = 'Reskit\Sales'
  AccessRights = 'FullControl'
}
Add-NTFSAccess @AHT3
```

12. Get the updated ACL for the folder:

```
Get-NTFSAccess -Path C:\Secure1 |
  Format-Table -AutoSize
```

13. View the updated ACL on the file:

```
Get-NTFSAccess -Path C:\Secure1\Secure.Txt |
  Format-Table -AutoSize
```

How it works...

In *step 1*, you download and install the NTFSSecurity module from the PowerShell Gallery on the internet, which produces no output. In *step 2*, you use the Get-Command cmdlet to view the commands inside the NTFSSecurity module, which looks like this:

```
PS C:\Foo> Get-Command -Module NTFSSecurity

CommandType  Name                            Version  Source
-----------  ----                            -------  ------
Cmdlet       Add-NTFSAccess                  4.2.4    NTFSSecurity
Cmdlet       Add-NTFSAudit                   4.2.4    NTFSSecurity
Cmdlet       Clear-NTFSAccess                4.2.4    NTFSSecurity
Cmdlet       Clear-NTFSAudit                 4.2.4    NTFSSecurity
Cmdlet       Copy-Item2                      4.2.4    NTFSSecurity
Cmdlet       Disable-NTFSAccessInheritance   4.2.4    NTFSSecurity
Cmdlet       Disable-NTFSAuditInheritance    4.2.4    NTFSSecurity
Cmdlet       Disable-Privileges              4.2.4    NTFSSecurity
Cmdlet       Enable-NTFSAccessInheritance    4.2.4    NTFSSecurity
Cmdlet       Enable-NTFSAuditInheritance     4.2.4    NTFSSecurity
Cmdlet       Enable-Privileges               4.2.4    NTFSSecurity
Cmdlet       Get-ChildItem2                  4.2.4    NTFSSecurity
Cmdlet       Get-DiskSpace                   4.2.4    NTFSSecurity
Cmdlet       Get-FileHash2                   4.2.4    NTFSSecurity
Cmdlet       Get-Item2                       4.2.4    NTFSSecurity
Cmdlet       Get-NTFSAccess                  4.2.4    NTFSSecurity
Cmdlet       Get-NTFSAudit                   4.2.4    NTFSSecurity
Cmdlet       Get-NTFSEffectiveAccess         4.2.4    NTFSSecurity
Cmdlet       Get-NTFSHardLink                4.2.4    NTFSSecurity
Cmdlet       Get-NTFSInheritance             4.2.4    NTFSSecurity
Cmdlet       Get-NTFSOrphanedAccess          4.2.4    NTFSSecurity
Cmdlet       Get-NTFSOrphanedAudit           4.2.4    NTFSSecurity
Cmdlet       Get-NTFSOwner                   4.2.4    NTFSSecurity
Cmdlet       Get-NTFSSecurityDescriptor      4.2.4    NTFSSecurity
Cmdlet       Get-NTFSSimpleAccess            4.2.4    NTFSSecurity
Cmdlet       Get-Privileges                  4.2.4    NTFSSecurity
Cmdlet       Move-Item2                      4.2.4    NTFSSecurity
Cmdlet       New-NTFSHardLink                4.2.4    NTFSSecurity
Cmdlet       New-NTFSSymbolicLink            4.2.4    NTFSSecurity
Cmdlet       Remove-Item2                    4.2.4    NTFSSecurity
Cmdlet       Remove-NTFSAccess               4.2.4    NTFSSecurity
Cmdlet       Remove-NTFSAudit                4.2.4    NTFSSecurity
Cmdlet       Set-NTFSInheritance             4.2.4    NTFSSecurity
Cmdlet       Set-NTFSOwner                   4.2.4    NTFSSecurity
Cmdlet       Set-NTFSSecurityDescriptor      4.2.4    NTFSSecurity
Cmdlet       Test-Path2                      4.2.4    NTFSSecurity
```

In *step 3*, you create a new folder, `C:\Secure1`, and a file within that folder (`C:\Secure1\Secure.Txt`) that looks like this:

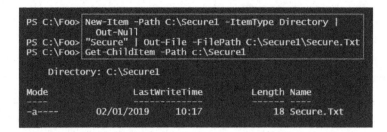

In *step 4*, you use the `Get-NTFSAccess` cmdlet to view the ACL for the `C:\Secure1` folder, which looks like this:

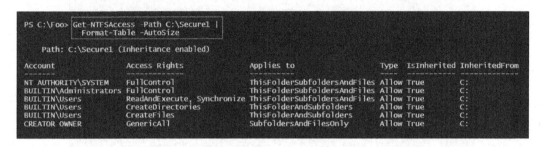

In *step 5*, you use the `Get-NTFSAccess` cmdlet to view the ACL on the `C:\Secure1\Secure.txt` file, which looks like this:

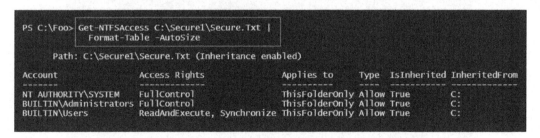

In *step 6*, you create a global group (`Sales`) in the `Reskit.Org` domain (if the group doesn't already exist). Whether or not the global group exists, this step produces no output. In *step 7*, you view the `Sales` global group, which looks like this:

```
PS C:\Foo> Get-ADGroup -Identity Sales

DistinguishedName : CN=Sales,CN=Users,DC=Reskit,DC=Org
GroupCategory     : Security
GroupScope        : Global
Name              : Sales
ObjectClass       : group
ObjectGUID        : 9224cc13-d897-428a-a04f-a91ef3dae7af
SamAccountName    : Sales
SID               : S-1-5-21-3496687451-3124355039-3783943179-1605
```

In *step 8*, you add an explicit ACE that gives the members of the `Domain Admins` group full control. In *step 9*, you remove the access ACE for `Builtin\Users` from the file's ACL. And in *step 10*, you remove the ACE entries on the `C:\Secure1\Secure.txt` file that were initially inherited from the `C:\Secure1` folder. In *step 11*, you add an ACL that gives full control to members of the `Reskit\Sales` global group. These four steps produce no output.

In *step 12*, you use the `Get-NTFSAccess` cmdlet to review the ACL for the `C:\Secure1` folder, which looks like this:

```
PS C:\Foo> Get-NTFSAccess -Path C:\Secure1 |
             Format-Table -AutoSize

    Path: C:\Secure1 (Inheritance disabled)

Account                  Access Rights Applies to                     Type  IsInherited InheritedFrom
-------                  ------------- ----------                     ----  ----------- -------------
RESKIT\Domain Admins FullControl   ThisFolderSubfoldersAndFiles Allow False
RESKIT\Sales             FullControl   ThisFolderSubfoldersAndFiles Allow False
```

In *step 13*, you view the ACL on the `C:\Secure1\Secure.Txt` file, which looks like this:

```
PS C:\Foo> Get-NTFSAccess -Path C:\Secure1\Secure.Txt |
             Format-Table -AutoSize

    Path: C:\Secure1\Secure.Txt (Inheritance enabled)

Account                  Access Rights Applies to        Type  IsInherited InheritedFrom
-------                  ------------- ----------        ----  ----------- -------------
RESKIT\Domain Admins FullControl   ThisFolderOnly Allow True        C:\Secure1
RESKIT\Sales             FullControl   ThisFolderOnly Allow True        C:\Secure1
```

There's more...

In *step 3*, you create a folder (`C:\Secure1`) and a file (`C:\Secure1\Secure.Txt`). In later steps, you adjust the ACLs on the file and folder to support the organization's security policy.

In *step 6*, you ensure that a global group, `Sales`, exists in the AD that you use to set ACLs. If the global group already exists (for example, if you've used other recipes in this book that make use of that group) then this step does nothing.

In *step 8*, you add a full control ACE to the folder for the `Reskit\Domain Admins` group. This means that, since you are logged on as a member of that group, when you remove the default ACE for `Builtin\Users` in *step 9*, you still have access to the folder and folder contents to continue the recipe.

After you adjust the ACL to the folder, you can see, in *step 12* and *step 13*, that the `C:\Secure1` folder no longer inherits ACE entries from the parent folder. Additionally, you can see that the file's ACL includes an ACE inherited from the folder.

In a production environment, it might be appropriate to remove the permissions for the `Domain Admins` account once the users are able to access and use the folder successfully. If a Domain Administrator does need to change the ACL, they could just take ownership of the folder, give themselves full control of the folder, and then perform any needed management (and removing any temporary access once this maintenance is complete).

See also

This recipe shows you how to use the `NTFSSecurity` module to manage aspects of file and folder ACLs. The module was first announced in 2014 and has been improved since. See `https://blogs.technet.microsoft.com/fieldcoding/2014/12/05/ntfssecurity-tutorial-1-getting-adding-and-removing-permissions/` for more details on the module.

Managing Storage Replica

Storage Replica (**SR**) is a feature of Windows Server 2019 that replicates storage volumes to other systems. SR is only available with the Windows Server 2019 Datacentre edition.

Getting ready

This recipe makes use of additional disk volumes on SRV1 and SRV2. In the *Managing physical disks and disk volumes* recipe, you added two additional disks to SRV1. In this recipe, you need to have two additional disks added to SRV2 that form the basis for storage replication. This recipe requires two additional hard disks for SRV2—you can use the Add-DiskstoSrv1+2.ps1 script to create the disks used in this and other recipes in this chapter. You can find the script on this book's GitHub repository (https://github.com/DoctorDNS/PowerShellCookBook2019/blob/master/Chapter%2004%20-%20Managing%20Storage/Add-DiskstoSRV1%2B2.ps1).

Run this recipe on SRV1 with SRV2 and DC1 online:

1. Create content on the F: drive in SRV1:

   ```
   1..100 | ForEach {
     $NF = "F:\CoolFolder$_"
     New-Item -Path $NF -ItemType Directory | Out-Null
     1..100 | ForEach {
       $NF2 = "$NF\CoolFile$_"
       "Cool File" | Out-File -PSPath $NF2
     }
   }
   ```

2. Show what's on F: locally on SRV1:

   ```
   Get-ChildItem -Path F:\ -Recurse | Measure-Object
   ```

3. Examine the same drives remotely on SRV2:

   ```
   $SB = {
     Get-ChildItem -Path F:\ -Recurse |
       Measure-Object
   }
   Invoke-Command -ComputerName SRV2 -ScriptBlock $SB
   ```

4. Add a Storage Replica feature to SRV1:

   ```
   Add-WindowsFeature -Name Storage-Replica
   ```

5. Restart SRV1 to finish the installation process:

   ```
   Restart-Computer
   ```

6. Add a storage-replica feature to SRV2:

```
$SB= {
   Add-WindowsFeature -Name Storage-Replica | Out-Null
}
Invoke-Command -ComputerName SRV2 -ScriptBlock $SB
```

7. Restart SRV2 and wait until the restart is complete:

```
$RSHT = @{
   ComputerName = 'SRV2'
   Force        = $true
}
Restart-Computer @RSHT -Wait -For PowerShell
```

8. Create a Storage Replica by replicating from F: on SRV1 to F: on SRV2:

```
$SRHT =  @{
   SourceComputerName      = 'SRV1'
   SourceRGName            = 'SRV1RG'
   SourceVolumeName        = 'F:'
   SourceLogVolumeName     = 'G:'
   DestinationComputerName = 'SRV2'
   DestinationRGName       = 'SRV2RG'
   DestinationVolumeName   = 'F:'
   DestinationLogVolumeName = 'G:'
   LogSizeInBytes          = 2gb
}
New-SRPartnership @SRHT -Verbose
```

9. View the storage replication partnership:

```
Get-SRPartnership
```

10. Examine the same drives remotely on SRV2:

```
$SB = {
   Get-Volume |
     Sort-Object -Property DriveLetter |
        Format-Table
}
Invoke-Command -ComputerName SRV2 -ScriptBlock $SB
```

11. Reverse the replication:

```
$SRHT2 = @{
  NewSourceComputerName   = 'SRV2'
  SourceRGName            = 'SRV2RG'
  DestinationComputerName = 'SRV1'
  DestinationRGName       = 'SRV1RG'
  Confirm                 = $False
}
Set-SRPartnership @SRHT2
```

12. View the replication partnership after reversing:

```
Get-SRPartnership
```

13. Examine the same drives remotely on SRV2:

```
$SB = {
  Get-ChildItem -Path F:\ -Recurse |
    Measure-Object
}
Invoke-Command -ComputerName SRV2 -ScriptBlock $SB
```

How it works...

In *step 1*, you create 100 folders on the F: of SRV1. Inside each folder, you also create 100 files. Each file contains some content. This step produces no output. In *step 2*, you view what you just created, which looks like this:

```
PS C:\Foo> Get-ChildItem -Path F:\ -Recurse | Measure-Object

Count    : 10100
Average  :
Sum      :
Maximum  :
Minimum  :
Property :
```

In *step 3*, you view the `F:` drive on `SRV2` (which contains no files yet). The output from *step 3* looks like this:

```
PS C:\Foo> $SB = {
               Get-ChildItem -Path F:\ -Recurse |
               Measure-Object
           }
PS C:\Foo> Invoke-Command -ComputerName SRV2 -ScriptBlock $SB


Count          : 0
Average        :
Sum            :
Maximum        :
Minimum        :
Property       :
PSComputerName : SRV2
```

In *step 4*, you add the `Storage Replica` feature to `SRV1`, which looks like this:

```
PS C:\Foo> Add-WindowsFeature -Name Storage-Replica

Success Restart Needed Exit Code        Feature Result
------- --------------- ----------        --------------
True    Yes             SuccessRest...   {Storage Replica}
WARNING: You must restart this server to finish the installation process.
```

In *step 5*, you reboot `SRV1`. In *step 6* and *step 7*, you add the `Storage Replica` feature to `SRV2` then reboot `SRV2`. These three steps produce no output.

In *step 8*, you create a Storage Replica partnership, replicating the contents of `F:` on `SRV1` to `F:` on `SRV2` (with the `G:` drive on both servers serving as a log file folder for storage replication). The output from this step looks like this:

```
PS C:\Foo> $SRHT = @{
               SourceComputerName      = 'SRV1'
               SourceRGName            = 'SRV1RG'
               SourceVolumeName        = 'F:'
               SourceLogVolumeName     = 'G:'
               DestinationComputerName = 'SRV2'
               DestinationRGName       = 'SRV2RG'
               DestinationVolumeName   = 'F:'
               DestinationLogVolumeName = 'G:'
               LogSizeInBytes          = 2gb
           }
PS C:\Foo> New-SRPartnership @SRHT -Verbose


DestinationComputerName : SRV2
DestinationRGName       : SRV2RG
Id                      : 4fef9369-6c57-4edc-aa78-cfe1b4f4422b
SourceComputerName      : SRV1
SourceRGName            : SRV1RG
PSComputerName          :
```

In *step 9*, you use the `Get-SRPartnership` cmdlet to view the now-reversed replication partnership, which looks like this:

```
PS C:\Foo> Get-SRPartnership

DestinationComputerName : SRV2  ⟵————————
DestinationRGName       : SRV1RG
Id                      : 4fef9369-6c57-4edc-aa78-cfe1b4f4422b
SourceComputerName      : SRV1  ⟵————————
SourceRGName            : SRV2RG
PSComputerName          :
```

In *step 10*, you examine the volumes available on `SRV2`, which look like this:

```
PS C:\Foo> $SB = {
             Get-Volume |
               Sort-Object -Property DriveLetter |
                 Format-Table
           }
PS C:\Foo> Invoke-Command -ComputerName SRV2 -ScriptBlock $SB

DriveLetter FriendlyName        FileSystemType DriveType HealthStatus OperationalStatus SizeRemaining     Size
----------- ------------        -------------- --------- ------------ ----------------- -------------     ----
                                 NTFS           Fixed     Healthy      OK                349.61 MB     816 MB
A                                Unknown        Removable Healthy      Unknown               0 B        0 B
C                                NTFS           Fixed     Healthy      OK                117.34 GB  127.2 GB
D           SSS_X64FRE_EN-US_DV9 Unknown        CD-ROM    Healthy      OK                    0 B     4.51 GB
F                                Unknown        Fixed     Healthy      Unknown               0 B        0 B
G           Log                  NTFS           Fixed     Healthy      OK                 1.97 GB       4 GB
H           GDShow               NTFS           Fixed     Healthy      OK                 5.95 GB    5.98 GB
```

Thus far, you're replicating from `SRV1` to `SRV2`. In *step 11*, you reverse the replication, which generates no output. With *step 12*, you can see that the replication is now reversed, replicating from files on `SRV2` to `SRV1`. The output from this step looks like this:

```
PS C:\Foo> Get-SRPartnership

DestinationComputerName : SRV1  ⟵————————
DestinationRGName       : SRV1RG
Id                      : 4fef9369-6c57-4edc-aa78-cfe1b4f4422b
SourceComputerName      : SRV2  ⟵————————
SourceRGName            : SRV2RG
PSComputerName          :
```

In the final step, *step 13*, you count the files now available on SRV2, which looks like this:

```
PS C:\Foo> $SB = {
             Get-ChildItem -Path F:\ -Recurse |
               Measure-Object
           }
PS C:\Foo> Invoke-Command -ComputerName SRV2 -ScriptBlock $SB

Count           : 10100 ◄────
Average         :
Sum             :
Maximum         :
Minimum         :
Property        :
PSComputerName  : SRV2   ◄────
```

There's more...

In this recipe, you create a set of 100 folders and 10,000 files on SRV1, which you replicate to SRV2. After the replication starts, you can't actually see anything useful on SRV2 since the volume is being used by SR itself. As you can see in *step 10*, the replicated data isn't viewable on SRV2—the partition into SR is replicating has no apparent filesystem. Once you reverse the replication, as you can see in *step 11* and *step 12*, the files and folders on SRV2 are now viewable (and those on SRV1 wouldn't be viewable). This is a feature of SR that prevents accidentally storing data on the replicated disk.

Managing Filestore quotas

The FSRM is a feature of the Windows server that assists you in managing file servers. FSRM has three key features:

- **Quota management**: With FSRM, you can set soft or hard quotas on volumes and folders. A soft quota allows a user to exceed an allowance, while hard quotas stop a user from exceeding an allowance. You can configure a quota with thresholds and threshold actions. If a user exceeds 65% of the quota allowance, FSRM can send an email, while at 90%, you log an event in the event log or run a program. You have different actions for different quota levels. This recipe shows how to use quotas.

- **File screening**: You can set up a file screen and stop a user from saving screened files. For example, you could screen for .MP3, or FLAC files—should a user then attempt to save a file (say, jg75-02-28D1T1.flac), the file screen rejects the request and doesn't allow the user to save the file.

- **Reporting**: FSRM enables you to create a wealth of storage reports that can be highly useful for management purposes.

In this recipe, you install FSRM, perform some general configuration, and then work with soft and hard quotas.

Getting ready

This recipe makes use of an email server so that FSRM can send email to the admin. To test the email-related components of this recipe, you need have an SMTP server or an email-forwarder. The resultant emails generated by this recipe were sent to SRV1, then forwarded to a free email service at `https://www.sendgrid.com`. With a SendGrid account in place, you can add the SMTP service to a server in your environment and then configure it to forward mail to SendGrid to then send the emails onward.

How to do it...

1. Install the FSRM feature:

```
$IHT = @{
  Name                   = 'FS-Resource-Manager'
  IncludeManagementTools = $True
}
Install-WindowsFeature @IHT
```

2. Set the SMTP settings in FSRM:

```
$MHT = @{
  SmtpServer       = 'SRV1.Reskit.Org'   # Previously setup
  FromEmailAddress = 'FSRM@Reskit.Org'
  AdminEmailAddress = 'Doctordns@Gmail.Com'
}
Set-FsrmSetting @MHT
```

3. Send a test email to check the setup:

```
$MHT = @{
  ToEmailAddress = 'DoctorDNS@gmail.com'
  Confirm        = $false
}
Send-FsrmTestEmail @MHT
```

4. Create a new FSRM quota template for a 10 MB quota:

```
$QHT1 = @{
  Description = 'Quota of 10MB'
  Name        = 'TenMB Limit'
  Size        = 10MB
}
New-FsrmQuotaTemplate @QHT1
```

5. Create another quota template for a quota of 5 MB:

```
$QHT2 = @{
  Name        = 'Soft 5MB Limit'
  Description = 'Soft Quota of 5MB'
  Size        = 5MB
  SoftLimit   = $True
}
New-FsrmQuotaTemplate @QHT2
```

6. View the available FSRM quota templates:

```
Get-FsrmQuotaTemplate |
  Format-Table -Property Name, Description, Size, SoftLimit
```

7. Create two new folders on which to place quotas:

```
If (-Not (Test-Path C:\Quota)) {
  New-Item -Path C:\Quota -ItemType Directory  |
    Out-Null
}
If (-Not (Test-Path C:\QuotaS)) {
  New-Item -Path C:\QuotaS -ItemType Directory  |
    Out-Null
}
```

8. Create an FSRM action for when the threshold is exceeded:

```
$Body = @'
User [Source Io Owner] has exceeded the [Quota Threshold]% quota
threshold for the quota on [Quota Path] on server [Server].
The quota limit is [Quota Limit MB] MB, and [Quota Used MB] MB
currently is in use ([Quota Used Percent]% of limit).
'@
$NAHT = @{
Type       = 'Email'
```

```
MailTo    = 'Doctordns@gmail.Com'
Subject   = 'FSRM Over limit [Source Io Owner]'
Body      = $Body
}
$Action1 = New-FsrmAction @NAHT
```

9. Create an FSRM action for when the soft threshold is exceeded:

```
$Thresh = New-FsrmQuotaThreshold -Percentage 85 -Action $Action1
```

10. Create a soft **10 MB** quota on the `C:\Quotas` folder with a threshold:

```
$NQHT1 = @{
  Path      = 'C:\QuotaS'
  Template  = 'Soft 5MB Limit'
  Threshold = $Thresh
}
New-FsrmQuota @NQHT1
```

11. Now test the 85% soft quota limit on `C:\QuotaS`:

```
Get-ChildItem c:\quotas -Recurse | Remove-Item -Force
$S = '42'
1..24 | foreach {$s = $s + $s}
$S | Out-File -FilePath C:\QuotaS\Demos.txt
Get-ChildItem -Path C:\QuotaS\Demos.txt
```

12. Check if you received a notification email via Outlook or another mail client.

13. Create a second threshold action to log to the application log:

```
$Action2 = New-FsrmAction -Type Event -EventType Error
$Action2.Body = $Body
```

14. Create two quota thresholds for a new quota:

```
$Thresh2 = New-FsrmQuotaThreshold -Percentage 65
$Thresh3 = New-FsrmQuotaThreshold -Percentage 85
$Thresh2.Action = $Action2
$Thresh3.Action = $Action2  # same action details
```

15. Create a hard quota, with two thresholds and related threshold actions, based on an FSRM quota template:

```
$NQHT = @{
Path        = 'C:\Quota'
Template    = 'TenMB Limit'
Threshold   = ($Thresh2, $Thresh3)
Description = 'Hard Threshold with2 actions'
}
New-FsrmQuota @NQHT
```

16. Remove existing files, if any:

```
Get-ChildItem C:\Quota -Recurse | Remove-Item -Force
```

17. Test a hard limit on C:\Quota from a different user:

```
$URK = "ThomasL@Reskit.Org"
$PRK = ConvertTo-SecureString 'Pa$$w0rd' -AsPlainText -Force
$CredRK = New-Object system.management.automation.PSCredential
$URK,$PRK
$SB = {
  $S = '42'
  1..27 | foreach {$s = $s + $s}
  $S | Out-File -FilePath C:\Quota\Demos.Txt -Encoding ascii
  $Len = (Get-ChildItem -Path C:\Quota\Demos.Txt).Length}
$ICMHT = @{
  ComputerName = 'SRV1'
  Credential   = $CredRK
  ScriptBlock  = $SB}
Invoke-Command @ICMHT
```

18. View the event log entries related to the overuse of the quota:

```
Get-EventLog -LogName Application -Source SRMSVC |
    Format-Table -AutoSize -Wrap
```

How it works...

In *step 1*, you install the FSRM feature on SRV1, which looks like this:

```
PS C:\Foo> $IHT = @{
              Name                   = 'FS-Resource-Manager'
              IncludeManagementTools = $True
           }
PS C:\Foo> Install-WindowsFeature @IHT

Success Restart Needed Exit Code Feature Result
------- -------------- --------- --------------
True    No             Success   {File Server Resource Manager}
```

In *step 2*, you set SMTP server settings for FSRM, which generates no output. The assumption is that you've configured SRV1 to be an email forwarder, forwarding mail to SendMail.Com for onward transmission. This step produces no output.

In *step 3*, you test the SMTP service by using the Send-FsrmTestEmail cmdlet. There's no output as such from this step, but the resultant email looks like this:

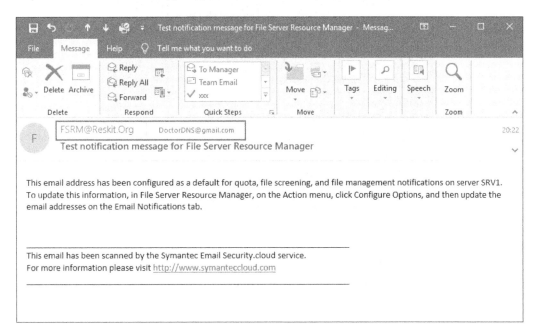

With *step 4*, you create an FSRM quota template, which looks like this:

```
PS C:\Foo> $QHT1 = @{
            Description = 'Quota of 10 MB'
            Name        = 'TenMB Limit'
            Size        = 10mb
          }
PS C:\Foo> New-FsrmQuotaTemplate @QHT1

Description             : Quota of 10 MB
Name                    : TenMB Limit
Size                    : 10485760
SoftLimit               : False
Threshold               :
UpdateDerived           : False
UpdateDerivedMatching   : False
PSComputerName          :
```

In *step 5*, you create an additional FSRM quota template, this time for 5 MB, which looks like this:

```
PS C:\foo> $QHT2 = @{
            Name        = 'Soft 5MB Limit'
            Description = 'Soft Quota of 5MB'
            Size        = 5MB
            SoftLimit   = $True
          }
PS C:\foo> New-FsrmQuotaTemplate @QHT2

Description             : Soft Quota of 5MB
Name                    : Soft 5MB Limit
Size                    : 5242880
SoftLimit               : True
Threshold               :
UpdateDerived           : False
UpdateDerivedMatching   : False
PSComputerName          :
```

In *step 6*, you review the FSRM templates available on SRV1. This includes templates added when you installed the FSRM feature, plus the ones you created in *step 4* and *step 5*. The available templates look like this:

```
PS C:\foo> Get-FsrmQuotaTemplate |
              Format-Table -Property Name, Description, Size, SoftLimit


Name                                Description              Size SoftLimit
----                                -----------              ---- ---------
100 MB Limit                                             104857600     False
200 MB Limit Reports to User                             209715200     False
Monitor 200 GB Volume Usage                           214748364800      True
Monitor 500 MB Share                                     524288000      True
200 MB Limit with 50 MB Extension                        209715200     False
250 MB Extended Limit                                    262144000     False
2 GB Limit                                              2147483648     False
5 GB Limit                                              5368709120     False
10 GB Limit                                            10737418240     False
Monitor 3 TB Volume Usage                            3298534883328      True
Monitor 5 TB Volume Usage                            5497558138880      True
Monitor 10 TB Volume Usage                          10995116277760      True
TenMB Limit                         Quota of 10 MB        10485760     False
Soft 5MB Limit                      Soft Quota of 5mb      5242880      True
```

In *step 7*, you create two new folders on SRV1 to assist in testing soft and hard Filestore
quotas. In *step 8* and *step 9*, you create two new FSRM quota-exceeded actions. These three
steps produce no output.

In *step 10*, you create a new soft quota on C:\QuotaS, which looks like this:

```
PS C:\foo> $NQHT1 = @{
              Path         = 'C:\QuotaS'
              Description  = 'Soft 5MB quota'
              Template     = 'Soft 5MB Limit'
           }
PS C:\foo> New-FsrmQuota @NQHT1

Description    : Soft 5MB quota
Disabled       : False
MatchesTemplate : True
Path           : C:\QuotaS
PeakUsage      : 4200448
Size           : 5242880
SoftLimit      : True
Template       : Soft 5MB Limit
Threshold      :
Usage          : 4200448
PSComputerName :
```

In *step 11*, you test the soft quota by building a large string and outputting the string to a file that exceeds the soft quota. The output from this step is as follows:

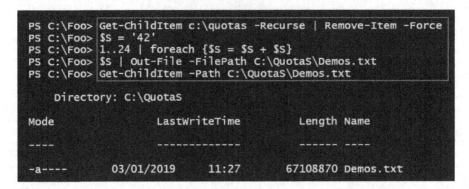

```
PS C:\Foo> Get-ChildItem c:\quotas -Recurse | Remove-Item -Force
PS C:\Foo> $S = '42'
PS C:\Foo> 1..24 | foreach {$S = $S + $S}
PS C:\Foo> $S | Out-File -FilePath C:\QuotaS\Demos.txt
PS C:\Foo> Get-ChildItem -Path C:\QuotaS\Demos.txt


    Directory: C:\QuotaS


Mode                 LastWriteTime         Length Name

----                 -------------         ------ ----

-a----        03/01/2019     11:27       67108870 Demos.txt
```

Exceeding the soft quota generates an email message, which looks like this:

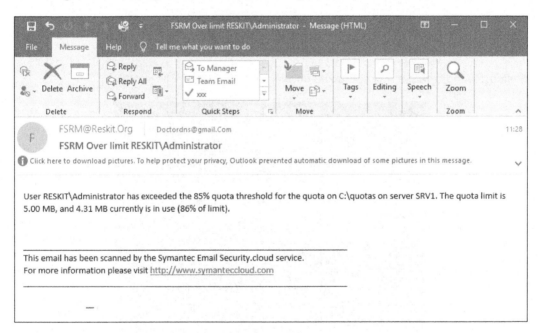

In *step 13*, you create a second threshold action to log to the application event log. In *step 14*, you create two new FSRM quota thresholds (for 65% of the quota exceeded, and 85% of the quota exceeded). These two steps produce no output.

In *step 15*, you create a hard quota for C:\Quota, which has the two threshold actions you set in the two previous steps. The output from this step looks like this:

```
PS C:\Foo> $NQHT = @{
PS C:\Foo> Path      = 'C:\Quota'
PS C:\Foo> Template  = 'TenMB Limit'
PS C:\Foo> Threshold = $Thresh2,$Thresh3
PS C:\Foo> Description= 'Hard Threshold (2 actions)'
PS C:\Foo> }
PS C:\Foo> New-FsrmQuota @NQHT


Description    : Hard Threshold (2 actions)
Disabled       : False
MatchesTemplate : False
Path           : C:\Quota
PeakUsage      : 10487808
Size           : 10485760
SoftLimit      : False
Template       : TenMB Limit
Threshold      : {MSFT_FSRMQuotaThreshold, MSFT_FSRMQuotaThreshold}
Usage          : 10487808
PSComputerName :
```

In *step 16*, you remove any existing files in C:\Quota, which produces no output. In *step 17*, you test the hard quota, which looks like this:

```
PS C:\Foo> URK = "ThomasL@reskit.org"
PS C:\Foo> $PRK = ConvertTo-SecureString 'Pa$$w0rd' -AsPlainText -Force
PS C:\Foo> $CredRK = New-Object system.management.automation.PSCredential $URK,$PRK
PS C:\Foo> $SB = {
             $S = '42'
             1..27 | foreach {$s = $s + $s}
             $S | Out-File -FilePath C:\Quota\Demos.Txt -Encoding ascii
             $Len = (Get-ChildItem -Path C:\Quota\Demos.Txt).Length
           }
PS C:\Foo> $ICMHT = @{
             ComputerName = 'SRV1'
             Credential   = $CredRK
             ScriptBlock  = $SB
           }
PS C:\Foo> Invoke-Command -ComputerName SRV1 -Credential $CredRK -ScriptBlock $SB
There is not enough space on the disk.
    + CategoryInfo          : NotSpecified: (:) [out-lineoutput], IOException
    + FullyQualifiedErrorId : System.IO.IOException,Microsoft.PowerShell.Commands.OutLineOutputCommand
    + PSComputerName        : SRV1
```

Finally, in *step 18*, you view the Application log events that FSRM logged when the two quota thresholds were exceeded (that is, when the quota threshold exceeded 65% and 85%). The output looks like this:

```
PS C:\Foo> Get-EventLog -LogName Application -Source SRMSVC |
             Format-Table -AutoSize -Wrap

Index Time         EntryType Source InstanceID Message
----- ----         --------- ------ ---------- -------
  813 Jan 03 12:54 Error     SRMSVC 2147758117 User RESKIT\ThomasL has exceeded the 85% quota
                                                threshold for the quota on C:\Quota on server
                                                SRV1.  The quota limit is 10.00 MB,and 8.50 MB
                                                currently is in use (85% of limit).
  812 Jan 03 12:54 Error     SRMSVC 2147758117 User RESKIT\ThomasL has exceeded the 65% quota
                                                threshold for the quota on C:\Quota on server
                                                SRV1.  The quota limit is 10.00 MB, and 6.50 MB
                                                currently is in use (65% of limit).
```

There's more...

In this recipe, you set up and tested both a soft and a hard FSRM quota. With the soft quota, you configured FSRM to send an email to inform the recipient that a quota has been exceeded. With the hard quota, you logged two event-log messages (when the quota has been exceeded by 65% and 85%). While the soft quota means a user can exceed the quota, with a hard quota, the user can only save up to the quota limit. As you can see in *step 17*, the file saved in `C:\Quota` was limited to just 10 MB.

The quotas set in this recipe were extremely small and would probably not be of much use in production. But a simple change from, say, `10 MB` to `10 GB`, would be simple to make.

Also, for the soft quota, the quota exceeded the action results in the email being sent, while for the hard quota, FSRM just writes `Application` event-log entries. In production, you might want to send email to either or both an administrator and the user who has exceeded the quota thresholds.

In *step 14*, you create two quota thresholds (one invoked at 65%, and the second at 85%). For both thresholds, you apply the same text, which gets posted when either threshold is exceeded. You can see these two messages in *step 18*.

Using filesystem reporting

A useful feature of the FSRM component is reporting. FSRM defines a number of basic report types that you can request. The reports can either be generated immediately (also known as interactive) or at a scheduled time. The latter causes FSRM to generate reports on a weekly or monthly basis.

Getting ready

Run this recipe on `SRV1`, after installing the FSRM feature. You did this in the *Managing Filestore quotas* recipe. That recipe also created two largish files. If you haven't run that recipe, consider creating a few large files on `SRV1` before running this recipe.

How to do it...

1. Create a new interactive Storage Report for large files on C:\ on SRV1:

```
$NRHT = @{
  Name            = 'Large Files on SRV1'
  NameSpace       = 'C:\'
  ReportType      = 'LargeFiles'
  LargeFileMinimum = 10MB
  Interactive     = $True
  }
New-FsrmStorageReport @NRHT
```

2. Get the current FSRM reports:

```
Get-FsrmStorageReport *
```

3. After the large file storage report is run, view the results in the filestore:

```
$Path = 'C:\StorageReports\Interactive'
Get-ChildItem -Path $Path
```

4. View the HTML report:

```
$Rep = Get-ChildItem -Path $path\*.html
Invoke-item -Path $Rep
```

5. Extract key information from the XML:

```
$XF   = Get-ChildItem -Path $Path\*.xml  # Find the XML file
$XML  = [XML] (Get-Content -Path $XF)     # Load file as XML
$Files = $XML.StorageReport.ReportData.Item # Get large files
$Files | Where-Object Path -NotMatch '^Windows|^Program|^Users'|
  Format-Table -Property Name, Path,
        @{Name        ='Sizemb'
          Expression = {(([int]$_.size)/1mb).ToString('N2')}
          },
          DaysSinceLastAccessed -AutoSize
```

6. Create a monthly FSRM task in the task scheduler:

```
$Date = Get-Date
$NTHT = @{
  Time    = $Date
  Monthly = 1
}
$Task = New-FsrmScheduledTask @NTHT
$NRHT = @{
  Name             = 'Monthly Files by files group report'
  Namespace        = 'C:\'
  Schedule         = $Task
  ReportType       = 'FilesbyFileGroup'
  FileGroupINclude = 'text files'
  LargeFileMinimum = 25MB
}
New-FsrmStorageReport @NRHT | Out-Null
```

7. Get the details of the task:

```
Get-ScheduledTask |
  Where-Object Taskname -Match 'Monthly' |
    Format-Table -AutoSize
```

8. Start the scheduled task:

```
Get-ScheduledTask -TaskName '*Monthly*' |
  Start-ScheduledTask
Get-ScheduledTask -TaskName '*Monthly*'
```

9. View the report:

```
$Path = 'C:\StorageReports\Scheduled'
$Rep = Get-ChildItem -Path $path\*.html
Invoke-item -Path $Rep
```

How it works...

In *step 1*, you use the `New-FsrmStorageReport` to create a report to report any files over 10 MB on `C:\`, which generates the following output:

```
PS C:\Foo> $NRHT = @{
    Name            = 'Large Files on SRV1'
    NameSpace       = 'C:\'
    ReportType      = 'LargeFiles'
    LargeFileMinimum = 10MB
    Interactive     = $true
    }
New-FsrmStorageReport @NRHT

FileGroupIncluded         :
FileOwnerFilePattern      :
FileOwnerUser             :
FileScreenAuditDaysSince  : 0
FileScreenAuditUser       :
FolderPropertyName        :
Interactive               : True
LargeFileMinimum          : 10485760
LargeFilePattern          :
LastError                 :
LastReportPath            :
LastRun                   :
LeastAccessedFilePattern  :
LeastAccessedMinimum      : 0
MailTo                    :
MostAccessedFilePattern   :
MostAccessedMaximum       : 0
Name                      : Large Files on SRV1
Namespace                 : {C:\}
PropertyFilePattern       :
PropertyName              :
QuotaMinimumUsage         : 0
ReportFormat              : {DHtml, XML}
ReportType                : LargeFiles
Schedule                  :
Status                    : Queued
PSComputerName            :
```

In *step 2*, you view the existing FSRM reports, which looks like this:

```
PS C:\Foo> Get-FsrmStorageReport *

FileGroupIncluded         :
FileOwnerFilePattern      :
FileOwnerUser             :
FileScreenAuditDaysSince  : 0
FileScreenAuditUser       :
FolderPropertyName        :
Interactive               : True
LargeFileMinimum          : 10485760
LargeFilePattern          :
LastError                 :
LastReportPath            :
LastRun                   :
LeastAccessedFilePattern  :
LeastAccessedMinimum      : 0
MailTo                    :
MostAccessedFilePattern   :
MostAccessedMaximum       : 0
Name                      : Large Files on SRV1
Namespace                 : {C:\}
PropertyFilePattern       :
PropertyName              :
QuotaMinimumUsage         : 0
ReportFormat              : {DHtml, XML}
ReportType                : LargeFiles
Schedule                  :
Status                    : Running  <----
PSComputerName            :
```

After the large file storage report is run, in *step 3*, you view the results in the filestore, which looks like this:

```
PS C:\foo> $Path = 'C:\StorageReports\Interactive'
PS C:\foo> Get-ChildItem -Path $Path

    Directory: C:\StorageReports\Interactive

Mode                LastWriteTime         Length Name
----                -------------         ------ ----
d-----        09/01/2019     12:01               LargeFiles13_2019-01-09_12-01-27_files
-a----        09/01/2019     12:01        192947 LargeFiles13_2019-01-09_12-01-27.html
-a----        09/01/2019     12:01        352904 LargeFiles13_2019-01-09_12-01-27.xml
```

In *step 4*, you view the HTML report, which looks like this:

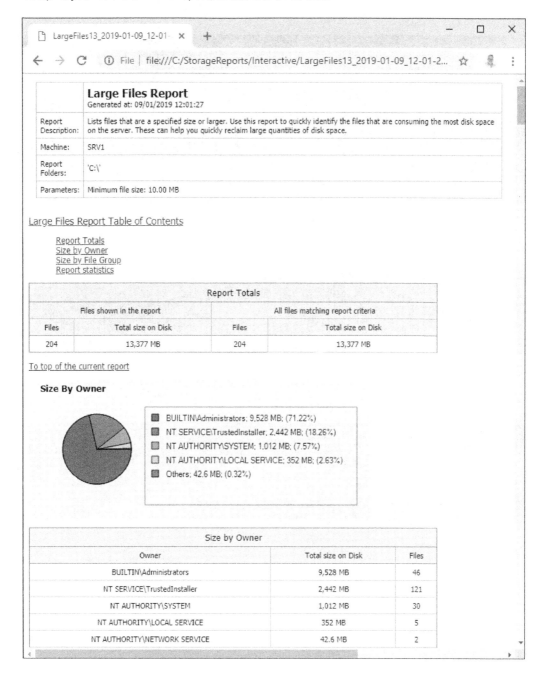

In *step 5*, you extract information from the XML version of the interactive large-file FSRM report, which looks like this:

```
PS C:\Foo> $XF   = Get-ChildItem -Path $Path\*.xml
PS C:\Foo> $XML  = [XML] (Get-Content -Path $XF)
PS C:\Foo> $Files = $x.StorageReport.ReportData.Item
PS C:\Foo> $Files | Where-Object Path -NotMatch '^Windows|^Program|^Users'|
PS C:\Foo>    Format-Table -Property name, path,
                @{ name ='Sizemb'
                   expression = {(([int]$_.size)/1mb).tostring('N2')}},
                   DaysSinceLastAccessed -AutoSize

Name                                     Path                       Sizemb DaysSinceLastAccessed
----                                     ----                       ------ ---------------------
5{3808876b-c176-4e48-b7ae-04046e6cc752} System Volume Information        0
pagefile.sys                                                              6
Demos.txt                                quotas                     64.00  6
Demos.Txt                                Quota                      10.00  5
```

In *step 6*, you set up a scheduled report that produces no output. In *step 7*, you view the details of the report:

```
PS C:\foo> Get-ScheduledTask |
               Where-Object taskname -Match 'Monthly' |
               Format-Table -AutoSize

TaskPath                                          TaskName                                  State
--------                                          --------                                  -----
\Microsoft\Windows\File Server Resource Manager\ StorageReport-Monthly Files by files group report Ready
```

In *step 8*, you start the task you defined in *step 7*, and view that this report is running, which looks like this:

```
PS C:\foo> Get-ScheduledTask -Taskname '*monthly*' |
               Start-ScheduledTask

PS C:\foo> Get-ScheduledTask -Taskname '*monthly*'

TaskPath                                          TaskName                                  State
--------                                          --------                                  -----
\Microsoft\Windows\File Server Resource Man... StorageReport-Monthly Files by... Running
```

In *step 9*, you view the report of files by file groups, which looks like this:

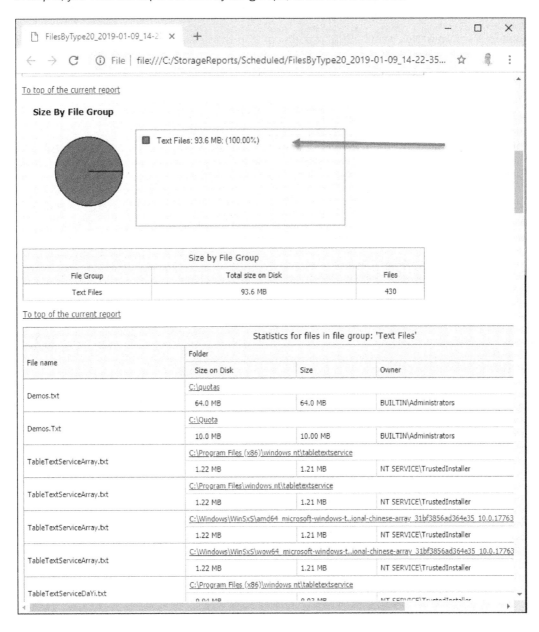

There's more...

In *step 2*, you view the current FSRM reports using the `Get-FsrmStorageReport` cmdlet. This shows all active FSRM reports (scheduled or interactive), although once FSRM completes an interactive report, the report is no longer visible using `Get-FsrmStorageReport`.

In *step 3*, you review the output FSRM generated for the interactive storage report. As you can see, there's both an HTML and an XML file. The HTML output looks good (as you see in *step 4*), but the format is fixed and can't be changed. However, the XML gives you all the information contained in the HTML report. You can use the XML to format the results exactly as you want. The XML file structure is pretty simple and you can pull out the basic information from the XML to create the details you might be interested in, as shown in *step 5*.

In *step 9*, you view the second report—a report on files by file group. In this case, the only file group reported is for text files. Were there other files belonging to other file groups, these would be reported.

5
Managing Shared Data

In this chapter, we cover the following recipes:

- ▸ Setting up and securing an SMB file server
- ▸ Creating and securing SMB shares
- ▸ Accessing data on SMB shares
- ▸ Creating an iSCSI target
- ▸ Using an iSCSI target
- ▸ Configuring a DFS Namespace
- ▸ Configuring DFS Replication

Introduction

Sharing data with other users on your network has been a feature of computer operating systems from the very earliest days of networking. This chapter looks at Windows Server 2019 features that enable you to share files and folders and to use the data that you've shared. This chapter follows on from *Chapter 4, Managing Windows Storage*.

Microsoft's LAN Manager was the company's first network offering. It enabled client computers to create, manage, and share files in a secure manner. The protocol that LAN Manager used to provide this client/server functionality was an early version of the **Server Message Block** (**SMB**) protocol.

SMB is a file-level storage protocol running over TCP/IP. SMB enables you to share files and folders securely and reliably. To increase reliability for SMB servers, you can install a cluster and cluster the file server role. This is an active-passive solution and works great as long as the underlying data is accessible.

This chapter shows you how to implement and leverage the features of sharing data between systems, including SMB contained in Windows Server 2016. In the recipes in this chapter, you'll begin by creating and using basic SMB file sharing. Then you build an iSCSI infrastructure, which you'll leverage when building an SOFS.

You finish by looking at the **Distributed File System** (**DFS**). With DFS, you can provide the means to connect to multiple shared folders, held on a variety of servers through DFS Namespace. A DFS Namespace is the virtual view of the files and folders with a DFS installation.

In the first recipe, *Securing an SMB file server*, you harden the security on your SMB file server. Then, in the *Creating and securing SMB shares* and *Accessing SMB shares* recipes, you set up simple file-folder sharing and access the shared files. With the *Creating an iSCSI target* recipe, you create an iSCSI target on the SRV2 server, while in the *Using an iSCSI target* recipe, you make use of that shared iSCSI disk from FS1. iSCSI is a popular **Storage Area Networking** (**SAN**) technology, and these recipes show you how to use the Microsoft iSCSI initiator and target features.

There are two separate features under the banner of the DFS. **DFS Namespaces** allows you to create a logical folder structure that you distribute across multiple computers. **DFS Replication** replicates data held on DFS target folders to provide a transparent, fault-tolerant, and load-balancing DFS implementation. Note that DFS Replication is separate from the Storage Replica feature discussed in *Chapter 4, Managing Windows Storage*.

In the *Configuring a DFS Namespace* recipe, you'll set up a domain-based DFS Namespace. And then, you'll configure and set up DFS Replication in the *Configuring DFS Replication* recipe.

There are a number of servers involved in the recipes in this chapter—each recipe describes the specific server you use for that recipe. As with other chapters, all the servers are members of the Reskit.Org domain.

Setting up and securing an SMB file server

The first step in creating a file server is to install the necessary features to the server, then harden it. You use the Add-WindowsFeature cmdlet to add the features necessary for a file server. You can then use the Set-SmbServerConfiguration cmdlet to improve the configuration.

Since your file server can contain sensitive information, you must take reasonable steps to avoid some of the common attack mechanisms and adopt best security practices. Security is a good thing but, as always, be careful! By locking down your SMB file server too hard, you can lock some users out of the server. SMB 1.0 has a number of weaknesses and, in general, should be removed. But, if you disable SMB 1.0, you may find that older computers (for example, those running Windows XP) lose the ability to access shared data. Before you lock down any of the server configurations, be sure to test your changes carefully.

Getting ready

Run this recipe on FS1, a new server in the Reskit.Org domain.

How to do it...

1. Add the FileServer features and RSAT tools to FS1:

```
$Features = 'FileAndStorage-Services','File-Services',
            'FS-FileServer','RSAT-File-Services'
Add-WindowsFeature -Name $Features
```

2. Retrieve the SMB Server settings:

```
Get-SmbServerConfiguration
```

3. Turn off SMB1:

```
$CHT = @{
   EnableSMB1Protocol = $false
   Confirm            = $false
}
Set-SmbServerConfiguration @CHT
```

4. Turn on SMB signing and encryption:

```
$SHT1 = @{
   RequireSecuritySignature = $true
   EnableSecuritySignature  = $true
   EncryptData              = $true
   Confirm                  = $false
}
Set-SmbServerConfiguration @SHT1
```

5. Turn off the default server and workstations shares:

```
$SHT2 = @{
  AutoShareServer        = $false
  AutoShareWorkstation   = $false
  Confirm                = $false
}
Set-SmbServerConfiguration @SHT2
```

6. Turn off server announcements:

```
$SHT3 = @{
  ServerHidden    = $true
  AnnounceServer  = $false
  Confirm         = $false
}
Set-SmbServerConfiguration @SHT3
```

7. Restart the service with the new configuration:

```
Restart-Service lanmanserver
```

How it works...

In *step 1*, you add four features to the FS1 server (FileAndStorage-Services, File-Services, FS-FileServer, RSAT-File-Services), which looks like this:

```
PS C:\Foo> $Features = 'FileAndStorage-Services','File-Services',
                       'FS-FileServer','RSAT-File-Services'
PS C:\Foo> Add-WindowsFeature -Name $Features

Success Restart Needed Exit Code    Feature Result
------- -------------- ---------    --------------
True    No             Success      {File and iSCSI Services, File Server, Rem...
```

In *step 2*, after adding the necessary features to FS1, you get the SMB server configuration using the Get-SMBServerConfiguration cmdlet. This returns 43 separate configuration properties. You can change some of these to harden your SMB server or to accommodate unique aspects of your infrastructure. Some of these properties, however, are relatively obscure—if you don't know what they do, consider leaving them at their default values.

The output of this step looks like this:

```
PS C:\Foo> Get-SmbServerConfiguration

AnnounceComment                       :
AnnounceServer                        : False
AsynchronousCredits                   : 512
AuditSmb1Access                       : False
AutoDisconnectTimeout                 : 15
AutoShareServer                       : True
AutoShareWorkstation                  : True
CachedOpenLimit                       : 10
DurableHandleV2TimeoutInSeconds       : 180
EnableAuthenticateUserSharing         : False
EnableDownlevelTimewarp               : False
EnableForcedLogoff                    : True
EnableLeasing                         : True
EnableMultiChannel                    : True
EnableOplocks                         : True
EnableSecuritySignature               : False
EnableSMB1Protocol                    : False
EnableSMB2Protocol                    : True
EnableStrictNameChecking              : True
EncryptData                           : False
IrpStackSize                          : 15
KeepAliveTime                         : 2
MaxChannelPerSession                  : 32
MaxMpxCount                           : 50
MaxSessionPerConnection               : 16384
MaxThreadsPerQueue                    : 20
MaxWorkItems                          : 1
NullSessionPipes                      :
NullSessionShares                     :
OplockBreakWait                       : 35
PendingClientTimeoutInSeconds         : 120
RejectUnencryptedAccess               : True
RequireSecuritySignature              : False
ServerHidden                          : True
Smb2CreditsMax                        : 8192
Smb2CreditsMin                        : 512
SmbServerNameHardeningLevel           : 0
TreatHostAsStableStorage              : False
ValidateAliasNotCircular              : True
ValidateShareScope                    : True
ValidateShareScopeNotAliased          : True
ValidateTargetName                    : True
```

In *step 3*, you turn off SMB1. In *step 4*, you configure the server to sign all SMB packets and to encrypt data transferred via SMB. SMB signing is particularly useful to reduce the risk of a man-in-the-middle attack. Requiring data encryption increases the security of your organization's data as it travels between server and client computers. Another benefit of using SMB encryption versus something such as IPSec is that deployment is just a matter of adjusting SMB server configuration.

Windows has a set of administrative shares it creates by default. In most cases, you can disable these. In *step 5*, you turn off the default server/workstation shares. It's important to note that when setting up DFS Replication, the DFS Replication cmdlets require access to these administrative shares.

With *step 6*, you also turn off server announcements, which reduces the visibility of your file server to hackers.

With those configuration items updated, in *step 7*, you restart the file server service `lanmanserver`. Note that restarting the service closes any active connections. Ensure you restart during a scheduled maintenance outage or when you're certain the server is inactive.

These final five steps created no output. After you update these configuration settings, you can use `Get-SMBServerConfiguration` to confirm the correct server settings are in place.

There's more...

In this recipe, you hardened a full installation of Windows Server 2019. To further harden your file server, consider using Server Core for your hosts.

In *step 3*, you disabled **SMB1**. **SMB1** is an older and less secure version of the SMB protocol and could represent an attack vector. The downside of disabling it is that older client computers only support **SMB1** and could cease to access shared data if you disable **SMB1**. Older clients include Windows XP and Windows Server 2003. Windows Vista/Server 2008 and later versions of Windows have built-in support for **SMB2**. So, as long as you're running fully-supported clients and server systems, you should be able to turn off **SMB1**.

For large organizations, you should consider using the `AuditSmb1Access` configuration setting. This setting logs access your server via **SMB1**. To discover any older SMB clients that would be affected by disabling **SMB1**, you can search the SMB event log.

Creating and securing SMB shares

With your file server service set up, the next step in deploying a file server is to create SMB shares and secure them. For decades, administrators have used the `net.exe` command to set up shared folders and to do a lot more. These continue to work, but you may find the new cmdlets easier to use, particularly if you're automating large-scale SMB server deployments.

This recipe looks at creating and securing shares on a Server 2019 platform using the PowerShell `SMBServer` module. You also use cmdlets from the `NTFSSecurity` module (a third-party module you download from the PS Gallery).

Getting ready

You run this recipe on the file server (FS1) that you set up and hardened in the *Setting up and securing your SMB server* recipe. In this recipe, you share a folder (C:\Foo) on the file server. You created this folder previously. Then, you create a file in the C:\Foo folder you just shared and set the ACL for the files to be the same as for the share. You use the Set-SMBPathAcl cmdlet to do this. You then review the ACL for both the folder and the file.

This recipe uses a global security group, Sales, which you create in the Reskit.Org domain. See the introduction section in *Chapter 7, Managing Printers*, for the script snippet you can use to create the groups, users, and group memberships used by this recipe.

In this recipe, you use the Get-NTFSAccess cmdlet from NTFSSecurity, a third-party module that you downloaded from the PowerShell Gallery. See the *Managing NTFS permissions* recipe for more details about this module and for instructions on how to download it.

How to do it...

1. Discover existing shares and access rights:

```
Get-SmbShare -Name * |
  Get-SmbShareAccess |
    Format-Table -GroupBy Name
```

2. Share a folder:

```
New-SmbShare -Name Foo -Path C:\Foo
```

3. Update the share to have a description:

```
$CHT = @{Confirm=$False}
Set-SmbShare -Name Foo -Description 'Foo share for IT' @CHT
```

4. Set folder enumeration mode:

```
$CHT = @{Confirm = $false}
Set-SMBShare -Name Foo -FolderEnumerationMode AccessBased @CHT
```

5. Set encryption on the Foo share:

```
Set-SmbShare -Name Foo -EncryptData $True @CHT
```

6. Remove all access to the `Foo` share:

```
$AHT1 = @{
    Name         =  'Foo'
    AccountName = 'Everyone'
    Confirm      =  $false
}
Revoke-SmbShareAccess @AHT1 | Out-Null
```

7. Add `Reskit\Administrator` to have Read access to the share:

```
$AHT2 = @{
    Name         = 'foo'
    AccessRight  = 'Read'
    AccountName  = 'Reskit\ADMINISTRATOR'
    ConFirm      = $false
}
Grant-SmbShareAccess @AHT2 | Out-Null
```

8. Add Full access for the OS:

```
$AHT3 = @{
    Name          = 'foo'
    AccessRight   = 'Full'
    AccountName   = 'NT Authority\SYSTEM'
    Confirm       = $False
}
Grant-SmbShareAccess  @AHT3 | Out-Null
```

9. Set Creator/Owner to have Full access:

```
$AHT4 = @{
    Name          = 'foo'
    AccessRight   = 'Full'
    AccountName   = 'CREATOR OWNER'
    Confirm       = $False
}
Grant-SmbShareAccess @AHT4  | Out-Null
```

10. Grant `Sales` administrators Read access, and grant `SalesAdmins` Full access:

```
$AHT5 = @{
    Name         = 'Foo'
    AccessRight = 'Read'
    AccountName = 'Sales'
```

```
        Confirm    = $false
}
Grant-SmbShareAccess @AHT5 | Out-Null
$AHT6 = @{
    Name        = 'Foo'
    AccessRight = 'Full'
    AccountName = 'SalesAdmins'
    Confirm     = $false
}
Grant-SmbShareAccess  @AHT6 | Out-Null
```

11. Review the ACL on the Foo share:

```
Get-SmbShareAccess -Name Foo |
  Sort-Object AccessRight
```

12. Set the ACL file to be same as the shared ACL:

```
Set-SmbPathAcl -ShareName 'Foo'
```

13. Create a file in C\Foo:

```
'foo' | Out-File -FilePath C:\Foo\Foo.Txt
```

14. Set the ACL file to be same as the shared ACL:

```
Set-SmbPathAcl -ShareName 'Foo'
```

15. View the ACL folder using Get-NTFSAccess:

```
Get-NTFSAccess -Path C:\Foo |
  Format-Table -AutoSize
```

16. View the ACL file:

```
Get-NTFSAccess -Path C:\Foo\Foo.Txt |
  Format-Table -AutoSize
```

How it works...

In *step 1*, you look at the existing shares and access rights, which looks like this:

```
PS C:\Foo> Get-SmbShare -Name * |
              Get-SmbShareAccess |
                Format-Table -GroupBy Name

    Name: IPC$

Name ScopeName AccountName                AccessControlType AccessRight
---- --------- -----------                ----------------- -----------
IPC$ *         BUILTIN\Administrators     Allow             Full
IPC$ *         BUILTIN\Backup Operators   Allow             Full
IPC$ *         NT AUTHORITY\INTERACTIVE   Allow             Full
```

In *step 2*, you create a new SMB share (`Foo`) on the `C:\Foo` folder, which looks like this:

```
PS C:\Foo> New-SmbShare -Name Foo -Path C:\Foo

Name ScopeName Path     Description
---- --------- ----     -----------
Foo  *         C:\Foo
```

With *step 3*, you add a description to the share. In *step 4*, you set the share enumeration mode to `AccessBased`. In *step 5*, you set encryption for data sent to/from the `Foo` share. With *step 6*, you explicitly remove all access to the `Foo` share. In *step 7*, you enable `Reskit\Administrator` to have read-only access to the share. In *step 8*, you enable the OS to have full access to the share, while in *step 9*, you allow the creator or owner full access to files or folders in the share. In *step 10*, you grant all members of the `Sales` group read access to data on the share, and you grant members of the `SalesAdmins` group full access to the share. *Step 3* through *step 10* produce no output.

After configuring access to the share, in *step 11*, you use the `Get-SMBShareAccess` cmdlet to view the `Foo` share's ACL, which looks like this:

```
PS C:\Foo> Get-SmbShareAccess -Name Foo |
              Sort-Object AccessRight

Name ScopeName AccountName            AccessControlType AccessRight
---- --------- -----------            ----------------- -----------
Foo  *         CREATOR OWNER          Allow             Full
Foo  *         NT AUTHORITY\SYSTEM    Allow             Full
Foo  *         RESKIT\SalesAdmins     Allow             Full
Foo  *         RESKIT\administrator   Allow             Read
Foo  *         RESKIT\Sales           Allow             Read
```

In *step 12*, you set the NTFS ACL file/folder to be same as the ACL for the share, which produces no output. With *step 13*, you create a new file in the `C:\Foo` folder. These two steps produce no output.

In *step 14*, you view the updated ACL on the `C:\Foo` folder itself, which looks like this:

```
PS C:\foo> Get-NTFSAccess -Path C:\Foo |
           Format-Table -AutoSize

   Path: C:\Foo (Inheritance enabled)

Account                    Access Rights               Applies to                           Type  IsInherited InheritedFrom
-------                    -------------               ----------                           ----  ----------- -------------
CREATOR OWNER              FullControl                 SubfoldersAndFilesOnly               Allow False
NT AUTHORITY\SYSTEM        FullControl                 ThisFolderSubfoldersAndFiles         Allow False
BUILTIN\Administrators     FullControl                 ThisFolderOnly                       Allow False
RESKIT\administrator       ReadAndExecute, Synchronize ThisFolderSubfoldersAndFiles         Allow False
RESKIT\SalesAdmins         FullControl                 ThisFolderSubfoldersAndFiles         Allow False
RESKIT\Sales               ReadAndExecute, Synchronize ThisFolderSubfoldersAndFiles         Allow False
NT AUTHORITY\SYSTEM        FullControl                 ThisFolderSubfoldersAndFiles         Allow True        C:
BUILTIN\Administrators     FullControl                 ThisFolderSubfoldersAndFiles         Allow True        C:
BUILTIN\Users              ReadAndExecute, Synchronize ThisFolderSubfoldersAndFiles         Allow True        C:
BUILTIN\Users              CreateDirectories           ThisFolderAndSubfolders              Allow True        C:
BUILTIN\Users              CreateFiles                 ThisFolderAndSubfolders              Allow True        C:
CREATOR OWNER              GenericAll                  SubfoldersAndFilesOnly               Allow True        C:
```

Finally, in *step 15*, you view the ACL for the file you created in *step 13*, which looks like this:

```
PS C:\foo> Get-NTFSAccess -Path C:\Foo\Foo.Txt |
           Format-Table -AutoSize

   Path: C:\Foo\Foo.Txt (Inheritance enabled)

Account                    Access Rights               Applies to      Type  IsInherited InheritedFrom
-------                    -------------               ----------      ----  ----------- -------------
BUILTIN\Administrators     FullControl                 ThisFolderOnly  Allow True        C:\Foo
NT AUTHORITY\SYSTEM        FullControl                 ThisFolderOnly  Allow True        C:\Foo
RESKIT\administrator       ReadAndExecute, Synchronize ThisFolderOnly  Allow True        C:\Foo
RESKIT\SalesAdmins         FullControl                 ThisFolderOnly  Allow True        C:\Foo
RESKIT\Sales               ReadAndExecute, Synchronize ThisFolderOnly  Allow True        C:\Foo
BUILTIN\Users              ReadAndExecute, Synchronize ThisFolderOnly  Allow True        C:
```

There's more...

In *step 1*, you examined the existing SMB shares. This step is run on the `FS1` file server after you've hardened it (see the *Creating and securing an SMB file server* recipe). Thus, all the default shares (except the `IPC$` share) aren't present on `FS1`.

The `IPC$` share is also known as the null session connection. This session connection enables anonymous users to enumerate the names of domain accounts and network shares. The `lanmanserver` service creates this share by default, although you can turn it off. The `IPC$` share is also used to support named pipe connections to your server.

In *step 4,* you set the enumeration mode on the `Foo` share to `AccessBased`. This means that when you're browsing folders and files within this share, you only see the objects you have access to. There is an improvement in security (as people can't see files they have no access to), but this does introduce a small performance penalty.

In *step 5*, you set up this share to encrypt data sent to/from the share. This overrides the overall server configuration you set in the *Setting up and securing an SMB file server* recipe.

In *step 14* and *step 15*, you examined the ACLs on the underlying folder and file after setting NTFS permissions on `C:\Foo` to be the same as for the `Foo` share. Since you didn't remove inheritance from the `C:\Foo` folder in this recipe, you can see that some users still have access (due to inheritance) to the files and files in the folder. To further secure this folder, you should remove NTFS inheritance from the `C:\Foo` folder.

See Also

For details about `IPC$` share, see `https://support.microsoft.com/en-in/help/3034016/ipc-share-and-null-session-behavior-in-windows`. Be careful if you chose to turn off the `IPC$` share—test the resulting configuration very carefully.

Accessing data on SMB shares

In the *Creating and securing SMB shares* recipe, you created a share on FS1. Files shared using SMB act and feel like local files when you access the share, for example, via Explorer.

In this recipe, you access the `Foo` share on FS1 from the CL1 Windows 10 system you created in *Chapter 1, Establishing a PowerShell Administrative Environment*.

Getting ready

You should have completed the *Creating and securing SMB shares* recipe. Additionally, you should have the CL1 Windows 10 system up and working—you created this system in *Chapter 1, Establishing a PowerShell Administrative Environment*.

You should run this recipe in an elevated console.

How to do it...

1. Examine the SMB client's configuration:

    ```
    Get-SmbClientConfiguration
    ```

2. Set SMB signing from the client:

    ```
    $CHT = @{Confirm=$false}
    Set-SmbClientConfiguration -RequireSecuritySignature $True @CHT
    ```

3. Examine the SMB client's network interface:

    ```
    Get-SmbClientNetworkInterface |
      Format-Table Friendlyname, RSS*, RD*, Speed, IpAddresses
    ```

4. Examine the shares provided by FS1:

    ```
    $FS1CS = New-CimSession -ComputerName FS1
    Get-SmbShare -CimSession $FS1CS
    ```

5. Create a drive mapping, mapping R: to the share on the FS1 server:

    ```
    New-SmbMapping -LocalPath R: -RemotePath \\FS1.Reskit.Org\Foo
    ```

6. View the shared folder mapping on CL1:

    ```
    Get-SmbMapping
    ```

7. View the shared folder's contents:

    ```
    Get-ChildItem -Path R:
    ```

8. View the existing connections:

    ```
    Get-SmbConnection
    ```

9. Show what files and folders are open on FS1:

    ```
    Notepad R:\Foo.Txt   # created in an earlier recipe
    Get-SmbOpenFile -CimSession $FS1CS
    ```

How it works...

In *step 1*, you view the SMB client configuration, which looks like this:

```
PS C:\Foo> Get-SmbClientConfiguration

ConnectionCountPerRssNetworkInterface : 4
DirectoryCacheEntriesMax              : 16
DirectoryCacheEntrySizeMax            : 65536
DirectoryCacheLifetime                : 10
DormantFileLimit                      : 1023
EnableBandwidthThrottling             : True
EnableByteRangeLockingOnReadOnlyFiles : True
EnableInsecureGuestLogons             : False
EnableLargeMtu                        : True
EnableLoadBalanceScaleOut             : True
EnableMultiChannel                    : True
EnableSecuritySignature               : True
ExtendedSessionTimeout                : 1000
FileInfoCacheEntriesMax               : 64
FileInfoCacheLifetime                 : 10
FileNotFoundCacheEntriesMax           : 128
FileNotFoundCacheLifetime             : 5
KeepConn                              : 600
MaxCmds                               : 50
MaximumConnectionCountPerServer       : 32
OplocksDisabled                       : False
RequireSecuritySignature              : False
SessionTimeout                        : 60
UseOpportunisticLocking               : True
WindowSizeThreshold                   : 8
```

In *step 2*, you explicitly set the SBM to require the signing of SMB packets. This step creates no output.

In *step 3*, you look at the SMB client's network interface details, which look something like this:

```
PS C:\Foo> Get-SmbClientNetworkInterface |
             Format-Table Friendlyname, RSS*, RD*, Speed, IpAddresses

Friendlyname              RssCapable RdmaCapable Speed IpAddresses
------------              ---------- ----------- ----- -----------
Ethernet                  True       False             {fe80::340b:dd6d:1a00:e5bd, 10.10.10.181}
vSwitch (Default Switch)  False      False             {}
vEthernet (Default Switch) True      False             {fe80::85b6:3013:a25f:a9dc, 192.168.145.145}
```

In *step 4*, you set up a CIM session to FS1, then use that session to determine the shares being offered by FS1, which looks like this:

```
PS C:\Foo> $FS1CS = New-CimSession -ComputerName FS1
PS C:\Foo> Get-SmbShare -CimSession $FS1CS

Name ScopeName Path   Description      PSComputerName
---- --------- ----   -----------      --------------
Foo  *         C:\Foo Foo share for IT FS1
IPC$ *                Remote IPC       FS1
```

In *step 5*, you create a new client-side drive mapping, mapping the R: drive on CL1 to the
\\FS1\Foo share. The output looks like this:

```
PS C:\Foo> New-SmbMapping -LocalPath R: -RemotePath \\FS1.Reskit.Org\Foo

Status Local Path Remote Path
------ ---------- -----------
OK     R:         \\FS1.Reskit.Org\Foo
```

In *step 6*, you view the client-side drive mappings, which looks like this:

```
PS C:\Foo> Get-SmbMapping

Status Local Path Remote Path
------ ---------- -----------
OK     R:         \\FS1.Reskit.Org\Foo
```

In *step 7*, you use the Get-ChildItem cmdlet to view the contents of the R: drive, and see
what files exist on the Foo share of FS1. The output of this step looks like this:

```
PS C:\Foo> Get-ChildItem -Path R:

    Directory: r:\

Mode                LastWriteTime         Length Name
----                -------------         ------ ----
-a----        12/01/2019     10:29            12 Foo.Txt
```

In *step 8*, you open a file on R: in the Notepad drive and then use the CIM session (which you
created in *step 4*) to view the open connections to FS1. The output looks like this:

```
PS C:\Foo> Get-SmbConnection

ServerName       ShareName UserName            Credential                 Dialect NumOpens
----------       --------- --------            ----------                 ------- --------
FS1.Reskit.Org   Foo       RESKIT\administrator RESKIT.ORG\Administrator   3.1.1   1
```

In the final step, *step 9*, you view the files and folders that are open on FS1, which looks like this:

```
PS C:\Foo> Get-SmbOpenFile -CimSession $FS1CS

FileId       SessionId    Path                ShareRelativePath ClientComputerName ClientUserName       PSComputerName
------       ---------    ----                ----------------- ------------------ --------------       --------------
34359738397 34359738373 C:\Foo\                               10.10.10.181       RESKIT\Administrator FS1
34359738401 34359738373 C:\Foo\Foo.Txt Foo.Txt                10.10.10.181       RESKIT\Administrator FS1
```

There's more...

In *step 4*, you create a CIM session from CL1 to FS1, and check which shares are provided by FS1. There's no cmdlet equivalent of the net view <servername> command.

In *step 7*, since you have set permissions, a regular domain admin account has no access. It needs to be part of the Sales or Salesadmin groups.

In *step 9*, you used Get-SmbOpenFile to see the files open on FS1. As you can see, details of the open file and the computer making the connection are clearly shown. You get both a full path for each open file or folder, as well as a share-relative path. What the output shows is that R:\Foo.Txt from CL1 is C:\Foo\Foo.Txt on FS1.

Creating an iSCSI target

iSCSI is an industry-standard protocol that implements block storage over a TCP/IP network. With iSCSI, the server, or initiator, provides a volume shared via iSCSI. Effectively, the shared volumes are iSCSI logical unit numbers. The iSCSI client then sees that disk as locally attached. From the iSCSI client, you can manage the disk just like locally-attached storage.

Windows Server 2019 includes both iSCSI target (server) and iSCSI initiator (client) features. You set up an iSCSI target on a server and then use an iSCSI initiator on a client system to access the iSCSI target. You can use both Microsoft and third-party initiators and targets, although if you mix and match, you need to test very carefully that the combination works in your environment.

With iSCSI, a target is a single disk that the client accesses using the iSCSI Client. An iSCSI target server hosts one or more targets, where each iSCSI target is equivalent to a LUN on a **Fiber Channel SAN**. The iSCSI initiator is a built-in component of Windows Server 2019 (and Windows 10). The iSCSI target feature is one you install optionally on Windows Server 2019.

You could use iSCSI in a cluster of Hyper-V servers. The servers in the cluster can use the iSCSI initiator to access an iSCSI target. Used via the **Cluster Shared Volume**, the shared iSCSI target is shared between nodes in a failover cluster that enables the VMs in that cluster to be highly available.

Getting ready

In this recipe, you create an iSCSI target on the SRV1 server. Run this recipe from SRV1.

How to do it...

1. Install the iSCSI target feature on SRV1:

```
Install-WindowsFeature FS-iSCSITarget-Server
```

2. Explore the iSCSI target server settings:

```
Get-IscsiTargetServerSetting
```

3. Create a folder on SRV1 to hold the iSCSI virtual disk:

```
$NIHT = @{
   Path        = 'C:\iSCSI'
   ItemType    = 'Directory'
   ErrorAction = 'SilentlyContinue'
}
New-Item @NIHT | Out-Null
```

4. Create an iSCSI disk (that is, a LUN):

```
$LP = 'C:\iSCSI\SalesData.Vhdx'
$LN = 'SalesTarget'
$VDHT = @{
   Path        = $LP
   Description = 'LUN For Sales'
   SizeBytes   = 100MB
 }
New-IscsiVirtualDisk @VDHT
```

5. Create the iSCSI target:

```
$THT = @{
   TargetName    = $LN
   InitiatorIds = 'DNSNAME:FS1.Reskit.Org'
}
New-IscsiServerTarget @THT
```

6. Create the iSCSI disk target mapping:

```
Add-IscsiVirtualDiskTargetMapping -TargetName $LN -Path $LP
```

How it works...

In *step 1*, you add the FS-iSCSITarget-Server feature to SRV1, which looks like this:

```
PS C:\Foo> Install-WindowsFeature FS-iSCSITarget-Server

Success Restart Needed Exit Code     Feature Result
------- -------------- ---------     --------------
True    No             Success       {iSCSI Target Server}
```

In *step 2*, you get the iSCSI target server settings for SRV1, which looks like this:

```
PS C:\Foo> Get-IscsiTargetServerSetting

ComputerName             : SRV1.Reskit.Org
IsClustered              : False
Version                  : 10.0
DisableRemoteManagement  : False
Portals                  : {+10.10.1.11:3260,  -[fe80::1cba:c89e:66da:928c%3]:3260...}
```

In *step 3*, which creates no output, you ensure you have a folder on SRV1 to hold the new iSCSI disk volume. In *step 4*, you create the iSCSI virtual disk, which looks like this:

```
PS C:\foo> $LP = 'C:\iSCSI\SalesData.Vhdx'
PS C:\foo> $LN = 'SalesTarget'
PS C:\foo> $VDHT = @{
             Path        = $LP
             Description = 'LUN For Sales'
             SizeBytes   = 100MB
           }
PS C:\Foo> New-IscsiVirtualDisk @VDHT


ClusterGroupName    :
ComputerName        : SRV1.Reskit.Org
Description         : LUN For Sales
DiskType            : Dynamic
HostVolumeId        : {883A5313-0000-0000-0000-100000000000}
LocalMountDeviceId  :
OriginalPath        :
ParentPath          :
Path                : C:\iSCSI\SalesData.Vhdx
SerialNumber        : 883E576D-1FAB-4AEB-9AE4-9CEEC4F98311
Size                : 104857600
SnapshotIds         :
Status              : NotConnected
VirtualDiskIndex    : 214536525
```

In *step 5*, you create the iSCSI target on SRV1, which looks like this:

```
PS C:\Foo> $THT = @{
             TargetName   = $LN
             InitiatorIds = 'DNSNAME:FS1.Reskit.Org'
           }
PS C:\Foo> New-IscsiServerTarget @THT


ChapUserName                   :
ClusterGroupName               :
ComputerName                   : SRV1.Reskit.Org
Description                    :
EnableChap                     : False
EnableReverseChap              : False
EnforceIdleTimeoutDetection    : True
FirstBurstLength               : 65536
IdleDuration                   : 00:00:00
InitiatorIds                   : {DnsName:FS1.Reskit.Org}
LastLogin                      :
LunMappings                    : {}
MaxBurstLength                 : 262144
MaxReceiveDataSegmentLength    : 65536
ReceiveBufferCount             : 10
ReverseChapUserName            :
Sessions                       : {}
Status                         : NotConnected
TargetIqn                      : iqn.1991-05.com.microsoft:fs1-salestarget-target
TargetName                     : SalesTarget
```

In *step 6*, you complete the creation of the iSCSI target by adding an iSCSI virtual disk target mapping.

There's more...

In *step 3*, you create the new LUN, using `New-IscsiVirtualDisk`. When using this command, you must specify a VHDX file extension. Windows Server 2019 doesn't support VHD files for new iSCSI targets. If you have older VHD files you want to use as an iSCSI virtual disk, you can create a target that points to it. You just can't create new iSCSI virtual disks.

The virtual disk you created in *step 4* is uninitialized and contains no filesystem. In order to use the iSCSI disk, you use the iSCSI initiator to mount and manage the drive as if it were local. You'll see this in the *Using an iSCSI target* recipe.

You can also increase security by using **Challenge Handshake Authentication Protocol (CHAP)** authentication. You can specify the CHAP username and password on both the initiator and the target to authenticate the connection to an iSCSI target. If the security of iSCSI traffic is an issue, you could consider securing iSCSI traffic using IPSec.

See Also

If you aren't familiar with iSCSI and iSCSI targets, see `https://docs.microsoft.com/en-us/windows-server/storage/iscsi/iscsi-target-server` for an overview. And for more information on iSCSI, see `https://en.wikipedia.org/wiki/ISCSI`.

Using an iSCSI target

Once you have an iSCSI target defined, as you did in the *Creating an iSCSI target* recipe, you can use it. Essentially, to use the disk, you connect to the iSCSI target server (that is, `SRV1`). Once you're connected, the `Get-Disk` cmdlet returns the iSCSI disk as though it were a local disk. You can then format and use the iSCSI disk as though it were local.

Getting ready

This recipe uses the iSCSI target you created in the *Creating an iSCSI target* recipe. You use `SRV1` as the iSCSI target and access the target from the iSCSI initiator (`FS1`).

How to do it...

1. On FS1, set the iSCSI service to start automatically, then start the service:

```
Set-Service MSiSCSI -StartupType 'Automatic'
Start-Service MSiSCSI
```

2. Set up the portal to SRV1:

```
$PHT = @{
  TargetPortalAddress     = 'SRV1.Reskit.Org'
  TargetPortalPortNumber  = 3260
}
New-IscsiTargetPortal @PHT
```

3. Find and view the SalesTarget on the portal:

```
$Target   = Get-IscsiTarget |
                Where-Object NodeAddress -Match 'SalesTarget'
$Target
```

4. Connect to the target on SRV1:

```
$CHT = @{
  TargetPortalAddress = 'SRV1.Reskit.Org'
  NodeAddress         = $Target.NodeAddress
}
Connect-IscsiTarget  @CHT
```

5. View the iSCSI disk on SRV1 from FS1:

```
$ISD =  Get-Disk |
  Where-Object BusType -eq 'iscsi'
$ISD |
  Format-Table -AutoSize
```

6. Turn the disk online and set it to read/write:

```
$ISD |
  Set-Disk -IsOffline $False
$ISD |
  Set-Disk -Isreadonly $False
```

7. Create a volume on the iSCSI disk on `FS1`:

```
$NVHT = @{
  FriendlyName = 'SalesData'
  FileSystem   = 'NTFS'
  DriveLetter  = 'I'
}
$ISD |
  New-Volume @NVHT
```

8. Use the drive as a local drive:

```
Set-Location -Path I:
New-Item -Path I:\  -Name SalesData -ItemType Directory |
  Out-Null
'Testing 1-2-3' |
  Out-File -FilePath I:\SalesData\Test.Txt
Get-ChildItem -Path I:\SalesData
```

How it works...

In *step 1*, you set the Microsoft iSCSI service to automatically start, then you start it. This step produces no output.

In *step 2*, you create a portal to the iSCSI server on `SRV1`, which looks like this:

```
PS C:\Foo> $PHT = @{
             TargetPortalAddress    = 'SRV1.Reskit.Org'
             TargetPortalPortNumber = 3260
           }
PS C:\Foo> New-IscsiTargetPortal @PHT

InitiatorInstanceName :
InitiatorPortalAddress :
IsDataDigest          : False
IsHeaderDigest        : False
TargetPortalAddress   : SRV1.Reskit.Org
TargetPortalPortNumber : 3260
PSComputerName        :
```

In *step 3*, you use the portal just created to get the `SalesTarget` iSCSI target on `SRV1`, which looks like this:

```
PS C:\Foo> $Target   = Get-IscsiTarget |
             Where-Object NodeAddress -Match 'SalesTarget'
PS C:\Foo> $Target

IsConnected NodeAddress                                          PSComputerName
----------- -----------                                          --------------
      False iqn.1991-05.com.microsoft:srv1-salestarget-target
```

In *step 4*, you connect to the iSCSI target on SRV1, which looks like this:

```
PS C:\Foo> $CHT = @{
             TargetPortalAddress = 'SRV1.Reskit.Org'
             NodeAddress         = $Target.NodeAddress
           }
PS C:\Foo> Connect-IscsiTarget  @CHT

AuthenticationType     : NONE
InitiatorInstanceName  : ROOT\ISCSIPRT\0000_0
InitiatorNodeAddress   : iqn.1991-05.com.microsoft:fs1.reskit.org
InitiatorPortalAddress : 0.0.0.0
InitiatorSideIdentifier : 400001370000
IsConnected            : True
IsDataDigest           : False
IsDiscovered           : False
IsHeaderDigest         : False
IsPersistent           : False
NumberOfConnections    : 1
SessionIdentifier      : ffffa48758373010-4000013700000002
TargetNodeAddress      : iqn.1991-05.com.microsoft:srv1-salestarget-target
TargetSideIdentifier   : 0100
PSComputerName         :
```

Once you've connected to the iSCSI target, you can view the disk drive provided via iSCSI, which looks like this:

```
PS C:\Foo> $ISD =  Get-Disk |
             Where-Object BusType -eq 'iscsi'
PS C:\Foo> $ISD |
             Format-Table -AutoSize

Number Friendly Name    Serial Number                          HealthStatus OperationalStatus Total Size Partition Style
------ -------------    -------------                          ------------ ----------------- ---------- ---------------
1      MSFT Virtual HD  3F123A44-45F7-4918-8294-7517058FEE36 Healthy      Online              500 MB RAW
```

In *step 6*, you turn the disk online and make it read/write. This step produces no output. In *step 7*, you create a new volume on this disk, which looks like this:

```
PS C:\Foo> $NVHT = @{
        FriendlyName = 'SalesData'
        FileSystem   = 'NTFS'
        DriveLetter  = 'I'
        }
PS C:\Foo> $ISD |
        New-Volume @NVHT

DriveLetter FriendlyName FileSystemType DriveType HealthStatus OperationalStatus SizeRemaining     Size
----------- ------------ -------------- --------- ------------ ----------------- -------------     ----
I           SalesData    NTFS           Fixed     Healthy      OK                467.78 MB 483.93 MB
```

In the final step, *step 8*, you use the iSCSI disk just like it was a local one, which looks like this:

```
PS C:\Foo> Set-Location -Path I:
PS I: > New-Item -Path I:\ -Name SalesData -ItemType Directory |
        Out-Null
PS I: > 'Testing 1-2-3' |
        Out-File -FilePath I:\SalesData\Test.Txt
PS I: > Get-ChildItem I:\SalesData

    Directory: I:\SalesData

Mode            LastWriteTime       Length Name
----            -------------       ------ ----
-a----      14/01/2019    10:06         32 Test.Txt
```

There's more...

This recipe enabled you to use the Microsoft iSCSI initiator to connect to a Microsoft iSCSI-provided target. These built-in features work and are fine for simple use.

The iSCSI initiator and the iSCSI target features with Windows Server 2019 have seen little development or improvement since they were first released over a decade ago. You may find independent third-party iSCSI vendors that are more appropriate depending on your requirements.

Configuring a DFS Namespace

The **Distributed File System** (**DFS**) is a set of services in Windows that enables you to create a structured replicated filestore on two or more servers within your organization. Microsoft first released DFS as an add-on to Windows NT 4.0. DFS has improved significantly since then.

In Windows Server 2019, DFS has two separate components. The first is **DFS Namespace** (**DFSN**). DFSN enables you to create a single contiguous namespace that refers to shares held on multiple servers. The second component, **DFS Replication** (**DFSR**), replicates data between DFS nodes in the DFS Namespace.

With DFS Namespaces, you can make use of shared folders stored on computers throughout the organization to create a single logically-structured namespace. This namespace appears to the user as a continuous and well-organized set of folders and subfolders, even though the actual shared data may be in a variety of independently-named shares on one or more computers in the organization.

Before you build your DFS Namespace, you need to create the shared folders that you wish to add to your DFS Namespace. The namespace design then determines which folder goes where within the namespace hierarchy. You also define the names of the folders in the namespace, and these can be different from the underlying file shares. When you view the DFS Namespace, the folders appear to reside on a single share that has multiple folders and subfolders. You navigate through the DFS Namespace and avoid needing to know the names of the actual servers and shares that physically hold the actual data.

It's important to note that using DFSN does not replicate any data between targets. Typically, you would use DFS Replication. If you need to replicate data, there are a variety of other tools available that may be more appropriate for your needs. For more information on file-synchronization tools, check out the following link: `https://en.wikipedia.org/wiki//Comparison_of_file_synchronization_software`.

Both DFSN and DFSR have a supporting PowerShell module. The DFSN module helps you to manage the DFS Namespaces in your DFS implementation. You manage DFSR replication using the DFSR module.

In this recipe, you set up and configure a domain-based DFS Namespace on the SRV1 and SRV2 servers. You create additional DFS Namespace targets on other computers, and add these to the DFS Namespace. In a later recipe, *Configuring DFS Replication*, you set up replication using DFSR.

Getting ready

This recipe uses several systems: DC1, DC2, FS1, FS2, SRV1, and SRV2. Each of these systems hosts one or more shares that you create and use in this recipe as targets for the DFSN Namespace. You run this recipe from the CL1 Windows 10 (1809) system.

> If your CL1 system is running an earlier edition of Windows 10, *step 1* may not work for you, as the mechanism for adding RSAT tools has changed with 1809. If you're using Windows 10 1709 or 1803, check out https://tfl09.blogspot.com/2018/10/installing-rsat-tools.html for details on how to add the RSAT tools. If you're using any earlier version of Windows 10 for your testing, consider downloading an evaluation version ISO image of Windows Server 2019 and creating a VM using that ISO image.

In this recipe, you create a DFS Namespace, as set out in this table:

Folder in DFSN Namespace	Target SMB share
\\Reskit.Org\ShareData\IT	n/a
\\Reskit.Org\ShareData\IT\ITData	\\FS1\ITData\
	\\FS2\ITData\
\\Reskit.Org\ShareData\IT\ITManagement	\\DC1\ITManagement
	\\DC2\Mananagement

How to do it...

1. Add the DFSN RSAT Tools to CL1:

```
Get-WindowsCapability -Online -Name *FileServices.Tools* |
  Add-WindowsCapability -Online |
    Out-Null
```

2. Install DFS Namespace, DFS Replication, and the related management tools:

```
$IHT = @{
  Name                  = 'FS-DFS-Namespace'
  IncludeManagementTools = $True
}
Install-WindowsFeature @IHT -ComputerName SRV1
Install-WindowsFeature @IHT -ComputerName SRV2
```

3. View the DFSN module and the DFSN cmdlets:

```
Get-Module -Name DFSN -ListAvailable
```

4. Create folders and shares for DFS Root:

```
$SB = {
  New-Item -Path C:\ShareData -ItemType Directory -Force |
    Out-Null
  $ACCESS = @{FullAccess = 'Everyone'}
  New-SmbShare -Name ShareData -Path C:\ShareData @ACCESS
}
Invoke-Command -ComputerName SRV1, SRV2 -ScriptBlock $SB |
  Out-Null
```

5. Create a DFS Namespace Root that points to \\SRV1\ShareData:

```
$NSHT = @{
    Path        = '\\Reskit.Org\ShareData'
    TargetPath  = '\\SRV1\ShareData'
    Type        = 'DomainV2'
    Description = 'Reskit Shared Data DFS Root'
}
New-DfsnRoot @NSHT
```

6. Add a second target and view the results:

```
$NSHT2 = @{
    Path        = '\\Reskit.Org\ShareData'
    TargetPath  = '\\SRV2\ShareData'
}
New-DfsnRootTarget @NSHT2 | Out-Null
Get-DfsnRootTarget -Path \\Reskit.Org\ShareData
```

7. Create additional IT data shares and populate:

```
# Create FS1 folders/shares
$SB = {
    # Create folder on FS1
    New-Item -Path C:\IT2 -ItemType Directory | Out-Null
    # Create share on FS1
    New-SmbShare -Name 'ITData' -Path C:\IT2 -FullAccess Everyone
    # Create a file in both the folder and therefore the share
    'Root' | Out-File -FilePath C:\IT2\Root.Txt
}
```

```
Invoke-Command -ScriptBlock $SB -Computer FS1 | Out-Null
# Create FS2 folders/shares
$SB = {
  New-Item -Path C:\IT2 -ItemType Directory | Out-Null
  New-SmbShare -Name 'ITData' -Path C:\IT2 -FullAccess Everyone
  'Root' | Out-File -FilePath c:\IT2\Root.Txt
}
Invoke-Command -ScriptBlock $SB -Computer FS2 | Out-Null
# Create DC1 folders/shares
$SB = {
    New-Item -Path C:\ITM -ItemType Directory | Out-Null
    New-SmbShare -Name 'ITM' -Path C:\ITM -FullAccess Everyone
    'Root' | Out-File -Filepath c:\itm\root.txt
}
Invoke-Command -ScriptBlock $SB -Computer DC1 | Out-Null
# Create DC2 folders/shares
$SB = {
    New-Item C:\ITM -ItemType Directory | Out-Null
    New-SmbShare -Name 'ITM' -Path C:\ITM -FullAccess Everyone
    'Root' | Out-File -FilePath c:\itm\root.txt
}
Invoke-Command -ScriptBlock $SB -Computer DC2
```

8. Create the DFS Namespace and set DFS targets:

```
$NSHT1 = @{
  Path               = '\\Reskit\ShareData\IT\ITData'
  TargetPath         = '\\FS1\ITData'
  EnableTargetFailback = $True
  Description        = 'IT Data'
}
New-DfsnFolder @NSHT1 | Out-Null
$NSHT2 = @{
    Path       = '\\Reskit\ShareData\IT\ITData'
    TargetPath = '\\FS2\ITData'
}
New-DfsnFolderTarget @NSHT2 | Out-Null
$NSHT3 = @{
    Path               = '\\Reskit\ShareData\IT\ITManagement'
    TargetPath         = '\\DC1\ITM'
    EnableTargetFailback = $true
    Description        = 'IT Management Data'
}
```

```
New-DfsnFolder @NSHT3 | Out-Null
$NSHT4 = @{
    Path        = '\\Reskit\ShareData\IT\ITManagement'
    TargetPath = '\\DC2\ITM'
}
New-DfsnFolderTarget @NSHT4 | Out-Null
```

9. View the hierarchy:

```
Get-ChildItem -Path \\Reskit.Org\ShareData\IT -Recurse
```

How it works...

In *step 1*, you add the RSAT tools needed for DFSN (and DFS Replication), which creates no output. In *step 2*, you install the DFS Namespace feature to both SRV1 and SRV2, which looks like this:

```
PS C:\foo> $IHT = @{
    Name                    = 'FS-DFS-Namespace'
    IncludeManagementTools = $True
}
PS C:\foo> $Install-WindowsFeature @IHT -ComputerName SRV1
PS C:\foo> $Install-WindowsFeature @IHT -ComputerName SRV2


Success Restart Needed Exit Code     Feature Result
------- --------------- ---------     --------------
True    No              Success       {DFS Namespaces}
True    No              Success       {File and iSCSI Services, DFS Namespaces, ...
```

In *step 3*, you view the DFSN module, containing the key DFSN cmdlets, which looks like this:

```
PS C:\foo> Get-Module -Name DFSN -ListAvailable

    Directory: C:\WINDOWS\system32\WindowsPowerShell\v1.0\Modules

ModuleType Version  Name   ExportedCommands
---------- -------  ----   ----------------
Manifest   1.0      DFSN   {Get-DfsnRoot, Remove-DfsnRoot, Set-DfsnRoot, New-DfsnRoot...}
```

In *step 4*, you create the folders and shares needed to support the DFSN you're about to create. This step creates no output.

In *step 5,* you create the DFSN root that points to \\SRV1\ShareData. The output from this step looks like this:

```
PS C:\foo> $NSHT = @{
            Path        = '\\Reskit.Org\ShareData'
            TargetPath  = '\\SRV1\ShareData'|
            Type        = 'DomainV2'
            Description = 'Reskit Shared Data DFS Root'
          }
PS C:\foo> New-DfsnRoot @NSHT

Path                     Type       Properties TimeToLiveSec State  Description
----                     ----       ---------- ------------- -----  -----------
\\Reskit.Org\ShareData Domain V2               300           Online Reskit Shared Data DFS Root
```

In *step 6,* you create a second target for the DFS root. Then you get the details of the DFSN root target. The output from this step looks like this:

```
PS C:\Foo> $NSHT2 = @{
            Path       = '\\Reskit.Org\ShareData'
            TargetPath = '\\SRV2\ShareData'
          }
PS C:\Foo> New-DfsnRootTarget @NSHT2 | Out-Null
PS C:\Foo> Get-DfsnRootTarget -Path \\Reskit.Org\ShareData

New-DfsnRootTarget : The requested object could not be found.
At line:5 char:1
+ New-DfsnRootTarget @NSHT2 | Out-Null
+ ~~~~~~~~~~~~~~~~~~~~~~~~~~~~~~~~~~~~~
    + CategoryInfo          : ObjectNotFound: (MSFT_DfsNamespaceRootTarget:ROOT\Microsoft\...spaceRootTarget)
                              [New-DfsnRootTarget], CimException
    + FullyQualifiedErrorId : MI RESULT 6,New-DfsnRootTarget


Path                   TargetPath                      State  ReferralPriorityClass ReferralPriorityRank
----                   ----------                      -----  --------------------- --------------------
\\Reskit.Org\ShareData \\SRV1.Reskit.Org\ShareData Online sitecost-normal       0
\\Reskit.Org\ShareData \\SRV2.Reskit.Org\ShareData Online sitecost-normal       0
```

In *step 7,* you create several additional shares and add data to the shares. In *step 8,* you create DFS Namespace targets for the newly-created shares. These two steps produce no output.

In *step 9,* you view the folders/files under the newly-created DFSN root, which look like this:

```
PS C:\foo> Get-ChildItem -Path \\Reskit.Org\ShareData\IT -Recurse

    Directory: \\Reskit.Org\ShareData\IT

Mode                LastWriteTime         Length Name
----                -------------         ------ ----
d----l         14/01/2019     22:42              ITData
d----l         14/01/2019     22:42              ITManagement

    Directory: \\Reskit.Org\ShareData\IT\ITData

Mode                LastWriteTime         Length Name
----                -------------         ------ ----
-a----         14/01/2019     22:37             14 root.txt

    Directory: \\Reskit.Org\ShareData\IT\ITManagement

Mode                LastWriteTime         Length Name
----                -------------         ------ ----
-a----         14/01/2019     22:40             14 root.txt
```

There's more...

In *step 1*, you add the RSAT tools needed for DFSN (and DFS Replication). The methods for adding RSAT tools on Windows 10 have evolved. The technique used in the recipe is valid for Windows 10, version 1809 or later. If you're using an earlier version (such as 1803 or 1709), see https://tfl09.blogspot.com/2018/10/installing-rsat-tools.html.

In *step 6*, you create a second target. As you can see from the screenshot, this step creates the second DFSN root target, but it generates a CIM Exception. However, this error appears benign and, despite the error, the step does work successfully. This is an issue with the cmdlet, as reported here: https://github.com/MicrosoftDocs/windows-powershell-docs/issues/541.

Configuring DFS Replication

DFSR is an efficient file-replication engine built into Windows Server 2019. You can use DFS Replication to replicate DFSN targets in an efficient manner, especially across low-bandwidth connections.

In DFSR, a replication group is a collection of computers, known as **members**. Each replication group member hosts replicated folders. Replicated folders are folders that DFSR ensures are synchronized. With DFS Replication groups, you can replicate the folders contained in your DFS Namespace.

A DFS replicated folder is a folder that DFSR keeps synchronized on each member. In the *Configuring a DFS Namespace* recipe, you created some folders that you need to replicate between each server. As the data changes in each replicated folder, DFSR replicates the changes across connections between the members of the replication group. The connections you set up between the members forms the replication topology.

Creating multiple replicated folders in a single replication group simplifies the process of deploying replicated folders because DFSR applies the topology, schedule, and bandwidth-throttling from the replication group to each replicated folder. Each replicated folder has many properties. These include file and subfolder filters that enable you to filter out different files and subfolders from each replicated folder.

In this recipe, you set up replication of the DFSN shared folders, created in the *Configuring a DFS Namespace* recipe. Then you'll test the replication in action.

Getting ready

This recipe uses the same systems you used in the *Configuring DFS Namespace* recipe and assumes you have completed that recipe successfully. It sets up DFS Replication on the folders you created in the earlier recipe. You run this recipe on the Windows 10 system, `CL1`, that you set up in *Chapter 1, Establishing a PowerShell Administrative Environment*.

How to do it...

1. Install the `DFS-Replication` feature on the key servers:

```
$SB = {
  $IHT = @{
    Name                  ='FS-DFS-Replication'
    IncludeManagementTools = $true
  }
  Add-WindowsFeature @IHT
}
$ICHT = @{
  ScriptBlock    = $SB
  ComputerName   = 'DC1', 'DC2', 'FS1', 'FS2', 'SRV1', 'SRV2'
}
Invoke-Command @ICHT |
  Format-Table -Property PSComputername, FeatureResult, Success
```

2. Turn on the administrative shares:

```
$SB2 = {
  $SCHT = @{
    AutoShareServer      = $true
    AutoShareWorkstation = $true
    Confirm              = $false
  }
  Set-SmbServerConfiguration @SCHT
  "Restarting LanmanServer on $(hostname)"
  Stop-Service -Name  LanManServer -Force
  Start-Service -Name  LanManServer
}
$CN = @('DC1','DC2','FS1','FS2','SRV1','SRV2')
Invoke-Command -ScriptBlock $SB2 -ComputerName $CN
```

3. View the DFS cmdlets:

```
Get-Module -Name DFSR -ListAvailable
Get-Command -Module DFSR | Measure-Object
```

4. Create replication groups:

```
$RGHT1 = @{
  GroupName   = 'FSShareRG'
  DomainName  = 'Reskit.org'
  Description = 'Replication Group for FS1, FS2 shares'
}
$RGHT2 = @{
  GroupName   = 'DCShareRG'
  DomainName  = 'Reskit.Org'
  Description = 'Replication Group for DC1, DC2 shares'
}
New-DfsReplicationGroup @RGHT1 | Out-Null
New-DfsReplicationGroup @RGHT2 | Out-Null
```

5. Get replication groups in Reskit.Org:

```
Get-DfsReplicationGroup -DomainName Reskit.Org |
  Format-Table
```

6. Add replication group members to `FSShareRG`:

```
$MHT1 = @{
  GroupName    = 'FSShareRG'
  Description  = 'ITData on FS1/2'
  ComputerName = ('FS1','FS2')
  DomainName   = 'Reskit.Org'
}
Add-DfsrMember @MHT1
```

7. Add the DFSN folder to the `FSShareRG` replication group, thus replicating the \
   `ITData` share:

```
$RFHT1 = @{
GroupName   = 'FSShareRG'
FolderName  = 'ITData'
Domain      = 'Reskit.Org'
Description = 'ITData on FS1/2'
DfsnPath    = '\\Reskit.Org\ShareData\IT\ITData'
}
New-DfsReplicatedFolder @RFHT1 | Out-Null
```

8. Add replication group members to `DCShareRG`:

```
$MHT2 = @{
GroupName    = 'DCShareRG'
Description  = 'DC Server members'
ComputerName = ('DC1','DC2')
DomainName   = 'Reskit.Org'
}
Add-DfsrMember @MHT2 |
  Out-Null
```

9. Add DFSN folders to the `DCShareRG` replication group:

```
$RFHT2 = @{
GroupName   = 'DCShareRG'
FolderName  = 'ITManagement'
Domain      = 'Reskit.Org'
Description = 'IT Management Data'
DfsnPath    = '\\Reskit.Org\ShareData\IT\ITManagement'
}
New-DfsReplicatedFolder @RFHT2 |
  Out-Null
```

10. View the replicated folders:

```
Get-DfsReplicatedFolder |
  Format-Table -Property DomainName, GroupName,
                         FolderName, Description
```

11. Set the membership for the `FSShareRG` replication group:

```
$DMHT1 = @{
  GroupName     = 'FSShareRG'
  FolderName    = 'ITData'
  ComputerName  = 'FS1'
  ContentPath   = 'C:\IT2'
  PrimaryMember = $true
  Force         = $true
}
Set-DfsrMembership @DMHT1 | Out-Null
$DMHT2 = @{
  GroupName     = 'FSShareRG'
  FolderName    = 'ITData'
  ComputerName  = 'FS2'
  ContentPath   = 'C:\IT2'
  PrimaryMember = $false
  Force         = $true
}
Set-DfsrMembership @DMHT2 | Out-Null
```

12. Set the membership for the `DCShareRG` replication group:

```
$DMHT3 = @{
    GroupName     = 'DCShareRG'
    FolderName    = 'ITManagement'
    ComputerName  = 'DC1'
    ContentPath   = 'C:\ITM'
    PrimaryMember = $true
    Force         = $true
}
Set-DfsrMembership @DMHT3 | Out-Null
$DMHT4 = @{
    GroupName     = 'DCShareRG'
    FolderName    = 'ITManagement'
    ComputerName  = 'DC2'
    ContentPath   = 'C:\ITM'
    Force         = $true
}
Set-DfsrMembership @DMHT4 | Out-Null
```

13. View the DFSR membership of the two replication groups:

```
Get-DfsrMembership -GroupName FSShareRG -ComputerName FS1, FS2 |
   Format-Table -Property GroupName, ComputerName,
                     ComputerDomainName, ContentPath,
                     Enabled
Get-DfsrMembership -GroupName DCShareRG -ComputerName DC1, DC2 |
   Format-Table -Property GroupName, ComputerName,
                     ComputerDomainName, ContentPath,
                     Enabled
```

14. Add replication connections for both replication groups:

```
$RCHT1 = @{
   GroupName               = 'FSShareRG'
   SourceComputerName      = 'FS1'
   DestinationComputerName = 'FS2'
   Description             = 'FS1-FS2 connection'
   DomainName              = 'Reskit.Org'
}
Add-DfsrConnection @RCHT1| Out-Null
$RCHT2 = @{
   GroupName               = 'DCShareRG'
   SourceComputerName      = 'DC1'
      DestinationComputerName = 'DC2'
      Description            = 'DC1-DC2 connection'
      DomainName             = 'Reskit.Org'
}
Add-DfsrConnection @RCHT2 | Out-Null
```

15. Get the DFSR Membership and view it:

```
Get-DfsrMember |
   Format-Table -Property Groupname, DomainName,
                     DNSName, Description
```

16. Update the DFSR configuration:

```
Update-DfsrConfigurationFromAD -ComputerName DC1, DC2, FS1, FS2
```

17. Check the existing folders to discover what's currently in the DFS share:

```
$Path  = '\\Reskit.Org\ShareData\IT\ITManagement'
$Path1 = '\\DC1\itm'
$Path2 = '\\DC2\itm'
```

```
Get-ChiLditem -Path $Path
Get-ChiLditem -Path $Path1
Get-ChildItem -Path $Path2
```

18. Create files in the DFS share and re-check the underlying shares:

```
1..100 | foreach { "foo" |
  Out-File \\Reskit.Org\ShareData\IT\ITManagement\Stuff$_.txt}
$P  = (Get-ChildItem -Path $Path  | Measure-Object).count
$P1 = (Get-ChildItem -Path $Path1 | Measure-Object).count
$P2 = (Get-ChildItem -Path $Path2 | Measure-Object).count
"$P objects in DFS root"
"$P1 objects on \\DC1"
"$P2 objects on \\DC2"
```

How it works...

In *step 1*, you install the DFS Replication feature on several servers, which looks like this:

```
PS C:\Foo> $SB = {
              $IHT = @{
                Name                    ='FS-DFS-Replication'
                IncludeManagementTools = $true
              }
              Add-WindowsFeature @IHT
           }
PS C:\Foo> $ICHT = @{
              ScriptBlock   = $SB
              ComputerName  = 'DC1', 'DC2', 'FS1', 'FS2', 'SRV1', 'SRV2'
           }
PS C:\Foo> Invoke-Command @ICHT |
              Format-Table -Property PSComputername,FeatureResult, Success

PSComputerName FeatureResult                                                        Success
-------------- -------------                                                        -------
DC1            {DFS Replication, DFS Management Tools, File Services Tools}         True
DC2            {DFS Replication, DFS Management Tools, File Services Tools}         True
FS1            {DFS Replication, DFS Management Tools}                              True
FS2            {DFS Replication, Remote Server Administration Tools, DFS...         True
SRV1           {DFS Replication}                                                    True
SRV2           {DFS Replication}                                                    True
```

In *step 2*, after installing the DFSR feature, you configure Windows to update the SMB server configuration and then restart the target servers, which looks like this:

```
PS C:\Foo> $SB2 = {
             $SCHT = @{
               AutoShareServer      = $true
               AutoShareWorkstation = $true
               Confirm              = $false
             }
             Set-SmbServerConfiguration @SCHT
             "Restarting LanmanServer on $(hostname)"
             Restart-Service -Name  LanManServer -Force
           }
PS C:\foo> $CN = @('DC1','DC2','FS1','FS2','SRV1','SRV2')
PS C:\foo> Invoke-Command -ScriptBlock $SB2 -ComputerName $CN

Restarting LanmanServer on DC1
Restarting LanmanServer on DC2
Restarting LanmanServer on SRV1
Restarting LanmanServer on SRV2
Restarting LanmanServer on FS2
Restarting LanmanServer on FS
```

In *step 3*, you view the DFS module and see how many cmdlets are provided by the module. The output looks like this:

```
PS C:\foo> Get-Module -Name DFSR -ListAvailable
PS C:\foo> Get-Command -Module DFSR | Measure-Object

    Directory: C:\WINDOWS\system32\WindowsPowerShell\v1.0\Modules

ModuleType Version   Name    ExportedCommands
---------- -------   ----    ----------------
Binary     2.0.0.0   DFSR    {New-DfsReplicationGroup, Get-DfsReplicationGroup, ...}

Count      : 45   ◄
Average    :
Sum        :
Maximum    :
Minimum    :
Property   :
```

In *step 4*, which produces no output, you define the replication groups (`FSShareRG` and `DCShareRG`). In *step 5*, you view the domain-based DFSR replication groups, which look like this:

```
PS C:\foo> Get-DfsReplicationGroup -DomainName Reskit.Org |
             Format-Table

GroupName DomainName Identifier                           Description                              State
--------- ---------- ----------                           -----------                              -----
FSShareRG Reskit.Org d47c204f-a9f3-441e-8fe9-b4a50a309d27 Replication Group for FS1, FS2 shares Normal
DCShareRG Reskit.Org 2a271234-0902-46b5-af16-975f2b4e5b4b Replication Group for DC1, DC2 shares Normal
```

In *step 6*, you populate the `FSShareRG` replication group, which looks like this:

```
PS C:\foo> $MHT1 = @{
             GroupName    = 'FSShareRG'
             Description  = 'ITData on FS1/2'
             ComputerName = ('FS1','FS2')
             DomainName   = 'Reskit.Org'
           }
PS C:\foo> Add-DfsrMember @MHT1


GroupName                       : FSShareRG
ComputerName                    : FS1
DomainName                      : Reskit.Org
Identifier                      : 4f91e7a4-cbf0-4b10-83f0-0347dcb25999
Description                     : ITData on FS1/2
DnsName                         : FS1.Reskit.Org
Site                            : Default-First-Site-Name
NumberOfConnections             : 0
NumberOfInboundConnections      : 0
NumberOfOutboundConnections     : 0
NumberOfInterSiteConnections    : 0
NumberOfIntraSiteConnections    : 0
IsClusterNode                   : False
State                           : Normal

GroupName                       : FSShareRG
ComputerName                    : FS2
DomainName                      : Reskit.Org
Identifier                      : 93ba0e66-cfb3-4cec-b5e8-48fc99764325
Description                     : ITData on FS1/2
DnsName                         : FS2.Reskit.Org
Site                            : Default-First-Site-Name
NumberOfConnections             : 0
NumberOfInboundConnections      : 0
NumberOfOutboundConnections     : 0
NumberOfInterSiteConnections    : 0
NumberOfIntraSiteConnections    : 0
IsClusterNode                   : False
State                           : Normal
```

In *step 7*, you add the DFSN folder to the replication group, which produces no output.

In *step 8*, you add the `Add` replication group members for `DCShareRG` and in *step 9*, you add the DFSN folders to the `DCShareRG` replication group. These two steps produce no output.

In *step 10*, you view the replicated folders in the `Reskit.Org` domain, which looks like this:

```
PS C:\foo> Get-DfsReplicatedFolder |
             Format-Table -Property DomainName, GroupName,
                                    FolderName, Description

DomainName GroupName FolderName    Description
---------- --------- ----------    -----------
Reskit.Org FSShareRG ITData        ITData on FS1/2
Reskit.Org DCShareRG ITManagement  IT Management Data
```

In *step 11*, you set the membership for the `FSShareRG` replication group, and in *step 12*, you set the membership for the `DCShareRG` replication group—these two steps produce no output.

In *step 13*, you view the DFSR membership of the two replication groups, which looks like this:

```
PS C:\foo> Get-DfsrMembership -GroupName FSShareRG -ComputerName FS1, FS2 |
            Format-Table -Property GroupName, ComputerName,
                              ComputerDomainName, ContentPath, Enabled

GroupName ComputerName ComputerDomainName ContentPath Enabled
--------- ------------ ------------------ ----------- -------
FSShareRG FS1          Reskit.Org         C:\IT2      True
FSShareRG FS2          Reskit.Org         C:\IT2      True


PS C:\foo> Get-DfsrMembership -GroupName DCShareRG -ComputerName DC1, DC2 |
            Format-Table -Property GroupName, ComputerName,
                              ComputerDomainName, ContentPath, Enabled

GroupName ComputerName ComputerDomainName ContentPath Enabled
--------- ------------ ------------------ ----------- -------
DCShareRG DC1          Reskit.Org         C:\ITM      True
DCShareRG DC2          Reskit.Org         C:\ITM      True
```

In *step 14*, you add connections for both replication groups, which produces no output. In *step 15*, you get the DFSR memberships of the groups in `Reskit.Org` and format the key properties, which looks like this:

```
PS C:\foo> Get-DfsrMember |
            Format-Table -Property Groupname, DomainName,
                              DNSName, Description

GroupName DomainName DnsName         Description
--------- ---------- -------         -----------
FSShareRG Reskit.Org FS1.Reskit.Org  ITData on FS1/2
FSShareRG Reskit.Org FS2.Reskit.Org  ITData on FS1/2
DCShareRG Reskit.Org DC1.Reskit.Org  DC Server members
DCShareRG Reskit.Org DC2.Reskit.Org  DC Server members
```

In *step 16*, you force an update to the DFSR configuration, which produces no output. In *step 17*, you check to see that there are no files in the DFS share—this step produces no output.

In *step 18,* you test DFS Replication by creating a number of files on the DFS share
(`\\Reskit.Org\ShareData`) and observe the number of files present in the underlying
shares. The output, which is likely to vary, looks like this:

```
PS C:\Foo> 1..100 | foreach { "foo" |
               Out-File \\Reskit.Org\ShareData\IT\ITManagement\Stuff$_.txt}
PS C:\Foo> $P  = (Get-ChildItem -Path $Path  | Measure-Object).count
PS C:\Foo> $P1 = (Get-ChildItem -Path $Path1 | Measure-Object).count
PS C:\Foo> $P2 = (Get-ChildItem -Path $Path2 | Measure-Object).count
PS C:\Foo> "$P objects in DFS root"
PS C:\Foo> "$P1 objects on \\DC1"
PS C:\Foo> "$P2 objects on \\DC2"

100 objects in DFS root
92 objects on \\DC1
100 objects on \\DC2
```

There's more...

In *step 2,* you turn on the administrative shares. This is a requirement for setting up DFS
Replication. Once you've set up replication, you may wish to turn off these administrative shares.

In *step 8,* for each shared folder in the `FSShareRG` replication group, you identify a primary
member. Should a document be changed by multiple different members in the replication
group, then DFS considers the copy on the primary master as definitive.

In *step 11,* you set up simple DFS Replication connections. DFS enables you to manage rich
replication topologies and supports your configuring-replication schedules and bandwidth
constraints.

For a comparison of DFS Replication and Storage Replica, see `https://www.petri.com/
windows-server-2016-dfs-r-vs-storage-replica`.

In *step 17,* you check to see what files exist in the DFS share (that is, none). Then in *step
18,* you test the DFSR replication by creating 100 new files on the DFSN share, and then
observe how many files exist in the two underlying shares. As you can see from the output,
100 files exist both on the DFS share and on `DC1`, but at the time of execution, only 92 files
had replicated. If you'd waited a few more seconds after creating the files, you would have
observed complete replication.

See also....

The recipe sets up a simple set of replicated folders—four replicated folders on four servers based on the DFS Namespace created earlier. To extend this recipe, you could add other folders to the replication groups that weren't part of the DFS Namespace.

DFS Replication is one way to replicate files in an organization. DFS was designed for use over lower-bandwidth networks, thus in larger networks, DFS replicas might be out of sync. Also, DFS only replicates a file after it has been closed. With Server 2019, the Storage Replica feature is an alternative to DFSR. SR works at the block level, unlike DFSR, which operates at the file level. As a result, SR can replicate the changes to open files.

6
Managing Windows Update

In this chapter, we cover the following recipes:

- ▶ Installing Windows Server Update Services
- ▶ Configuring WSUS update synchronization
- ▶ Configuring the Windows Update Client
- ▶ Creating computer target groups
- ▶ Configuring WSUS automatic approvals
- ▶ Managing WSUS updates

Introduction

Keeping your systems, client and server, up to date with patches and updates is an important task undertaken by Windows administrators. **Windows Server Update Services** (**WSUS**) is a feature of Windows Server 2019 that enables you to manage the download and distribution of updates to your organization's computers.

In addition to updating Windows itself, WSUS also enables you to manage patches and updates for a wide variety of Microsoft software products. Thus, an update you download from Microsoft and distribute via WSUS may apply to Windows itself as well as Office and a huge range of other Microsoft software products.

In this chapter, you see how to install and configure both WSUS server and WSUS client computers. The recipes examine the management, approval, and installation of updates, and how you can report on the status of update installation.

Installing Windows Update Services

WSUS is a feature within Windows Server 2019. To use Windows Update Services, you first install the WSUS Windows feature and then do basic configuration and setup. In this recipe, you install WSUS and review the results of that installation.

Getting ready

This recipe uses the WSUS1 server, a member server in the Reskit.Org domain. At the start of this recipe, WSUS1 has no additional features or software loaded.

How to do it...

1. Install the Windows Update feature and tools:

```
$IFHT = @{
  Name                  = 'UpdateServices'
  IncludeManagementTools = $true
}
Install-WindowsFeature @IFHT
```

2. Determine the features installed on the WSUS1 server after installation of WSUS:

```
Get-WindowsFeature | Where-Object Installed
```

3. Create a folder for WSUS update content:

```
$WSUSDir = 'C:\WSUS'
If (-Not (Test-Path -Path $WSUSDir -ErrorAction SilentlyContinue))
    {New-Item -Path $WSUSDir -ItemType Directory| Out-Null}
```

4. Perform post-installation configuration using WsusUtil.Exe:

```
$CMD ="$env:ProgramFiles\" + 'Update Services\Tools\WsusUtil.exe'
& $CMD Postinstall CONTENT_DIR=$WSUSDir
```

5. View the post-installation log file:

```
$LOG = "$env:localappdata\temp\WSUS_Post*.log"
Get-ChildItem -Path $LOG
```

6. View the WSUS website created on WSUS1:

```
Get-Website -Name ws* | Format-Table -AutoSize
```

7. View the cmdlets in the UpdateServices module:

```
Get-Command -Module UpdateServices
```

8. Inspect TypeName and properties of the WSUS1 server:

```
$WSUSServer = Get-WsusServer
$WSUSServer.GetType().Fullname
$WSUSServer | Select-Object -Property *
```

9. Examine the methods available:

```
($WSUSServer | Get-Member -MemberType Method).count
$WSUSServer | Get-Member -MemberType Method
```

10. Examine the configuration of the WSUS1 server:

```
$WSUSServer.GetConfiguration() |
    Select-Object -Property SyncFromMicrosoftUpdate,LogFilePath
```

11. View product categories after initial install:

```
$WSUSProducts = Get-WsusProduct -UpdateServer $WSUSServer
$WSUSProducts.Count
$WSUSProducts
```

12. Display subscription information:

```
$WSUSSubscription = $WSUSServer.GetSubscription()
$WSUSSubscription | Select-Object -Property * |
    Format-List
```

13. Update the categories of products available:

```
$WSUSSubscription.StartSynchronization()
Do {
    Write-Output $WSUSSubscription.GetSynchronizationProgress()
    Start-Sleep -Seconds 5
}
While ($WSUSSubscription.GetSynchronizationStatus() -ne
                                        'NotProcessing')
```

14. Once synchronization is complete, check the results of the synchronization:

```
$WSUSSubscription.GetLastSynchronizationInfo()
```

15. Examine the categories available after synchronization:

```
$WSUSProducts = Get-WsusProduct -UpdateServer $WSUSServer
$WSUSProducts.Count
$WSUSProducts
```

How it works...

In *step 1*, you install the Windows Update Services feature and the associated tools, which looks like this:

```
PS C:\foo> $IFHT = @{
                Name                 = 'UpdateServices'
                IncludeManagementTools = $true
            }
PS C:\foo> Install-WindowsFeature @IFHT

Success Restart Needed Exit Code     Feature Result
------- -------------- ---------     --------------
True    No             Success       {ASP.NET 4.7, HTTP Activation, Remote Serv...
WARNING: Additional configuration may be required. Review the article Managing WSUS Using
PowerShell at TechNet Library (http://go.microsoft.com/fwlink/?LinkId=235499) for more
information on the recommended steps to perform WSUS installation using PowerShell.
```

Adding the Update Services feature adds a number of additional related services, as you can see in *step 2*, which looks like this:

```
PS C:\foo> Get-WindowsFeature | Where-Object Installed

Display Name                                        Name                      Install State
------------                                        ----                      -------------
[X] File and Storage Services                       FileAndStorage-Services      Installed
    [X] Storage Services                            Storage-Services             Installed
[X] Web Server (IIS)                                Web-Server                   Installed
    [X] Web Server                  ◀──────────     Web-WebServer                Installed
        [X] Common HTTP Features                    Web-Common-Http              Installed
            [X] Default Document                    Web-Default-Doc              Installed
            [X] Static Content                      Web-Static-Content           Installed
        [X] Performance                             Web-Performance              Installed
            [X] Dynamic Content Compression         Web-Dyn-Compression          Installed
        [X] Security                                Web-Security                 Installed
            [X] Request Filtering                   Web-Filtering                Installed
            [X] Windows Authentication              Web-Windows-Auth             Installed
        [X] Application Development                 Web-App-Dev                  Installed
            [X] .NET Extensibility 4.7              Web-Net-Ext45                Installed
            [X] ASP.NET 4.7                         Web-Asp-Net45                Installed
            [X] ISAPI Extensions                    Web-ISAPI-Ext                Installed
            [X] ISAPI Filters                       Web-ISAPI-Filter             Installed
    [X] Management Tools                            Web-Mgmt-Tools               Installed
        [X] IIS Management Console                  Web-Mgmt-Console             Installed
        [X] IIS 6 Management Compatibility          Web-Mgmt-Compat              Installed
            [X] IIS 6 Metabase Compatibility        Web-Metabase                 Installed
[X] Windows Server Update Services  ◀──────────     UpdateServices               Installed
    [X] WID Connectivity                            UpdateServices-WidDB         Installed
    [X] WSUS Services                               UpdateServices-Services      Installed
[X] .NET Framework 4.7 Features                     NET-Framework-45-Fea...      Installed
    [X] .NET Framework 4.7                          NET-Framework-45-Core        Installed
    [X] ASP.NET 4.7                 ◀──────         NET-Framework-45-ASPNET      Installed
    [X] WCF Services                                NET-WCF-Services45           Installed
        [X] HTTP Activation                         NET-WCF-HTTP-Activat...      Installed
        [X] TCP Port Sharing                        NET-WCF-TCP-PortShar...      Installed
[X] Remote Server Administration Tools              RSAT                         Installed
    [X] Role Administration Tools                   RSAT-Role-Tools              Installed
        [X] Windows Server Update Services Tools ◀  UpdateServices-RSAT          Installed
            [X] API and PowerShell cmdlets          UpdateServices-API           Installed
            [X] User Interface Management Console   UpdateServices-UI            Installed
[X] System Data Archiver            ◀──────         System-DataArchiver          Installed
[X] Windows Defender Antivirus                      Windows-Defender             Installed
[X] Windows Internal Database                       Windows-Internal-Dat...      Installed
[X] Windows PowerShell                              PowerShellRoot               Installed
    [X] Windows PowerShell 5.1                      PowerShell                   Installed
    [X] Windows PowerShell ISE                      PowerShell-ISE               Installed
[X] Windows Process Activation Service              WAS                          Installed
    [X] Process Model                               WAS-Process-Model            Installed
    [X] Configuration APIs                          WAS-Config-APIs              Installed
[X] WoW64 Support                                   WoW64-Support                Installed
[X] XPS Viewer                                      XPS-Viewer                   Installed
```

In *step 3*, you create, silently, a folder that you are going to use to hold WSUS content. In *step 4*, you perform the post-installation task using the `wsusutil.exe` console command, which also produces no output.

The `wsusutil.exe` application creates an output log file containing details of the actions taken by the application. In *step 5*, you look at the log file that `wsusutil.exe` created in *step 4*:

```
PS C:foo> $LOG = "$env:localappdata\temp\WSUS_Post*.log"
PS C:foo> Get-ChildItem -Path $LOG

    Directory: C:\Users\administrator\AppData\Local\temp

Mode              LastWriteTime         Length Name

----              -------------         ------ ----

-a----        15/09/2018     19:33       61095 WSUS_PostInstall_20180915T183157.log
```

The WSUS installer also installs a website on a WSUS to communicate with WSUS clients. In *step 6*, you view the site, as you can see here:

```
PS C:\foo> Get-Website -Name ws* | Format-Table -AutoSize

Name               ID         State   Physical Path                                    Bindings
----               --         -----   -------------                                    --------
WSUS Administration 1774618519 Started C:\Program Files\Update Services\WebServices\Root\ http :8530:
                                                                                         https :8531: sslFlags=0
```

In *step 7*, you examine the commands contained in the `UpdateServices` module that you installed as part of *step 1*. The output of this step looks like this:

```
PS C:\foo> Get-Command -Module UpdateServices

CommandType     Name                             Version    Source

-----------     ----                             -------    ------

Cmdlet          Add-WsusComputer                 2.0.0.0    UpdateServices
Cmdlet          Add-WsusDynamicCategory          2.0.0.0    UpdateServices
Cmdlet          Approve-WsusUpdate               2.0.0.0    UpdateServices
Cmdlet          Deny-WsusUpdate                  2.0.0.0    UpdateServices
Cmdlet          Get-WsusClassification           2.0.0.0    UpdateServices
Cmdlet          Get-WsusComputer                 2.0.0.0    UpdateServices
Cmdlet          Get-WsusDynamicCategory          2.0.0.0    UpdateServices
Cmdlet          Get-WsusProduct                  2.0.0.0    UpdateServices
Cmdlet          Get-WsusServer                   2.0.0.0    UpdateServices
Cmdlet          Get-WsusUpdate                   2.0.0.0    UpdateServices
Cmdlet          Invoke-WsusServerCleanup         2.0.0.0    UpdateServices
Cmdlet          Remove-WsusDynamicCategory       2.0.0.0    UpdateServices
Cmdlet          Set-WsusClassification           2.0.0.0    UpdateServices
Cmdlet          Set-WsusDynamicCategory          2.0.0.0    UpdateServices
Cmdlet          Set-WsusProduct                  2.0.0.0    UpdateServices
Cmdlet          Set-WsusServerSynchronization    2.0.0.0    UpdateServices
```

You examine the status of your WSUS server, in *step 8*, by using the `Get-WsusServer` cmdlet, which returns an `UpdateServer` object, which looks like this:

```
PS C:\foo> $WSUSServer = Get-WsusServer
PS C:\foo> $WSUSServer.GetType().Fullname
PS C:\foo> $WSUSServer | Select-Object -Property *

Microsoft.UpdateServices.Internal.BaseApi.UpdateServer

WebServiceUrl                        : http://WSUS1:8530/ApiRemoting30/WebS
BypassApiRemoting                    : False
IsServerLocal                        : True
Name                                 : WSUS1
Version                              : 10.0.17733.1000
IsConnectionSecureForApiRemoting     : True
PortNumber                           : 8530
PreferredCulture                     : en
ServerName                           : WSUS1
UseSecureConnection                  : False
ServerProtocolVersion                : 1.20
```

The $WSUSServer object you instantiated in *step 8* contains a large number of methods you can call to manage aspects of the WSUS server. As you can see from the output of *step 9*, there are 77 methods—to save space, only a few are listed, as shown here:

```
PS C:\foo> ($WSUSServer | Get-Member -MemberType Method).count
77  <----

PS C:\foo> $WSUSServer | Get-Member -MemberType Method


    TypeName: Microsoft.UpdateServices.Internal.BaseApi.UpdateServer

Name                         MemberType Definition
----                         ---------- ----------
AddDynamicCategories         Method     void AddDynamicCategories
AddDynamicCategory           Method     void AddDynamicCategory(M
CancelAllDownloads           Method     void CancelAllDownloads()
CreateComputerTargetGroup    Method     Microsoft.UpdateServices.
CreateDynamicCategory        Method     Microsoft.UpdateServices.
CreateInstallApprovalRule    Method     Microsoft.UpdateServices.
CreateObjRef                 Method     System.Runtime.Remoting.O
...   {more methods - removed}
```

WSUS also generates an important log file, SoftwareDistribution.log, that can be invaluable for troubleshooting. You can see the filename, in *step 10*, which looks like this:

```
PS C:\foo> $WSUSServer.GetConfiguration() |
           Select-Object -Property SyncFromMicrosoftUpdate,LogFilePat

SyncFromMicrosoftUpdate LogFilePath
----------------------- -----------
                   True C:\Program Files\Update Services\LogFiles\Softw
```

Following the initial installation and configuration done so far, in *step 11*, you can see that the WSUS1 server now is to get updates for a small set of products (17 in total), as you can see here:

```
PS C:\foo> $WSUSProducts = Get-WsusProduct -UpdateServer $WSUSServer
PS C:\foo> $WSUSProducts.Count
17   ⟵

PS C:\foo> $WSUSProducts

Title                                          ID
-----                                          --
Exchange 2000 Server                           83a83e29-7d55-44a0-afed-aea164b
Exchange Server 2003                           3cf32f7c-d8ee-43f8-a0da-8b88a6f
Exchange                                       352f9494-d516-4b40-a21a-cd24160
Local Publisher                                7c40e8c2-01ae-47f5-9af2-6e75a05
Locally published packages                     5cc25303-143f-40f3-a2ff-803a1db
Microsoft Corporation                          56309036-4c77-4dd9-951a-99ee9c2
Office 2003                                     1403f223-a63f-f572-82ba-c923912
Office XP                                       6248b8b1-ffeb-dbd9-887a-2acf53b
Office                                          477b856e-65c4-4473-b621-a8b230b
SQL Server                                      7145181b-9556-4b11-b659-0162fa9
SQL                                            0a4c6c73-8887-4d7f-9cbe-d08fa8f
Windows 2000 family                            3b4b8621-726e-43a6-b43b-37d07ec
Windows Server 2003 family                     dbf57a08-0d5a-46ff-b30c-7715eb9
Windows Server 2003, Datacenter Edition        7f44c2a7-bc36-470b-be3b-c01b6dc
Windows XP 64-Bit Edition Version 2003         a4bedb1d-a809-4f63-9b49-3fe3196
Windows XP family                              558f4bc3-4827-49e1-accf-ea79fd7
Windows                                        6964aab4-c5b5-43bd-a17d-ffb4346
```

In *step 12*, you retrieve and view the WSUS server's subscription details, which looks like this:

```
PS C:\foo> $WSUSSubscription = $WSUSServer.GetSubscription()
PS C:\foo> $WSUSSubscription | Select-Object -Property * | Format-List

UpdateServer                        : Microsoft.UpdateServices.Internal.B
SynchronizeAutomatically            : False
SynchronizeAutomaticallyTimeOfDay   : 21:19:02
LastModifiedTime                    : 15/09/2018 18:35:36
LastModifiedBy                      : RESKIT\administrator
LastSynchronizationTime             : 01/01/0001 00:00:00
Anchor                              : 0,2000-01-01 00:00:01.000
DeploymentAnchor                    :
NumberOfSynchronizationsPerDay      : 1
IsCategoryOnlySync                  : False
```

In *step 13*, you perform a full synchronization by invoking the StartSynchronization() method of the WSUS server object. This is an asynchronous operation—when you call the method, WSUS carries out the server update process in the background. You can call the GetSynchronizationStatus() method to view the status, as you can see in *step 13*. The synchronization process is not overly fast and can take several hours to complete. Truncated for brevity, the output of this step looks something like this:

```
PS C:\foo> $WSUSSubscription.StartSynchronization()
PS C:\foo> Do {
             Write-Output $WSUSSubscription.GetSynchronizationProgress()
             Start-Sleep -Seconds 5
         }
         While ($WSUSSubscription.GetSynchronizationStatus() -ne `
                'NotProcessing')

TotalItems  ProcessedItems          Phase
----------  --------------          -----
         0               0 NotProcessing
         0               0 NotProcessing
      3377               0    Categories
      3377            3377    Categories
     95059              59       Updates
     95059             420       Updates
     95059            7859       Updates
     95059           18224       Updates
     95059           48196       Updates
     95059           57677       Updates
     95059           84730       Updates
     95059           94994       Updates
```

Once the synchronization has completed, in *step 14*, you review a summary of the results, which looks like this:

```
PS C:\foo> $WSUSSubscription.GetLastSynchronizationInfo()

Id              : 5b8cf0f0-1301-44db-ad58-088b2fe028ec
StartTime       : 15/09/2018 19:04:35
EndTime         : 15/09/2018 23:23:02
StartedManually : True
Result          : Succeeded
Error           : NotApplicable
ErrorText       :
```

Now that this first full synchronization has taken place, WSUS is able to support a larger number of Microsoft products, as you can see in the output from *step 15*:

```
PS C:\foo> $WSUSProducts = Get-WsusProduct -UpdateServer $WSUSServer
PS C:\foo> $WSUSProducts.Count
307

PS C:\foo> $WSUSProducts
Title                                                      D
-----                                                      --
Active Directory Rights Management Services Client 2.0     fdcfda10-5b1f-4e57-8298-c744257e30db
Active Directory                                           57742761-615a-4e06-90bb-008394eaea47
Antigen for Exchange/SMTP                                  5d6a452a-55ba-4e11-adac-85e180bda3d6
Antigen                                                    116a3557-3847-4858-9f03-38e94b977456
ASP.NET Web and Data Frameworks                           4756f399-b049-8e6e-94e9-ff63d0e236a7
ASP.NET Web Frameworks                                     fa5ef799-b817-439e-abf7-c76ba0cacb75
Azure File Sync agent updates for Windows Server 2012 R2   fb08c71c-dbe9-40ab-8302-fb0231b1c814
Azure File Sync agent updates for Windows Server 2016      7ff1d901-fd38-441b-aaba-36d7b0ebf264
Azure File Sync                                            9d6f2556-534f-047e-5ec9-91bf0da81a75
...                      More titles - snipped
Writer Installation and Upgrades                          a13d331b-ce8f-40e4-8a18-227bf18f22f3
```

There's more...

In *step 2*, you can see that installing WSUS also installs the web-server (Internet Information Server) along with ASP.NET 4.7 on WSUS1.

In *step 3*, you create a folder to hold downloaded updates that you intend to review then deploy to your organization. This folder can get large, especially when you implement multi-language updates. You should hold your updates on a volume that is likely to have adequate space going forward. Making the volume fault-tolerant is also important as you plan and deploy WSUS.

In *step 13*, you perform a full sync with the Windows Update servers. This can take several hours. You may wish to change the value used in the Start-Sleep command to a larger value (otherwise you could end up with thousands of lines of output!).

In this recipe, you installed WSUS on a single server. You can use WSUS on multiple servers, which is appropriate for supporting larger networks. You can set up a WSUS server to synchronize from other WSUS servers on the network, you can use web proxies, and you can work with SQL Server instead of the Windows Internal Database.

See also

The WSUS server requirements and deployment scenarios are documented at https://docs.microsoft.com/en-us/windows-server/administration/windows-server-update-services/plan/plan-your-wsus-deployment.

The commands in the UpdateServices module are useful, but many of the tasks you are going to perform in PowerShell make use of the UpdateServer and Subscription objects and their methods.

MSDN contains documentation on the objects inside the Microsoft.UpdateServices. Administration namespace. You can view the documentation at https://docs.microsoft.com/en-us/previous-versions/windows/desktop/ms748969(v=vs.85).

Configuring WSUS update synchronization

After you install WSUS and do a basic synchronization, you configure WSUS to identify the products for which your organization requires product updates as well as the classifications of updates WSUS should download.

Once these are defined, you can synchronize updates manually or you can build an update schedule. This enables your WSUS server to download only the updates for the product categories and update classifications you have selected, both at a time of your choosing. The first initial synchronization can take hours, depending on your selections. Subsequent synchronizations pull only the newest updates since the last synchronization.

Getting ready

This recipe configures the WSUS1 WSUS server, which is a domain-joined system. This recipe assumes you are starting with the just-installed WSUS as performed in the *Installing Windows Update Services* recipe.

How to do it...

1. Discover the versions of Windows Server supported by Windows Update:

```
Get-WsusProduct |
  Where-Object -FilterScript {$_.Product.Title -match
                             '^Windows Server'}
```

2. Also, get update titles for Windows 10:

```
Get-WsusProduct -TitleIncludes 'Windows 10'
```

3. Create and view a list of software product titles to include:

```
$CHP =
 (Get-WsusProduct |
   Where-Object -FilterScript {$_.product.title -match
                              '^Windows Server'}).Product.Title
$CHP += @('Microsoft SQL Server 2016','Windows 10')
$CHP
```

4. Assign the desired products to include in Windows Update:

```
Get-WsusProduct |
    Where-Object {$PSItem.Product.Title -in $CHP} |
        Set-WsusProduct
```

5. Get a list of the distinct categories of updates you can retrieve from Windows Update for distribution to your client hosts:

```
Get-WsusClassification
```

6. Create and view a list of desired update classifications to make available on your WSUS server:

```
$CCL = @('Critical Updates',
         'Definition Updates',
         'Security Updates',
         'Service Packs',
         'Update Rollups',
         'Updates')
```

7. Now set the list of desired update classifications in WSUS:

```
Get-WsusClassification |
    Where-Object {$_.Classification.Title -in
                      $CCL} |
        Set-WsusClassification
```

8. Get current subscriptions:

```
$WSUSServer = Get-WsusServer
$WSUSSubscription = $WSUSServer.GetSubscription()
```

9. Start synchronizing available updates based on configured categories:

```
$WSUSSubscription.StartSynchronization()
```

10. Next, loop and wait for synchronization to complete:

```
$IntervalSeconds = 5
$NP = 'NotProcessing'
Do {
  $WSUSSubscription.GetSynchronizationProgress()
  Start-Sleep -Seconds $IntervalSeconds
} While ($WSUSSubscription.GetSynchronizationStatus() -eq $NP)
```

11. Synchronize the updates; this can take a long while to complete:

```
$IntervalSeconds = 1
$NP = 'NotProcessing'
#   Wait for synchronizing to start
Do {
Write-Output $WSUSSubscription.GetSynchronizationProgress()
Start-Sleep -Seconds $IntervalSeconds
}
While ($WSUSSubscription.GetSynchronizationStatus() -eq $NP)
#    Wait for all phases of process to end
```

```
Do {
Write-Output $WSUSSubscription.GetSynchronizationProgress()
Start-Sleep -Seconds $IntervalSeconds
}
Until ($WSUSSubscription.GetSynchronizationStatus() -eq $NP)
```

12. When the final loop is complete, check the results of the synchronization:

```
$WSUSSubscription.GetLastSynchronizationInfo()
```

13. Finally, going forward, ensure that synchronization happens once a day:

```
$WSUSSubscription = $WSUSServer.GetSubscription()
$WSUSSubscription.SynchronizeAutomatically = $true
$WSUSSubscription.NumberOfSynchronizationsPerDay = 1
$WSUSSubscription.Save()
```

How it works...

In *step 1*, you examine the product updates available:

```
PS C:\foo> Get-WsusProduct |
         Where-Object -FilterScript {$_.product.title -match
                      '^Windows Server'}

Title                                                     ID
-----                                                     --
Windows Server 2003, Datacenter Edition                   7f44c2a7-bc36-470b-be3b-c01b6dc5dd4e
Windows Server 2003                                       dbf57a08-0d5a-46ff-b30c-7715eb9498e9
Windows Server 2008 R2                                    fdfe8200-9d98-44ba-a12a-772282bf60ef
Windows Server 2008 Server Manager Dynamic Installer      ec9aaca2-f868-4f06-b201-fb8eefd84cef
Windows Server 2008                                       ba0ae9cc-5f01-40b4-ac3f-50192b5d6aaf
Windows Server 2012 Language Packs                        26cbba0f-45de-40d5-b94a-3cbe5b761c9d
Windows Server 2012 R2  and later drivers                 f3c2263d-b256-4c49-a246-973c0e366449
Windows Server 2012 R2 Drivers                            bfd3e48c-c96b-43fd-8b09-9&cdc89dc77e
Windows Server 2012 R2 Language Packs                     8b4e84f6-595f-41ed-854f-4ca886e317a5
Windows Server 2012 R2                                    d31bd4c3-d872-41c9-a2e7-231f372588cb
Windows Server 2012                                       a105a108-7c9b-4518-bbbe-73f0fe30012b
Windows Server 2016 and Later Servicing Drivers           3c54bb6c-66d1-4a79-884c-8a0c96fa20d1
Windows Server 2016                                       569e8e8f-c6cd-42c8-92a3-efbb20a0f6f5
Windows Server Drivers                                    323cceaf-b60b-4a0d-8a8a-3069efde76bf
Windows Server Manager - Windows Server Update Services ....  4e487029-f550-4c22-8b31-9173f3f95786
Windows Server Solutions Best Practices Analyzer 1.0      eef074e9-61d6-4dac-b102-3dbe15fff3ea
Windows Server Technical Preview Language Packs           0b378f2d-bff3-47dd-9b7f-5c9f966bdd81
```

In *step 2*, you review the version of Windows 10 that you can update using WSUS and Windows Update, like this:

```
PS C:\foo> Get-WsusProduct -TitleIncludes 'Windows 10'

Title                                                                    ID
-----                                                                    --
Windows 10 and later drivers                                             05eebf61-148b-43cf-80da-1c99ab0b8699
Windows 10 and later upgrade & servicing drivers                         34f268b4-7e2d-40e1-8966-8bb6ea3dad27
Windows 10 Anniversary Update and Later Servicing Drivers                bab879a4-c1af-4b52-9617-0f9ae1286fb6
Windows 10 Anniversary Update and Later Upgrade & Servicing Drivers      0ba562e6-a6ba-490d-bdce-93a770ba8d21
Windows 10 Creators Update and Later Servicing Drivers                   cfe7182c-14a0-4d7e-9f5e-505d5c3a66f6
Windows 10 Creators Update and Later Servicing Drivers                   f5b5092c-d05e-4eb1-8a6a-919770378ff6
Windows 10 Creators Update and Later Upgrade & Servicing Drivers         06da2f0c-7937-4e28-b46c-a37317eade73
Windows 10 Dynamic Update                                                e4b04398-adbd-4b69-93b9-477322331cd3
Windows 10 Fall Creators Update and Later Servicing Drivers              876dad18f-f41d-442a-ac64-f5c5ce74cc83
Windows 10 Fall Creators Update and Later Upgrade & Servicing Drivers    c70f1038-66ac-443d-9e58-ac22e891e4fb
Windows 10 Feature On Demand                                             e104dd76-2895-41c4-9eb5-c483a61e9427
Windows 10 GDR-DU FOD                                                    3efabf46-3037-4c85-a752-3189e574b621
Windows 10 GDR-DU LP                                                     6111a83d-7a6b-4a2c-a7c2-f222eebcabf4
Windows 10 GDR-DU                                                        abc45868-0c9c-4bc0-a36d-03d54113baf4
Windows 10 Language Interface Packs                                      7d247b99-caa2-45e4-9c8f-6d60d0aae35c
Windows 10 Language Packs                                                fc7c9913-7a1e-4b30-b602-3c62fffd9b1a
Windows 10 LTSB                                                          d2085b71-5f1f-43a9-880d-ed159016d5c6
Windows 10 S and Later Servicing Drivers                                 c1006636-eab4-4b0b-b1b0-d50282c0377e
Windows 10 S Version 1709 and Later Servicing Drivers for testing        bb06ba08-3df8-4221-8794-18effb79156a
Windows 10 S Version 1709 and Later Upgrade & Servicing Drivers for testing b7f52cfb-c9e9-4481-9bc0-c8b4e208ba39
Windows 10 S Version 1803 and Later Servicing Drivers                    e727f134-a089-4b23-83f1-3004e054f658
Windows 10 S Version 1803 and Later Upgrade & Servicing Drivers          761370fd-6dbb-427f-899e-c19d56e22a9b
Windows 10 version 1803 and Later Servicing Drivers                      8570b1a2-0551-42c8-a3e7-d3783c3d36d4
Windows 10 Version 1803 and Later Upgrade   & Servicing Drivers          29e060d2-aa33-4784-9b50-2021bb84cc18
Windows 10                                                               a3c2375d-0c8a-42f9-bce0-28333e198407
```

In most cases, you probably do not want to support all Microsoft products. To achieve that, you begin, in *step 3*, by creating a list of the products you do want to support. In this step, you include all versions of Windows Server, SQL Server 2016, and all versions of Windows 10, which looks like this:

```
PS C:\foo> $CHP =
            (Get-WsusProduct |
            Where-Object -FilterScript {$_.product.title -match
                                        '^Windows Server'}).Product.Title
PS C:\foo> $CHP += @('Microsoft SQL Server 2016','Windows 10')
PS C:\foo> $CHP

Windows Server 2003, Datacenter Edition
Windows Server 2003
Windows Server 2008 R2
Windows Server 2008 Server Manager Dynamic Installer
Windows Server 2008
Windows Server 2012 Language Packs
Windows Server 2012 R2  and later drivers
Windows Server 2012 R2 Drivers
Windows Server 2012 R2 Language Packs
Windows Server 2012 R2
Windows Server 2012
Windows Server 2016 and Later Servicing Drivers
Windows Server 2016
Windows Server Drivers
Windows Server Manager - Windows Server Update Services (WSUS) Dynamic Installer
Windows Server Solutions Best Practices Analyzer 1.0
Windows Server Technical Preview Language Packs
Microsoft SQL Server 2016
Windows 10
```

In *step 4*, you specify that your WSUS server should get updates for the products in the `$CHP` array. There is no output from this step.

For any given product supported, Windows Update can provide a number of different kinds, classifications, of updates. In *step 6*, you get the classifications of update types available, which looks like this:

```
PS C:\foo> Get-WsusClassification

Title            ID
-----            --
Applications     5c9376ab-8ce6-464a-b136-22113dd69801
Critical Updates e6cf1350-c01b-414d-a61f-263d14d133b4
Definition Updates e0789628-ce08-4437-be74-2495b842f43b
Driver Sets      77835c8d-62a7-41f5-82ad-f28d1af1e3b1
Drivers          ebfc1fc5-71a4-4f7b-9aca-3b9a503104a0
Feature Packs    b54e7d24-7add-428f-8b75-90a396fa584f
Security Updates 0fa1201d-4330-4fa8-8ae9-b877473b6441
Service Packs    68c5b0a3-d1a6-4553-ae49-01d3a7827828
Tools            b4832bd8-e735-4761-8daf-37f882276dab
Update Rollups   28bc880e-0592-4cbf-8f95-c79b17911d5f
Updates          cd5ffd1e-e932-4e3a-bf74-18bf0b1bbd83
Upgrades         3689bdc8-b205-4af4-8d4a-a63924c5e9d5
```

You may not want all these kinds of updates. To achieve this, in *step 6*, you build a list of the update classifications you do wish to support. In *step 7*, you configure your WSUS server with this list. In *step 8*, you obtain the synchronization status of `WSUS1`, and in *step 9*, you initiate synchronization of update categories of `WSUS1` from Windows Update. These three steps produce no output.

In *step 10*, you initiate a loop that gets the category synchronization status and, if it's still processing, wait a bit longer. This synchronization takes a long time—and looks like this (but with significant trimming!):

```
TotalItems ProcessedItems         Phase
---------- --------------         -----
         0             0 NotProcessing
     27438           800 Updates
```

Next, in *step 11*, you now synchronize the updates available based on previous configuration, which, slightly trimmed to avoid pages of output, looks like this:

```
PS C:\foo> $IntervalSeconds = 1
          $NP= 'NotPrcessing'
          #    Wait for synchronizing to start
          Do {
              Write-Output $WSUSSubscription.GetSynchronizationProgress()
              Start-Sleep -Seconds $IntervalSeconds
              }
          While ($WSUSSubscription.GetSynchronizationStatus() -eq $NP)
          #    Wait for all phases of process to end
          Do {
           Write-Output $WSUSSubscription.GetSynchronizationProgress()
           Start-Sleep -Seconds $IntervalSeconds
          }
          Until ($WSUSSubscription.GetSynchronizationStatus() -eq $NP)


TotalItems ProcessedItems    Phase
---------- --------------    -----
     27438          2288 Updates
...
     27438         22704 Updates
```

Once this synchronization is complete, in *step 12*, you can view the synchronization status, which now looks like this:

```
PS C:\foo> $WSUSSubscription.GetLastSynchronizationInfo()

Id              : fafeeffa-4375-4425-95e5-d1b6a8c526e4
StartTime       : 17/09/2018 11:19:55
EndTime         : 17/09/2018 12:40:36
StartedManually : True
Result          : Succeeded
Error           : NotApplicable
ErrorText       :
UpdateErrors    : {}
```

In *step 13*, you configure WSUS1 to download new updates every day, for those products and classifications you previously specified. This step produces no output.

There's more...

In *step 1*, you examined the updates available for all versions of Windows Server. As you can see, this even includes very old versions of Windows Server, such as Windows Server 2003, which is now out of support and hopefully no longer being used in your organization. Inevitably, there are some organizations still running Windows Server 2003, hopefully for good business reasons. It's comforting to know that updates are still available even if the product should have been replaced years ago. You can also see that, as of the time of writing, Windows Update has no updates for Server 2019.

WSUS supports a range of products and different classifications of updates. Consider carefully what products you wish to get updates for and what update types to support. You could err on the side of caution, but that involves a lot of files and a very large number of updates you may never need.

Configuring the Windows Update Client

By default, Windows computers, both the server and client version, download updates from Microsoft's Windows Update servers on the internet. In order to configure Windows hosts to take updates from an internal WSUS server, you need to update the configuration of the Windows Update Client that is built into Windows.

The easiest method of configuring the Windows Update Client is to use Group Policy. You create a **Group Policy Object** (**GPO**), configure the policy with server names, and so on, and then assign the policy.

You can apply a single GPO to the domain as a whole (configuring Windows Update Client on every domain-joined host) or apply policies at the site or OU level, depending on the complexity of your WSUS implementation. A small company located in a single site might apply just one policy at the domain level. Large multinational organizations may have multiple WSUS servers around the globe and might need multiple Windows Update policies applied throughout a large multi-forest network.

Getting ready

You run this recipe from your client host, *CL1*, as configured by the *Installing RSAT Tools on Windows 10 and Windows Server 2019* recipe.

How to do it...

1. Create the WSUS server URL using the properties returned from the Get-WsusServer cmdlet:

```
$WSUSServer = Get-WsusServer -Name WSUS1.Reskit.Org -Port 8530
$FS = "http{2}://{0}:{1}"
$N  = $WSUSServer.Name
$P  = 8530 # default port
$WSUSServerURL = $FS -f $n, $p,
                    ('','s')[$WSUSServer.UseSecureConnection]
$WSUSServerURL
```

2. Create a **GPO** and link it to the domain:

```
$PolicyName = 'Reskit WSUS Policy'
New-GPO -Name $PolicyName
New-GPLink -Name $PolicyName -Target 'DC=RESKIT,DC=Org'
```

3. Add registry key settings to the Group Policy to assign the WSUS server:

```
# Set computer to use WSUS not WU:
$KEY1 = 'HKLM\Software\Policies\Microsoft\Windows\WindowsUpdate\AU'
$RVHT1 = @{
  Name        = $PolicyName
  Key         = $KEY1
  ValueName   = 'UseWUServer'
  Type        = 'DWORD'
  Value       = 1}
Set-GPRegistryValue @RVHT1 | Out-Null
# Set AU options:
$KEY2 = 'HKLM\Software\Policies\Microsoft\Windows\WindowsUpdate\AU'
$RVHT2 = @{
  Name      = $PolicyName
  Key       = $KEY2
  ValueName = 'AUOptions'
  Type      = 'DWORD'
  Value     = 2}
Set-GPRegistryValue  @RVHT2 | Out-Null
# Set WSUS Server URL:
$KEY3 = 'HKLM\Software\Policies\Microsoft\Windows\WindowsUpdate'
$RVHT3 = @{
Name      = $PolicyName
Key       = $KEY3
ValueName = 'WUServer'
Type      = 'String'
Value     = $WSUSServerURL}
Set-GPRegistryValue @RVHT3 | Out-Null
# Set WU Status server URL:
$KEY4 = 'HKLM\Software\Policies\Microsoft\Windows\WindowsUpdate'
$RVHT4 = @{
Name       = $PolicyName
Key        = $KEY4
ValueName  = 'WUStatusServer'
Type       = 'String'
Value      = $WSUSServerURL}
Set-GPRegistryValue @RVHT4 | Out-Null
```

4. Get a report on the GPO and view it:

```
$RHT = @{
  Name       = $PolicyName
  ReportType = 'Html'
  Path       = 'C:\Foo\Out.htm'}
Get-GPOReport @RHT
Invoke-Item -Path $RHT.Path
```

How it works...

In *step 1*, you instantiate a WSUS server object that is used in later steps in the recipe. Then you use that object to create the URL that Windows Update Clients use to contact your WSUS server. There is no output from this step.

In *step 2*, you create a new GPO policy (`Reskit WSUS Policy`) and assign that policy to the `Reskit.Org` domain. This means that every domain-joined computer in the `Reskit.Org` domain is to get updates from `WSUS1.Reskit.Org`. This step produces output like this:

```
PS C:\Foo> $PolicyName = 'Reskit WSUS Policy'
PS C:\Foo> New-GPO -Name $PolicyName

DisplayName       : Reskit WSUS Policy
DomainName        : Reskit.Org
Owner             : RESKIT\Domain Admins
Id                : 33cff7e9-3fa7-4442-aa0a-4cf185de4488
GpoStatus         : AllSettingsEnabled
Description       :
CreationTime      : 18/09/2018 00:47:03
ModificationTime  : 18/09/2018 00:48:03
UserVersion       : AD Version: 0, SysVol Version: 0
ComputerVersion   : AD Version: 0, SysVol Version: 0
WmiFilter         :


PS C:\Foo> New-GPLink -Name $PolicyName -Target 'DC=RESKIT,DC=Org'

DisplayName   : Reskit WSUS Policy
GpoId         : 33cff7e9-3fa7-4442-aa0a-4cf185de4488
Enabled       : True
Enforced      : False
Order         : 2
Target        : DC=Reskit,DC=Org
GpoDomainName : Reskit.Org
```

In *step 4*, you set values for the WSUS policy GPO. This configures the GPO with the necessary information to enable Windows Update to make use of WSUS in the organization. There is no output from this step.

In *step 5*, you view a GPO report of the WSUS policy GPO, which looks like this:

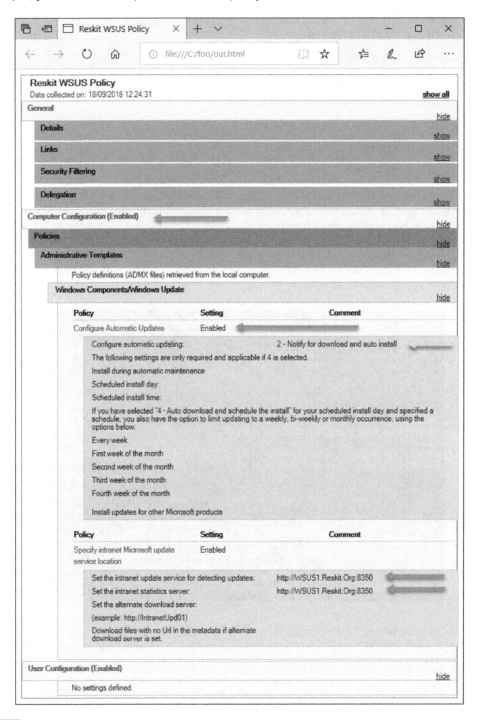

There's more...

In *step 2*, you created the WSUS policy and linked it to the domain. For very large organizations, separate policies may be appropriate, each linked to separate OUs or sites in your AD. You may even wish, for very large organizations, multiple WSUS implementations around the world.

In *step 3*, you configured the GPO object with 4 registry-based settings. The recipe used Out-Null to limit the amount of output. If you experiment with this recipe, consider removing the pipe to null to see the output generated.

Creating computer target groups

With the recipes so far in this chapter, you have set up a WSUS Server and created a GPO to configure the Windows Update Client on your computers. The next step is to create target groups—groups of computers you plan to use when targeting WSUS updates.

In any organization, different groups of hosts can have different update requirements. Your Windows client hosts run software such as Microsoft Office that is rarely seen on a server. Your mission critical servers might require a separate testing and sign-off process for updates that are approved for use.

For efficient management of updates, you define target groups (for example, **domain controllers** (**DCs**), SQL Servers, and so on) and then define the computers in the target group. In this recipe, you create a target group for DCs (that is, DC1, DC2).

Getting ready

This recipe runs in the WSUS1 WSUS server. In the preceding recipes in this chapter, you have set up the WSUS server, configured WSUS updates, and configured the Windows Update Client computers via a GPO.

How to do it...

1. Create a WSUS computer target group for the DCs:

    ```
    $WSUSServer = Get-WsusServer -Name WSUS1 -port 8530
    $WSUSServer.CreateComputerTargetGroup('Domain Controllers')
    ```

2. Examine existing target groups and view the new one:

```
$WSUSServer.GetComputerTargetGroups() |
   Format-Table -Property Name
```

3. Find the DCs that have registered with WSUS1:

```
Get-WsusComputer -NameIncludes DC
```

4. Add DC1 and DC2 to the Domain Controllers target group:

```
Get-WsusComputer -NameIncludes DC |
   Add-WsusComputer -TargetGroupName 'Domain Controllers'
```

5. Get the Domain Controllers target computer group:

```
$DCGroup = $WSUSServer.GetComputerTargetGroups() |
              Where-Object Name -eq 'Domain Controllers'
```

6. Display the computers in the group:

```
Get-WsusComputer |
   Where-Object ComputerTargetGroupIDs -Contains $DCGroup.id |
      Sort-Object -Property FullDomainName |
         Format-Table -Property FullDomainName, ClientVersion,
                                LastSyncTime
```

How it works...

In *step 1*, you create a new computer target group called Domain Controllers, which looks like this:

```
PS C:\foo> $WSUSServer = Get-WsusServer
PS C:\foo> $WSUSServer.CreateComputerTargetGroup('Domain Controllers')

UpdateServer                                                  Id                                    Name
------------                                                  --                                    ----
Microsoft.UpdateServices.Internal.BaseApi.UpdateServer        30f5d153-7ad3-4bd7-96b4-9caad12b52f8  Domain Controllers
```

In *step 2*, you use the $WSUSServer object to get and then display the current target groups, including the one you just created, which looks like this:

```
PS C:\foo> $WSUSServer.GetComputerTargetGroups() |
              Format-Table -Property Name

Name
----
All Computers
Domain Controllers    ⟵
Unassigned Computers
```

In *step 3*, you retrieve the computers whose name contains DC and that have registered with the WSUS server, which looks like this:

```
PS C:\foo> Get-WsusComputer -NameIncludes DC

Computer        IP Address   Operating System           Last Status Report
--------        ----------   ----------------           ------------------
dc2.reskit.org 10.10.10.11 Windows Server Datacenter 01/01/0001 00:00:00
dc1.reskit.org 10.10.10.10 Windows Server Datacenter 01/01/0001 00:00:00
```

In *step 4*, which creates no output, you add the two DCs to the Domain Controllers computer target group. In *step 5*, which also creates no output, you get the target group from the WSUS computer.

Finally, in *step 6,* you examine the computers, their OS version, and the last synchronization time (with time in UTC), which looks like this:

```
PS C:\foo> Get-WsusComputer |
      Where-Object ComputerTargetGroupIDs -Contains $DCGroup.id |
        Sort-Object -Property FullDomainName |
          Format-Table -Property FullDomainName, ClientVersion,
                          LastSyncTime

FullDomainName ClientVersion   LastSyncTime
-------------- -------------   ------------
dc1.reskit.org 10.0.17733.1000 18/09/2018 15:30:07
dc2.reskit.org 10.0.17733.1000 18/09/2018 14:25:05
```

There's more...

In *step 6*, you display the computers in the Domain Controllers computer target group. Once you create the GPO object, it can take 24 hours or longer to have all the computers in your domain begin to work with WSUS for the computers in the Domain Controllers target group. Because of the time it can take to set up a WSUS server, it's a task possibly for a long weekend.

Configuring WSUS automatic approvals

Microsoft's Windows Update can produce a large number of updates for you to manage (inspect, accept/decline, and deploy). Some update types, or example critical updates, may be ones you want to automatically approve, so as soon as you receive one of these, you can start deploying it.

Getting ready

This recipe assumes you have a WSUS server, `WSUS1`, set up as per the previous recipes in this chapter. You can also use your own WSUS server, adapting this recipe as appropriate.

How to do it...

1. Create the auto-approval rule:

```
$WSUSServer   = Get-WsusServer
$ApprovalRule =
   $WSUSServer.CreateInstallApprovalRule('Critical Updates')
```

2. Define a deadline for the rule:

```
$Type = 'Microsoft.UpdateServices.Administration.' +
         'AutomaticUpdateApprovalDeadline'
$RuleDeadLine = New-Object -Typename $Type
$RuleDeadLine.DayOffset = 3
$RuleDeadLine.MinutesAfterMidnight = 180
$ApprovalRule.Deadline = $RuleDeadLine
```

3. Add update classifications to the rule:

```
$UC = $ApprovalRule.GetUpdateClassifications()
$C  = $WSUSServer.GetUpdateClassifications() |
         Where-Object -Property Title -eq 'Critical Updates'
$UC.Add($C)
$D = $WSUSServer.GetUpdateClassifications() |
         Where-Object -Property Title -eq 'Definition Updates'
$UC.Add($D)
$ApprovalRule.SetUpdateClassifications($UpdateClassification)
```

4. Assign the rule to a computer target group:

```
$Type = 'Microsoft.UpdateServices.Administration.'+
        'ComputerTargetGroupCollection'
$TargetGroups = New-Object $Type
$TargetGroups.Add(($WSUSServer.GetComputerTargetGroups() |
  Where-Object -Property Name -eq "Domain Controllers"))
$ApprovalRule.SetComputerTargetGroups($TargetGroups)
```

5. Enable and save the rule:

```
$ApprovalRule.Enabled = $true
$ApprovalRule.Save()
```

6. Get a list of approval rules:

```
$WSUSServer.GetInstallApprovalRules()   |
  Format-Table -Property Name, Enabled, Action
```

How it works...

In this recipe, you configured auto approval for some updates. This rule automatically approves updates that are either critical updates or definition updates. Any updates of these two types are automatically approved for use by clients.

In *step 1*, you create an in-memory object for an approval rule. Next, in *step 2*, you define a deadline for the rule. In *step 3*, you add some update classifications to the rule. Then, in *step 4,* you assign the rule to a computer target group. In *step 5*, you enable this new approval rule and save it. These five steps produce no output.

In *step 6*, you view the approval rules in place on your WSUS server, which looks like this:

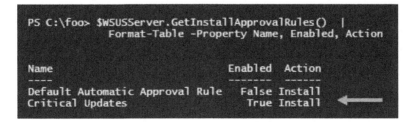

There's more...

This recipe uses the WSUS Server object and the many methods that the object provides. This is not dissimilar to older-style COM-object type programming. Other Windows features use cmdlets to perform management operations whereas here you are using object method calls. PowerShell's built-in help system does not provide much assistance for discovering details about the methods and how to use them. There is not much current up-to-date documentation on the methods and objects either.

Managing WSUS updates

Each PowerShell module developer team, which includes the various feature teams inside the overall Windows Server product team, approach their problem domains slightly differently. Their product, their PowerShell module, has a certain usage style.

An important stylistic difference is the balance between cmdlets and object method calls. For some modules, you manage the service totally through cmdlets. The DNSServer and DHCPServer modules are examples of this.

The Windows Update module, on the other hand, makes use of method calls to perform the desired administrative task, such as approving or declining a specific update. Thus, many administrative functions are performed via method calls rather than cmdlets.

This recipe shows you how you can make use of the UpdateServer object and its rich collections of methods.

Getting ready

This recipe runs on WSUS1, a WSUS server that you set up in the previous recipes in this chapter. You can certainly adapt this recipe to use your own local WSUS server.

How to do it...

1. On WSUS1, open a session on the WSUS1 host and check overall status:

```
$WSUSServer = Get-WsusServer
$WSUSServer.GetStatus()
```

2. View the computer targets:

```
$WSUSServer.GetComputerTargets() |
  Sort-Object -Property FullDomainName |
    Format-Table -Property FullDomainName, IPAddress, Last*
```

3. Search the WSUS server for updates with titles containing Windows Server 2016 that are classified as security updates, then use `Get-Member`, reviewing the properties and methods of the `Microsoft.UpdateServices.Internal.BaseApi.Update` object:

```
$ST = 'Windows Server 2016'
$SU = 'Security Updates'
$SecurityUpdates = $WSUSServer.SearchUpdates($ST) |
  Where-Object UpdateClassificationTitle -eq $SU |
    Sort-Object -Property CreationDate -Descending
```

4. View the first 10 security updates on `WSUS1`:

```
$SecurityUpdates |
  Sort-Object -Property Title |
    Select-Object -First 10 |
      Format-Table -Property Title, Description
```

5. Select one of the updates to approve based on the KB article ID:

```
$SelectedUpdate = $SecurityUpdates |
  Where-Object KnowledgebaseArticles -eq 3194798
```

6. Define the computer target group where you approve this update:

```
$DCTargetGroup = $WSUSServer.GetComputerTargetGroups() |
  Where-Object -Property Name -eq 'Domain Controllers'
```

7. Approve the update for installation in the target group:

```
$SelectedUpdate.Approve('Install',$DCTargetGroup)
```

8. Select one of the updates to decline based on a KB article ID:

```
$DeclinedUpdate = $SecurityUpdates |
  Where-Object -Property KnowledgebaseArticles -eq 4020821
```

9. Decline the update:

```
$DeclinedUpdate.Decline($DCTargetGroup)
```

How it works...

In *step 1,* you use the `Get-WsusServer` cmdlet to return an `UpdateServer` object. This object and its methods are at the core of automating WSUS. You then use the `GetStatus()` method to return the status of your WSUS server, which looks like this:

```
PS C:\foo> $WSUSServer = Get-WsusServer
PS C:\foo> $WSUSServer.GetStatus()

UpdateCount                                               : 20041
DeclinedUpdateCount                                       : 414
ApprovedUpdateCount                                       : 17
NotApprovedUpdateCount                                    : 19610
UpdatesWithStaleUpdateApprovalsCount                      : 0
ExpiredUpdateCount                                        : 0
CriticalOrSecurityUpdatesNotApprovedForInstallCount       : 11275
WsusInfrastructureUpdatesNotApprovedForInstallCount       : 0
UpdatesWithClientErrorsCount                              : 0
UpdatesWithServerErrorsCount                              : 0
UpdatesNeedingFilesCount                                  : 0
UpdatesNeededByComputersCount                             : 6
UpdatesUpToDateCount                                      : 0
CustomComputerTargetGroupCount                            : 1
ComputerTargetCount                                       : 5
ComputerTargetsNeedingUpdatesCount                        : 2
ComputerTargetsWithUpdateErrorsCount                      : 0
ComputersUpToDateCount                                    : 0
UnrecognizedClientRequestedTargetGroupNames               : {}
ShouldDeleteUnneededRevisions                             : False
```

In *step 2,* you use the `GetComputerTargets()` method to get the host computers served by your WSUS server, which looks like this:

```
PS C:\foo> $WSUSServer.GetComputerTargets() |
             Sort-Object -Property FullDomainName |
               Format-Table -Property FullDomainName, IPAddress, Last*

FullDomainName      IPAddress               LastSyncTime          LastSyncResult LastReportedStatusTime LastReportedInventoryTime
--------------      ---------               ------------          -------------- ---------------------- -------------------------
dc1.reskit.org      10.10.10.10             21/09/2018 16:48:18    Succeeded 21/09/2018 16:57:03    01/01/0001 00:00:00
dc2.reskit.org      10.10.10.11             21/09/2018 16:44:56    Succeeded 21/09/2018 16:53:08    01/01/0001 00:00:00
srv1.reskit.org     10.10.10.50             21/09/2018 16:48:36    Succeeded 21/09/2018 16:56:51    01/01/0001 00:00:00
ssrv2.reskit.org    10.10.10.112            21/09/2018 16:48:34    Succeeded 21/09/2018 16:56:48    01/01/0001 00:00:00
wsus1.reskit.org    fe80::1c4f:ede7:333a:dfc%4 21/09/2018 15:10:49    Succeeded 21/09/2018 15:19:35    01/01/0001 00:00:00
```

In *step 3,* you use the `SearchUpdates()` method to get the security updates for hosts running Windows Server 2016. This step produces no output.

In *step 4,* you review the first 10 security updates, which looks like this:

```
PS C:\foo> $SecurityUpdates |
    Sort-Object -Property Title |
      Select-Object -First 10 |
        Format-Table -Property Title, Description

Title                                                                                        Description
-----                                                                                        -----------
2017-05 Cumulative Update for Windows Server 2016 for x64-based Systems (KB4019472)          A security issue has been identified in a Micros...
2017-05 Security Update for Adobe Flash Player for Windows Server 2016 for x64-based Systems (KB4020821) A security issue has been identified in a Micros...
2017-06 Cumulative Update for Windows Server 2016 for x64-based Systems (KB4022715)          A security issue has been identified in a Micros...
2017-06 Security Update for Adobe Flash Player for Windows Server 2016 for x64-based Systems (KB4022730) A security issue has been identified in a Micros...
2017-07 Cumulative Update for Windows Server 2016 for x64-based Systems (KB4025339)          A security issue has been identified in a Micros...
2017-07 Security Update for Adobe Flash Player for Windows Server 2016 for x64-based Systems (KB4025376) A security issue has been identified in a Micros...
2017-08 Cumulative Update for Windows Server 2016 for x64-based Systems (KB4034658)          A security issue has been identified in a Micros...
2017-08 Security Update for Adobe Flash Player for Windows Server 2016 for x64-based Systems (KB4034662) A security issue has been identified in a Micros...
2017-09 Cumulative Update for Windows Server 2016 for x64-based Systems (KB4038782)          A security issue has been identified in a Micros...
2017-09 Security Update for Adobe Flash Player for Windows Server 2016 for x64-based Systems (KB4038806) A security issue has been identified in a Micros...
```

In *step 5*, which produces no output, you select a specific update, based on a KB article number. In *step 6*, you define a target group to which to apply the selected update. This step produces no output.

In *step 7*, you approve this selected patch for installation for all `Domain Controllers` computer target group. The output of this step looks like this:

```
PS C:\foo> $SelectedUpdate.Approve('Install',$DCTargetGroup)

UpdateServer          : Microsoft.UpdateServices.Internal.BaseApi.UpdateServer
Id                    : c0c86518-f5c3-4314-99d3-979351114fb9
CreationDate          : 16/10/2018 14:28:32
Action                : Install
GoLiveTime            : 16/10/2018 14:28:32
Deadline              : 31/12/9999 23:59:59
IsOptional            : False
State                 : Pending
AdministratorName     : RESKIT\Administrator
UpdateId              : Microsoft.UpdateServices.Administration.UpdateRevisionId
ComputerTargetGroupId : 30f5d153-7ad3-4bd7-96b4-9caad12b52f8
IsAssigned            : True
```

In *step 8*, you select an update that you wish not to install. This step produces no output. In *step 9*, you decline the update for the `Domain Controllers` computer target group.

There's more...

In *step 3*, you examined the security updates for Windows Server 2016. You could also have looked for any `Updates` or `Critical Updates`. You can also vary the value of the `$ST` parameter to search for different targets, such as `Windows 10` or `Office`.

In *step 5*, you selected a specific update. If you are an IT Pro responsible for Windows Update Services inside your organization, you need to keep up to date on critical updates so you can deploy urgent patches as quickly as possible.

In *step 9*, you declined a specific update for one computer target group. As you administer WSUS, you are likely to discover certain updates that can be declined since they do not impact certain target groups. Keeping on top of which patches to approve or decline can be a lot of work, but is vital to ensure that your systems are updated promptly.

7
Managing Printing

In this chapter, we cover the following recipes:

- ▶ Installing and sharing printers
- ▶ Publishing a printer
- ▶ Changing the spool directory
- ▶ Changing printer drivers
- ▶ Printing a test page
- ▶ Managing printer security
- ▶ Creating a printer pool

Introduction

Printing is a feature that has been incorporated into various versions of the Windows operating system, and has evolved over the years. Printer configuration and management in Windows Server 2019 hasn't changed much from earlier versions, and provides you with the ability to create print servers that you can share with users in your organization.

When printing in Windows, the physical device that renders output onto paper is known as a **print device**. A **printer** is a queue for a print device. A **print server** can support multiple printers.

Each printing device has an associated **printer driver** that converts your documents to the printed form on a given print device. Some drivers come with Windows—others you need to obtain from the printer vendor. In some cases, these drivers are downloadable from the internet; in other cases, you may need to download and run a driver installation program to add the correct drivers to your print server.

Printers print to the print device by using a **printer port** (such as USB, parallel, or network). For network printers, you need to define the port before you can create a Windows printer.

Microsoft hasn't changed the basic print architecture with Windows Server 2019. Windows Server 2012 introduced a new driver architecture that Windows Server 2019 supports. This driver model enables you to make use of two different driver types: printer class drivers and model-specific drivers. The former provides a single driver for a variety of specific printing device models, whereas the latter is used for just a single model. Increasingly, print device manufacturers are implementing more generic drivers that can simplify the organizational rollout of shared printing.

Another change in Windows Server 2012, carried into Windows Server 2019, is that you no longer use the print server to distribute printer drivers (which is especially relevant for network printers). You can use tools, such as the System Center Configuration Manager or Group Policies, to distribute print drivers to clients in such cases.

This chapter covers installing, managing, and updating printers, print drivers, and printer ports on a Windows Server 2019 server. You may find that some of the administration tools used in this chapter aren't available on Windows Server Core systems. To enable full management, you need to have the full GUI (including the Desktop Experience) for any GUI utilities.

In the *Installing and sharing printers* recipe, you install a printer and share it for others to use. In the *Publishing a printer* recipe, you'll publish the printer to Active Directory (AD), enabling users in the domain to search AD to find the printer.

When you create a print server (adding printer ports, printers, and so on), the default spool folder (underneath `C:\Windows`) may not be in an ideal location. In the *Changing the spool directory* recipe, you change the default location for the printer spool.

Sometimes, a printer can have an associated print device swapped for a different printer model. In the *Changing printer drivers* recipe, you change the driver for the printer you created earlier. A useful troubleshooting step when working with printers is to print a test page, as you can see in the *Printing a test page* recipe.

Printers, like files, can have Access Control Lists (ACL) to specify who can use the printer. In the *Reporting on printer security* recipe, you report on the access enabled for a printer. You can also modify the ACL, as shown in the *Modifying printer* security recipe. In many organizations, print devices are a shared resource. In the *Deploying shared printers* recipe, you'll see how to deploy a shared printer.

In Windows, a **printer pool** is a printer that has two or more associated printing devices. This means having two or more physical printers (print devices on separate ports) that users see as just a single printer. This could be useful in situations where users create large numbers of printed documents. In the *Creating a printer pool* recipe, you see how you can automate the creation of a printer pool, using RunDLL32.Exe.

This chapter makes use of a sales team inside Reskit.Org, which has a number of users and groups contained in an organizational unit (OU). You create these AD resources as follows:

```
# Create-SaleTeam.ps1
# Creates the OU, groups, users and group memberships
# used in Reskit.Org

# Create Sales OU
$OUPath = 'DC=Reskit,DC=Org'
New-ADOrganizationalUnit -Name Sales -Path $OUPath

# Setup for creating users for sales
$OUPath = 'OU=Sales,DC=Reskit,DC=Org'
$Password   = 'Pa$$w0rd'
$PHT = @{
  String      = $Password
  AsPlainText = $true
  Force       = $true
}
$PasswordSS = ConvertTo-SecureString @PHT
$NewUserHT   = @{
  AccountPassword       = $PasswordSS;
  Enabled               = $true;
  PasswordNeverExpires  = $true;
  ChangePasswordAtLogon = $false
  Path                  = $OUPath
}

# Create Sales users Nigel, Samantha, Pippa, Jeremy
$NewUserHT.SamAccountName   = 'Nigel'
$NewUserHT.UserPrincipalName = 'Nigel@Reskit.Org'
$NewuserHT.Name             = 'Nigel'
$NewUserHT.DisplayName   = 'Nigel Hwathorn-Smyth'
New-ADUser @NewUserHT

$NewUserHT.SamAccountName   = 'Samantha'
$NewUserHT.UserPrincipalName = 'Samantha@Reskit.Org'
$NewuserHT.Name             = 'Samantha'
$NewUserHT.DisplayName   = 'Samantha Rhees-Jenkins'
```

```
New-ADUser @NewUserHT

$NewUserHT.SamAccountName    = 'Pippa'
$NewUserHT.UserPrincipalName = 'Pippa@Reskit.Org'
$NewuserHT.Name              = 'Pippa'
$NewUserHT.DisplayName  = 'Pippa van Spergel'
New-ADUser @NewUserHT

$NewUserHT.SamAccountName    = 'Jeremy'
$NewUserHT.UserPrincipalName = 'Jeremy@Reskit.Org'
$NewuserHT.Name              = 'Jeremy'
$NewUserHT.DisplayName  = 'Jeremy Cadwalender'
New-ADUser @NewUserHT

# Create Sales Groups
$GSHT = @{GroupScope = 'Global'}
$OUPath = 'OU=Sales,DC=Reskit,DC=Org'
New-ADGroup -Name Sales -Path $OUPath @GSHT
New-ADGroup -Name SalesAdmins -Path $OUPath @GSHT
New-ADGroup -Name SalesPrinterUsers -Path $OUPath @GSHT


# Add users to the groups
Add-ADGroupMember -Identity Sales -Members Nigel, Samantha
Add-ADGroupMember -Identity Sales -Members Pippa, Jeremy
Add-ADGroupMember -Identity SalesAdmins -Members Nigel, Samantha
Add-AdgroupMember -Identity SalesPrinterUsers -Members Sales
Add-AdgroupMember -Identity SalesPrinterUsers -Members ThomasL
```

You can find this script in the GitHub repository for this book. The script name is `Create-SalesTeam.ps1`. You can find this script at `https://github.com/doctordns/PowerShellCookBook2019/blob/master/Chapter%2007%20-%20Managing%20Printers/Create-SalesTeam.ps1`.

Installing and sharing printers

The first step in creating a print server for your organization involves installing the print server feature, printer drivers, and printer ports. With those installed, you can create and share a printer for others to access. You can also, as you see in the *Deploying shared printers* recipe, push out the printer details to client computers.

In this recipe, you download and install two Xerox printer drivers. One of the drivers is used in this recipe; the other is used in the *Changing printer drivers* recipe. This download comes as a ZIP archive that you need to extract before you can use the drivers.

> If you're adapting this recipe to use other printer makes and models, this recipe may have to be adapted. In some cases (such as with Hewlett Packard printers), the printer drivers are installed via a downloadable executable that wasn't designed to be automated. You need run the downloaded executable and then run it on your print server to add the drivers.

Getting ready

In this recipe, you install the **Print-Server** feature to set up a print server on PSRV, and then set up a TCP/IP printer. PSRV is a domain-joined Windows 2019 server with only the default features installed. This server is used throughout this chapter.

How to do it...

1. Install the `Print-Server` feature on PSRV, along with the `Print Management` RSAT tools:

   ```
   Install-WindowsFeature -Name Print-Server, RSAT-Print-Services
   ```

2. Create a folder on PSRV for the Xerox printer drivers:

   ```
   $NIHT = @{
      Path        = 'C:\Foo\Xerox'
      ItemType    = 'Directory'
      Force       = $true
      ErrorAction = "SilentlyContinue"
   }
   New-Item @NIHT | Out-Null
   ```

3. Download the printer drivers for Xerox printers:

   ```
   $URL='Http://Download.Support.Xerox.Com/pub/drivers/6510/'+
        'drivers/win10x64/ar/6510_5.617.7.0_PCL6_x64.zip'
   $Target='C:\Foo\Xerox\Xdrivers.zip'
   Start-BitsTransfer -Source $URL -Destination $Target
   ```

4. Expand the archive into the `C:\Foo\Xerox\Drivers` folder:

    ```
    $Drivers = 'C:\Foo\Xerox\Drivers'
    Expand-Archive -Path $Target -DestinationPath $Drivers
    ```

5. Install the two Xerox printer drivers:

    ```
    $M1 = 'Xerox Phaser 6510 PCL6'
    $P  = 'C:\Foo\Xerox\Drivers\6510_5.617.7.0_PCL6_x64_Driver.inf\'+
          'x3NSURX.inf'
    rundll32.exe printui.dll,PrintUIEntry /ia /m "$M1"  /f "$P"
    $M2 = 'Xerox WorkCentre 6515 PCL6'
    rundll32.exe printui.dll,PrintUIEntry /ia /m "$M2"  /f "$P"
    ```

6. Add an IP address-based `PrinterPort` for a new printer:

    ```
    $PPHT = @{
      Name              = 'SalesPP'
      PrinterHostAddress = '10.10.10.61'
    }
    Add-PrinterPort @PPHT
    ```

7. Add the printer to `PSRV`:

    ```
    $PRHT = @{
      Name = 'SalesPrinter1'
      DriverName = $M1          # Xerox Phaser 6510 PCL6
      PortName   = 'SalesPP'
    }
    Add-Printer @PRHT
    ```

8. Share the printer:

    ```
    Set-Printer -Name SalesPrinter1 -Shared $True
    ```

9. Review the printer port, printer driver, and printer you just created:

    ```
    Get-PrinterPort -Name SalesPP |
      Format-Table -Autosize -Property Name, Description,
                    PrinterHostAddress, PortNumber
    Get-PrinterDriver -Name xerox* |
      Format-Table -Property Name, Manufacturer,
                    DriverVersion, PrinterEnvironment
    Get-Printer -ComputerName PSRV -Name SalesPrinter1 |
      Format-Table -Property Name, ComputerName,
                    Type, PortName, Location, Shared
    ```

How it works...

In *step 1*, you install the Print-Server feature on PSRV, along with the management tools, which looks like this:

```
PS C:\Foo> Install-WindowsFeature -Name Print-Server, RSAT-Print-Services


Success Restart Needed Exit Code     Feature Result
------- --------------- ---------     --------------
True    No              Success       {Print Server, Print and Document Services...
```

In *step 2*, you ensure that there's a folder to hold the drivers. With *step 3*, you use the BITS service to download the drivers. In *step 4*, you extract the downloaded driver archive. In *step 5*, you install one print driver. In *step 6*, you add a printer port for a networked printer. In *step 7*, you create the networked printer based on the printer port and printer driver you just added. Finally, in *step 8*, you share the printer. These steps produce no output.

In *step 9*, you examine the printer port, printer driver, and the printer created in this recipe, which looks like this:

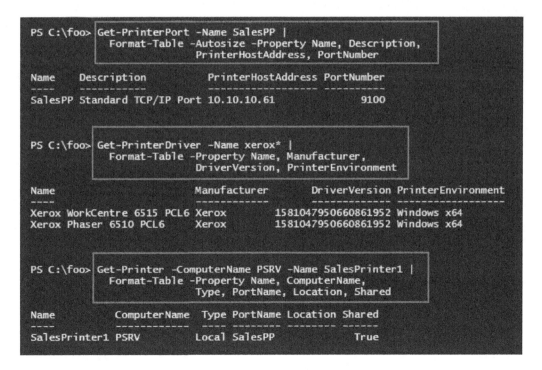

```
PS C:\foo> Get-PrinterPort -Name SalesPP |
             Format-Table -Autosize -Property Name, Description,
                           PrinterHostAddress, PortNumber

Name    Description         PrinterHostAddress PortNumber
----    -----------         ------------------ ----------
SalesPP Standard TCP/IP Port 10.10.10.61            9100


PS C:\foo> Get-PrinterDriver -Name xerox* |
             Format-Table -Property Name, Manufacturer,
                           DriverVersion, PrinterEnvironment

Name                      Manufacturer    DriverVersion      PrinterEnvironment
----                      ------------    -------------      ------------------
Xerox WorkCentre 6515 PCL6 Xerox          1581047950660861952 Windows x64
Xerox Phaser 6510 PCL6     Xerox          1581047950660861952 Windows x64


PS C:\foo> Get-Printer -ComputerName PSRV -Name SalesPrinter1 |
             Format-Table -Property Name, ComputerName,
                           Type, PortName, Location, Shared

Name          ComputerName  Type  PortName Location Shared
----          ------------  ----  -------- -------- ------
SalesPrinter1 PSRV          Local SalesPP           True
```

There's more...

In *step 5*, you use `PrintUI.DLL` and `RunDLL32.EXE`. `PrintUI.DLL` is a library of printer-management functionalities. If you use the Printer Management GUI tool to manage printers, the GUI calls this DLL to perform your chosen action. That can often result in displaying another Windows form (as opposed to generating text output).

`RunDLL32.EXE` allows you to run the same functions within `PrintUI.DLL`. In many cases, using `PrintUI.DLL` generates a pop-up form for you to use, which is useful, but not so helpful in terms of automation.

In practice, sometimes you may see curious errors when using `PrintUI.DLL`. The solution is to reboot the server.

A further downside to using `PrintUI.DLL` is that the error messages aren't very actionable, should you make errors with the complex syntax involved. You can get help information by opening a PowerShell console window and running the following command:

```
rundll32 printui.dll PrintUIEntry
```

In this recipe, you downloaded and installed two drivers, although you only used one to create the `SalesPrinter1` printer. You use the second driver in the *Changing printer drivers* recipe later in this chapter.

Publishing a printer

After you create and share a printer, as shown in the previous recipe, you can also publish it to the Active Directory. When you publish a printer, you can also specify a physical location for the printer. Your users can then search for published printers based on location, as well as on capabilities (such as color printers). In this recipe, you publish the printer you created in the previous recipe and examine the results.

Getting ready

Before running this recipe, you need to have the PSRV printer server set up (you did this in the *Installing and sharing printers* recipe). Additionally, you need `SalesPrinter1` created.

How to do it...

1. Get the printer to publish:

   ```
   $Printer = Get-Printer -Name SalesPrinter1
   ```

2. Display the publication status:

   ```
   $Printer | Format-Table -Property Name, Published
   ```

3. Set the printer details and publish the printer to AD:

   ```
   $Printer | Set-Printer -Location '10th floor 10E4'
   $Printer | Set-Printer -Shared $true -Published $true
   ```

4. View the updated publication status:

   ```
   Get-Printer -Name SalesPrinter1 |
       Format-Table -Property Name, Location, Drivername, Published
   ```

5. See the shared printer status:

   ```
   Get-SmbShare -Name SalesPrinter1
   ```

How it works...

In *step 1*, you retrieved the printer details for the `SalesPrinter1` printer that you set up in the *Installing and sharing printers* recipe. There's no output from this step.

In *step 2*, you display the printer details and can see that the printer is unpublished, which looks like this:

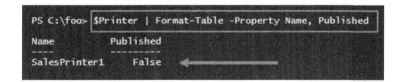

In *step 3*, you use the `Set-Printer` cmdlet to set the location details for the printer and publish the printer in AD. This step updates the printer details in the AD and produces no output.

In *step 4*, you view the details of the printer, which looks like this:

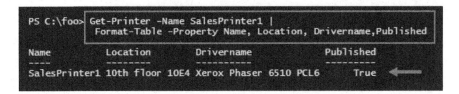

```
PS C:\foo> Get-Printer -Name SalesPrinter1 |
           Format-Table -Property Name, Location, Drivername,Published

Name        Location         Drivername               Published
----        --------         ----------               ---------
SalesPrinter1 10th floor 10E4 Xerox Phaser 6510 PCL6   True
```

There's more...

Publishing a printer to AD allows users to locate printers near them using the **Add Printer** dialog to search for published printers. For example, if you log into the client computer, `CL1`, you can get to this dialog by clicking **Start | Settings | Devices | Printers & scanners** to bring up the **Add printers & scanners** dialog. From this dialog box, click **Add a printer or scanner**. Wait until the search is complete, then click on **The printer that I want isn't listed**, which brings up the **Add Printer** dialog, like this:

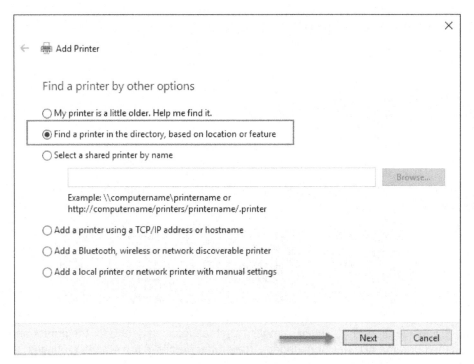

From this dialog box, click on **Next** to bring up the **Find Printers** dialog, which looks like this:

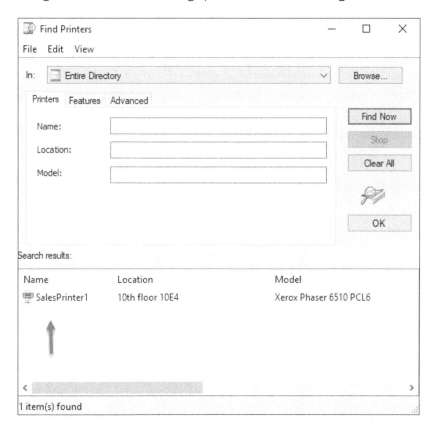

Changing the spool directory

During the printing process, the Windows printer spooler in Windows uses an on-disk folder to hold the temporary files that have been created. If multiple users each print large documents to a single printer, the print queue can get quite large. By default, this folder is `C:\Windows\System32\spool\PRINTERS`. For a busy print server with multiple printers, you may wish to change the default spool folder.

Getting ready

This recipe uses the `PSRV` printer server that was set up as per the *Installing and sharing printers* recipe.

How to do it...

1. Load the `System.Printing` namespace and classes:

    ```
    Add-Type -AssemblyName System.Printing
    ```

2. Define the required permissions—that is, the ability to administrate the server:

    ```
    $Permissions =
        [System.Printing.PrintSystemDesiredAccess]::
                AdministrateServer
    ```

3. Create a `PrintServer` object (in memory) with the required permissions:

    ```
    $NOHT = @{
      TypeName     = 'System.Printing.PrintServer'
      ArgumentList = $Permissions
    }
    $PS = New-Object @NOHT
    ```

4. Create a new spool path:

    ```
    $NIHT = @{
        Path        = 'C:\SpoolPath'
        ItemType    = 'Directory'
        Force       = $true
        ErrorAction = 'SilentlyContinue'
    }
    New-Item @NIHT | Out-Null
    ```

5. Update the default spool folder path on the in-memory object:

    ```
    $Newpath = 'C:\SpoolPath'
    $PS.DefaultSpoolDirectory = $Newpath
    ```

6. Commit the change:

    ```
    $Ps.Commit()
    ```

7. Restart the spooler, which now uses the new `Spooler` folder:

    ```
    Restart-Service -Name Spooler
    ```

8. Once the spooler has restarted, view the results:

    ```
    New-Object -TypeName System.Printing.PrintServer |
        Format-Table -Property Name, DefaultSpoolDirectory
    ```

Another way to set the Spooler directory is by directly editing the registry as follows:

1. Stop the Spooler service:

```
Stop-Service -Name Spooler
```

2. Create a new spool folder for the print server to use:

```
$SPL = 'C:\SpoolViaRegistry'
$NIHT2 = @{
  Path        = $SPL
  Itemtype    = 'Directory'
  ErrorAction = 'SilentlyContinue'
}
New-Item  @NIHT2 | Out-Null
```

3. Set the details in the registry:

```
$RPath = 'HKLM:\SYSTEM\CurrentControlSet\Control\' +
         'Print\Printers'
$Spooldir = 'C:\SpoolViaRegistry' # Folder should exist
$IP = @{
  Path    = $RPath
  Name    = 'DefaultSpoolDirectory'
  Value   = $SPL
}
Set-ItemProperty @IP
```

4. Restart the Spooler:

```
Start-Service -Name Spooler
```

5. View the results:

```
New-Object -TypeName System.Printing.PrintServer |
  Format-Table -Property Name, DefaultSpoolDirectory
```

How it works...

In *step 1*, you loaded the `System.Printing` assembly to provide additional .NET classes that relate to printing and print servers. In *step 2*, you created an object that defines the permissions needed to administrate the printer server. In *step 3*, you created an in-memory print server object using the permissions object you just instantiated. In *step 4*, you created a new folder to serve as the spooler folder. In *step 5*, you updated the default spooler path to the in-memory spooler object. In *step 6*, you committed the changes you just made to the spooler object, and then in *step 7*, you restarted the `Spooler` service. These first seven steps produced no output.

In *step 8*, after the `Spooler` service restarted, you viewed the properties of the print server, including the default printer spool directory you just updated. It looks like this:

```
PS C:\foo> New-Object -TypeName System.Printing.PrintServer |
              Format-Table -Property Name, DefaultSpoolDirectory

Name    DefaultSpoolDirectory
----    ---------------------
\\PSRV  C:\SpoolPath   ◄─────────────
```

Then, you updated the spooler folder by directly editing the registry. In *step 9*, you stopped the spooler service. In *step 10*, you created a second spooler folder, and in *step 11*, you set the relevant registry setting for the printer spooler folder. Then, in *step 12*, you restarted the spooler service. *Step 9* through *step 12* produced no output.

In *step 13*, you looked at the updated printer spooler properties, which looks like this:

```
PS C:Foo> New-Object -TypeName System.Printing.PrintServer |
              Format-Table -Property Name, DefaultSpoolDirectory

Name    DefaultSpoolDirectory
----    ---------------------
\\PSRV  C:\SpoolViaRegistry  ◄─────────────
```

There's more...

In this recipe, you used two different mechanisms to change the spooler folder. One uses a .NET object (which isn't loaded by default), while the other involves directly editing the registry. Needless to say, if you're rolling out printers using scripts, particularly ones that edit the registry, careful testing is vital.

Many of the steps in this recipe produce no output. This is normal when you're dealing directly with .NET classes and methods, and when editing the registry.

Changing printer drivers

On occasion, it may be necessary to change the printer driver for a printer. For example, you might be replacing an existing print device with a new or different model. In this case, you want the printer name to remain the same, but you need to update the actual driver. In the *Installing and sharing a printer* recipe, you downloaded and installed two Xerox printer drivers. You used the first driver, `Xerox Phaser 6510 PCL6`, when you defined the `SalesPrinter1` printer.

In this recipe, you change the driver for the printer and use the other previously-installed driver, the `Xerox Phaser 6515 PCL6`.

The assumption behind this recipe is that the printer name and printer port (including the printer's IP address and port number) don't change, only the driver.

Getting ready

Run this recipe on the `PSRV1` printer, set up as per the *Installing and sharing printers* recipe.

How to do it...

1. Add the print driver for the new printing device:

```
$M2 = 'Xerox WorkCentre 6515 PCL6'
Add-PrinterDriver -Name $M2
```

2. Get the Sales group printer object and store it in `$Printer`:

```
$Printern = 'SalesPrinter1'
$Printer = Get-Printer -Name $Printern
```

3. Update the driver using the `Set-Printer` cmdlet:

```
$Printer | Set-Printer -DriverName $M2
```

4. Observe the result:

```
Get-Printer -Name $Printern |
   Format-Table -Property Name, DriverName, PortName,
                   Published, Shared
```

How it works...

In *step 1*, you added a printer driver for the Xerox 6515 device. In *step 2*, you instantiated an in-memory printer object that represents the print server on PSRV. In *step 3*, you updated SalesPrinter1 with the details of the updated driver name. These steps produced no output.

In *step 4*, you reviewed the changes made, which look like this:

```
PS C:\Foo> Get-Printer -Name $Printern |
              Format-Table -Property Name, DriverName, PortName,
                                       Published,Shared

Name           DriverName                  PortName Published Shared
----           ----------                  -------- --------- ------
SalesPrinter1  Xerox WorkCentre 6515 PCL6  SalesPP       True   True
```

Printing a test page

There are occasions when you may wish to print a test page on a printer; for example, after you change the toner or printer ink on a physical printer or after changing the print driver (as shown in the *Changing printer drivers* recipe). In those cases, the test page helps you to ensure that the printer is working properly.

Getting ready

This recipe uses the PSRV print server that you set up in the *Installing and sharing printers* recipe.

How to do it...

1. Get the printer objects from WMI:

    ```
    $Printers = Get-CimInstance -ClassName Win32_Printer
    ```

2. Display the number of printers defined on PSRV:

```
'{0} Printers defined on this system' -f $Printers.Count
```

3. Get the sales group printer WMI object:

```
$Printer = $Printers |
  Where-Object Name -eq "SalesPrinter1"
```

4. Display the printer's details:

```
$Printer | Format-Table -AutoSize
```

5. Print a test page:

```
Invoke-CimMethod -InputObject $Printer -MethodName PrintTestPage
```

How it works...

In *step 1*, you used `Get-CimInstance` to return all the printers defined on this system. There's no output from this step.

In *step 2*, you displayed the total printers defined, which looks like this:

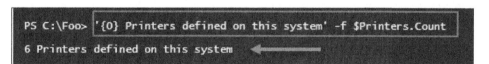

In *step 3*, you got the printer object that corresponds to the sales group LaserJet printer, which generates no output. In *step 4*, you displayed the details of this printer, which looks like this:

In *step 5*, you invoked the `PrintTestPage` method on the sales group printer
(`SalesPrinter1`) to generate a test page on the printer. Using the printer MMC snap-in,
generating a test page looks like this:

Managing printer security

Every Windows printer has a discretionary **access control list** (**ACL**). The ACL contains one or
more **access control entries** (**ACEs**). Each ACE defines a specific permission for some specific
group or user. You could define a group (such as `SalesAdmins`) and give that group the
permission to manage documents, while you give another group (`Sales`) access to print to
the printer.

By default, when you create a printer, Windows adds some ACEs to the printer's ACL. This
includes giving the `Everyone` group the permission to print to the printer. For some printers,
this may not be appropriate. For this reason, you may need to adjust the ACL, as shown in
this recipe.

The `PrintManagement` module contains a number of cmdlets that help you manage the
printers; there are no cmdlets for managing ACLs on printers. You can always use .NET directly
to manage the ACL, or you can use a third-party script that does the job for you. But the code
for that is complex (and easy to mess up). For simplicity in this case, you're going to download
and use a script, `Set-PrintPermissions.ps1`, available on TechNet.

The `SetPrintPermissions.ps1` script enables you to grant or deny printer permissions to
AD users or groups. In this recipe, you use this script to remove the permission for members
of the everyone group, then enable print, document, and print management to members of
a different group. The script uses permission names that are familiar to IT pros, making this
script easy to adapt.

A downside to this script is that there's no feature in the script to display the permissions on a printer object. You can always use .NET security classes to delve into the permissions, or (as you do in this recipe) just use the GUI to verify the actual permissions.

 During the development of Windows Server 2019, printers that are created with the recipes in this chapter have some interesting ACEs set. One ACE is set with an SID that relates to the SID that belongs to `'defaultuser0'`. To avoid confusion, the graphics in the *How it works...* section don't show these ACEs.

Getting ready

This recipe uses AD accounts to set permissions based on the `Create-SalesGroup.ps1` script . You need the `PSRV` print server and the `DC1` domain controller. To test the permissions, you can use `CL1`.

How to do it...

1. Download the `Set-PrinterPermissions.ps1` script:

```
$URL = 'https://gallery.technet.microsoft.com/scriptcenter/' +
        'Modify-Printer-Permissions-149ae172/file/116651/1/' +
        'Set-PrinterPermissions.ps1'
$Target = 'C:\Foo\Set-PrinterPermissions.ps1'
Start-BitsTransfer -Source $URL -Destination $Target
```

2. Get help on the script:

```
Get-Help $Target
```

3. Use `PrintUI.DLL` to bring up the printer properties GUI:

```
rundll32.exe printui.dll,PrintUIEntry /p /nSalesprinter1
```

4. From the GUI, click on **Security** to view the initial ACL.

5. Remove the `Everyone` ACE from the ACL for `SalesPrinter1`:

```
$SPHT1 = @{
  ServerName        = 'PSRV'
  Remove            = $True
  AccountName       = 'EVERYONE'
  SinglePrinterName = 'SalesPrinter1'
}
C:\foo\Set-PrinterPermissions.ps1 @SPHT1
```

6. Enable the members of the `Sales` group to print to this printer:

```
$SPHT2 = @{
  ServerName        = 'PSRV'
  AccountName       = 'Reskit\Sales'
  AccessMask        = 'Print'
  SinglePrinterName = 'SalesPrinter1'
}
C:\foo\Set-PrinterPermissions.ps1 @SPHT2
```

7. Give `SalesAdmins` permission to manage the documents:

```
$SPHT3 = @{
  ServerName        = 'PSRV'
  AccountName       = 'Reskit\SalesAdmins'
  AccessMask        = 'ManageDocuments'
  SinglePrinterName = 'SalesPrinter1'
}
C:\foo\Set-PrinterPermissions.ps1 @SPHT3
```

8. Bring up the Printer GUI:

```
rundll32.exe printui.dll,PrintUIEntry /p /nSalesprinter1
```

9. Click the **Security** tab and view the updated ACL.

How it works...

In *step 1*, you used the BITS service to download the `Set-PrinterPermissions` script. This step generates no output.

The `Set-PrinterPermissions` script has comment-based help, which provides usage assistance. In *step 2*, you used `Get-Help` to view the basic help information, which looks like this:

```
PS C:\foo> Get-Help $Target

NAME
    C:\Foo\Set-PrinterPermissions.ps1

SYNOPSIS
    Purpose:  Modifies Printer Permissions.

SYNTAX
    C:\Foo\Set-PrinterPermissions.ps1 [[-ServerName] <String>] [-AccountName] <String> [[-SinglePrinterName] <String>]
    [[-AccessMask] <String>] [[-Deny]] [[-Remove]] [[-AceFlag] <Int32>] [[-IntAccessMask] <UInt32>] [[-NoLog]]
    [[-LogFile] <String>] [<CommonParameters>]

DESCRIPTION
    This script was created to modify the DACL of printer objects.  It can be
    used to add specific permissions or remove permissions from printers on
    the localhost or a specified server.

    See -full help for example usage.  If no parameters are set, aside from the
    mandatory AccountName, it will set the "Print" permission on all printers
    of the host it is ran on.

    As an alternative to this script, something like SubInACL.exe can be used
    to alter printer permissions.

RELATED LINKS

REMARKS
    To see the examples, type: "get-help C:\Foo\Set-PrinterPermissions.ps1 -examples".
    For more information, type: "get-help C:\Foo\Set-PrinterPermissions.ps1 -detailed".
    For technical information, type: "get-help C:\Foo\Set-PrinterPermissions.ps1 -full".
```

In *step 3*, you used `PrintUI.DLL` to bring up the properties of the `Salesprinter1` printer. In *step 4*, you viewed the initial ACL for the printer, which looks like this:

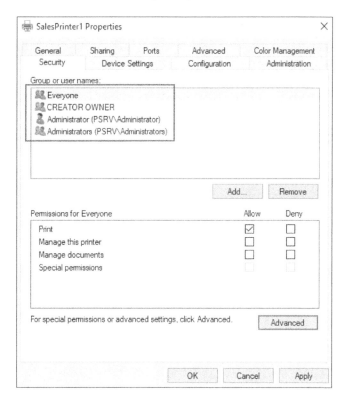

In *step 5*, you used the `Set-Printerpermissions` script to remove the default ACE, allowing everyone to print to the printer. In *step 6*, you enabled the members of the sales group to print to the printer, and in *step 7*, you enabled the members of the sales admins group to manage the printer. These steps produced no output to the console.

In *step 8*, you printed the printer UI to view the updated ACL, which looks like this:

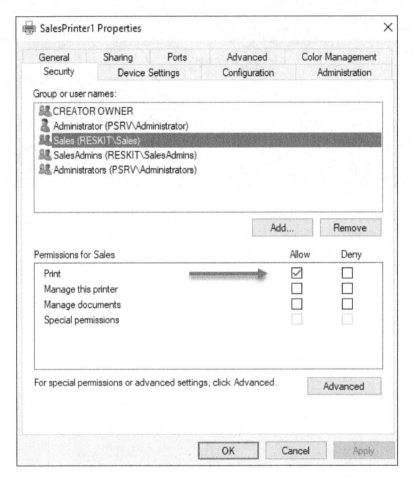

If you click on **Sales**, you can see their permissions, like this:

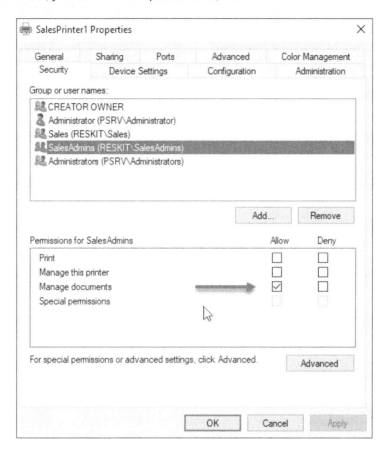

There's more...

In *step 1,* you used the BITS service to download the `Set-PrinterPermissions` script using the URL of the script. Alternatively, you could have used your search engine and downloaded it directly. The script isn't available on PowerShell Gallery.

In *step 3* and *step 8,* you used `PrintUI.DLL` to display a print-management GUI from which you can view the updated ACL for this printer. As you can see, the members of the `Sales` group are able to print, and members of the **SalesAdmins** group can manage the printer.

Creating a printer pool

Windows allows you to create a **printer pool**, which is a printer with two or more print devices (that is, printer ports) available. Windows sends a given print job to any of the printers in the pool. This feature is useful in environments where users do a lot of printing and need the speed that additional printers can provide, without having to ask the user to choose a specific print device to use.

There are no PowerShell cmdlets to enable you to create a printer pool. Also, WMI does not provide a mechanism to create a printer pool. As with other recipes in this chapter, you make use of `PrintUI.DLL` and `RunDLL32` to deploy a printer pool. This is another example of utilizing older console applications to achieve your objective.

Getting ready

Run this recipe on the PSRV print server. This recipe uses the printer and port you created in the *Installing and sharing printers* recipe.

How to do it...

1. Add an additional port for the `SalesPrinter1` printer:

   ```
   $P = 'SalesPP2'         # new port name
   Add-PrinterPort -Name $P -PrinterHostAddress 10.10.10.62
   ```

2. Create the printer pool for `SalesPrinter1`:

   ```
   $P1='SalesPP'
   $P2='SalesPP2'
   rundll32.exe printui.dll,PrintUIEntry /Xs /n $p Portname $P1,$P2
   ```

3. View the resulting details, which show both printer ports:

   ```
   $P = 'SalesPrinter1'
   Get-Printer $P |
       Format-Table -Property Name, Type, DriverName, PortName
   ```

How it works...

In *step 1*, you added a new printer port (SalesPP2) to serve as a second printer port for the SalesPrinter1 printer. In *step 2*, you set the two printer ports for SalesPrinter1, thus creating the printer pool. These steps produced no output.

In *step 3*, you can see the result of the first two steps. Notice that the SalesPrinter1 printer now has two available printer ports, as can be seen here:

```
PS C:\foo> Get-Printer $P |
           Format-Table -Property Name, Type, DriverName, PortName

Name                 Type  DriverName              PortName
----                 ----  ----------              --------
SalesPrinter1        Local Xerox Phaser 6510 PCL6  SalesPP,SalesPP2
```

There's more...

In creating a printer pool, it's important to ensure that all print devices in a pool are the same, or at least can use the same driver. For example, you can use HP drivers for many printers. Having identical models and matching drivers is preferable.

8
Introducing Containers

In this chapter, we cover the following recipes:

- ▶ Configuring a container host
- ▶ Deploying a hello world sample
- ▶ Deploying IIS in a container
- ▶ Using a Dockerfile to create and use a container

Introduction

As a method of Unix virtualization, containers have been around for quite a while. To a large degree, containers serve as an approach for deploying applications popularized by the open source Docker initiative. With Windows 2019, Windows Server supports Docker and Docker containerization integrated with Hyper-V.

Most of the administration you are likely to do with containers in Windows Server 2019 is done not by cmdlets, but by a command-line tool called `docker.exe`. For those used to PowerShell's object-oriented and task-focused approach, you may find this application hard to use. I daresay you are not alone. The `docker.exe` application works in PowerShell and you can, of course, use PowerShell to wrap the command.

With containers in Windows Server 2019, you need to download and install a number of components. In the *Deploying a hello world sample* recipe, you download and make use of OS base images. These require an internet connection.

Containers provide scalability by enabling you to run multiple containers directly on top of Windows Server 2019. This takes up considerably fewer resources than if each container was contained in its own separate **virtual machine** (**VM**).

This approach has a theoretical security vulnerability whereby malware enables bad actors to access one container's contents from another. To reduce those risks, you can run containers inside Hyper-V. With Hyper-V containers, the container is run inside a completely virtualized environment that provides additional hardware-level security, albeit at the price of performance. Hyper-V containers are useful in a shared tenant environment, where one container host can run containers belonging to different organizations.

Once you have configured a container host, it's a great idea to test that you can run containers successfully. There are a number of sample containers you can download to test out the basic container functionality (and the use of `docker.exe`). You use these in the *Deploying a hello world sample* recipe, as well as look at using containers with Hyper-V virtualization.

With containers, you package applications inside a container, which then makes use of a shared kernel. The (single) shared kernel provides kernel-level features for all the containers deployed on a container host. The container then runs an application making use of the shared kernel.

To deploy containers in Windows Server 2019, you need to provide both a container host (to run the container) and one or more images, which Docker can run as a container. You can also download base operating system images from the Docker repository and build your own images on top.

You build and deploy containers using `docker.exe` (and in some cases, Hyper-V), as you see in this chapter. In the *Deploying a hello world sample* recipe, you will explore and download key base images.

An application you can easily containerize is IIS. This is pretty simple, as you can see in the *Deploying IIS in a container* recipe.

If you are deploying containers, you can use a Dockerfile, a simple text file with build instructions. Docker uses this file to build a customized container image, which you can then deploy. You look at creating and using an image using a Dockerfile in the snappily-named *Using a Dockerfile to create and use a container* recipe.

This chapter provides only an introduction to containers, images, `docker.exe`, and Dockerfile files. There is much more to explore with containers. Topics including Docker networking, Docker Swarm, and more are outside the scope of this book. To discover more about containers than we can fit here, look at Packt's book: *Learning Windows Server Containers* by *Srikanth Machiraju*. And, for more on the endearingly awful `docker.exe` application, take a look at *Docker on Windows* by Elton Stoneman.

For more information on Windows containers, see this link: `https://docs.microsoft.com/en-us/virtualization/windowscontainers/about/`.

The recipes in this chapter use the command-line tool docker.exe. For those familiar and comfortable with all of PowerShell's awesomeness, this is going to come as a bit of a shock. docker.exe has no tab completion, all output is minimal text blobs (no objects), parameter names seem random and curious, the online help is not very helpful, and the error reporting is downright atrocious. docker.exe is not all that easy to get to grips with, is less easy to automate than other Windows features, and feels very, very slow even on a well-equipped workstation. Containers as a feature are awesome—if you plan to adopt them, consider spending some time building a good framework and framework tools for your environment. Additionally, using major search engines to discover aspects of containers tends to yield a lot of useful pages, but focused on Linux as a container host and is used in a container.

Configuring a container host

The first step in containerization is to configure a container host. The container host is a machine (virtual or physical) running Windows Server 2019 with the necessary container-related services and prerequisites installed and running. You can also run containers on Windows 10, but this is outside the scope of this chapter.

In this recipe, you install the components necessary for containers, including loading the Docker components.

Getting ready

This recipe uses a new Windows Server 2019 system, named CH1. At the start of this chapter and this recipe, CH1 contains only the base-installed Windows features and has not been used for other recipes in this book.

How to do it...

1. Install the nuget provider:

```
Install-PackageProvider -Name nuget -Force
```

2. Install the Docker provider:

```
$IHT1 = @{
  Name       = 'DockerMSFTProvider'
  Repository = 'PSGallery'
  Force      = $True
}
Install-Module @IHT1
```

3. Install the latest version of the Docker package. This also enables the containers feature in Windows Server:

```
$IHT2 = @{
  Name         = 'Docker'
  ProviderName = 'DockerMSFTProvider'
  Force        = $True
}
Install-Package @IHT2
```

4. Ensure Hyper-V and the Hyper-V management tools are installed:

```
Install-WindowsFeature -Name Hyper-V -IncludeManagementTools |
  Out-Null
```

5. Remove Windows Defender as it can interfere with Docker:

```
Remove-WindowsFeature -Name Windows-Defender |
  Out-Null
```

6. Restart the computer to enable Docker and Windows Containers:

```
Restart-Computer
```

7. Check that the Windows Containers and Hyper-V features are installed on CH1:

```
Get-WindowsFeature -Name Containers, Hyper-v
```

8. Next, check the Docker service:

```
Start-Service -Name Docker
Get-Service -Name Docker
```

9. Check the Docker version information:

```
docker version
```

10. Display the Docker configuration information:

```
docker info
```

How it works...

In *step 1*, you add the `nuget` package provider. The output of that step looks like this:

```
PS C:\Foo> Install-PackageProvider -Name nuget -Force

Name        Version     Source          Summary

----        -------     ------          -------

nuget       2.8.5.208   https://onege... NuGet provider for the OneGet meta-package manager
```

In *step 2*, which produces no output, you install the `DockerMSFTProvider` provider. Next, in *step 3*, you install the latest version of the Docker packages. This step produces the following output:

```
PS C:\Foo> Install-Package -Name Docker -ProviderName DockerMsftProvider -Force
WARNING: A restart is required to enable the containers feature. Please restart your machine.

Name      Version   Source         Summary
----      -------   ------         -------
Docker    18.09.1   DockerDefault  Contains Docker EE for use with Windows Server.
```

In *step 4*, you install the Hyper-V feature and related management tools. In *step 5*, you remove Windows Defender, which can interfere with Docker. In *step 6*, you reboot the system to complete the installation of the core container features. These three steps produce no output.

After CH1 has restarted, in *step 7*, you check on the containers and Hyper-V Windows features, which looks like this:

```
PS C:\Foo> Get-WindowsFeature -Name Containers, Hyper-v

Display Name        Name           Install State
------------        ----           -------------
[X] Hyper-V         Hyper-V            Installed
[X] Containers      Containers         Installed
```

In *step 8*, you check to ensure that the Docker service is running, which looks like this:

```
PS C:\Foo> Get-Service -Name Docker

Status    Name    DisplayName
------    ----    -----------
Running   Docker  Docker
```

In *step 9*, you use the `docker.exe` command to check the Docker client and server version details, which looks like this:

```
PS C:\Foo> docker version

Client:
 Version:           18.09.1
 API version:       1.39
 Go version:        go1.10.6
 Git commit:        20b67756d0
 Built:             unknown-buildtime
 OS/Arch:           windows/amd64
 Experimental:      false

Server:
 Engine:
  Version:          18.09.1
  API version:      1.39 (minimum version 1.24)
  Go version:       go1.10.6
  Git commit:       20b67756d0
  Built:            01/09/2019 17:09:57
  OS/Arch:          windows/amd64
  Experimental:     false
```

In *step 10*, you view the Docker configuration details, which looks like this:

```
PS C:\Foo> docker info
Containers: 0
  Running: 0
  Paused: 0
  Stopped: 0
Images: 0
Server Version: 18.09.1
Storage Driver: windowsfilter
  Windows:
Logging Driver: json-file
Plugins:
  Volume: local
  Network: ics l2bridge l2tunnel nat null overlay transparent
  Log: awslogs etwlogs fluentd gelf json-file local logentries splunk syslog
Swarm: inactive
Default Isolation: process
Kernel Version: 10.0 17763 (17763.1.amd64fre.rs5_release.180914-1434)
Operating System: Windows Server 2019 Datacenter Version 1809 (OS Build 17763.107)
OSType: windows
Architecture: x86_64
CPUs: 2
Total Memory: 1024MiB
Name: CH1
ID: HVEI:VJEV:PYWA:OQLZ:DUYS:NUTN:OHIT:3FDW:73XV:GRJC:OU52:RTA4
Docker Root Dir: C:\ProgramData\docker
Debug Mode (client): false
Debug Mode (server): false
Registry: https://index.docker.io/v1/
Labels:
Experimental: false
Insecure Registries:
  127.0.0.0/8
Live Restore Enabled: false
```

There's more...

In `step 1`, you download and install the NuGet provider. This enables you to get the Docker provider and the Docker application package from the PowerShell Gallery. For more details on NuGet, see: `https://docs.microsoft.com/en-us/nuget/what-is-nuget`.

Deploying a hello world sample

Once you have a container host configured, you need to ensure that your environment has been configured successfully and can utilize containers. A really simple way to check that all is well on your container host is by downloading and running an application. Running this containerized application successfully shows that you have containers and Docker set up.

There are a few simple applications you can utilize that test the container environment on CH1 (which you set up in the *Configuring a container host* recipe). You use a few of them in this recipe.

Before you can run a container, you must acquire a container image. There are several ways to obtain images as you see in this chapter. Docker maintains an online registry that contains a variety of container images for you to leverage. Using the `docker` command, you can search and download images either to use directly or to use as the basis of a custom-built container (for example, as you can see in the *Using a Dockerfile to create and use a container* recipe). In this recipe, you download several images, run them as containers, and then clean up your environment.

This recipe demonstrates using the Docker registry to obtain images, and then using those images locally. This recipe looks at some basic container management tasks and shows some methods to automate the `docker.exe` command.

Getting ready

This recipe needs a configured container host, CH1. You set up this host in the *Configuring a container host* recipe.

How to do it...

1. Find any `hello-world` containers at the Docker registry:

    ```
    docker search hello-world
    ```

2. Pull the official Docker `hello-world` container image:

    ```
    docker pull hello-world
    ```

3. List the images on CH1:

    ```
    docker image ls
    ```

4. Run the `hello-world` container image:

    ```
    docker run hello-world
    ```

5. Look for Microsoft images in the Docker registry:

    ```
    docker search microsoft
    ```

6. Get the `nanoserver` base image:

   ```
   docker image pull mcr.microsoft.com/windows/nanoserver:1809
   ```

7. Run the `nanoserver` base image:

   ```
   docker run mcr.microsoft.com/windows/nanoserver:1809
   ```

8. Check the images available now on `CH1`:

   ```
   docker image ls
   ```

9. Inspect the first image:

   ```
   $Images = docker image ls
   $Image = (($Images[1]).Split(' ')|where {$_.Length -ge 1})[2]
   docker inspect $image | ConvertFrom-Json
   ```

10. Get another (older) image and try to run it:

    ```
    docker image pull microsoft/nanoserver | Out-Null
    docker run microsoft/nanoserver
    ```

11. Now, run the image with Hyper-V isolation:

    ```
    docker run --isolation=hyperv microsoft/nanoserver
    ```

12. Examine the differences in runtimes with Hyper-V:

    ```
    # Run the container with no isolation
    $S1 = Get-Date
    docker run hello-world | Out-Null
    $E1 = Get-Date
    $T1 = ($E1-$S1).TotalMilliseconds
    # Run the same container with isolation
    $S2 = Get-Date
    docker run --isolation=hyperv hello-world | Out-Null
    $E2 = get-date
    $T2 = ($E2-$S2).TotalMilliseconds
    # display the difference
    "Without isolation, took : $T1 milliseconds"
    "With isolation, took    : $T2 milliseconds"
    ```

13. Remove all container images:

```
docker rmi $(docker images -q) -f | out-Null
```

14. View the remaining images and verify that the containers have been removed:

```
docker image ls
docker container ls
```

How it works...

In *step 1*, you search the Docker registry for `hello-world` images, like this:

```
PS C:\Foo> docker search hello-world
NAME                                          DESCRIPTION                                      STARS   OFFICIAL  AUTOMATED
hello-world                                   Hello World! (an example of minimal Dockeriza€¦  816     [OK]
kitematic/hello-world-nginx                   A light-weight nginx container that demonstra€¦  120
tutum/hello-world                             Image to test docker deployments. Has Apachea€¦  59                [OK]
dockercloud/hello-world                       Hello World!                                     14                [OK]
crccheck/hello-world                          Hello World web server in under 2.5 MB           6                 [OK]
hypriot/armhf-hello-world                     Hello World! (an example of minimal Dockeriza€¦  6
marcells/aspnet-hello-world                   ASP.NET vNext - Hello World                      5                 [OK]
armhf/hello-world                             Hello World! (an example of minimal Dockeriza€¦  5
bonomat/nodejs-hello-world                    a simple nodejs hello world container            3                 [OK]
kornkitti/express-hello-world                 Node.js Express Hello World : https://githuba€¦  3
ppc64le/hello-world                           Hello World! (an example of minimal Dockeriza€¦  2
hello-seattle                                 Hello from DockerCon 2016 (Seattle)!             2       [OK]
arm32v7/hello-world                           Hello World! (an example of minimal Dockeriza€¦  1
microsoft/mcr-hello-world                     Hello World! (an example of minimal Dockeriza€¦  1
carinamarina/hello-world-app                  This is a sample Python web application, runâ€¦  1                 [OK]
mcrflowtest/mcr-hello-world                   Hello World! (an example of minimal Dockeriza€¦  0
s390x/hello-world                             Hello World! (an example of minimal Dockeriza€¦  0
infrastructureascode/hello-world              A tiny "Hello World" web server with a healtâ€¦  0                 [OK]
gscrivano/hello-world                         hello world example system container             0                 [OK]
ansibleplaybookbundle/hello-world-db-apb      An APB which deploys a sample Hello World! aâ€¦   0                 [OK]
markmnei/hello-world-java                     Automated build of Hello World Java              0                 [OK]
burdz/hello-world-k8s                         To provide a simple webserver that can have â€¦  0                 [OK]
kevindockercompany/hello-world                                                                 0
ansibleplaybookbundle/hello-world-apb         An APB which deploys a sample Hello World! aâ€¦   0                 [OK]
winamd64/hello-world                          Hello World! (an example of minimal Dockeriza€¦  0
```

In *step 2*, you pull the official Docker `hello-world` image and download it to your container host, which looks like this:

```
PS C:\Foo> docker pull hello-world
...  {docker download progress - snipped}
Digest: sha256:2557e3c07ed1e38f26e389462d03ed943586f744621577a99efb77324b0fe535
Status: Downloaded newer image for hello-world:latest
```

In *step 3*, you use the `docker` command to list the images on CH1, which looks like this:

```
PS C:\Foo> docker image ls
REPOSITORY     TAG        IMAGE ID       CREATED       SIZE
hello-world    latest     7dddd19ddc59   5 weeks ago   333MB
```

In *step 4*, you run the Docker `hello-world` image, which produces the following output:

```
PS C:\Foo> docker run hello-world

Hello from Docker!
This message shows that your installation appears to be working correctly.

To generate this message, Docker took the following steps:
 1. The Docker client contacted the Docker daemon.
 2. The Docker daemon pulled the "hello-world" image from the Docker Hub.
    (windows-amd64, nanoserver-1809)
 3. The Docker daemon created a new container from that image which runs the
    executable that produces the output you are currently reading.
 4. The Docker daemon streamed that output to the Docker client, which sent it
    to your terminal.

To try something more ambitious, you can run a Windows Server container with:
 PS C:\> docker run -it mcr.microsoft.com/windows/servercore powershell

Share images, automate workflows, and more with a free Docker ID:
 https://hub.docker.com/

For more examples and ideas, visit:
 https://docs.docker.com/get-started/
```

In *step 5*, your search for Microsoft images in the online Docker registry, which produces output like this:

```
PS C:\Foo> docker search microsoft

NAME                                      DESCRIPTION                                    STARS  OFFICIAL  AUTOMATED
microsoft/dotnet                          Official images for .NET Core and ASP.NET Coâ€¦  1414             [OK]
microsoft/mssql-server-linux              Official images for Microsoft SQL Server on â€¦  1084
microsoft/aspnet                          Microsoft IIS images                            823             [OK]
microsoft/windowsservercore               The official Windows Server Core base image     651
microsoft/aspnetcore                      Official images for running compiled ASP.NETâ€¦   583             [OK]
microsoft/nanoserver                      The official Nano Server base image             477
microsoft/iis                             Microsoft IIS images                            359
microsoft/mssql-server-windows-developer  Official Microsoft SQL Server Developer Editâ€¦  290
microsoft/mssql-server-windows-express    Official Microsoft SQL Server Express Editioâ€¦  283
microsoft/aspnetcore-build                Official images for building ASP.NET Core apâ€¦  273             [OK]
microsoft/azure-cli                       Official images for Microsoft Azure CLI         156             [OK]
microsoft/powershell                      PowerShell for every system!                    146             [OK]
microsoft/vsts-agent                      Official images for the Visual Studio Team Sâ€¦  119
microsoft/dynamics-nav                    Official images for Microsoft Dynamics NAV oâ€¦  108
microsoft/dotnet-samples                  .NET Core Docker Samples                         74             [OK]
microsoft/bcsandbox                       Business Central Sandbox                         53
microsoft/mssql-tools                     Official images for Microsoft SQL Server Comâ€¦   51
microsoft/oms                             Monitor your containers using the Operationsâ€¦   41             [OK]
microsoft/cntk                            CNTK images from github.com/Microsoft/CNTK-dâ€¦   38             [OK]
microsoft/wcf                             Microsoft WCF images                            29
microsoft/dotnet-nightly                  Preview images for the .NET Core SDK            23             [OK]
microsoft/dotnet-framework-build          The .NET Framework build images have moved tâ€¦   17             [OK]
microsoft/mmlspark                        Microsoft Machine Learning for Apache Spark      7
microsoft/aspnetcore-build-nightly        Images to build preview versions of ASP.NET â€¦    4             [OK]
microsoft/cntk-nightly                    CNTK nightly image from github.com/Microsoftâ€¦    2
```

In *step 6*, you download another base image from the Docker registry with output like this:

```
PS C:\Foo> docker image pull mcr.microsoft.com/windows/nanoserver:1809
... {docker download status - omitted}
Digest: sha256:cd875087d08dad4c5bf6ba6273e8d506bcec604c2c7c96c56d68f4f0c81ff1a0
Status: Downloaded newer image for mcr.microsoft.com/windows/nanoserver:1809
```

In *step 7,* you run the `nanoserver:1809` image, which looks like this:

```
PS C:\> docker run mcr.microsoft.com/windows/nanoserver:1809
Microsoft Windows [Version 10.0.17763.253]
(c) 2018 Microsoft Corporation. All rights reserved.
```

In *step 8,* you look at the images you have downloaded so far, which now looks like this:

```
PS C:\> docker image ls

REPOSITORY                                   TAG    IMAGE ID       CREATED       SIZE
mcr.microsoft.com/windows/nanoserver         1809   e265050d95bf   4 weeks ago   340MB
hello-world                                  latest 7dddd19ddc59   5 weeks ago   333MB
```

In *step 9,* you use the `docker inspect` command to get more information about the `nanoserver` image, which looks like this:

```
PS C:\Foo\> $Images = docker image ls
PS C:\Foo\> $Rxs = '(\w+)  +(\w+)  +(\w+)  '
PS C:\Foo\> $OK = $Images[1] -Match $Rxs
PS C:\Foo\> $Image = $Matches[1]  # grab the image name
PS C:\Foo\> docker inspect $image | ConvertFrom-Json

Id              : sha256:e265050d95bf517dc4a24f9c72eebf9d45a9952b0d5a58da91f66c
                  6c2093176e
RepoTags        : {mcr.microsoft.com/windows/nanoserver:1809}
RepoDigests     : {mcr.microsoft.com/windows/nanoserver@sha256:cd875087d08dad4c
                  5bf6ba6273e8d506bcec604c2c7c96c56d68f4f0c81ff1a0}
Parent          :
Comment         :
Created         : 2019-01-08T13:11:40.5723426-08:00
Container       :
ContainerConfig : @{Hostname=; Domainname=; User=; AttachStdin=False;
                  AttachStdout=False; AttachStderr=False; Tty=False;
                  OpenStdin=False; StdinOnce=False; Env=; Cmd=; Image=;
                  Volumes=; WorkingDir=; Entrypoint=; OnBuild=; Labels=}
DockerVersion   :
Author          :
Config          : @{Hostname=; Domainname=; User=ContainerUser;
                  AttachStdin=False; AttachStdout=False; AttachStderr=False;
                  Tty=False; OpenStdin=False; StdinOnce=False; Env=;
                  Cmd=System.Object[]; Image=; Volumes=; WorkingDir=;
                  Entrypoint=; OnBuild=; Labels=}
Architecture    : amd64
Os              : windows
OsVersion       : 10.0.17763.253
Size            : 339692504
VirtualSize     : 339692504
GraphDriver     : @{Data=; Name=windowsfilter}
RootFS          : @{Type=layers; Layers=System.Object[]}
Metadata        : @{LastTagTime=0001-01-01T00:00:00Z}
```

In *step 10,* you download and run a container that needs isolation, which generates a Docker error, as follows:

```
PS C:\Foo> docker image pull microsoft/nanoserver | Out-Null
PS C:\Foo> docker run microsoft/nanoserver powershell

docker : C:\Program Files\Docker\docker.exe: Error response from daemon:
CreateComputeSystem
b0decd7d5b2e44557f26d1dc8a4df8110f5e085a557001ca33b26ebce4fcf34d: The
container operating system does not match the host operating system.
At line:1 char:1
+ docker run microsoft/nanoserver
+ ~~~~~~~~~~~~~~~~~~~~~~~~~~~~~~~~~
    + CategoryInfo          : NotSpecified: (C:\Program File...erating system.
   :String) [], RemoteException
    + FullyQualifiedErrorId : NativeCommandError

(extra info: {"SystemType":"Container","Name":"b0decd7d5b2e44557f26d1dc8a4df811
0f5e085a557001ca33b26ebce4fcf34d","Owner":"docker","VolumePath":"\\\\?\\Volume{
0d8b4cc0-8550-46c9-9c89-6d99207c926d}","IgnoreFlushesDuringBoot":true,"LayerFol
derPath":"C:\\ProgramData\\docker\\windowsfilter\\b0decd7d5b2e44557f26d1dc8a4df
8110f5e085a557001ca33b26ebce4fcf34d","Layers":[{"ID":"16479008-564b-5cb6-8c54-e
08e47855223","Path":"C:\\ProgramData\\docker\\windowsfilter\\4cd4a5785de2cef21c
284e495379f819a7c062e320f4fd9b507d8aacbf94740"},{"ID":"ffaeea14-d23b-5cb9-b507
-569a0161e9f9","Path":"C:\\ProgramData\\docker\\windowsfilter\\3b99905d28d71be0
74ead47331c1f993f5b0aab50806b01405ed212f668d196a"}],"HostName":"b0decd7d5b2e","
HvPartition":false,"EndpointList":["78665804-DBE9-444C-B158-4EA9AC01EFBC"],"All
owUnqualifiedDNSQuery":true}).
```

In *step 11,* you run this same image, but this time using Hyper-V isolation. The results are more like what you might expect, as shown in the following screenshot:

```
PS C:\Foo> docker run --isolation=hyperv  microsoft/nanoserver

Microsoft Windows [Version 10.0.14393]
(c) 2016 Microsoft Corporation. All rights reserved.

C:\>
```

In *step 12,* you examine the performance impact of using Hyper-V isolation, which looks like this:

```
PS C:\Foo> # run with no isolation
PS C:\Foo> $S1 = Get-Date
PS C:\Foo> docker run hello-world |
             Out-Null
PS C:\Foo> $E1 = Get-Date
PS C:\Foo> $T1 = ($E1-$S1).TotalMilliseconds
PS C:\Foo> # run with isolation
PS C:\Foo> $S2 = Get-Date
PS C:\Foo> docker run --isolation=hyperv hello-world | Out-Null
PS C:\Foo> $E2 = get-date
PS C:\Foo> $T2 = ($E2-$S2).TotalMilliseconds
PS C:\Foo> "Without isolation, took : $T1 milliseconds"
PS C:\Foo> "With isolation, took    : $T2 milliseconds"

Without isolation, took : 16165.5532 milliseconds
With isolation, took    : 41120.4256 milliseconds
```

In *step 13*, you remove all the container images on CH1, which produces no output. In *step 14*, you list the current images and containers on CH1, which looks like this:

```
PS C:\> docker image ls
PS C:\> docker container ls

REPOSITORY      TAG     IMAGE ID CREATED  SIZE
CONTAINER ID    IMAGE   COMMAND  CREATED  STATUS   PORTS NAMES
```

There's more...

In *step 4*, you run the hello-world container you downloaded in *step 2*. This container prints out some text, then exits. This is a great demonstration that your container host is up, running, and able to host containers.

In *step 7*, you download the nanoserver image. By using the :1809 tag in the image name, you ensure that docker.exe downloads an image which corresponds to the kernel in Windows Server 2019 (and Windows 10 1809).

In *step 9*, you use the docker image command to get all the images on the container host (CH1). Docker.exe returns the images on the system as an array of strings (that is, **not** objects!). The first ($Images[0]) entry is a string of the line of column headers. The next two entries in the $Images array relate to the nanoserver and hello-world images, respectively. You create the $Image value by using a regular expression to pull the Docker image name from the string returned by docker. Those more experienced in the dark arts of regular expressions could no doubt improve this step.

In *step 10*, you download and attempt to run a container whose built-in base OS is a different version to the OS running on the container host (CH1). This is to be expected, and you have two alternatives. The first is to use a more up-to-date container image—one that matches yours (or create an updated image as shown in the *Using a Dockerfile to create and use a container* recipe). The other alternative is to use Hyper-V isolation, which works fine, as you saw in *step 11*.

Using isolation, however, has a performance implication. The approach does provide added security, which may be appropriate in a share-hosting environment. There is, however, a significant startup performance hit. The good news is that the overhead of running a container using the isolation provided by Hyper-V is not huge once the container is up and running.

In *step 13*, you start up a detached container. In doing so, you tell Docker to map the local host's port 80 to port 80 in the container. So, when you browse to http://CH1, you see the standard IIS startup screen, which comes from IIS running in the container. We look at doing a bit more with IIS in the *Deploying IIS in a container* and *Using a Dockerfile to create and use a container* recipes.

See also

For more information around getting started with Docker, see this link: `https://docs.docker.com/get-started/`.

Deploying IIS in a container

In the *Deploying a hello-world sample* recipe, you downloaded and ran multiple container images. One of those images was the `microsoft/iis` image. This image contains IIS with only the default website set up and working. When you run this image, IIS is loaded in the container, and with port mapping in place, you can easily see the website in the container, even though IIS is not loaded on the container host.

For this recipe to work as written, the container has to have the same base OS image as your container host. This recipe, therefore, assumes that the host you are using for the recipes in this chapter is 1809 (for both Windows 10 and Server 2019). If you run this recipe on an older OS, for example, 1709 or Server 2016, Docker would not run the container and you get an error, so ensure that the kernel versions on the container host and the container itself are the same (or use Hyper-V isolation).

Getting ready

This recipe uses the CH1 host, which you configured in the *Configuring a container host* recipe.

How to do it...

1. Create the `C:\Reskitapp` folder:

```
$EA = @{ErrorAction='SilentlyContinue'}
New-Item -Path C:\ReskitApp -ItemType Directory @EA
```

2. Create a web page:

```
$Fn = 'C:\Reskitapp\Index.htm'
$Index = @"
<!DOCTYPE html>
<html><head><title>
ReskitApp Container Application</title></head>
```

```
<body><p><center><b>
HOME PAGE FOR RESKITAPP APPLICATION</b></p>
Running in a container in Windows Server 2019<p>
</center><br><hr></body></html>
"@
$Index | Out-File -FilePath $Fn
```

3. Get a server core with a server core image (with IIS loaded) from the Docker registry:

```
docker pull mcr.microsoft.com/windows/servercore/iis |
   Out-Null
```

4. Run the image as a container named `rkwebc`:

```
$image = 'mcr.microsoft.com/windows/servercore/iis'
docker run -d -p 80:80 --name rkwebc "$image"
```

5. Copy our file into the container:

```
Set-Location -Path C:\Reskitapp
docker cp .\index.htm rkwebc:c:\inetpub\wwwroot\index.htm
```

6. View the page:

```
Start-Process "Http://CH1.Reskit.Org/Index.htm"
```

7. Clean up:

```
docker rm rkwebc -f | Out-Null
docker image rm  mcr.microsoft.com/windows/servercore/iis |
   Out-Null
```

How it works...

In *step 1*, you create a folder on CH1 to hold a web page. In *step 2*, you create a very simple **home** HTML page. In *step 3*, you download a server core image that contains IIS. These first three steps produce no output.

In *step 4*, you run the image as a container named `rkwebc` and bridge the local port 80 to the container's port 80, which looks like this:

```
PS C:\Foo> $Image = 'mcr.microsoft.com/windows/servercore/iis'
PS C:\Foo> docker run -d -p80:80 --name rkwebc "$Image"
e34fbaee99b9370f2e793dc45e3dd707ff0a82b9609b6dc1a7ea9c723201b5db
```

In *step 5,* you copy the web page HTML file from CH1 into the container, which produces no output. In *step 6,* you view the container's web page, which looks like this:

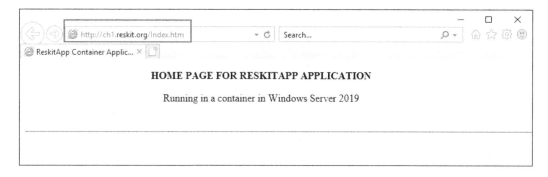

Finally, in *step 7,* you forcibly stop the container and remove the container image, which produces no output.

There's more...

This recipe creates a new web page (in *step 1* and *step 2)* on the CH1 host, then copies that file into the running container (*step 5*). When you run the container, you use port forwarding to instruct Docker to forward port 80 on the container host to port 80 in the container. This means that although you do not have IIS loaded on CH1, it is loaded, active, and runs a website *inside* the container. In this recipe, you are making use of the existing network address/name (that is, of the CH1 host) to access the container's website. You can see another method to push data into a container in the *Using a Dockerfile to create and use a container* recipe.

In *step 5,* you use the docker cp command to copy files from the container host into the container. In this recipe, you only add (and in *step 6,* view) a single page to the existing default website that was loaded by installing IIS. You can use the docker exec command to create a new website inside the container and run that, much like you did in the recipes in the IIS chapter. You could also copy all the files and other resources that are necessary for a rich website, set up SSL, and make use of host headers to support multiple containers.

In this recipe, you forwarded traffic inbound to port 80 on the container host to port 80 in the container. This is a very simple way to use containers and container networking. You could also create a Docker network and give your container unique IP settings. For more on Docker networking, see the following: http://rafalgolarz.com/blog/2017/04/10/networking_golang_app_with_docker_containers/ and https://docs.docker.com/v17.09/engine/userguide/networking/. You can, as ever, use your search engine to discover more about containers and networking. One thing to keep in mind as you search is that much of the search results relate to running containers on Linux, where the networking stack is quite different, and differently managed.

See also

This recipe uses the `docker cp` command to copy a file into the container. There are other ways to transfer information between your container and other hosts in your environment. See `https://markheath.net/post/transfer-files-docker-windows-containers` to take a look at some methods you can use to transfer data into and out of your containers.

Using a Dockerfile to create and use a container

Containers can be used in a variety of ways. In most cases, you are going to want to build your own custom images, complete with an operating system, OS features, and applications. A great way to build your image is to use a Dockerfile containing the instructions for building a new image, and then use the `docker build` command to create a customized container you can then run.

Getting ready

In this recipe, you use the container host, CH1, that you set up in the *Configuring a container host* recipe.

How to do it...

1. Create a folder and `Set-Location` to the folder on CH1:

```
$SitePath = 'C:\RKWebContainer'
$NIHT = @{
  Path          = $SitePath
  ItemType      = 'Directory'
 ErrorAction   = 'SilentlyContinue'
}
New-Item @NIHT | Out-Null
Set-Location -Path $NIHT.Path
```

2. Create a script to run in the container to create a new site in the container:

```
$SB = {
# 2.1 create folder in the container
$SitePath = 'C:\RKWebContainer'
```

```
$NIHT = @{
  Path          = $SitePath
  ItemType      = 'Directory'
  ErrorAction   = 'SilentlyContinue'
}
New-Item @NIHT | Out-Null
Set-Location -Path $NIHT.Path
# 2.2 Create a page for the site
$PAGE = @'
<!DOCTYPE html>
<html>
<head><title>Main Page for RKWeb.Reskit.Org</title></head>
<body><p><center><b>
HOME PAGE FOR RKWEBr.RESKIT.ORG</b></p>
Containers and PowerShell Rock!
</center/</body></html>
'@
$PAGE | Out-File $SitePath\Index.html | Out-Null
# 2.3 Create a new web site in the container that uses Host
headers
$WSHT = @{
  PhysicalPath = $SitePath
  Name         = 'RKWeb'
  HostHeader   = 'RKWeb.Reskit.Org'
}
New-Website @WSHT
} # End of $SB script block
```

3. Save the script block to the file:

```
$SB | Out-File $SitePath\Config.ps1
```

4. Create and test a new A record for our soon-to-be containerized site:

```
Invoke-Command -Computer DC1.Reskit.Org -ScriptBlock {
  $DNSHT = @{
    ZoneName  = 'Reskit.Org'
    Name      = 'RKWeb'
    IpAddress = '10.10.10.221'
  }
  Add-DnsServerResourceRecordA @DNSHT
}
Resolve-DnsName -Name Rkweb.Reskit.Org
```

5. Create a Dockerfile that contains build instructions:

```
$DF = @"
FROM mcr.microsoft.com/windows/servercore:1809
LABEL Description="RKWEB Container" Vendor="PS Partnership"
Version="1.0.0.42"
RUN powershell -Command Add-WindowsFeature Web-Server
WORKDIR C:\\RKWebContainer
COPY Config.ps1 Config.ps1
RUN powershell -Command .\config.ps1
"@
$DF | Out-File -FilePath .\Dockerfile -Encoding ASCII
```

6. Build the image:

```
docker build -t rkwebc .
```

7. Run the image:

```
docker run -d -t --name rkwebc -p 80:80 rkwebc | Out-Null
```

8. Check that the rkwebc container is running:

```
docker ps
```

9. Get the page using Invoke-WebRequest:

```
Invoke-WebRequest -UseBasicParsing HTTP://RKweb.Reskit.Org
```

10. View the page using a browser:

```
Start-Process 'HTTP://RKWeb.Reskit.Org'
```

11. Clean up forcibly:

```
docker container rm rkwebc -f | Out-Null
```

How it works...

In *step 1*, you create a folder, C:\RKWebContainer in CH1, to all the files needed in this recipe. In *step 2*, you create a script block that you later use to create a website in the container. In *step 3*, you save this script block to a file on CH1. In *step 4*, you set up a new DNS A record for RKweb.Reskit.Org that points to the same IP address as the CH1 host. In *step 5*, you create a file, Dockerfile, that contains the Docker image-building instructions. These steps produce no output.

In *step 6,* you use the docker build command to build a customized image, rkwebc, on CH1. The output looks like this:

```
PS C:\RKWebContainer> docker build -t rkwebc .
Sending build context to Docker daemon  4.096kB
Step 1/6 : FROM mcr.microsoft.com/windows/servercore:1809
 ---> 17b224ab9b3a
Step 2/6 : LABEL Description="RKWEB Container" Vendor="PS Partnership" Version="1.0.0.42"
 ---> Using cache
 ---> 576cac5f0f90
Step 3/6 : RUN powershell -Command Add-WindowsFeature Web-Server
 ---> Using cache
 ---> 5a063146e711
Step 4/6 : WORKDIR C:\\RKWebContainer
 ---> Using cache
 ---> 5539d494af69
Step 5/6 : COPY Config.ps1 Config.ps1
 ---> Using cache
 ---> 9967eb0d1cdc
Step 6/6 : RUN powershell -Command .\config.ps1
 ---> Using cache
 ---> 3e4b28a3f75f
Successfully built 3e4b28a3f75f
Successfully tagged rkwebc:latest
```

With your image created, in *step 7,* you run the image as a container, which produces no output. In *step 8,* you use the docker ps command to view the rkwebc container running on CH1, which looks like this:

```
PS C:\RKWebContainer> docker ps
CONTAINER ID   IMAGE    COMMAND                CREATED          STATUS           PORTS                 NAMES
efd0e3cd79eb   rkwebc   "c:\\windows\\system32â€¦"   36 seconds ago   Up 34 seconds    0.0.0.0:80->80/tcp    rkwebc
```

In *step 9,* you use Invoke-WebRequest to view the newly created website. The output looks like this:

```
PS C:\RKWebContainer> Invoke-WebRequest -UseBasicParsing HTTP://RKWeb.Reskit.Org

StatusCode        : 200
StatusDescription : OK
Content           : <!DOCTYPE html>
                    <html>
                    <head><title>Main Page for RKWeb.Reskit.Org</title></head>
                    <body><p><cen...
RawContent        : HTTP/1.1 200 OK
                    Accept-Ranges: bytes
                    Content-Length: 416
                    Content-Type: text/html
                    Date: Sun, 10 Feb 2019 19:23:36 GMT
                    ETag: "ec999cb973c1d41:0"
                    Last-Modified: Sun, 10 Feb 2019 19:06:28 GMT
                    Serve...
Forms             :
Headers           : {[Accept-Ranges, bytes], [Content-Length, 416], [Content-Type, text/html], [Date, Sun, 10 Feb 2019 19:23:36 GMT]...}
Images            : {}
InputFields       : {}
Links             : {}
ParsedHtml        :
RawContentLength  : 416
```

In *Step 10*, you view the site in the browser, which looks like:

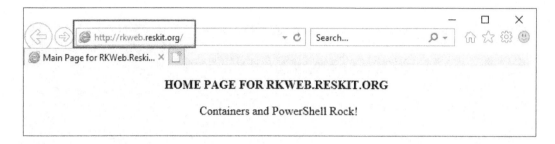

There's more...

In this recipe, you use a base container image that you have to download from the Docker registry (`mcr.microsoft.com/windows/servercore:1809`). Then, you build a container that has the web server feature added and in which you can run the `Config.ps1` file to configure the container to run your website. For more information on Dockerfiles, see this link: `https://docs.docker.com/engine/reference/builder/`.

See also

In this recipe, you build and run a Dockerfile to create an image. In the Dockerfile, you use the `RUN` instruction to run PowerShell twice during the building of the image. To optimize the container, you could run the two commands (to add the Windows feature and to run the `Config.Ps1` script) as a single Docker image. For some tips on how to build container images, see `https://cloud.google.com/blog/products/gcp/7-best-practices-for-building-containers`.

9
Managing Windows Internet Information Server

In this chapter, we cover the following recipes:

- ▸ Installing IIS
- ▸ Configuring IIS for SSL
- ▸ Managing TLS cipher suites
- ▸ Configuring a central certificate store
- ▸ Configuring IIS bindings
- ▸ Managing IIS logging and log files
- ▸ Managing IIS applications and application pools
- ▸ Analyzing IIS log files
- ▸ Managing and monitoring Network Load Balancing

Introduction

Internet Information Services (IIS) is a Windows feature that implements an extensible web server. IIS was first introduced as an add-on for Windows NT 4.0, and has been the focus of substantial development ever since. IIS is an add-on feature that Microsoft has built into both Windows Server 2019 and Windows 10.

With IIS in Windows Server, you can deploy both internet-facing public websites and sites on your internal intranet. You can integrate IIS with enterprise applications, including SharePoint, Exchange, and System Center.

IIS provides a platform for a variety of web-based applications. With IIS, you can provide a simple, HTML-based static website, as well as rich, multi-tiered applications. You can combine the applications running on IIS with backend databases, such as Microsoft SQL Server.

Like other Windows Server features, there is good PowerShell cmdlet coverage for IIS. You can make use of two PowerShell modules: the `WebAdministration` module, introduced in earlier versions of Windows Server, and the `IISAdministration` module, which provides additional cmdlets. While many PowerShell modules work well in PowerShell Core, neither of the IIS modules work in PowerShell Core. As a workaround (if you are using PowerShell Core), you can use PowerShell remoting to run these cmdlets on the remote IIS server.

This chapter covers how to install, configure, manage, and maintain IIS on Windows Server 2019. While you can load and use IIS in Windows 10, the focus, in this chapter, is on Windows Server 2019.

Installing IIS

Before you can use IIS, you must install it onto your host. Like other roles and features of Windows Server 2019 that are covered in this book, you install IIS by using the `Install-WindowsFeature` cmdlet. Once you have installed the web server, you can take a look at the host.

Getting ready

This recipe uses `SRV1` and assumes a fresh installation. If you have used `SRV1` to test previous recipes, you may need to remove the `Web-Server` feature before you run this recipe. Also, you should have the Windows Server 2019 installation DVD in the `D:` drive of `SRV1`.

How to do it...

1. Add the `Web-Server` feature, sub-features, and tools to `SRV1`, as follows:

```
$FHT = @{
   Name                  = 'Web-Server'
   IncludeAllSubFeature  = $true
```

```
    IncludeManagementTools = $true
    Source                 = "D:\sources\sxs"
}
Install-WindowsFeature  @FHT
```

2. See what features are installed:

```
Get-WindowsFeature -Name Web*  | Where-Object Installed
```

3. Check the IIS administration modules:

```
$Modules = @('WebAdministration', 'IISAdministration')
Get-Module -Name $Modules -ListAvailable
```

4. Get a count of how many commands are in each module:

```
$C1 = (Get-Command -Module WebAdministration |
        Measure-Object |
            Select-Object -Property Count).Count
$C2 = (Get-Command -Module IISAdministration |
        Measure-Object |
            Select-Object -Property Count).Count
"$C1 commands in WebAdministration Module"
"$C2 commands in IISAdministration Module"
```

5. Get details of the IIS provider contained in the WebAdministration module:

```
Import-Module -Name WebAdministration
Get-PSProvider -PSProvider WebAdministration
```

6. You can find out what is in the IIS: drive with the following command:

```
Get-ChildItem -Path IIS:\
```

7. You can find out what is in the Sites folder with the following command:

```
Get-Childitem -Path IIS:\Sites
```

8. Look at the default website, as follows:

```
$IE  = New-Object -ComObject InterNetExplorer.Application
$URL = 'HTTP://SRV1'
$IE.Navigate2($URL)
$IE.Visible = $true
```

How it works...

In *step 1,* you use the `Install-WindowsFeature` cmdlet to install IIS, as well as a number of the web server sub-features and management tools, which look like this:

```
PS C:\Foo> $FHT = @{
             Name                  = 'Web-Server'
             IncludeAllSubFeature  = $true
             IncludeManagementTools = $true
           }
PS C:\Foo> Install-WindowsFeature  @FHT

Success Restart Needed Exit Code     Feature Result
------- -------------- ---------     --------------
True    No             Success       {Application Development, Application Init...
```

In *step 2,* you use the `Get-WindowsFeature` cmdlet to retrieve the web server related features installed on `SRV1`, the output for which looks like this:

```
PS C:\Foo> Get-WindowsFeature -Name web* | Where-Object Installed

Display Name                                        Name                    Install State
------------                                        ----                    -------------
[X] Web Server (IIS)                                Web-Server              Installed
    [X] Web Server                                  Web-WebServer           Installed
        [X] Common HTTP Features                    Web-Common-Http         Installed
            [X] Default Document                    Web-Default-Doc         Installed
            [X] Directory Browsing                  Web-Dir-Browsing        Installed
            [X] HTTP Errors                         Web-Http-Errors         Installed
            [X] Static Content                      Web-Static-Content      Installed
            [X] HTTP Redirection                    Web-Http-Redirect       Installed
            [X] WebDAV Publishing                   Web-DAV-Publishing      Installed
        [X] Health and Diagnostics                  Web-Health              Installed
            [X] HTTP Logging                        Web-Http-Logging        Installed
            [X] Custom Logging                      Web-Custom-Logging      Installed
            [X] Logging Tools                       Web-Log-Libraries       Installed
            [X] ODBC Logging                        Web-ODBC-Logging        Installed
            [X] Request Monitor                     Web-Request-Monitor     Installed
            [X] Tracing                             Web-Http-Tracing        Installed
        [X] Performance                             Web-Performance         Installed
            [X] Static Content Compression          Web-Stat-Compression    Installed
            [X] Dynamic Content Compression         Web-Dyn-Compression     Installed
        [X] Security                                Web-Security            Installed
            [X] Request Filtering                   Web-Filtering           Installed
            [X] Basic Authentication                Web-Basic-Auth          Installed
            [X] Centralized SSL Certificate Support Web-CertProvider        Installed
            [X] Client Certificate Mapping Authentic... Web-Client-Auth     Installed
            [X] Digest Authentication               Web-Digest-Auth         Installed
            [X] IIS Client Certificate Mapping Authe... Web-Cert-Auth       Installed
            [X] IP and Domain Restrictions          Web-IP-Security         Installed
            [X] URL Authorization                   Web-Url-Auth            Installed
            [X] Windows Authentication              Web-Windows-Auth        Installed
        [X] Application Development                 Web-App-Dev             Installed
            [X] .NET Extensibility 3.5              Web-Net-Ext             Installed
            [X] .NET Extensibility 4.7              Web-Net-Ext45           Installed
            [X] Application Initialization          Web-AppInit             Installed
            [X] ASP                                 Web-ASP                 Installed
            [X] ASP.NET 3.5                         Web-Asp-Net             Installed
            [X] ASP.NET 4.7                         Web-Asp-Net45           Installed
            [X] CGI                                 Web-CGI                 Installed
            [X] ISAPI Extensions                    Web-ISAPI-Ext           Installed
            [X] ISAPI Filters                       Web-ISAPI-Filter        Installed
            [X] Server Side Includes                Web-Includes            Installed
            [X] WebSocket Protocol                  Web-websockets          Installed
    [X] FTP Server                                  Web-Ftp-Server          Installed
        [X] FTP Service                             Web-Ftp-Service         Installed
        [X] FTP Extensibility                       Web-Ftp-Ext             Installed
    [X] Management Tools                            Web-Mgmt-Tools          Installed
        [X] IIS Management Console                  Web-Mgmt-Console        Installed
        [X] IIS 6 Management Compatibility          Web-Mgmt-Compat         Installed
            [X] IIS 6 Metabase Compatibility        Web-Metabase            Installed
            [X] IIS 6 Management Console            Web-Lgcy-Mgmt-Console   Installed
            [X] IIS 6 Scripting Tools               Web-Lgcy-Scripting      Installed
            [X] IIS 6 WMI Compatibility             Web-WMI                 Installed
        [X] IIS Management Scripts and Tools        Web-Scripting-Tools     Installed
        [X] Management Service                      Web-Mgmt-Service        Installed
```

In *step 3*, you get the IIS-related modules on SRV1, which produces the following output:

```
PS C:\Foo> $Modules = @('WebAdministration', 'IISAdministration')
PS C:\Foo> Get-Module -Name $Modules -ListAvailable

    Directory: C:\WINDOWS\system32\windowsPowerShell\v1.0\Modules

ModuleType Version   Name               ExportedCommands
---------- -------   ----               ----------------
Script     1.1.0.0   IISAdministration  {Start-IISSite, Start-IISCommitDelay, Get-IISConfigCollectionElement, ...}
Manifest   1.0.0.0   WebAdministration  {Start-WebCommitDelay, Stop-WebCommitDelay, Get-WebConfigurationLock, ...}
```

In *step 4*, you get a count of the number of commands in the WebAdministration and IISAdministrtion modules, as follows:

```
PS C:\Foo> $C1 = (Get-Command -Module WebAdministration |
                    Measure-Object |
                      Select-Object -Property Count).Count
PS C:\Foo> $C2 = (Get-Command -Module IISAdministration |
                    Measure-Object |
                      Select-Object -Property Count).Count
PS C:\Foo> "$C1 commands in WebAdministration Module"
PS C:\Foo> "$C2 commands in IISAdministration Module"

79 commands in WebAdministration Module
34 commands in IISAdministration Module
```

In *step 5*, you import the WebAdministration module, which loads the IIS provider. Then you get details of the provider, as follows:

```
PS C:\Foo> Import-Module -Name WebAdministration
PS C:\Foo> Get-PSProvider -PSProvider WebAdministration

Name               Capabilities     Drives
----               ------------     ------
WebAdministration  ShouldProcess    {IIS}
```

In *step 6*, you use the provider to view the contents of IIS:, which looks as follows:

```
PS C:\Foo> Get-ChildItem -Path IIS:\

Name
----
AppPools
Sites
SslBindings
```

In *step 7*, you view the contents of IIS:\Sites, which looks like this:

```
PS C:\Foo> Get-Childitem -Path IIS:\Sites

Name                 ID    State     Physical Path                   Bindings
----                 --    -----     -------------                   --------
Default Web Site 1   Started   %SystemDrive%\inetpub\wwwroot   http *:80:
```

In *step 8*, you use Internet Explorer to view the web service on SRV1, which looks like this:

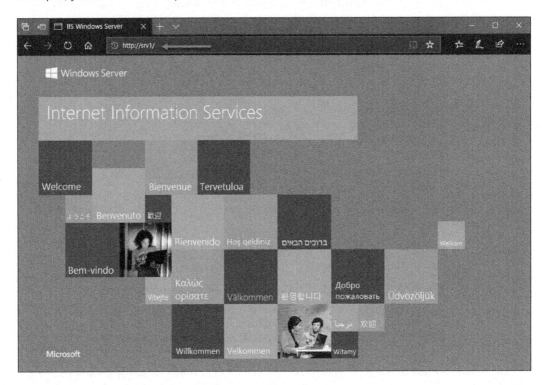

There's more...

In *step 1*, you installed the IIS management tools. These tools include the IIS GUI tool, plus the WebAddministration and IISAdministration PowerShell modules.

In *step 5*, you import the `WebAdministration` module manually. In addition to loading the cmdlets/functions contained in the module, when you import the module, PowerShell loads the `WebAdministration` PowerShell provider. This provider enables you to browse aspects of the web server, including the sites, application pools, and SSL bindings on the host. You use this feature in later recipes in this chapter. When you use any of the cmdlets in the `WebAdministration` module, PowerShell, by default, auto-loads the module. But if you only want to use the provider, you have to manually load the module first, as shown in this recipe.

In *step 8*, you view the default website that the installation process adds for you. Browsing to the server is a great way to determine that IIS is loaded and is running on `SRV1`.

Configuring IIS for SSL

Traffic between a web browser and a web server on the internet, or even within a corporate intranet, is open, and can be intercepted. To avoid the data being compromised, you can make use of protocols built into your web browser, along with IIS, to provide encryption, as well as authentication.

In the 1990s, Netscape Communications developed a protocol that provided some necessary security, in the form of the **Secure Socket Layer** (**SSL**) protocol. SSL 1.0 was never commercially released, while SSL 2.0 and SSL 3.0 were developed and released, but are now deprecated as unsafe.

Transport Layer Security (**TLS**) was developed openly as the next version of SSL. TLS 1.0 is essentially SSL 3.1. In 2014, Google identified a serious vulnerability in both SSL 3.0 and TLS 1.0. That leaves TLS 2.0 as the best protocol to deploy, and it is the only one installed by default with IIS in Windows Server 2019.

These days, SSL, as a protocol, is being deprecated in favor of TLS. Most major websites no longer actually use the SSL protocol. Nevertheless, we refer to such websites as using SSL, and we continue to use the HTTPS scheme, since end users cannot explicitly choose between SSL and TLS.

When the user specifies a URL beginning with `HTTPS:`, the browser contacts the server on port `443`. The browser and server then negotiate which security protocol to use (for example, TLS 2.0) and which cipher suite to use to protect the data being transferred. A cipher suite is a distinct set of algorithms to provide for key exchange and the encryption algorithms to be used for both bulk encryption and hashing.

In order to set up IIS for secure transfer, first, you need a certificate. The certificate identifies the server by name and specifies what the certificate can be used for. Public and private keys are associated with the certificate.

If you are setting up IIS as an internal web server, then you should use your internal **Certificate Authority** (**CA**) to create the web server certificate. If your web server is to be internet-facing, then you should get a certificate from a public CA. Remember that the certificate should be issued (and signed) by a CA that is explicitly trusted by any client accessing the secure site. Many public CAs around the world are automatically trusted by most modern browsers. Additionally, you can configure workstations and servers to enroll the root CA certificate for your internal CA automatically.

In this recipe, you use self-signed certificates. This works wonderfully in a test environment, but should never be used in production. The technique that you use in this recipe first generates a self-signed certificate, which you then copy into the local machine's trusted root store. This action makes the local machine trust the self-signed certificate. Should you access the server from any other host, the browser generates certificate errors, since those other machines do not trust the certificate.

Getting ready

You need to run this recipe on SRV1, after you have installed IIS, as you did in the *Installing IIS* recipe.

How to do it...

1. Import the WebAdministration module:

    ```
    Import-Module -Name WebAdministration
    ```

2. Create a self-signed certificate:

    ```
    $CHT = @{
      CertStoreLocation = 'CERT:\LocalMachine\MY'
      DnsName           = 'SRV1.Reskit.Org'
    }
    $SSLCert = New-SelfSignedCertificate @CHT
    ```

3. Copy the certificate to the root store on SRV1:

```
$C = 'System.Security.Cryptography.X509Certificates.X509Store'
$AL = 'Root', 'LocalMachine'
$Store = New-Object -TypeName $C -ArgumentList $AL
$Store.Open('ReadWrite')
$Store.Add($SSLcert)
$Store.Close()
```

4. Create a new SSL binding on the Default Web Site:

```
New-WebBinding -Name 'Default Web Site' -Protocol https -Port 443
```

5. Assign the certificate that was created earlier to this new binding:

```
$SSLCert | New-Item -Path IIS:\SslBindings\0.0.0.0!443
```

6. View the site using HTTPS:

```
$IE  = New-Object -ComObject InterNetExplorer.Application
$URL = 'https://SRV1.Reskit.Org'
$IE.Navigate2($URL)
$IE.Visible = $true
```

How it works...

In *step 1*, you import the web administration module manually. In *step 2*, you create a self-signed certificate for SRV1, and in *step 3*, you copy that newly created certificate to the local machine's root certificate store. In *step 4*, you create a new binding for port 443 on the default website. These steps produce no output.

In *step 5*, you assign your self-signed certificate to the default website, which looks like this:

In *step 6*, you use HTTPS to view the default website on SRV1, which looks like this:

There's more...

In this recipe, you manually import the WebAdministration module (in *step 1*). You need to do this because in *step 5*, you use the IIS Provider to bind the certificate to the SSL/TLS port (that is, 443). Since you were not using any of the cmdlets in the module, you have to import the module before you can use the provider.

In *step 3*, you use the .NET framework to copy the self-signed certificate into the local server's trusted root certificate store. This enables SRV1 to trust the self-signed certificate. You have to use .NET because the PowerShell certificate provider does not support a copy operation. As an alternative, you could use the Export-Certificate and Import-Certificate to export the certificate to a file, and then re-import it.

The output shown for *step 6* in this recipe is identical to the output for *step 8* in the *Install IIS* recipe, except that in this recipe, you used TLS to view the web page.

Managing TLS cipher suites

A cipher suite is a specific set of methods or algorithms that provide functions, including key exchange, bulk encryption, hashing, and creating message digests. Numerous Windows services, such as TLS, SSH, and IPSEC, make use of cipher suites when communicating with other hosts. With TLS, you can use the TLS cipher suite cmdlets to manage the cipher suites that your IIS web server is going to negotiate (or not).

Once the browser connects to the web server, the web server and the browser negotiate and choose the best cipher suite that both sides can support. If the browser only asks for cipher suites that the web server does not support, then the server terminates the communication.

By default, Windows Server 2019 supports 31 cipher suites, providing different algorithms and key lengths. In this recipe, you retrieve the cipher suites on Windows Server 2019, and both enable and disable a specific cipher suite.

Getting ready

This recipe makes use of SRV1, after you have run the *Installing IIS* recipe.

How to do it...

1. Get the cipher suites on SRV1 and display them, as follows:

```
Get-TlsCipherSuite |
  Format-Table Name, Exchange, Cipher, Hash, Certificate
```

2. Find the cipher suites that support 3DES with the following command:

```
Get-TlsCipherSuite -Name 3DES |
  Format-Table Name, Exchange, Cipher, Hash, Certificate
```

3. Disable the 3DES-based cipher suites:

```
Foreach ($CS in (Get-TlsCipherSuite -Name '3DES'))
  {Disable-TlsCipherSuite -Name $CS.Name}
```

4. Check whether any cipher suites that support 3DES remain:

```
Get-TlsCipherSuite 3DES |
  Format-Table Name, Exchange, Cipher, Hash, Certificate
```

5. Re-enable the 3DES-based cipher suite:

    ```
    Enable-TlsCipherSuite -Name TLS_RSA_WITH_3DES_EDE_CBC_SHA
    ```

6. Check for enabled cipher suites that support 3DES:

    ```
    Get-TlsCipherSuite 3DES |
      Format-Table -Property Name, Exchange, Cipher, Hash, Certificate
    ```

How it works...

In *step 1*, you get the available cipher suites on SRV1, which looks like this:

```
PS C:\Foo> Get-TlsCipherSuite |
             Format-Table Name, Exchange, Cipher, Hash, Certificate

Name                                         Exchange Cipher Hash   Certificate
----                                         -------- ------ ----   -----------
TLS_AES_256_GCM_SHA384                                AES
TLS_AES_128_GCM_SHA256                                AES
TLS_ECDHE_ECDSA_WITH_AES_256_GCM_SHA384
TLS_ECDHE_ECDSA_WITH_AES_128_GCM_SHA256      ECDH     AES           ECDSA
TLS_ECDHE_RSA_WITH_AES_256_GCM_SHA384        ECDH     AES           RSA
TLS_ECDHE_RSA_WITH_AES_128_GCM_SHA256        ECDH     AES           RSA
TLS_DHE_RSA_WITH_AES_256_GCM_SHA384          DH       AES           RSA
TLS_DHE_RSA_WITH_AES_128_GCM_SHA256          DH       AES           RSA
TLS_ECDHE_ECDSA_WITH_AES_256_CBC_SHA384
TLS_ECDHE_ECDSA_WITH_AES_128_CBC_SHA256      ECDH     AES    SHA256 ECDSA
TLS_ECDHE_RSA_WITH_AES_256_CBC_SHA384        ECDH     AES    SHA384 RSA
TLS_ECDHE_RSA_WITH_AES_128_CBC_SHA256        ECDH     AES    SHA256 RSA
TLS_ECDHE_ECDSA_WITH_AES_256_CBC_SHA         ECDH     AES    SHA1   ECDSA
TLS_ECDHE_ECDSA_WITH_AES_128_CBC_SHA         ECDH     AES    SHA1   ECDSA
TLS_ECDHE_RSA_WITH_AES_256_CBC_SHA           ECDH     AES    SHA1   RSA
TLS_ECDHE_RSA_WITH_AES_128_CBC_SHA           ECDH     AES    SHA1   RSA
TLS_RSA_WITH_AES_256_GCM_SHA384              RSA      AES           RSA
TLS_RSA_WITH_AES_128_GCM_SHA256              RSA      AES           RSA
TLS_RSA_WITH_AES_256_CBC_SHA256              RSA      AES    SHA256 RSA
TLS_RSA_WITH_AES_128_CBC_SHA256              RSA      AES    SHA256 RSA
TLS_RSA_WITH_AES_256_CBC_SHA                 RSA      AES    SHA1   RSA
TLS_RSA_WITH_AES_128_CBC_SHA                 RSA      AES    SHA1   RSA
TLS_RSA_WITH_3DES_EDE_CBC_SHA                RSA      3DES   SHA1   RSA
TLS_RSA_WITH_NULL_SHA256                     RSA             SHA256 RSA
TLS_RSA_WITH_NULL_SHA                        RSA             SHA1   RSA
TLS_PSK_WITH_AES_256_GCM_SHA384
TLS_PSK_WITH_AES_128_GCM_SHA256              PSK      AES
TLS_PSK_WITH_AES_256_CBC_SHA384              PSK      AES    SHA384
TLS_PSK_WITH_AES_128_CBC_SHA256              PSK      AES    SHA256
TLS_PSK_WITH_NULL_SHA384                     PSK             SHA384
TLS_PSK_WITH_NULL_SHA256                     PSK             SHA256
```

In *step 2*, you discover which cipher suites utilize 3DES, which looks like this:

```
PS C:\Foo> Get-TlsCipherSuite -Name 3DES |
            Format-Table Name, Exchange, Cipher, Hash, Certificate

Name                         Exchange Cipher Hash Certificate
----                         -------- ------ ---- -----------
TLS_RSA_WITH_3DES_EDE_CBC_SHA RSA      3DES   SHA1 RSA
```

In *step 3*, you disable any cipher suites based on 3DES, which produces no output. In *step 4*, you re-query to check for any 3DES based cipher suites—having just removed that suite, this step produces no output. In *step 5*, you re-enable the cipher suite named TLS_RSA_WITH_3DES_EDE_CBC_SHA (which you previously disabled). This step also produces no output.

In the final step, *step 6*, you check to see which TLS cipher suites are enabled that support 3DES, which looks like this:

```
PS C:\Foo> Get-TlsCipherSuite 3DES |
            Format-Table Name, -Property Exchange, Cipher, Hash, Certificate
Name                          Exchange Cipher Hash Certificate
----                          -------- ------ ---- -----------
TLS_RSA_WITH_3DES_EDE_CBC_SHA RSA      3DES   SHA1 RSA
```

There's more...

In *step 5*, you re-enabled the 3DES-based cipher suite that you disabled in *step 3*. You enabled the cipher suite using its full name. There is no cmdlet that can show you which cipher suites you have on your system that are now disabled—you can only see which ones are specifically enabled, so **be careful** when disabling cipher suites you may subsequently need to re-enable!

See also

For more details on cipher suites in Windows, see https://docs.microsoft.com/en-us/windows/desktop/secauthn/cipher-suites-in-schannel.

The 3DES cryptographic algorithm uses a block cipher mechanism based on 64-bit blocks. The Sweet32 Birthday attacks show the vulnerability potential of using block ciphers with small block sizes, which includes 3DES. For this reason, and especially if you are using IIS on a large-scale, internet-facing server, you should consider disabling the 3DES-based cipher, as shown in the recipe. For more information on block ciphers and the Sweet32 Birthday attacks, see `https://sweet32.info/`.

Configuring a central certificate store

If you host multiple secure servers at the internet scale, you may find that certificate management can be challenging. Each time you add a new IIS host into your infrastructure, you need to ensure that all of the correct certificates are in place on that host and the correct web binding (binding the certificates to IIS) is in place for each secure site. To add to the workload, you need to deal with certificate expiration and the renewal of certificates across each IIS server that utilizes those certificates.

Windows 2019 includes a feature, the **Central Certificate Store** (**CCS**), that simplifies managing certificates. With CCS, you store certificates in a central location, such as on an SMB file share, and use IIS to load certificates from the central CCS share.

In this recipe, you configure SRV1 to use a new share on DC1, which holds the CCS SMB share. You create the certificate store, create a new certificate for SRV1, and move that certificate to the central certificate share on DC1. You then configure IIS to make use of the central store, rather than using the local certificate stores, like you did in the *Configuring IIS for SSL* recipe.

Getting ready

This recipe uses two servers: SRV1 is an IIS server and DC1 is configured to hold the SSL CCS. You should have both servers up and running. Also, this recipe assumes that you have IIS at least partly loaded and set up for SSL (in other words, you should have run the *Install IIS* and *Configure IIS for SSL* recipes in advance). This recipe does check and ensure that the needed features are added to SRV1. You should also ensure that the **Active Directory** (**AD**) cmdlets are loaded on SRV1.

How to do it...

1. Remove the existing certificates from SRV1:

```
Get-ChildItem Cert:\localmachine\My |
  Where-Object Subject -Match 'SRV1.Reskit.Org' |
```

```
          Remove-Item -ErrorAction SilentlyContinue
Get-ChildItem Cert:\localmachine\root |
  Where-Object Subject -match 'SRV1.Reskit.Org' |
    Remove-Item
```

2. Remove SSL web bindings, if any exist:

```
Import-Module -Name WebAdministration
Get-WebBinding |
  Where-Object protocol -EQ 'https' |
    Remove-WebBinding
Get-ChildItem IIS:\SslBindings |
  Where-Object Port -eq 443 |
      Remove-Item
```

3. Create a shared folder and share it on DC1:

```
$SB = {
  If ( -NOT (Test-Path c:\SSLCerts)) {
     New-Item  -Path c:\SSLCerts -ItemType Directory |
                   Out-Null}
  $SHAREHT= @{
    Name        = 'SSLCertShare'
    Path        = 'C:\SSLCerts'
    FullAccess  = 'Everyone'
    Description = 'SSL Certificate Share'
  }
  New-SmbShare @SHAREHT
  'SSL Cert Share' | Out-File C:\SSLCerts\Readme.Txt
}
Invoke-Command -ScriptBlock $SB -ComputerName DC1 |
  Out-Null
```

4. Check the share on DC1:

```
New-SmbMapping -LocalPath X: -RemotePath \\DC1\SSLCertShare |
    Out-Null
Get-ChildItem -Path X:
```

5. Add new SSL certificates to the root certificate store on SRV1:

```
$SSLHT = @{
  CertStoreLocation = 'CERT:\LocalMachine\MY'
  DnsName           = 'SRV1.Reskit.Org'
}
```

```
$SSLCert = New-SelfSignedCertificate @SSLHT
$C = 'System.Security.Cryptography.X509Certificates.X509Store'
$NOHT = @{
  TypeName     = $C
  ArgumentList = 'Root','LocalMachine'
}
$Store = New-Object @NOHT
$Store.Open('ReadWrite')
$Store.Add($SSLcert)
$Store.Close()
```

6. Export the certificate to a PFX file:

```
$CertPW    = 'SSLCerts101!'
$SSHT = @{
  String      = $CertPW
  Force       = $true
  AsPlainText = $True
}
$Certpwss = ConvertTo-SecureString @SSHT
$CertHT = @{
    Cert     = $SSLCert
    FilePath = 'C:\SRV1.Reskit.Org.pfx'
    Password = $Certpwss
}
Export-PfxCertificate @CertHT
```

7. Move the certificate to the SSLCertShare share on DC1:

```
$MHT = @{
    Path        = 'C:\SRV1.Reskit.Org.pfx'
    Destination = '\\DC1\SSLCertShare\SRV1.Reskit.Org.Pfx'
    Force       = $True
}
Move-Item @MHT
```

8. Install the CCS feature on SRV1:

```
Install-WindowsFeature Web-CertProvider | Out-Null
```

9. Create a new user for the certificate sharing:

```
$User        = 'Reskit\SSLCertShare'
$Password    = 'Pa$$w0rd'
$SSHT2 = @{
```

```
  String      = $Password
  AsPlainText = $true
  $Force      = $True
}
$PSS = ConvertTo-SecureString  @SSHT2
$NewUserHT  = @{
  AccountPassword       = $PSS
  Enabled               = $true
  PasswordNeverExpires  = $true
  ChangePasswordAtLogon = $false
  SamAccountName        = 'SSLCertShare'
  UserPrincipalName     = 'SSLCertShare@Reskit.Org'
  Name                  = 'SSLCertShare'
  DisplayName           = 'SSL Cert Share User'
}
New-ADUser @NewUserHT
```

10. Configure the SSL CSS in the registry:

```
$IPHT = @{
  Path   = 'HKLM:\SOFTWARE\Microsoft\IIS\CentralCertProvider\'
  Name   = 'Enabled'
  Value  = 1
}
Set-ItemProperty @IPHT
$IPHT.Name  = 'CertStoreLocation'
$IPHT.Value = '\\DC1\SSLCertShare'
Set-ItemProperty @IPHT
```

11. Enable the SSL CCS, as follows:

```
$WCHT = @{
    CertStoreLocation  = '\\DC1\SSLCertShare'
    UserName           = $User
    Password           = $Password
    PrivateKeyPassword = $Certpw
}
Enable-WebCentralCertProvider @WCHT
$CPHT = @{
    UserName           = 'Reskit\SSLCertShare'
    Password           = $Password
    PrivateKeyPassword = $Certpw
}
Set-WebCentralCertProvider @CPHT
```

12. Set up SSL for a default site:

```
New-WebBinding -Name 'Default Web Site' -Protocol https -Port 443
$SslCert | New-Item -Path IIS:\SslBindings\0.0.0.0!443
```

13. Remove the certificate from SRV1:

```
Get-ChildItem Cert:\LocalMachine\My    |
  Where-Object Subject -Match 'SRV1.RESKIT.ORG' |
    Remove-Item -Force
```

14. Now, view the website with SSL, as follows:

```
$IE  = New-Object -ComObject InterNetExplorer.Application
$URL = 'HTTPS://SRV1.Reskit.Org/'
$IE.Navigate2($URL)
$IE.Visible = $true
```

How it works...

In *step 1*, you remove all certificates from the LocalMachine's MY certificate store. In *step 2*, you remove any SSL bindings for SRV1. In *step 3*, you create a new folder to hold centrally provided certificates, and share it on DC1. These three steps produce no output.

In *step 4*, you check the contents of the \\DC1\SSLCertShare share, which looks like this:

```
PS Foo:\> New-SmbMapping -LocalPath X: -RemotePath \\dc1\SSLCertShare |
          Out-Null
PS Foo:\> Get-ChildItem -Path X:

    Directory: X:\

Mode            LastWriteTime     Length Name
----            -------------     ------ ----
-a----    24/01/2019    11:08         34 Readme.Txt
```

In *step 5*, you create a self-signed certificate in the `LocalMachine\MY` certificate store. This certificate is then copied into the `LocalMachine\Root` certificate share. This step produces no output.

In *step 6*, you export the newly created self-signed certificate to a PFX file, which looks like this:

```
PS Foo:\> $Certpw   = 'SSLCerts101!'
PS Foo:\> $Certpwss = ConvertTo-SecureString -String $Certpw -Force -AsPlainText
PS Foo:\> $CertHT = @{
            Cert       = $SSLCert
            FilePath   = 'C:\Srv1.Reskit.Org.pfx'
            Password   = $Certpwss
          }
PS Foo:\> Export-PfxCertificate @CertHT


    Directory: C:\

Mode                LastWriteTime     Length Name
----                -------------     ------ ----
-a----     24/01/2019     11:22         2669 Srv1.Reskit.Org.pfx
```

In *step 7*, you move the PFX file containing the certificate to the `SSLCertShare` share on `DC1`. In *step 8*, you install the `Web-Cert Provider` feature to `SRV1`. In *step 9*, you create a new user in the AD for certificate sharing. In *step 10*, you configure the SSL CCS in the registry on `SRV1`. Then, in *step 11*, you enable the SSL CCS. These five steps produce no output.

In *step 12*, you set an initial web binding, which looks like this:

```
PS C:\Foo> New-WebBinding -Name 'Default Web Site' -Protocol https -Port 443
PS C:\Foo> $SslCert | New-Item -Path IIS:\SslBindings\0.0.0.0!443

IP Address          Port    Host Name     Store     Sites
----------          ----    ---------     -----     -----
0.0.0.0             443                   MY        Default Web Site
```

With *step 13*, you remove the certificate from the local certificate store, producing no output. Finally, in *step 14*, you use Internet Explorer to navigate to the default website on SRV1 using HTTPS:, which looks like this:

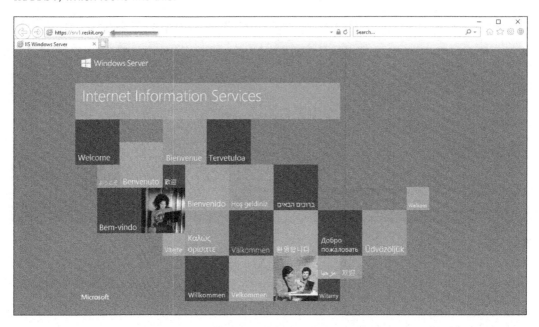

There's more...

In *step 5*, you created a self-signed certificate in the LocalMachine\MY certificate store; then, you copied this certificate into the LocalMachine\Root certificate share. The copy operation has the effect of making SRV1 trust the newly created certificate. In production, you would create a certificate from a trusted Certificate Authority and avoid copying the certificate (since the system would already trust that CA).

Configuring IIS bindings

In IIS, a binding consists of an IP address, a port, and a host header on which the web server listens for requests made to that website. The binding tells IIS how to route inbound HTTP/HTTPS requests.

In this recipe, you create a new website on SRV1 and add bindings to enable the site. In this recipe, you only bind for HTTP.

Getting ready

You need to run this recipe on SRV1 after installing IIS (which you did in the _Installing IIS_ recipe).

How to do it...

1. Import the WebAdministration module:

```
Import-Module -Name WebAdministration
```

2. Create and populate a new page:

```
$SitePath = 'C:\inetpub\www2'
New-Item $SitePath -ItemType Directory | Out-Null
$page = @'
<!DOCTYPE html>
<html>
<head><title>Main Page for WWW2.Reskit.Org</title></head>
<body><p><center>
<b>HOME PAGE FOR WWW2.RESKIT.ORG</b></p>
This is the root page for this site
</body></html>
'@
$PAGE | Out-File -FilePath $SitePath\INDEX.HTML | Out-Null
```

3. Create a new website that uses host headers:

```
$WSHT = @{
PhysicalPath = $SitePath
Name         = 'WWW2'
HostHeader   = 'WWW2.Reskit.Org'
}
New-Website @WSHT
```

4. Create a DNS record on DC1 for WWW2.Reskit.Org:

```
Invoke-Command -Computer DC1.Reskit.Org -ScriptBlock {
  $DNSHT = @{
    ZoneName  = 'Reskit.Org'
    Name      = 'www2'
    IpAddress = '10.10.10.50'
  }
  Add-DnsServerResourceRecordA @DNSHT
}
```

5. Finally, show the site, as follows:

```
$IE  = New-Object -ComObject InterNetExplorer.Application
$URL = 'Http://WWW2.Reskit.Org'
$IE.Navigate2($URL)
$IE.Visible = $true
```

How it works...

In *step 1*, you import the `WebAdministration` module explicitly, in order to load the IIS provider. In *step 2*, you create a new page on `SRV1` that serves as the new site's home page. These two steps produce no output.

In *step 3*, you create a new IIS website on `SRV1`; namely, `WWW2.Reskit.Org`. The output of this step looks like this:

```
PS C:\Foo> $WSHT = @{
             PhysicalPath = $SitePath
             name         = 'www2'
             HostHeader   = 'www2.reskit.org'
             }
PS C:\Foo> New-Website @WSHT

Name   ID   State     Physical Path     Bindings

----   --   -----     -------------     --------

www2   2    Started   C:\inetpub\www2   http *:80:www2.reskit.org
```

In *step 4*, you create a new DNS record to point to this new site, which produces no output. In *step 5*, you use Internet Explorer to navigate to the new site, which looks like this:

There's more...

By default, while you can have as many HTTP-based sites as you want on a given machine, you can only have one HTTPS site. This is because the details of the site that the browser is asking for are inside the encrypted content, and thus, can only be actioned once decrypted.

To overcome this limitation, IIS uses a TLS feature known as **Server Name Indication** (**SNI**). SNI allows the name of the hostname being contacted to be specified during the SSL/TLS handshake. This, in turn, enables IIS to support more than one secure site. To use SNI, the browser or web client, as well as the web server, must support SNI. Modern web browsers support SNI, which has been a feature of IIS on Windows Server for many versions.

In *step 4*, you created a DNS A record that points to the site at `10.10.10.50`. If your site is on a different IP address, change this input accordingly.

See also

SNI has been a feature of IIS for some time. See `https://docs.microsoft.com/en-us/iis/get-started/whats-new-in-iis-8/iis-80-server-name-indication-sni-ssl-scalability` for details of the SNI feature in IIS in Windows Server. You can find more details on SNI in general at `http://en.wikipedia.org/wiki/Server_Name_Indication`.

Managing IIS logging and log files

By default, every time IIS receives a request from a client, it logs that request to a log file. You can use PowerShell to modify this behavior. You can turn off logging, change the logging frequency, or changing the folder where IIS stores its log files.

Log files are a great place to look when troubleshooting a web server or when analyzing your website's traffic. IIS web server logs are also useful for capacity planning and to help you to analyze the behavior of the traffic (for example, where is it coming from, what clients are being used, which sites/pages are being accessed, and so on).

By default, IIS creates a separate log file every day. This has advantages, but on a busy web server with many sites, managing log files can become a challenge. A web server that has been up and running for a month would have 30 separate log files. You may wish to change log files less frequently.

Also, since IIS puts log files inside the `C:\Windows` folder by default, you may wish to change the location of log files. You could move the log files to a separate folder in your `C:\` drive, or to a separate drive altogether, depending on the sizes of your IIS logs.

In this recipe, you configure logging in IIS using PowerShell and the IIS provider that you load from the `WebAdministration` module. This technique uses `Set-ItemProperty` to configure IIS logging.

Getting ready

This recipe assumes that you have installed IIS, as per the *Installing IIS* recipe.

How to do it...

1. Import the web administration module to ensure that the IIS provider is loaded:

    ```
    Import-Module WebAdministration
    ```

2. Look at where you are currently storing log files:

    ```
    $IPHT1 = @{
      Path  = 'IIS:\Sites\Default Web Site'
      Name  =  'logfile.directory'
    }
    $LogfileLocation = (Get-ItemProperty @IPHT1).value
    $LF = [System.Environment]::ExpandEnvironmentVariables("$LF")
    Get-ChildItem $LogFileFolder -Recurse
    ```

3. Change the folder to `C:\IISLogs`:

    ```
    $IPHT2 = @{
      Path  = 'IIS:\Sites\Default Web Site'
      Name  = 'logfile.directory'
    }
    Set-ItemProperty @IPHT2 -Value 'C:\IISLogs'
    New-Item -Path C:\IISLogs -ItemType Directory |
      Out-Null
    ```

4. Change the logging style, as follows:

    ```
    $IPHT3 = @{
      Path = 'IIS:\Sites\Default Web Site'
      Name = 'logFile.logFormat'
    }
    Set-ItemProperty @IPHT3 -Value 'W3C'
    ```

5. Change logging change file frequency:

```
$IPHT3 = @{
  Path = 'IIS:\Sites\Default Web Site'
  Name = 'logFile.period'
}
Set-ItemProperty @IPHT3 -Value Weekly
```

6. Change the logging to use a maximum log size:

```
$IPHT4 = @{
  Path = 'IIS:\Sites\Default Web Site'
  Name = 'logFile.period'
}
Set-ItemProperty @IPHT4 -Value 'MaxSize'
$Size = 1GB
$IPHT5 = @{
  Path = 'IIS:\Sites\Default Web Site'
  Name = 'logFile.truncateSize'
}
Set-ItemProperty @IPHT5 -Value $size
```

7. Disable logging, as follows:

```
$IPHT5 = @{
  Path = 'IIS:\Sites\Default Web Site'
  Name = 'logFile.enabled'
}
Set-ItemProperty @IPHT5 -Value $False
```

8. Delete all of the log files over 30 days old, as shown here:

```
$LogDirs = Get-ChildItem -Path IIS:\Sites |
            Get-ItemProperty -Name logFile.directory.value |
              Select -Unique
$Age = 30                               # days to keep log files
$DaysOld = (Get-Date).AddDays(-$Age)    # how long ago that was
Foreach ($LogDir in $LogDirs){
 $Dir = [Environment]::ExpandEnvironmentVariables($LogDir)
 Get-ChildItem -Path $Dir -Recurse -ErrorAction SilentlyContinue |
   Where-Object LastWriteTime -lt $DaysOld  |
     Remove-Item
}
```

How it works...

In *step 1*, you import the `WebAdministration` module explicitly, which loads the IIS provider, creates an `IIS:` PSDrive on your system, and produces no output.

In *step 2*, you use the IIS provider to retrieve the location of IIS logs for `SRV1` and display the existing log files. Depending on how much you have used the two websites created in this chapter's recipes (that is, the default website created in the *Installing IIS* recipe and the `WWW2` site created in the *Configuring IIS bindings* recipe), the output might look like this:

```
PS C:\Foo> $IPHT1 = @{
               Path  = 'IIS:\Sites\Default Web Site'
               Name  = 'logfile.directory'
           }
PS C:\Foo> $LogfileLocation = (Get-ItemProperty @IPHT1).Value
PS C:\Foo> $LogFileFolder = [System.Environment]::ExpandEnvironmentVariables("$LogfileLocation")
PS C:\Foo> Get-ChildItem $LogFileFolder -Recurse

    Directory: C:\inetpub\logs\LogFiles

Mode            LastWriteTime      Length Name
----            -------------      ------ ----
d-----    24/01/2019     10:48            W3SVC1
d-----    24/01/2019     13:14            W3SVC2
-a----    20/01/2019     20:44      6059  AllLogs.tmp

    Directory:  C:\inetpub\logs\LogFiles\W3SVC1

Mode            LastWriteTime      Length Name
----            -------------      ------ ----
-a----    21/01/2019     12:26     13888  AllLogs.tmp
-a----    18/01/2019     18:05      1326  u_ex190118.log
-a----    19/01/2019     21:19      4943  u_ex190119.log
-a----    20/01/2019     21:11      6795  u_ex190120.log
-a----    21/01/2019     12:25      3301  u_ex190121.log
-a----    23/01/2019     22:44      6344  u_ex190123.log
-a----    24/01/2019     12:05      2496  u_ex190124.log

    Directory:  C:\inetpub\logs\LogFiles\W3SVC2

Mode            LastWriteTime      Length Name
----            -------------      ------ ----
-a----    20/01/2019     21:02      1398  u_ex190120.log
-a----    23/01/2019     16:51       555  u_ex190123.log
-a----    24/01/2019     13:15       544  u_ex190124.log
```

In *step 3*, you create a folder at `C:\IISLogs` and change the log file folder to this one. In *step 4*, you change the logging type to `W3C`; in *step 5*, you set the frequency that IIS uses to change log files, and in *step 6*, you set a maximum log file size. In *step 7*, you disable logging for the default website. Finally, in *step 8*, you remove any log files over 30 days old. These six steps produce no output.

There's more...

In *step 2*, you look at the log files created so far. Your output is likely to be different, depending on how many clients you have used to access the two websites created in the recipes in this chapter. In the output, you may notice that the logging file folder root (`C:\inetpub\logs\LogFiles`) has two sub-folders that both contain individual daily log files. The log files that you see in the `W3SVC1` sub-folder relate to the default website, while the log files in the `W3SVC2` sub-folder relate to the `WWW2.Reskit.Org` site.

In *step 3*, you changed the folder that holds the IIS logs. In production, you may choose to hold IIS log files on separate disks, which is a best practice.

In *step 4*, you adjusted the log file format for IIS logging to `W3C`. You have several options for log file formats. See `https://docs.microsoft.com/en-us/iis/manage/provisioning-and-managing-iis/configure-logging-in-iis` for more information on IIS log file formats.

In *step 6*, you change the logging to use a maximum size log file. This does keep the size of log files in check, but means that you may not record all events.

In *step 7*, you disable logging for the default website. This would enable your IIS server to be a little more efficient (due to not having to log events) and means that runaway disk space usage is less likely. As with most Windows logging, IIS logging is turned on by default, but you can easily turn it off or reconfigure it, based on your requirements.

In *step 8*, you deleted any log files over 30 days old. Instead of deleting them, you may wish to copy them to a central site for more in-depth analysis. The regular logs are great for simple analysis, but for longer term capacity planning, having more data could be useful.

You may also want to keep your log files on your web servers for less than 30 days. To avoid the logs from clogging up your web servers, you can update this recipe to copy the oldest log file(s) to a central repository.

Log files can consume a significant amount of space. You might also consider saving them to a folder that you compress using NTFS file compression, or by using something like WinZIP or WinRAR to compress the files (and decompress them, if you need to do more analysis).

See also

For more information on how to resolve application issues using IIS log files, see `https://www.sumologic.com/blog/log-management-analysis/iis-logs-troubleshooting/`.

Managing IIS applications and application pools

In the earliest versions of IIS, all of the web pages and sites on a given system ran in a single Windows process. This meant that one application, if not written well, could cause issues with other applications. An application with a memory or handle leak would eventually require a restart of the single process (or even a reboot of the server).

In later versions of IIS, Microsoft added the concept of web applications and application pools to IIS. With IIS, a web application is a set of one or more URLs (web pages). For example, the pages for the WWW2.Reskit.Org example that you created in the *Configuring IIS bindings* recipe are stored in C:\inetpub\www2 on SRV1. You can configure IIS to run different web applications inside of independent worker processes. This means that your default website and the WWW2 site could run inside of totally different worker processes, and issues with one are not going to affect the other.

An application pool is a set of worker processes that IIS uses to run a specific application. You can run one or more applications within a given application pool, or run each application in separate application pools. Technically, a website and a web application are not the same, but in many cases, different websites end up being distinct applications.

The application pool feature provides application isolation, enabling you to run possibly unstable applications independently of others. And since you can configure an application pool to run more than one worker process, application pools provide a degree of scalability (taking use of multiple cores on modern processors).

With application pools, IIS can spawn numerous threads in each worker process that IIS runs in parallel, which takes advantage of today's multi-core processors. IIS can create and destroy worker processes on demand, adding more when the workload is higher, and destroying them when they are not needed.

You can also set up the worker processes to be recycled by IIS (that is, stop, then restart). Thus, if an unstable application contains a memory leak (something quite possible when using older ISAPI technologies, for example), recycling the process returns the leaked resources back to the OS. Thus, even a very poorly written application can run reasonably well inside IIS.

There are a variety of conditions that you can set to trigger recycling on an application pool. You can set a schedule of when to recycle; you can recycle if the private memory exceeds a predetermined value (for example, 1 GB), or after a certain number of requests (such as recycling the application pool after 1 million hits).

For fuller details, see https://technet.microsoft.com/en-us/library/cc745955.aspx.

This page relates to IIS 7, but the details are still the same for the version of IIS shipped both with Windows 10 and Server 2019. Another nice feature of application pools is that you can configure each application pool with separate credentials, which provides increased security of IIS applications. For example, an HR application could run using the credentials Reskit\HRApp, while you could configure an accounting web application to run as Reskit\ AccountApp. You could then set up Access Control Lists on various resources (files, SQL databases, and so on) based on these user IDs.

In this recipe, you create a new IIS web application based on the WWW2 site that you created in the *Configuring* recipe. The recipe also creates and configures an application pool that hosts the application/website.

Getting ready

You need to run this recipe on SRV1, which you configured with IIS (created in the *Installing IIS* recipe) and with the WWW2 site (created in the *Configuring IIS bindings* recipe).

How to do it...

1. Import the web administration module:

   ```
   Import-Module -Name WebAdministration
   ```

2. Create a new application pool:

   ```
   New-WebAppPool -Name WWW2Pool
   ```

3. Create a new application in the pool:

   ```
   $WAHT = @{
       Name            = 'WWW2'
       Site            = 'WWW2'
       ApplicationPool = 'WWW2Pool'
       PhysicalPath    = 'C:\inetpub\WWW2'
   }
   New-WebApplication @WAHT
   ```

4. View the application pools on SRV1:

   ```
   Get-IISAppPool
   ```

5. Set the application pool restart time, as follows:

```
$IPHT1 = @{
  Path = 'IIS:\AppPools\WWW2Pool'
  Name = 'Recycling.periodicRestart.schedule'
}
Clear-ItemProperty  @IPHT1
$RestartAt = @('07:55', '19:55')
New-ItemProperty @IPHT1 -Value $RestartAt
```

6. Set the application pool maximum private memory, as follows::

```
$IPHT2 = @{
  Path = 'IIS:\AppPools\WWW2Pool'
  Name = 'Recycling.periodicRestart.privatememory'
}
Clear-ItemProperty @IPHT2
[int32] $PrivMemMax = 150mb
Set-ItemProperty -Path 'IIS:\AppPools\WWW2Pool' `
                 -Name Recycling.periodicRestart.privateMemory `
                 -Value $PrivMemMax
```

7. Set the maximum number of requests before a recycle and view, as follows:

```
$IPHT3 = @{
  Path = 'IIS:\AppPools\WWW2Pool'
  Name = 'Recycling.periodicRestart.requests'
}
Clear-ItemProperty @IPHT3
[int32] $MaxRequests = 104242
Set-ItemProperty @IPHT3 -Value $MaxRequests
Get-ItemProperty @IPHT3
```

8. Recycle the application pool immediately:

```
$Pool = Get-IISAppPool -Name WWW2Pool
$Pool.Recycle()
```

How it works...

In *step 1*, you import the `WebAdministration` module explicitly. This loads the IIS provider, creates an `IIS:` PSDrive on your system, and produces no output.

In *step 2*, you create a new application pool (WWW2Pool). This application pool points to the WWW2 site that you created earlier. While that site is currently just a single page, you could extend it, in which case the application would encompass all pages in the folder. This step has output that looks like this:

```
PS C:\Foo> New-WebAppPool -Name WWW2Pool

Name         State        Applications
----         -----        ------------
WWW2Pool     Started
```

Once you have created the application pool, you can create a new web application to host the WWW2 site created earlier. In *step 3*, you create an application within the just created application pool. The output looks like this:

```
PS C:\Foo> $WAHT = @{
              Name            = 'WWW2'
              Site            = 'WWW2'
              ApplicationPool = 'WWW2Pool'
              PhysicalPath    = 'C:\inetpub\WWW2'
          }
PS C:\Foo> New-WebApplication @WAHT

Name    Application pool    Protocols    Physical Path
----    ----------------    ---------    -------------
WWW2    WWW2Pool            http
```

In *step 4*, you review the existing web application pools on SRV1 (including the WWW2Pool that you just created). The output for this looks like the following:

```
PS C:\Foo> Get-IISAppPool

Name                    Status     CLR Ver    Pipeline Mode    Start Mode
----                    ------     -------    -------------    ----------
DefaultAppPool          Started    v4.0       Integrated       OnDemand
Classic .NET AppPool    Started    v2.0       Classic          OnDemand
.NET v2.0 Classic       Started    v2.0       Classic          OnDemand
.NET v2.0               Started    v2.0       Integrated       OnDemand
.NET v4.5 Classic       Started    v4.0       Classic          OnDemand
.NET v4.5               Started    v4.0       Integrated       OnDemand
WWW2Pool                Started    v4.0       Integrated       OnDemand
```

In *step 5*, you configure IIS to recycle the application pool at 07:55, and again at 19:55. In *step 6*, you configure the application to have a maximum size of 150 MB. In *step 7*, you specify that after a certain number of requests, IIS should automatically recycle the app pool. These three steps produce no output.

In *step 7*, you set the maximum requests to 100,042 to trigger an application pool recycle and view the result, which looks like this:

```
PS C:\Foo>  $IPHT1 = @{
                Path = 'IIS:\AppPools\WWW2Pool'
                Name = 'Recycling.periodicRestart.schedule'
            }
PS C:\Foo> Clear-ItemProperty  @IPHT1
PS C:\Foo> [int32] $MaxRequests = 100042
PS C:\Foo> Set-ItemProperty @IPHT3 -Value $MaxRequests
PS C:\Foo> Get-ItemProperty @IPHT3

PSPath                      : WebAdministration::\\SRV1\AppPools\WWW2Pool
PSParentPath                : WebAdministration::\\SRV1\AppPools
PSChildName                 : WWW2Pool
PSDrive                     : IIS
PSProvider                  : WebAdministration
IsInheritedFromDefaultValue : False
IsProtected                 : False
Name                        : requests
TypeName                    : System.Int64
Schema                      : Microsoft.IIs.PowerShell.Framework.ConfigurationAttributeSchema
Value                       : 100042
IsExtended                  : False
```

Finally, in *step 8*, you recycle the pool immediately. This produces the following output:

```
PS C:\Foo> $Pool = Get-IISAppPool -Name WWW2Pool
PS C:\Foo> $Pool.Recycle()
Started
```

There's more...

In *step 2*, you create a new application pool using the `New-WebAppPool` cmdlet. However, there is no `Get-WebAppPool` cmdlet to enable you to view the application pools. Instead, as you can see in *step 4*, you use the `Get-IISAppPool` cmdlet. That's because the `Get-IISAppPool` comes from the IISAdministration module—so much for consistency.

In *step 4*, you can see a variety of existing web pools. These show the IIS application pools created both by default, and by other recipes in this book. The application pool is an important feature to enable you to run multiple web applications on a single server and avoid application interference. As a part of deploying IIS, you might consider removing all but the necessary application pools.

In *step 5*, *step 6*, and *step 7*, you configure the application pool properties. You achieve this by setting the item properties within the IIS provider. Where you want to configure pool properties, you set the relevant item property on the application pool item for the pool.

These steps make use of the `WebAdministration` provider. The item properties that you set are translated by the provider into the XML that actually drives IIS. For more information on the `WebAdministration` provider, see `https://technet.microsoft.com/en-us/library/ee909471(v=ws.10).aspx`.

Analyzing IIS log files

IIS logs each request that it receives from a client. If someone uses a browser to navigate to `HTTP://SRV1.Reskit.Org`, then details of that interaction are logged to a text file. By default, IIS stores log entries in files within the `C:\inetpub\logs\LogFiles` folder, but you can change the location, as you saw in the *Managing IIS logging and log files* recipe.

The log files that IIS generates are therefore a great source of information about who is using your web servers, and for what. Details such as the client's IP address, the HTTP verb (GET, POST, and so on), the page requested, and more, are all in the log.

In this recipe, you process the logs on `SRV1` to see which clients are connecting to your server and what client software they are using.

Getting ready

You run this recipe on/against `SRV1`, a web server that you have configured and used in other recipes in this chapter. In order to get useful data from this recipe, you need log files, and that means using one (and preferably more) client to access the web server on `SRV1`. You can use any of the other **virtual machines** (**VMs**) that you have to access the default IIS website on `SRV1`.

How to do it...

1. Define the location of the log files and a temporary filename:

```
$LogFolder = 'C:\inetpub\logs\LogFiles\W3SVC1'
$LogFiles = Get-ChildItem $LogFolder\*.log -Recurse
$LogTemp = "C:\inetpub\logs\LogFiles\W3SVC1\AllLogs.tmp"
```

2. Create a ($Logs) array to hold each useful line of each log file:

```
$Logs = @()                     # Create empty array
# Remove the comment lines
$LogFiles |
  ForEach { Get-Content $_ |
    Where-Object {$_ -notLike "#[D,F,S,V]*" } |
      Foreach { $Logs += $_ }  # add log entry to $Logs array
}
```

3. Build a better CSV file header:

```
$LogColumns = ( $LogFiles |
                Select-Object -First 1 |
                  Foreach { Get-Content $_ |
                    Where-Object {$_ -Like "#[F]*" } } )
$LogColumns = $LogColumns -replace "#Fields: ", ""
$LogColumns = $LogColumns -replace "-",""
$LogColumns = $LogColumns -replace "\(",""
$LogColumns = $LogColumns -replace "\)",""
```

4. Save the updated log entries to the temporary file:

```
$NL = [Environment]::NewLine
$P  = [System.String]::Join( [Environment]::NewLine, $Logs)
$S = "{0}{1}{2}" -f  $LogColumns, $NL,$P
Set-Content -Path $LogTemp -Value  $S
```

5. Read the reformatted logs as a CSV file:

```
$Logs = Import-Csv -Path $LogTemp -Delimiter " "
```

6. View the client IP addresses:

```
$Logs |
  Sort-Object -Property cip |
    Select-Object -Property CIP -Unique
```

7. View the user agent instances used to communicate with SRV1:

```
$Logs |
  Sort-Object -property csUserAgent |
    Select-Object -Property csUserAgent -Unique
```

8. View the access frequency of each user agent:

```
$Logs |
  Sort-Object -Property csUserAgent |
    Group-Object csuseragent |
      Sort-object -Property Count -Desc |
        Format-Table -Property Count, Name
```

9. Who is using what:

```
$Logs |
  Select-Object -Property CIP, CSUserAgent -Unique |
    Sort-Object -Property CIP
```

How it works...

In *step 1*, you define the location of the IIS log files that you are interested in and collect the logs for the specific website (that is, the default website on SRV1). You also create the name of a temporary file that you use to hold the log details.

In *step 2*, you build an array ($Logs), which contains all of the actual log events, with the comments stripped out.

In *step 3*, you build a more useful header line for the temporary log file.

Next, in *step 4*, you save the actual log events, along with the updated header, into the temporary CSV file.

Then, in *step 5*, you read in the temporary CSV file. These first five steps produce no output.

In *step 6*, you extract the different client IP addresses representing the individual clients that accessed SRV1, which looks like this:

```
PS C:\Foo> $Logs |
             Sort-Object -Property cip |
               Select-Object -Property CIP -Unique

cip
---
10.10.10.10
10.10.10.150
10.10.10.181
10.10.10.201
10.10.10.202
10.10.10.60
fe80::295c:a764:6ffe:4ec7%7
```

In *step 7*, you extract the names of the different user agents (browsers, and so on) that were used by clients to access `http://SRV1`. The output of this step looks like this:

```
PS C:\Foo> $Logs |
             Sort-Object -property csUserAgent |
             Select-Object -Property csUserAgent -Unique

csUserAgent
-----------
Mozilla/4.0+(compatible;+MSIE+7.0;+Windows+NT+10.0;+WOW64;+Trident/7.0;+.NET...
Mozilla/4.0+(compatible;+MSIE+7.0;+Windows+NT+10.0;+WOW64;+Trident/7.0;+.NET...
Mozilla/5.0+(Windows+NT+10.0;+Win64;+x64)+AppleWebKit/537.36+(KHTML,+like+Ge...
Mozilla/5.0+(Windows+NT+10.0;+Win64;+x64)+AppleWebKit/537.36+(KHTML,+like+Ge...
Mozilla/5.0+(Windows+NT+10.0;+Win64;+x64)+AppleWebKit/537.36+(KHTML,+like+Ge...
Mozilla/5.0+(Windows+NT+10.0;+WOW64;+Trident/7.0;+rv:11.0)+like+Gecko
```

In *step 8*, you examine the frequency of user agent usage, which looks like this:

```
PS C:\Foo> $Logs |
             Sort-Object -Property csUserAgent |
             Group-Object csuseragent |
             Sort-object -Property Count -Desc |
             Format-Table -Property Count, Name

Count Name
----- ----
   29 Mozilla/5.0+(Windows+NT+10.0;+Win64;+x64)+AppleWebKit/537.36+(KHTML,+1...
   12 Mozilla/4.0+(compatible;+MSIE+7.0;+Windows+NT+10.0;+WOW64;+Trident/7.0...
   11 Mozilla/4.0+(compatible;+MSIE+7.0;+Windows+NT+10.0;+WOW64;+Trident/7.0...
    7 Mozilla/5.0+(Windows+NT+10.0;+Win64;+x64)+AppleWebKit/537.36+(KHTML,+1...
    4 Mozilla/5.0+(Windows+NT+10.0;+WOW64;+Trident/7.0;+rv:11.0)+like+Gecko
    2 Mozilla/5.0+(Windows+NT+10.0;+Win64;+x64)+AppleWebKit/537.36+(KHTML,+1...
```

Finally, in *step 9*, you look at what IP address is using which user agent, which looks like this:

```
PS C:\Foo> $Logs |
             Select-Object -Property CIP, CSUserAgent -Unique |
             Sort-Object -Property CIP

cip                       csUserAgent
---                       -----------
10.10.10.10               Mozilla/5.0+(Windows+NT+10.0;+Win64;+x64)+AppleWebKit/537.36...
10.10.10.150              Mozilla/5.0+(Windows+NT+10.0;+Win64;+x64)+AppleWebKit/537.36...
10.10.10.150              Mozilla/5.0+(Windows+NT+10.0;+Win64;+x64)+AppleWebKit/537.36...
10.10.10.181              Mozilla/5.0+(Windows+NT+10.0;+Win64;+x64)+AppleWebKit/537.36...
10.10.10.181              Mozilla/4.0+(compatible;+MSIE+7.0;+Windows+NT+10.0;+WOW64;+T...
10.10.10.201              Mozilla/4.0+(compatible;+MSIE+7.0;+Windows+NT+10.0;+WOW64;+T...
10.10.10.202              Mozilla/4.0+(compatible;+MSIE+7.0;+Windows+NT+10.0;+WOW64;+T...
10.10.10.60               Mozilla/4.0+(compatible;+MSIE+7.0;+Windows+NT+10.0;+WOW64;+T...
fe80::295c:a764:6ffe:4ec7%7 Mozilla/4.0+(compatible;+MSIE+7.0;+Windows+NT+10.0;+WOW64;+T...
fe80::295c:a764:6ffe:4ec7%7 Mozilla/5.0+(Windows+NT+10.0;+WOW64;+Trident/7.0;+rv:11.0)+1...
fe80::295c:a764:6ffe:4ec7%7 Mozilla/5.0+(Windows+NT+10.0;+Win64;+x64)+AppleWebKit/537.36...
```

There's more...

In the *Managing IIS logging and log files* recipe, you might have changed the location of the IIS log files. If so, you may need to adjust the value of `$LogFolder` set in *step 1*.

In *step 3*, you create an updated and more useful CSV header line. This, amongst other things, gives the data columns more helpful names, which simplifies the processing you do, in *step 6*, *step 7*, and *step 8*. You could augment the updates to column names to be even more useful in your environment.

In the last three steps, you examine the user agent names supplied to `SRV1` when the client systems connected. At connection time, each web client provides the name of the user agent, which is what IIS logs. In *step 7*, you see the different agent names, while in *step 8*, you look at how often each user agent is used. Finally, in *step 9*, you examine which IP address uses which user agent.

In *step 8*, you sort the user agent usage by IP address. Since PowerShell stores the IP address as a string, you can see that `10.10.10.202` comes before `10.10.10.60`, which is, of course, how string sorting works in PowerShell. Additionally, you could extend this step to perform a DNS lookup (using `Resolve-DnsName`) to get the hostname and add the hostname to the output.

Managing and monitoring Network Load Balancing

Network Load Balancing (**NLB**) is a feature of Windows and IIS that allows for multiple hosts to host the same website. The NLB cluster distributes all traffic to the cluster on the individual hosts.

NLB provides both scalability and fault tolerance. If you add additional nodes, the cluster is able to handle more traffic. And if a node should fail, the remaining nodes take the traffic, albeit at a potentially lower performance level.

NLB is a versatile feature. You can use NLB to load balance traffic from the web, over FTP, firewalls, proxies, and VPNs. Performance is acceptable, although many users prefer to use hardware load balancers.

In this recipe, you create a new NLB cluster (`ReskitNLB`) that load balances between two hosts (`NLB1`, `NLB2`). The recipe creates a simple, single-page site on each system, and then provides load balancing and failover of the NLB site.

In this recipe, you create a single-document site. The single document differs on each server, which is useful to show which server accepted and processed any given request. In production, you would want all of the nodes to have the same content, providing a seamless experience.

You run the first part of this recipe on NLB1. Once you have the NLB cluster, you can view it from another host (in this case, DC1).

Getting ready

This recipe uses two new Windows 2019 servers: NLB1 and NLB2. You also use the server DC1, which is the domain controller in the Reskit.Org domain, and is also a DNS server for the domain. Each server is required to have static IP addresses; otherwise, you see an error when attempting to create the NLB cluster.

How to do it...

1. Install the Web-Server (and .NET 3.5) feature on NLB1, NLB2:

```
$IHT1 = @{
    Name                 = 'Web-Server'
    IncludeManagementTools = $True
    IncludeAllSubFeature   = $True
    Source               = 'D:\sources\sxs'
}
Install-WindowsFeature @IHT1 -ComputerName NLB1
Install-WindowsFeature @IHT1 -ComputerName NLB2
```

2. Now, add the NLB feature to NLB1, NLB2:

```
$IHT2 = @{
    Name                 = 'NLB'
    IncludeManagementTools = $True
    IncludeAllSubFeature   = $True
}
Install-WindowsFeature @IHT -ComputerName NLB1 | Out-Null
Install-WindowsFeature @IHT -ComputerName NLB2 | Out-Null
```

3. Confirm that the `NLB` and `Web-Server` features are loaded on both NLB systems:

```
$SB = {
  Get-WindowsFeature Web-Server, NLB
}
Invoke-Command -ScriptBlock $SB -ComputerName NLB1, NLB2 |
  Format-table -Property DisplayName,PSComputername,Installstate
```

4. Create the NLB cluster, beginning with `NLB1`:

```
$NLBHT1 = @{
  InterFaceName     = 'Ethernet'
  ClusterName       = 'ReskitNLB'
  ClusterPrimaryIP  = '10.10.10.55'
  SubnetMask        = '255.255.255.0'
  OperationMode     = 'Multicast'
}
New-NlbCluster @NLBHT1
```

5. Add `NLB2` to the `ReskitNLB` cluster:

```
$NLBHT2 = @{
  NewNodeName      = 'NLB2.Reskit.Org'
  NewNodeInterface = 'Ethernet'
  InterfaceName    = 'Ethernet'
}
Add-NlbClusterNode @NLBHT2
```

6. Create the following network firewall rule:

```
$SB = {
  $NFTHT =@{
    DisplayGroup = 'File and Printer Sharing'
    Enabled      = 'True'
  }
  Set-NetFirewallRule @NFTHT
}
Invoke-Command -ScriptBlock $SB -ComputerName NLB1
Invoke-Command -ScriptBlock $SB -ComputerName NLB2
```

7. Create a default document, with different content on each machine:

```
'NLB Cluster: Hosted on NLB1' |
    Out-File -FilePath C:\inetpub\wwwroot\Index.Html
'NLB Cluster: Greetings from NLB2' |
    Out-File -FilePath \\NLB2\C$\inetpub\wwwroot\Index.Html
```

8. Check the VIP address for the NLB cluster:

```
Get-NlbClusterVip
```

9. Add a DNS A record for the cluster:

```
$SB = {
  $NAHT = @{
    Name        = 'ReskitNLB'
    IPv4Address = '10.10.10.55'
    ZoneName    = 'Reskit.Org'
  }
  Add-DnsServerResourceRecordA @NAHT
}
Invoke-Command -ComputerName DC1 -ScriptBlock $SB

#    DO REMAINDER OF THIS RECIPE FROM DC1
```

10. View the NLB cluster node details from DC1:

```
Get-NlbClusterNode -HostName NLB1.Reskit.Org
```

11. View the NLB site from DC1, as follows:

```
Start-Process 'HTTP://ReskitNLB.Reskit.Org'
```

12. Stop one node (the one that responded in *step 11*):

```
Stop-NlbClusterNode -HostName NLB1
Clear-DnsClientCache
```

13. View the cluster node details on NLB1:

```
Get-NlbClusterNode -HostName NLB1
```

14. View the site again (from DC1):

```
Start-Process 'HTTP://ReskitNLB.Reskit.Org'
```

How it works...

In *step 1*, you add the web service, tools, and sub-features to NLB1 and NLB2, which looks like this:

```
PS C:\Foo> $IHT1 = @{
             Name  = 'Web-Server'
             IncludeManagementTools = $True
             IncludeAllSubFeature   = $True
             Source                 = 'D:\sources\sxs'
           }
PS C:\Foo> Install-WindowsFeature @IHT1 -ComputerName NLB1
PS C:\Foo> Install-WindowsFeature @IHT1 -ComputerName NLB2


Success Restart Needed Exit Code     Feature Result
------- -------------- ---------     --------------
True    No             Success       {ASP.NET 4.7, .NET Framework 3.5 (includes...
True    No             Success       {ASP.NET 4.7, .NET Framework 3.5 (includes...
```

In *step 2*, you also install the web server feature on NLB1 and NLB2, which produces no output.

In *step 3*, you check to see whether IIS and NLB are loaded on both NLB1 and NLB2, which looks like this:

```
PS C:\Foo> $SB = {
             Get-WindowsFeature Web-Server, NLB
           }
PS C:\Foo> Invoke-Command -ScriptBlock $SB -ComputerName NLB1, NLB2 |
             Format-table -Property DisplayName,PSComputername,Installstate

DisplayName               PSComputerName InstallState
-----------               -------------- ------------
Web Server (IIS)          NLB2           Installed
Network Load Balancing    NLB2           Installed
Web Server (IIS)          NLB1           Installed
Network Load Balancing    NLB1           Installed
```

In *step 4,* you configure NLB to run on `NLB1`, which looks like this:

```
PS C:\Foo> $NLBHT1 = @{
             InterFaceName    = 'Ethernet'
             ClusterName      = 'ReskitNLB'
             ClusterPrimaryIP = '10.10.10.55'
             SubnetMask       = '255.255.255.0'
             OperationMode    = 'Multicast'
           }
PS C:\Foo> New-NlbCluster @NLBHT1

Name      IPAddress    SubnetMask     Mode
----      ---------    ----------     ----
ReskitNLB 10.10.10.55 255.255.255.0 MULTICAST
```

In *step 5,* you add `NLB2.Reskit.Org` to the `ReskitNLB` cluster. In *step 6,* you create firewall rules for the cluster. In *step 7,* you create the contents of the default document for both `NLB1` and `NLB2`. These three steps produce no output.

In *step 8,* with the configuration of the NLB cluster, you retrieve the cluster's VIP address, which looks like this:

```
PS C:\Foo> Get-NlbClusterVip

IPAddress    SubnetMask
---------    ----------
10.10.10.55 255.255.255.0
```

In *step 9,* you complete the configuration of the NLB cluster on `NLB1` by creating an A record for the cluster name, which produces no output.

Once these steps have been completed, you have set up the NLB cluster. To test it, run the remaining steps in this recipe on `DC1`.

In *step 10,* you view the cluster node status, as follows:

```
PS C:\Foor> Get-NlbClusterNode -HostName NLB1.Reskit.Org

Name State              Interface HostID
---- -----              --------- ------
NLB1 Converged(default) Ethernet  1
NLB2 Converged          Ethernet  2
```

In *step 11*, you view the NLB site from DC1, which looks like this:

In *step 12*, you stop NLB on NLB1, which produces no output. In *step 13*, you get the NLB cluster node details for the NLB cluster, showing that NLB1 is down, which looks like this:

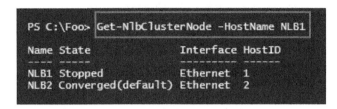

After shutting down NLB, you re-browse on DC1 to the cluster, in order to see the following:

There's more...

This recipe uses two new servers (NLB1 and NLB2). You could also run this recipe on other servers, as appropriate; for example, the SRV1 and SRV2 servers that are used elsewhere in this book.

In *step 3*, you create the NLB cluster. Because NLB1 and NLB2 have just one network adapter, you create the cluster with an operation mode of multicast. Had you used unicast, Windows would have effectively killed off the normal connection to these systems. In production, you would probably want two NICs inside each NLB cluster member.

In *step 12*, you stop a node in the `ReskitNLB` load balancing cluster. You then view (in *step 13*) the status of the nodes in the cluster by using the `Get-NlbClusterNode` cmdlet. After stopping `NLB1`, you can review the cluster to see the document from `NLB2` (in *step 14*).

In *step 7*, you create the contents of the default document for both `NLB1` and `NLB2`. In this recipe, you deliberately create different content for each document on both NLB cluster members. This shows you which host is handling the request for the default document on the NLB cluster.

If you need to take a node down (for example, to install a patch), you might want to do this during a maintenance window, when no one would be using the website provided by the cluster. If necessary, you can take one node down, perform any maintenance, and then restore the cluster member. All the while, the cluster continues to work. While a node is not part of the cluster, the cluster is less performant, but this is a fact to consider when deciding to maintain a live cluster (that is, during the day) or by waiting until your next setting any maintenance window.

In *step 11*, you view the site via the NLB cluster (from `DC1`), which shows that `NLB1` is supplying the page. If you are testing this, you may find that `NLB2` responds to the initial request (*step 11*); if so, in *step 12*, shut down `NLB2` instead.

> If you run these tests on either of the cluster members, NLB resolves the cluster to the local site. Thus, running this from `NLB1` would always pick `NLB1`, whereas running it from another host, such as `DC1`, you would see the desired behavior.

10
Managing Desired State Configuration

In this chapter, we cover the following recipes:

- Using DSC and built-in DSC resources
- Parameterizing the DSC configuration
- Finding and installing DSC resources
- Using DSC with resources from PS Gallery
- Configuring the DSC local configuration manager
- Implementing an SMB DSC pull server
- Implementing a web-based DSC pull server
- Using DSC partial configurations

Introduction

Desired State Configuration (**DSC**) is a management platform within Windows Server, and is implemented with Windows PowerShell. DSC enables you to define a computer's desired state declaratively and have PowerShell ensure that the computer is configured accordingly, and that it remains so. This is simpler than writing complex scripts to configure a particular computer.

With DSC, you define a configuration that describes the details of how a given node (computer) is to be configured. The configuration defines a series of resources to be invoked on the node and how these resources should be configured.

A DSC resource is a PowerShell module that is instructed to configure a given object residing on a node. If you are planning on using a specific DSC resource, you need the related PowerShell module on the computer on which you author the DSC configurations and on the target node.

As an example, you could define a node and specify that the `WindowsFeature` resource should be configured to ensure that the `Web-Server` feature (a subset of the full installation of **Internet Information Service (IIS)**) is installed. You could also use the DSC `File` resource to ensure that a set of files—which are available from somewhere in your network or the internet—are present on the target node. This could dramatically simplify the process of configuring a web farm and ensure that it stays configured properly.

Resources come from a variety of sources. Microsoft has a few resources built in to PowerShell, and these ship inside Windows Server 2019. But you can also get additional DSC resources from the internet, or you can develop your own DSC resources. For more information on developing DSC resources, refer to `https://docs.microsoft.com/en-us/powershell/dsc/resources/authoringResource`.

 PowerShell V6 and later versions do not currently support DSC. If you want to leverage DSC, you are going to need to use PowerShell V4 or later versions (preferably PowerShell version 5.1).

The first step with DSC is defining a configuration statement. A configuration statement, which is not dissimilar to a function, defines the desired state of a node. It states how you wish certain resources on the target node to be configured.

The next step is to execute the configuration statement. This is a lot like functions in PowerShell. When you execute your function, you are compiling it and creating a managed object format (MOF) file as output.

You can parameterize configuration statements to make it simple to create different MOF files based on the parameter values. For example, a configuration statement could take a node name and the name of a Windows feature that should be present on the node. When you run the configuration, you specify values for the node name (for example, `DC1`), and the name of the Windows feature you want loaded (for example, `Web-Server`). The generated MOF file instructs DSC to ensure that the `Web-Server` feature is present on `DC1`.

When you run the configuration statement, PowerShell compiles the DSC configuration into a PowerShell function. When you invoke this generated function, PowerShell creates a MOF file based on the specified configuration. A MOF file tells PowerShell precisely how the resource is to be configured on a specific node.

Microsoft chose to use the MOF file in addition to the configuration statement to define the configuration. MOF is standardized and well supported, although it is more complex in terms of syntax and content. Separating the specification of the configuration from the details involved in deploying it can feel like additional overhead (create the PowerShell configuration statement, then create and deploy the MOF file).

Microsoft thought that someone could create a DSC-workbench-type product that enabled you to use a GUI and define the configuration graphically. Then, at the click of a button, this as-yet unbuilt tool would generate the necessary MOF file and deploy it automatically. Even though this GUI has never been built, the approach does allow you to define security boundaries between defining a configuration and deploying it.

Once you have generated the MOF files, you deploy the configuration. DSC uses the MOF file to ensure that the specified DSC resources are correctly configured on the target node. Subsequently, you can check that the node is correctly configured, with the service and files in place, and remedy any unapproved changes to the target node, referred to as configuration drift.

You can also use DSC to have a node pull configuration details from a centralized pull server. The pull server is a server that makes DSC configuration files (that is, the MOF files) and the resources available to target nodes. A target node is set up to regularly contact the pull server and pull configuration information (and any required resources) from the pull server. You can have two types of pull server—a web pull server or an SMB pull server. The latter is simpler to set up.

With a pull server, you configure the target node's **local configuration manager** (**LCM**) with a GUID and the location of the pull server. The LCM uses that GUID to locate the configuration information that you want to be applied to the node on the pull server. This enables you to configure multiple servers—for example a multinode web farm—identically by just giving them the same GUID.

A DSC partial configuration is a configuration statement that defines part of a node's overall configuration. This enables you to combine different configuration statements and have DSC add them together as it configures the node. In larger organizations, different teams can determine a part of a node's configuration independently. Partial configurations allow you to deploy the partial configurations from the different teams to the relevant nodes.

In this chapter, you first look at the built-in resources and the basics of DSC deployment. Then you learn how to get more resources, how to set up a pull server, and finally, how to implement partial configurations.

Using DSC and built-in resources

This recipe shows you how to use DSC in **push mode**. With this mode, you create a configuration document on one system—in this case SRV1—and push the configuration to the target node (SRV2). You can also use DSC in **pull mode**, which you look at in greater detail in the *Implementing an SMB DSC pull server* and *Implementing a web-based DSC pull server* recipes.

With pull mode, you create a configuration definition and execute it to produce a MOF file. In this recipe, you use the built-in File resource to specify the files that should be on the target node (and where to find them if they are not).

Getting ready

In this recipe, you examine the Windows Server 2019 built-in resources and use these to create and compile a configuration statement on server SRV1. You use this configuration statement to then deploy the Web-Server feature on a second server, SRV2.

This recipe relies on two files being created and shared from DC1. The two files are Index.Htm and Page2.Htm. These two files are created and shared as \\DC1\ReskitApp. You can use the following code to achieve this, which you can run on SRV1:

```
# Setup for DSC Recipe
# Create folder/share on DC1
$SB = {
  New-Item C:\ReskitApp -ItemType Directory
  New-SMBShare -Name ReskitApp -Path C:\ReskitApp
}
Invoke-Command -ComputerName DC1 -ScriptBlock $SB |
  Out-Null
# Create Index.Htm on DC1
$HP     = '\\DC1.Reskit.Org\C$\ReskitApp\Index.htm'
$P2     = '\\DC1.Reskit.Org\C$\ReskitApp\Page2.htm'

$Index = @"
<!DOCTYPE html>
<html><head><title>
Main Page - ReskitApp Application</title></head>
<body><p><center><b>
HOME PAGE FOR RESKITAPP APPLICATION</b></p>
This is the root page of the RESKITAPP application
<br><hr>
Pushed via DSC</p><br><hr>
```

```
<a href="http://SRV2/ReskitApp/Page2.htm">
Click to View Page 2</a>
</center>
<br><hr></body></html>
"@
$Index |
  Out-File -FilePath $HP -Force
# Create Page2.htm on DC1
$Page2 = @"
<!DOCTYPE html>
<html>
<head><title>ReskitApp Application - Page 2</title></head>
<body><p><center>
<b>Page 2 For the ReskitApp Web Application</b></p>
<a href="http://SRV2/ReskitApp/Index.htm">
Click to Go Home</a>
<hr></body></html>
"@
$Page2 |
  Out-File -FilePath $P2 -Force
```

You can use (and embellish) this code and HTML. Alternatively, the GitHub repository supporting this book has both of these files, which you can download. See `https://github.com/doctordns/PowerShellCookBook2019/tree/master/Chapter%2010%20-%20Implementing%20Desired%20State%20Configuration` for the HTML for these two pages, and for this script, see `https://github.com/doctordns/PowerShellCookBook2019/blob/master/Chapter%2010%20-%20Implementing%20Desired%20State%20Configuration/Setup-DSCWebApp.ps1`.

> The recipe just uses DSC to ensure that these two files reside on SRV2, and if they do not, they are copied from the share on DC1. This recipe does not create a web server on SRV2 or create a website using these two files.

You run this recipe on SRV1.

How to do it...

1. Discover DSC resources on SRV1 using the following code:

```
Get-DscResource |
  Format-Table -Property Name, ModuleName, Version
```

2. Examine the DSC `File` resource using the following code:

```
Get-DscResource -Name File |
    Format-List -Property *
```

3. Get the DSC `File` resource syntax using the following code:

```
Get-DscResource -Name File -Syntax
```

4. Create/compile a configuration block using the following code:

```
Configuration PrepareSRV2 {
    Import-DscResource –ModuleName 'PSDesiredStateConfiguration'
    Node SRV2
    {
      File  BaseFiles
      {
        DestinationPath = 'C:\ReskitApp\'
        SourcePath      = '\\DC1\ReskitApp\'
        Ensure          = 'Present'
        Recurse         = $True
      }
    }
}
```

5. View the configuration function using the following code:

```
Get-Item -Path Function:\PrepareSRV2
```

6. Create an output folder for DSC using the following code:

```
$Conf = {
  $EASC = @{ErrorAction = 'SilentlyContinue'}
  New-Item -Path C:\ReskitApp -ItemType Directory @EASC
}
Invoke-command -ComputerName SRV2 -ScriptBlock $Conf |
    Out-Null
```

7. Run the following function to produce a MOF file:

```
PrepareSRV2 -OutputPath C:\DSC
```

8. View the MOF file, as follows:

```
Get-Content -Path C:\DSC\SRV2.mof
```

9. Make it so, Mr. Riker!

```
Start-DscConfiguration -Path C:\DSC -Wait -Verbose
```

10. Observe the results using the following code:

```
Get-ChildItem -Path '\\SRV2\C$\ReskitApp'
```

11. Induce a configuration drift using the following code:

```
Remove-Item -Path \\SRV2\C$\ReskitApp\Index.htm
```

12. Fix the configuration drift using the following code:

```
Start-DscConfiguration -Path C:\DSC\ -Wait -Verbose
```

13. What happens if there is no configuration drift?

```
Start-DscConfiguration -Path C:\dsc\ -Wait -Verbose
```

How it works...

In *step 1*, you discover the DSC resources on SRV1, which looks like this:

```
PS C:\FOO> Get-DscResource |
            Format-Table -Property Name, ModuleName, Version

Name                         ModuleName                    Version
----                         ----------                    -------
File
SignatureValidation
PackageManagement            PackageManagement             1.0.0.1
PackageManagement            PackageManagement             1.1.7.2
PackageManagementSource      PackageManagement             1.1.7.2
PackageManagementSource      PackageManagement             1.0.0.1
Archive                      PSDesiredStateConfiguration   1.1
Environment                  PSDesiredStateConfiguration   1.1
Group                        PSDesiredStateConfiguration   1.1
GroupSet                     PSDesiredStateConfiguration   1.1
Log                          PSDesiredStateConfiguration   1.1
Package                      PSDesiredStateConfiguration   1.1
ProcessSet                   PSDesiredStateConfiguration   1.1
Registry                     PSDesiredStateConfiguration   1.1
Script                       PSDesiredStateConfiguration   1.1
Service                      PSDesiredStateConfiguration   1.1
ServiceSet                   PSDesiredStateConfiguration   1.1
User                         PSDesiredStateConfiguration   1.1
WaitForAll                   PSDesiredStateConfiguration   1.1
WaitForAny                   PSDesiredStateConfiguration   1.1
WaitForSome                  PSDesiredStateConfiguration   1.1
WindowsFeature               PSDesiredStateConfiguration   1.1
WindowsFeatureSet            PSDesiredStateConfiguration   1.1
WindowsOptionalFeature       PSDesiredStateConfiguration   1.1
WindowsOptionalFeatureSet    PSDesiredStateConfiguration   1.1
WindowsPackageCab            PSDesiredStateConfiguration   1.1
WindowsProcess               PSDesiredStateConfiguration   1.1
```

In *step 2*, you use the `Get-DSCResource` to discover more information about the in-built file DSC resource. The output from this step is shown in the following screenshot:

```
PS C:\Foo> Get-DscResource -Name File |
           Format-List -Property *

ResourceType   : MSFT_FileDirectoryConfiguration
Name           : File
FriendlyName   : File
Module         :
ModuleName     :
Version        :
Path           :
ParentPath     : C:\WINDOWS\system32\Configuration\Schema\MSFT_FileDirectoryConfiguration
ImplementedAs  : Binary
CompanyName    :
Properties     : {DestinationPath, Attributes, Checksum, Contents...}
```

In *step 3*, you use the `Get-DSCResouce` cmdlet to determine the syntax for the `File` DSC resource, as follows:

```
PS C:\Foo> Get-DscResource -Name File -Syntax
File [String] #ResourceName
{
    DestinationPath = [string]
    [Attributes = [string[]]{ Archive | Hidden | ReadOnly | System }]
    [Checksum = [string]{ CreatedDate | ModifiedDate | SHA-1 | SHA-256 | SHA-512 }]
    [Contents = [string]]
    [Credential = [PSCredential]]
    [DependsOn = [string[]]]
    [Ensure = [string]{ Absent | Present }]
    [Force = [bool]]
    [MatchSource = [bool]]
    [PsDscRunAsCredential = [PSCredential]]
    [Recurse = [bool]]
    [SourcePath = [string]]
    [Type = [string]{ Directory | File }]
}
```

In *step 4*, you define a configuration block. When you execute this configuration block, PowerShell compiles it into a function. There is no output from this step.

In *step 5*, you view the function definition for this compiled configuration block, which looks like this:

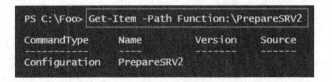

```
PS C:\Foo> Get-Item -Path Function:\PrepareSRV2

CommandType     Name            Version     Source
-----------     ----            -------     ------
Configuration   PrepareSRV2
```

In *step 6*, you create a folder on SRV2. This folder is where you want the DSC process to place the files specified in the configuration block. There is no output from this step.

In *step 7*, you execute the PrepareSRV2 function, which creates a MOF file corresponding to the configuration. The output looks like this:

```
PS C:\Foo> PrepareSRV2 -OutputPath C:\DSC

    Directory: C:\DSC

Mode            LastWriteTime     Length Name
----            -------------     ------ ----
-a----   25/01/2019     20:42       2016 SRV2.mof
```

In *step 8*, you view the MOF file that PowerShell generated in *step 7*, which looks like this:

```
PS C:\Foo> Get-Content -Path C:\DSC\SRV2.mof
/*
@TargetNode='SRV2'
@GeneratedBy=Administrator
@GenerationDate=01/25/2019 20:42:49
@GenerationHost=SRV1
*/
instance of MSFT_FileDirectoryConfiguration as $MSFT_FileDirectoryConfiguration1ref {
ResourceID = "[File]BaseFiles";
 Ensure = "Present";
 DestinationPath = "C:\\ReskitApp\\";
 ModuleName = "PSDesiredStateConfiguration";
 SourceInfo = "::5::5::File";
 Recurse = True;
 SourcePath = "\\\\DC1\\ReskitApp\\";

ModuleVersion = "1.0";

 ConfigurationName = "PrepareSRV2";

};
instance of OMI_ConfigurationDocument {
  Version="2.0.0";
  MinimumCompatibleVersion = "1.0.0";
  CompatibleVersionAdditionalProperties= {"Omi_BaseResource:ConfigurationName"};
  Author="Administrator";
  GenerationDate="01/25/2019 20:42:49";
  GenerationHost="SRV1";
  Name="PrepareSRV2";
};
```

In *step 9*, you push the DSC configuration to SRV2. You use the -Wait and -Verbose switches to create rich output, which looks like this:

```
PS C:\Foo> Start-DscConfiguration -Path C:\DSC -Wait -Verbose

VERBOSE: Perform operation 'Invoke CimMethod' with following parameters,
      'methodName' = SendConfigurationApply,'className' = MSFT_DSCLocalConfigurationManager,
      'namespaceName' = root/Microsoft/Windows/DesiredStateConfiguration'.
VERBOSE: An LCM method call arrived from computer SRV1 with user sid S-1-5-21-3496687451-3124355039-3783943179-500.
VERBOSE: [SRV2]: LCM:   [ Start  Set      ]
VERBOSE: [SRV2]: LCM:   [ Start  Resource ] [[File]BaseFiles]
VERBOSE: [SRV2]: LCM:   [ Start  Test     ] [[File]BaseFiles]
VERBOSE: [SRV2]:                            [[File]BaseFiles] The system cannot find the file specified.
VERBOSE: [SRV2]:                            [[File]BaseFiles] The related file/directory is: \\DC1\ReskitApp.
VERBOSE: [SRV2]:                            [[File]BaseFiles] Building file list from cache.
VERBOSE: [SRV2]: LCM:   [ End    Test     ] [[File]BaseFiles]  in 0.1100 seconds.
VERBOSE: [SRV2]: LCM:   [ Start  Set      ] [[File]BaseFiles]
VERBOSE: [SRV2]:                            [[File]BaseFiles] The system cannot find the file specified.
VERBOSE: [SRV2]:                            [[File]BaseFiles] The related file/directory is: \\DC1\ReskitApp.
VERBOSE: [SRV2]:                            [[File]BaseFiles] Building file list from cache.
VERBOSE: [SRV2]:                            [[File]BaseFiles] Copying file \\DC1\ReskitApp\Index.htm to C:\ReskitApp\Index.htm.
VERBOSE: [SRV2]:                            [[File]BaseFiles] Copying file \\DC1\ReskitApp\Page2.htm to C:\ReskitApp\Page2.htm.
VERBOSE: [SRV2]: LCM:   [ End    Set      ] [[File]BaseFiles]  in 0.0620 seconds.
VERBOSE: [SRV2]: LCM:   [ End    Resource ] [[File]BaseFiles]
VERBOSE: [SRV2]: LCM:   [ End    Set      ]
VERBOSE: [SRV2]: LCM:   [ End    Set      ]      in  0.6900 seconds.
VERBOSE: Operation 'Invoke CimMethod' complete.
VERBOSE: Time taken for configuration job to complete is 1.007 seconds
```

After pushing the new configuration to SRV2 in *step 9* and *step 10*, you examine the effect. The output from this step looks like this:

```
PS C:\Foo> Get-ChildItem -Path '\\SRV2\C$\ReskitApp'

    Directory: \\SRV2\C$\ReskitApp

Mode                LastWriteTime     Length Name
----                -------------     ------ ----
-a----    25/01/2019     20:18        688 Index.htm
-a----    25/01/2019     20:18        352 Page2.htm
```

In *step 11*, you delete a file on SRV2, thereby introducing configuration drift. This step produces no output. With step 12, you rerun Start-DSCConfiguration to correct the configuration drift, which looks this:

```
PS C:\Foo> Start-DscConfiguration -Path C:\DSC\ -Wait -Verbose

VERBOSE: Perform operation 'Invoke CimMethod' with following parameters,
                'methodName' = SendConfigurationApply,'className' = MSFT_DSCLocalConfigurationManager,
                'namespaceName' = root/Microsoft/Windows/DesiredStateConfiguration'.
VERBOSE: An LCM method call arrived from computer SRV1 with user sid S-1-5-21-3496687451-3124355039-3783943179-500.
VERBOSE: [SRV2]: LCM:   [ Start  Set      ]
VERBOSE: [SRV2]: LCM:   [ Start  Resource ] [[File]BaseFiles]
VERBOSE: [SRV2]: LCM:   [ Start  Test     ] [[File]BaseFiles]
VERBOSE: [SRV2]:                            [[File]BaseFiles] The system cannot find the file specified.
VERBOSE: [SRV2]:                            [[File]BaseFiles] The related file/directory is: \\DC1\ReskitApp.
VERBOSE: [SRV2]:                            [[File]BaseFiles] Building file list from cache.
VERBOSE: [SRV2]: LCM:   [ End    Test     ] [[File]BaseFiles]  in 0.0310 seconds.
VERBOSE: [SRV2]: LCM:   [ Start  Set      ] [[File]BaseFiles]
VERBOSE: [SRV2]:                            [[File]BaseFiles] The system cannot find the file specified.
VERBOSE: [SRV2]:                            [[File]BaseFiles] The related file/directory is: \\DC1\ReskitApp.
VERBOSE: [SRV2]:                            [[File]BaseFiles] Building file list from cache.
VERBOSE: [SRV2]:                            [[File]BaseFiles] Copying file \\DC1\ReskitApp\Index.htm to C:\ReskitApp\Index.htm.
VERBOSE: [SRV2]:                            [[File]BaseFiles] The destination object was found and no action is required.
VERBOSE: [SRV2]: LCM:   [ End    Set      ] [[File]BaseFiles]  in 0.0320 seconds.
VERBOSE: [SRV2]: LCM:   [ End    Resource ] [[File]BaseFiles]
VERBOSE: [SRV2]: LCM:   [ End    Set      ]
VERBOSE: [SRV2]: LCM:   [ End    Set      ]      in  0.2810 seconds.
VERBOSE: Operation 'Invoke CimMethod' complete.
VERBOSE: Time taken for configuration job to complete is 0.446 seconds
```

In *step 13*, you observe the results of running Start-DSCResource in the case where there is no configuration drift. This looks like the following:

```
PS C:\Foo> Start-DscConfiguration -Path C:\DSC\ -Wait -Verbose

VERBOSE: Perform operation 'Invoke CimMethod' with following parameters,
                            ''methodName' = SendConfigurationApply,
                            'className' = MSFT_DSCLocalConfigurationManager,
                            'namespaceName' = root/Microsoft/Windows/DesiredStateConfiguration'.
VERBOSE: An LCM method call arrived from computer SRV1 with user sid S-1-5-21-3496687451-3124355039-3783943179-500.
VERBOSE: [SRV2]: LCM:  [ Start  Set      ]
VERBOSE: [SRV2]: LCM:  [ Start  Resource ] [[File]BaseFiles]
VERBOSE: [SRV2]: LCM:  [ Start  Test     ] [[File]BaseFiles]
VERBOSE: [SRV2]:                            [[File]BaseFiles] The system cannot find the file specified.
VERBOSE: [SRV2]:                            [[File]BaseFiles] The related file/directory is: \\DC1\ReskitApp.
VERBOSE: [SRV2]:                            [[File]BaseFiles] Building file list from cache.
VERBOSE: [SRV2]:                            [[File]BaseFiles] The destination object was found and no action is required.
VERBOSE: [SRV2]: LCM:  [ End    Test     ] [[File]BaseFiles]  in 0.0310 seconds.
VERBOSE: [SRV2]: LCM:  [ Skip   Set      ] [[File]BaseFiles]
VERBOSE: [SRV2]: LCM:  [ End    Resource ] [[File]BaseFiles]
VERBOSE: [SRV2]: LCM:  [ End    Set      ]
VERBOSE: [SRV2]: LCM:  [ End    Set      ]      in  0.1250 seconds.
VERBOSE: Operation 'Invoke CimMethod' complete.
VERBOSE: Time taken for configuration job to complete is 0.213 seconds
```

There's more...

In this recipe, you push the DSC configuration to the target node (SRV2) using the Start-DscConfiguration cmdlet. Using the -Wait and -Verbose switches produces some great output that helps you to trace precisely what DSC is doing. In *step 9*, DSC could not find the files on SRV2, and so it copies them from DC1. In *step 12*, DSC discovers a missing file and corrects that.

With Start-DscConfiguration, if you do not specify the -Wait switch, PowerShell runs the DSC configuration silently as a background job. If you do not specify the -Verbose switch specified, PowerShell produces minimal output. You should use both parameters when you are learning DSC.

In *step 1*, you discover the DSC resources on SRV1. As you can see, there are not many built into Windows Server 2019. The good news is that there is a wealth of additional DSC resources that you can leverage, as you can see in the *Using DSC with resources from the PS Gallery* recipe.

In *step 4*, when you execute the configuration block, PowerShell compiles in a similar way to how PowerShell compiles a function. With configurations, PowerShell creates a function of the same name, as you can see in *step 5*.

In *step 8*, you view the MOF generated by running the function created by running the configuration. Fortunately, IT pros do not need to understand the MOF file format as it is automatically generated by PowerShell. Further, PowerShell uses the MOF file to apply the DSC configuration on the target node. All you need to do is to keep track of the MOF files themselves.

Parameterizing DSC configuration

As with functions, you can create configuration blocks with parameters. These enable you to produce different MOF files by varying the parameter values that are used when you execute the configuration.

For example, suppose you wanted to add a feature to a node. You could create a specific configuration where you hard code the feature name and the node name. This is not dissimilar to how you copied specific files from DC1 to SRV1 in the *Using DSC and built-in resources* recipe.

With parameterization, you create a configuration that takes the node name and the service name as parameters. When you run the configuration, PowerShell creates a MOF file that adds the specified service to the specified node. This recipe demonstrates that approach.

This approach throws up the problem that, by default, you can only send a single MOF file to a given node; therefore, if you used the earlier recipe and copied files to SRV2, attempting to send a second MOF file to the system results in an error. There are three solutions to this, as described in the following list:

▸ Have a single MOF file generated for each target node. This means larger MOF files, and files that are used for larger organizations sometimes require hard-to-achieve coordination between the different groups that create the overall configuration for a node.

▸ Use DSC partial configurations, which enables you to send multiple configurations to a node. You configure the node to pull different configuration blocks from potentially multiple DSC pull servers, and then the DSC's local configuration manager combines and then applies them. The *Using DSC partial configuration* recipe shows you how to use partial configurations.

▸ Push a configuration to a node, remove the node's MOF files, and send another configuration. This recipe demonstrates this—you remove the MOF files on SRV2 that DSC created when you pushed the configuration. By removing the files from the node, DSC is happy to apply another configuration.

Getting ready

This recipe uses SRV1 and SRV2, as configured in the *Using DSC and built-in resources* recipe.

How to do it...

1. Check the status of DNS on SRV2 using the following code:

```
Get-WindowsFeature DNS -ComputerName SRV2
```

2. Create a configuration document using the following code:

```
Configuration ProvisionServices
{
  param (
    [Parameter(Mandatory=$true)]  $NodeName,
    [Parameter(Mandatory=$true)]  $FeatureName
  )
Import-DscResource -ModuleName 'PSDesiredStateConfiguration'
Node $NodeName  {
  WindowsFeature $FeatureName   {
      Name                = $FeatureName
      Ensure              = 'Present'
      IncludeAllSubFeature = $true
  } # End Windows Feature
  }  # End Node configuration
}   # End of Configuration document
```

3. Ensure that an empty DSC folder exists, then create MOF file using the following code:

```
$NIHT = @{
  Path        = 'C:\DSC '
  ItemType    = 'Directory'
  ErrorAction = 'SilentlyContinue'
}
New-Item  @NIHT| Out-Null
Get-ChildItem -Path C:\DSC | Remove-Item -Force | Out-Null
```

4. Clear any existing configuration documents on SRV2 using the following code:

```
$RIHT =@{
  Path        = '\\SRV2\C$\Windows\System32\configuration\*.mof'
  ErrorAction = 'SilentlyContinue'
}
Get-Childitem '\\SRV2\C$\Windows\System32\configuration\*.MOF' |
  Remove-Item @RIHT -Force
```

5. Now run the `ProvisionServices` function to create the MOF to provision DNS on SRV2, using the following code:

```
$PSHT = @{
   OutputPath  = 'C:\DSC'
   NodeName    = 'SRV2'
   FeatureName = 'DNS'
}
ProvisionServices @PSHT
```

6. And make it so:

```
Start-DscConfiguration -Path C:\DSC -Wait -Verbose
```

7. Check the results on SRV2 using the following code:

```
Get-Service -Name DNS -ComputerName SRV2
```

How it works...

In *step 1*, you check to see whether the DNS server service is installed on SRV2. The output showing that DNS is not installed looks like this:

In *step 2*, you create a parameterized configuration (`ProvisionServices`) that takes a feature name and a node name as parameters. In *step 3*, you ensure that C:\DSC is created on SRV1 and is empty (that is, with no MOF files left over from earlier recipes!). In *step 4*, you clear out any MOF files on SRV2. These steps produce no output.

In *step 5*, you create a MOF file, specifying the name of the feature (DNS) you wish to install on the node (SRV2). The output looks like this:

```
PS C:\Foo> $PSHT = @{
               OutputPath  = 'C:\DSC'
               NodeName    = 'SRV2'
               FeatureName = 'DNS'
           }
PS C:\Foo> $ProvisionServices @PSHT

     Directory: C:\DSC

Mode                 LastWriteTime         Length Name
----                 -------------         ------ ----
-a----     26/01/2019     13:24              1914 SRV2.mof
```

In *step 6*, you use `Start-DscConfiguration` to push the configuration to SRV2, which
looks like this:

```
PS C:\Foo> Start-DscConfiguration -Path C:\DSC -Wait -Verbose

VERBOSE: Perform operation 'Invoke CimMethod' with following parameters,
                       'methodName' = SendConfigurationApply,'className' = MSFT_DSCLocalConfigurationManager,
                       'namespaceName' = root/Microsoft/Windows/DesiredStateConfiguration'.
VERBOSE: An LCM method call arrived from computer SRV1 with user sid S-1-5-21-3496687451-3124355039-3783943179-500.
VERBOSE: [SRV2]: LCM:  [ Start  Set      ]
VERBOSE: [SRV2]: LCM:  [ Start  Resource ]  [[WindowsFeature]DNS]
VERBOSE: [SRV2]: LCM:  [ Start  Test     ]  [[WindowsFeature]DNS]
VERBOSE: [SRV2]:                             [[WindowsFeature]DNS] The operation 'Get-WindowsFeature' started: DNS
VERBOSE: [SRV2]:                             [[WindowsFeature]DNS] The operation 'Get-WindowsFeature' succeeded: DNS
VERBOSE: [SRV2]: LCM:  [ End    Test     ]  [[WindowsFeature]DNS]  in 1.9530 seconds.
VERBOSE: [SRV2]: LCM:  [ Start  Set      ]  [[WindowsFeature]DNS]
VERBOSE: [SRV2]:                             [[WindowsFeature]DNS] Installation started...
VERBOSE: [SRV2]:                             [[WindowsFeature]DNS] Continue with installation?
VERBOSE: [SRV2]:                             [[WindowsFeature]DNS] Prerequisite processing started...
VERBOSE: [SRV2]:                             [[WindowsFeature]DNS] Prerequisite processing succeeded.
VERBOSE: [SRV2]:                             [[WindowsFeature]DNS] Installation succeeded.
VERBOSE: [SRV2]:                             [[WindowsFeature]DNS] Successfully installed the feature DNS.
VERBOSE: [SRV2]: LCM:  [ End    Set      ]  [[WindowsFeature]DNS]  in 27.9380 seconds.
VERBOSE: [SRV2]: LCM:  [ End    Resource ]  [[WindowsFeature]DNS]
VERBOSE: [SRV2]: LCM:  [ End    Set      ]
VERBOSE: [SRV2]: LCM:  [ End    Set      ]  in  30.8710 seconds.
VERBOSE: Operation 'Invoke CimMethod' complete.
VERBOSE: Time taken for configuration job to complete is 31.03 seconds
```

In the final step, *step 7*, you recheck the DNS Server service on SRV2 to find out whether it
is installed and running, which looks like this:

```
PS C:\Foo> Get-Service -Name DNS -ComputerName SRV2

Status   Name      DisplayName
------   ----      -----------
Running  DNS       DNS Server
```

There's more...

In *step 2*, you create a simple parameterized configuration statement. This configuration takes
two parameters: a feature name and a node name. The purpose of the configuration block is
to add a named feature (for example, DNS) to a named node (SRV2). With this configuration,
you can create the necessary MOF file to add any feature to any node.

In *step 4*, you clear any previously created MOF files from `SRV2`. If you delete a previously pushed MOF file, the configuration set by those configuration MOF files does not change. This enables you to use `SRV2` to test different configurations or multiple DSC recipes.

Finding and installing DSC resources

A DSC resource is a specially crafted PowerShell module that enables DSC to configure various aspects of a node. The `WindowsFeature` DSC resource, for example, enables you to ensure that a particular node has a particular Windows feature installed. You can also specify that a particular Windows feature should not be present (in which case, DSC removes the feature if it were already installed).

As you saw in the *Using DSC and built-in resources* recipe, Microsoft does not ship very many DSC resources natively with Windows Server 2019. This is intentional—you use the PowerShell Gallery to get the DSC resources you need to do your job and not hundreds or thousands of DSC resources you never need.

The built-in DSC resources with Windows Server 2019 do not provide broad coverage, and are not sufficient for most organizations. For example, you can use the built-in `File` resource to copy the source files for a small web application onto a new server, as you did in the *Using DSC and built-in resources* recipe. But the built-in resources do not allow you to specify the application's settings (what the application's name is, which application pool it runs in, and so on). This is where add-on DSC resources from the PS Gallery come in.

In this recipe, you use the PS Gallery to find, install, and explore third-party DSC resources. In the next recipe, *Using DSC with resources from PS Gallery*, you use the newly installed resources.

Getting ready

In this recipe, you find, download, and install DSC resources.

How to do it...

1. Find available repositories using the following code:

    ```
    Get-PSRepository
    ```

2. See what DSC resources you can find using the following code:

    ```
    Find-DscResource -Repository 'PSGallery' |
      Measure-Object
    ```

3. See what IIS-related resources might exist using the following code:

```
Find-DscResource |
  Where-Object ModuleName -match 'web|iis' |
    Select-Object -Property ModuleName, Version -Unique |
      Sort-Object -Property ModuleName
```

4. Examine the xWebAdministration module using the following code:

```
Find-DscResource -ModuleName 'xWebAdministration'
```

5. Install the xWebAdministration module (on SRV1) using the following code:

```
Install-Module -Name 'xWebAdministration' -Force
```

6. See the local module details using the following code:

```
Get-Module -Name xWebAdministration -ListAvailable
```

7. See what DSC resources are contained in the module using the following code:

```
Get-DscResource -Module xWebAdministration
```

8. Examine what is in the module using the following code:

```
$Mod = Get-Module -Name xWebAdministration -ListAvailable
$P   = $Mod.Path
$FP  = Split-Path -Parent $P
Get-ChildItem -Path $FP, $FP\DSCResources
```

How it works...

In *step 1*, you examine any configured repositories on your system. Depending on the recipes you have performed on SRV1, the output of this step looks like this:

```
PS C:\Foo> Get-PSRepository

Name        InstallationPolicy   SourceLocation
----        ------------------   --------------
PSGallery   Trusted              https://www.powershellgallery.com/api/v2/
RKRepo      Trusted              \\SRV1\RKRepo
```

In *step 2*, you use the `Find-DSCResource` cmdlet to examine how many DSC resources are in the gallery (at the time of writing!), which looks like this:

```
PS C:\Foo> Find-DscResource -Repository 'PSGallery' |
              Measure-Object

Count     : 1371
Average   :
Sum       :
Maximum   :
Minimum   :
Property  :
```

In *step 3*, you query the PS Gallery to find DSC resources that might be helpful to manage IIS. The output looks like this:

```
PS C:\Foo> Find-DscResource |
              Where-Object ModuleName -match 'web|iis' |
                Select-Object -Property ModuleName,Version -Unique |
                  Sort-Object -Property ModuleName

ModuleName                         Version
----------                         -------
cAspNetIisRegistration             1.0.0
cEPRSDeployAzureWebsite            1.0
cEPRSWebDirProperties              1.0
cEPRSWebProperties                 1.0
cIBMWebSphereAppServer             1.1.3
cIBMWebSpherePortal                1.0.1
cWebManagementService              1.0.1
DSCPullServerWeb                   1.1.0
PSWebAccessAuthorization           0.5.0.0
WebAdministrationDsc               0.1.0.0
WebApplicationProxyDSC             1.1.0.0
xIISApplicationPoolIdentityType    1.0.0.2
xIISCertSBinding                   1.0.0.1
xIISMachineKey                     1.0.0.1
xIISMail                           1.0.0.1
xIISSession                        1.0.0.0
xIISWebBinding                     1.0.0.1
xWebAdministration                 2.4.0.0
xWebDeploy                         1.2.0.0
```

In *step 4*, you look at the DSC resources in the `xWebAdministration` module on the PS Gallery. The output looks like this:

```
PS C:\Foo> Find-DscResource -ModuleName 'xWebAdministration'

Name                            Version  ModuleName         Repository
----                            -------  ----------         ----------
WebApplicationHandler           2.4.0.0  xWebAdministration PSGallery
xIisFeatureDelegation           2.4.0.0  xWebAdministration PSGallery
xIisHandler                     2.4.0.0  xWebAdministration PSGallery
xIisLogging                     2.4.0.0  xWebAdministration PSGallery
xIisMimeTypeMapping             2.4.0.0  xWebAdministration PSGallery
xIisModule                      2.4.0.0  xWebAdministration PSGallery
xSSLSettings                    2.4.0.0  xWebAdministration PSGallery
xWebApplication                 2.4.0.0  xWebAdministration PSGallery
xWebAppPool                     2.4.0.0  xWebAdministration PSGallery
xWebAppPoolDefaults             2.4.0.0  xWebAdministration PSGallery
xWebConfigKeyValue              2.4.0.0  xWebAdministration PSGallery
xWebConfigProperty              2.4.0.0  xWebAdministration PSGallery
xWebConfigPropertyCollection    2.4.0.0  xWebAdministration PSGallery
xWebsite                        2.4.0.0  xWebAdministration PSGallery
xWebSiteDefaults                2.4.0.0  xWebAdministration PSGallery
xWebVirtualDirectory            2.4.0.0  xWebAdministration PSGallery
```

In *step 5*, you install the module on SRV1. This step produces no output. In *step 6*, you examine the details of the newly installed module, which looks like this:

```
PS C:\Foo> Get-Module -Name xWebAdministration -ListAvailable

    Directory: C:\Program Files\WindowsPowerShell\Modules

ModuleType Version   Name                 ExportedCommands
---------- -------   ----                 ----------------
Manifest   2.4.0.0   xWebAdministration
```

In *step 7*, you use the Get-DscResource cmdlet to discover the specific DSC resources contained in the xWebAdministration module, which looks like this:

```
PS C:\Foo> Get-DscResource -Module xWebAdministration

ImplementedAs  Name                    ModuleName          Version  Properties
-------------  ----                    ----------          -------  ----------
PowerShell     WebApplicationHandler   xWebAdministration  2.4.0.0  {Name, Path, AllowPathInfo, DependsOn...}
PowerShell     xIisFeatureDelegation   xWebAdministration  2.4.0.0  {Filter, OverrideMode, Path, DependsOn...}
PowerShell     xIisHandler             xWebAdministration  2.4.0.0  {Ensure, Name, DependsOn, PsDscRunAsCredential}
PowerShell     xIisLogging             xWebAdministration  2.4.0.0  {LogPath, DependsOn, LogCustomFields, LogFlags...}
PowerShell     xIisMimeTypeMapping     xWebAdministration  2.4.0.0  {ConfigurationPath, Ensure, Extension, MimeType...
PowerShell     xIisModule              xWebAdministration  2.4.0.0  {Name, Path, RequestPath, Verb...}
PowerShell     xSSLSettings            xWebAdministration  2.4.0.0  {Bindings, Name, DependsOn, Ensure...}
PowerShell     xWebApplication         xWebAdministration  2.4.0.0  {Name, PhysicalPath, WebAppPool, Website...}
PowerShell     xWebAppPool             xWebAdministration  2.4.0.0  {Name, autoShutdownExe, autoShutdownParams, aut...
PowerShell     xWebAppPoolDefaults     xWebAdministration  2.4.0.0  {ApplyTo, DependsOn, IdentityType, ManagedRunti...
PowerShell     xWebConfigKeyValue      xWebAdministration  2.4.0.0  {ConfigSection, Key, WebsitePath, DependsOn...}
PowerShell     xWebConfigProperty      xWebAdministration  2.4.0.0  {Filter, PropertyName, WebsitePath, DependsOn...}
PowerShell     xWebConfigPropertyC...  xWebAdministration  2.4.0.0  {CollectionName, Filter, ItemKeyName, ItemKeyVa...
PowerShell     xWebsite                xWebAdministration  2.4.0.0  {Name, ApplicationPool, ApplicationType, Authen...
PowerShell     xWebSiteDefaults        xWebAdministration  2.4.0.0  {ApplyTo, AllowSubDirConfig, DefaultApplication...
PowerShell     xWebVirtualDirectory    xWebAdministration  2.4.0.0  {Name, PhysicalPath, WebApplication, Website...}
```

In the last step, *step 8,* you view the files that make up the xWebAdministration module. The output looks like this:

```
PS C:\Foo> $Mod = Get-Module -Name xWebAdministration -ListAvailable
PS C:\Foo> $P   = $Mod.Path
PS C:\Foo> $FP  = Split-Path -Parent $P
PS C:\Foo> Get-ChildItem -Path $FP, $FP\DSCResources

    Directory: C:\Program Files\WindowsPowerShell\Modules\xWebAdministration\2.4.0.0

Mode            LastWriteTime     Length Name
----            -------------     ------ ----
d-----     26/01/2019     19:51          DSCResources
d-----     26/01/2019     19:51          Examples
d-----     26/01/2019     19:51          Tests
-a----     10/01/2019     00:23     4704 HighQualityResourceKitPlan.md
-a----     10/01/2019     00:23     1108 LICENSE
-a----     10/01/2019     00:23    66323 README.md
-a----     10/01/2019     00:23     1856 xWebAdministration.psd1

    Directory: C:\Program Files\WindowsPowerShell\Modules\xWebAdministration\2.4.0.0\DSCResources

Mode            LastWriteTime     Length Name
----            -------------     ------ ----
d-----     26/01/2019     19:51          MSFT_WebApplicationHandler
d-----     26/01/2019     19:51          MSFT_xIisFeatureDelegation
d-----     26/01/2019     19:51          MSFT_xIIsHandler
d-----     26/01/2019     19:51          MSFT_xIisLogging
d-----     26/01/2019     19:51          MSFT_xIisMimeTypeMapping
d-----     26/01/2019     19:51          MSFT_xIisModule
d-----     26/01/2019     19:51          MSFT_xSSLSettings
d-----     26/01/2019     19:51          MSFT_xWebApplication
d-----     26/01/2019     19:51          MSFT_xWebAppPool
d-----     26/01/2019     19:51          MSFT_xWebAppPoolDefaults
d-----     26/01/2019     19:51          MSFT_xWebConfigKeyValue
d-----     26/01/2019     19:51          MSFT_xWebConfigProperty
d-----     26/01/2019     19:51          MSFT_xWebConfigPropertyCollection
d-----     26/01/2019     19:51          MSFT_xWebsite
d-----     26/01/2019     19:51          MSFT_xWebSiteDefaults
d-----     26/01/2019     19:51          MSFT_xWebVirtualDirectory
-a----     10/01/2019     00:23     7454 Helper.psm1
```

There's more...

This recipe describes how to obtain DSC resources from the PowerShell Gallery repository, but there are many other places that you can find DSC resources. One other repository you might consider is Chocolatey (https://www.chocolatey.org).

In *step 3*, you query the PS Gallery to discover DSC resources that might be useful. In this step, you find any DSC resource whose name contains either web or iis. Depending on what DSC resource you are looking for, you may need to adjust this regular expression string.

In *step 8*, you view the files that make up the xWebAdministration module. To learn more about how to develop DSC resources, you should examine the files in this module in more detail.

See also

In *step 8*, you examine the files making up the `xWebAdministration` module. For more information about what is inside a DSC resource module, see `https://docs.microsoft.com/en-us/powershell/dsc/resources/resources`.

If you cannot find the DSC resources you need, you can always create your own customized resources. There are two main methods that IT pros can use to write their own resources. You can use the traditional approach, where you both write the PowerShell code and create a MOF schema. With PowerShell 5, Microsoft introduced a much simpler method of creating a DSC resource based on PowerShell classes. For more details about the older mechanism, see `https://docs.microsoft.com/en-us/powershell/dsc/resources/authoringresourcemof`, and for more details about creating a DSC resource using PowerShell classes, see `https://docs.microsoft.com/en-us/powershell/dsc/resources/authoringresourceclass`. And finally, for the hard core folks, you can implement the resource in C# (`https://docs.microsoft.com/en-us/powershell/dsc/resources/authoringresourcemofcs`).

If you do decide to develop your own DSC resources, take a look at using the **Resource Designer** tool—a set of cmdlets that make creating DSC resources easier. See `https://docs.microsoft.com/en-us/powershell/dsc/resources/authoringresourcemofdesigner` for more details about this tool.

Using DSC with resources from PS Gallery

In the *Finding and installing DSC resources* recipe, you discovered and installed some additional DSC resources. The `xWebAdministration` module you installed contains a number of DSC resources that enable you to define the configuration of an IIS website.

In this recipe, you are going to make use of this module to create, configure, and view a new website on `SRV2`, based on the files created in the *Using DSC and built-in resources* recipe. This recipe uses the DSC resources contained in the `xWebAdministration` module (which you downloaded in the *Finding and installing DSC resources* recipe).

Getting ready

In this recipe, you use `SRV1` to manage DSC resources and configurations, `SRV2` as the target node that DSC is going to control, and `DC1` as both the DC in the domain and the source of the initial files that make up the application you deploy. You run this recipe on `SRV1`.

How to do it...

1. Copy the `xWebAdministration` module to `SRV2` using the following code:

```
$CIHT = @{
  Path        = 'C:\Program Files\WindowsPowerShell\' +
                'Modules\xWebAdministration'
  Destination = '\\SRV2\C$\Program Files\WindowsPowerShell\'+
                'Modules'
  Recurse     = $True
}
Copy-Item @CIHT
```

2. Clear any existing configuration documents on `SRV2` and local MOF files on `SRV1` using the following code:

```
$RIHT =@{
  Path        = '\\SRV2\C$\Windows\System32\configuration\*.mof'
  ErrorAction = 'SilentlyContinue'
}
Get-Childitem @RIHT |
  Remove-Item @RIHT -Force
Remove-Item C:\DSC\* -Recurse -Force
```

3. Create a new configuration document based on DSC resources in the `xWebAdministration` module using the following code:

```
Configuration  RKAppSRV2 {
  Import-DscResource -ModuleName xWebAdministration
  Import-DscResource -ModuleName PSDesiredStateConfiguration
  Node SRV2 {
    Windowsfeature IISSRV2 {
      Ensure = 'Present'
      Name = 'Web-Server'
    }
    Windowsfeature IISSrvTools {
      Ensure = 'Present'
      Name = 'Web-Mgmt-Tools'
      DependsOn = '[WindowsFeature] IISSRV2'
    }
    File RKAppFiles {
      Ensure = 'Present'
      Checksum = 'ModifiedDate'
      Sourcepath = '\\DC1\ReskitApp\'
      Type = 'Directory'
```

```
        Recurse = $true
        DestinationPath = 'C:\ReskitApp\'
        DependsOn = '[Windowsfeature]IISSRV2'
        MatchSource = $true
      }
    xWebAppPool ReskitAppPool {
      Name = 'RKAppPool'
      Ensure = 'Present'
      State = 'Started'
      DependsOn = '[File]RKAppFiles'
      }
    xWebApplication ReskitAppPool {
      Website = 'Default Web Site'
      WebAppPool = 'RKAppPool'
      Name = 'ReskitApp'
      PhysicalPath = 'C:\ReskitApp\'
      Ensure = 'Present'
      DependsOn = '[xWebAppPool]ReskitAppPool'
      }
    Log Completed {
      Message = 'Finished Configuring ReskitAp via DSC'
      }
    } # End of SRV2 Configuration
} # End of Configuration
```

4. Run the configuration block to compile it to C:\DSC on SRV1 using the following code:

```
RKAppSRV2 -OutputPath C:\DSC
```

5. Deploy the configuration to SRV2 using the following code:

```
Start-DscConfiguration -Path C:\DSC  -Verbose -Wait
```

6. Test the result using the following code:

```
Start-Process 'HTTP://SRV2.Reskit.Org/ReskitApp/'
```

How it works...

In *step 1*, you copy the xAdministration module to SRV2, then in *step 2*, you clear out any MOF files on SRV2 and SRV1. These two steps produce no output.

In *step 3*, you create a configuration document, `RKAppSRV2`. This step also produces no screen output.

In *step 4*, you create the MOF file for this recipe by executing the `RKAppSRV2` function, which should yield the output shown in the following screenshot:

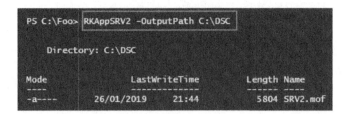

In *step 5*, you deploy this new configuration to `SRV2` using the `-Wait` and `-Verbose` switches, producing an output like the following:

```
PS C:\Foo> Start-DSCConfiguration -Path C:\DSC -Verbose -Wait

VERBOSE: Perform operation 'Invoke CimMethod' with following parameters, ''methodName' = SendConfigurationApply,
                                                                            'className' = MSFT_DSCLocalConfigurationManager,
                                                                            'namespaceName' = root/Microsoft/Windows/DesiredStateConfiguration'.
VERBOSE: An LCM method call arrived from computer SRV1 with user sid S-1-5-21-3496687451-3124355039-3783943179-500.
VERBOSE: [SRV2]: LCM:  [ Start  Set     ]
VERBOSE: [SRV2]: LCM:  [ Start  Resource ]  [[WindowsFeature]IISSrv2]
VERBOSE: [SRV2]: LCM:  [ Start  Test     ]  [[WindowsFeature]IISSrv2]
VERBOSE: [SRV2]:                            [[WindowsFeature]IISSrv2]  The operation 'Get-WindowsFeature' started: Web-Server
VERBOSE: [SRV2]:                            [[WindowsFeature]IISSrv2]  The operation 'Get-WindowsFeature' succeeded: Web-Server
VERBOSE: [SRV2]: LCM:  [ End    Test     ]  [[WindowsFeature]IISSrv2]  in 1.3750 seconds.
VERBOSE: [SRV2]: LCM:  [ Start  Set      ]  [[WindowsFeature]IISSrv2]
VERBOSE: [SRV2]:                            [[WindowsFeature]IISSrv2]  Installation started...
VERBOSE: [SRV2]:                            [[WindowsFeature]IISSrv2]  Continue with installation?
VERBOSE: [SRV2]:                            [[WindowsFeature]IISSrv2]  Prerequisite processing started...
VERBOSE: [SRV2]:                            [[WindowsFeature]IISSrv2]  Prerequisite processing succeeded.
VERBOSE: [SRV2]:                            [[WindowsFeature]IISSrv2]  Installation succeeded.
VERBOSE: [SRV2]:                            [[WindowsFeature]IISSrv2]  Successfully installed the feature Web-Server.
VERBOSE: [SRV2]: LCM:  [ End    Set      ]  [[WindowsFeature]IISSrv2]  in 54.7750 seconds.
VERBOSE: [SRV2]: LCM:  [ End    Resource ]  [[WindowsFeature]IISSrv2]
VERBOSE: [SRV2]: LCM:  [ Start  Resource ]  [[WindowsFeature]IISSrvTools]
VERBOSE: [SRV2]: LCM:  [ Start  Test     ]  [[WindowsFeature]IISSrvTools]
VERBOSE: [SRV2]:                            [[WindowsFeature]IISSrvTools]  The operation 'Get-WindowsFeature' started: Web-Mgmt-Tools
VERBOSE: [SRV2]:                            [[WindowsFeature]IISSrvTools]  The operation 'Get-WindowsFeature' succeeded: Web-Mgmt-Tools
VERBOSE: [SRV2]: LCM:  [ End    Test     ]  [[WindowsFeature]IISSrvTools]  in 1.7810 seconds.
VERBOSE: [SRV2]: LCM:  [ Start  Set      ]  [[WindowsFeature]IISSrvTools]
VERBOSE: [SRV2]:                            [[WindowsFeature]IISSrvTools]  Installation started...
VERBOSE: [SRV2]:                            [[WindowsFeature]IISSrvTools]  Continue with installation?
VERBOSE: [SRV2]:                            [[WindowsFeature]IISSrvTools]  Prerequisite processing started...
VERBOSE: [SRV2]:                            [[WindowsFeature]IISSrvTools]  Prerequisite processing succeeded.
VERBOSE: [SRV2]:                            [[WindowsFeature]IISSrvTools]  Installation succeeded.
VERBOSE: [SRV2]:                            [[WindowsFeature]IISSrvTools]  Successfully installed the feature Web-Mgmt-Tools.
VERBOSE: [SRV2]: LCM:  [ End    Set      ]  [[WindowsFeature]IISSrvTools]  in 29.4140 seconds.
VERBOSE: [SRV2]: LCM:  [ End    Resource ]  [[WindowsFeature]IISSrvTools]
VERBOSE: [SRV2]: LCM:  [ Start  Resource ]  [[File]RKAppFiles]
VERBOSE: [SRV2]: LCM:  [ Start  Test     ]  [[File]RKAppFiles]
VERBOSE: [SRV2]:                            [[File]RKAppFiles]  The system cannot find the file specified.
VERBOSE: [SRV2]:                            [[File]RKAppFiles]  The related file/directory is: \\DC1\ReskitApp.
VERBOSE: [SRV2]:                            [[File]RKAppFiles]  Building file list without using cache.
VERBOSE: [SRV2]:                            [[File]RKAppFiles]  The destination object was found and no action is required.
VERBOSE: [SRV2]: LCM:  [ End    Test     ]  [[File]RKAppFiles]  in 0.0940 seconds.
VERBOSE: [SRV2]: LCM:  [ Skip   Set      ]  [[File]RKAppFiles]
VERBOSE: [SRV2]: LCM:  [ End    Resource ]  [[File]RKAppFiles]
VERBOSE: [SRV2]: LCM:  [ Start  Resource ]  [[xWebAppPool]ReskitAppPool]
VERBOSE: [SRV2]: LCM:  [ Start  Test     ]  [[xWebAppPool]ReskitAppPool]
VERBOSE: [SRV2]:                            [[xWebAppPool]ReskitAppPool]  Application pool "RKAppPool" was not found.
VERBOSE: [SRV2]:                            [[xWebAppPool]ReskitAppPool]  The "Ensure" state of application pool "RKAppPool" does not match the desired state.
VERBOSE: [SRV2]:                            [[xWebAppPool]ReskitAppPool]  The target resource is not in the desired state.
VERBOSE: [SRV2]: LCM:  [ End    Test     ]  [[xWebAppPool]ReskitAppPool]  in 3.3590 seconds.
VERBOSE: [SRV2]: LCM:  [ Start  Set      ]  [[xWebAppPool]ReskitAppPool]
VERBOSE: [SRV2]:                            [[xWebAppPool]ReskitAppPool]  Performing the operation "Set-TargetResource" on target "RKAppPool".
VERBOSE: [SRV2]:                            [[xWebAppPool]ReskitAppPool]  Application pool "RKAppPool" was not found.
VERBOSE: [SRV2]:                            [[xWebAppPool]ReskitAppPool]  Creating application pool "RKAppPool".
VERBOSE: [SRV2]:                            [[xWebAppPool]ReskitAppPool]  Application pool "RKAppPool" was found.
VERBOSE: [SRV2]: LCM:  [ End    Set      ]  [[xWebAppPool]ReskitAppPool]  in 0.3910 seconds.
VERBOSE: [SRV2]: LCM:  [ End    Resource ]  [[xWebAppPool]ReskitAppPool]
VERBOSE: [SRV2]: LCM:  [ Start  Resource ]  [[xWebApplication]ReskitAppPool]
VERBOSE: [SRV2]: LCM:  [ Start  Test     ]  [[xWebApplication]ReskitAppPool]
VERBOSE: [SRV2]:                            [[xWebApplication]ReskitAppPool]  Web application "ReskitApp" is absent and should not absent.
VERBOSE: [SRV2]: LCM:  [ End    Test     ]  [[xWebApplication]ReskitAppPool]  in 0.0940 seconds.
VERBOSE: [SRV2]: LCM:  [ Start  Set      ]  [[xWebApplication]ReskitAppPool]
VERBOSE: [SRV2]:                            [[xWebApplication]ReskitAppPool]  Creating new Web application "ReskitApp".
VERBOSE: [SRV2]: LCM:  [ End    Set      ]  [[xWebApplication]ReskitAppPool]  in 0.2030 seconds.
VERBOSE: [SRV2]: LCM:  [ End    Resource ]  [[xWebApplication]ReskitAppPool]
VERBOSE: [SRV2]: LCM:  [ Start  Resource ]  [[Log]Completed]
VERBOSE: [SRV2]: LCM:  [ Start  Test     ]  [[Log]Completed]
VERBOSE: [SRV2]: LCM:  [ End    Test     ]  [[Log]Completed]  in 0.0000 seconds.
VERBOSE: [SRV2]: LCM:  [ Start  Set      ]  [[Log]Completed]
VERBOSE: [SRV2]:                            [[Log]Completed]  Finished Configuring ReskitAp via DSC against SRV2
VERBOSE: [SRV2]: LCM:  [ End    Set      ]  [[Log]Completed]  in 0.0000 seconds.
VERBOSE: [SRV2]: LCM:  [ End    Resource ]  [[Log]Completed]
VERBOSE: [SRV2]: LCM:  [ End    Set      ]  in 93.0180 seconds.
VERBOSE: Operation 'Invoke CimMethod' complete.
VERBOSE: Time taken for configuration job to complete is 93.207 seconds
```

Finally, in *step 6*, you view the web pages created by the earlier steps. If you first navigate to the home page of the application, using *step 6*. You should see the following:

From this page, if you click to page 2, you should see this:

There's more...

In *step 3*, you created a configuration block that does the following:

► Configures SRV2 with two Windows features (Web-Server and Web-Mgmt-Tools)
► Copies the application's source files from DC1 to SRV2
► Creates an application pool, RKAppPool
► Creates an IIS web application, ReskitApp

This step also demonstrates the dependency mechanism in DSC. A dependency allows you to state that a particular resource configuration can only be performed after some other resource configuration has completed. For example, this configuration does not create a ReskitApp application until the RKAppPool application pool exists and does not do either until the WindowsFeature resource has finished installing IIS.

This recipe uses the push model for DSC deployment. In this recipe, you manually copy the `xWebAdministration` module to `SRV2` as part of the recipe. If you use a pull server model to deploy DSC, target nodes can download the necessary resources from the pull server, which greatly simplifies deployment of DSC resources. The two recipes later in this chapter (*Implement an SMB pull server* and *Implement a DSC web pull server*) show you how to configure a pull server.

Configuring the DSC local configuration manager

The LCM is a key component of DSC. LCM is a Windows service that runs on each DSC target node, and is responsible for receiving configuration information and ensuring that the node is configured in the desired state (and remains that way).

DSC has two mechanisms for the desired state delivery: push and pull. The earlier recipes in this chapter demonstrated the push model: you create a configuration and its related MOF file on one node and push that configuration to another node. In the pull model, you configure the node with details of where and how to find a pull server. Once configured, a node can pull configurations from the configured pull server. In both cases, it is the LCM that performs the actual configuration.

The way the LCM works changed in PowerShell version 5. In this recipe, which you run on `SRV2`, you configure the LCM (based on the PowerShell V5 mechanism) on `SRV2` and set up `SRV2` to pull the DSC configuration from `SRV1` which you set up as an SMB pull server. You set up `SRV1` itself in the next recipe, *Implementing an SMB pull server*.

Getting ready

In this recipe, you use a special type of configuration known as a metaconfiguration. You use the metaconfiguration statement to configure DSC on a node. You run this recipe on the target node, `SRV2`.

How to do it...

1. Remove the local MOF files and configurations on `SRV2` and ensure that `C:\DSC` exists using the following code:

```
$RIHT =@{
  Path       = 'C:\Windows\System32\configuration\*.mof'
  ErrorAction = 'SilentlyContinue'
```

```
}
Get-Childitem @RIHT |
  Remove-Item @RIHT -Force
$EASC = @{
  ErrorAction = 'SilentlyContinue'}
New-Item -Path c:\DSC -ItemType Directory @EASC |
  Out-Null
```

2. Get the default settings for LCM using the following code:

```
Get-DscLocalConfigurationManager |
  Format-List -Property ActionafterReboot,
                        AllowModuleOverwrite,
                        Configuration*,
                        LCMState,
                        PartialConfigurations,
                        Reboot*,
                        Refresh*,
                        Report*,
                        Resource*
```

3. Create the metaconfiguration for this host using the following code:

```
Configuration SRV2LcmConfig {
  Node Localhost{
    LocalConfigurationManager {
      ConfigurationMode             = 'ApplyOnly'
      RebootNodeIfNeeded            = $true
    }
  }
}
```

4. Run the configuration and create the MOF file using the following code:

```
SRV2LcmConfig -OutputPath C:\DSC
```

5. Update the LCM configuration based on the MOF using the following code:

```
Set-DscLocalConfigurationManager -Path c:\DSC -Verbose
```

6. Check the updated properties for the LCM using the following code:

```
Get-DscLocalConfigurationManager |
   Format-List -Property ActionafterReboot,
                         AllowModuleOverwrite,
                         Configuration*,
                         LCMState,
                         PartialConfigurations,
                         Reboot*,
                         Refresh*,
                         Report*,
                         Resource*
```

How it works

In *step 1*, you remove any existing DSC configuration MOF files for this node and ensure that the C:\DSC folder exists on SRV2. There is no output from this step.

In *step 2*, you retrieve and view some of the properties of the DSC LCM on SRV2, which looks like this:

```
PS C:\Foo> Get-DscLocalConfigurationManager |
           Format-List -Property ActionafterReboot,
                                 AllowModuleOverwrite,
                                 Configuration*,
                                 LCMState,
                                 PartialConfigurations,
                                 Reboot*,
                                 Refresh*,
                                 Report*,
                                 Resource*


ActionafterReboot                 : ContinueConfiguration
AllowModuleOverwrite              : False
ConfigurationDownloadManagers     : {}
ConfigurationID                   :
ConfigurationMode                 : ApplyAndMonitor
ConfigurationModeFrequencyMins    : 15
LCMState                          : Idle
PartialConfigurations             :
RebootNodeIfNeeded                : False
RefreshFrequencyMins              : 30
RefreshMode                       : PUSH
ReportManagers                    : {}
ResourceModuleManagers            : {}
```

In *step 3*, you create a configuration statement to configure the LCM of SRV2. There is no output from this step.

In *step 4*, you execute the configuration to create the MOF file, which looks like this:

```
PS C:\Foo> SRV2LcmConfig -OutputPath C:\DSC   -VERBOSE

        Directory: C:\DSC

Mode                LastWriteTime   Length Name
----                -------------   ------ ----
-a----    28/01/2019       17:32     1068 Localhost.meta.mof
```

In *step 5*, you apply the LCM's configuration and, using the -Verbose switch. You get the following output:

```
PS C:\Foo> Set-DscLocalConfigurationManager -Path c:\DSC -Verbose

VERBOSE: Performing the operation "Start-DscConfiguration: SendMetaConfigurationApply" on
        target "MSFT_DSCLocalConfigurationManager".
VERBOSE: Perform operation 'Invoke CimMethod' with following parameters,
                ''methodName' = SendMetaConfigurationApply,
                'className' = MSFT_DSCLocalConfigurationManager,
                'namespaceName' = root/Microsoft/Windows/DesiredStateConfiguration'.
VERBOSE: An LCM method call arrived from computer SRV2 with
        user sid S-1-5-21-3496687451-3124355039-3783943179-500.
VERBOSE: [SRV2]: LCM:  [ Start  Set      ]
VERBOSE: [SRV2]: LCM:  [ Start  Resource ] [MSFT_DSCMetaConfiguration]
VERBOSE: [SRV2]: LCM:  [ Start  Set      ] [MSFT_DSCMetaConfiguration]
VERBOSE: [SRV2]: LCM:  [ End    Set      ] [MSFT_DSCMetaConfiguration]  in 0.0470 seconds.
VERBOSE: [SRV2]: LCM:  [ End    Resource ] [MSFT_DSCMetaConfiguration]
VERBOSE: [SRV2]: LCM:  [ End    Set      ]  in  0.1720 seconds.
VERBOSE: Operation 'Invoke CimMethod' complete.
VERBOSE: Set-DscLocalConfigurationManager finished in 0.262 seconds.
```

In the final step of this recipe, *step 6*, you review the key properties of the LCM of SRV2, which looks like this:

```
PS C:\Foo> Get-DscLocalConfigurationManager |
            Format-List -Property ActionafterReboot,
                                  AllowModuleOverwrite,
                                  Configuration*,
                                  LCMState,
                                  PartialConfigurations,
                                  Reboot*,
                                  Refresh*,
                                  Report*,
                                  Resource*


ActionafterReboot             : ContinueConfiguration
AllowModuleOverwrite          : False
ConfigurationDownloadManagers : {}
ConfigurationID               :
ConfigurationMode             : ApplyOnly     <----
ConfigurationModeFrequencyMins : 15
LCMState                      : Idle
PartialConfigurations         :
RebootNodeIfNeeded            : True      <----
RefreshFrequencyMins          : 30
RefreshMode                   : PUSH
ReportManagers                : {}
ResourceModuleManagers        : {}
```

This recipe demonstrated the basics of configuring the LCM on a node. To set up a pull server, as you see in the remaining recipes in this chapter, you need to update the LCM further.

Implementing an SMB DSC pull server

There are two different types of DSC pull server that you can implement: SMB-based and web-based. The SMB-based pull server approach is most useful on a private routable network, one where all nodes can reach the centralized configuration and resource pull server shares. For high availability, you could set up an SMB pull server on a clustered, scaled-out file server.

DSC uses MOF to communicate the desired state to a node. The LCM on a node, in effect, configures the node based on whatever the MOF file says. MOF files are, at rest, just plaintext documents, and are not encrypted or signed. If your private network is secure, then the SMB pull server is easier to set up and configure. If security is an issue, consider using the web server pull server approach and configure it with HTTPS (which you do in the *Implementing a web-based DSC pull server* recipe).

Since you may have used other recipes in this chapter—such as the *Configuring the DSC local configuration manager* recipe where you configured a node—you first need to clean out any existing DSC configuration details before carrying out this recipe.

When you deploy an SMB-based pull server, you place the configuration documents on the SMB share for the target nodes to pull and use. You also configure the LCM on a node to tell the node where and how to get the MOF files. To enable a node to identify which configuration document it should download and use, the node is configured with a GUID (the ConfigurationID) and an SMB share path where the LCM can find configuration MOF files. The MOF file that you deploy to a node is named using the GUID (that is, <guid>.mof).

In this recipe, you configure the LCM on SRV2 with a ConfigurationID set to 5d79ee6e-0420-4c98-9cc3-9f696901a816. The LCM configuration also specifies that the LCM on SRV2 should pull configurations from the SMB pull server located at \\SRV1\DSCConfiguration. In this case, the LCM on SRV2 would look for the file named \\SRV1\DSCConfiguration\5d79ee6e-0420-4c98-9cc3-9f696901a816.mof plus the related checksum file.

This recipe uses another PS Gallery sourced module, the xSMBShare module. This module is used to create a DSC configuration that creates necessary shares. In this case, you use DSC with this module to configure two shares on SRV1, which DSC nodes (that is, SRV2) use to pull configuration documents.

Getting ready

This recipe is run on SRV1 and provides a DSC configuration for SRV2.

 This recipe removes any DSC configuration documents on both SRV1 and SRV2. Any configuration that was performed using previous recipes, for example adding the DNS Server service to SRV2, remain in place with DSC only concerning itself with the new configuration document(s) you add to the pull server.

How to do it...

1. Ensure that the xSMBShare module is installed on SRV1 and SRV2 and ensure that C:\DSC exists using the following code:

```
$SB1 = {
  Install-Module xSMBShare -Force |
    Out-Null
}
Invoke-Command -ComputerName SRV1 -ScriptBlock $SB1
Invoke-Command -ComputerName SRV2 -ScriptBlock $SB1
```

2. Remove the existing MOF files and DSC configuration on SRV1 and SRV2 using the following code:

```
$SB2 = {
  $RIHT = @{
    Path        = 'C:\Windows\System32\configuration\*.mof'
    ErrorAction = 'SilentlyContinue'
  }
  Get-Childitem @RIHT |
    Remove-Item @RIHT -Force
  $EASC = @{
    ErrorAction = 'SilentlyContinue'
  }
  New-Item -Path c:\DSC -ItemType Directory @EASC |
    Out-Null
  Remove-DscConfigurationDocument -Stage Current
  }
Invoke-Command -ComputerName SRV1 -ScriptBlock $SB2
Invoke-Command -ComputerName SRV2 -ScriptBlock $SB2
```

3. Create a script block to set the LCM configuration for SRV2 that configures SRV2 to pull from SRV1 using the following code:

```
$SB3 = {
  [DSCLocalConfigurationManager()]
  Configuration SetSRV2PullMode {
    Node localhost {
      Settings  {
        ConfigurationModeFrequencyMins = '30'
        ConfigurationMode              = 'ApplyAndAutoCorrect'
        RebootNodeIfNeeded             = $true
        ActionAfterReboot              = 'ContinueConfiguration'
        RefreshMOde                    = 'Pull'
        RefreshFrequencyMins           = '30'
        AllowModuleOverwrite           = $true
        ConfigurationID                = '5d79ee6e-0420-4c98-'+
                                         '9cc3-9f696901a816'
      }
      ConfigurationRepositoryShare PullServer  {
        SourcePath = '\\SRV1\DSCConfiguration'
      }
      ResourceRepositoryShare ResourceServer {
        SourcePath = '\\SRV1\DSCResource'
      }
    }
  }
}
  SetSRV2PullMode -OutputPath 'C:\DSC' |
    Out-Null
```

4. Create the MOF file for SRV2 LCM using the following code:

```
$DHT = @{
  Path  = 'C:\DSC'
}
Set-DscLocalConfigurationManager -Path C:\DSC
Get-DscLocalConfigurationManager
```

5. Configure SRV2 to pull via SMB from SRV1 using the following code:

```
Invoke-Command -ScriptBlock $SB3 -ComputerName SRV2
```

6. Create a DSC configuration to configure SRV1 as a DSC pull server using the following code:

```
Configuration PullSrv1
{
  Import-DscResource -ModuleName PSDesiredStateConfiguration
  Import-DscResource -ModuleName xSmbShare
  File ConfigFolder {
    DestinationPath = 'C:\DSCConfiguration'
    Type        = 'Directory'
    Ensure      = 'Present'
  }
  File ResourceFolder  {
    DestinationPath = 'C:\DscResource'
   Type         = 'Directory'
    Ensure      = 'Present'
  }
  xSmbShare DscConfiguration {
    Name        = 'DSCConfiguration'
    Path        = 'C:\DscConfiguration\'
    DependsOn   = '[File]ConfigFolder'
        Description = 'DSC Configuration Share'
        Ensure      = 'Present'
    }
  xSmbShare DscResource {
    Name        = 'DSCResource'
    Path        = 'C:\DscResource'
    DependsOn   = '[File]ResourceFolder'
    Description = 'DSC Resource Share'
    Ensure      = 'Present' }
}
```

7. Create a MOF file to configure SRV1 as a pull server using the following code:

```
PullSRV1 -OutputPath C:\DSC |
  Out-Null
```

8. Use DSC to configure SRV1 as a pull server using the following code:

```
Start-DscConfiguration -Path C:\DSC -Wait -Verbose -Force
```

9. Get shares on SRV1 using the following code:

```
Get-SMBShare -Name DSC*
```

10. Create a new configuration for SRV2 to pull from SRV1 that configures SRV2 to have a Telnet client feature using the following code:

```
Configuration  TelnetSRV2
{
  Import-DscResource -ModuleName 'PSDesiredStateConfiguration'
  Node SRV2
  {
    WindowsFeature TelnetSRV2
    { Name      = 'Telnet-Client'
      Ensure    = 'Present'  }
  }
}
```

11. Create a MOF file to configure SRV2 to have the Telnet client using the following code:

```
TelnetSRV2 -OutputPath C:\DSCConfiguration
```

12. Rename the MOF file with the GUID name using the following code:

```
$Guid = '5d79ee6e-0420-4c98-9cc3-9f696901a816'
$RIHT = @{
  Path     = 'C:\DSCConfiguration\SRV2.mof'
  NewName = "C:\DSCConfiguration\$Guid.MOF"
}
Rename-Item  @RIHT
```

13. Create a MOF checksum for the new MOF file using the following code:

```
New-DscChecksum -Path C:\DSCConfiguration
```

14. View the MOF and checksum files using the following code:

```
Get-ChildItem -Path C:\DSCConfiguration
```

15. View the current configuration on SRV2 using the following code:

```
Get-WindowsFeature -Name Telnet-Client -ComputerName SRV2
```

16. Set it to sleep for a while and check it again using the following code:

```
Start-Sleep -Seconds (30*60)
Get-WindowsFeature -Name Telnet-Client -ComputerName SRV2
```

How it works...

In *step 1*, you ensure that the xSMBShare module is installed on SRV1 and SRV2. In *step 2*, you remove both any existing MOF files and any DSC configurations from both SRV1 and SRV2. In *step 3*, you create a script block that creates and deploys an LCM configuration that sets the LCM configuration and creates the related MOF file. These three steps produce no output, although depending on what other recipes you have run, you may get prompted to install the NuGet provider in *Step 2*.

In *step 4*, you create a script to run the script block you just created that configures the LCM on SRV2 (based on the configuration block you created in *step 3*) and returns the LCM configuration, which looks like this:

```
PS C:\Foo> Invoke-Command -ScriptBlock $SB3 -ComputerName SRV2

ActionAfterReboot                : ContinueConfiguration
AgentId                          : A37E7738-20E2-11E9-B24B-00155D012A6C
AllowModuleOverwrite             : True
CertificateID                    :
ConfigurationDownloadManagers    : {[ConfigurationRepositoryShare]PullServer}
ConfigurationID                  : 5d79ee6e-0420-4c98-9cc3-9f696901a816
ConfigurationMode                : ApplyAndAutoCorrect
ConfigurationModeFrequencyMins   : 30
Credential                       :
DebugMode                        : {NONE}
DownloadManagerCustomData        :
DownloadManagerName              :
LCMCompatibleVersions            : {1.0, 2.0}
LCMState                         : Idle
LCMStateDetail                   :
LCMVersion                       : 2.0
StatusRetentionTimeInDays        : 10
SignatureValidationPolicy        : NONE
SignatureValidations             : {}
MaximumDownloadSizeMB            : 500
PartialConfigurations            :
RebootNodeIfNeeded               : True
RefreshFrequencyMins             : 30
RefreshMode                      : PUSH
ReportManagers                   : {}
ResourceModuleManagers           : {[ResourceRepositoryShare]ResourceServer}
PSComputerName                   : SRV2
PSComputerName                   : SRV2
```

In *step 5*, you create and compile a configuration statement that configures SRV1 to be a DSC pull server. In *step 6*, you generate the MOF for this configuration. In *step 7*, you run the configuration block to produce the relevant MOF file These three steps produce no output.

In *step 8*, you run `Start-DscConfiguration` to configure `SRV1` based on the just-compiled MOF file, which looks like this:

```
PS C:\DSC> Start-DscConfiguration -Path C:\DSC -Wait -Verbose -Force
VERBOSE: Perform operation 'Invoke CimMethod' with following parameters,
                          'methodName' = SendConfigurationApply,
                          'className' = MSFT_DSCLocalConfigurationManager,
                          'namespaceName' = root/Microsoft/Window
s/DesiredStateConfiguration'.
VERBOSE: An LCM method call arrived from computer SRV2 with user sid S-1-5-21-3496687451-3124355039-3783943179-500.
VERBOSE: [SRV2]: LCM:  [ Start  Set      ]
VERBOSE: [SRV2]: LCM:  [ Start  Resource ] [[File]ConfigFolder]
VERBOSE: [SRV2]: LCM:  [ Start  Test     ] [[File]ConfigFolder]
VERBOSE: [SRV2]:                            [[File]ConfigFolder] The destination object was found and no action is required.
VERBOSE: [SRV2]: LCM:  [ End    Test     ] [[File]ConfigFolder]  in 0.0470 seconds.
VERBOSE: [SRV2]: LCM:  [ Skip   Set      ] [[File]ConfigFolder]
VERBOSE: [SRV2]: LCM:  [ End    Resource ] [[File]ConfigFolder]
VERBOSE: [SRV2]: LCM:  [ Start  Resource ] [[File]ResourceFolder]
VERBOSE: [SRV2]: LCM:  [ Start  Test     ] [[File]ResourceFolder]
VERBOSE: [SRV2]:                            [[File]ResourceFolder] The destination object was found and no action is required.
VERBOSE: [SRV2]: LCM:  [ End    Test     ] [[File]ResourceFolder]  in 0.0150 seconds.
VERBOSE: [SRV2]: LCM:  [ Skip   Set      ] [[File]ResourceFolder]
VERBOSE: [SRV2]: LCM:  [ End    Resource ] [[File]ResourceFolder]
VERBOSE: [SRV2]: LCM:  [ Start  Resource ] [[xSmbShare]DscConfiguration]
VERBOSE: [SRV2]: LCM:  [ Start  Test     ] [[xSmbShare]DscConfiguration]
VERBOSE: [SRV2]:                            [[xSmbShare]DscConfiguration] Share with name DSCConfiguration does not exist
VERBOSE: [SRV2]:                            [[xSmbShare]DscConfiguration]  in 0.1250 seconds.
VERBOSE: [SRV2]: LCM:  [ End    Test     ] [[xSmbShare]DscConfiguration]
VERBOSE: [SRV2]: LCM:  [ Start  Set      ] [[xSmbShare]DscConfiguration]
VERBOSE: [SRV2]:                            [[xSmbShare]DscConfiguration] Creating share DSCConfiguration to ensure it is Present
VERBOSE: [SRV2]: LCM:  [ End    Set      ] [[xSmbShare]DscConfiguration]  in 0.1880 seconds.
VERBOSE: [SRV2]: LCM:  [ End    Resource ] [[xSmbShare]DscConfiguration]
VERBOSE: [SRV2]: LCM:  [ Start  Resource ] [[xSmbShare]DscResource]
VERBOSE: [SRV2]: LCM:  [ Start  Test     ] [[xSmbShare]DscResource]
VERBOSE: [SRV2]:                            [[xSmbShare]DscResource] Share with name DSCResource does not exist
VERBOSE: [SRV2]: LCM:  [ End    Test     ] [[xSmbShare]DscResource]  in 0.0470 seconds.
VERBOSE: [SRV2]: LCM:  [ Start  Set      ] [[xSmbShare]DscResource]
VERBOSE: [SRV2]:                            [[xSmbShare]DscResource] Creating share DSCResource to ensure it is Present
VERBOSE: [SRV2]: LCM:  [ End    Set      ] [[xSmbShare]DscResource]  in 0.1400 seconds.
VERBOSE: [SRV2]: LCM:  [ End    Resource ] [[xSmbShare]DscResource]
VERBOSE: [SRV2]: LCM:  [ End    Set      ]
VERBOSE: [SRV2]: LCM:  [ End    Set      ]  in  0.7500 seconds.
VERBOSE: Operation 'Invoke CimMethod' complete.
VERBOSE: Time taken for configuration job to complete is 0.879 seconds
```

In *step 9*, you get the SMB shares—created in the previous step—on `SRV1`, which looks like this:

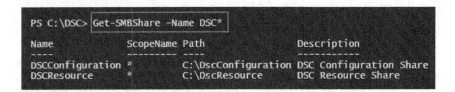

```
PS C:\DSC> Get-SMBShare -Name DSC*

Name              ScopeName Path                 Description
----              --------- ----                 -----------
DSCConfiguration  *         C:\DscConfiguration  DSC Configuration Share
DSCResource       *         C:\DscResource       DSC Resource Share
```

In *step 10*, you create the first partial configuration block, `TelnetSRV2`, which creates no output. In *step 11*, you run this configuration block to produce `SRV2.mof`, which looks like this:

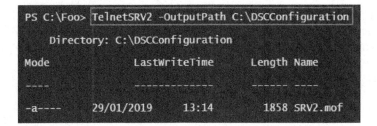

```
PS C:\Foo> TelnetSRV2 -OutputPath C:\DSCConfiguration

    Directory: C:\DSCConfiguration

Mode              LastWriteTime        Length Name
----              -------------        ------ ----
-a----    29/01/2019     13:14           1858 SRV2.mof
```

In *step 12*, you rename the MOF file with the GUID name, and then in *step 13*, you create a MOF checksum file. These two steps produce no output.

In *step 14*, you view the MOF and checksum files, which looks like this:

```
PS C:\Foo> Get-ChildItem C:\DSCConfiguration

    Directory: C:\DSCConfiguration

Mode            LastWriteTime     Length Name
----            -------------     ------ ----
-a----     29/01/2019     13:14     1858 5d79ee6e-0420-4c98-9cc3-9f696901a816.MOF
-a----     29/01/2019     13:17       64 5d79ee6e-0420-4c98-9cc3-9f696901a816.MOF.checksum
```

In *step 15*, you view the current (uninstalled) state of the `Telnet-client` on SRV2, which looks like this:

```
PS C:\Foo> Get-WindowsFeature -Name Telnet-Client -ComputerName SRV2

Display Name        Name          Install State
------------        ----          -------------
[ ] Telnet Client   Telnet-Client     Available
```

In *step 16*, you wait for DSC operations to happen, then review the state of `Telnet-Client` on SRV2, which now looks like this:

```
PS C:\Foo> Start-Sleep -Seconds (30*60)
PS C:\Foo> Get-WindowsFeature -Name Telnet-Client -ComputerName SRV2

Display Name                                    Name           Install State
------------                                    ----           -------------
[X] Telnet Client   <------                     Telnet-Client      Installed
```

There's more...

In the last two steps in this recipe, you look at the state of the Telnet client on SRV2. In *step 15*, you can see that DSC has not yet run the SRV2 configuration, and so the client is not installed. After waiting, in *step 16*, you can see that the Telnet client is now installed on SRV2. Note that if adding this feature had required a reboot, SRV2 would have been rebooted some time after *step 15* completed.

See also

Setting up a pull server and getting it to configure another server is straightforward, although typos are often a challenge to troubleshoot. By default, Windows Server does not perform detailed DSC event logging; however, it is simple to turn logging on using the following code:

```
wevtutil.exe set-log "Microsoft-Windows-Dsc/Analytic" /q:true /e:true
wevtutil.exe set-log "Microsoft-Windows-Dsc/Debug" /q:True /e:true
```

Once you turn on DSC analytic and debug logging, every DSC activity is logged in detail. In earlier recipes, you examined the verbose output of `Start-DscConfiguration`, which shows the LCM getting and performing a configuration. That same amount of information, and more, is available from the event logs. From these logs, you can trace DSC's activities, see the configuration blocks and resources that are being downloaded, and see DSC enforce the configuration. For more detail on using DSC event logging for troubleshooting, see `https://docs.microsoft.com/en-us/powershell/dsc/troubleshooting/troubleshooting`.

Implementing a web-based DSC pull server

Deploying a DSC web-based pull server is more complex than deploying an SMB pull server. Deploying the SMB-based pull server is simple: just create the two shares that you need and place the relevant files on that share. The web server approach requires you to also load IIS, install the DSC service, and configure the service, as well as place the MOF files, resources, and any relevant checksums on the web server. Of course, in both cases, you need to configure each node's LCM.

You deploy a web-based pull server to provide a pull client with both resources and configuration MOF files. Unlike an SMB-based pull server, a web-based pull server also provides reporting capabilities, enabling a pull client to report the status back to the reporting server.

Reporting is not available using an SMB-based pull server. To simplify the creation of a web-based DSC pull server, you can use the `xPSDesiredStateConfiguration` module DSC resource. You download this resource from PS Gallery, which greatly simplifies the process of configuring a node to be a DSC pull server (and to be a reporting server).

As with SMB-based pull servers, once you have set up a DSC web pull server, you need to configure the clients to pull configurations/resources from the pull server and send reporting information to the report servers.

The details of setting up a DSC web-based pull server changed with PowerShell V5 (and later versions). This recipe is based on the PowerShell V5 approach.

Getting ready

This recipe uses two servers: SRV1 and SRV2. SRV1 is the pull server. This recipe configures the DSC web service on SRV1 and configures SRV2 to pull configurations and resources from the pull server.

How to do it...

1. Install the xPSDesiredStateConfiguration module from the PS Gallery on SRV1 and SRV2 using the following code:

```
$SB = {
   Install-Module  -Name xPSDesiredStateConfiguration
}
Invoke-Command -ComputerName SRV1 -ScriptBlock $SB
Invoke-Command -ComputerName SRV2 -ScriptBlock $SB
```

2. Remove the existing certificates for SRV1, then create a self-signed certificate for SRV1 using the following code:

```
Get-ChildItem cert:\LocalMachine\root |
   Where Subject -EQ 'CN=SRV1.reskit.org' |
      Remove-Item -Force
Get-ChildItem cert:\LocalMachine\my |
   Where Subject -EQ 'CN=SRV1.reskit.org' |
      Remove-Item -Force
$CHT = @{
    CertStoreLocation = 'CERT:\LocalMachine\MY'
    DnsName           = 'SRV1.Reskit.Org'
}
$DscCert = New-SelfSignedCertificate @CHT
```

3. Copy the certificate to the root store on SRV2 and SRV1 using the following code:

```
$SB1 = {
   Param ($Rootcert)
   $C = 'System.Security.Cryptography.X509Certificates.X509Store'
   $Store = New-Object -TypeName $C `
                       -ArgumentList 'Root','LocalMachine'
   $Store.Open('ReadWrite')
   $Store.Add($Rootcert)
   $Store.Close()
}
```

```
$ICHT1 = @{
  ScriptBlock   = $SB1
  ComputerName = 'SRV2.Reskit.Org'
  Verbose       = $True
  ArgumentList = $DscCert
}
# run script block on SRV2
Invoke-Command @ICHT1
# and copy it to root on SRV1
$ICHT2= @{
  ScriptBlock   = $SB1
  ComputerName = 'SRV1.Reskit.Org'
  Verbose       = $True
  ArgumentList = $DscCert
}
Invoke-Command @ICHT2
```

4. Check that the certificate is properly installed on SRV2 using the following code:

```
$SB2 = {
  Get-ChildItem Cert:\LocalMachine\root |
    Where-Object Subject -Match 'SRV1.Reskit.Org'
}
Invoke-Command -ScriptBlock $SB2 -ComputerName SRV2
```

5. Remove the existing DSC configuration on SRV1 and SRV2 using the following code:

```
$SB3 = {
  $RIHT = @{
    Path         = 'C:\Windows\System32\configuration\*.mof'
    ErrorAction = 'SilentlyContinue'
  }
  Get-Childitem @RIHT |
    Remove-Item @RIHT -Force
  $EASC = @{
    ErrorAction = 'SilentlyContinue'
  }
  New-Item -Path c:\DSC -ItemType Directory @EASC |
    Out-Null
  Remove-DscConfigurationDocument -Stage Current
}
Invoke-Command -ComputerName SRV1 -ScriptBlock $SB3
Invoke-Command -ComputerName SRV2 -ScriptBlock $SB3
```

6. Create a DSC Service `Configuration` block to make SRV1 a web pull server using the following code:

```
Configuration WebPullSRV1 {
  Param ([String] $CertThumbPrint)
  Import-DscResource -Module PSDesiredStateConfiguration
  Import-DscResource -Module xPSDesiredStateConfiguration
  $Regfile= 'C:\Program Files\WindowsPowerShell\DscService\'+
            'RegistrationKeys.txt'
Node SRV1 {
  $Key = '5d79ee6e-0420-4c98-9cc3-9f696901a816'
  WindowsFeature IIS1 {
    Ensure           = 'Present'
    Name             = 'Web-Server'
  }
  File DSCConfig-Folder {
    DestinationPath  = 'C:\DSCConfiguration'
    Ensure           = 'Present'
    Type             = 'Directory' }
  File DSCResource-Folder{
    DestinationPath  = 'C:\DSCResource'
    Ensure           = 'Present'
    Type             = 'Directory' }
  WindowsFeature DSCService {
    DependsOn        = '[WindowsFeature]IIS1'
    Ensure           = 'Present'
    Name             = 'DSC-Service' }
  xDscWebService WebPullSRV1 {
    Ensure           = 'Present'
    EndpointName     = 'PSDSCPullServer'
    Port             = 8080
    PhysicalPath     = 'C:\inetpub\PSDSCPullServer'
    CertificateThumbPrint = $CertThumbPrint
    ConfigurationPath = 'C:\DSCConfiguration'
    ModulePath       = 'C:\DSCResource'
    State            = 'Started'
    UseSecurityBestPractices = $true
    DependsOn        =
             '[WindowsFeature]DSCService','[WindowsFeature]IIS1'
  }
  File RegistrationKeyFile {
    Ensure               = 'Present'
    Type                 = 'File'
```

```
          DestinationPath        = $Regfile
          Contents               = $Key   }
   } # End of Node configuration
} # End of Configuration
```

7. Create a MOF file to configure SRV1 using the following code:

```
$TP = $DscCert.Thumbprint
WebPullSRV1 -OutputPath C:\DSC  -CertThumbPrint $TP |
   Out-Null
```

8. Use DSC to configure SRV1 to host the DSC web service using the following code:

```
Start-DscConfiguration -Path C:\DSC -Wait -Verbose
$DscCert | Set-Item -Path IIS:\SslBindings\0.0.0.0!8080
```

9. Check on the results using the following code:

```
$URI = 'https://SRV1.reskit.org:8080/PSDSCPullServer.svc/'
Start-Process -FilePath $URI
```

10. Create a metaconfiguration to make SRV2 pull two partial configuration blocks from SRV1 using the following code:

```
[DSCLocalConfigurationManager()]
Configuration SRV2WebPullPartial {
Node SRV2 {
  Settings {
    RefreshMode           = 'Pull'
    ConfigurationModeFrequencyMins = 30
    ConfigurationMode     = 'ApplyandAutoCorrect'
    RefreshFrequencyMins = 30
    RebootNodeIfNeeded    = $true
    AllowModuleOverwrite = $true
  }
  ConfigurationRepositoryWeb DSCPullSrv {
    ServerURL = 'https://SRV1.Reskit.Org:8080/PSDSCPullServer.svc'
    RegistrationKey = '5d79ee6e-0420-4c98-9cc3-9f696901a816'
    ConfigurationNames = @('NFSConfig','SMBConfig')
  }
  PartialConfiguration NFSConfig {
    Description = 'NFS Client Configuration'
     Configurationsource =
                  @('[ConfigurationRepositoryWeb]DSCPullSrv')
  }
```

```
PartialConfiguration SMBConfig {
        Description = 'FS-SMB1 Client Removal'
        Configurationsource = @('[ConfigurationRepositoryWeb]
DSCPullSrv')
        DependsOn    = '[PartialConfiguration]NFSConfig'}
    }
} # End of Configuration block
```

11. Create a MOF to configure DSC LCM on SRV2 using the following code:

```
SRV2WebPullPartial -OutputPath C:\DSC | Out-Null
```

12. Configure LCM on SRV2 using the following code:

```
$CSSrv2 = New-CimSession -ComputerName SRV2
$LCMHT = @{
  CimSession = $CSSrv2
  Path       = 'C:\DSC'
  Verbose    = $true
}
Set-DscLocalConfigurationManager @LCMHT
```

13. Create a partial configuration to ensure that the NFS client is present using the following code:

```
Configuration  TFTPSRV2 {
  Import-DscResource -ModuleName 'PSDesiredStateConfiguration'
  Node SRV2 {
    WindowsFeature TFTPClient {
      Name = 'TFTP-Client'
      Ensure = 'Present'
    }
  }
}
```

14. Create the MOF file for this configuration and place the MOF file into the configuration folder using the following code:

```
Remove-Item -Path C:\DSCConfiguration -Rec -Force
TFTPSRV2 -OutputPath C:\DSCConfiguration |
  Out-Null
```

15. Rename the file and create the checksum using the following code:

```
$RIHT = @{
    Path    = 'C:\DSCConfiguration\SRV2.mof'
    NewName = "C:\DSCConfiguration\$Guid.MOF"
}
Rename-Item @RIHT
New-DscChecksum  -Path C:\DSCConfiguration
Get-ChildItem C:\DSCConfiguration
```

16. Wait a while, then review the details using the following code:

```
Start-Sleep -Seconds (30*60)
$Session = New-CimSession -ComputerName SRV2
Get-DscConfiguration -CimSession $Session
```

17. Check on the feature on SRV2 using the following code:

```
Get-WindowsFeature -Name TFTP-Client -ComputerName SRV2
```

How it works...

In *step 1*, you ensure that the xDesiredStateConfiguration module is loaded on both SRV1 and SRV2. In *step 2*, you remove the existing certificates for SRV1 then create a new self-signed certificate. In *step 3*, you copy the newly created self-signed certificate to the root store of SRV2, thereby enabling SRV2 to trust the self-signed certificate. These three steps produce no output.

In *step 4*, you check to ensure that the certificate is properly installed on SRV2, which looks like this:

```
PS C:\foo> $S1B = {
            Get-ChildItem Cert:\LocalMachine\root |
              Where-Object Subject -Match 'SRV1.Reskit.Org'
          }
PS C:\foo> Invoke-Command -ScriptBlock $SB1 -ComputerName SRV2


   PSParentPath: Microsoft.PowerShell.Security\Certificate::LocalMachine\root

Thumbprint                                Subject                 PSComputerName
----------                                -------                 --------------
8F8B5546CA0C4AA9EE6081141AF337E03BBFA57C  CN=SRV1.Reskit.Org      SRV2
```

In *step 5*, you forcibly remove any DSC configuration information from both SRV1 and SRV2. In *step 6*, you create a configuration to configure SRV1. Then, in *step 7*, you run the configuration to produce the MOF file to configure SRV1 to be a pull. These three steps produce no output.

In *step 8*, you use the Start-DscConfiguration cmdlet to set the DSC configuration for SRV1, which looks like this:

```
PS C:\Foo> Start-DscConfiguration -Path C:\DSC -Wait -Verbose
VERBOSE: Perform operation 'Invoke CimMethod' with following parameters,
        ''methodName' = SendConfigurationApply,
        'className' = MSFT_DSCLocalConfigurationManager,
        'namespaceName' = root/Microsoft/Windows/DesiredStateConfiguration'.
VERBOSE: An LCM method call arrived from computer SRV1 with user sid S-1-5-21-3496687451-3124355039-3783943179-500.
VERBOSE: Operation 'Invoke CimMethod' complete.
VERBOSE: [SRV1]: LCM:  [ Start  Set      ]
VERBOSE: [SRV1]: LCM:  [ Start  Resource ]  [[File]DSCConfig-Folder]
VERBOSE: [SRV1]: LCM:  [ Start  Test     ]  [[File]DSCConfig-Folder]
VERBOSE: [SRV1]:                            [[File]DSCConfig-Folder] The destination object was found and no action is required.
VERBOSE: [SRV1]: LCM:  [ End    Test     ]  [[File]DSCConfig-Folder]  in 0.3280 seconds.
VERBOSE: [SRV1]: LCM:  [ Skip   Set      ]  [[File]DSCConfig-Folder]
VERBOSE: [SRV1]: LCM:  [ End    Resource ]  [[File]DSCConfig-Folder]
VERBOSE: [SRV1]: LCM:  [ Start  Resource ]  [[File]DSCResource-Folder]
VERBOSE: [SRV1]: LCM:  [ Start  Test     ]  [[File]DSCResource-Folder]
VERBOSE: [SRV1]:                            [[File]DSCResource-Folder] The destination object was found and no action is required.
VERBOSE: [SRV1]: LCM:  [ End    Test     ]  [[File]DSCResource-Folder]  in 0.0780 seconds.
VERBOSE: [SRV1]: LCM:  [ Skip   Set      ]  [[File]DSCResource-Folder]
VERBOSE: [SRV1]: LCM:  [ End    Resource ]  [[File]DSCResource-Folder]
VERBOSE: [SRV1]: LCM:  [ Start  Resource ]  [WindowsFeature]DSCService]
VERBOSE: [SRV1]: LCM:  [ Start  Test     ]  [WindowsFeature]DSCService]
VERBOSE: [SRV1]:                            [WindowsFeature]DSCService] The operation 'Get-WindowsFeature' started: DSC-Service
VERBOSE: [SRV1]:                            [WindowsFeature]DSCService] The operation 'Get-WindowsFeature' succeeded: DSC-Service
VERBOSE: [SRV1]: LCM:  [ End    Test     ]  [WindowsFeature]DSCService]  in 1.9220 seconds.
VERBOSE: [SRV1]: LCM:  [ Start  Set      ]  [WindowsFeature]DSCService]
VERBOSE: [SRV1]:                            [WindowsFeature]DSCService] Installation started...
VERBOSE: [SRV1]:                            [WindowsFeature]DSCService] Continue with installation?
VERBOSE: [SRV1]:                            [WindowsFeature]DSCService] Prerequisite processing started...
VERBOSE: [SRV1]:                            [WindowsFeature]DSCService] Prerequisite processing succeeded.
VERBOSE: [SRV1]:                            [WindowsFeature]DSCService] Installation succeeded.
VERBOSE: [SRV1]:                            [WindowsFeature]DSCService] Successfully installed the feature DSC-Service.
VERBOSE: [SRV1]: LCM:  [ End    Set      ]  [WindowsFeature]DSCService]  in 34.1530 seconds.
VERBOSE: [SRV1]: LCM:  [ End    Resource ]  [WindowsFeature]DSCService]
VERBOSE: [SRV1]: LCM:  [ Start  Resource ]  [[xDSCWebService]WebPullSRV1]
VERBOSE: [SRV1]: LCM:  [ Start  Test     ]  [[xDSCWebService]WebPullSRV1]
VERBOSE: [SRV1]:                            [[xDSCWebService]WebPullSRV1] Check Ensure
VERBOSE: [SRV1]:                            [[xDSCWebService]WebPullSRV1] The Website PSDSCPullServer is not present
VERBOSE: [SRV1]: LCM:  [ End    Test     ]  [[xDSCWebService]WebPullSRV1]  in 0.9370 seconds.
VERBOSE: [SRV1]: LCM:  [ Start  Set      ]  [[xDSCWebService]WebPullSRV1]
VERBOSE: [SRV1]:                            [[xDSCWebService]WebPullSRV1] Create the IIS endpoint
VERBOSE: [SRV1]:                            [[xDSCWebService]WebPullSRV1] Setting up endpoint at ~ https://SRV1:8080/PSDSCPullServer.svc
VERBOSE: [SRV1]:                            [[xDSCWebService]WebPullSRV1] Verify that the certificate with the provided thumbprint
                                            exists in CERT:\LocalMachine\MY\
VERBOSE: [SRV1]:                            [[xDSCWebService]WebPullSRV1] Checking IIS requirements
VERBOSE: [SRV1]:                            [[xDSCWebService]WebPullSRV1] Delete the App Pool if it exists
VERBOSE: [SRV1]:                            [[xDSCWebService]WebPullSRV1] Remove the site if it already exists
VERBOSE: [SRV1]:                            [[xDSCWebService]WebPullSRV1] Create the bin folder for deploying custom dependent binaries
                                            required by the endpoint
VERBOSE: [SRV1]:                            [[xDSCWebService]WebPullSRV1] Adding App Pool
VERBOSE: [SRV1]:                            [[xDSCWebService]WebPullSRV1] Set App Pool Properties
VERBOSE: [SRV1]:                            [[xDSCWebService]WebPullSRV1] Add and Set Site Properties
VERBOSE: [SRV1]:                            [[xDSCWebService]WebPullSRV1] pll
VERBOSE: [SRV1]:                            [[xDSCWebService]WebPullSRV1] Enabling firewall exception for port 8080
VERBOSE: [SRV1]:                            [[xDSCWebService]WebPullSRV1] Disable Inbound Firewall Notification
VERBOSE: [SRV1]:                            [[xDSCWebService]WebPullSRV1] Add Firewall Rule for port 8080
VERBOSE: [SRV1]:                            [[xDSCWebService]WebPullSRV1] Set values into the web.config that define the
                                            repository later than BLUE OS
VERBOSE: [SRV1]:                            [[xDSCWebService]WebPullSRV1] Only ESENT is supported on Windows Server 2016
VERBOSE: [SRV1]:                            [[xDSCWebService]WebPullSRV1] Pull Server: Set values into the web.config that indicate
                                            the location of repository, configuration, modules
VERBOSE: [SRV1]:                            [[xDSCWebService]WebPullSRV1] Enabling Pull Server to run in a 64 bit process
VERBOSE: [SRV1]: LCM:  [ End    Set      ]  [[xDSCWebService]WebPullSRV1]  in 5.3680 seconds.
VERBOSE: [SRV1]: LCM:  [ End    Resource ]  [[xDSCWebService]WebPullSRV1]
VERBOSE: [SRV1]: LCM:  [ Start  Resource ]  [[File]RegistrationKeyFile]
VERBOSE: [SRV1]: LCM:  [ Start  Test     ]  [[File]RegistrationKeyFile]
VERBOSE: [SRV1]:                            [[File]RegistrationKeyFile] The system cannot find the path specified.
VERBOSE: [SRV1]:                            [[File]RegistrationKeyFile] The related file/directory is:
                                            C:\ProgramFiles\WindowsPowerShell\DscService\RegistrationKeys.txt.
VERBOSE: [SRV1]: LCM:  [ End    Test     ]  [[File]RegistrationKeyFile]  in 0.0160 seconds.
VERBOSE: [SRV1]: LCM:  [ Start  Set      ]  [[File]RegistrationKeyFile]
VERBOSE: [SRV1]:                            [[File]RegistrationKeyFile] The system cannot find the path specified.
VERBOSE: [SRV1]:                            [[File]RegistrationKeyFile] The related file/directory is:
                                            C:\ProgramFiles\WindowsPowerShell\DscService\RegistrationKeys.txt.
VERBOSE: [SRV1]: LCM:  [ End    Set      ]  [[File]RegistrationKeyFile]  in 0.0000 seconds.
VERBOSE: [SRV1]: LCM:  [ End    Resource ]  [[File]RegistrationKeyFile]
VERBOSE: [SRV1]: LCM:  [ End    Set      ]  in 44.8180 seconds.
VERBOSE: Operation 'Invoke CimMethod' complete.
VERBOSE: Time taken for configuration job to complete is 45.069 seconds
PS C:\Foo> $DscCert | Set-Item -Path IIS:\SslBindings\0.0.0.0!8080
```

In *step 9*, you use the browser to check on the configuration of SRV1 as a DSC pull server, which looks like this:

In *step 10*, you create an LCM configuration document to make SRV2 pull DSC partial configurations from SRV1 via HTTPS. In *step 11*, you use the configuration statement to create the required MOF file. These two steps produce no output.

In *step 12*, you use `Set-DSCLocalConfigurationManager` to configure the LCM on `SRV2`. The output from this step, created by using the `-Verbose` and `-Wait` switches, looks like this:

```
PS C:\Foo> $LCMHT = @{
              ComputerName = 'SRV2'
              Path         = 'C:\DSC'
              Verbose      = $True
           }
PS C:\Foo> Set-DscLocalConfigurationManager @LCMHT

VERBOSE: Performing the operation "Start-DscConfiguration: SendMetaConfigurationApply"
         on target "MSFT_DSCLocalConfigurationManager".
VERBOSE: Perform operation 'Invoke CimMethod' with following parameters,
                       ''methodName' = SendMetaConfigurationApply,
                       'className' = MSFT_DSCLocalConfigurationManager,
                       'namespaceName' = root/Microsoft/Windows/DesiredStateConfiguration'.
VERBOSE: An LCM method call arrived from computer SRV1 with user sid S-1-5-21-3496687451-3124355039-3783943179-500.
VERBOSE: [SRV2]: LCM:  [ Start  Set        ]
VERBOSE: [SRV2]: LCM:  [ Start  Resource ]  [MSFT_DSCMetaConfiguration]
VERBOSE: [SRV2]: LCM:  [ Start  Set        ]  [MSFT_DSCMetaConfiguration]
VERBOSE: [SRV2]: LCM:  [ End    Set        ]  [MSFT_DSCMetaConfiguration]  in 0.0270 seconds.
VERBOSE: [SRV2]: LCM:  [ End    Resource ]  [MSFT_DSCMetaConfiguration]
VERBOSE: [SRV2]: LCM:  [ End    Set        ]
VERBOSE: [SRV2]: LCM:  [ End    Set        ]  in  0.0550 seconds.
VERBOSE: Operation 'Invoke CimMethod' complete.
VERBOSE: Set-DscLocalConfigurationManager finished in 1.611 seconds.
```

In *step 13*, you create a partial configuration to ensure that the NFS client is present, and then in *step 14*, you run the configuration to create the MOF file. You send the MOF file to the `C:\DSCConfiguration` folder. There is no output from these two steps.

In *step 15*, you rename the MOF file, create the DSC checksum file, and view the contents of the `DSCConfiguration` folder, which looks like this:

```
PS C:\Foo> $RIHT = @{
              Path     = 'C:\DSCConfiguration\SRV2.mof'
              NewName  = "C:\DSCConfiguration\$Guid.MOF"
           }
PS C:\Foo> Rename-Item @RIHT
PS C:\Foo> New-DscChecksum   -Path C:\DSCConfiguration
PS C:\Foo> Get-ChildItem C:\DSCConfiguration


    Directory: C:\DSCConfiguration


Mode            LastWriteTime   Length Name
----            -------------   ------ ----
-a----     03/02/2019    18:19    1846 5d79ee6e-0420-4c98-9cc3-9f696901a816.MOF
-a----     03/02/2019    18:21      64 5d79ee6e-0420-4c98-9cc3-9f696901a816.MOF.checksum
```

In *step 16*, you wait for SRV2 to contact SRV1, and then pull the configuration and apply it. Then you can get the DSC configuration for SRV2, which looks like this.

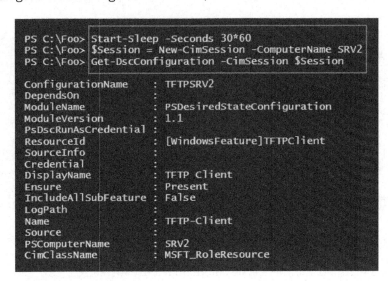

```
PS C:\Foo> Start-Sleep -Seconds 30*60
PS C:\Foo> $Session = New-CimSession -ComputerName SRV2
PS C:\Foo> Get-DscConfiguration -CimSession $Session

ConfigurationName    : TFTPSRV2
DependsOn            :
ModuleName          : PSDesiredStateConfiguration
ModuleVersion       : 1.1
PsDscRunAsCredential :
ResourceId          : [WindowsFeature]TFTPClient
SourceInfo          :
Credential          :
DisplayName         : TFTP Client
Ensure              : Present
IncludeAllSubFeature : False
LogPath             :
Name                : TFTP-Client
Source              :
PSComputerName      : SRV2
CimClassName        : MSFT_RoleResource
```

In *step 17*, you check for the presence of the TFTP client on SRV2, which looks like this:

```
PS C:\Foo> Get-WindowsFeature -Name TFTP-Client -ComputerName SRV2

Display Name              Name          Install State
------------              ----          -------------
[X] TFTP Client           TFTP-Client       Installed
```

There's more...

In *step 5*, you remove all DSC configurations from both SRV1 and SRV2. After doing that, running some of the DSC cmdlets, such as Get-DSCConfiguration, may result in an error, as there is no configuration. This error is to be expected. In later steps in the recipe, you push a configuration to SRV1 and enable SRV2 to pull its configuration from the DSC pull server on SRV1. Once those steps are complete (and SRV2 gets around to pulling the two partial configurations from SRV1), the DSC cmdlets work as expected. Also, if you examine the DSC event logs, events happening just after you wipe the DSC configuration can show odd dates and times in the event log entries. This is also to be expected.

In *step 9*, you viewed the output from the **SRV1's** DSC web service over HTTPS. If the system you run this step on trusts the certificate, you see the page as shown. If, for some reason, you have not copied the self-signed certificate in the local machine's root certificate store, you see certificate errors when navigating to the DSC service.

If you run the step on another computer, say DC1, then you see a certificate error, since that computer does not trust the self-signed certificate.

Using DSC partial configurations

PowerShell V5 introduced a new extension to DSC known as partial configurations. A partial configuration is a DSC configuration that makes up part of a given node's overall desired state. Each node can then pull (and apply) some or all of those partial configurations.

Partial configurations allow you to share the configuration of a node between multiple teams. For example, you might want the central IT team to define the basic configuration of a node. Another team could be responsible for deploying a web application to that same node. The alternative is to have a single MOF document fully describing a node's desired state, which can be organizationally challenging.

To support partial configurations, you configure a node's LCM to define the partial configurations that the node should pull and how the node is to be configured. Each partial configuration can be either pushed or pulled as appropriate. This provides considerable flexibility in deploying DSC partial configurations.

In this recipe, you configure SRV2 to pull two partial configurations from SRV1.

Getting ready

In this recipe, you use two servers, SRV1 and SRV2, which you used in the other recipes in this chapter.

How to do it...

1. Remove the existing certificates for SRV1, then create a self-signed certificate for the FQDN SRV1.Reskit.Org using the following code:

```
Get-ChildItem Cert:\LocalMachine\root |
  Where Subject -EQ 'CN=SRV1.Reskit.Org' |
    Remove-Item -Force
```

```
Get-ChildItem Cert:\LocalMachine\my |
  Where Subject -EQ 'CN=SRV1.Reskit.Org' |
    Remove-Item -Force
$CHT = @{
    CertStoreLocation = 'Cert:\LocalMachine\MY'
    DnsName           = 'SRV1.Reskit.Org'
}
$DscCert = New-SelfSignedCertificate @CHT
```

2. Copy the certificate to the root store on SRV2 and SRV1 using the following code:

```
$SB1 = {
  Param ($Rootcert)
  $C = 'System.Security.Cryptography.X509Certificates.X509Store'
  $Store = New-Object -TypeName $C `
                      -ArgumentList 'Root','LocalMachine'
  $Store.Open('ReadWrite')
  $Store.Add($Rootcert)
  $Store.Close()
}
$ICHT1 = @{
  ScriptBlock  = $SB1
  ComputerName = 'SRV2.Reskit.Org'
  Verbose      = $True
  ArgumentList = $DscCert
}
# run script block on SRV2
Invoke-Command @ICHT1
# and copy it to root on SRV1
$ICHT3= @{
  ScriptBlock  = $SB1
  ComputerName = 'SRV1.Reskit.Org'
  Verbose      = $True
  ArgumentList = $DscCert
}
Invoke-Command @ICHT3
```

3. Check the certificate in the root certificate store on SRV2 using the following code:

```
$SB2 = {
  Get-ChildItem Cert:\LocalMachine\root |
    Where-Object Subject -Match 'SRV1.Reskit.Org'
}
Invoke-Command -ScriptBlock $SB2 -ComputerName SRV2
```

4. Remove the existing DSC configuration on SRV1 and SRV2 using the following code:

```
$SB3 = {
  $RIHT = @{
    Path        = 'C:\Windows\System32\configuration\*.mof'
    ErrorAction = 'SilentlyContinue'
  }
  Get-Childitem @RIHT |
    Remove-Item @RIHT -Force
  $EASC = @{
    ErrorAction = 'SilentlyContinue'
  }
  New-Item -Path c:\DSC -ItemType Directory @EASC |
    Out-Null
  Remove-DscConfigurationDocument -Stage Current
}
Invoke-Command -ComputerName SRV1 -ScriptBlock $SB3
Invoke-Command -ComputerName SRV2 -ScriptBlock $SB3
```

5. Ensure that the xPsDesiredStateConfiguration module is installed on both SRV1 and SRV2 using the following code:

```
$SB2 = {
  Install-Module -Name xPSDesiredStateConfiguration -Force
}
Invoke-Command -Computer SRV1 -ScriptBlock $SB2
Invoke-Command -Computer SRV2 -ScriptBlock $SB2
```

6. Create the desired state configuration for SRV1 using the following code:

```
Configuration WebPullSrv1 {
  Param ([String] $CertThumbPrint)
  Import-DscResource -Module PSDesiredStateConfiguration
  Import-DscResource -Module xPSDesiredStateConfiguration
  $Regfile= 'C:\Program Files\WindowsPowerShell\DscService\'+
            'RegistrationKeys.txt'
  Node SRV1 {
   $Key = '5d79ee6e-0420-4c98-9cc3-9f696901a816'
   WindowsFeature IIS1 {
     Ensure        = 'Present'
     Name          = 'Web-Server'
   }
    File DSCConfig-Folder {
    DestinationPath   = 'C:\DSCConfiguration'
    Ensure            = 'Present'
```

```
         Type              = 'Directory'
      }
      File DSCResource-Folder{
         DestinationPath   = 'C:\DSCResource'
         Ensure            = 'Present'
         Type              = 'Directory'
      }
      WindowsFeature DSCService {
         DependsOn         =   '[WindowsFeature]IIS1'
         Ensure            =   'Present'
         Name              =   'DSC-Service'
      }
      xDscWebService WebPullSRV1 {
         Ensure            = 'Present'
         EndpointName      = 'PSDSCPullServer'
         Port              = 8080
         PhysicalPath      = 'C:\inetpub\PSDSCPullServer'
         CertificateThumbPrint = $CertThumbPrint
         ConfigurationPath = 'C:\DSCConfiguration'
         ModulePath        = 'C:\DSCResource'
         State             = 'Started'
         UseSecurityBestPractices = $true
         DependsOn         =
                 '[WindowsFeature]DSCService','[WindowsFeature]IIS1'}
      File RegistrationKeyFile {
         Ensure              = 'Present'
         Type                = 'File'
         DestinationPath     = $Regfile
         Contents            = $Key  }
   } # End of Node configuration
 } # End of Configuration
```

7. Remove any existing MOF files on SRV1, then create an MOF file for SRV1 using the following code:

```
Get-ChildItem -Path C:\DSC -ErrorAction SilentlyContinue |
    Remove-Item -Force | Out-Null
$TP = $DscCert.Thumbprint
WebPullSrv1 -OutputPath C:\DSC  -CertThumbPrint $TP
```

8. Configure SRV1 to host the DSC web service using the following code:

```
Start-DscConfiguration -Path C:\DSC -Wait -Verbose
$DscCert | Set-Item -Path IIS:\SslBindings\0.0.0.0!8080
```

9. Check on the results using the browser with the following code:

```
$URI = 'https://SRV1.reskit.org:8080/PSDSCPullServer.svc/'
Start-Process -FilePath $URI
```

10. Create a metaconfiguration to make SRV2 pull two partial configuration blocks from SRV1 using the following code:

```
[DSCLocalConfigurationManager()]
Configuration SRV2WebPullPartial {
Node SRV2 {
  Settings
    {  RefreshMode             = 'Pull'
       ConfigurationModeFrequencyMins = 30
       ConfigurationMode       = 'ApplyandAutoCorrect'
       RefreshFrequencyMins    = 30
       RebootNodeIfNeeded      = $true
       AllowModuleOverwrite    = $true }
  ConfigurationRepositoryWeb DSCPullSrv {
    ServerURL = 'HTTPS://SRV1.Reskit.Org:8080/PSDSCPullServer.svc'
    RegistrationKey = '5d79ee6e-0420-4c98-9cc3-9f696901a816'
    ConfigurationNames = @('NFSConfig','SMBConfig') }
  PartialConfiguration NFSConfig {
    Description = 'NFS Client Configuration'
    Configurationsource =
                @('[ConfigurationRepositoryWeb]DSCPullSrv') }
  PartialConfiguration SMBConfig {
    Description = 'FS-SMB1 Client Removal'
    Configurationsource =
                @('[ConfigurationRepositoryWeb]DSCPullSrv')
    DependsOn    = '[PartialConfiguration]NFSConfig'
  }
 } # End Node 2 Configuration
}
```

11. Run the configuration to create the MOF file to configure DSC LCM on SRV2 using the following code:

```
SRV2WebPullPartial -OutputPath C:\DSC | Out-Null
```

12. Configure the LCM on SRV2 with the updated configuration using the following code:

```
$CSSrv2 = New-CimSession -ComputerName SRV2
$LCMHT = @{
  CimSession = $CSSrv2
```

```
        Path        = 'C:\DSC'
        Verbose     = $true
    }
    Set-DscLocalConfigurationManager @LCMHT
```

13. Create the NFS client partial configuration and related build MOF file, then rename the partial configuration using the following code:

```
$Guid = '5d79ee6e-0420-4c98-9cc3-9f696901a816'
$ConfigData = @{
    AllNodes  = @(
        @{ NodeName = '*' ; PsDscAllowPlainTextPassword = $true},
        @{ NodeName = $Guid }
    )
}
Configuration  NFSConfig {
    Import-DscResource -ModuleName PSDesiredStateConfiguration
    Node $Allnodes.NodeName {
        WindowsFeature NFSClientPresent {
            Name     = 'NFS-Client'
            Ensure   = 'Present'
        }
    }
}
$CHT1 = @{
    ConfigurationData = $ConfigData
    OutputPath        = 'C:\DSCConfiguration'
}
NFSConfig @CHT1
$RIHT = @{
    Path     = "C:\DSCConfiguration\$Guid.mof"
    Newname  = 'C:\DSCConfiguration\NFSConfig.MOF'
}
Rename-Item  @RIHT
```

14. Create and compile the SMB client partial configuration, which ensures that SMB is **not** installed, using the following code:

```
$Guid = '5d79ee6e-0420-4c98-9cc3-9f696901a816'
$ConfigData = @{
    AllNodes = @(
        @{ NodeName = '*' ; PsDscAllowPlainTextPassword = $true},
        @{ NodeName = $Guid }
    )
}
```

```
Configuration  SMBConfig {
  Import-DscResource -ModuleName 'PSDesiredStateConfiguration'
  Node $AllNodes.NodeName {
  WindowsFeature SMB1 {
    Name    = 'FS-SMB1'
    Ensure = 'Absent'
  }
}
}
$SMBHT = @{
  ConfigurationData = $ConfigData
  OutputPath        = 'C:\DSCConfiguration\'
}
SMBConfig @SMBHT  |  Out-Null
$RIHT =  @{
  Path    = "C:\DSCConfiguration\$Guid.mof"
  NewName = 'C:\DSCConfiguration\SMBConfig.MOF'
}
Rename-Item  @RIHT
```

15. Create DSC checksums for the two partial configurations using the following code:

```
New-DscChecksum -Path C:\DSCConfiguration
```

16. Observe the configuration documents and checksum using the following code:

```
Get-ChildItem -Path C:\DSCConfiguration
```

17. Wait, then check the status of the features on SRV2 using the following code:

```
Start-Sleep -Seconds (30*60)  # wait for 30 minutes
$FeatureNames = @('FS-SMB1', 'NFS-Client')
Get-WindowsFeature -ComputerName SRV2 -Name $FeatureNames
```

18. Test the DSC configuration for SRV2 using the following code:

```
Test-DscConfiguration -ComputerName SRV2  -Verbose
```

How it works...

In *step 1*, you remove any existing certificates for SRV1.Reskit.Org, then you create a new self-signed certificate that you store in the local machine's MY certificate store. In *step 2*, you copy that certificate to the local machine's ROOT certificate store on SRV1 and SRV2. These two steps produce no output.

In *step 3*, you examine the certificate in the local machine's ROOT certificate store on SRV2, which looks like this:

```
PS C:\Foo> $SB2 = {
              Get-ChildItem Cert:\LocalMachine\root |
                Where-Object Subject -Match 'SRV1.Reskit.Org'
           }
PS C:\Foo> Invoke-Command -ScriptBlock $SB2 -ComputerName SRV2


   PSParentPath: Microsoft.PowerShell.Security\Certificate::LocalMachine\root

Thumbprint                                Subject                PSComputerName
----------                                -------                --------------
5BE4B8AE5ECE496652E42FB861525E79B6B65A3B  CN=SRV1.Reskit.Org     SRV2
```

In *step 4*, you remove all DSC configurations from both SRV1 and SRV2. In *step 5*, you ensure that the xPsDesiredStateConfiguration module is installed on both SRV1 and SRV2. In *step 6*, you create a DSC Configuration block for SRV1. These three steps produce no output.

In *step 7*, you remove any old MOF files in C:\DSC on SRV1, then create the MOF file to configure SRV1 to be a pull server. This step produces output like this:

```
PS C:\Foo> Get-ChildItem -Path C:\DSC -ErrorAction SilentlyContinue |
             Remove-Item -Force | Out-Null
PS C:\Foo> WebPullSrv1 -OutputPath C:\DSC  -CertThumbPrint $DscCert.Thumbprint

    Directory: C:\DSC

ode            LastWriteTime        Length Name
----           -------------        ------ ----
-a----    31/01/2019      16:03       6292 SRV1.mof
```

In *step 8*, you use Start-DSCConfiguration to configure SRV1 to be a pull server. This produces output like this:

```
PS C:\Foo> Start-DscConfiguration -Path C:\DSC -Wait -Verbose

VERBOSE: Perform operation 'Invoke CimMethod' with following parameters,
                'methodName' = SendConfigurationApply,
                'className' = MSFT_DSCLocalConfigurationManager,
                'namespaceName' = root/Microsoft/Windows/DesiredStateConfiguration'.
VERBOSE: An LCM method call arrived from computer SRV1 with user sid S-1-5-21-3496687451-3124355039-3783943179-500.
VERBOSE: [SRV1]: LCM:  [ Start  Set      ]
VERBOSE: [SRV1]: LCM:  [ Start  Resource ]  [[WindowsFeature]IIS1]
VERBOSE: [SRV1]: LCM:  [ Start  Test     ]  [[WindowsFeature]IIS1]
VERBOSE: [SRV1]:                            [[WindowsFeature]IIS1]  The operation 'Get-WindowsFeature' started: Web-Server
VERBOSE: [SRV1]:                            [[WindowsFeature]IIS1]  The operation 'Get-WindowsFeature' succeeded: Web-Server
VERBOSE: [SRV1]: LCM:  [ End    Test     ]  [[WindowsFeature]IIS1]  in 1.9840 seconds.
VERBOSE: [SRV1]: LCM:  [ Start  Set      ]  [[WindowsFeature]IIS1]
VERBOSE: [SRV1]:                            [[WindowsFeature]IIS1]  Installation started...
VERBOSE: [SRV1]:                            [[WindowsFeature]IIS1]  Continue with installation?
VERBOSE: [SRV1]:                            [[WindowsFeature]IIS1]  Prerequisite processing started...
VERBOSE: [SRV1]:                            [[WindowsFeature]IIS1]  Prerequisite processing succeeded.
VERBOSE: [SRV1]:                            [[WindowsFeature]IIS1]  Installation succeeded.
VERBOSE: [SRV1]:                            [[WindowsFeature]IIS1]  Successfully installed the feature Web-Server.
VERBOSE: [SRV1]: LCM:  [ End    Set      ]  [[WindowsFeature]IIS1]  in 46.0680 seconds.
VERBOSE: [SRV1]: LCM:  [ End    Resource ]  [[WindowsFeature]IIS1]
VERBOSE: [SRV1]: LCM:  [ Start  Resource ]  [[File]DSCConfig-Folder]
VERBOSE: [SRV1]: LCM:  [ Start  Test     ]  [[File]DSCConfig-Folder]
VERBOSE: [SRV1]:                            [[File]DSCConfig-Folder]  The destination object was found and no action is required.
VERBOSE: [SRV1]: LCM:  [ End    Test     ]  [[File]DSCConfig-Folder]  in 0.0780 seconds.
VERBOSE: [SRV1]: LCM:  [ Skip   Set      ]  [[File]DSCConfig-Folder]
VERBOSE: [SRV1]: LCM:  [ End    Resource ]  [[File]DSCConfig-Folder]
VERBOSE: [SRV1]: LCM:  [ Start  Resource ]  [[File]DSCResource-Folder]
VERBOSE: [SRV1]: LCM:  [ Start  Test     ]  [[File]DSCResource-Folder]
VERBOSE: [SRV1]:                            [[File]DSCResource-Folder]  The destination object was found and no action is required.
VERBOSE: [SRV1]: LCM:  [ End    Test     ]  [[File]DSCResource-Folder]  in 0.0160 seconds.
VERBOSE: [SRV1]: LCM:  [ Skip   Set      ]  [[File]DSCResource-Folder]
VERBOSE: [SRV1]: LCM:  [ End    Resource ]  [[File]DSCResource-Folder]
VERBOSE: [SRV1]: LCM:  [ Start  Resource ]  [[WindowsFeature]DSCService]
VERBOSE: [SRV1]: LCM:  [ Start  Test     ]  [[WindowsFeature]DSCService]
VERBOSE: [SRV1]:                            [[WindowsFeature]DSCService]  The operation 'Get-WindowsFeature' started: DSC-Service
VERBOSE: [SRV1]:                            [[WindowsFeature]DSCService]  The operation 'Get-WindowsFeature' succeeded: DSC-Service
VERBOSE: [SRV1]: LCM:  [ End    Test     ]  [[WindowsFeature]DSCService]  in 0.7810 seconds.
VERBOSE: [SRV1]: LCM:  [ Start  Set      ]  [[WindowsFeature]DSCService]
VERBOSE: [SRV1]:                            [[WindowsFeature]DSCService]  Installation started...
VERBOSE: [SRV1]:                            [[WindowsFeature]DSCService]  Continue with installation?
VERBOSE: [SRV1]:                            [[WindowsFeature]DSCService]  Prerequisite processing started...
VERBOSE: [SRV1]:                            [[WindowsFeature]DSCService]  Prerequisite processing succeeded.
VERBOSE: [SRV1]:                            [[WindowsFeature]DSCService]  Installation succeeded.
VERBOSE: [SRV1]:                            [[WindowsFeature]DSCService]  Successfully installed the feature DSC-Service.
VERBOSE: [SRV1]: LCM:  [ End    Set      ]  [[WindowsFeature]DSCService]  in 42.9020 seconds.
VERBOSE: [SRV1]: LCM:  [ End    Resource ]  [[WindowsFeature]DSCService]
VERBOSE: [SRV1]: LCM:  [ Start  Resource ]  [[xDSCWebService]webPullSRV1]
VERBOSE: [SRV1]: LCM:  [ Start  Test     ]  [[xDSCWebService]webPullSRV1]
VERBOSE: [SRV1]:                            [[xDSCWebService]webPullSRV1]  Check Ensure
VERBOSE: [SRV1]:                            [[xDSCWebService]webPullSRV1]  Check Port
VERBOSE: [SRV1]:                            [[xDSCWebService]webPullSRV1]  Check Binding
VERBOSE: [SRV1]:                            [[xDSCWebService]webPullSRV1]  Check Physical Path property
VERBOSE: [SRV1]:                            [[xDSCWebService]webPullSRV1]  Physical Path of Website PSDSCPullServer does not match the
                                                                           desired state.
VERBOSE: [SRV1]: LCM:  [ End    Test     ]  [[xDSCWebService]webPullSRV1]  in 0.7500 seconds.
VERBOSE: [SRV1]: LCM:  [ Start  Set      ]  [[xDSCWebService]webPullSRV1]
VERBOSE: [SRV1]:                            [[xDSCWebService]webPullSRV1]  Create the IIS endpoint
VERBOSE: [SRV1]:                            [[xDSCWebService]webPullSRV1]  Setting up endpoint at - https://SRV1:8080/PSDSCPullServer.svc
VERBOSE: [SRV1]:                            [[xDSCWebService]webPullSRV1]  Verify that the certificate with the provided thumbprint exists
                                                                           in CERT:\LocalMachine\MY\
VERBOSE: [SRV1]:                            [[xDSCWebService]webPullSRV1]  Checking IIS requirements
VERBOSE: [SRV1]:                            [[xDSCWebService]webPullSRV1]  Delete the App Pool if it exists
VERBOSE: [SRV1]:                            [[xDSCWebService]webPullSRV1]  Remove the site if it already exists
VERBOSE: [SRV1]:                            [[xDSCWebService]webPullSRV1]  p11
VERBOSE: [SRV1]:                            [[xDSCWebService]webPullSRV1]  Create the bin folder for deploying custom dependent binaries
                                                                           required by the endpoint
VERBOSE: [SRV1]:                            [[xDSCWebService]webPullSRV1]  Adding App Pool
VERBOSE: [SRV1]:                            [[xDSCWebService]webPullSRV1]  Set App Pool Properties
VERBOSE: [SRV1]:                            [[xDSCWebService]webPullSRV1]  Add and Set Site Properties
VERBOSE: [SRV1]:                            [[xDSCWebService]webPullSRV1]  p11
VERBOSE: [SRV1]:                            [[xDSCWebService]webPullSRV1]  Enabling firewall exception for port 8080
VERBOSE: [SRV1]:                            [[xDSCWebService]webPullSRV1]  Disable Inbound Firewall Notification
VERBOSE: [SRV1]:                            [[xDSCWebService]webPullSRV1]  Add Firewall Rule for port 8080
VERBOSE: [SRV1]:                            [[xDSCWebService]webPullSRV1]  Set values into the web.config that define the repository later
                                                                           than BLUE OS
VERBOSE: [SRV1]:                            [[xDSCWebService]webPullSRV1]  Only ESENT is supported on Windows Server 2016
VERBOSE: [SRV1]:                            [[xDSCWebService]webPullSRV1]  Pull Server: Set values into the web.config that indicate the
                                                                           location of repository, configuration, modules
VERBOSE: [SRV1]:                            [[xDSCWebService]webPullSRV1]  Enabling Pull Server to run in a 64 bit process
VERBOSE: [SRV1]: LCM:  [ End    Set      ]  [[xDSCWebService]webPullSRV1]  in 4.1610 seconds.
VERBOSE: [SRV1]: LCM:  [ End    Resource ]  [[xDSCWebService]webPullSRV1]
VERBOSE: [SRV1]: LCM:  [ Start  Resource ]  [[File]RegistrationKeyFile]
VERBOSE: [SRV1]: LCM:  [ Start  Test     ]  [[File]RegistrationKeyFile]
VERBOSE: [SRV1]:                            [[File]RegistrationKeyFile]  The system cannot find the file specified.
VERBOSE: [SRV1]:                            [[File]RegistrationKeyFile]  The related file/directory is:
                                                                         C:\Program Files\WindowsPowerShell\DscService\RegistrationKeys.txt.
VERBOSE: [SRV1]: LCM:  [ End    Test     ]  [[File]RegistrationKeyFile]  in 0.0160 seconds.
VERBOSE: [SRV1]: LCM:  [ Start  Set      ]  [[File]RegistrationKeyFile]
VERBOSE: [SRV1]:                            [[File]RegistrationKeyFile]  The system cannot find the file specified.
VERBOSE: [SRV1]:                            [[File]RegistrationKeyFile]  The related file/directory is:
                                                                         C:\Program Files\WindowsPowerShell\DscService\RegistrationKeys.txt.
VERBOSE: [SRV1]: LCM:  [ End    Set      ]  [[File]RegistrationKeyFile]  in 0.0470 seconds.
VERBOSE: [SRV1]: LCM:  [ End    Resource ]  [[File]RegistrationKeyFile]
VERBOSE: [SRV1]: LCM:  [ End    Set      ]
VERBOSE: [SRV1]: LCM:  [ End    Set      ]  in  98.5990 seconds.
VERBOSE: Operation 'Invoke CimMethod' complete.
VERBOSE: Time taken for configuration job to complete is 98.889 seconds
```

In *step 9*, you check to see whether the DSC web-based pull service is running on SRV1, which looks like this:

In *step 10*, you create a metaconfiguration to make SRV2 pull two partial configuration blocks from SRV1. In *step 11*, you create the MOF file for SRV2. These steps produce no output.

In *step 12*, you configure SRV2 to pull partial configurations from SRV1, which looks like this:

```
PS C:\Foo> $CSSrv2 = New-CimSession -ComputerName SRV2
PS C:\Foo> $LCMHT = @{
             CimSession = $CSSrv2
             Path       = 'C:\DSC'
             Verbose    = $true
           }
PS C:\Foo> Set-DscLocalConfigurationManager @LCMHT

VERBOSE: Performing the operation "Start-DscConfiguration: SendMetaConfigurationApply"
         on target "MSFT_DSCLocalConfigurationManager".
VERBOSE: Perform operation 'Invoke CimMethod' with following parameters,
                  ''methodName' = SendMetaConfigurationApply,
                  'className' = MSFT_DSCLocalConfigurationManager,
                  'namespaceName' = root/Microsoft/Windows/DesiredStateConfiguration'.
VERBOSE: An LCM method call arrived from computer SRV2 with user sid S-1-5-21-3496687451-3124355039-37839
43179-500.
VERBOSE: [SRV2]: LCM:  [ Start  Set      ]
VERBOSE: [SRV2]: LCM:  [ Start  Resource ]  [MSFT_DSCMetaConfiguration]
VERBOSE: [SRV2]: LCM:  [ Start  Set      ]  [MSFT_DSCMetaConfiguration]
VERBOSE: [SRV2]: LCM:  [ End    Set      ]  [MSFT_DSCMetaConfiguration]  in 0.0240 seconds.
VERBOSE: [SRV2]: LCM:  [ End    Resource ]  [MSFT_DSCMetaConfiguration]
VERBOSE: [SRV2]:                            [] Registration of the Dsc Agent with the server
                                               https://SRV1.Reskit.Org:8080/PSDSCPullServer.svc
                                               was successful.
VERBOSE: [SRV2]: LCM:  [ End    Set      ]
VERBOSE: [SRV2]: LCM:  [ End    Set      ]  in  0.5300 seconds.
VERBOSE: Operation 'Invoke CimMethod' complete.
VERBOSE: Set-DscLocalConfigurationManager finished in 0.666 seconds.
```

In *step 13*, you create a partial configuration to install the NSF client. In *step 14*, you create and compile another partial configuration to ensure that SMB1 is absent. In *step 15*, you create DSC checksum files for these two configurations. These three steps produce no output.

In *step 16*, you examine the configuration information available in the C:\DSCConfiguration folder (which is now available to nodes via the DSC pull service). The output looks like this:

```
PS C:\Foo> Get-ChildItem -Path C:\DSCConfiguration


    Directory: C:\DSCConfiguration


Mode                LastWriteTime         Length Name
----                -------------         ------ ----
-a----        31/01/2019     17:07          1926 NFSConfig.MOF
-a----        31/01/2019     17:08            64 NFSConfig.MOF.checksum
-a----        31/01/2019     17:08          1894 SMBConfig.Mof
-a----        31/01/2019     17:08            64 SMBConfig.Mof.checksum
```

Once you have completed deploying the partial configurations, you wait for the LCM in SRV2 to recheck its configuration and deploy the two partial configurations. In *step 18*, you examine the state of the two features on SRV2 (now configured as per the partial configurations), which looks like this:

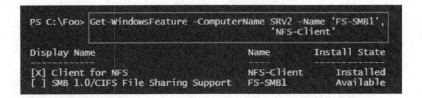

```
PS C:\Foo> Get-WindowsFeature -ComputerName SRV2 -Name 'FS-SMB1',
                                                    'NFS-Client'

Display Name                              Name          Install State
------------                              ----          -------------
[X] Client for NFS                        NFS-Client        Installed
[ ] SMB 1.0/CIFS File Sharing Support     FS-SMB1           Available
```

In *step 18*, you test the DSC configuration on SRV2 (to see whether the node is in the desired state), which looks like this:

```
PS C:\Foo> Test-DscConfiguration -ComputerName SRV2
True
```

There's more...

In *step 1*, you create a self-signed certificate that you make trusted on SRV1, and in *step 2*, you make this certificate trusted on SRV2. In an ideal world, you should create an enterprise **certificate authority (CA)**, then issue certificates signed by that CA. With an enterprise CA, your root certificates can be autopublished, making the SRV1 server's certificate trusted by everyone.

In *step 2*, you use .NET to copy the certificate to SRV2. The certificate provider in PowerShell does not support a copy operation, allowing you to use Copy-Item to copy the certificate between certificate stores on SRV1 and SRV2. But .NET provides a mechanism to copy the certificate to SRV2.

With *step 3*, you view the certificate contained in the SRV2 server's local machine's trusted root certificate store. Note that the thumbprint is the same as the thumbprint shown in *step 2*. In effect, what you have done is to make the certificate in the local machine's personal certificate store trusted on SRV2 (and, using *step 1*, on SRV1).

Note that you could set DSC up to not use SSL (and therefore require certificates). This is, in general, not a good idea as it does not protect us from a man-in-the-middle attack. It also means that the MOF documents transmitted from a pull server are in plain text. For configurations that contain credentials or other internal secrets, the best practice is to use SSL.

In *step 5*, you ensure that the DSC resources that you need (which are contained in the (xPSDesiredStateConfiguration module) have been copied to SRV2. You could also have placed it on the pull server (SRV1) to enable the pull client to download it. This is probably a better approach for production use—just put all the resources in one place, and let the nodes pull that module when necessary.

In *step 17*, you check that DSC has configured SRV2. Depending on how long you take between *step 16* and *step 17*, you may not see SRV2 being in the desired state. As was the case in the *Implementing a web-based DSC pull server* recipe, you need to wait until the LCM in SRV2 checks the consistency (and applies the partial configurations). One way to speed this up would be to reboot SRV2 after *step 16*. After the reboot, SRV2 would check for DSC consistency without waiting.

11
Managing Hyper-V

In this chapter, we cover the following recipes:

- ▸ Installing and configuring Hyper-V
- ▸ Creating a virtual machine
- ▸ Using PowerShell Direct
- ▸ Working with VM groups
- ▸ Configuring VM hardware
- ▸ Configuring Hyper-V networking
- ▸ Implementing nested Hyper-V
- ▸ Managing VM state
- ▸ Configuring VM and storage movement
- ▸ Configuring VM replication
- ▸ Managing VM checkpoints

Introduction

Hyper-V is Microsoft's **virtual machine** (**VM**) hypervisor. Both Windows Server 2019 and Windows 10 include Hyper-V as an option you can install. The Hyper-V feature is included in all versions of Windows Server 2019, as well as in the Enterprise, Professional, and Education editions of Windows 10.

Hyper-V was first released with Server 2008 and has been improved with each successive version of Windows Server. Improvements include additional features, support of the latest hardware, and scalability.

Hyper-V supports nested Hyper-V, the ability to run Hyper-V inside a Hyper-V VM. Nested Hyper-V has some great use cases, such as in training—give each student a VM on a large blade in which are the VMs needed for the course labs. Nested Hyper-V also provides an additional layer of security that might be useful in multi-tenant scenarios.

Microsoft also ships a free version of Hyper-V, the Microsoft Hyper-V Server. The Hyper-V Server runs virtual machines with no GUI. You configure and manage remotely using recipes like the ones in this chapter.

This chapter focuses solely on Hyper-V inside Windows Server 2019, although you can manage Hyper-V Server using the tools used in this chapter's recipes. References to your Hyper-V servers refer to your Windows 2019 servers that have the Hyper-V feature added.

Hyper-V's management tools enable you to configure and manage both the Hyper-V service and the virtual machines running on your Hyper-V servers. This chapter starts with installing and configuring the Hyper-V feature. Later in the chapter, you create and manage virtual machines, and use `PSDirect`.

Installing and configuring Hyper-V

With Windows Server 2019, to add Hyper-V to your server, you install the Hyper-V feature. This recipe installs Hyper-V on two servers: `HV1` and `HV2`, which are domain-joined Windows 2019 servers with no added features.

Getting ready

In this recipe, you do the set up remotely from a client machine, `CL1`, using the Hyper-V cmdlets and PowerShell's remoting capabilities. `CL1` is a domain-joined Windows 10 system with the RSAT tools installed. You previously set up the `CL1` client in the *Installing RSAT tools on Windows 10 and Windows Server 2019* recipe.

How to do it...

1. From `CL1`, install the Hyper-V feature on `HV1` and `HV2`:

    ```
    $Sb = {
      Install-WindowsFeature -Name Hyper-V -IncludeManagementTools
    }
    Invoke-Command -ComputerName HV1, HV2 -ScriptBlock $Sb
    ```

2. Reboot both servers to complete the installation:

```
Restart-Computer -ComputerName HV1, HV2 -Force
```

3. Create a `PSSession` with both HV servers (after the restart has completed):

```
$S = New-PSSession HV1, HV2
```

4. Create and set the location for VMs and VHDs on `HV1` and `HV2`, then view the results:

```
$Sb = {
    New-Item -Path C:\Vm -ItemType Directory -Force |
        Out-Null
    New-Item -Path C:\Vm\Vhds -ItemType Directory -Force |
        Out-Null
    New-Item -Path C:\Vm\VMs -ItemType Directory -force |
        Out-Null
    Get-ChildItem -Path C:\Vm }
Invoke-Command -ScriptBlock $Sb -Session $S
```

5. Set default paths for Hyper-V VM hard disks and VM configuration information:

```
$SB = {
  $VMs  = 'C:\Vm\Vhds'
  $VHDs = 'C:\Vm\VMs\Managing Hyper-V'
  Set-VMHost -ComputerName Localhost -VirtualHardDiskPath $VMs
  Set-VMHost -ComputerName Localhost -VirtualMachinePath $VHDs
}
Invoke-Command -ScriptBlock $SB -Session $S
```

6. Set up NUMA spanning:

```
$SB = {
  Set-VMHost -NumaSpanningEnabled $true
}
Invoke-Command -ScriptBlock $SB -Session $S
```

7. Set up `EnhancedSessionMode`:

```
$SB = {
 Set-VMHost -EnableEnhancedSessionMode $true
}
Invoke-Command -ScriptBlock $SB -Session $S
```

8. Set up host resource metering on HV1, HV2:

```
$SB = {
 $RMInterval = New-TimeSpan -Hours 0 -Minutes 15
   Set-VMHost -ResourceMeteringSaveInterval $RMInterval
}
Invoke-Command -ScriptBlock $SB -Session $S
```

9. Review key VMHost settings:

```
$SB = {
  Get-VMHost
  }
$P = 'Name', 'V*Path','Numasp*', 'Ena*','RES*'
Invoke-Command -ScriptBlock $SB -Session $S |
  Format-Table -Property $P
```

How it works...

In *step 1*, you use the Install-WindowsFeature cmdlet to install Hyper-V on HV1 and HV2 remotely, which looks like this:

```
PS C:\foo> $Sb = {
             Install-WindowsFeature -Name Hyper-V -IncludeManagementTools
           }
PS C:\foo> Invoke-Command -ComputerName HV1, HV2 -ScriptBlock $Sb


Success Restart Needed Exit Code     Feature Result                              PSComputerName
------- -------------- ---------     --------------                              --------------
True    Yes            SuccessRest... {Hyper-V, Hyper-V Module for Windows Power... HV1  <----
WARNING: You must restart this server to finish the installation process.
True    Yes            SuccessRest... {Hyper-V, Hyper-V Module for Windows Power... HV2  <----
WARNING: You must restart this server to finish the installation process.
```

In *step 2*, you reboot HV1 and HV2, which completes the process of installing Hyper-V on both servers. There is no output from this step.

After the reboot, in *step 3*, you create a remoting session on both HV1 and HV2. You use this in the following steps, but there is no output.

In *step 4*, you create new folders to hold virtual machines and virtual hard drives on both servers. The output of this step looks like this:

```
PS C:\foo> $Sb = {
               New-Item -Path C:\Vm -ItemType Directory -Force |
                  Out-Null
               New-Item -Path C:\Vm\Vhds -ItemType Directory -Force |
                  Out-Null
               New-Item -Path C:\Vm\VMs -ItemType Directory -force |
                  Out-Null
               Get-ChildItem -Path C:\Vm
             }
PS C:\foo> Invoke-Command -ComputerName HV1, HV2 -ScriptBlock $Sb

    Directory: C:\Vm


Mode                LastWriteTime       Length Name      PSComputerName
----                -------------       ------ ----      --------------
d-----        20/11/2018     23:09             Vhds      HV2
d-----        20/11/2018     23:09             VMs       HV2
d-----        20/11/2018     23:09             Vhds      HV1
d-----        20/11/2018     23:09             VMs       HV1
```

In *step 5*, you configure Hyper-V to save VMs and VHDs in the newly created folder on both servers. In *step 6*, you configure Hyper-V to support NUMA. In *step 7*, you configure EnhancedSessionMode. In *step 8*, you configure host resource metering. These four steps produce no output.

In *step 9*, you look to see how HV1 and HV2 are configured, which looks like this:

```
PS C:\foo> $SB = {
             Get-VMHost
           }
PS C:\foo> $P = 'Name', 'V*Path','Numasp*', 'Ena*','RES*'
PS C:\foo> Invoke-Command -Scriptblock $SB -Session $S |
             Format-Table -Property $P

Name VirtualHardDiskPath VirtualMachinePath              NumaSpanningEnabled EnableEnhancedSessionMode ResourceMeteringSaveInterval
---- ------------------- ------------------              ------------------- ------------------------- ----------------------------
HV1  C:\Vm\Vhds          C:\Vm\VMs\Managing Hyper-V                     True                           True 01:00:00
HV2  C:\Vm\Vhds          C:\Vm\VMs\Managing Hyper-V                     True                           True 01:00:00
```

There's more...

In *step 1*, you install the Hyper-V feature on two servers. You can only do this successfully if the host you are using supports the necessary virtualization capabilities and you have enabled them in your system's BIOS. To ensure if your system is capable, see this link: http://mikefrobbins.com/2012/09/06/use-powershell-to-check-for-processor-cpu-second-level-address-translation-slat-support/. Additionally, ensure you double-check the BIOS to ensure virtualization is enabled prior to running this step.

In *step 2*, you restart both servers. You could have allowed `Install-WindowsFeature` (used in *step 1*) to restart the servers automatically by using the `-Restart` switch. In automation terms, this could have meant that the system started rebooting before the remote script had completed, which could cause `Invoke-Command` to error out. The recipe avoids this by not rebooting after the installation of the Hyper-V features, then rebooting in a controlled way. Once the restart has completed, your script can carry on managing the servers.

In *step 5* through *step 8*, you set up one aspect of the VM hosts. You could have combined these steps and just called `Set-VMHost` once with all of the properties specified.

See also

You can find more information on some of the Hyper-V features used in this recipe (details of which are outside the scope of this book), as follows:

Features	Links for more information
Connecting to a VM, including enhanced session mode	`https://docs.microsoft.com/en-us/windows-server/virtualization/hyper-v/learn-more/use-local-resources-on-hyper-v-virtual-machine-with-vmconnect`
Understanding the hard disk options	`https://www.altaro.com/hyper-v/understanding-working-vhdx-files/`
Hyper-V and NUMA	`https://blogs.technet.microsoft.com/pracheta/2014/01/22/numa-understand-it-its-usefulness-with-windows-server-2012/`
Configuring Hyper-V Resource Metering	`https://redmondmag.com/articles/2013/08/15/hyper-v-resource-metering.aspx`

Creating a VM

Creating a Hyper-V virtual machine is relatively straightforward and consists of a few simple steps.

First, you need to create the VM itself inside Hyper-V. Then, you create the VM's virtual hard drive, and add it to the VM. You may also wish to adjust the number of processors and memory for the VM and set the contents of the VM's DVD drive.

Once you have created your VM, you need to install the VM's operating system. You have a number of options in terms of how you deploy Windows (or Linux) in a Hyper-V VM.

The Windows Assessment and Deployment Kit, a free product from Microsoft, contains a variety of tools to assist in the automation of deploying Windows. These include **Deployment Image Servicing and Management (DISM)**, **Windows Imaging and Configuration Designer (Windows ICD)**, **Windows System Image Manager (Windows SIM)**, **User State Migration Tool (USMT)**, and a lot more. For more information on the tools and deploying Windows, see `https://docs.microsoft.com/en-us/windows/deployment/windows-deployment-scenarios-and-tools`.

Another way to install the OS into a VM is to just create the VM (either with PowerShell or the **Hyper-V Manager**) and attach the operating system's ISO image into the VM's DVD drive. After starting the VM, you do a manual installation and once the OS is installed, you can use the recipes in this book to configure the server to your needs.

In this recipe, you create a VM, `PSDirect`, which has a hostname of `Tiger`. In building the VM, you assign the Windows Server 2019 DVD to the VM's DVD drive. This ensures that, when you start the VM, Windows commences the GUI setup process, ending up with a fully installed OS inside the VM. The details of performing the actual installation are outside the scope of this recipe.

Two small issues using the GUI to install Windows Server 2019 are that the machine name is randomly generated by Windows and the VM is set up as a workgroup computer and not joined to the domain. You can easily script both renaming the server and joining the domain.

The scripts used to generate the VM farm used in this book are examples of how to deploy Windows Server 2019 in a more automated fashion using a `SETUP.XML` file that specifies the details of the installation. The scripts that create the VMs used are available online at GitHub. See `https://github.com/doctordns/ReskitBuildScripts` for the scripts and documentation on them.

Getting ready

You run this this recipe on the VM host `HV1` that you created in the *Installing and configuring Hyper-V* recipe. You also need the Windows Server 2019 ISO image. For testing purposes, this could be an evaluation version, or a full retail edition.

How to do it...

1. Set up the VM name and paths for this recipe:

```
$VMName       = 'PSDirect'
$VMLocation   = 'C:\Vm\VMs'
$VHDlocation  = 'C:\Vm\Vhds'
$VhdPath      = "$VHDlocation\PSDirect.Vhdx"
$ISOPath      = 'C:\builds\windows_server_2019_x64_dvd.iso'
```

2. Create a new VM:

```
New-VM -Name $VMName -Path $VMLocation -MemoryStartupBytes 1GB
```

3. Create a virtual disk file for the VM:

```
New-VHD -Path $VhdPath -SizeBytes 128GB -Dynamic | Out-Null
```

4. Add the virtual hard drive to the VM:

```
Add-VMHardDiskDrive -VMName $VMName -Path $VhdPath
```

5. Set the ISO image in the VM's DVD drive:

```
$IHT = @{
  VMName            = $VMName
  ControllerNumber  = 1
  Path              = $ISOPath
}
Set-VMDvdDrive @IHT
```

6. Start the VM:

```
Start-VM -VMname $VMname
```

7. View the results:

```
Get-VM -Name $VMname
```

8. Use the VM connect tool from the Hyper-V console and complete the OS installation of the VM using the GUI setup tool.

How it works...

In *step 1*, you create a number of variables representing values you use in this recipe. This step produces no output.

In *step 2*, you use the `New-VM` cmdlet to create a new Hyper-V VM, which produces the following output:

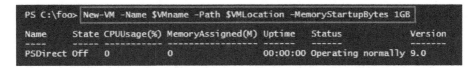

In *step 3*, you create a new VHDX file, which is to serve as the VM's `C:` drive. In *step 4*, you add the newly created VHDX to the `PSDirect` VM. In *step 5*, you add the Windows Server 2019 ISO image to the VM. Then, in *step 6*, you start the VM. These four steps produce no output.

In *step 7*, you use the `Get-VM` cmdlet to see the newly created VM, which looks like this:

Using the VMConnect feature of the Hyper-V GUI, in *step 8*, you can view the VM. Initially, you see something like this:

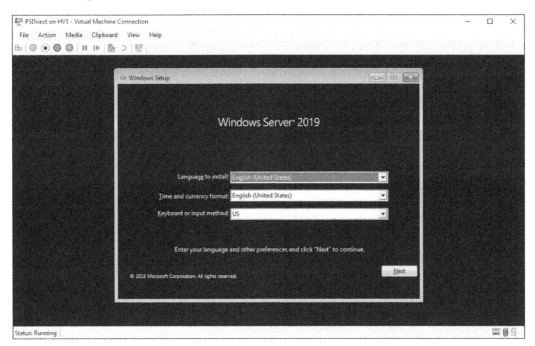

From that screen, you click **Next**, and so on, to complete the GUI installation process. To get the VM ready for the next step, you should rename the VM (`Tiger`) and join the domain.

There's more...

In *step 1*, you use the Windows 2019 Server ISO image, saved on `HV1` as `C:\builds\windows_server_2019_x64_dvd.iso`. Depending on where you obtain the image, the file name may differ.

In *step 8*, you view the VM, which should have started and have reached the initial dialog in the setup process. From here, you can use the GUI to complete the installation of Windows Server 2019. The details of Windows Server setup are outside the scope of this book and are left as an exercise for the reader.

Using PowerShell Direct

PowerShell Direct (**PSD**) is a new feature with Windows Server 2016 (and on Windows 10 Anniversary Update or later). PSD enables you to use PowerShell remoting to access a Hyper-V VM without needing to set up networking and firewall settings inside the VM. With PSD, you use `Invoke-Command`, specifying either the VM's name or the VM's VMID (the VMID is a GUID used internally by Hyper-V to identify a VM) rather than the VM's hostname. You can also use the VM name or VMID to enter a remote session using `Enter-PSSession`.

In earlier versions of Hyper-V, you needed a networking connection between your Hyper-V host and the guest OS in order to remote into the guest. This meant setting up and establishing network connectivity. With PSD, you can use the VM's name or ID and remote straight in. This is useful when a VM is misconfigured and its network connectivity is unavailable.

Getting ready

For this recipe, you need the Hyper-V host that you set up in the *Installing and configuring Hyper-V* recipe. You also need the VM setup in the *Creating a virtual machine* recipe. The VM has a VM name of `PSDirect`, but has a hostname of `Tiger`.

To ensure security, you need to specify credentials when you call `Invoke-Command` or `Enter-PSSession`. You can either specify the `-Credential` parameter or let either cmdlet prompt for credentials. With Hyper-V and `PSDirect`, the VM name and the hostname of the OS running inside the VM do not need to be the same.

Getting ready

This recipe uses the HV1 host you created in the *Installing and configuring VM* recipe, along with a Windows Server VM running on HV1. This VM has a VM name of PSDirect, a hostname of Tiger, and a local administrator password of Pa$$w0rd. You can use the *Creating a VM recipe*, suitably adapted, to create the PSDirect VM.

How to do it...

1. Create a credential object for the local administrator on PSDirect:

```
$RKAn    = 'Administrator'
$PS      = 'Pa$$w0rd'
$RKP     = ConvertTo-SecureString -String $PS -AsPlainText -Force
$T       = 'System.Management.Automation.PSCredential'
$RKCred  = New-Object -TypeName $T -ArgumentList $RKAn,$RKP
```

2. Retrieve and display the details of the PSDirect VM:

```
Get-VM -Name PSDirect
```

3. Invoke a command on the VM, specifying the VM name:

```
$SBHT = @{
  VMName      = 'PSDirect'
  Credential  = $RKCred
  ScriptBlock = {hostname}
}
Invoke-Command @SBHT
```

4. Invoke a command based on VMId:

```
$VMID = (Get-VM -VMName PSDirect).VMId.Guid
$ICMHT = @{
  VMid        = $VMID
  Credential  = $RKCred
  ScriptBlock = {hostname}
}
Invoke-Command @ICMHT
```

5. Enter a PS remoting session with the `PSDirect` VM:

```
Enter-PSSession -VMName PSDirect -Credential $RKCred
Get-CimInstance -Class Win32_ComputerSystem
Exit-PSSession
```

How it works...

In *step 1*, you create a credential object for the local administrator of the `PSDirect` virtual machine. This step creates no output.

In *step 2*, you retrieve the details of the `PSDirect` virtual machine, which looks like this:

```
PS C:\foo> Get-VM -Name PSDirect

Name      State    CPUUsage(%) MemoryAssigned(M) Uptime             Status             Version
----      -----    ----------- ----------------- ------             ------             -------
PSDirect  Running  1           1132              02:33:05.3120000   Operating normally 9.0
```

In *step 3*, you use the PSD feature and invoke a command inside the `PSDirect` VM using just the virtual machine name, which looks like this:

```
PS C:\foo> $SBHT = @{
             VMName      = 'PSDirect'
             Credential  = $RKCred
             ScriptBlock = {hostname}
           }
PS C:\foo> Invoke-Command @SBHT

Tiger
```

In *step 4*, you invoke a command inside the `PSDirect` virtual machine but using the VM's VMID value, like this:

```
PS C:\foo> $VMID = (Get-VM -VMName PSDirect).VMId.Guid
PS C:\foo> $ICMHT = @{
             VMid        = $VMID
             Credential  = $RKCred
             ScriptBlock = {hostname}
           }
PS C:\foo> Invoke-Command @ICMHT

Tiger
```

In *step 5*, you enter a PS remoting session with the PSDirect VM, which looks like this:

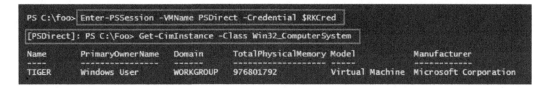

There's more...

In *step 3* and *step 4*, you make use of PSD by invoking a command using either the VM's name or the VM's VMID value. In *step 5*, you use Enter-PSSession and enter a PowerShell session in the PSDirect VM, and as you can see, the hostname of that VM is Tiger.

Working with VM groups

VM groups are a feature of Hyper-V that allow you to group VMs for the purposes of automation. With Hyper-V, there are two types of VM groups: a VMCollectionType and a ManagementCollectionType. A VMCollectionType VM group contains VMs, while the ManagementCollectionType VM group contains VMCollectionType VM groups.

The might enable you to have two VMCollectionType VM groups, SQLAccVMG (that contains the VMs SQLAcct1, SQLAcct2, and SQLAcct3) and a group, SQLAccVMG, that contains the VMs SQLMfg1 and SQLMfg2.

You could then create a ManagementCollectionType VM group, VM-All, containing the two VMCollectionType VM groups.

Getting ready

You run this recipe on the HV2 Hyper-V server, which you created in the *Installing and configuring Hyper-V* recipe. This Hyper-V server has a number of VMs defined. For the purposes of this recipe, you can create the necessary VMs using the following:

```
# Create HV2 VMs for Hyper-V Chapter
$VMLocation  = 'C:\Vm\VMs'
# Create VM1
$VMN1        = 'SQLAcct1'
New-VM -Name $VMN1 -Path "$VMLocation\$VMN1"
# Create VM2
```

```
$VMN2          = 'SQLAcct2'
New-VM -Name $VMN2 -Path "$VMLocation\$VMN2"
# Create VM3
$VMN3          = 'SQLAcct3'
New-VM -Name $VMN3 -Path "$VMLocation\$VMN3"
# Create VM4
$VMN4          = 'SQLMfg1'
New-VM -Name $VMN4 -Path "$VMLocation\$VMN4"
# Create VM5
$VMN5          = 'SQLMfg2'
New-VM -Name $VMN5 -Path "$VMLocation\$VMN5"
```

How to do it...

1. Set up Hyper-V VM groups and display them:

    ```
    $VHGHT1 = @{
      Name      = 'SQLAccVMG'
      GroupType = 'VMCollectionType'
    }
    $VMGroupACC = New-VMGroup @VHGHT1
    $VHGHT2 = @{
      Name      = 'SQLMfgVMG'
      GroupType = 'VMCollectionType'
    }
    $VMGroupMFG = New-VMGroup @VHGHT2
    ```

2. Create arrays of group member VM names:

    ```
    $ACCVMs = 'SQLAcct1', 'SQLAcct2','SQLAcct3'
    $MFGVms = 'SQLMfg1', 'SQLMfg2'
    ```

3. Add members to the accounting SQL VM group:

    ```
    Foreach ($Server in $ACCVMs) {
        $VM = Get-VM -Name $Server
        Add-VMGroupMember -Name SQLAccVMG -VM $VM
    }
    ```

4. Add members to the manufacturing SQL VM group:

```
Foreach ($Server in $MfgVMs) {
    $VM = Get-VM -Name $Server
    Add-VMGroupMember -Name  SQLMfgVMG  -VM $VM
}
```

5. Create a management collection VM group:

```
$VMGHT = @{
  Name      = 'VMMGSQL'
  GroupType = 'ManagementCollectionType'
}
$VMMGSQL = New-VMGroup  @VMGHT
```

6. Add the two VM collection type groups to the VM management group:

```
Add-VMGroupMember -Name VMMGSQL -VMGroupMember $VMGroupACC,
                                              $VMGroupMFG
```

7. Set `FormatEnumerationLimit` to a higher value, then view the VM groups:

```
$FormatEnumerationLimit = 99
Get-VMGroup |
   Format-Table -Property Name, GroupType, VMGroupMembers,
                          VMMembers
```

8. Stop all the SQL VMs:

```
Foreach ($VM in ((Get-VMGroup VMMGSQL).VMGroupMembers.vmmembers))
{
  Stop-VM -Name $vm.name -WarningAction SilentlyContinue
}
```

9. Set the CPU count in all SQL VMs to 4:

```
Foreach ($VM in ((Get-VMGroup VMMGSQL).VMGroupMembers.VMMembers))
{
  Set-VMProcessor -VMName $VM.name -Count 4
}
```

10. Set accounting SQL VMs to have 6 processors:

```
Foreach ($VM in ((Get-VMGroup SQLAccVMG).VMMembers)) {
  Set-VMProcessor -VMName $VM.name -Count 6
}
```

11. Check processor counts for all VMs sorted by CPU count:

```
$VMS = (Get-VMGroup -Name VMMGSQL).VMGroupMembers.VMMembers
Get-VMProcessor -VMName $VMS.Name |
   Sort-Object -Property Count -Descending |
      Format-Table -Property VMName, Count
```

12. Remove VMs from VM groups:

```
$ACCVMs = (Get-VMGroup -Name SQLAccVMG).VMMEMBERS
Foreach ($VM in $ACCVMS) {
   $X = Get-VM -VMName $VM.name
   Remove-VMGroupMember -Name SQLAccVMG -VM $x
   }
$MFGVMs = (Get-VMGroup -Name SQLMfgVMG).VMMEMBERS
Foreach ($VM in $MFGVMS) {
   $X = Get-VM -VMName $VM.Name
   Remove-VMGroupMember -Name SQLMfgVMG -VM $x
}
```

13. Remove all the VM groups from VM management groups:

```
$VMGS = (Get-VMGroup -Name VMMGSQL).VMMembers
Foreach ($VMG in $VMGS) {
   $X = Get-VMGroup -VMName $VMG.Name
   Remove-VMGroupMember -Name VMMGSQL -VMGroupName $x
}
```

14. Remove all the VM groups:

```
Remove-VMGroup SQLAccVMG -Force
Remove-VMGroup SQLMfgVMG -Force
Remove-VMGroup VMMGSQL -Force
```

How it works...

In the first part of this recipe, you create and populate two VM collection type VM groups and a VM management type VM group. Then, you use these VM groups in some management activities—in this case, updating the VM configuration for several VMs.

In *step 1,* you create two VM groups: SQLAccVMG and SQLMfgVMG. In *step 2,* you create two arrays of VM names. In *step 3* and *step 4,* you add the VMs to the two VM collection type VM groups. In *step 5,* you create a ManagementCollectionType VM group and in *step 6,* you populate the VM management collection type group with the two VM collection type VM groups. There is no output from these steps.

In *step 7,* you view the VM groups and their members, which looks like this:

```
PS C:\foo> $FormatEnumerationLimit = 99
PS C:\foo> Get-VMGroup |
            Format-Table -Property Name, GroupType, VMGroupMembers,
                            VMMembers


Name       GroupType VMGroupMembers           VMMembers
----       --------- --------------           ---------
VMMGSQL    ManagementCollectionType {SQLMfgVMG, SQLAccVMG}
SQLMfgVMG          VMCollectionType           {SQLMfg1, SQLMfg2}
SQLAccVMG          VMCollectionType           {SQLAcct3, SQLAcct1, SQLAcct2}
```

In *step 8,* you use the management collection type VM group to stop all the SQL VMs. In *step 9,* you set all of the SQL VMs to have four virtual processors, and in *step 10,* you set the VMs in the SQLAccVMG to have four CPUs. These three steps produce no output.

In *step 11,* you view the processor counts for all the SQL VMs, which looks like this:

```
PS C:\foo> $VMS = (Get-VMGroup -Name VMMGSQL).VMGroupMembers.VMMembers
PS C:\foo> Get-VMProcessor -VMName $VMS.name |
             Sort-Object -Property Count -Descending |
             Format-Table -Property VMName, Count

VMName    Count
------    -----
SQLAcct3      6
SQLAcct1      6
SQLAcct2      6
SQLMfg1       4
SQLMfg2       4
```

In *step 12,* you remove the VMs from the VM collection type VM groups, and in *step 13* you remove the VM collection type VM groups from the VM management groups. Finally, in *step 14,* you remove all the VM groups from HV2. There is no output from these three steps.

There's more...

In *step 12* and *step 13,* you explicitly remove members from the three VM groups before, in *step 14,* you remove the three VM groups. If you attempt to remove the VM groups that still have members, the cmdlet fails.

The VM group is a feature of Hyper-V that feels only partly finished. The distinction between VM collection groups and VM management groups seems unnecessary. It might be better if there were just one group type (VM collection) that collected VMs and VM collections. Additionally, it would be useful to add a -VMGroup parameter to most of the cmdlets as an alternative to VMName, VMID, and so on—that way, the cmdlet would apply to **all** the VMs in the specified VM group and not just a single VM.

See also

In this recipe, you updated the CPU count for several VMs. See the *Configuring VM hardware* recipe for more on configuring the VM's virtual hardware.

Configuring VM hardware

Configuring hardware in your virtual machine is very much like configuring a physical computer—just without the need for a screwdriver. With a physical computer, you can adjust the CPUs and BIOS settings. You can also adjust physical RAM, network interfaces, disk interfaces and disk devices, and DVD drives (with/without a loaded DVD), and so on. Each of these physical components is provided within a Hyper-V VM, and the PowerShell cmdlets make it simple to configure the virtual hardware available to any Hyper-V VM.

In this recipe, you adjust the VM's BIOS, CPU count, and memory, and then add a SCSI controller. You then create a virtual disk and assign it to the SCSI controller. Then, you view the results.

Just like in most physical servers, not all of these components can be changed while the server is running. You run this recipe from HV1 and turn the PSDirect VM off before configuring the virtual hardware.

This recipe does not cover the VM's virtual NIC. By default, Virtual Machines (such as you created in the *Creating a virtual machine* recipe) contain a single virtual NIC. But you can always add additional NICs. Configuring the VM's networking is covered in the *Configuring Hyper-V networking* recipe.

Getting ready

This recipe uses the VM you created in the *Creating a virtual machine* recipe. The VM is called PSDirect.

How to do it...

1. Turn off the `PSDirect` VM:

```
Stop-VM -VMName PSDirect
Get-VM  -VMName PSDirect
```

2. Set the `StartupOrder` in the VM's BIOS:

```
$Order = 'IDE','CD','LegacyNetworkAdapter','Floppy'
Set-VMBios -VmName PSDirect -StartupOrder $Order
Get-VMBios PSDirect
```

3. Set and view CPU count for `PSDirect`:

```
Set-VMProcessor -VMName PSDirect -Count 2
Get-VMProcessor -VmName PSDirect |
   Format-Table VMName, Count
```

4. Configure `PSDirect` memory settings:

```
$VMHT = [ordered] @{
  VMName               = 'PSDirect'
  DynamicMemoryEnabled = $true
  MinimumBytes         = 512MB
  StartupBytes         = 1GB
  MaximumBytes         = 2GB
}
Set-VMMemory @VMHT
Get-VMMemory -VMName PSDirect
```

5. Add a SCSI controller to `PSDirect` and view the controllers available in the VM:

```
Add-VMScsiController -VMName PSDirect
Get-VMScsiController -VMName PSDirect
```

6. Restart the VM:

```
Start-VM -VMName PSDirect
Wait-VM -VMName PSDirect -For IPAddress
```

7. Create a new VHDX file:

```
$VHDPath = 'C:\Vm\Vhds\PSDirect-D.VHDX'
New-VHD -Path $VHDPath -SizeBytes 8GB -Dynamic
```

8. Add the VHD to the SCSI controller:

```
$VHDHT = @{
    VMName              = 'PSDirect'
    ControllerType      = 'SCSI'
    ControllerNumber    = 0
    ControllerLocation  = 0
    Path                = $VHDPath
}
Add-VMHardDiskDrive @VHDHT
```

9. Get volumes from `PSDirect` VM:

```
Get-VMScsiController -VMName PSDirect |
    Select-Object -ExpandProperty Drives
```

How it works...

In *step 1*, you turn off the `PSDirect` VM, then get the VM's details, as follows:

```
PS C:\foo> Stop-VM -VMName PSDirect
PS C:\foo> Get-VM -VMName PSDirect

Name     State CPUUsage(%) MemoryAssigned(M) Uptime   Status              Version
----     ----- ----------- ----------------- ------   ------              -------
PSDirect Off   0           0                 00:00:00 Operating normally  9.0
```

In *step 2*, you adjust then view the startup order in the VM's virtual BIOS, which looks like this:

```
PS C:\foo> $Order = 'IDE','CD','LegacyNetworkAdapter','Floppy'
PS C:\foo> Set-VMBios -VmName PSDirect -StartupOrder $Order
PS C:\foo> Get-VMBios PSDirect

VMName    StartupOrder                              NumLockEnabled
------    ------------                              --------------
PSDirect  {IDE, CD, LegacyNetworkAdapter, Floppy}   False
```

In *step 3*, you set and then view the CPU count for the `PSDirect` VM, which looks like this:

```
PS C:\foo> Set-VMProcessor -VMName PSDirect -Count 2
PS C:\foo> Get-VMProcessor -VmName PSDirect |
             Format-Table VMName, Count

VMName    Count
------    -----
PSDirect  2
```

In *step 4,* you adjust and view the VM's memory settings, which looks like this:

```
PS C:\foo> $VMHT = [ordered] @{
              VMName              = 'PSDirect'
              DynamicMemoryEnabled = $true
              MinimumBytes        = 512MB
              StartupBytes        = 1GB
              MaximumBytes        = 2GB
           }
PS C:\foo> Set-VMMemory @VMHT
PS C:\foo> Get-VMMemory -VMName PSDirect

VMName    DynamicMemoryEnabled Minimum(M) Startup(M) Maximum(M)
------    -------------------- ---------- ---------- ----------
PSDirect  True                 512        1024       2048
```

In *step 5,* you add a new SCSI controller to the PSDirect VM, then view the controllers, which looks like this:

```
PS C:\foo> Add-VMScsiController -VMName PSDirect
PS C:\foo> Get-VMScsiController -VMName PSDirect

VMName    ControllerNumber Drives
------    ---------------- ------
PSDirect  0                {}
PSDirect  1                {}
```

In *step 6,* you restart the PSDirect VM, which produces no output. Once the VM has restarted, in *step 7,* you create a new virtual hard drive, that looks like this:

```
PS C:\foo> $VHDPath = 'C:\Vm\Vhds\PSDirect-D.VHDX'
PS C:\foo> New-VHD -Path $VHDPath -SizeBytes 8GB -Dynamic

ComputerName            : HV1
Path                    : C:\Vm\Vhds\PSDirect-D.VHDX
VhdFormat               : VHDX
VhdType                 : Dynamic
FileSize                : 4194304
Size                    : 8589934592
MinimumSize             :
LogicalSectorSize       : 512
PhysicalSectorSize      : 4096
BlockSize               : 33554432
ParentPath              :
DiskIdentifier          : 8A3493A2-B6E6-4ECD-B7A1-B721896D2527
FragmentationPercentage : 0
Alignment               : 1
Attached                : False
DiskNumber              :
IsPMEMCompatible        : False
AddressAbstractionType  : None
Number                  :
```

In *step 8*, you add the VHDX to the VM, which produces no output. In *step 9*, you view the details of the virtual hard drive in the SCSI controller in the `PSDirect` VM, which looks like this:

```
PS C:\foo> Get-VMScsiController -VMName PSDirect |
             Select-Object -ExpandProperty Drives

VMName    ControllerType ControllerNumber ControllerLocation DiskNumber Path
------    -------------- ---------------- ------------------ ---------- ----
PSDirect  SCSI                0                 0                        C:\Vm\Vhds\PSDirect-D.VHDX
```

There's more...

In addition to the hardware components covered in this recipe, you can also manage a VM's COM ports and diskette drives. While you cannot directly connect a VM's COM port to the host's COM port, you can configure a VM to communicate with the physical computer via a named pipe on the host computer. A typical use for this is kernel debugging—probably something most IT pros rarely ever do. For more information on named pipes, see https://docs.microsoft.com/en-us/windows/desktop/ipc/named-pipes.

You can also use a virtual floppy drive in a VM. There is no cmdlet support to create a virtual floppy drive file (a `.vfd` file) in the Hyper-V module, nor is there support for mounting a VFD file in Windows. You can create VFD files using Hyper-V Manager and then use `Set-VMFloppyDiskDrive` to attach the VFD file as a floppy disk drive in the VM.

Configuring Hyper-V networking

Each VM is essentially another host in your infrastructure. It's important therefore to set up networking for your Hyper-V hosts. There are three basic types of networking:

- **External**: This enables a VM to share the host's physical NIC and participate in host-to-host networking
- **VM to VM only**: This is a secure network that enables traffic between VMs only
- **VM to VM and VM Host**: This is a fairly secure network that shares traffic between VMs and the VM host

You start the configuration process by creating a VM switch. If you create either an external or VM to VM and VM host switch, then Windows adds a NIC into the VM host to enable the host to communicate via the VM Switch. Once you have the VM switch(es) set up, you can configure a VM's NIC to use a specific switch. This recipe shows some of the basic steps involved in getting started with Hyper-V networking.

Getting ready

You run this recipe on HV1, which you set up in the *Installing and configuring the Hyper-V feature recipe*. HV1 has no switch defined—you create a virtual switch in this recipe. Additionally, this Hyper-V server has a VM, PSDirect, which you have set up and configured in earlier recipes in this chapter. This VM has a hostname of Tiger. Also, the local administrator has a password of Pa$$w0rd.

How to do it...

1. Get NIC details and IP address from the PSDirect VM:

    ```
    Get-VMNetworkAdapter -VMName PSDirect
    ```

2. Create a credential, then get VM networking details:

    ```
    $RKAn    = 'localhost\Administrator'
    $PS      = 'Pa$$w0rd'
    $RKP     = ConvertTo-SecureString -String $PS -AsPlainText -Force
    $T       = 'System.Management.Automation.PSCredential'
    $RKCred = New-Object -TypeName $T -ArgumentList $RKAn, $RKP
    $VMHT = @{
      VMName      = 'PSDirect'
      ScriptBlock = {Get-NetIPConfiguration }
      Credential  = $RKCred
    }
    Invoke-Command @VMHT | Format-List
    ```

3. Create a virtual switch on HV1:

    ```
    $VSHT = @{
      Name            = 'External'
      NetAdapterName  = 'Ethernet'
      Notes           = 'Created on HV1'
    }
    New-VMSwitch @VSHT
    ```

4. Connect PSDirect to the switch:

    ```
    Connect-VMNetworkAdapter -VMName PSDirect -SwitchName External
    ```

5. See the VM's network adapter information:

    ```
    Get-VMNetworkAdapter -VMName PSDirect
    ```

6. With `PSDirect` now in the network, observe the IP address in the VM:

```
$NCHT = @{
    VMName      = 'PSDirect'
    ScriptBlock = {Get-NetIPConfiguration}
    Credential  = $RKCred
}
Invoke-Command @NCHT
```

7. View the hostname on `PSDirect`, reusing the hash table from *step 6*:

```
$NCHT.ScriptBlock = {hostname}
Invoke-Command @NCHT
```

8. Change the name of the host in `VM1`, making use of the hash table from *step 6* and *step 7*:

```
$NCHT.ScriptBlock = {Rename-Computer -NewName Wolf -Force}
Invoke-Command @NCHT
```

9. Reboot and wait for the restarted `PSDirect`:

```
Restart-VM -VMName PSDirect -Wait -For IPAddress -Force
```

10. Get the hostname of the `PSDirect` VM:

```
$NCHT.ScriptBlock = {hostname}
Invoke-Command @NCHT
```

How it works...

In *step 1*, you get the NIC details and IP addresses assigned to the `PSDirect` VM, which looks like this:

```
PS C:\foo> Get-VMNetworkAdapter -VMName PSDirect

Name             IsManagementOs VMName   SwitchName MacAddress    Status IPAddresses
----             -------------- ------   ---------- ----------    ------ -----------
Network Adapter  False          PSDirect            00155D0AC900  {Ok}   {169.254.141.180, fe80::d93a:d509:6135:8db4}
```

In *step 2*, you create a credential object for the `PSDirect` virtual machine. Then, you use this to execute a script block on `PSDirect`, which returns the host's network IP configuration, and looks like this:

```
PS C:\foo> $RKAn = 'localhost\Administrator'
PS C:\foo> $PS = 'Pa$$w0rd'
PS C:\foo> $RKP = ConvertTo-SecureString -String $PS -AsPlainText -Force
PS C:\foo> $T = 'System.Management.Automation.PSCredential'
PS C:\foo> $RKCred = New-Object -TypeName $T -ArgumentList $RKAn, $RKP
PS C:\foo> $VMHT = @{
    VMName      = 'PSDirect'
    ScriptBlock = {Get-NetIPConfiguration}
    Credential  = $RKCred
    }
PS C:\foo> Invoke-Command @VMHT | Format-List

InterfaceAlias       : Ethernet
InterfaceIndex       : 2
InterfaceDescription : Microsoft Hyper-V Network Adapter
NetAdapter.Status    :
PSComputerName       : PSDirect
```

In *step 3*, you create a new virtual switch on HV1 with the switch name set to External. The output of this step looks like this:

```
PS C:\foo> $VSHT = @{
    Name            = 'External'
    NetAdapterName  = 'Ethernet'
    Notes           = 'Created on HV1'
    }
PS C:\foo> New-VMSwitch @VSHT

Name     SwitchType NetAdapterInterfaceDescription
----     ---------- ------------------------------
External External   Microsoft Hyper-V Network Adapter
```

In *step 4*, you add the NIC in the PSDirect VM to the new External switch. This step produces no output.

With the VM now having network connectivity, in *step 5*, you look at the VM's networking details, which look like this:

```
PS C:\foo> Get-VMNetworkAdapter -VMName PSDirect

Name            IsManagementOs VMName   SwitchName MacAddress   Status IPAddresses
----            -------------- ------   ---------- ----------   ------ -----------
Network Adapter False          PSDirect External   00155D0AC900 {Ok}   {10.10.10.150, fe80::d93a:d509:6135:8db4}
```

In *step 6*, you get the host's networking details, showing the IP address and DNS servers (obtained from the DHCP server), like this:

```
PS C:\foo> $NCHT = @{
              VMName      = 'PSDirect'
              ScriptBlock = {Get-NetIPConfiguration}
              Credential  = $RKCred
          }
PS C:\foo> Invoke-Command @NCHT

InterfaceAlias       : Ethernet
InterfaceIndex       : 2
InterfaceDescription : Microsoft Hyper-V Network Adapter
NetAdapter.Status    :
NetProfile.Name      : Reskit.Org
IPv4Address          : 10.10.10.150
IPv6DefaultGateway   :
IPv4DefaultGateway   :
DNSServer            : 10.10.10.10
                       10.10.10.11
PSComputerName       : PSDirect
```

In *step 7*, you view the hostname of the PSDirect VM, which looks like this:

```
PS C:\foo> $NCHT.ScriptBlock = {hostname}
PS C:\foo> Invoke-Command @NCHT
Tiger
```

In *step 8*, you change the name of the PSDirect VM to Wolf, which looks like this:

```
PS C:\foo> $NCHT.ScriptBlock = {Rename-Computer -NewName Wolf -Force}
PS C:\foo> Invoke-Command @NCHT
WARNING: The changes will take effect after you restart the computer Tiger.
```

In *step 9*, you restart the PSDirect VM, producing no output. In *step 10*, you re-check the PSDirect VM's hostname, which looks like this:

```
PS C:\foo> $NCHT.ScriptBlock = {hostname}
PS C:\foo> Invoke-Command @NCHT
Wolf
```

There's more...

In *step 1*, you use the `Get-VMNetworkAdapter` for the `PSDirect` VM. The output from this step shows that the virtual NIC inside the `PSDirect` VM is not connected to any switch. It also shows that the VM has assigned an IPV4 **Automatic Private IP Address** (**APIPA**) address to the NIC (in this case, `169.254.141.180`). Since the address chosen by Windows is random, you may see a different address in the `169.254.0.0/16` network. Note that even though Windows has an IP address for the NIC, since you have not connected the VM's NIC to a Hyper-V switch, no networking is possible with the VM until you execute the subsequent steps that resolve that issue. In such cases, using PowerShell Direct, as shown in the *Using PowerShell Direct* recipe, is useful.

In *step 3*, you create a new switch. If you already have an `External` switch created on your Hyper-V host, you can use it in this recipe as opposed to the `External` switch created in this step.

In *step 5* and *step 6,* you view the `PSDirect` VM's networking configuration after you created the `External` VM switch and added the NIC in the `PSDirect` VM to the switch. The initial IP address, which you saw in *step 1,* was automatically assigned when the VM was unable to obtain a DHCP address. After connecting the VM to the network, the VM was able to contact the DHCP server that you set up in the *Installing and authorizing a DHCP server* recipe, and configured in the *Configuring DHCP Scopes* recipe. This DHCP server is used to get an IP address for the `PSDirect` VM.

In *step 7*, you obtain the VM's configured hostname. If you created the VM simply from the default installation via the product DVD, Windows automatically creates a hostname, such as `WIN-O5LPHTHBB5U`. In the *Using PowerShell Direct* recipe, you installed Windows Server 2019 to the PSDirect VM and gave the VM a host name of `Tiger`. In this recipe, regardless of the current hostname, you update the hostname to `Wolf`.

Implementing nested Hyper-V

Nested Hyper-V is a cool feature of Windows 2019 and Windows 10 (Anniversary Update and later). Nested Hyper-V enables a Hyper-V VM to host VMs that also have virtualization enabled. You could, for example, take a physical host (say, `HV1`) and on that host run a VM (`PSDirect`). With nested Hyper-V, you could install Hyper-V in the `PSDirect` VM to enable that VM to host further VMs.

Nested VMs have a number of uses. First, nested VMs hosted in one VM are provided hardware isolation from nested VMs run in other VMs. This provides a further level of security for virtual machines. Nested Hyper-V is also useful for testing and education/training. In a training course, you could give a student one VM (running in a large blade server) and enable the student to create additional VMs as part of the course. You could, for example, run the recipes in this chapter using nested VMs.

Enabling nested Hyper-V is very simple. First, you must update the virtual CPU in the VM you want to support nesting. Therefore, in this recipe, you adjust the virtual CPU in the `PSDirect` VM to expose the virtualization extensions. This has to be done while the VM is turned off. After you restart the VM, you install the Hyper-V feature and create the `NestedVM` VM. This recipe does not show the details of configuring the `NestedVM`, which are left as an exercise for the reader.

Getting ready

This recipe uses the `PSDirect` VM running on the `HV1` Windows Server 2019 system with Hyper-V loaded. You created the Hyper-V server in the *Installing and configuring Hyper-V* recipe. You also make use of the `PSDirect` VM, which you created in the *Creating a virtual machine* recipe. You also updated the VM's hostname (to `Wolf`) in the *Configuring Hyper-V networking* recipe.

How to do it...

1. Stop the `PSDirect` VM:

   ```
   Stop-VM -VMName PSDirect
   ```

2. Change and view the VM's processor to support virtualization:

   ```
   $VMHT = @{
       VMName                        = 'PSDirect'
       ExposeVirtualizationExtensions = $true
   }
   Set-VMProcessor @VMHT
   Get-VMProcessor -VMName PSDirect |
       Format-Table -Property Name, Count,
                            ExposeVirtualizationExtensions
   ```

3. Start the `PSDirect` VM:

   ```
   Start-VM -VMName PSDirect
   Wait-VM  -VMName PSDirect -For Heartbeat
   Get-VM   -VMName PSDirect
   ```

4. Create credentials for the `PSDirect` machine. Note that this assumes the VM has been renamed `Wolf`:

```
$User = 'Wolf\Administrator'
$PHT = @{
  String      = 'Pa$$w0rd'
  AsPlainText = $true
  Force       = $true
}
$PSS  = ConvertTo-SecureString @PHT
$Type = 'System.Management.Automation.PSCredential'
$CredRK = New-Object -TypeName $Type -ArgumentList $User,$PSS
```

5. Create a script block for remote execution:

```
$SB = {
  Install-WindowsFeature -Name Hyper-V -IncludeManagementTools
}
```

6. Install Hyper-V inside the `PSDirect` VM:

```
$Session = New-PSSession -VMName PSDirect -Credential $CredRK
$IHT = @{
  Session     = $Session
  ScriptBlock = $SB
}
Invoke-Command @IHT
```

7. Restart the VM to finish adding Hyper-V to the `PSDirect` VM:

```
Stop-VM  -VMName PSDirect
Start-VM -VMName PSDirect
Wait-VM  -VMName PSDirect -For IPAddress
```

8. Create a nested VM inside the `PSDirect` VM:

```
$SB2 = {
  $VMname = 'NestedVM'
  New-VM -Name $VMname -MemoryStartupBytes 1GB
}
$IHT2 = @{
  VMName = 'PSDirect'
  ScriptBlock = $SB2
}
Invoke-Command @IHT2 -Credential $CredRK
```

How it works...

This recipe stops, reconfigures, then restarts the PSDirect VM. Once the VM is running, you create an embedded VM (NestedVM) inside the PSDirect VM.

In *step 1*, you stop the PSDirect VM on the HV1 server, which produces no output.

In *step 2*, you update the virtual CPU in the PSDirect VM to expose the virtualization extensions (in the PSDirect VM), which looks like this:

```
PS C:\foo> $VMHT = @{
               VMName                         = 'PSDirect'
               ExposeVirtualizationExtensions = $true
           }
PS C:\foo> Set-VMProcessor @VMHT
PS C:\foo> Get-VMProcessor -VMName PSDirect |
               Format-Table -Property Name, Count,
                                      ExposeVirtualizationExtensions

Name        Count ExposeVirtualizationExtensions
----        ----- ------------------------------
Processor     2                             True   ⟵
```

In *step 3*, you restart the PSDirect VM, which looks like this:

```
PS C:\foo> Start-VM -VMName PSDirect
PS C:\foo> Wait-VM  -VMName PSDirect -For Heartbeat
PS C:\foo> Get VM   -VMName PSDirect


Name      State   CPUUsage(%) MemoryAssigned(M) Uptime            Status             Version
----      -----   ----------- ----------------- ------            ------             -------
PSDirect  Running 15          1024              00:00:30.2800000  Operating normally 9.0
```

In *step 4,* you create a credentials object. In *step 5*, you create a script block for execution on PSDirect. These two steps produce no output.

In *step 6*, you install the Hyper-V feature inside the PSDirect VM, adding the management tools, which looks like this:

```
PS C:\foo> $Session = New-PSSession -VMName PSDirect -Credential $CredRK
PS C:\foo> $IHT = @{
               Session     = $Session
               ScriptBlock = $SB
           }
PS C:\foo> Invoke-Command @IHT

Success Restart Needed Exit Code     Feature Result                 PSComputerName
------- -------------- ---------     --------------                 --------------
True    Yes            SuccessRest... {Hyper-V, Hyper-V Module..}   PSDirect
WARNING: You must restart this server to finish the installation process.
```

In *step 7*, after you install the Hyper-V to the `PSDirect` virtual machine, you reboot the VM, then wait for it to start. There is no output from this step.

In *step 8*, you create a VM, `NestedVM`, inside the `PSDirect` VM, which looks like this:

```
PS C:\foo> $SB2 = {
             $VMname = 'NestedVM'
             New-VM -Name $VMname -MemoryStartupBytes 1GB
           }
PS C:\foo> $IHT2 = @{
             VMName      = 'PSDirect'
             ScriptBlock = $SB2
             Credential  = $CredRK
           }
PS C:\foo> Invoke-Command @IHT2

Name     State CPUUsage(%) MemoryAssigned(M) Uptime   Status             Version PSComputerName
----     ----- ----------- ----------------- ------   ------             ------- --------------
NestedVM Off   0           0                 00:00:00 Operating normally 9.0     PSDirect
```

There's more...

In *step 2*, you look at the properties of the virtual CPU(s) in the `PSDirect` VM. If you have not yet executed the *Configuring VM hardware* recipe previously, you may see a different CPU count.

In *step 5*, you stopped then started the `PSDirect` VM. As an alternative, you could have used the `Restart-VM` cmdlet.

In *step 6*, you create a new VM, but you have not loaded an operating system or configured the VM. Naturally, you can use the techniques in this chapter to configure your new VM as needed.

Managing VM state

Managing the VM state involves stopping and starting, or pausing and resuming, a VM. You can also save and restore, as shown in this recipe.

Getting ready

This recipe uses the `PSDirect` VM created in the *Creating a virtual machine* recipe. This recipe assumes the `PSDirect` VM is stopped when you start this recipe. If this VM is running, then first stop it using the `Stop-VM` cmdlet.

How to do it...

1. Get the VM's state to check if whether is off:

    ```
    Stop-VM -Name PSDirect -WarningAction SilentlyContinue
    Get-VM -Name PSDirect
    ```

2. Start the VM, get its status, then wait until the VM has an IP address assigned and the networking stack is working, then examine the VM's state:

    ```
    Start-VM -VMName PSDirect
    Wait-VM  -VMName PSDirect -For IPAddress
    Get-VM   -VMName PSDirect
    ```

3. Suspend and view the `PSDirect` VM:

    ```
    Suspend-VM -VMName PSDirect
    Get-VM -VMName PSDirect
    ```

4. Resume the VM:

    ```
    Resume-VM -VMName PSDirect
    Get-VM -VMName PSDirect
    ```

5. Save the VM and check its status:

    ```
    Save-VM -VMName PSDirect
    Get-VM -VMName PSDirect
    ```

6. Resume the saved VM and view the status:

    ```
    Start-VM -VMName PSDirect
    Get-Vm -VMName PSDirect
    ```

7. Restart the VM:

    ```
    Restart-VM -VMName PSDirect -Force
    Get-VM      -VMName PSDirect
    ```

8. Wait for the VM to get an IP address:

    ```
    Wait-VM    -VMName PSDirect -For IPaddress
    Get-VM     -VMName PSDirect
    ```

9. Perform a hard power off on the VM:

```
Stop-VM -VMName PSDirect -TurnOff
Get-VM  -VMname PSDirect
```

How it works...

This recipe shows you how to manage VM state. In *step 1*, you view the properties of the VM, which is not running. As you can see from the screenshot, the PSDirect VM is turned off and is not running (and has an uptime of 00:00:00), as follows:

```
PS C:\foo> Stop-VM -Name PSDirect -WarningAction SilentlyContinue
PS C:\foo> Get-VM   -Name PSDirect

Name     State CPUUsage(%) MemoryAssigned(M) Uptime   Status             Version
----     ----- ----------- ----------------- ------   ------             -------
PSDirect Off   0           0                 00:00:00 Operating normally 9.0
```

With *step 2*, you start the PSDirect VM and retrieve the VM's status, which looks like this:

```
PS C:\foo> Start-VM -VMName PSDirect
PS C:\foo> Wait-VM  -VMName PSDirect -For IPAddress
PS C:\foo> Get-Vm   -VMName PSDirect

Name     State   CPUUsage(%) MemoryAssigned(M) Uptime              Status             Version
----     -----   ----------- ----------------- ------              ------             -------
PSDirect Running 0           1024              00:00:00.0460000    Operating normally 9.0
```

Next, in *step 3*, you suspend the PSDirect VM, which looks like this:

```
PS C:\foo> Suspend-VM -VMName PSDirect
PS C:\foo> Get-VM -VMName PSDirect

Name     State  CPUUsage(%) MemoryAssigned(M) Uptime              Status             Version
----     -----  ----------- ----------------- ------              ------             -------
PSDirect Paused 0           1024              00:02:55.5310000    Operating normally 9.0
```

In *step 4*, you resume the PSDirect VM, which looks like this:

```
PS C:\foo> Resume-VM -VMName PSDirect
PS C:\foo> Get-VM -VMName PSDirect

Name     State   CPUUsage(%) MemoryAssigned(M) Uptime              Status             Version
----     -----   ----------- ----------------- ------              ------             -------
PSDirect Running 0           1024              00:02:55.5770000    Operating normally 9.0
```

With *step 5*, you save a VM and view the status, like this:

```
PS C:\foo> Save-VM -VMName PSDirect
PS C:\foo> Get-VM  -VMName PSDirect

Name     State CPUUsage(%) MemoryAssigned(M) Uptime   Status             Version
----     ----- ----------- ----------------- ------   ------             -------
PSDirect Saved 0           0                 00:00:00 Operating normally 9.0.
```

With *step 6*, you start the saved `PSDirect` VM and view the VM's details, which looks like this:

```
PS C:\foo> Start-VM -VMName PSDirect
PS C:\foo> Get-Vm   -VMName PSDirect

Name     State   CPUUsage(%) MemoryAssigned(M) Uptime              Status             Version
----     -----   ----------- ----------------- ------              ------             -------
PSDirect Running 0           1024              00:00:00.0330000    Operating normally 9.0
```

With *step 7*, you forcibly shut down the VM, which looks like this:

```
PS C:\foo> Wait-VM  -VMName PSDirect -For IPaddress
PS C:\foo> Get-VM   -VMName PSDirect

Name     State   CPUUsage(%) MemoryAssigned(M) Uptime              Status             Version
----     -----   ----------- ----------------- ------              ------             -------
PSDirect Running 23          1024              00:00:35.7500000    Operating normally 9.0
```

In *step 8*, you wait until the `PSDirect` VM is up and running to re-view the VM's status, which looks like this:

```
PS C:\foo> Stop-VM -VMName PSDirect -TurnOff
PS C:\foo> Get-VM  -VMname PSDirect

Name     State CPUUsage(%) MemoryAssigned(M) Uptime   Status             Version
----     ----- ----------- ----------------- ------   ------             -------
PSDirect Off   0           0                 00:00:00 Operating normally 9.0
```

There's more...

With *step 2*, you start the VM and retrieve the VM's status. Next, in *step 3*, you suspend then resume a VM.

With *step 3* and *step 4*, you suspend then resume the `PSDirect` VM. While the VM is suspended, the VM is not active and therefore receives and sends no network traffic. The VM's memory is maintained, as is the current state, and the VM can be resumed at any moment.

In *step 6* you save the `PSDirect` VM. When you save a VM, Hyper-V saves the VM's memory to disk and the VM's virtual disks are not used. Saving a VM is similar to pausing it, except that with a saved VM, all the VM's memory is written to disk then released.

In *step 7*, you perform a forced shutdown of the `PSDirect` VM. This is equivalent to pulling the power from a running computer then restarting it. When you do this, all VM state is lost, and it is possible to introduce disk corruption due to data being still in memory and not written to disk prior to the power off. While Windows and the most-used Windows filesystems (NTFS and ReFS) are fairly resilient to errors, you should avoid hard shutdown if possible.

Configuring VM and storage movement

Hyper-V enables you to move VM details and VM storage to a new location. Moving a VM and moving a VM's storage are two important features you can use to manage your Hyper-V hosts.

Getting ready

In this recipe, you are going to move configuration details for the `PSDirect` VM within the `HV1` server. Then, you move the entire VM to another server, `HV2`, and view the results. The two Hyper-V servers, `HV1` and `HV2`, were set up in the *Installing and configuring the Hyper-V* recipe. The VM, `PSDirect`, was created in the *Create a virtual machine* recipe.

How to do it...

1. View the `PSDirect` VM on `HV1` and verify that it is turned off:

   ```
   Get-VM -Name PSDirect -Computer HV1
   ```

2. Get the VM configuration location:

   ```
   (Get-VM -Name PSDirect).ConfigurationLocation
   ```

3. Get virtual hard drive locations:

   ```
   Get-VMHardDiskDrive -VMName PSDirect |
       Format-Table -Property VMName, ControllerType, Path
   ```

4. Move the VM's storage to the `C:\PSDirectNew` folder:

```
$MHT = @{
  Name                = 'PSDirect'
  DestinationStoragePath = 'C:\PSDirectNew'
}
Move-VMStorage @MHT
```

5. View the configuration details after moving the VM's storage:

```
(Get-VM -Name PSDirect).ConfigurationLocation
Get-VMHardDiskDrive -VMName PSDirect |
  Format-Table -Property VMName, ControllerType, Path
```

6. Get the VM details for the VMs from `HV2`:

```
Get-VM -ComputerName HV2
```

7. Enable VM migration from both `HV1` and `HV2`:

```
Enable-VMMigration -ComputerName HV1, HV2
```

8. Configure VM migration on both hosts:

```
$SVHT = @{
  UseAnyNetworkForMigration             = $true
  ComputerName                          = 'HV1', 'HV2'
  VirtualMachineMigrationAuthenticationType = 'Kerberos'
  VirtualMachineMigrationPerformanceOption = 'Compression'
}
Set-VMHost @SVHT
```

9. Move the VM to `HV2`:

```
$Start = Get-Date
$VMHT = @{
    Name                = 'PSDirect'
    ComputerName        = 'HV1'
    DestinationHost     = 'HV2'
    IncludeStorage      = $true
    DestinationStoragePath = 'C:\PSDirect' # on HV2
}
Move-VM @VMHT
$Finish = Get-Date
```

10. Display the time taken to migrate:

```
$OS = "Migration took: [{0:n2}] minutes"
($OS -f ($($Finish-$Start).TotalMinutes))
```

11. Check which VMs on are on HV1:

```
Get-VM -ComputerName HV1
```

12. Check the VMs on HV2:

```
Get-VM -ComputerName HV2
```

13. Look at the details of the moved VM:

```
((Get-VM -Name PSDirect -Computer HV2).ConfigurationLocation)
Get-VMHardDiskDrive -VMName PSDirect -Computer HV2  |
  Format-Table -Property VMName, Path
```

How it works...

In *step 1*, you ensure that the PSDirect VM is stopped, which looks like this:

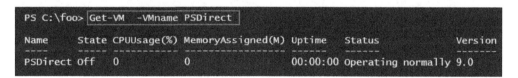

In *step 2*, you view the VM configuration location for the PSDirect VM, which looks like this:

```
PS C:\foo> (Get-VM -Name PSDirect).ConfigurationLocation
C:\Vm\VMs\PSDirect\PSDirect
```

With *step 3*, you view the details of the two virtual disk drives used by the PSDirect VM. You created one drive when you installed the PSDirect virtual machine (using the *Creating a virtual machine* recipe), and you created the second drive based on the *Configuring VM hardware* recipe. The output of this step looks like this:

```
PS C:\foo> Get-VMHardDiskDrive -VMName PSDirect |
            Format-Table -Property VMName, ControllerType, Path

VMName      ControllerType Path
------      -------------- ----
PSDirect               IDE C:\Vm\Vhds\PSDirect.vhdx        ⟵
PSDirect              SCSI C:\Vm\Vhds\PSDirect-D.VHDX      ⟵
```

In *step 4*, you move the PSDirect VM and the VMs hard drives to the C:\PSDirectNew folder. There is no output from this step.

With *step 5*, you get the new location for the PSDirect VM's configuration files and get the details of the VM's disks, including their new location, which looks like this:

```
PS C:\foo> (Get-VM -Name PSDirect).ConfigurationLocation
C:\PSDirectNew     ⟵

PS C:\foo> Get-VMHardDiskDrive -VMName PSDirect |
            Format-Table -Property VMName, ControllerType, Path

VMName      ControllerType Path
------      -------------- ----
PSDirect    ⟶          IDE C:\PSDirectNew\Virtual Hard Disks\PSDirect.vhdx
PSDirect    ⟶         SCSI C:\PSDirectNew\Virtual Hard Disks\PSDirect-D.VHDX
```

Before you migrate the PSDirect VM, in *step 6*, you view the VMs currently residing on HV2, which looks like this:

```
PS C:\foo> Get-VM -ComputerName HV2

Name      State CPUUsage(%) MemoryAssigned(M) Uptime   Status              Version
----      ----- ----------- ----------------- ------   ------              -------
SQLAcct1  Off   0           0                 00:00:00 Operating normally  9.0
SQLAcct2  Off   0           0                 00:00:00 Operating normally  9.0
SQLAcct3  Off   0           0                 00:00:00 Operating normally  9.0
SQLMfg1   Off   0           0                 00:00:00 Operating normally  9.0
SQLMfg2   Off   0           0                 00:00:00 Operating normally  9.0
```

In *step 7*, you enable VM migration on both HV1 and HV2. In *step 8*, you configure VM migration on both servers. In *step 9*, you perform a migration of the PSDirect VM from HV1 to HV2. These three steps produce no output. In *step 10*, you display how long the migration took, which looks like this:

```
PS C:\foo> $OS = "Migration took: [{0:n2}] minutes"
PS C:\foo> ($os -f ($($finish-$start).TotalMinutes))
Migration took: [5.22] minutes  ←
```

With the migration of the PSDirect VM to HV2 completed, in *step 11*, you get the VMs on HV1. Since the PSDirect VM has been migrated, you have no VMs running in HV1, thus there is no output from this step.

In *step 12*, you get the VMs running on HV2, which shows the PSDirect VM is now running on this server (in addition to the five VMs you saw in *step 6*), as follows:

```
PS C:\foo> Get-VM -ComputerName HV2

Name     State   CPUUsage(%) MemoryAssigned(M) Uptime            Status              Version
PSDirect Running 1           2048              00:07:05.4840000  Operating normally  9.0
SQLAcct1 Off     0           0                 00:00:00          Operating normally  9.0
SQLAcct2 Off     0           0                 00:00:00          Operating normally  9.0
SQLAcct3 Off     0           0                 00:00:00          Operating normally  9.0
SQLMfg1  Off     0           0                 00:00:00          Operating normally  9.0
SQLMfg2  Off     0           0                 00:00:00          Operating normally  9.0
```

In the final step, you examine the configuration location for the PSDirect VM (on HV2), and the disk details for this VM's two disks, which looks like this:

```
PS C:\foo> ((Get-VM -Name PSDirect -Computer HV2).ConfigurationLocation)
C:\PSDirect  ←

PS C:\foo> Get-VMHardDiskDrive -VMName PSDirect -Computer HV2 |
              Format-Table -Property VMName, Path

VMName    Path
------    ----
PSDirect  C:\PSDirect\Virtual Hard Disks\PSDirect.vhdx  ←
PSDirect  C:\PSDirect\Virtual Hard Disks\PSDirect-D.VHDX
```

There's more...

In this recipe, you first view the storage location details of a VM, before moving the VM and again after. You first move the PSDirect VM within the HV1 VM, then you move the VM to a different server, HV2.

In *step 3*, you moved the storage for the PSDirect VM. If you had an RDP connection open to the PSDirect VM, you would have seen the VM functioning normally during the migration. You may have seen a brief flicker as the VM movement completes and Hyper-V begins to use the new VM details.

In this recipe, HV1 and HV2 are two non-clustered systems. In *step 8*, you move the PSDirect VM from HV1 to HV2. In this case, since there is no shared storage involved with the VMs, Hyper-V needs to perform a full storage migration migrating the storage between the two servers. If you store the VM on shared storage, for example, using an SMB **Scale-Out File Server** or storing VHDX files on an iSCSI server, moving a VM between cluster nodes is significantly faster.

At the completion of the VM movement in *step 8*, Hyper-V drops connectivity to the VM on HV1 and establishes it on HV2. This means that for a moment, you lose connectivity to the VM. If you open an RDP connection into the PSDirect VM before you move the VM, you can see that as the movement finishes, the connection stops for a moment, then reappears with the VM running on HV2. Using VMConnect would mean having to reopen the connection on the other Hyper-V host.

You could also open up a PowerShell window on another system, say DC1, and ping the VM continuously during the movement of the VM. You may notice a moment of dropped pings, before they pick up again once the live migration has completed. An application running on the PSDirect VM would be unaffected by the momentary loss of connectivity during the move.

Configuring VM replication

Hyper-V VM replication is a disaster recovery feature that creates a replica of a VM on a remote Hyper-V server and keeps the replica up to date. The VM replica on the remote host is not active, but can be made active should the VM's host fail for some reason.

With Hyper-V replication, the source VM host bundles up any changes in a running VM's VHD file(s) and sends them to the replica server on a regular basis. The replica server then applies those changes to the dormant replica.

Once you have a replica established, you can test the replica to ensure it can start should you need it. Also, you can failover to the replica—bringing the replicated VM up based on the most recently replicated data. If the source VM host becomes inoperable before it can replicate changes on the source VM, there is a risk of those changes being lost.

In this recipe, you create and use a replica of a VM, PSDirect, that you have running on your HV1 server. The recipe sets up the replica on the HV2 server.

Getting ready

This recipe replicates the PSDirect VM running in HV2 to HV1. This assumes you have used the *Creating a virtual machine* recipe to create the VM, and used the *Configuring VM and storage movement* recipe; you need to move the PSDirect VM to HV2.

How to do it...

1. Configure HV1 and HV2 to be trusted for delegation in AD on DC1:

```
$SB1 = {
   Set-ADComputer -Identity HV1 -TrustedForDelegation $True
}
Invoke-Command -ComputerName DC1 -ScriptBlock $SB1
$SB2 = {
   Set-ADComputer -Identity HV2 -TrustedForDelegation $True}
Invoke-Command -ComputerName DC1 -ScriptBlock $SB2
```

2. Reboot the HV1 and HV2 servers:

```
Restart-Computer -ComputerName HV1 -Force
Restart-Computer -ComputerName HV2 -Force
```

3. Once both systems are restarted, log back on to HV2, and set up both servers as a replication server:

```
$VMRHT = @{
   ReplicationEnabled               = $true
   AllowedAuthenticationType        = 'Kerberos'
   KerberosAuthenticationPort       = 42000
   DefaultStorageLocation           = 'C:\Replicas'
   ReplicationAllowedFromAnyServer  = $true
   ComputerName                     = 'HV1', 'HV2'
}
Set-VMReplicationServer @VMRHT
```

4. Enable PSDirect on HV2 to be a replica source:

```
$VMRHT = @{
  VMName             = 'PSDirect'
  Computer           = 'HV2' # from server
  ReplicaServerName  = 'HV1' # to server
  ReplicaServerPort  = 42000
  AuthenticationType = 'Kerberos'
  CompressionEnabled = $true
  RecoveryHistory    = 5
}
Enable-VMReplication  @VMRHT
```

5. View the replication status of HV2:

    ```
    Get-VMReplicationServer -ComputerName HV2
    ```

6. Check the PSDirect VM's status on HV2:

    ```
    Get-VM -ComputerName HV2 -VMName PSDirect
    ```

7. Start the initial replication:

    ```
    Start-VMInitialReplication -VMName PSDirect -ComputerName HV2
    ```

8. Examine the initial replication state on HV1 just after you start the initial replication:

    ```
    Measure-VMReplication -ComputerName HV2
    ```

9. Wait for replication to finish, then examine the replication status on HV2:

    ```
    Measure-VMReplication -ComputerName HV2
    ```

10. Test PSDirect failover to HV1:

    ```
    $SB = {
      $VM = Start-VMFailover -AsTest -VMName PSDirect -Confirm:$false
      Start-VM $VM
    }
    Invoke-Command -ComputerName HV1 -ScriptBlock $SB
    ```

11. View the status of VMs on HV1:

    ```
    Get-VM -ComputerName HV1
    ```

12. Stop the failover test on HV1:

    ```
    $SB = {
      Stop-VMFailover -VMName PSDirect
    }
    Invoke-Command -ComputerName HV1 -ScriptBlock $SB
    ```

13. View the status of VMs on HV1 and HV2 after failover stopped:

    ```
    Get-VM -ComputerName HV1
    Get-VM -ComputerName HV2
    ```

14. Stop PSDirect on HV2 prior to performing a planned failover:

    ```
    Stop-VM PSDirect -ComputerName HV2
    ```

15. Start VM failover from `HV1`:

```
$STHT = @{
  VMName        = 'PSDirect'
  ComputerName = 'HV1'
  Confirm       = $false
}
Start-VMFailover @STHT
```

16. Complete the failover:

```
$CHT = @{
  VMName        = 'PSDirect'
  ComputerName = 'HV1'
  Confirm       = $false
}
Complete-VMFailover @CHT
```

17. Start the replicated VM on `HV1`:

```
Start-VM -VMname PSDirect -ComputerName HV1
```

18. View the VMs on `HV1` and `HV2` after the failover:

```
Get-VM -ComputerName HV1
Get-VM -ComputerName HV2
```

How it works...

In *step 1*, you configure `HV1` and `HV2` to be trusted for delegation in AD on `DC1`. After configuring delegation, in *step 2*, you restart both servers to enable the delegation trust. With *step 3*, you set replication settings, and in *step 4*, you complete establishing replication between `HV2` an `HV1`. These four steps produce no output.

In *step 5*, you view the replication status on `HV2`, which looks like this:

```
PS C:\Foo> Get-VMReplicationServer -ComputerName HV2

RepEnabled AuthType KerbAuthPort CertAuthPort AllowAnyServer
---------- -------- ------------ ------------ --------------
True       Kerb     42000        443          True
```

In *step 6*, you view the VM details of the `PSDirect` VM, running on `HV2`, which looks like this:

In *step 7*, you start the replication of `PSDirect` from `HV2` to `HV1`. This produces no output. In *step 8*, just after you started replication, you take another look at the replication status, which looks like this:

After the VM replication has completed, in *step 9*, you re-check the replication status, which looks like this:

In *step 10*, you test a failover of `PSDirect` between the Hyper-V servers. This step produces no output. In *step 11*, you view the status of the failover test on `HV1`, which looks like this:

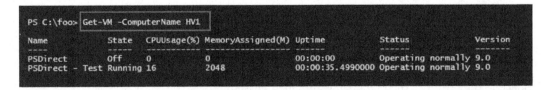

In *step 12*, you stop the failover test, which produces no output. In *step 13*, you view the status of VMs on both `HV1` and `HV2`, which looks like this:

```
PS C:\foo> Get-VM -ComputerName HV1

Name      State CPUUsage(%) MemoryAssigned(M) Uptime    Status             Version
----      ----- ----------- ----------------- ------    ------             -------
PSDirect  Off   0           0                 00:00:00  Operating normally 9.0


PS C:\foo> Get-VM -ComputerName HV2

Name     State   CPUUsage(%) MemoryAssigned(M) Uptime              Status             Version
----     -----   ----------- ----------------- ------              ------             -------
PSDirect Running 0           2048              00:25:28.7040000    Operating normally 9.0
SQLAcct1 Off     0           0                 00:00:00            Operating normally 9.0
SQLAcct2 Off     0           0                 00:00:00            Operating normally 9.0
SQLAcct3 Off     0           0                 00:00:00            Operating normally 9.0
SQLMfg1  Off     0           0                 00:00:00            Operating normally 9.0
SQLMfg2  Off     0           0                 00:00:00            Operating normally 9.0
```

In *step 14,* you shut down the PSDirect VM on HV2 in preparation for a failover. In *step 15,* you begin the failover. In *step 16,* you complete the failover. After the VM failover has completed, in *step 17,* you start the PSDirect VM on HV1. These three steps produce no output. The result of these four steps, which produce no output, is that the PSDirect VM is now running on HV1. You can view this in *step 18,* where you review the VMs running on both Hyper-V servers. The output of this step looks like this:

```
PS C:\foo> Get-VM -ComputerName HV1

Name     State   CPUUsage(%) MemoryAssigned(M) Uptime              Status             Version
----     -----   ----------- ----------------- ------              ------             -------
PSDirect Running 7           2048              00:00:31.1560000    Operating normally 9.0


PS C:\foo> Get-VM -ComputerName HV2

Name     State CPUUsage(%) MemoryAssigned(M) Uptime    Status             Version
----     ----- ----------- ----------------- ------    ------             -------
PSDirect Off   0           0                 00:00:00  Operating normally 9.0
SQLAcct1 Off   0           0                 00:00:00  Operating normally 9.0
SQLAcct2 Off   0           0                 00:00:00  Operating normally 9.0
SQLAcct3 Off   0           0                 00:00:00  Operating normally 9.0
SQLMfg1  Off   0           0                 00:00:00  Operating normally 9.0
SQLMfg2  Off   0           0                 00:00:00  Operating normally 9.0
```

There's more...

In *step 2,* you restart both Hyper-V hosts (HV1 and HV2). Since you run this recipe from the HV2 machine, the second command in this step reboots the HV2 system you are working on immediately (there is no prompt to ask you if you are sure or to save any work). If you test this recipe, make sure you have any files saved before you reboot.

In *step 3*, you configure HV1 to accept inbound replication from any Hyper-V system. If you have not configured the host firewalls (or turned them off) you may see errors trying to invoke replication.

You may also wish to configure HV2 to accept replication only from a specific server, such as HV1. To do this, you would have to set up the replication server to not accept replication from any server. Then, you use the Hyper-V cmdlet New-VMReplicationAuthorizationEntry to specify that HV2 can only receive replicas from the HV1 server. To set this up, you would do the following:

```
$RHT = @{
  AllowedPrimaryServer    = 'HV1'
  ReplicaStorageLocation  = 'C:\Replica'
  ComputerName            = 'HV2'
}
Set-VMReplicationAuthorizationEntry @RHT
```

In *step 12*, you view the status of VMs on both HV1 and HV2. As you can see, the PSDirect VM is up and running (on HV2) with a replica VM on HV1, which is turned off.

In *step 11*, you view the details of the test version of the PSDirect VM running. If you were to open up a VMConnect window on this test VM, you see that both the hostname and the IP address are not the same as the VM running on.

After *step 17*, if you looked inside PSDirect, running this time on HV1, you would find the same issue. The impact is that after a real-life failover, you may need to reset the hostname and reset the IP configuration details. If you are using Hyper-V replica in production, it would be a great idea to develop a script to fix these two issues in an automated fashion.

In *step 18*, you see that the PSDirect VM is running on HV1 and stopped on HV2. However, if you look inside the PSDirect VM running on HV1, you see it has a hostname that is **not** PSDirect and has no networking setup. If you were to fail over and wanted to run the failed-over VM, you would need to deal with these two issues, which typically involves re-booting the PSDirect VM and possibly running a script to ensure the hostname and the IP configuration details are correct for your environment.

Managing VM checkpoints

With Hyper-V in Server 2019, a checkpoint captures the state of a VM into a restore point. Hyper-V then enables you to roll back a VM to a checkpoint. Windows Server 2008's version of Hyper-V first provided this feature. With Server 2008, these restore points were called **snapshots**. With Server 2012, Microsoft also changed the name to **checkpoint**. This made the terminology consistent with System Center, and avoided confusion with respect to the **Volume Shadow Copy Service** (**VSS**) snapshots used by backup systems.

While the Hyper-V team did change the terminology, some of the cmdlet names remain unchanged. To restore a VM to a checkpoint, you use the `Restore-VMSnapShot` cmdlet.

When you create a checkpoint, Hyper-V temporarily pauses the VM. It then creates a new differencing disk (AVHD). Hyper-V then resumes the VM, which writes all data to the differencing disk. You can create multiple checkpoints for a VM.

Checkpoints are great for a variety of scenarios. They can be useful for troubleshooting. For example, if you are troubleshooting, you can get the VM to the point where some bug is triggered, then take a checkpoint. With the checkpoint taken, you can try a fix. If the fix does not work, you can just roll back to the checkpoint and try some other fix. Checkpoints are also useful for training. You could create a VM for a course, and create a checkpoint after each successful lab. That way, the student can make a mistake in a lab, and skip forward to a later checkpoint and carry on.

Using checkpoints in production is a different matter. In general, you should avoid using checkpoints on your production systems for a number of reasons. If your servers use any sort of replication or transaction-based applications, the impact of resetting the clock to an earlier time can be bad. Since checkpoints rely on differencing disks that feature constantly growing physical disk files, the use of checkpoints can result in poor performance.

Checkpoints have their place—but should not be used as a backup strategy. In this recipe, you create a snapshot of `PSDirect`, then you create a file in the VM. You take a further checkpoint and create a second file, after reverting back to the first snapshot, observing that there are no files created. Then, you roll forward to the second snapshot to see that the first file is there but not the second (because you created the second file after the snapshot was taken). Then, you remove all the snapshots. After each key checkpoint operation, you observe the VHDX and AVHD files, which support the `PSDirect` VM.

Getting ready

This recipe, which you run on `HV1`, uses the `PSDirect` VM you created and used earlier in this chapter. The VHDX files for the VM reside in `C:\Vm\Vhds\PSDirect`. Depending on which other recipes you have run from this chapter, the virtual disks may be in a different folder, but the recipe copes with the disk files being in any folder (known to Hyper-V).

How to do it...

1. Create credentials for `PSDirect`:

```
$RKAn   = 'Wolf\Administrator'
$PS     = 'Pa$$w0rd'
$RKP    = ConvertTo-SecureString -String $PS -AsPlainText -Force
$T      = 'System.Management.Automation.PSCredential'
$RKCred = New-Object -TypeName $T -ArgumentList $RKAn,$RKP
```

2. Look at `C\:` in the `PSDirect` VM at the start:

```
$SB = { Get-ChildItem -Path C:\ }
$ICHT = @{
  VMName       = 'PSDirect'
  ScriptBlock  = $SB
  Credential   = $RKCred
}
Invoke-Command @ICHT
```

3. Create a snapshot of the `PSDirect` VM on HV1:

```
$CPHT = @{
  VMName       = 'PSDirect'
  ComputerName = 'HV1'
  SnapshotName = 'Snapshot1'
}
Checkpoint-VM @CPHT
```

4. Look at the files created to support the checkpoints:

```
$Parent = Split-Path -Parent (Get-VM -Name PSDirect |
            Select-Object -ExpandProperty HardDrives).Path |
              Select -First 1
Get-ChildItem -Path $Parent
```

5. Create some content in a file on `PSDirect` and display it:

```
$SB = {
   $FileName1 = 'C:\File_After_Checkpoint_1'
   Get-Date | Out-File -FilePath $FileName1
   Get-Content -Path $FileName1
}
$ICHT = @{
  VMName       = 'PSDirect'
  ScriptBlock  = $SB
```

```
      Credential   = $RKCred
   }
   Invoke-Command @ICHT
```

6. Take a second checkpoint of the PSDirect VM:

```
$SNHT = @{
   VMName         = 'PSDirect'
   ComputerName   = 'HV1'
   SnapshotName   = 'Snapshot2'
}
Checkpoint-VM @SNHT
```

7. Get the VM checkpoint details for PSDirect:

```
Get-VMSnapshot -VMName PSDirect
```

8. Look at the files supporting the two checkpoints:

```
Get-ChildItem -Path $Parent
```

9. Create and display another file in PSDirect (after you have taken Snapshot2):

```
$SB = {
   $FileName2 = 'C:\File_After_Checkpoint_2'
   Get-Date | Out-File -FilePath $FileName2
   Get-ChildItem -Path C:\ -File
}
$ICHT = @{
   VMName      = 'PSDirect'
   ScriptBlock = $SB
   Credential  = $RKCred
}
Invoke-Command @ICHT
```

10. Restore the PSDirect VM back to the checkpoint named Snapshot1:

```
$Snap1 = Get-VMSnapshot -VMName PSDirect -Name Snapshot1
Restore-VMSnapshot -VMSnapshot $Snap1 -Confirm:$false
Start-VM -Name PSDirect
Wait-VM -For IPAddress -Name PSDirect
```

11. See what files we now have on `PSDirect`:

```
$SB = {
  Get-ChildItem -Path C:\
}
$ICHT = @{
  VMName      = 'PSDirect'
  ScriptBlock = $SB
  Credential  = $RKCred
}
Invoke-Command @ICHT
```

12. Roll forward to `Snapshot2`:

```
$Snap2 = Get-VMSnapshot -VMName PSdirect -Name Snapshot2
Restore-VMSnapshot -VMSnapshot $Snap2 -Confirm:$false
Start-VM -Name PSDirect
Wait-VM -For IPAddress -Name PSDirect
```

13. Observe the files you now have in the `PSDirect` VM:

```
$SB = {
    Get-ChildItem -Path C:\
}
$ICHT = @{
  VMName      = 'PSDirect'
  ScriptBlock = $SB
  Credential  = $RKCred
}
Invoke-Command @ICHT
```

14. Restore the VM to `Snapshot1`:

```
$Snap1 = Get-VMSnapshot -VMName PSDirect -Name Snapshot1
Restore-VMSnapshot -VMSnapshot $Snap1 -Confirm:$false
Start-VM -Name PSDirect
Wait-VM -For IPAddress -Name PSDirect
```

15. Check snapshots and VM data files again:

```
Get-VMSnapshot -VMName PSDirect
Get-ChildItem -Path $Parent
```

16. Remove all the snapshots from HV1:

```
Get-VMSnapshot -VMName PSDirect |
  Remove-VMSnapshot
```

17. Check VM data files again:

```
Get-ChildItem -Path $Parent
```

How it works...

In *step 1*, you create a credentials object for the PSDirect VM's local administrator account. There is no output from this step.

In *step 2*, you examine the C:\ drive in the PSDirect VM, which looks like this:

```
PS C:\foo> $SB = { Get-ChildItem -Path C:\ }
PS C:\foo> $ICHT = @{
              VMName     = 'PSDirect'
              ScriptBlock = $SB
              Credential  = $RKCred
           }
PS C:\foo> Invoke-Command @ICHT

    Directory: C:\

Mode              LastWriteTime     Length Name                    PSComputerName
----              -------------     ------ ----                    --------------
d-----     15/09/2018     08:19            PerfLogs                PSDirect
d-r---     27/11/2018     10:24            Program Files           PSDirect
d-----     15/09/2018     10:06            Program Files (x86)     PSDirect
d-r---     21/11/2018     15:14            Users                   PSDirect
d-----     21/11/2018     16:29            Windows                 PSDirect
```

In *step 3*, you create a checkpoint of PSDirect on HV1, which produces no output. With *step 4*, examine the files supporting the PSDirect VM after the checkpoint is taken, which looks like this:

```
PS C:\foo> $Parent = Split-Path -Parent (Get-VM -Name PSdirect |
              Select-Object -ExpandProperty HardDrives).Path |
              Select -First 1
PS C:\foo> Get-ChildItem -Path $Parent

    Directory: C:\Vm\Vhds\psdirect

Mode              LastWriteTime       Length Name
----              -------------       ------ ----
-a----     29/11/2018     17:45     138412032 PSDirect-D.VHDX
-a----     29/11/2018     17:45      37748736 PSDirect-D_809AE0CD-40E2-4352-894D-0C036D488D28.avhdx
-a----     29/11/2018     17:45   10372513792 PSDirect.vhdx
-a----     29/11/2018     17:46      71303168 PSDirect_A1EA773E-AF68-4C42-869C-60780990340D.avhdx
```

In *step 5*, you create a file (after the first checkpoint is taken) and file contents, then view the file, which looks like this:

```
PS C:\foo> $SB = {
               $FileName1 = 'C:\File_After_Checkpoint_1'
               Get-Date | Out-File -FilePath $FileName1
               Get-Content -Path $FileName1
           }
PS C:\foo> $ICHT = @{
               VMName      = 'PSDirect'
               ScriptBlock = $SB
               Credential  = $RKCred
           }
PS C:\foo> Invoke-Command @ICHT

29 November 2018 17:47:54   <-----
```

After creating the file, in *step 6*, you take another checkpoint for the PSDirect VM, which produces no output. With *step 7*, you view the VM snapshots available for the PSDirect VM, which looks like this:

```
PS C:\foo> Get-VMSnapshot -VMName PSDirect

VMName    Name      SnapshotType  CreationTime         ParentSnapshotName
------    ----      ------------  ------------         ------------------
PSDirect  Snapshot1 Standard      29/11/2018 17:45:46
PSDirect  Snapshot2 Standard      29/11/2018 17:50:57  Snapshot1
```

In *step 8*, you again view the files supporting the PSDirect VM, which looks like this:

```
PS C:\foo> Get-ChildItem -Path $Parent

    Directory: C:\Vm\Vhds\psdirect

Mode           LastWriteTime          Length Name
----           -------------          ------ ----
-a----    29/11/2018     17:45      138412032 PSDirect-D.VHDX
-a----    29/11/2018     17:50        9437184 PSDirect-D_809AE0CD-40E2-4352-894D-0C036D488D28.avhdx
-a----    29/11/2018     17:51       37748736 PSDirect-D_CF60F23A-4E97-4E16-9F31-8E783486213C.avhdx
-a----    29/11/2018     17:45    10372513792 PSDirect.vhdx
-a----    29/11/2018     17:51       71303168 PSDirect_04D9E6B1-8D0C-4B1D-AB4B-AE2924FFDB9D.avhdx
-a----    29/11/2018     17:50      277872640 PSDirect_A1EA773E-AF68-4C42-869C-60780990340D.avhdx
```

After reverting the PSDirect VM back to the first checkpoint, in *step 9*, you create a further file in the C:\ folder inside the PSDirect VM, which looks like this:

```
PS C:\foo> $SB = {
              $FileName2 = 'C:\File_After_Checkpoint_2'
              Get-Date | Out-File -FilePath $FileName2
              Get-ChildItem -Path C:\ -File
              }
PS C:\foo> $ICHT = @{
              VMName      = 'PSDirect'
              ScriptBlock = $SB
              Credential  = $RKCred
              }
PS C:\foo> Invoke-Command @ICHT


    Directory: C:\


Mode                LastWriteTime     Length Name                        PSComputerName
----                -------------     ------ ----                        --------------
-a----     29/11/2018      17:47          68 File_After_Checkpoint_1     PSDirect
-a----     29/11/2018      17:52          68 File_After_Checkpoint_2     PSDirect
```

Without saving any work done, in *step 10*, you revert the PSDirect VM back to the first
snapshot, Snapshot1, which creates no output. Once the PSDirect VM is restarted from
Snapshot1, in *step 11*, you look at the files now in the PSDirect VM's C:\ drive, which looks
like this:

```
PS C:\foo> $SB = {
              Get-ChildItem -Path C:\
              }
PS C:\foo> $ICHT = @{
              VMName      = 'PSDirect'
              ScriptBlock = $SB
              Credential  = $RKCred
              }
PS C:\foo> Invoke-Command @ICHT

    Directory: C:\

Mode                LastWriteTime     Length Name                  PSComputerName
----                -------------     ------ ----                  --------------
d-----     15/09/2018      08:19             PerfLogs              PSDirect
d-r---     27/11/2018      10:24             Program Files         PSDirect
d-----     15/09/2018      10:06             Program Files (x86)   PSDirect
d-r---     21/11/2018      15:14             Users                 PSDirect
d-----     21/11/2018      16:29             Windows               PSDirect
```

In *step 12*, you roll the VM forward to the second checkpoint, `Snapshot2`. This step produces no output. With *step 13*, you view the files in the root of the `C:` drive of the `PSDirect` VM, which looks like this:

```
PS C:\foo> $SB = {
              Get-ChildItem -Path C:\
           }
PS C:\foo> $ICHT = @{
              VMName      = 'PSDirect'
              ScriptBlock = $SB
              Credential  = $RKCred
           }
PS C:\foo> Invoke-Command @ICHT


    Directory: C:\

Mode            LastWriteTime    Length  Name                         PSComputerName
----            -------------    ------  ----                         --------------
d-----    15/09/2018     08:19           PerfLogs                     PSDirect
d-r---    27/11/2018     10:24           Program Files                PSDirect
d-----    15/09/2018     10:06           Program Files (x86)          PSDirect
d-r---    21/11/2018     15:14           Users                        PSDirect
d-----    21/11/2018     16:29           Windows                      PSDirect
-a----    29/11/2018     17:47       68  File_After_Checkpoint_1      PSDirect
```

In *step 14*, you re-restore the `PSDirect` VM back to the first snapshot, `Snapshot1`, then wait until the VM is restarted. This step produces no output. In *step 15*, you re-view the `PSDirect` VM's snapshots and the snapshot files, which looks like this:

```
PS C:\foo> Get-VMSnapshot -VMName PSDirect

VMName    Name       SnapshotType CreationTime          ParentSnapshotName
------    ----       ------------ ------------          ------------------
PSDirect  Snapshot1  Standard     29/11/2018 17:45:46
PSDirect  Snapshot2  Standard     29/11/2018 17:50:57   Snapshot1


PS C:\foo> Get-ChildItem -Path $Parent


    Directory: C:\Vm\Vhds\psdirect


Mode            LastWriteTime          Length  Name
----            -------------          ------  ----
-a----    29/11/2018     17:45      138412032  PSDirect-D.VHDX
-a----    29/11/2018     18:01       37748736  PSDirect-D_39205D64-8905-473D-82D5-156385B593D4.avhdx
-a----    29/11/2018     17:50        9437184  PSDirect-D_809AE0CD-40E2-4352-894D-0C036D488D28.avhdx
-a----    29/11/2018     17:45    10372513792  PSDirect.vhdx
-a----    29/11/2018     17:50      277872640  PSDirect_A1EA773E-AF68-4C42-869C-60780990340D.avhdx
-a----    29/11/2018     18:01      406847488  PSDirect_DDD59F37-1C50-4E7C-B1F7-B50A271B7D06.avhdx
```

In *step 16,* you remove all the snapshots from the PSDirect virtual machine, which produces no output. In *step 17,* you view the VHDX files for the PSDirect VM (now that all snapshots are removed), which looks like this:

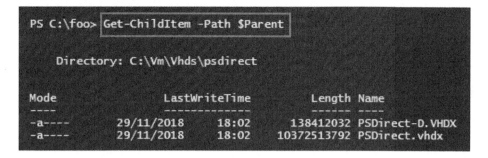

```
PS C:\foo> Get-ChildItem -Path $Parent


    Directory: C:\Vm\Vhds\psdirect


Mode                 LastWriteTime         Length Name
----                 -------------         ------ ----
-a----         29/11/2018     18:02      138412032 PSDirect-D.VHDX
-a----         29/11/2018     18:02    10372513792 PSDirect.vhdx
```

There's more...

In *step 10,* you revert the PSDirect VM back to an earlier snapshot. Any file activity in the VM after you took the second snapshot, and before reverting to the earlier snapshot, is now lost. In *step 12,* you roll forward the PSDirect VM to the second snapshot. This loses all work you might have done after reverting to Snapshot1 and before rolling forward to Snapshot2. Be very careful when reverting to earlier snapshots or rolling forward.

12
Managing Azure

In this chapter, we cover the following recipes:

- ▸ Using PowerShell with Azure
- ▸ Creating core Azure resources
- ▸ Exploring your storage account
- ▸ Creating an Azure SMB file share
- ▸ Create an Azure website
- ▸ Creating an Azure VM

Introduction

Azure is Microsoft's cloud computing platform and is a competitor to Amazon's Amazon Web Services and other public cloud providers, Azure provides you with access to a huge range of features. Organizations can literally move their entire on-premises infrastructure into the cloud.

Azure features come from three levels:

- ▸ **Infrastructure as a Service (IaaS)**
- ▸ **Platform as a Service (PaaS)**
- ▸ **Software as a Service (SaaS)**

IaaS is, in effect, an instant computing infrastructure that you can provision, manage, and use over the internet or via a private network connection. IaaS includes the basic computing infrastructure components (servers, storage, networking, firewalls, and security), plus the physical plant that's required to run these components (power, air conditioning, and so on). In an IaaS environment, the servers are all Azure virtual machines (effectively Hyper-V VMs) and interact with the networking, security, and storage components.

PaaS is a complete deployment environment in the cloud, including the operating system, storage, and other infrastructure. One key PaaS offering in Azure is the Azure SQL Database. Things like the OS and SQL server patching, which you would have to deal with if you deploy SQL in an IaaS environment, are all managed by Azure. This provides a complete SQL service, all managed by Azure. This, of course, means there are some things you can't do—actions that are reserved for the platform owner (that is, Microsoft). For example, with SQL running inside an IaaS Azure VM, you can use database mirroring—the SQL PaaS service does not provide that feature for you to use.

With SaaS, you just use an application that the vendor has placed in the cloud. One key example of SaaS is Office 365 (O365), which bundles Exchange Online, SharePoint Online, Skype For Business Online, OneDrive for Business, and Microsoft Teams. Strictly speaking, Office 365 is not an Azure offering—you purchase it directly from either the Office 365 website or via a Microsoft Partner. In terms of purchase, Office 365 is a single offering with many different plans (combinations of services that also include a downloadable version of the Office applications, such as Word and Excel). In terms of using PowerShell to manage Office 365, each of the included applications has its own unique approach. With Exchange Online, for example, you use PowerShell Implicit Remoting to manage the exchange component of your Office 365 subscription.

To provide authentication for software running within Azure and for other SaaS applications, you can make use of **Azure Active Directory** (**AAD**). With AAD, you can create a cloud-only directory or you can synchronize the AAD with your on-premises Active Directory. AAD can also be used to provide authentication for a range of other third-party SaaS applications. Full details in terms of managing both AAD and Office 365 components are outside the scope of this chapter.

In this chapter, we begin with the first recipe: *Using PowerShell with Azure*. In this recipe, we look at setting up a basic environment that we can manage Azure and the Office 365 SaaS components. This recipe also shows how to download the AAD cmdlets.

The *Creating core Azure resources* recipe guides you through creating a few of the core resources you need to create and manage other Azure resources. These include a resource group and a storage account. Every Azure resource you create with the ARM API must be contained in a resource group. Also, any storage you may require, such as VHD files for an Azure VM, need to be stored in a storage group. While the recipes in this chapter use a single resource group and a single storage account, large-scale Azure deployments may require multiple instances of these key resources.

In the *Creating Azure storage* recipe, we look at setting up Azure storage using the storage account we created earlier. The *Creating and using an Azure SMB file share* recipe shows you how you can create an SMB file share that you can access from client applications across the internet. Instead of having an application point to an on-premises file share, you can now host the share in Azure. This might be useful if you use Azure IaaS VM to host an application that utilizes a shared folder for its data. You could also use it as a file share in the cloud.

The *Creating and using Azure websites* recipe shows you how you can set up a simple website. The recipe sets up a WordPress blog using PowerShell. This feature enables you to set up a simple website, say for a short-term marketing campaign, as well as build internet-scale websites that you can have Azure scale dynamically according to load.

The next recipe, *Creating and using Azure virtual machines*, examines how to create an Azure VM and access it. This includes creating a virtual network and setting the VM up to enable you to manage it with PowerShell or connect via RDP. This chapter is only a taster for using Azure with PowerShell. There is so much more that you can do that could not fit into this book.

Using PowerShell with Azure

There are two key things you need to do before you can start managing Azure features using PowerShell. The first is to obtain an Azure subscription. The second is to get access to the cmdlets you need to be able to access Azure (and Office 365's features).

Azure is a commercial service—each feature you use has a cost attached. Azure charges are based on resource usage. With an Azure VM, for example, you would pay to have the VM running, with additional charges for the storage the VM uses and for any network traffic.

The charges for Office 365, on the other hand, are user-based—a given user can use lots of email, for example, without incurring any additional charges. For details on costs for Azure, see `https://azure.microsoft.com/pricing/`, and for details of Office 365 charges, see `https://products.office.com/business/compare-office-365-for-business-plans`.

To use Azure's IaaS and PaaS features, you need to have an Azure subscription. There are many ways you can get an Azure subscription, including via an MSDN subscription, an Action Pack subscription, or by outright purchase. Naturally, you need to ensure that any systems are properly licensed.

Microsoft also provides a one-month free trial subscription. This subscription provides you with full access to Azure features up to a financial limit, which, at the time of writing, is $200 US dollars or similar in other currencies. These limits may have changed by the time you read this book. Having said that, the trial subscription should be sufficient to enable you to learn how to use PowerShell with Azure.

If you do not have an existing subscription to Azure, navigate to `https://azure.microsoft.com/free/`, where you can create a trial subscription.

Note that a free trial requires you to submit a credit card number. There is no charge for the subscription; the credit card number is used only to identify verification—plus it keeps the lawyers happier.

If you take out an Azure trial and you want to keep your Azure resources running after the trial expires, you have to move it to a pay as you go subscription. You will receive an email shortly before the trial expires to transition it, which prevents downtime if you are using the trial for production.

To use PowerShell with Azure's various features, you need to obtain cmdlets that Microsoft does not provide in Windows Server 2019, Windows PowerShell 5.0/5.1, or PowerShell Core. You get the relevant modules from the PowerShell Gallery using the cmdlets in the `PowerShellGet` module to find and download them.

Azure has had PowerShell support almost since the very start of the service. These cmdlet sets have changed as Azure has matured (and expanded in scope). In 2019, the Azure PowerShell team released a new module, the `Az` module, to serve as the basis for automating Azure operations with PowerShell. The `Az` module is actually a set of modules containing over 2,500 cmdlets, a few of which you explore in this chapter.

Getting ready

To run this recipe, and all the recipes in this chapter, on CL1, which you initially configured in the *Installing RSAT Tools on Windows 10 and Windows Server 2019* recipe in *Chapter 1, Establishing a PowerShell Administrative Environment*.

How to do it...

1. Find the core `AZ` module:

   ```
   Find-Module -Name Az
   ```

2. Install the `AZ` modules:

   ```
   Install-Module -Name Az -Force
   ```

3. Discover Azure modules and how many cmdlets each contains:

```
$HT = @{ Label ='Cmdlets'
         Expression = {(Get-Command -module $_.name).count}}
Get-Module Az* -ListAvailable |
  Sort {(Get-command -Module $_.Name).Count} -Descending |
    Format-Table -Property Name,Version,Author,$HT -AutoSize
```

4. Find the Azure AD cmdlets:

```
Find-Module AzureAD |
  Format-Table -Property Name,Version,Author -AutoSize -Wrap
```

5. Download and install the `AzureAD` module:

```
Install-Module -Name AzureAD -Force
```

6. Discover the `AzureAD` module:

```
$FTHT = @{
  Property = 'Name', 'Version', 'Author', 'Description'
  AutoSize = $true
  Wrap     = $true
}
Get-Module -Name AzureAD -ListAvailable |
  Format-Table @FTHT
```

7. Log in to Azure:

```
$CredAZ = Get-Credential
$Subscription = Login-AzAccount -Credential $CredAZ
```

8. Obtain the Azure subscription details:

```
$SubID = $Subscription.Context.Subscription.SubscriptionId
Get-AzSubscription -SubscriptionId $SubId |
  Format-List -Property *
```

9. Get Azure locations:

```
Get-AzLocation | Sort-Object Location |
  Format-Table Location, Displayname
```

10. Get Azure environments:

```
Get-AzEnvironment |
  Format-Table -Property name, ManagementPortalURL
```

How it works...

In *step 1*, you used the `Find-Module` cmdlet to search the PowerShell Gallery for the `AZ` module, which produces the following output:

```
PS C:\Foo> Find-Module -Name Az

Version   Name   Repository   Description
-------   ----   ----------   -----------
1.2.1     Az     PSGallery    Microsoft Azure PowerShell - Cmdlets to manage resources...
```

In *step 2*, you downloaded and installed the `AZ` modules, which generates no output.
In *step 3*, you looked at the downloaded modules, which look like this:

```
PS C:\Foo> Get-Module Az* -ListAvailable  -ov m|
           Sort {(Get-command -Module $_.Name).Count} -Descending |
           Format-Table -Property Name,Version,Author,$HT -AutoSize

Name                    Version Author                  Cmdlets
----                    ------- ------                  -------
Az.Network              1.1.0   Microsoft Corporation   410
Az.Compute              1.2.0   Microsoft Corporation   187
Az.Sql                  1.1.0   Microsoft Corporation   169
Az.RecoveryServices     1.0.1   Microsoft Corporation   165
Az.Resources            1.1.1   Microsoft Corporation   104
Az.ApiManagement        1.0.0   Microsoft Corporation   100
Az.Storage              1.0.2   Microsoft Corporation    96
Az.Automation           1.1.0   Microsoft Corporation    88
Az.DataLakeStore        1.0.2   Microsoft Corporation    82
Az.Batch                1.0.0   Microsoft Corporation    73
Az.DataFactory          1.0.1   Microsoft Corporation    73
Az.DataLakeAnalytics    1.0.0   Microsoft Corporation    62
Az.KeyVault             1.0.1   Microsoft Corporation    61
Az.Websites             1.1.0   Microsoft Corporation    50
Az.LogicApp             1.1.0   Microsoft Corporation    43
Az.HDInsight            1.0.0   Microsoft Corporation    41
Az.OperationalInsights  1.0.0   Microsoft Corporation    41
Az.ServiceBus           1.0.0   Microsoft Corporation    38
Az.Accounts             1.2.1   Microsoft Corporation    37
Az.IotHub               1.0.2   Microsoft Corporation    36
Az.Monitor              1.0.0   Microsoft Corporation    36
Az.Cdn                  1.0.1   Microsoft Corporation    29
Az.AnalysisServices     1.0.1   Microsoft Corporation    28
Az.EventHub             1.0.0   Microsoft Corporation    24
Az.TrafficManager       1.0.1   Microsoft Corporation    22
Az.MachineLearning      1.0.0   Microsoft Corporation    22
Az.StreamAnalytics      1.0.0   Microsoft Corporation    21
Az.RedisCache           1.0.0   Microsoft Corporation    21
Az.NotificationHubs     1.0.0   Microsoft Corporation    21
Az.Relay                1.0.0   Microsoft Corporation    20
Az.ContainerRegistry    1.0.1   Microsoft Corporation    16
Az.ServiceFabric        1.0.1   Microsoft Corporation    16
Az.PowerBIEmbedded      1.0.0   Microsoft Corporation    13
Az.Billing              1.0.0   Microsoft Corporation    13
Az.ApplicationInsights  1.0.0   Microsoft Corporation    12
Az.EventGrid            1.1.0   Microsoft Corporation    11
Az.Dns                  1.0.0   Microsoft Corporation    11
Az.DevTestLabs          1.0.0   Microsoft Corporation    10
Az.CognitiveServices    1.0.0   Microsoft Corporation     9
Az.Media                1.0.0   Microsoft Corporation     9
Az.PolicyInsights       1.0.0   Microsoft Corporation     7
Az.Aks                  1.0.1   Microsoft Corporation     7
Az.SignalR              1.0.2   Microsoft Corporation     5
Az.ContainerInstance    1.0.0   Microsoft Corporation     4
Az.MarketplaceOrdering  1.0.0   Microsoft Corporation     2
```

In *step 4*, you found the `Azure AD` module, which generates output like this:

```
PS C:\Foo> Find-Module AzureAD

Version    Name      Repository   Description
-------    ----      ----------   -----------
2.0.2.4    AzureAD   PSGallery    Azure Active Directory V2 General Availability Module....
```

In *step 5*, you installed the `Azure AD` module, which generates no output. After you installed the module, in *step 6*, you examined the module, which generated the following output:

```
PS C:\Foo> $FTHT = @{
              Property = 'Name', 'Version', 'Author', 'Description'
              AutoSize = $true
              Wrap     = $true
           }
PS C:\Foo> Get-Module -Name AzureAD -ListAvailable |
              Format-Table @FTHT

Name     Version Author                Description
----     ------- ------                -----------
AzureAD 2.0.2.4 Microsoft Corporation Azure Active Directory V2 General Availability Module.
                                      This is the General Availability release of Azure
                                      Active Directory V2 PowerShell Module.
                                      For detailed information on how to install and run
                                      this module from the PowerShell Gallery including
                                      prerequisites, please refer to
                                      https://msdn.microsoft.com/powershell/gallery/readme
```

In *step 7*, you used your subscription logon information and logged on to Azure. This step produced output. In *step 8*, you got the details of your subscription, which looks like this:

```
PS C:\Foo> $SubID = $Subscription.Context.Subscription.SubscriptionId
PS C:\Foo> Get-AzSubscription -SubscriptionId $SubId |
              Format-List -Property *

Id                        : 0bc29420-0222-4599-b91e-e8699f760742
Name                      : MSDN Platforms
State                     : Enabled
SubscriptionId            : 0bc29420-0222-4599-b91e-e8699f760742
TenantId                  : c1a6d420-6960-42e1-9104-65669aabc420
CurrentStorageAccountName :
ExtendedProperties        : {[Account, thomas_lee@msn.com], [Tenants, c1a6d420-6960-42e1-9104-65669aabc420], [Environment, AzureCloud]}
CurrentStorageAccount     :
```

In *step 9*, you used the `Get-AzLocation` cmdlet to discover the current Azure locations, which produces output like this:

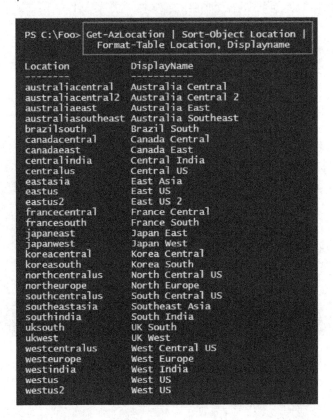

```
PS C:\Foo> Get-AzLocation | Sort-Object Location |
           Format-Table Location, Displayname

Location            DisplayName
--------            -----------
australiacentral    Australia Central
australiacentral2   Australia Central 2
australiaeast       Australia East
australiasoutheast  Australia Southeast
brazilsouth         Brazil South
canadacentral       Canada Central
canadaeast          Canada East
centralindia        Central India
centralus           Central US
eastasia            East Asia
eastus              East US
eastus2             East US 2
francecentral       France Central
francesouth         France South
japaneast           Japan East
japanwest           Japan West
koreacentral        Korea Central
koreasouth          Korea South
northcentralus      North Central US
northeurope         North Europe
southcentralus      South Central US
southeastasia       Southeast Asia
southindia          South India
uksouth             UK South
ukwest              UK West
westcentralus       West Central US
westeurope          West Europe
westindia           West India
westus              West US
westus2             West US
```

In the final step, *step 10*, you viewed the different public Azure clouds that are run by Microsoft. The output of this step looks like this:

```
PS C:\Foo> Get-AzEnvironment |
           Format-Table -Property name, ManagementPortalURL

Name                 ManagementPortalUrl
----                 -------------------
AzureChinaCloud      https://go.microsoft.com/fwlink/?LinkId=301902
AzureCloud           https://go.microsoft.com/fwlink/?LinkId=254433
AzureGermanCloud     https://portal.microsoftazure.de/
AzureUSGovernment    https://manage.windowsazure.us
```

There's more...

In *step 3*, you examined the modules you downloaded. Possibly confusingly, you downloaded the `Az` module, which actually downloads the 46 separate modules you can see in the preceding screenshots.

In *step 9*, you viewed the current Azure public cloud locations. Each of these 30 locations provide a range of services, although not all services are necessarily in every location. In *step 10*, you viewed the current Azure environments. Each of these four environments are totally separate and unrelated cloud offerings. The recipes in this chapter should run unchanged on each of the four Azure cloud environments, but no testing has been undertaken in this regard. You should also be aware that Azure is a very fast changing set of products. By the time you read this book, Azure may well have expanded.

See also

To keep up to date about new Azure product updates as well as roadmap announcements, see the Azure updates page at `https://azure.microsoft.com/en-gb/updates/`. The recipes in this chapter make use of Azure data centers in Europe. Depending on where you live, you may find that these data centers are further away from locations nearer to you. To discover network latency between you and the Azure locations, see `https://www.AzureSpeed.com`.

Creating core Azure resources

In the previous recipe, you created and used the basic Azure management environment by downloading the key modules, logging in to Azure, and having a brief look around. In this recipe, you create certain key Azure assets, including a resource group, a storage account, and tags.

With Azure, all Azure resources are created within a `resource group`. A resource group is a grouping of Azure resources. Any storage you create within Azure resides in a storage account, a fundamental building block within Azure.

All storage you use with any Azure feature always exists within a storage account. You create a storage account within one of the Azure regions you saw in the *Using PowerShell with Azure* recipe. When you create your storage account, you also specify the level of resiliency and durability that's provided. There are several levels of replication provided within Azure, which provide for multiple copies of the data that are replicated automatically in both the local Azure data center but also in other data centers. The extra resilience, which does come at a price, provides greater levels of recovery should the unthinkable happen and an entire data center somehow fails in a catastrophic way.

You can provision a storage account as either standard or premium. A standard storage account allows you to store any kind of data (as you see in the *Exploring your storage account* recipe). A premium storage account provides extra features, but at a cost.

Tags are name/value pairs that allow you to organize your resources within your subscription. For more details on how you can use tags to organize your Azure resources, see `https://docs.microsoft.com/en-us/azure/azure-resource-manager/resource-group-using-tags/`.

Getting ready

This recipe requires you to have an Azure account and that you have your system configured with the `Az` module, which was done in the *Using PowerShell with Azure* recipe.

How to do it...

1. Set values for key variables:

```
$Locname    = 'uksouth'      # location name
$RgName     = 'packt_rg'     # resource group we are using
$SAName     = 'packt42sa'    # Storage account name
```

2. Log in to your Azure account:

```
$CredAZ = Get-Credential
Login-AzAccount -Credential $CredAZ
```

3. Create a resource group and tag it:

```
$RGTag  = [Ordered] @{Publisher='Packt'}
$RGTag +=            @{Author='Thomas Lee'}
$RGHT = @{
  Name     = $RgName
  Location = $Locname
  Tag      = $RGTag
}
$RG = New-AzResourceGroup @RGHT
$RG
```

4. View the `Resource Group` details:

```
Get-AzResourceGroup -Name $RGName |
  Format-List -Property *
```

5. Test to see if a `Storage Account` name is available:

```
Get-AzStorageAccountNameAvailability $SAName
```

6. Create a new `Storage Account` within our newly created resource group:

```
$SAHT = @{
    Name              = $SAName
    SkuName           = 'Standard_LRS'
    ResourceGroupName = $RgName
    Tag               = $RGTag
    Location          = $Locname
}
New-AzStorageAccount @SAHT
```

7. Get an overview of the `Storage Account` in this `Resource Group`:

```
$SA = Get-AzStorageAccount -ResourceGroupName $RgName
$SA |
    Format-List -Property *
```

8. Get primary endpoints for the `Storage Account`:

```
$SA.PrimaryEndpoints
```

9. Review `SKU` for this `Storage Account`:

```
$SA.Sku
```

10. View the value of the `C` property of your `Storage Account`:

```
$SA.Context
```

How it works...

In *step 1*, you set the value of a number of key variables that are used in this recipe. In *step 2*, you logged in to your Azure account. Neither of these steps produce output.

In *step 3*, you created a new Azure Resource Group and gave it some nice tags. This step produces output like this:

```
PS C:\Foo> $RG = New-AzResourceGroup @$RGHT
PS C:\Foo> $RG

ResourceGroupName : packt_rg
Location          : uksouth
ProvisioningState : Succeeded
Tags              :
                    Name       Value
                    ========   ==========
                    Publisher  Packt
                    Author     Thomas Lee

ResourceId        : /subscriptions/0bc29420-0222-4599-b91e-e8699f760742/resourceGroups/packt_rg
```

In *step 4*, you got the `Resource Group` and viewed its properties, as follows:

```
PS C:\Foo> Get-AzResourceGroup -Name $RGName |
             Format-List -Property *

ResourceGroupName : packt_rg
Location          : uksouth
ProvisioningState : Succeeded
Tags              : {Publisher, Author}
TagsTable         :
                    Name       Value
                    ========   ==========
                    Publisher  Packt
                    Author     Thomas Lee

ResourceId        : /subscriptions/0bc29250-0222-4599-b91e-e8aa9f760794/resourceGroups/packt_rg
```

To create a Storage Account, you needed to check that the name was available, as shown in *step 5*:

```
PS C:\Foo> Get-AzStorageAccountNameAvailability $SAName

NameAvailable Reason Message
------------- ------ -------
         True
```

In *step 6*, you created a new `Storage Account`:

```
PS C:\Foo> $SAHT = @{
              Name              = $SAName
              SkuName           = 'Standard_LRS'
              ResourceGroupName = $RgName
              Tag               = $RGTag
              Location          = $Lorname
           }
PS C:\Foo> New-AzStorageAccount @SAHT

StorageAccountName ResourceGroupName Location SkuName     Kind    AccessTier CreationTime         ProvisioningState EnableHttpsTrafficOnly
------------------ ----------------- -------- -------     ----    ---------- ------------         ----------------- ----------------------
packt42sa          packt_rg          uksouth  StandardLRS Storage            13/02/2019 08:54:37  Succeeded         False
```

In *step 7*, you used the `Get-AzStorageAccount` cmdlet to view details of the `Storage Account`, which looks like this:

```
PS C:\Foo> $SA = Get-AzStorageAccount -ResourceGroupName $RgName
PS C:\Foo> $SA |
          Format-List -Property *

ResourceGroupName           : packt_rg
StorageAccountName          : packt42sa
Id                          : /subscriptions/0bc29250-0222-4599-b91e-e8aa9f760794/resourceGroups/packt_rg/
                              providers/Microsoft.Storage/storageAccounts/packt42sa
Location                    : uksouth
Sku                         : Microsoft.Azure.Management.Storage.Models.Sku
Kind                        : Storage
Encryption                  : Microsoft.Azure.Management.Storage.Models.Encryption
AccessTier                  :
CreationTime                : 13/02/2019 08:54:37
CustomDomain                :
Identity                    :
LastGeoFailoverTime         :
PrimaryEndpoints            : Microsoft.Azure.Management.Storage.Models.Endpoints
PrimaryLocation             : uksouth
ProvisioningState           : Succeeded
SecondaryEndpoints          :
SecondaryLocation           :
StatusOfPrimary             : Available
StatusOfSecondary           :
Tags                        : {[Publisher, Packt], [Author, Thomas Lee]}
EnableHttpsTrafficOnly      : False
EnableHierarchicalNamespace :
NetworkRuleSet              : Microsoft.Azure.Commands.Management.Storage.Models.PSNetworkRuleSet
Context                     : Microsoft.WindowsAzure.Commands.Common.Storage.LazyAzureStorageContext
ExtendedProperties          : {}
```

In *step 8*, you examined the key endpoints for your newly created `Storage Account`, which looks like this:

```
PS C:\Foo> $SA.PrimaryEndpoints

Blob  : https://packt42sa.blob.core.windows.net/
Queue : https://packt42sa.queue.core.windows.net/
Table : https://packt42sa.table.core.windows.net/
File  : https://packt42sa.file.core.windows.net/
Web   :
Dfs   :
```

In *step 9*, you viewed the SKU for your `Storage Account`, like this:

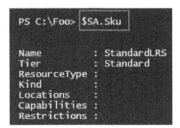

```
PS C:\Foo> $SA.Sku

Name         : StandardLRS
Tier         : Standard
ResourceType :
Kind         :
Locations    :
Capabilities :
Restrictions :
```

In *step 10*, you viewed the details of the Storage Account's `Context` property, which looks like this:

```
PS C:\Foo> $SA.Context

BlobEndPoint        : https://packt42sa.blob.core.windows.net/
TableEndPoint       : https://packt42sa.table.core.windows.net/
QueueEndPoint       : https://packt42sa.queue.core.windows.net/
FileEndPoint        : https://packt42sa.file.core.windows.net/
StorageAccount      : BlobEndpoint=https://packt42sa.blob.core.windows.net/;QueueEndpoint=https://packt42sa
                      .queue.core.windows.net/;TableEndpoint=https://packt42sa.table.core.windows.net/;File
                      Endpoint=https://packt42sa.file.core.windows.net/;AccountName=packt42sa;AccountKey=[k
                      ey hidden]
StorageAccountName  : packt42sa
Context             : Microsoft.WindowsAzure.Commands.Common.Storage.LazyAzureStorageContext
Name                : packt42sa
EndPointSuffix      : core.windows.net/
ConnectionString    : BlobEndpoint=https://packt42sa.blob.core.windows.net/;QueueEndpoint=https://packt42sa
                      .queue.core.windows.net/;TableEndpoint=https://packt42sa.table.core.windows.net/;File
                      Endpoint=https://packt42sa.file.core.windows.net/;AccountName=packt42sa;AccountKey=mQ
                      hkCIh8suJdcTY7TLuCa4diYK8qMN2i2tVuYx+9l952JFHhSde3/wwEdDYeG9/K2Cz2vRflYA4cwDxu37ii1A=
                      =
ExtendedProperties  : {}
```

There's more...

With *step 1*, you created some variables and gave them the appropriate values. When you go to replicate these recipes, you may find that some of the names that are used here are already in use by other Azure customers. To run this and other recipes in this chapter, you may need to adjust these values. For example, the `Storage Account` name that was used in the previous edition of this book has been taken by someone so it cannot be used!

In *step 2*, you used `Login-AzAccount` to log in to Azure. In earlier versions of the Azure cmdlets, this cmdlet was somewhat restricted and did not support Microsoft accounts (for example, accounts that end in @MSN.Com). That shortcoming is eliminated in the Az cmdlets.

In *step 6*, you created a new Storage Account, but only after you determined the storage account name was valid. With Azure, the Storage Name (an important part of the URIs that PowerShell uses to connect to Azure) must be globally unique. Thus, no two Azure customers in the world can use the same storage account names. To ensure that your account is valid, in *step 5*, you used the cmdlet `Get-AzStorageAccountNameAvailability` to test that the name was indeed allowed. If the name was not valid, you would have to choose another storage account name and amend the recipe accordingly.

See also

Resource groups are a fundamental part of the Azure Resource Management API. For a good introduction to the Azure Resource Management API, see `https://docs.microsoft.com/ en-us/azure/storage/common/storage-introduction`.

Storage in Azure is both complex and somewhat different to on-premise storage solutions. Take a look at `https://docs.microsoft.com/en-us/azure/storage/common/storage-introduction` for an introduction to Azure Storage.

Exploring your storage account

Many Azure resources use Azure Storage. When you create an Azure VM, for example, you store the VHD file in Azure Storage. Azure Storage accounts can hold a variety of data, with different mechanisms for managing each data type.

Additionally, the storage account provides both scalability and data durability and resiliency. Azure Storage manages five distinct types of data:

- **Binary large object (blob)**
- Table
- Queue
- File
- Disk

A `blob` is unstructured data that you store in Azure. Blob storage can hold any type of data in any form. This could include MP4 movies, ISO images, VHD drives, JPG files, and so on. Individual blobs reside within blob `containers,` which are equivalent to file store folders, but with very limited nesting capability.

Blobs come in three types: block blobs, append blobs, and page blobs. Block blobs are physically optimized for storing documents to the cloud and for streaming applications. Append blobs are optimized for append operations and are useful for logging. Page blobs are optimized for read/write operations—Azure VHDs, for example, are always of the page blob type. For more information about blob types, take a look at `https://docs.microsoft.com /azure/storage/blobs/storage-blobs-introduction`.

An Azure table is a non-relational storage system that utilizes key-value pairs. You can use Azure tables for storing unstructured or semi-structured data. This contrasts with an SQL table, which holds highly normalized data. A table consists of a grouping of entities. See `https://azure.microsoft.com/services/storage/tables/` for more information about Azure table storage.

An Azure queue is a durable message queuing feature that's used to implement scalable applications. With message queues, one part of an application can write a transaction to the queue for another part to process. A queue enables you to decouple application components for independent scaling and to provide greater resiliency. For more details on Azure queues, see `https://azure.microsoft.com/services/storage/queues/`.

The Azure file feature provides simple cross-platform file storage that you can access using SMB. This enables you to create and use SMB file shares in the cloud and access them, just like you would access on-premises SMB shares. Azure files support SMB 2.1 and 3.0, which makes it simple and easy for you to migrate legacy applications that rely on file shares. For more information on Azure files, see `https://azure.microsoft.com/services/storage/files/`.

Azure's disk storage provides persistent, highly secure disk options, particularly for Azure VMs. Azure disks are designed for low latency and high throughput. You can provision both traditional spinning disks as well as SSD disks that provide better I/O performance for I/O intensive applications. For more details on Azure disk storage, see `https://azure.microsoft.com/services/storage/disks/`.

Storage features continue to evolve with more options available as time goes by. For more details on Azure storage as a whole, see `https://docs.microsoft.com/azure/storage/common/storage-introduction`.

As we noted earlier, you name your storage account based on a global naming scheme which is based on HTTPS URLs. The Azure REST API relies on URLs to manage the Azure resources in your resource groups. All storage accounts are named by specifying the storage account, data type, container name, and filename. The format for a blob is as follows:

```
https://<storageaccountname>.<datatype>.core.windows.net/...
```

Getting ready

Run this recipe on CL1, which you previously configured via the *Using PowerShell with Azure* recipe.

How to do it...

1. Define key variables:

```
$Locname    = 'uksouth'            # location name
$RgName     = 'packt_rg'           # resource group we are using
$SAName     = 'packt42sa'          # Storage account name
$CName      = 'packtcontainer'
$CName2     = 'packtcontainer2'
```

2. Log in to your Azure account:

```
$CredAz = Get-Credential
Login-AzAccount -Credential $CredAz
```

3. Ensure that the Resource Group and the Storage Account have been created:

```
$RGHT = @{
    Name  = $RgName
    ErrorAction =  'SilentlyContinue'
}
$RG = Get-AzResourceGroup  @RGHT
if (-not $RG) {
  $RGTag  = [Ordered] @{Publisher='Packt'}
  $RGTag +=            @{Author='Thomas Lee'}
  $RGHT2 = @{
    Name     = $RgName
    Location = $Locname
    Tag      = $RGTag
}
  $RG = New-AzureRmResourceGroup @RGHT2
  "RG $RgName created"
}
$SAHT = @{
    Name              = $SAName
    ResourceGroupName = $RgName
    ErrorAction       = 'SilentlyContinue'
}
$SA = Get-AzStorageAccount @SAHT
if (-not $SA) {
    $SATag = [Ordered] @{Publisher = 'Packt'}
    $SATag += @{Author = 'Thomas Lee'}
    $SAHT = @{
        Name              = $SAName
        ResourceGroupName = $RgName
        Location          = $Locname
        Tag               = $SATag
        SkuName           = 'Standard_LRS'
    }
    $SA = New-AzStorageAccount  @SAHT
    "SA $SAName created"
}
```

4. Get and display the Storage Account key:

```
$SAKHT = @{
    Name              = $SAName
    ResourceGroupName = $RgName
}
$Sak = Get-AzStorageAccountKey  @SAKHT
$Sak
```

5. Extract the first key's password:

```
$Key = ($Sak | Select-Object -First 1).Value
```

6. Get and view the Storage Account Context, which encapsulates credentials for the storage account:

```
$SCHT = @{
   StorageAccountName = $SAName
   StorageAccountKey = $Key
}
$SACon = New-AzStorageContext @SCHT
$SACon
```

7. Create two blob containers:

```
$CHT - @{
   Context    = $SACon
   Permission = 'Blob'
}
New-AzStorageContainer -Name $CName @CHT
New-AzStorageContainer -Name $CName2 @CHT
```

8. View the blob container:

```
Get-AzStorageContainer -Context $SACon |
   Select-Object -ExpandProperty CloudBlobContainer
```

9. Create a very small blob in Azure:

```
'This is a small Azure blob!!' | Out-File .\azurefile.txt
$BHT = @{
    Context = $SACon
    File = '.\azurefile.txt'
```

```
        Container = $CName
    }
    $Blob = Set-AzStorageBlobContent   @BHT
    $Blob
```

10. Construct and display the blob name:

```
    $BlobUrl = "$($Blob.Context.BlobEndPoint)$CName/$($Blob.name)"
    $BlobUrl
```

11. View the URL via IE:

```
    $IE = New-Object -ComObject InterNetExplorer.Application
    $IE.Navigate2($BlobUrl)
    $IE.Visible = $true
```

How it works...

In *step 1*, you defined the key variables that are used in the recipe and, in *step 2*, you logged in to your Azure account. These two steps produce no output.

In *step 3*, you ensured that the Resource Group and Storage Account were created and created them if not. Assuming you completed the previous recipe, *Creating core Azure resources*, this step produces no output. A message indicating that the resource group and/or storage account were not found and were created is issued if the resources were not found.

In *step 4*, you gathered and displayed the storage account key, which looks like this:

```
PS C:\Foo> $SAKHT = @{
               Name              = $SAName
               ResourceGroupName = $RgName
           }
PS C:\Foo> $Sak = Get-AzStorageAccountKey  @SAKHT
PS C:\Foo> $Sak

KeyName Value                                                                               Permissio
                                                                                            ns
------- -----                                                                               ---------
key1    vHVZzF8c3Bnvn/QTVOizWkgYOGNwvaUi841p5s3zIO16M7Sf2xExVBmY0+oTXdfcJmFtqtSRkqBIwyhSm3gpyg==  Full
key2    3ky2ulp77zswyRSMJo5RbDEKGj57WVxB3jFh3117fi+yb+1C2+M3iXrN6kOgsZWjFZkOQthahUGtNEmlPLlfZg==   Full
```

In *step 5*, you extracted the password from the first storage account key, which produces no output. Using that password, in *step 6*, you created and displayed the Storage Account context, which looks like this:

```
PS C:\Foo> $CHT = @{
              Context    = $SACon
              Permission = 'Blob'
          }
PS C:\Foo> New-AzStorageContainer -Name $CName @CHT
PS C:\Foo> New-AzStorageContainer -Name $CName2 @CHT

   Blob End Point: https://packt42sa.blob.core.windows.net/

Name              PublicAccess          LastModified
----              ------------          ------------
packtcontainer    Blob                  13/02/2019 19:53:46 +00:00
packtcontainer2   Blob                  13/02/2019 19:53:46 +00:00
```

In *step 7*, you used the Storage Account Context (which encapsulates the credentials) to create two Azure blob containers, as follows:

```
PS C:\Foo> $CHT = @{
              Context    = $SACon
              Permission = 'Blob'
          }
PS C:\Foo> New-AzStorageContainer -Name $CName @CHT
PS C:\Foo> New-AzStorageContainer -Name $CName2 @CHT

   Blob End Point: https://packt42sa.blob.core.windows.net/

Name              PublicAccess          LastModified
----              ------------          ------------
packtcontainer    Blob                  13/02/2019 19:53:46 +00:00
packtcontainer2   Blob                  13/02/2019 19:53:46 +00:00
```

In *step 8*, you viewed the two new blob containers, as follows:

```
PS C:\Foo> Get-AzStorageContainer -Context $SACon |
             Select-Object -ExpandProperty CloudBlobContainer

   Blob End Point: https://packt42sa.blob.core.windows.net/

Name              Uri                                                       LastModified
----              ---                                                       ------------
packtcontainer    https://packt42sa.blob.core.windows.net/packtcontainer    2019-02-13 19:53:46Z
packtcontainer2   https://packt42sa.blob.core.windows.net/packtcontainer2   2019-02-13 19:53:46Z
```

In *step 9*, you created a new Azure blob by using the `Set-AzStorageBlobContent` cmdlet. The output looks like this:

```
PS C:\Foo> 'This is a small Azure blob!!' | Out-File .\azurefile.txt
PS C:\Foo> $BHT = @{
             Context = $SACon
             File = '.\azurefile.txt'
             Container = $CName
           }
PS C:\Foo> $Blob = Set-AzStorageBlobContent  @BHT
PS C:\Foo> $Blob

   Container Uri: https://packt42sa.blob.core.windows.net/packtcontainer

Name          BlobType   Length  ContentType            LastModified         AccessTier SnapshotTime IsDeleted
----          --------   ------  -----------            ------------         ---------- ------------ ---------
azurefile.txt BlockBlob  62      application/octet-stream 2019-02-13 19:56:24Z Unknown                False
```

In *step 10*, you generated a URL for this blob, as follows:

```
PS C:\Foo> $BlobUrl = "$($Blob.Context.BlobEndPoint)$CName/$($Blob.name)"
PS C:\Foo> $BlobUrl

https://packt42sa.blob.core.windows.net/packtcontainer/azurefile.txt
```

In *step 11*, you viewed the blob's content using Internet Explorer, as follows:

```
https://packt42sa.blob.core.windows.net/packtcontainer/azurefile.txt

This is a small Azure blob!!
```

There's more...

In *step 4,* you retrieved the Storage Account keys for your Storage Account. Each key's value property is, in effect, a password for your Azure storage account. Having two keys enables you to regularly regenerate and rotate your key values. In *step 5*, you got this value for the first key.

In *step 6,* you got the storage account's storage context. This object encapsulates the details of the storage account, including the storage account key you created in the prior step.

In *step 7* and *step 8*, you created two blob containers and displayed their URLs. Containers are a single-level, folder-like object that contains your blobs. In *step 9*, you created a simple blob and, as you can see from the output, this is a block blob, with the content just comprising an octet stream.

Creating an Azure SMB file share

Azure provides you with the ability to create SMB shares with an Azure storage account. These SMB shares act the same as the local on-premises SMB shares you used in *Chapter 9, Managing Network Shares*. The key difference is how you create them and the credentials you use to access the shares.

Before an SMB client can access data held in an SMB share, the SMB client needs to authenticate with the SMB server. With Windows-based shares, you either use a user ID/password credential, or in a domain environment, the SMB client utilizes Kerberos to authenticate. With Azure, you use the storage account name as the user ID and the storage account key as the password.

The storage account key provides you with two keys (imaginatively named key1 and key2). The values of both keys are valid passwords for Azure SMB file shares. Having two keys enables you to do regular key rotation. If your application uses the value of key1, you can reconfigure your application to use the key2 value as the share's password and then regenerate the key1 value. Some time later, you repeat this—changing the application to use key1's value and then regenerate key2. This provides you with an immediate key update where you need it. Armed with the value of either key, you can easily create SMB shares that are directly addressed across the internet.

An Azure SMB share differs from Azure blobs with respect to how you access them. You access a blob via HTTP, whereas you access an Azure file share via the standard SMB networking commands that you used in, for example, *Chapter 5, Managing Shared Data*.

Blobs and files also differ in that with blobs, you only have a single level of a folder (the container). With Azure files, you can have as many folders as you need.

When using Azure SMB shares, the Storage Account key is the password for the share and the Storage Account name is the user ID. As with all credentials, you should exercise caution when including the account key in code.

In this recipe, you use the resource group and storage account we created earlier (in the *Create Core Azure resources* recipe). This recipe also checks to ensure that these exist and creates them if they are not available.

Getting ready

This recipe uses the CL1 host that you set up in the *Using PowerShell with Azure* recipe.

How to do it...

1. Define the variables:

```
$Locname    = 'uksouth'      # location name
$RgName     = 'packt_rg'     # resource group we are using
$SAName     = 'packt42sa'    # storage account name
$ShareName  = 'packtshare'   # must be lower case!
```

2. Log in to your Azure Account and ensure that the RG and SA have been created:

```
$CredAZ = Get-Credential
$Account = Login-AzAccount -Credential $CredAZ
```

3. Get a Storage account, Storage Account key, and context:

```
$SA = Get-AzStorageAccount -ResourceGroupName $Rgname
$SAKHT = @{
    Name               = $SAName
    ResourceGroupName  = $RgName
}
$Sak = Get-AzStorageAccountKey @SAKHT
$Key = ($Sak | Select-Object -First 1).Value
$SCHT = @{
    StorageAccountName = $SAName
    StorageAccountKey  = $Key
}
$SACon = New-AzStorageContext @SCHT
```

4. Add credentials to the local store:

```
$T = "$SAName.file.core.windows.net"
cmdkey /add:$T /user:"AZURE\$SAName" /pass:$Key
```

5. Create an Azure Files file share:

```
New-AzStorageShare -Name share2 -Context $SACon
```

6. Test that the share is reachable:

```
$TNCHT = @{
  ComputerName = "$SAName.file.core.windows.net"
  Port         = 445
}
Test-NetConnection @TNCHT
```

447

7. Mount the share as Z:

```
$Mount = 'Z:'
$Rshare = "\\$SaName.file.core.windows.net\$ShareName"
$SMHT = @{
    LocalPath  = $Mount
    RemotePath = $Rshare
    UserName   = $SAName
    Password   = $Key
}
New-SmbMapping @SMHT
```

8. View the share in Azure:

```
Get-AzStorageShare -Context $SACon  |
   Format-List -Property *
```

9. View the local SMB mapping:

```
Get-SmbMapping
```

10. Now, use the new share. Create a folder and a file in the share:

```
New-Item -Path Z:\Foo -ItemType Directory | Out-Null
'Azure and PowerShell Rock!!!' |
   Out-File -FilePath Z:\Foo\recipe.txt
```

11. Get the content from the file:

```
Get-Content -Path Z:\Foo\recipe.txt
```

How it works...

In *step 1*, you set the values for the variables that are to be used in this recipe. In *step 2*, you logged in to your Azure account. In *step 3*, you retrieved the Storage Account key and Storage Context. These three steps produce no output.

In *step 4*, you added the Azure Files credential details into the local store using cmdkey, exe, which looks like this:

```
PS C:\Foo> $T = "$SAName.file.core.windows.net"
PS C:\Foo> cmdkey /add:$T /user:"AZURE\$SAName" /pass:$Key

CMDKEY: Credential added successfully.
```

In *step 5*, you created a new Azure Files file share by using the `New-AzStorageShare` cmdlet:

```
PS C:\Foo> New-AzStorageShare -Name $ShareName -Context $SACon

   File End Point: https://packt42sa.file.core.windows.net/
Name           LastModified                      IsSnapshot  SnapshotTime
----           ------------                      ----------  ------------
packtshare     13/02/2019 23:41:47 +00:00        False
```

In *step 6*, you checked the connection over the SMB port (`445`) to the Azure storage server hosting the new share. The output looks like this:

```
PS C:\Foo> $TNCHT = @{
              ComputerName = "$SAName.file.core.windows.net"
              Port         = 445
           }
PS C:\Foo> Test-NetConnection @TNCHT

ComputerName      : packt42sa.file.core.windows.net
RemoteAddress     : 52.239.187.40
RemotePort        : 445
InterfaceAlias    : PureVPN
SourceAddress     : 10.2.48.34
TcpTestSucceeded  : True
```

Next, in *step 7*, you created an SMB Mapping, mapping the `Z:` drive to your new share, which looks like this:

```
PS C:\Foo> $Mount = 'Z:'
PS C:\Foo> $Rshare = "\\$SaName.file.core.windows.net\$ShareName"
PS C:\Foo> $SMHT = @{
              LocalPath  = $Mount
              RemotePath = $Rshare
              UserName   = $SAName
              Password   = $Key
           }
PS C:\Foo> New-SmbMapping @SMHT

Status Local Path Remote Path
------ ---------- -----------
OK     Z:         \\packt42sa.file.core.windows.net\packtshare
```

In *step 8*, you viewed the share in Azure, which looks like this:

```
PS C:\Foo> Get-AzStorageShare -Context $SACon  |
           Format-List -Property *

ServiceClient               : Microsoft.WindowsAzure.Storage.File.CloudFileClient
Uri                         : https://packt42sa.file.core.windows.net/packtshare
StorageUri                  : Primary = 'https://packt42sa.file.core.windows.net/packtshare'; Secondary = ''
SnapshotTime                :
IsSnapshot                  : False
SnapshotQualifiedUri        : https://packt42sa.file.core.windows.net/packtshare
SnapshotQualifiedStorageUri : Primary = 'https://packt42sa.file.core.windows.net/packtshare'; Secondary = ''
Name                        : packtshare
Metadata                    : {}
Properties                  : Microsoft.WindowsAzure.Storage.File.FileShareProperties
```

In *step 9*, you viewed the local SMB Mappings, which looks like this:

```
PS C:\foo> Get-SmbMapping

Status Local Path Remote Path
------ ---------- -----------
OK     Z:         \\packt42sa.file.core.windows.net\packtshare
```

In *step 10*, you created a folder in the new share and created a small file in the share. This step produces no output. In *step 11*, you used Get-Content to retrieve the contents of the file, which looks like this:

```
PS C:\Foo> Get-Content -Path Z:\Foo\recipe.txt
Azure and PowerShell Rock!!!
```

There's more...

In *step 1*, you created variables to hold the names of the Azure objects you were to use in this recipe. The $Locname variable holds the name of the Azure region in which you create your storage account, which you may wish to change to a more local Azure region.

In *step 3*, you created a storage context object. The context object encapsulates the credentials for your storage account.

You used cmdkey.exe in *step 4* to save credentials for Azure's storage account. You used cmdkey to store the username and password that Windows should use to access the Azure share. For more details on cmdkey, see https://technet.microsoft.com/en-us/library/cc754243(v=ws.11).aspx. You can use the cmdkey utility to list all the stored credentials (cmdkey /list).

Creating an Azure website

Azure provides a number of ways in which you can create rich web and mobile applications in the cloud. You could set up your own virtual machines, install IIS, and add your web application. If your application needs to store data, you can create a separate SQL Server VM (or use Azure's SQL database PASS offering).

A simpler way is to create an Azure Web App. Azure Web Apps enabled you to build, deploy, and manage rich websites and web applications. You can use frameworks such as .NET, Node. js, PHP, and Python in these applications and use any database software that's appropriate to your needs. An Azure Web App can be simple static HTML sites, or rich multi-tier applications that run on both web and mobile platforms. You have a lot of choices.

In this recipe, you create a simple single-page static website. You upload the page via FTP. The PSFTP third-party module makes the upload simple.

Getting ready

You run this on CL1, which you set up for Azure in the *Using PowerShell with Azure* recipe. This recipe uses the C:\Foo folder, which should have already been created on CL1.

How to do it...

1. Define the variables:

```
$Locname     = 'uksouth'       # location name
$RgName      = 'packt_rg'       # resource group we are using
$SAName      = 'packt42sa'     # storage account name
$AppSrvName  = 'packt42'
$AppName     = 'packt42website'
```

2. Log in to your Azure Account:

```
$CredAZ = Get-Credential
$Sccount = Login-AzAccount -Credential $CredAz
```

3. Ensure that the Resource Group has been created:

```
$RGHT1 = @{
  Name          = $RgName
  ErrorAction = 'Silentlycontinue'
}
```

```
$RG = Get-AzResourceGroup @RGHT1
if (-not $RG) {
  $RGTag  = [Ordered] @{Publisher='Packt'}
  $RGTag +=            @{Author='Thomas Lee'}
  $RGHT2 = @{
    Name     = $RgName
    Location = $Locname
    Tag      = $RGTag
  }
  $RG = New-AzResourceGroup @RGHT2
  Write-Host "RG $RgName created"
}
```

4. Ensure that the Storage Account has been created:

```
$SAHT = @{
  Name              = $SAName
  ResourceGroupName = $RgName
  ErrorAction       = 'SilentlyContinue'
}
$SA = Get-AzStorageAccount @SAHT
if (-not $SA) {
  $SATag  = [Ordered] @{Publisher='Packt'}
  $SATag +=            @{Author='Thomas Lee'}
  $SAHT = @{
    Name              = $SAName
    ResourceGroupName = $RgName
    Location          = $Locname
    Tag               = $SATag
    SkuName           = 'Standard_LRS'
  }
  $SA = New-AStorageAccount @SAHT
  "SA $SAName created"
}
```

5. Create an application service plan:

```
$SPHT = @{
    ResourceGroupName = $RgName
    Name              = $AppSrvName
    Location          = $Locname
    Tier              = 'Free'
}
New-AzAppServicePlan @SPHT | Out-Null
```

6. View the application service plan:

```
$PHT = @{
  ResourceGroupName = $RGname
  Name              = $AppSrvName
}
Get-AzAppServicePlan @PHT
```

7. Create the new Azure Web App using the application service plan:

```
$WAHT = @{
  ResourceGroupName = $RgName
  Name              = $AppName
  AppServicePlan    = $AppSrvName
  Location          = $Locname
}
New-AzWebApp @WAHT | Out-Null
```

8. View the application details:

```
$WebApp = Get-AzWebApp -ResourceGroupName $RgName -Name $AppName
$WebApp |
  Format-Table -Property Name, State, Hostnames, Location
```

9. Now, view the website:

```
$SiteUrl = "https://$($WebApp.DefaultHostName)"
$IE  = New-Object -ComObject InterNetExplorer.Application
$IE.Navigate2($SiteUrl)
$IE.Visible = $true
```

10. Install the PSFTP module:

```
Install-module PSFTP -Force | Out-Null
Import-Module PSFTP
```

11. Get the publishing profile XML and extract the FTP upload details:

```
$APHT = @{
  ResourceGroupName = $RgName
  Name              = $AppName
  OutputFile        = 'C:\Foo\pdata.txt'
}
$x = [xml] (Get-AzWebAppPublishingProfile @APHT)
$x.publishData.publishProfile[1]
```

12. Extract the credentials and site details:

```
$UserName = $x.publishData.publishProfile[1].userName
$UserPwd  = $x.publishData.publishProfile[1].userPWD
$Site     = $x.publishData.publishProfile[1].publishUrl
```

13. Connect to the FTP site:

```
$FTPSN  = 'FTPtoAzure'
$PS     = ConvertTo-SecureString $UserPWD -AsPlainText -Force
$T      = 'System.Management.automation.PSCredentiaL'
$Cred   = New-Object -TypeName $T -ArgumentList $UserName,$PS
$FTPHT  = @{
  Credentials = $Cred
  Server      = $Site
  Session     = $FTPSN
  UsePassive  = $true
}
Set-FTPConnection @FTPHT
$Session = Get-FTPConnection -Session $FTPSN
```

14. Create a web page and upload it:

```
'My First Azure Web Site' | Out-File -FilePath C:\Foo\Index.Html
$Filename = 'C:\foo\index.html'
$IHT = @{
  Path      = '/'
  LocalPath = 'C:\foo\index.html'
  Session   = $FTPSN
}
Add-FTPItem @IHT
```

15. Now, look at the site using the default browser (Chrome):

```
$SiteUrl = "https://$($WebApp.DefaultHostName)"
Start-Process -FilePath $SiteUrl
```

How it works...

In *step 1*, you set the variables you were going to use in this recipe. In *step 2*, you logged in to Azure. In *step 3*, you ensured that the Resource Group was created and in *step 4*, you made sure that the Storage Account was created. In *step 5*, you created a new Azure application service plan. These five steps produce no output.

In *step 6*, you viewed the Azure Application Service Plan, which looks like this:

```
PS C:\Foo> $PHT = @{
              ResourceGroupName = $RGname
              Name              = $AppSrvName
           }
PS C:\Foo> Get-AzAppServicePlan @PHT

WorkerTierName             :
Status                     : Ready
Subscription               : 0bc29420-0222-4599-b91e-e8699f760742
AdminSiteName              :
HostingEnvironmentProfile  :
MaximumNumberOfWorkers     : 1
GeoRegion                  : UK South
PerSiteScaling             : False
NumberOfSites              : 0
IsSpot                     : False
SpotExpirationTime         :
FreeOfferExpirationTime    :
ResourceGroup              : packt_rg
Reserved                   : False
IsXenon                    : False
TargetWorkerCount          : 0
TargetWorkerSizeId         : 0
ProvisioningState          : Succeeded
Sku                        : Microsoft.Azure.Management.WebSites.Models.SkuDescription
Id                         : /subscriptions/0bc29420-0222-4599-b91e-e8699f760742/
                           ; resourceGroups/packt_rg/providers/Microsoft.Web/
                           ; serverfarms/packt42
Name                       : packt42
Kind                       : app
Location                   : UK South
Type                       : Microsoft.Web/serverfarms
Tags                       :
```

In *step 7*, you created a new Azure Web App using the Application Service Plan you created in the previous step. This step produces no output. In *step 8*, you viewed some of the properties of the Azure Web App. The output of this step looks like this:

```
PS C:\Foo> $WebApp = Get-AzWebApp -ResourceGroupName $RgName -Name $AppName
PS C:\Foo> $WebApp |
              Format-Table -Property Name, State, Hostnames, Location

Name            State    HostNames                            Location
----            -----    ---------                            --------
packt42website  Running  {packt42website.azurewebsites.net}   UK South
```

In *step 9*, you looked at the new website using IE, which looks like this:

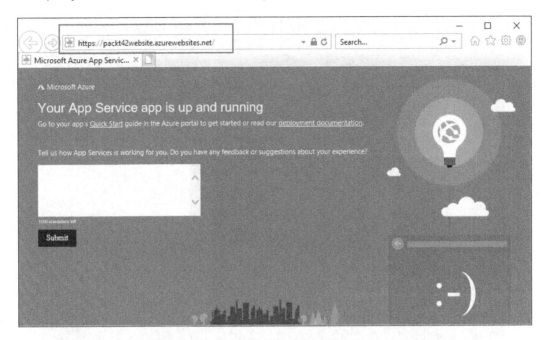

In *step 10*, you downloaded and installed the third-party PSFTP module, which helps to automate FTP operations. This step produces no output. In *step 11*, you got the Web App publishing profile, which contains the FTP credentials you need so that you can upload content to the Web App. The output of this step looks like this:

```
PS C:\Foo> $APHT = @{
               ResourceGroupName  = $RgName
               Name               = $AppName
               OutputFile         = 'C:\Foo\pdata.txt'
           }
PS C:\Foo> $x = [xml] (Get-AzWebAppPublishingProfile @APHT)
PS C:\Foo> $x.publishData.publishProfile[1]


profileName                  : packt42website - FTP
publishMethod                : FTP
publishUrl                   : ftp://waws-prod-ln1-021.ftp.azurewebsites.windows.net/site/wwwroot
ftpPassiveMode               : True
userName                     : packt42website\$packt42website
userPWD                      : lNPblfx3Htdl1HlGid3LcEqBytZCJDzA02u3Te420R9btaQaT6X9Rttzhb69
destinationAppUrl            : http://packt42website.azurewebsites.net
SQLServerDBConnectionString  :
mySQLDBConnectionString      :
hostingProviderForumLink     :
controlPanelLink             : http://windows.azure.com
webSystem                    : WebSites
databases                    :
```

In *step 12*, you extracted the FTP site's credentials from the Publishing Profile, creating no output. In *step 13*, you used cmdlets from the PSFTP module to open an FTP session with the Azure web app. The output looks like this:

```
PS C:\Foo> $FTPSN    = 'FTPtoAzure'
PS C:\Foo> $PS       = ConvertTo-SecureString $UserPWD -AsPlainText -Force
PS C:\Foo> $T        = 'System.Management.automation.PSCredentiaL'
PS C:\Foo> $Cred     = New-Object -TypeName $T -ArgumentList $UserName,$PS
PS C:\Foo> $FTPHT    = @{
               Credentials = $Cred
               Server      = $Site
               Session     = $FTPSN
               UsePassive  = $true
           }
PS C:\Foo> Set-FTPConnection @FTPHT
PS C:\Foo> $Session = Get-FTPConnection -Session $FTPSN


ContentLength               : -1
Headers                     : {}
SupportsHeaders             : True
ResponseUri                 : ftp://waws-prod-ln1-021.ftp.azurewebsites.windows.net/site/wwwroot
StatusCode                  : ClosingData
StatusDescription           : 226 Transfer complete.

LastModified                : 01/01/0001 00:00:00
BannerMessage               : 220 Microsoft FTP Service

WelcomeMessage              : 230 User logged in.

ExitMessage                 : 221 Goodbye.

IsFromCache                 : False
IsMutuallyAuthenticated     : False
ContentType                 :
```

In *step 14*, you created a very simple web page and uploaded it to Azure. The output looks like this:

```
PS C:\Foo> 'My First Azure Web Site' | Out-File -FilePath C:\Foo\Index.Html
PS C:\Foo> $IHT = @{
               Path      = '/'
               LocalPath = 'C:\Foo\Index.html'
               Session   = $FTPSN
           }
PS C:\Foo> Add-FTPItem @IHT

    Parent: ftp://waws-prod-ln1-021.ftp.azurewebsites.windows.net/site/wwwroot

Dir Right     Ln  User  Group  Size  ModifiedDate         Name
--- -----     --  ----  -----  ----  ------------         ----
-                              52B   02-17-19  07:35PM    index.html
```

In the final step, *step 15*, you viewed the site in your browser, as follows:

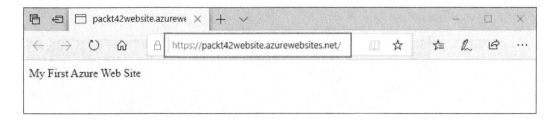

There's more...

In *step 5*, you created an application service plan. This plan basically tells Azure where to place your website and in which service tier. All Azure web apps run inside an Azure-managed VM. This recipe uses the Free Web App service tier, which is a site in a shared VM. This should provide more than adequate performance for testing and development. If you need better performance, you can scale up in terms of the processors available and scale out in terms of the number of VM instances running in your web app. For an overview of Azure App Service plans, see `https://docs.microsoft.com/en-gb/azure/app-service/overview`.

See also

This recipe uses the PSFTP third-party module. For more information about the module, see `https://gallery.technet.microsoft.com/scriptcenter/PowerShell-FTP-Client-db6fe0cb`. That web page is a little out of date and the latest version of the PSFTP module that was used in this recipe is later than shown.

Creating an Azure VM

Azure provides a range of on-demand computing resources, one of which is **virtual machines** (**VM**). An Azure VM is a good solution where you need more control over the computing environment than you might be able to obtain using a PaaS service.

An Azure VM is essentially a Hyper-V VM that you run within Azure. There are some differences between the Hyper-V VMs you create within Server 2019 (or Windows 10) and Azure VMs, but they are minor. The AZ cmdlets you use to manage Azure VMs are a little different in style to Hyper-V cmdlets, which may mean a bit of a learning curve.

Getting ready

You run this recipe on CL1, which you configured (in the *Using PowerShell with Azure* recipe) to work with Azure. Also, you should have already created an Azure Resource Group and an Azure Storage Account, but this recipe checks for these and creates the resources if needed.

How to do it...

1. Define the key variables:

```
$Locname = 'uksouth'          # Azure location name
$RgName  = 'packt_rg'         # Resource group name
$SAName  = 'packt42sa'        # Storage account name
$VNName  = 'packtvnet'        # Virtual Network Name
$CloudSN = 'packtcloudsn'     # Cloud subnet name
$NSGName = 'packt_nsg'        # NSG name
$Ports   = @(80, 3389)        # Ports to open in VBM
$IPName  = 'Packt_IP1'        # Private IP Address name
$User    = 'AzureAdmin'       # User Name
$UserPS  = 'JerryRocks42!'    # User Password
$VMName  = 'Packt42VM'        # VM Name
```

2. Log in to your Azure account:

```
$CredAZ = Get-Credential
Login-AzAccount -Credential $CredAZ
```

3. Ensure that the Resource Group has been created:

```
$RG = Get-AzResourceGroup -Name $RgName -ErrorAction
SilentlyContinue
if (-not $rg) {
    $RGTag = @{Publisher = 'Packt'}
    $RGTag += @{Author = 'Thomas Lee'}
    $RGHT1 = @{
        Name     = $RgName
        Location = $Locname
        Tag      = $RGTag
    }
    $RG = New-AzResourceGroup @RGHT1
    Write-Host  "RG $RgName created"
}
```

4. Ensure that the Storage Account has been created:

```
$SA = Get-AzStorageAccount -Name $SAName -ResourceGroupName
$RgName -ErrorAction SilentlyContinue
if (-not $SA) {
    $SATag = [Ordered] @{Publisher = 'Packt'}
    $SATag += @{Author = 'Thomas Lee'}
    $SAHT - @{
        Name                = $SAName
        ResourceGroupName   = $RgName
        Location            = $Locname
        Tag                 = $SATag
        $SkuName            = 'Standard_LRS'
    }
    $SA = New-AzStorageAccount @SAHT
    Write-Host "SA $SAName created"
}
```

5. Create the VM credentials:

```
$T = 'System.Management.Automation.PSCredential'
$P = ConvertTo-SecureString -String $UserPS -AsPlainText -Force
$VMCred = New-Object -TypeName $T -ArgumentList $User, $P
```

6. Create a VM:

```
$VMHT = @{
  ResourceGroupName   = $RgName
  Location            = $Locname
  Name                = $VMName
  VirtualNetworkName  = $VNName
  SubnetName          = $CloudSN
  SecurityGroupName   = $NSGName
  PublicIpAddressName = $IPName
  OpenPorts           = $Ports
  Credential          = $VMCred
}
New-AzVm @VMHT
```

7. Get and view the VM's external IP address:

```
$VMIP = Get-AzPublicIpAddress -ResourceGroupName $RGname
$VMIP = $VMIP.IpAddress
"VM Public IP Address: [$VMIP]"
```

8. Connect to and view the VM:

```
mstsc /v:"$VMIP"
```

How it works...

In *step 1*, you defined the variables to be used for this recipe. In *step 2*, you logged in to your Azure account. In *step 3*, you ensured that the resource group was created and, in *step 4*, you ensured that the Azure Storage Account for this recipe was created. In *step 5*, you created a PowerShell credential object that encapsulates the credentials for the VM. These steps produce no output.

In *step 6*, you used the `New-AzVm` cmdlet to create your new VM. This produces the following output:

```
PS C:\Foo> $VMHT = @{
              ResourceGroupName    = $RgName
              Location             = $Locname
              Name                 = $VMName
              VirtualNetworkName   = $VNName
              SubnetName           = $CloudSN
              SecurityGroupName    = $NSGName
              PublicIpAddressName  = $IPName
              OpenPorts            = $Ports
              Credential           = $VMCred
            }
PS C:\Foo> New-AzVm @VMHT

ResourceGroupName        : packt_rg
Id                       : /subscriptions/0bc29420-0222-4599-b91e-e8699f760742/
                           resourceGroups/packt_rg/providers/
                           Microsoft.Compute/virtualMachines/Packt42VM
VmId                     : 22d59b62-b220-41a8-94e4-300116e24033
Name                     : Packt42VM
Type                     : Microsoft.Compute/virtualMachines
Location                 : uksouth
Tags                     : {}
HardwareProfile          : {VmSize}
NetworkProfile           : {NetworkInterfaces}
OSProfile                : {ComputerName, AdminUsername, WindowsConfiguration, Secrets, AllowExtensionOperations}
ProvisioningState        : Succeeded
StorageProfile           : {ImageReference, OsDisk, DataDisks}
FullyQualifiedDomainName : packt42vm-3dbc7d.uksouth.cloudapp.azure.com
```

In *step 7*, you retrieved the new Azure VM's public IP address and displayed it, as follows:

```
PS C:\Foo> $VMIP = Get-AzPublicIpAddress -ResourceGroupName $RGname
PS C:\Foo> $VMIP = $VMIP.IpAddress
PS C:\Foo> "VM Public IP Address: [$VMIP]"

VM Public IP Address: [51.140.36.42]
```

In the final step, *step 8*, you used the `mstsc.exe` application to open up an RDS window into the VM, as follows:

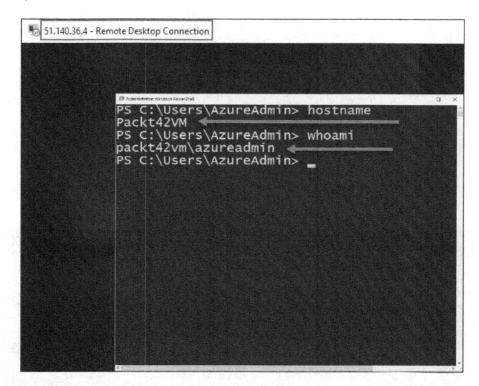

There's more...

In *step 6*, you used the `New-AzVm` cmdlet to create a new Azure VM. This method of creating the VM takes a number of defaults, including the version of the OS to install in the VM. This recipe takes a very simple approach to the creation of the VM—there is a lot more that you can do that is beyond the scope of this book.

See also

There is a lot of richness in terms of the VM and the networks you can create to access it that this recipe has not covered. For more details on Azure VMs, refer to the online documentation at `https://docs.microsoft.com/en-us/azure/virtual-machines/windows/`.

13
Managing Performance and Usage

In this chapter, we cover the following recipes:

- ▸ Retrieving performance counters using Get-Counter
- ▸ Using WMI to retrieve performance counters
- ▸ Creating and using PLA data collector sets
- ▸ Reporting on performance data
- ▸ Generating performance-monitoring graphs
- ▸ Creating a system diagnostic report
- ▸ Reporting on printer usage
- ▸ Monitoring Hyper-V utilization and performance

Introduction

Understanding how your infrastructure is being utilized is a key task for many IT pros today, and has been a challenge since the earliest days of computing. Windows NT 3.1 came with a marvelous tool, **Performance Monitor** (**perfmon**), that allowed you to see what the OS and applications are doing and what resources they are consuming. The Windows NT 3.1 Resource Kit even included an entire book on how to use perfmon and the various performance counters.

In addition to understanding how your individual servers are performing, you need to know what they are actually doing in terms of user work. Knowing, for example, the usage of printers is useful for capacity-planning purposes.

This chapter shows you how you can use PowerShell to obtain and display performance information and usage information using a variety of techniques, including cmdlets, WMI, and more.

Windows Server 2019 contains a subsystem known as **Performance Logging and Alerting** (**PLA**). PLA enables you to obtain performance details, logging information, and diagnostic data from local and remote computers (and more!).

PLA provides the underpinnings to familiar GUI tools such as **Performance Monitor** and **Task Manager**. These tools utilize the performance-monitoring framework built into Windows and help to visualize the outputs from PLA. You can also use PLA to generate data from which you can generate performance graphs.

In PLA, a `counter set` contains information about the performance of some aspect of your systems such as memory, disk devices, or network interfaces. A PLA counter set contains one or more individual `counters`. A counter provides a measurement of some aspect of the counter set. For example, the `Memory` counter set on Windows Server 2019 has 36 counters. Counters include `Pages/Sec` and `Available Bytes`.

A counter can be either single-instance or multi-instance. Counters such as `\Memory\Page/Sec` are single-instance counters, where each counter sample contains just one measurement (the current number of pages/second is being requested). Other counters, such as `\Processor(*)\% Processor Time`, are multi-instance counters, returning counter samples for each processor in the server, plus one for the total CPU being consumed (helpfully named `_total`). If your physical processor has hyper-threading enabled, you get two measurements for each physical core; thus, on a dual-processor hex-core system with hyper-threading, this counter would return 25 measurements (two measurements for each of the 12 cores plus one for total CPU utilization). A Hyper-V virtual machine with eight cores assigned would return nine counter samples (one for each virtual processor plus the total).

To get counter values from within a counter set, you use the `Get-Counter` cmdlet and specify the counter name (that is, the path) to the counter. The path is formatted as `\\<ServerName\<CounterSetName>\<CounterName>`. For example, the path to a counter on a remote server could look like this: `\\DC1\Memory\Page Faults/sec`. If you are getting counters on the local machine, you can omit the computer name prefix and just specify `\Memory\Page Faults/sec`. Note that the counter set and counter names can be long and can have spaces in the names. You often need to specify counter paths using PowerShell string quoting.

The `Get-Counter` cmdlet returns counter measurements as well as the available counter sets on a system. The `PerformanceCounterSampleSet` object, returned by `Get-Counter`, contains a `CounterSamples property`. This property contains one measurement of the counter (for single-instance counters) or an array of samples (for multi-instance counters).

In the *Retrieving performance counters using Get-Counter* recipe, you see how to use `Get-Counter` to return counter set details and counter measurements.

You can also use WMI to return performance counter details, as you can see in the *Using WMI to retrieve performance counters* recipe.

If you are using multiple counters and counter sets and plan to analyze performance data, using PLA data collector sets is the preferred approach. With the *Creating and using PLA data collector sets* recipe, you create and start a data collector set. The *Reporting on performance data* and *Generating performance monitoring graphs* recipes show how you can leverage the results from a PLA data collector.

PLA also has some built-in data collectors and predefined reports based on those collectors. You can easily get PLA to produce a Systems Diagnostic Report, as shown in the *Creating a systems diagnostic report* recipe. This report can provide insights into possible performance or other issues on your server.

When looking at the performance of a print server, it's useful to know how much usage a given printer is experiencing. The *Reporting on printer usage* recipe shows you how to retrieve printer usage information from your print server's event log and generate a report.

The final recipe in this chapter, *Monitoring Hyper-V utilization and performance*, demonstrates generating reports on your **virtual machines** (**VMs**) and VM servers. This recipe shows how to obtain basic performance information about a Hyper-V host and the VMs defined on the host.

Retrieving performance counters using Get-Counter

Within Windows, a performance counter set is a set of performance counters. Each counter in a counter set measures an aspect of your system related to that counter set. In this recipe, we explore counter sets and counters on several servers.

Getting ready

This recipe uses DC1, DC2, SRV1, SRV2, HV1, and HV2. These are servers that you have worked with in various recipes in this book. DC1 and DC2 are domain controllers, HV1 and HV2 host Hyper-V, and SRV1 and SRV2 are general-purpose Windows servers. All of these systems are running Windows 2019 Datacenter edition. Run this recipe from SRV1.

How to do it...

1. Discover performance counter sets on SRV1:

```
$CounterSets = Get-Counter -ListSet *
$CS1 = 'There are {0} counter sets on [{1}]'
$CS1 -f $CounterSets.Count,(hostname)
```

2. Discover performance counter sets on remote systems:

```
$Machines = 'DC1','DC2','HV1','HV2','SRV1','SRV2'
Foreach ($Machine in $Machines)
{
  $RCounters =  Get-Counter -ListSet * -ComputerName $Machine
  $CS2 = "There are {0} counters on [{1}]"
  $CS2 -f $RCounters.Count, $Machine
}
```

3. List key performance counter sets:

```
Get-Counter -ListSet Processor, Memory, Network*,*Disk |
  Sort-Object -Property CounterSetName |
    Format-Table -Property CounterSetName
```

4. Get a description of the memory counter set:

```
Get-Counter -ListSet Memory |
  Format-Table -Property Name, Description -Wrap
```

5. Get and display counters in the memory counter set on the localhost:

```
$CountersMem = (Get-Counter -ListSet Memory).Counter
'Memory counter set has [{0}] counters:' -f $CountersMem.Count
$CountersMem
```

6. Get and display a sample from each counter in the memory counter set:

```
$Counters = (Get-Counter -ListSet Memory).Counter
$FS = '{0,-19} {1,-60} {2,-10}'
$FS -f 'At', 'Counter', 'Value' # Display header row
foreach ($Counter in $Counters){
  $C = Get-Counter -Counter $Counter
  $T = $C.Timestamp                      # Time
  $N = $C.CounterSamples.Path.Trim()     # Counter Name
```

```
    $V = $C.CounterSamples.CookedValue        # Value
    '{0,-15}  {1,-59}  {2,-14}' -f $T, $N, $V
}
```

7. Explore counter set types for key performance counters:

```
Get-Counter -ListSet Processor, Memory, Network*, *Disk* |
  Select-Object -Property CounterSetName, CounterSetType
```

8. Explore a local performance counter sample set:

```
$Counter1 = '\Memory\Page Faults/sec'
$PFS      = Get-Counter -Counter $Counter1
$PFS
```

9. Look at a remote performance counter sample set on HV1:

```
$Counter2 = '\\HV1\Memory\Page Faults/sec'
$RPFS      = Get-Counter -Counter $Counter1
$RPFS
```

10. Look inside a counter sample set:

```
$PFS | Get-Member -MemberType *Property |
  Format-Table -Wrap
```

11. What is inside a local multi-value counter sample:

```
$Counter3 = '\Processor(*)\% Processor Time'
$CPU      =  Get-Counter -Counter $Counter3
$CPU
```

12. View a multi-value counter sample on HV2:

```
$Counter4 = '\\HV2\Processor(*)\% Processor Time'
$CPU      =  Get-Counter -Counter $Counter4
$CPU
```

How it works...

In *step 1*, you use the `Get-Counter` cmdlet to determine how many counter sets exist on
SRV1, which looks like this:

```
PS C:\Foo> $CounterSets = Get-Counter -ListSet *
PS C:\Foo> $CS = "There are {0} counter sets on [{1}]"
PS C:\Foo> $CS -f $CounterSets.count, (hostname)

There are 173 counter sets on [SRV1]    ⬅
```

With *step 2*, you determine how many performance counter sets exist on remote servers,
which looks like this:

```
PS C:\Foo> $Machines = 'DC1','DC2','HV1','HV2','SRV1','SRV2'
PS C:\Foo> Foreach ($Machine in $Machines)
           {
               $RCounters =   Get-Counter -ListSet * -ComputerName $Machine
               $CS2 = "There are {0} counters on [{1}]"
               $CS2 -f $RCounters.Count, $Machine
           }

There are 179 counters on [DC1]
There are 179 counters on [DC2]
There are 192 counters on [HV1]
There are 192 counters on [HV2]
There are 173 counters on [SRV1]
There are 166 counters on [SRV2]
```

In *step 3*, you retrieve and view key counter sets, which looks like this:

```
PS C:\Foo> Get-Counter -ListSet Processor, Memory, Network*,*Disk |
               Sort-Object -Property CounterSetName |
                   Format-Table -Property CounterSetName

CounterSetName
--------------
LogicalDisk
Memory
Network Adapter
Network Interface
Network QoS Policy
PhysicalDisk
Processor
Storage Spaces Virtual Disk
```

With *step 4*, you get a description of the `Memory` counter set:

```
PS C:\Foo> Get-Counter -ListSet Memory |
              Format-Table -Property Description -Wrap

Description
-----------
The Memory performance object consists of counters that describe the
behavior of physical and virtual memory on the computer.  Physical memory
is the amount of random access memory on the computer.  Virtual memory
consists of the space in physical memory and on disk.  Many of the memory
counters monitor paging, which is the movement of pages of code and data
between disk and physical memory.  Excessive paging, a symptom of a
memory shortage, can cause delays which interfere with all system
processes.
```

In *step 5*, you retrieve the counters in the `Memory` counter set (showing just the first few counters), which looks like this:

```
PS C:\Foo> $CountersMem = (Get-Counter -ListSet Memory).Counter
PS C:\Foo> 'Memory counter set has [{0}] counters:' -f $countersMem.Count
PS C:\Foo> $CountersMem

Memory counter set has [36] counters:
\Memory\Page Faults/sec
\Memory\Available Bytes
\Memory\Committed Bytes
\Memory\Commit Limit
\Memory\Write Copies/sec
\Memory\Transition Faults/sec
\Memory\Cache Faults/sec
\Memory\Demand Zero Faults/sec
\Memory\Pages/sec
...
```

In *step 6*, you use `Get-Counter` to retrieve counter data from the `Memory` counter set, which looks like this:

```
PS C:\Foo> $Counters = (Get-Counter -ListSet Memory).counter
PS C:\Foo> $FS = '{0,-19} {1,-60} {2,-10}'
PS C:\Foo> $FS -f 'At', 'Counter', 'Value'
PS C:\Foo> foreach ($Counter in $Counters) {
             $C = Get-Counter -Counter $Counter
             $T = $C.Timestamp                     # Time
             $N = $C.CounterSamples.Path.Trim()    # Name
             $V = $C.CounterSamples.CookedValue    # Value
             '{0,-15} {1,-59} {2,-14}' -f $T, $N, $V
           }

At                  Counter                                                  Value
02/12/2018 13:06:30 \\srv1\memory\page faults/sec                            4520.2914934334
02/12/2018 13:06:31 \\srv1\memory\available bytes                            707297280
02/12/2018 13:06:34 \\srv1\memory\committed bytes                           1698086912
02/12/2018 13:06:36 \\srv1\memory\commit limit                               5198368768
02/12/2018 13:06:42 \\srv1\memory\write copies/sec                           0
02/12/2018 13:06:45 \\srv1\memory\transition faults/sec                      29.6306690041123
02/12/2018 13:06:48 \\srv1\memory\cache faults/sec                           0
02/12/2018 13:06:52 \\srv1\memory\demand zero faults/sec                     3.90279236988481
02/12/2018 13:06:54 \\srv1\memory\pages/sec                                  0
02/12/2018 13:06:57 \\srv1\memory\pages input/sec                            0
02/12/2018 13:07:00 \\srv1\memory\page reads/sec                             0
02/12/2018 13:07:02 \\srv1\memory\pages output/sec                           0
02/12/2018 13:07:05 \\srv1\memory\pool paged bytes                           122318848
02/12/2018 13:07:08 \\srv1\memory\pool nonpaged bytes                        88764416
02/12/2018 13:07:10 \\srv1\memory\page writes/sec                            0
02/12/2018 13:07:13 \\srv1\memory\pool paged allocs                          0
02/12/2018 13:07:16 \\srv1\memory\pool nonpaged allocs                       0
02/12/2018 13:07:18 \\srv1\memory\free system page table entries             12299320
02/12/2018 13:07:21 \\srv1\memory\cache bytes                                87281664
02/12/2018 13:07:23 \\srv1\memory\cache bytes peak                           108310528
02/12/2018 13:07:26 \\srv1\memory\pool paged resident bytes                  104390656
02/12/2018 13:07:28 \\srv1\memory\system code total bytes                    4419584
02/12/2018 13:07:30 \\srv1\memory\system code resident bytes                 4145152
02/12/2018 13:07:33 \\srv1\memory\system driver total bytes                  15462400
02/12/2018 13:07:36 \\srv1\memory\system driver resident bytes               6303744
02/12/2018 13:07:39 \\srv1\memory\system cache resident bytes                85155840
02/12/2018 13:07:41 \\srv1\memory\% committed bytes in use                   33.0038212549416
02/12/2018 13:07:44 \\srv1\memory\available kbytes                           665704
02/12/2018 13:07:47 \\srv1\memory\available mbytes                           652
02/12/2018 13:07:50 \\srv1\memory\transition pages repurposed/sec            0
02/12/2018 13:07:53 \\srv1\memory\free & zero page list bytes                6344704
02/12/2018 13:07:56 \\srv1\memory\modified page list bytes                   35397632
02/12/2018 13:08:00 \\srv1\memory\standby cache reserve bytes                139522048
02/12/2018 13:08:03 \\srv1\memory\standby cache normal priority bytes        548347904
02/12/2018 13:08:09 \\srv1\memory\standby cache core bytes                   0
02/12/2018 13:08:12 \\srv1\memory\long-term average standby cache lifetime (s)  626
```

In *step 7*, you determine which counter set names produce single- or multi-instance counters, which looks like this:

```
PS C:\Foo> Get-Counter -ListSet Processor, Memory, Network*, *Disk* |
           Select-Object -Property CounterSetName, CounterSetType

CounterSetName                     CounterSetType
--------------                     --------------
Processor                          MultiInstance
Memory                             SingleInstance
Network QoS Policy                 SingleInstance
Network Interface                  MultiInstance
Network Adapter                    MultiInstance
FileSystem Disk Activity           SingleInstance
Storage Spaces Virtual Disk        SingleInstance
LogicalDisk                        MultiInstance
PhysicalDisk                       MultiInstance
```

In *step 8*, you retrieve a specific memory counter (page faults per second) from SRV1, which looks like this:

```
PS C:\Foo> $Counter1 = '\Memory\Page Faults/sec'
PS C:\Foo> $PFS      = Get-Counter -Counter $Counter1
PS C:\Foo> $PFS

Timestamp                      CounterSamples
---------                      --------------
02/12/2018 14:43:24            \\srv1\memory\page faults/sec :
                               289.226378092902
```

In *step 9*, you retrieve a counter value from a remote system, HV1, which looks like this:

```
PS C:\Foo> $Counter2 = '\\HV1\Memory\Page Faults/sec'
PS C:\Foo> $RPFS     = Get-Counter -Counter $Counter1
PS C:\Foo> $RPFS

Timestamp                      CounterSamples
---------                      --------------
02/12/2018 14:44:57            \\srv1\memory\page faults/sec :
                               72.5333566499923
```

In *step 10*, you view the properties of one counter, which looks like this:

```
PS C:\Foo> $PFS  | Get-Member -MemberType *Property |
           Format-Table -Wrap

    TypeName: Microsoft.PowerShell.Commands.GetCounter.PerformanceCounterSampleSet

Name           MemberType     Definition
----           ----------     ----------
CounterSamples Property       Microsoft.PowerShell.Commands.GetCounter.PerformanceCounterSample[] CounterSamples {get;set;}
Timestamp      Property       datetime Timestamp {get;set;}
Readings       ScriptProperty System.Object Readings {get=$strPaths = ""
                              foreach ($ctr in $this.CounterSamples)
                              {
                                  $strPaths += ($ctr.Path + " :" + "`n")
                                  $strPaths += ($ctr.CookedValue.ToString() + "`n`n")
                              }
                              return $strPaths;}
```

In *step 11*, you view a multi-value counter sample on the local machine, which looks like this:

```
PS C:\Foo>  $Counter3 = '\Processor(*)\% Processor Time'
PS C:\Foo>  $CPU      =  Get-Counter -Counter $Counter3
PS C:\Foo>  $CPU

Timestamp                        CounterSamples
---------                        --------------
02/12/2018 14:50:08              \\srv1\processor(0)\% processor time :
                                 6.93205772178016

                                 \\srv1\processor(_total)\% processor time :
                                 6.93205772178016
```

In *step 12*, you retrieve a multi-value counter from HV2, contains counter values for each processor in the HV1 computer, which looks like this:

```
PS C:\Foo>  $Counter4 = '\\HV2\Processor(*)\% Processor Time'
PS C:\Foo>  $CPU      =  Get-Counter -Counter $Counter4
PS C:\Foo>  $CPU

Timestamp                        CounterSamples
---------                        --------------
02/12/2018 14:49:33              \\HV2\processor(0)\% processor time :
                                 0.372123911818356

                                 \\HV2\processor(1)\% processor time :
                                 1.90486046702115

                                 \\HV2\processor(2)\% processor time :
                                 1.90486046702115

                                 \\HV2\processor(3)\% processor time :
                                 1.90486046702115

                                 \\HV2\processor(_total)\% processor time :
                                 1.52168123297742
```

There's more...

In *step 5*, you use Get-Counter to get the values of the counter on the Memory counter set (on SRV1). As you can see, this is not particularly fast. Using Get-Counter to retrieve larger numbers of counter values is not a great approach—using PLA data collector sets (as discussed in the *Creating and using PLA data collector sets* recipe) is much more efficient.

In *step 8*, you can see that the `PerformanceCounterSampleSet` object has both a `CounterSamples` property and a `Readings` script property, which returns the same basic information. The `PerformanceCounterSampleSet` object is a structured object with properties for counter path and counter values. The `Readings` script property is a small PowerShell script that returns a string made up of the path and the cooked data value. For viewing from the PowerShell console, use the `Readings` property, whereas for analysis, having a structured object can be useful.

In *step 11* and *step 12*, you look at two multi-valued processor counters. Each step returns one counter measurement for each CPU, plus a total for all CPUs in the system. In *step 11*, you view the processor usage on `SRV1`, which has just one CPU (and produces two counter values), while in *step 12*, `HV2` has four processors, so you see five counter samples (one for each processor plus a total).

Using WMI to retrieve performance counters

Another way to access performance information is via WMI. You can use either the WMI or the CIM cmdlets to access a large number of performance counters, as an alternative to using `Get-Counter`.

When using WMI, the naming structure for counter information is different from using `Get-Counter`. With WMI, counters are exposed via separate WMI classes whose names are slightly different from those you use with `Get-Counter`. Effectively, with WMI, each performance counter set is a WMI class.

You find the WMI performance counters in the `ROOT\CimV2` namespace; they have names that begin with `Win32_Perf`. For example, the `Memory` performance counter set contains 36 separate counters. The `Win32_PerfFormattedData_PerfOS_Memory` WMI class contains 46 properties, including the numerous individual performance counters.

With WMI, you get all the measurements back in one call to `Get-CimInstance`, whereas you would need to call `Get-Counter` for each counter sample. This provides better performance than you see with `Get-Counter`, but WMI is still fairly slow when compared to the PLA data collector sets you use in later recipes in this chapter.

This recipe gets performance counters from local and remote machines using the CIM cmdlet set. The CIM cmdlet set is preferable to the older WMI commands as it is a little faster, and it can make use of `WinRM` for remote sessions.

Getting ready

You run this recipe on SRV1. This recipe uses the CIM cmdlets. You could revise this recipe to make use of the WMI cmdlets, which might be useful in cases where you are communicating with an older system that does not have PowerShell remoting up and running.

How to do it...

1. Find performance-related counters in the Root\CimV2 namespace:

```
Get-CimClass -ClassName Win32*perf* | Measure-Object |
  Select-Object -Property Count
Get-CimClass -ClassName Win32*perfFormatted* | Measure-Object |
  Select-Object -Property Count
Get-CimClass -ClassName Win32*perfraw* | Measure-Object |
  Select-Object -Property Count
```

2. Find key performance classes for the OS:

```
Get-CimClass "win32_PerfFormatted*PerfOS*" |
  Select-Object -Property CimClassName
```

3. Find key performance classes for the disk:

```
Get-CimClass "Win32_PerfFormatted*Disk*" |
  Select-Object -Property CimClassName
```

4. Find key performance classes for the disk:

```
Get-CimInstance -ClassName Win32_PerfFormattedData_PerfOS_Memory |
  Select-Object -Property PagesPerSec, AvailableMBytes
```

5. Get CPU counter samples:

```
Get-CimInstance -ClassName
Win32_PerfFormattedData_PerfOS_Processor |
  Where-Object Name -eq '_Total' |
    Select-Object -Property Name, PercentProcessortime
```

6. Get CPU counter samples from a remote system:

```
$CHT = @{
    ClassName       = 'Win32_PerfFormattedData_PerfOS_Memory'
    ComputerName    = 'DC1'
}
Get-CimInstance @CHT |
  Select-Object -Property PSComputerName, PagesPerSec,
                          AvailableMBytes
```

How it works...

In *step 1*, you search for the performance-related counters in the Root\CIMV2 namespace, which looks like this:

```
PS C:\Foo> Get-CimClass -ClassName Win32*Perf* | Measure-Object |
           Select-Object -Property Count

Count
-----
  345  ←

PS C:\Foo> Get-CimClass -ClassName Win32*PerfFormatted* | Measure-Object |
           Select-Object -Property Count

Count
-----
  172  ←

PS C:\Foo> Get-CimClass -ClassName Win32*PerfRaw* | Measure-Object |
           Select-Object -Property Count

Count
-----
  172  ←
```

In *step 2*, you search for WMI classes relating to the OS performance, which looks like this:

```
PS C:\Foo> Get-CimClass "win32_PerfFormatted*PerfOS*" |
           Select-Object -Property CimClassName

CimClassName
------------
Win32_PerfFormattedData_PerfOS_Cache
Win32_PerfFormattedData_PerfOS_Memory
Win32_PerfFormattedData_PerfOS_NUMANodeMemory
Win32_PerfFormattedData_PerfOS_Objects
Win32_PerfFormattedData_PerfOS_PagingFile
Win32_PerfFormattedData_PerfOS_Processor
Win32_PerfFormattedData_PerfOS_System
```

In *step 3*, you search for WMI classes relating to disk performance, which looks like this:

```
PS C:\Foo> Get-CimClass "win32_PerfFormatted*Disk*" |
               Select-Object -Property CimClassName

CimClassName
------------
Win32_PerfFormattedData_Counters_FileSystemDiskActivity
Win32_PerfFormattedData_Counters_StorageSpacesVirtualDisk
Win32_PerfFormattedData_PerfDisk_LogicalDisk
Win32_PerfFormattedData_PerfDisk_PhysicalDisk
```

In *step 4*, you get two memory counters from SRV1, which looks like this:

```
PS C:\Foo> Get-CimInstance -ClassName Win32_PerfFormattedData_PerfOS_Memory |
               Select-Object -Property PagesPerSec, AvailableMBytes

PagesPerSec AvailableMBytes
----------- ---------------
        234             550
```

In *step 5*, you retrieve the PerfOS_Processor class and display just the name and the percentage of CPU time being used on SRV1, which looks like this:

```
PS C:\Foo> Get-CimInstance -ClassName Win32_PerfFormattedData_PerfOS_Processor |
               Where-Object Name -eq '_Total' |
               Select-Object -Property Name, PercentProcessortime

Name    PercentProcessortime
----    --------------------
_Total                    84
```

With *step 6*, you retrieve the memory performance information, but remotely from DC1, which looks like this:

```
PS C:\Foo> $CHT = @{
               ClassName    = 'Win32_PerfFormattedData_PerfOS_Memory'
               ComputerName = 'DC1'
           }
PS C:\Foo> Get-CimInstance @CHT |
               Select-Object -Property PSComputerName, PagesPerSec,
                                       AvailableMBytes

PSComputerName PagesPerSec AvailableMBytes
-------------- ----------- ---------------
DC1                    232             779
```

There's more...

In *step 1*, you saw there were 172 WMI classes containing formatted data and the same number containing uncooked values, out of a total of 345 performance classes in the Root\CIMV2 namespace on SRV1. The one additional class is Win32_Perf, which returns all the other performance class instances (on SRV1, using Get-CimInstance to return the class results in 2,891 entries).

Creating and using PLA data collector sets

In the previous two recipes, you retrieved individual counter objects either by using Get-Counter or via WMI. That works, but retrieving performance data is slow. It took over a minute and 40 seconds to retrieve the performance counters in a local machine's Memory counter set. Using these methods for large-scale performance data collection does not scale well.

The PLA subsystem provides an efficient mechanism to perform the data collection. PLA allows you to create a data collector set. This is an object representing the counters whose values you wish to collect. Once you create the data collector set, you can direct Windows to start collecting the data and to output it for later analysis. You have options as to how to output the data—you can use a binary log file, a comma-delimited file, and more. Once you have the data collected and output, you can analyze it, as you can see in the *Reporting on performance data* recipe.

There is no direct cmdlet support for setting up and using performance data collection. Instead, you use the PLA COM objects that are built into Windows.

Getting ready

You run this on SRV1, a domain-joined server.

How to do it...

1. Create and populate a new performance data collector set:

```
$Name    = 'SRV1 Collector Set'
$SRV1CS = New-Object -COM Pla.DataCollectorSet
$SRV1CS.DisplayName              = $Name
$SRV1CS.Duration                 = 12*3600  # 12 hours - 19:00
$SRV1CS.SubdirectoryFormat       = 1
```

```
$SRV1CS.SubdirectoryFormatPattern   = 'yyyy\-MM'
$JPHT = @{
  Path      = "$Env:SystemDrive"
  ChildPath = "\PerfLogs\Admin\$Name"
}
$SRV1CS.RootPath = Join-Path @JPHT
$SRV1Collector = $SRV1CS.DataCollectors.CreateDataCollector(0)
$SRV1Collector.FileName                = "$Name_"
$SRV1Collector.FileNameFormat          = 1
$SRV1Collector.FileNameFormatPattern   = "\-MM\-dd"
$SRV1Collector.SampleInterval          = 15
$SRV1Collector.LogFileFormat           = 3 # BLG format
$SRV1Collector.LogAppend               = $True
```

2. Define counters of interest:

```
$Counters = @(
      '\Memory\Pages/sec',
      '\Memory\Available MBytes',
      '\Processor(_Total)\% Processor Time',
      '\PhysicalDisk(_Total)\% Disk Time',
      '\PhysicalDisk(_Total)\Disk Transfers/sec' ,
      '\PhysicalDisk(_Total)\Avg. Disk Sec/Read',
      '\PhysicalDisk(_Total)\Avg. Disk Sec/Write',
      '\PhysicalDisk(_Total)\Avg. Disk Queue Length'
)
```

3. Add the counters to the collector:

```
$SRV1Collector.PerformanceCounters = $Counters
```

4. Create a schedule—start tomorrow morning at 07:00:

```
$StartDate =
  Get-Date -Day $((Get-Date).Day+1) -Hour 7 -Minute 0 -Second 0
$Schedule = $SRV1CS.Schedules.CreateSchedule()
$Schedule.Days = 127
$Schedule.StartDate = $StartDate
$Schedule.StartTime = $StartDate
```

5. Create, add, and start the collector set:

```
try
{
    $SRV1CS.Schedules.Add($Schedule)
```

```
        $SRV1CS.DataCollectors.Add($SRV1Collector)
        $SRV1CS.Commit("$Name" , $null , 0x0003) | Out-Null
        $SRV1CS.Start($false);
    }
    catch
    {
        Write-Host "Exception Caught starting PLA DC: " $_.Exception
        Return
    }
```

How it works...

In *step 1*, you create and configure a new data collector set object (on SRV1). In *step 2*, you specify the performance counters you wish the data collector to collect. With *step 3*, you add those counters to the data collector. In *step 4*, you create a schedule telling the data collector when it should collect data. Finally, in *step 5*, you save the data collection details and start the data collection.

None of these steps produce output.

There's more...

In *step 1*, you assign the data collector's LogFileFormat to be 1. This tells PLA to create a log in binary format. When you create a data collector set, you could alternatively output using comma-separated values or tab-separated values, or as SQL records.

Setting the data collector's LogFileFormat property to 1 creates data in a comma-separated value format, while setting the property to 2 results in a tab-separated value format. Depending on the tools you use to analyze the output, different formats may be more appropriate.

In the GitHub repository supporting this book, you can find alternatives to this recipe that store the logging data in comma-separated and tab-separated formats. Note that other recipes in this chapter use different log file formats.

Adding a counter set and activating it generates data, and that consumes disk space. After using a counter set to analyze an issue, you might wish to stop data collection and possibly remove the counter set; you could do that as follows:

```
# Stop data collection
$DCStRemote = New-Object -COM Pla.DataCollectorSet
$Name = 'SRV1 Collector Set'
$DCstRemote.Query($Name,'LocalHost')
```

```
$DCstRemote.Stop($true)
# Remove the counter set
$DCstRemote.Delete()
```

As noted, the steps in this recipe produce no output. Once you have completed the steps in this recipe, you can view the data collector inside perfmon, which looks like this:

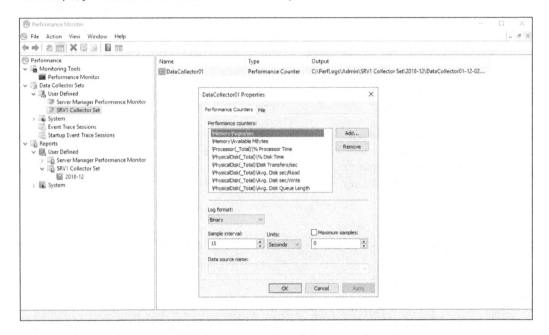

Reporting on performance data

Once you have created performance information using a PLA data collector set, you can use PowerShell to analyze the data.

In this recipe, you create a very simple report on the CPU usage of SRV1. The source of the report is the information logged as a result of the *Creating and using PLA data collection sets* recipe. As noted earlier, PLA can output the performance data in a variety of formats. In the *Creating and using PLA data collector sets* recipe, you used a binary log file format. This recipe, on the other hand, makes uses of a CSV format.

Getting ready

This recipe uses PLA data collection output logged in a CSV format from SRV1. To create CSV output, use the *Creating and using PLA data collector sets* recipe and change the value of the log file format to 1.

How to do it...

1. Import the CSV file of counter samples:

   ```
   $Folder = 'C:\PerfLogs\Admin'
   $File = Get-ChildItem -Path $Folder\*.csv -Recurse
   ```

2. Import the performance counters:

   ```
   $Counters = Import-Csv $File.FullName
   "$($Counters.Count) counters in $($File.FullName)"
   ```

3. Fix the issue with the first row in the counters:

   ```
   $Counters[0] = $Counters[1]
   ```

4. Obtain basic CPU stats:

   ```
   $CN = '\\SRV1\Processor(_Total)\% Processor Time'
   $HT = @{
      Name = 'CPU'
      Expression = {[System.Double] $_.$CN}
   }
   $Stats = $counters |
     Select-Object -Property *,$HT |
       Measure-Object -Property CPU -Average -Minimum -Maximum
   ```

5. Add the 95th percentile value of the CPU:

   ```
   $CN    = '\\SRV1\Processor(_Total)\% Processor Time'
   $Row   = [int]($Counters.Count * .95 )
   $CPU   = ($Counters.$CN | Sort-Object)
   $CPU95 = [double] $CPU[$Row]
   $AMHT  = @{
     InputObject = $Stats
     Name        = 'CPU95'
     MemberType  = 'NoteProperty'
   ```

```
    Value       = $CPU95
  }
  Add-Member @AMHT
```

6. Combine the results into a single report:

```
$Stats.CPU95   = $Stats.CPU95.ToString('n2')
$Stats.Average = $Stats.Average.ToString('n2')
$Stats.Maximum = $Stats.Maximum.ToString('n2')
$Stats.Minimum = $Stats.Minimum.ToString('n2')
```

7. Display the CPU performance summary:

```
$Stats |
  Format-Table -Property Property,Count,Maximum,CPU95,Minimum
```

How it works...

This recipe uses a CSV file of performance data created by using PLA. In *step 1*, you import the data in the CSV file. This step produces no output.

In *step 2*, you display the number of counter samples imported, which looks like this:

In *step 3*, you fix a known error with PLA affecting the first row returned (PLA returns an invalid first row). The fix is to assume the first two rows have identical values. That has the potential to introduce some degree of error into detailed calculations. The impact of such an error is small and mitigated by having a significant number of samples.

In *step 4*, you analyze the data sample and derive basic CPU usage statistics. In *step 5*, you create a 95th percentile value for CPU usage on SRV1.

With *step 6*, you work out an approximation of the 95th percentile CPU time. This is a good number to track, as it is a measure of how high, in general, the CPU load is on the computers that you are monitoring (95 percent of the time). It eliminates infrequent but high CPU measurements which might be misleading. You calculate this by first counting the total number of rows returned (sorted by CPU utilization), and then calculating an index that contains a value of 0.95 times the number of rows.

You then use this index to get that row from a list of sorted CPU values. With 100 rows of data returned, this calculation would return row 95 (that is, the 95th-highest CPU reading in the sample set).

Assuming you have a significant number of samples, this approach gets you the row that is a good approximation of the 95th-percentile CPU time measurement. At the end of this step, you add the value as a note property (CPU95).

In *step 7*, you display a summary of the CPU usage on SRV1, including a maximum, minimum, and 95th-percentile average CPU utilization, which looks like this:

```
PS C:\Foo> $stats |
            Format-Table -Property Property,Count,Maximum,CPU95,Minimum

Property Count Maximum CPU95 Minimum
-------- ----- ------- ----- -------
CPU       2881     100 27.26    0.45
```

There's more...

In this recipe, we reported on just one counter, the total CPU time on just one computer (SRV1). Although there was a maximum CPU utilization during the sampling of 100%, most of the time, CPU utilization was at or below 27.26%. That suggests SRV1 is not CPU-bound.

This recipe just reported on a single performance counter. It would be straightforward to update your data-collection process to include more counters, which enables you to report on more performance information. You could include counters for networking, storage counters, and more. These other counters may help you to understand just why CPU utilization is high.

You could also make use of data collector output from the different hosts in your infrastructure. You could then adjust this recipe to report on these additional counter values from all different hosts. Knowing that overall performance load is high on Hyper-V Host HV1 but low on the host HV2 might suggest moving a VM or two between the hosts.

Generating a performance-monitoring graph

In the *Reporting on performance data* recipe, you saw how you could take the data logged by a PLA data collector set and create a performance report. The report in that recipe showed CPU utilization of SRV1. That output is in the form of a table and is a summary of the performance of the server.

Another way to view the performance data is in the form of a graph. PowerShell does not have direct cmdlet support for displaying rich graphs, but the .NET Framework's `System. Windows.Forms.DataVisualization` namespace does.

This recipe uses the data visualization's `Chart` object to create a chart and save it as a **Portable Network Graphic** (**PNG**) file. You then display the graphic on your workstation.

Getting ready

You run this recipe on SRV1. This recipe uses the output of the PLA data collector set similar to the one you created and started in the *Creating and using PLA data collector sets* recipe. Note that the input to this recipe is a CSV file produced by PLA.

How to do it...

1. Load the assembly containing the `DataVisualization` classes:

   ```
   Add-Type -AssemblyName System.Windows.Forms.DataVisualization
   ```

2. Import the CSV data from earlier, and fix the row 0 issue:

   ```
   $CSVFile      = Get-ChildItem -Path C:\PerfLogs\Admin\*.csv -rec
   $Counters     = Import-Csv $CSVFile
   $Counters[0]  = $Counters[1]          # fix row 0 issue
   ```

3. Create a chart object:

   ```
   $Type = 'System.Windows.Forms.DataVisualization.Charting.Chart'
   $CPUChart = New-Object -TypeName $Type
   ```

4. Define the chart dimensions:

   ```
   $CPUChart.Width  = 1000
   $CPUChart.Height = 600
   $CPUChart.Titles.Add("SRV1 CPU Utilisation") | Out-Null
   ```

5. Create and define the chart area:

   ```
   $Type = 'System.Windows.Forms.DataVisualization.' +
           'Charting.ChartArea'
   $ChartArea              = New-Object -TypeName $Type
   $ChartArea.Name         = "SRV1 CPU Usage"
   $ChartArea.AxisY.Title  = "% CPU Usage"
   $CPUChart.ChartAreas.Add($ChartArea)
   ```

6. Get the date/time column:

```
$Name = ($counters[0] |
        Get-Member |
            Where-Object MemberType -EQ "NoteProperty")[0].Name
```

7. Add the counter sample values to the chart:

```
$CPUChart.Series.Add("CPUPerc")   | Out-Null
$CPUChart.Series["CPUPerc"].ChartType = "Line"
$CPUCounter = '\\SRV1\Processor(_Total)\% Processor Time'
$Counters |
  ForEach-Object {
$CPUChart.Series["CPUPerc"].Points.AddXY($_.$Name,$_.$CPUCounter)|
  Out-Null
}
```

8. Ensure the output folder exists, then save the chart image as a PNG file in the folder:

```
$NIHT = @{
  Path        = 'C:\Perflogs\Reports'
  ItemType    = 'Directory'
  ErrorAction = 'SilentlyContinue'
}
New-Item @NIHT  # create the folder if it does not exist
$CPUChart.SaveImage("C:\PerfLogs\Reports\Srv1CPU.Png", 'PNG')
```

9. Use the `mspaint.exe` application to view the chart image:

```
mspaint.exe C:\PerfLogs\Reports\SRV1cpu.Png
```

How it works...

Like the *Reporting on performance data recipe*, the steps in this recipe produce no output (except *step 9* where you view the chart). That is usual when you use many objects in the .NET Framework or when you use COM objects.

In *step 1*, you load the assembly containing the .NET classes you are using in this recipe. By default, this is an assembly that is not loaded by PowerShell.

With *step 2*, you import the PLA-created CPU data for SRV1. This file consists of a number of counter samples. You configured these details in the *Creating and using PLA data collector sets* recipe.

In *step 3*, you create a chart object, and in *step 4*, you define the chart's dimensions. In *step 5*, you create and configure a chart area object then add it to the chart.

In *step 6*, you get the name of the time and date column within the performance counters. *Step 7* adds the data to the chart. *Step 8* saves the chart as a PNG file.

Executing *step 9* invokes the `mspaint.exe` application, which displays the PNG file, as follows:

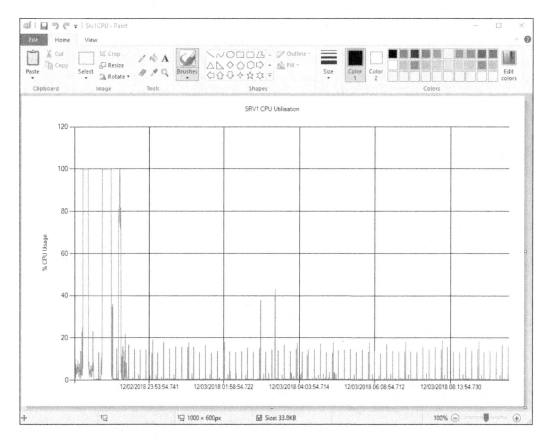

There's more...

This recipe showed you how to create a simple report graphing one counter, `CPUutilization`, across several hours of monitoring one server. You could add a second series, such as memory pages per second, to the chart. The result could be a customized graph that is similar to what you see in Performance Monitor. You could also incorporate data from more servers to the chart.

To support ongoing server monitoring, consider creating scheduled tasks to create the performance graphs and email the resultant output to those who need to know. Or have the scheduled task create a new web page on your intranet and drop the graphs into the page.

Creating a system diagnostic report

The PLA subsystem that you have been working with in this chapter has an additional system-defined report known as the System Diagnostic Report. This report monitors a system for a period then provides a detailed report on the server.

Getting ready

You use the SRV1 server that you have used in other recipes in this chapter.

How to do it...

1. Start the built-in data collector on the local system, which generates the report:

```
$PerfReportName="System\System Diagnostics"
$DataSet = New-Object -ComObject Pla.DataCollectorSet
$DataSet.Query($PerfReportName,$null)
$DataSet.Start($true)
```

2. Output a message, then wait for the data collector to finish:

```
"Sleeping for [$($Dataset.Duration)] seconds"
Start-Sleep -Seconds $Dataset.Duration
```

3. Get the report and save it as HTML:

```
$Dataset.Query($PerfReportName,$null)
$PerfReport = $Dataset.LatestOutputLocation + "\Report.html"
```

4. View the report:

```
& $PerfReport
```

How it works...

In *step 1*, you create a `DataCollectorSet` object, which starts the System Diagnostic Reporting process. With *step 2*, you wait for PLA to complete building the report, which looks like this:

```
PS C:\Foo> Start-Sleep -Seconds $Dataset.Duration
Sleeping for [600] seconds
```

In *step 3*, after the report has completed, you save it as HTML. Then, in *step 4*, you display it, which looks like this:

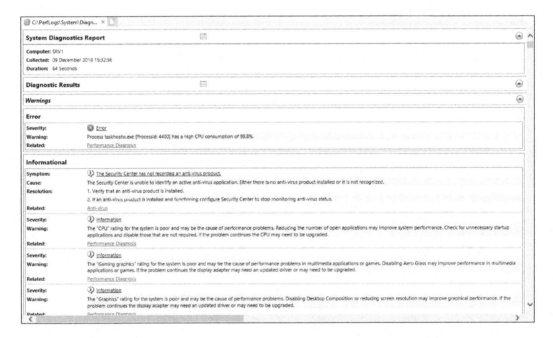

There's more...

In *step 4*, you view the report in your browser. You could adapt this recipe to run as a scheduled task on every server in your network once daily. Store the output in a central place and you can easily access it to begin troubleshooting a server.

Reporting on printer usage

Knowing who is using your printing devices and how much can be important in terms of capacity planning.

By default, Windows does not log printer usage information. But it is simple to turn on this logging and use the results.

Getting ready

You use this recipe on the PSRV host.

How to do it...

1. Run wevtutil.exe to turn on printer monitoring on the PSRV host:

```
$LogName = 'Microsoft-Windows-PrintService/Operational'
wevtutil.exe sl $LogName /enabled:true
```

2. Define a function that returns objects for each printer job completed on the server:

```
Function Get-PrinterUsage {
# 2.1 Get events from the print server event log
$LogName = 'Microsoft-Windows-PrintService/Operational'
$Dps = Get-WinEvent -LogName $LogName |
        Where-Object ID -eq 307
Foreach ($Dp in $Dps) {
# 2.2 Create an ordered hash table
    $Document            = [ordered] @{}
# 2.3 Populate the hash table with properties from the
# Event Log entry
    $Document.Id        = $Dp.Properties[0].value
    $Document.Type      = $Dp.Properties[1].value
    $Document.User      = $Dp.Properties[2].value
    $Document.Computer  = $Dp.Properties[3].value
    $Document.Printer   = $Dp.Properties[4].value
    $Document.Port      = $Dp.Properties[5].value
    $Document.Bytes     = $Dp.Properties[6].value
    $Document.Pages     = $Dp.Properties[7].value
```

```
# 2.4 Create an object for this printer usage entry
    $UEntry = New-Object -TypeName PSObject -Property $Document
# 2.5 And give it a more relecant tyhpe name
    $UEntry.PsTypeNames.Clear()
    $UEntry.PsTypeNames.Add('Reskit.PrintUsage')
# 2.6 Output the entry
    $UEntry
  } # End of foreach
}   # End of function
```

3. Set and use an alias to get printer usage:

    ```
    Get-PrinterUsage | Format-Table
    ```

How it works...

In *step 1*, which produces no output, you turn on event logging of completed printer jobs. By default, this logging is not enabled.

In *step 2*, you create a function that returns objects representing completed printer jobs. The function first combs the `Microsoft-Windows-PrintService/Operational` event log for printer job details. Turning on event logging results in an event log entry for each completed job. For each event log entry found, the function extracts the details of the print job, creates a custom object documenting the job, and returns that object. Before returning the object, the function also changes the object returned to be of the `Reskit.PrintUsage` type.

In *step 3*, you call the function to return output that looks like this:

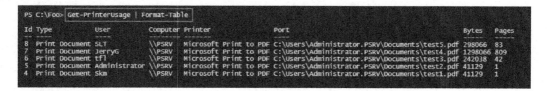

There's more...

In *step 2*, you created and returned a custom object for each event log entry found. In doing so, you change the type name used by PowerShell for this object. This enables you to create custom-display XML to display the object nicely. By default, the object would be displayed in a list. Your custom-display XML could force the output to be a table (much in the way the display XML for `Get-Process` is structured).

Monitoring Hyper-V utilization and performance

This report gathers information about a Hyper-V server and the VMs running on that server.

Getting ready

You run this recipe on the HV1 Hyper-V host.

How to do it...

1. Create a basic report hash table:

```
$ReportHT = [Ordered] @{}
```

2. Get the host details and add them to the report hash table:

```
$HostDetails = Get-CimInstance -ClassName Win32_ComputerSystem
$ReportHT.HostName = $HostDetails.Name
$ReportHT.Maker = $HostDetails.Manufacturer
$ReportHT.Model = $HostDetails.Model
```

3. Add the PowerShell version information to the report hash table:

```
$ReportHT.PSVersion = $PSVersionTable.PSVersion.ToString()
```

4. Add OS information to the report hash table:

```
$OS = Get-CimInstance -Class Win32_OperatingSystem
$ReportHT.OSEdition   = $OS.Caption
$ReportHT.OSArch      = $OS.OSArchitecture
$ReportHT.OSLang      = $OS.OSLanguage
$ReportHT.LastBootTime = $os.LastBootUpTime
$Now = Get-Date
$UTD = [float] ("{0:n3}" -f (($Now -
                            $OS.LastBootUpTime).Totaldays))
$ReportHT.UpTimeDays = $UTD
```

5. Add a count of processors in the host to the report hash table:

```
$PHT = @{
  ClassName  = 'MSvm_Processor'
  Namespace  = 'Root/Virtualization/v2'
}
$Proc = Get-CimInstance @PHT
$ReportHT.CPUCount = ($Proc |
  Where-Object ElementName -Match 'Logical Processor').Count
```

6. Add the current host CPU usage to the report hash table:

```
$Cname = '\\.\processor(_total)\% processor time'
$CPU = Get-Counter -Counter $Cname
$ReportHT.HostCPUUsage = $CPU.CounterSamples.CookedValue
```

7. Add the total host physical memory to the report hash table:

```
$Memory = Get-Ciminstance -Class Win32_ComputerSystem
$HostMemory = [float]("{0:n2}" -f
                             ($Memory.TotalPhysicalMemory/1GB))
$ReportHT.HostMemoryGB = $HostMemory
```

8. Add the memory allocated to VMs to the report hash table:

```
$Sum = 0
Get-VM | Foreach-Object {$sum += $_.MemoryAssigned + $Total}
$Sum = [float] ( "{0:N2}" -f ($Sum/1gb) )
$ReportHT.AllocatedMemoryGB = $Sum
```

9. Create the host report object from the hash table:

```
$Reportobj = New-Object -TypeName PSObject -Property $ReportHT
```

10. Create the report header:

```
$Report =  "Hyper-V Report for: $(hostname)`n"
$Report += "At: [$(Get-Date)]"
```

11. Add the report object to the report:

```
$Report += $Reportobj | Out-String
```

12. Get the VM details on the local VM host and create a container array for individual VM-related objects:

```
$VMs = Get-VM -Name *
$VMHT = @()   # to be an array of hash tables
```

13. Get VM details for each VM into an object added to the hash table container:

```
Foreach ($VM in $VMs) {
  # Create VM Report hash table for this VM
   $VMReport = [ordered] @{}
  # Add VM's Name
   $VMReport.VMName = $VM.VMName
  # Add Status
   $VMReport.Status = $VM.Status
  # Add current VM uptime
   $VMReport.Uptime = $VM.Uptime
  # Add VM CPU
   $VMReport.VMCPU = $VM.CPUUsage
  # Replication mode and status
   $VMReport.ReplMode = $VM.ReplicationMode
   $VMReport.ReplState = $Vm.ReplicationState
  # Create an object from Hash table and add to array
   $VMR = New-Object -TypeName PSObject -Property $VMReport
   $VMHT += $VMR
}
```

14. Convert the array of hash tables to a nice string, finishing the report creation:

```
$Report += $VMHT | Format-Table | Out-String
```

15. Display the report:

```
$Report
```

How it works...

This recipe creates a report that describes both the Hyper-V host and the VM on the host. In the first part, you build a hash table containing information about the host itself which you add to the report. Then, you report on the VMs running on this server (HV1).

In *step 1*, you create an ordered hash table ($ReportHT). You create an ordered hash table so that the order of rows is maintained. With *step 2*, you add basic host details to the hash table.

In *step 3*, you add details of the PowerShell version running on the host. With *step 4*, you add operating system details to the hash table along with (in *step 5*) a count of processors available in the host. Then you add current host CPU usage in *step 6*, and total host physical memory in *step 7*. In *step 8*, you calculate the total amount of memory assigned to VMs and add it to the hash table.

In *step 9*, you create a summary report object with properties coming from the hash table. In *step 10*, you create a basic report header to which, in *step 11*, you convert the report object to a string and add it the report.

With *step 12* and *step 13*, you retrieve details of each of the VMs assigned to HV1, and with *step 14*, you add those details to the report.

Finally, in *step 15*, you view the report, which looks like this:

```
Hyper-V Report for: HV1
At: [12/09/2018 20:33:16]

HostName          : HV1
Maker             : Dell Inc.
Model             : Precision WorkStation T7500
PSVersion         : 5.1.17733.1000
OSEdition         : Microsoft Windows Server 2019 Datacenter
OSArch            : 64-bit
OSLang            : 1033
LastBootTime      : 09/12/2018 19:01:10
UpTimeDays        : 42.064
CPUCount          : 16
HostCPUUsage      : 62.18224586418426
HostMemoryGB      : 96.00
AllocatedMemoryGB : 72


VMName   Status            Uptime              VMCPU ReplMode ReplState
------   ------            ------              ----- -------- ---------
VM2      Operating normally 12:29:43.4265000     12     None Disabled
OM1      Operating normally 22:42:18.1238263     20     None Disabled
SQL1     Operating normally 00:00:00              0     None Disabled
PSDirect Operating normally 01:29:46.1170000      0     None Disabled
SQL2     Operating normally 12:00:00             22     None Disabled
VM3      Operating normally 05:42:35:2420230      6     None Disabled
```

There's more...

In this recipe, you create and use two hash tables. The first hash table holds details about the VM host overall. If you were reporting on multiple Hyper-V servers, you could create hash tables relating to each server and then convert those two hash tables into objects to report on. If you are going to expand this recipe to cover multiple servers, using objects to report from is easier.

This recipe chose some basic performance and usage information to report. As ever with performance analysis, you could add more. For example, you could add network throughput, storage usage information to the report header. And you could expand the information reported on each VM to include more details. An important thing to consider is when to stop adding details to your reports.

14
Troubleshooting Windows Server

In this chapter, we cover the following recipes:

- Checking network connectivity
- Using Best Practices Analyzer
- Managing event logs

Introduction

Troubleshooting is the art and science of discovering the cause of some problem in your organization's computing estate and providing a solution that overcomes the problem. Troubleshooting encompasses a variety of tasks, many of which you can perform using PowerShell.

With applications and services increasingly being networked, network connectivity can be a problem in many organizations. In the first recipe, you look at some commands that can help you troubleshoot this area.

Microsoft has built a troubleshooting framework into both Windows 10 and into Server 2019. These troubleshoots enable common problems to be resolved by an IT pro just by running the troubleshooter.

Troubleshooting is not just what you do when an issue arises. It also involves being proactive to avoid small issues becoming major problems. Often, it also means ensuring that your systems and services are set up by way of accepted best practice. The Exchange and Office Communications Server (later known as Lync and Skype For Business) teams both produced **Best Practice Analyzer** (**BPA**) tools. These were applications that examined your Exchange or OCS (Lync/Skype for Business) environment and showed you places where you have not configured your application based on best practices. With Windows Server, many of the Windows features have their own BPA tools built around a common framework and are powered by PowerShell. The BPA tools can help you to ensure that the features installed on your Windows servers are operating according to best practices.

A great feature of Windows and Windows applications, roles, and services is the sheer amount of information that's logged. Windows NT (which is the basis for both Windows 10 and Windows Server 2019) initially came with a number of base event logs. In Windows Vista, Microsoft extended the amount of logging with the addition of application and service logs.

These event logs contain a wealth of additional information that is invaluable in terms of both troubleshooting after the fact and being proactive. It is certainly the case that getting information out of these logs is a bit like looking for a needle in a haystack. PowerShell has some great features for helping you find the information you need quickly and easily.

Checking network connectivity

One of the first things you can do in terms of troubleshooting is to determine whether you have network connectivity between your hosts.

Getting ready

This recipe uses servers in the `Reskit.Org` domain (`DC1`, `DC2`, `SRV1`, and `SRV2`) that you have previously installed. Run this recipe on `SRV1`.

How to do it...

1. Use `Test-Connection` to test the connection to `DC1`:

   ```
   Test-Connection -ComputerName DC1
   ```

2. Redo the test with a simple true/false return:

   ```
   Test-Connection -ComputerName DC1 -Quiet
   ```

3. Test multiple systems at once:

```
Test-Connection -ComputerName 'DC1','DC2','SRV2' -Count 1
```

4. Test the connectivity for SMB traffic with DC1:

```
Test-NetConnection -ComputerName DC1 -CommonTCPPort SMB
```

5. Get a detailed connectivity check by using DC1 with HTTP:

```
$TNCHT = @{
  ComputerName     = 'DC1'
  CommonTCPPort    = 'HTTP'
  InformationLevel = 'Detailed'
}
Test-NetConnection @TNCHT
```

6. Look for a particular port (that is, SMB on DC1):

```
Test-NetConnection -ComputerName DC1 -Port 445
```

7. Look for a host that does not exist:

```
Test-NetConnection -ComputerName 10.10.10.123
```

8. Look for a host that exists but a port/application that does not exist:

```
Test-NetConnection -ComputerName DC1 -PORT 9999
```

How it works...

In *step 1*, you checked the network connectivity from SRV1 to DC1 using the Test-NetConnection cmdlet, which looks like this:

```
PS C:\Foo> Test-Connection -ComputerName DC1

Source  Destination  IPV4Address   IPV6Address             Bytes  Time(ms)
------  -----------  -----------   -----------             -----  --------
SRV1    DC1          10.10.10.10   fd00::7d64:a4c:ff81:4d8b  32     0
SRV1    DC1          10.10.10.10   fd00::7d64:a4c:ff81:4d8b  32     0
SRV1    DC1          10.10.10.10   fd00::7d64:a4c:ff81:4d8b  32     1
SRV1    DC1          10.10.10.10   fd00::7d64:a4c:ff81:4d8b  32     1
```

In *step 2*, you repeated this test using the -Quiet switch, which looks like this:

```
PS C:\Foo> Test-Connection -ComputerName DC1 -Quiet
True ←——
```

In *step 3*, you used Test-Connection to test connections from SRV1 to multiple remote servers, which looks like this:

```
PS C:\Foo> Test-Connection -ComputerName 'DC1','DC2','SRV2' -Count 1

Source  Destination  IPV4Address   IPV6Address                   Bytes  Time(ms)
------  -----------  -----------   -----------                   -----  --------
SRV1    DC1          10.10.10.10   fd00::7d64:a4c:ff81:4d8b      32     0
SRV1    DC2          10.10.10.11                                 32     1
SRV1    SRV2         10.10.10.51                                 32     0
```

The Test-NetConnection cmdlet provides additional parameters. In *step 4*, you tested whether SRV1 can reach the SMB server service on DC1. SRV1 uses this port to download group policy details. The output looks like this:

```
PS C:\Foo> Test-NetConnection -ComputerName DC1 -CommonTCPPort SMB

ComputerName     : DC1
RemoteAddress    : 10.10.10.10
RemotePort       : 445
InterfaceAlias   : Ethernet
SourceAddress    : 10.10.10.50
TcpTestSucceeded : True ←——
```

You can also get a more detailed report of attempted connectivity. You can use the -InformationLevel parameter set to detailed so that you receive more information on the attempt to connect. In *step 5*, you checked whether SRV1 can create a HTTP connection with DC1, as follows:

```
PS C:\Foo> $TNCHT = @{
               ComputerName     = 'DC1'
               CommonTCPPort    = 'HTTP'
               InformationLevel = 'Detailed'
           }
PS C:\Foo> Test-NetConnection @TNCHT

ComputerName             : DC1
RemoteAddress            : 10.10.10.10
RemotePort               : 80
NameResolutionResults    : 10.10.10.10
                           fd00::7d64:a4c:ff81:4d8b
MatchingIPsecRules       :
NetworkIsolationContext  : Private Network
InterfaceAlias           : Ethernet
SourceAddress            : 10.10.10.50
NetRoute (NextHop)       : 0.0.0.0
PingSucceeded            : True
PingReplyDetails (RTT)   : 0 ms
TcpTestSucceeded         : False  ⬅
```

In *step 6*, you used `Test-NetConnection` to test the connectivity to a numbered port, port `389` on `DC1`. Port `389` is the LDAP port that an AD client uses to talk to a domain controller. The output of this step looks like this:

```
PS C:\Foo> Test-NetConnection -ComputerName DC1 -Port 389

ComputerName      : DC1
RemoteAddress     : 10.10.10.10
RemotePort        : 389
InterfaceAlias    : Ethernet
SourceAddress     : 10.10.10.50
TcpTestSucceeded  : True  ⬅
```

There's more...

In *step 2*, you used the `-Quiet` switch with `Test-NetConnection`. This directs the cmdlet to just return a true or false value after attempting to connect to the remote system. This can be useful in scripts where you only need to check whether a server is contactable.

Using the Best Practices Analyzer

A best practice is a way of doing things that is considered by others (generally more experienced in the area) to provide the best result. For example, a best practice is to always have at least two domain controllers in case one goes down.

Following a best practice can both solve existing issues and avoid future ones, but a bit of common sense is needed to ensure that you are following the advice that is relevant for you and your organization. In a small test lab of a few VMs, having a second DC may not be needed.

The BPA is an automated tool that's built into Windows. With BPA, a best practice model is a set of specific guidelines for a single area. BPA reviews your infrastructure and points out areas where the environment is not compliant with the best practice model.

The Windows BPA framework provides PowerShell support for managing the BPA process. Windows and applications come with a number of BPA models, generally built by the relevant product group within the Windows Team. The PowerShell cmdlets let you find the BPA models, invoke them, and then view the results. Since not all BPA model guidelines are relevant for all situations, the BPA feature also lets you ignore specific recommendations that are not relevant to you.

Getting ready

You run this recipe on SRV1, a server that was used in recipes earlier in this book. This recipe requires IIS (the web server feature) to be loaded. Refer to *Chapter 9, Managing Windows Internet Information Server,* the Installing IIS recipe for details on how to install the web server feature.

You also use DC1 in this recipe.

How to do it...

1. Get all BPA models on SRV1:

```
Get-BpaModel |
   Format-Table -Property Name, Id, LastScanTime -Wrap
```

2. Invoke a BPA model for the WebServer feature:

```
Invoke-BpaModel -ModelId Microsoft/Windows/WebServer
```

3. Get the results of the BPA run:

```
$Results = Get-BpaResult -ModelId Microsoft/Windows/webServer
```

4. Display how many tests/results are in the BPA model:

```
$Results.Count
```

5. How many errors and warnings were found?

```
$Errors = $Results | Where-Object Severity -eq 'Error'
$Warnings = $Results | Where-Object Severity -eq 'Warning'
"Errors found   : {0}" -f $Errors.Count
"Warnings found : {0}" -f $Warnings.Count
```

6. Look at other BPA results:

```
$Results  | Format-Table -Property Title, Compliance -Wrap
```

7. Use BPA remotely—what BPA models exist on DC1?

```
Invoke-Command -ComputerName DC1 -ScriptBlock {Get-BpaModel} |
   Format-Table -Property Name, Id
```

8. Run BPA Analyzer on DC1:

```
$ModelId = 'Microsoft/Windows/DirectoryServices'
$SB = {Invoke-BpaModel -ModelId $using:ModelId}
Invoke-Command -ComputerName DC1 -ScriptBlock $SB
```

9. Get the results of the `DirectoryServices` BPA model from DC1:

```
$SB = {Get-BpaResult -ModelId Microsoft/Windows/DirectoryServices}
$RRESULTS = Invoke-Command -ComputerName DC1 -ScriptBlock $SB
```

10. Review the results returned from the scan:

```
"Total results returned: $($RResults.Count)"
$RResults | Group-Object SEVERITY |
   Format-Table -Property Name, Count
```

11. View the error(s) from the scan:

```
$RResults |
   Where-Object Severity -EQ 'Error' |
     Format-List -Property Category,Problem,Impact,Resolution
```

How it works...

In *step 1*, you obtained and displayed the details about the BPA models on the SRV1 host, which looks like this:

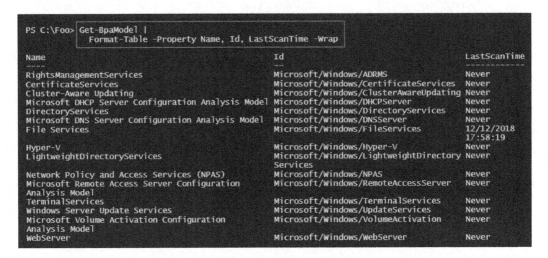

```
PS C:\Foo> Get-BpaModel |
             Format-Table -Property Name, Id, LastScanTime -Wrap

Name                                                    Id                                            LastScanTime
----                                                    --                                            ------------
RightsManagementServices                                Microsoft/Windows/ADRMS                       Never
CertificateServices                                     Microsoft/Windows/CertificateServices         Never
Cluster-Aware Updating                                  Microsoft/Windows/ClusterAwareUpdating        Never
Microsoft DHCP Server Configuration Analysis Model      Microsoft/Windows/DHCPServer                  Never
DirectoryServices                                       Microsoft/Windows/DirectoryServices           Never
Microsoft DNS Server Configuration Analysis Model       Microsoft/Windows/DNSServer                   Never
File Services                                           Microsoft/Windows/FileServices                12/12/2018
                                                                                                      17:58:19
Hyper-V                                                 Microsoft/Windows/Hyper-V                     Never
LightweightDirectoryServices                            Microsoft/Windows/LightweightDirectory        Never
                                                        Services
Network Policy and Access Services (NPAS)               Microsoft/Windows/NPAS                         Never
Microsoft Remote Access Server Configuration            Microsoft/Windows/RemoteAccessServer          Never
Analysis Model
TerminalServices                                        Microsoft/Windows/TerminalServices            Never
Windows Server Update Services                          Microsoft/Windows/UpdateServices              Never
Microsoft Volume Activation Configuration               Microsoft/Windows/VolumeActivation            Never
Analysis Model
WebServer                                               Microsoft/Windows/WebServer                   Never
```

As IIS is installed on SRV1, in *step 2*, you ran the BPA model for the Windows WebServer feature. The output looks like this:

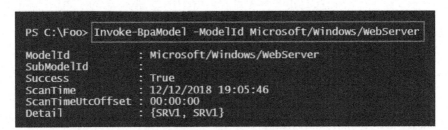

```
PS C:\Foo> Invoke-BpaModel -ModelId Microsoft/Windows/WebServer

ModelId           : Microsoft/Windows/WebServer
SubModelId        :
Success           : True
ScanTime          : 12/12/2018 19:05:46
ScanTimeUtcOffset : 00:00:00
Detail            : {SRV1, SRV1}
```

In *step 3*, you retrieved the results of the most recent invocation of the WebServer BPA model and stored it in $Results. This step produces no output.

In *step 4*, you displayed a count of the number of BPA results returned from the WebServer BPA scan, which looks like this:

```
PS C:\Foo> $Results.Count
4
```

Next, in *step 5*, you counted and displayed the number of error or warning results that were returned by the BPA scan, as follows:

```
PS C:\Foo> $Errors = $Results | Where-Object Severity -eq 'Error'
PS C:\Foo> $Warnings = $Results | Where-Object Severity -eq 'Warning'
PS C:\Foo> "Errors found   : {0}" -f $Errors.Count
PS C:\Foo> "Warnings found : {0}" -f $Warnings.Count
Errors found   : 0 ⟵
Warnings found : 0 ⟵
```

In *step 6*, you viewed the specific items that were tested by the `WebService` BPA model, and the compliance status of `SRV1`, which looks like this:

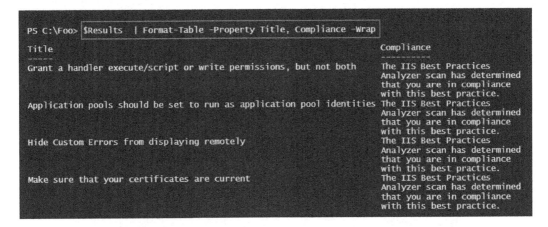

```
PS C:\Foo> $Results   | Format-Table -Property Title, Compliance -Wrap

Title                                                                        Compliance
-----                                                                        ----------
Grant a handler execute/script or write permissions, but not both            The IIS Best Practices
                                                                             Analyzer scan has determined
                                                                             that you are in compliance
                                                                             with this best practice.
Application pools should be set to run as application pool identities The IIS Best Practices
                                                                             Analyzer scan has determined
                                                                             that you are in compliance
                                                                             with this best practice.
Hide Custom Errors from displaying remotely                                  The IIS Best Practices
                                                                             Analyzer scan has determined
                                                                             that you are in compliance
                                                                             with this best practice.
Make sure that your certificates are current                                 The IIS Best Practices
                                                                             Analyzer scan has determined
                                                                             that you are in compliance
                                                                             with this best practice.
```

You can also use BPA models remotely. In *step7*, you viewed the BPA models on `DC1`, a domain controller, which looks like this:

```
PS C:\Foo> Invoke-Command -ComputerName DC1 -ScriptBlock {Get-BpaModel} |
           Format-Table -Property Name, Id

Name                                                       Id
----                                                       --
RightsManagementServices                                   Microsoft/Windows/ADRMS
CertificateServices                                        Microsoft/Windows/CertificateServices
Microsoft DHCP Server Configuration Analysis Model         Microsoft/Windows/DHCPServer
DirectoryServices                                          Microsoft/Windows/DirectoryServices
Microsoft DNS Server Configuration Analysis Model          Microsoft/Windows/DNSServer
File Services                                              Microsoft/Windows/FileServices
Hyper-V                                                     Microsoft/Windows/Hyper-V
LightweightDirectoryServices                               Microsoft/Windows/LightweightDirectoryServices
Network Policy and Access Services (NPAS)                  Microsoft/Windows/NPAS
Microsoft Remote Access Server Configuration Analysis Model Microsoft/Windows/RemoteAccessServer
TerminalServices                                           Microsoft/Windows/TerminalServices
Windows Server Update Services                             Microsoft/Windows/UpdateServices
Microsoft Volume Activation Configuration Analysis Model   Microsoft/Windows/VolumeActivation
WebServer                                                  Microsoft/Windows/WebServer
```

In *step 8*, you ran the `DirectoryServices` model remotely on `DC1`. The output looks like this:

```
PS C:\Foo> $ModelId = 'Microsoft/Windows/DirectoryServices'
PS C:\Foo> $SB = {Invoke-BpaModel -ModelId $using:ModelId}
PS C:\Foo> Invoke-Command -ComputerName DC1 -ScriptBlock $SB

ModelId             : Microsoft/Windows/DirectoryServices
SubModelId          :
Success             : True
ScanTime            : 13/12/2018 13:54:26
ScanTimeUtcOffset   :
Detail              : {DC1, DC1}
```

Having run the `DirectoryServices` BPA model on `DC1`, in *step 9*, you retrieved the results. This step produces no output.

In *step 10*, you examined the BPA results. You displayed the number of BPA results and what kinds of results the BPA scan of `DC1` reveals, which looks like this:

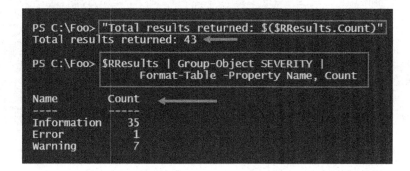

```
PS C:\Foo> "Total results returned: $($RRResults.Count)"
Total results returned: 43  ⟵

PS C:\Foo> $RRResults | Group-Object SEVERITY |
              Format-Table -Property Name, Count

Name             Count   ⟵
----             -----
Information       35
Error              1
Warning            7
```

The BPA results show one error and seven warnings out of **43** BPA checks on `DC1`. While you should investigate the warnings, you may find some of the BPA warnings can be ignored in your environment. The BPA error results should be prioritized. In our case, the error result, which you obtained in *step 11*, looks like this:

```
PS C:\Foo> $RResults | Where-Object Severity -EQ 'Error' |
           Format-List -Property Category,Problem,Impact,Resolution

Category   : Configuration
Problem    : The primary domain controller (PDC) emulator operations master in this
             forest is not configured to correctly synchronize time from a valid time
             source.
Impact     : If the PDC emulator master in this forest is not configured to correctly
             synchronize time from a valid time source, it might use its internal clock
             for time synchronization. If the PDC emulator master in this forest fails
             or otherwise becomes unavailable (and if you have not configured a
             reliable time server (GTIMESERV) in the forest root domain), other member
             computers and domain controllers in the forest will not be able to
             synchronize their time.
Resolution : Set the PDC emulator master in this forest to synchronize time with a
             reliable external time source. If you have not configured a reliable time
             server (GTIMESERV) in the forest root domain, set the PDC emulator master
             in this forest to synchronize time with a hardware clock that is installed
             on the network (the recommended approach). You can also set the PDC
             emulator master in this forest to synchronize time with an external time
             server by running the w32tm /config /computer:DC1.Reskit.Org
             /manualpeerlist:time.windows.com /syncfromflags:manual /update command. If
             you have configured a reliable time server (GTIMESERV) in the forest root
             domain, set the PDC emulator master in this forest to synchronize time
             from the forest root domain hierarchy by running w32tm /config
             /computer:DC1.Reskit.Org /syncfromflags:domhier /update.
```

There's more...

In *step 1*, you saw the BPA models on SRV1. Depending on which other features you added to SRV1, you may see more BPA models.

In *step 4*, you can observe that the + BPA model checks just four configuration settings for IIS. There are not a lot of BPA checks being done by this model. Other BPA models, such as the DirectoryServices model, which you used in *step 9*, are much more detailed.

In *step 11*, you can see that when you run the DirectoryServices BPA model on DC1, BPA reports an error. The error result object includes a description of the problem, the impact, and how to resolve the issue. In this case, the problem that was found was that there was a lack of time synchronization between your forest root DC (DC1.Reskit.Org) and an external (and reliable) time source. Since all hosts in your forest ultimately get their time settings from the forest root server, it is important that the forest root server is synchronized with a reliable, external time source.

Managing event logs

Event logs are an important troubleshooting asset. Windows and Windows applications can log a significant amount of information that can be invaluable in both troubleshooting and in the day-to-day administration of Windows Server 2019.

Windows computers maintain a set of event logs that document events that occur on a given machine. Any time an event occurs, the application or service can log events that can then be used to help in the debugging process.

In Windows, there are two types of event logs: Windows logs and application and services logs. Windows logs began with Windows NT 3.1 and continue in Windows Server 2019 and are important components in troubleshooting and system monitoring.

Windows Vista added a new category of logs, application and services logs. These logs contain events that are within a single application, service, or other Windows component. Windows comes, by default, with a set of application and service logs—adding components such as new Windows features or roles often results in additional application and service logs.

These logs give you a great picture of what your system is actually doing. Additionally, you can also add new event logs and enable scripts to log events that occur while the script is running.

PowerShell provides you with several useful cmdlets to help you comb the event log looking for key events. The `Get-EventLog` enables you to get details of the logs that exist as well as retrieving log events from the Windows logs. With `Get-WinEvent`, you can examine both the classic Windows logs and the new application and services logs. You use both these cmdlets in this recipe.

Getting ready

You run this recipe from `SRV1`, a domain joined server in the `Reskit.Org` domain. You also use the domain controller `DC1. Reskit.Org` in this recipe.

How to do it...

1. Get the core event logs on `SRV1`:

```
Get-EventLog -LogName *
```

2. Get the remote classic event logs from `DC1`:

```
Get-EventLog -LogName * -ComputerName DC1
```

3. Clear the application log on `DC1`:

```
Clear-EventLog -LogName Application -ComputerName DC1
```

4. Look at the types of events on `SRV1`:

```
Get-EventLog -LogName Application |
  Group-Object -Property EntryType |
    Format-Table -Property Name, Count
```

5. Examine which area created the events in the application log:

```
Get-EventLog -LogName System |
  Group-Object -Property Source |
    Sort-Object -Property Count -Descending |
      Select-Object -First 10 |
        Format-Table -Property Name, Count
```

6. Examine all the event logs on `SRV1`:

```
$LocEventLogs = Get-WinEvent -ListLog *
$LocEventLogs.Count
$LocEventLogs |
  Sort-Object -Property RecordCount -Descending |
    Select-Object -First 10
```

7. Examine all the event logs on `DC1`:

```
$RemEventLogs = Get-WinEvent -ListLog * -ComputerName DC1
$RemEventLogs.count
$RemEventLogs |
  Sort-Object -Property RecordCount -Descending |
    Select-Object -First 10
```

8. Look at the `WindowsUpdateClient` operational event log on the localhost and discover the updates that the WU client has found:

```
$LN = 'Microsoft-Windows-WindowsUpdateClient/Operational'
$Updates = Get-WinEvent -LogName $LN |
  Where-Object ID -EQ 41
$Out = foreach ($Update in $Updates) {
  $HT = @{}
```

```
$HT.Time = [System.DateTime] $Update.TimeCreated
$HT.Update = ($Update.Properties | Select-Object -First 1).Value
New-Object -TypeName PSObject -Property $HT
}
$Out | Sort -Property Time
  Sort-Object -Property TimeCreated |
      Format-Table -Wrap
```

How it works...

In *step 1*, you used the Get-EventLog cmdlet to display the core event logs on SRV1, which looks like this:

```
PS C:\Foo> Get-EventLog -LogName *

Max(K) Retain OverflowAction          Entries Log
------ ------ --------------          ------- ---
20,480      0 OverwriteAsNeeded           273 Application
20,480      0 OverwriteAsNeeded             0 HardwareEvents
   512      7 OverwriteOlder                0 Internet Explorer
20,480      0 OverwriteAsNeeded             0 Key Management Service
   512      7 OverwriteOlder               90 Microsoft-ServerManagementExperience
   512      7 OverwriteOlder                  Parameters
20,480      0 OverwriteAsNeeded         2,120 Security
   512      7 OverwriteOlder                  State
20,480      0 OverwriteAsNeeded         3,644 System
15,360      0 OverwriteAsNeeded         6,419 Windows PowerShell
```

In *step 2*, you retrieved the core event logs remotely on DC1, which looks like this:

```
PS C:\Foo> Get-EventLog -LogName * -ComputerName DC1

 Max(K) Retain OverflowAction          Entries Log
 ------ ------ --------------          ------- ---
    512      7 OverwriteOlder               50 Active Directory Web Services
 20,480      0 OverwriteAsNeeded           248 Application
 15,168      0 OverwriteAsNeeded           104 DFS Replication
    512      0 OverwriteAsNeeded           331 Directory Service
102,400      0 OverwriteAsNeeded            47 DNS Server
 20,480      0 OverwriteAsNeeded             0 HardwareEvents
    512      7 OverwriteOlder                0 Internet Explorer
 20,480      0 OverwriteAsNeeded             0 Key Management Service
    512      7 OverwriteOlder                  Parameters
 20,480      0 OverwriteAsNeeded        29,909 Security
    512      7 OverwriteOlder                  State
 20,480      0 OverwriteAsNeeded         3,354 System
 15,360      0 OverwriteAsNeeded         1,548 Windows PowerShell
```

In *step 3*, you cleared the application log remotely on DC1. There is no output from this step.

In *step 4*, you examined the event types that are in the event log on SRV1, which looks like this:

```
PS C:\Foo> Get-EventLog -LogName Application |
             Group-Object -Property EntryType |
             Format-Table -Property Name, Count

Name          Count
----          -----
Information    239
0                6
Warning         21
Error            7
```

In *step 5*, you looked at the Windows event logs, using Get-EventLog to get all the different Windows components that are logging events to the System log. This step then displays the ten areas that are logging the most entries on SRV1, which looks like this:

```
PS C:\Foo> $LocEventLogs = Get-WinEvent -ListLog *
PS C:\Foo> $LocEventLogs.Count
PS C:\Foo> $LocEventLogs |
             Sort-Object -Property RecordCount -Descending |
             Select-Object -First 10
417

LogMode    MaximumSizeInBytes RecordCount LogName
-------    ------------------ ----------- -------
Circular          314572800      506369 Microsoft-Windows-SystemDataArchiver/Diagnostic
Circular           10485760        8081 Microsoft-Windows-TaskScheduler/Operational
Circular            4194304        7748 Microsoft-Windows-GroupPolicy/Operational
Circular           15728640        6419 Windows PowerShell
Circular           20971520        3644 System
Circular            1052672        2450 Microsoft-Windows-Kernel-IO/Operational
Circular           20971520        2127 Security
Circular            1052672        2100 Microsoft-Windows-ServerManager-DeploymentProvider/Operational
Circular            1052672        2028 Microsoft-Windows-ServerManager-MultiMachine/Operational
Circular            1052672        1912 Microsoft-Windows-ServerManager-MgmtProvider/Operational
```

In *step 6*, you displayed the total number of event logs found by Get-WinEvent, and then you listed the 10 busiest extended logs, as follows:

```
PS C:\Foo> $LocEventLogs = Get-WinEvent -ListLog *
PS C:\Foo> $LocEventLogs.Count
417

PS C:\Foo> $LocEventLogs |
             Sort-Object -Property RecordCount -Descending |
             Select-Object -First 10

LogMode    MaximumSizeInBytes RecordCount LogName
-------    ------------------ ----------- -------
Circular          314572800      506369 Microsoft-Windows-SystemDataArchiver/Diagnostic
Circular           10485760        8081 Microsoft-Windows-TaskScheduler/Operational
Circular            4194304        7748 Microsoft-Windows-GroupPolicy/Operational
Circular           15728640        6419 Windows PowerShell
Circular           20971520        3644 System
Circular            1052672        2450 Microsoft-Windows-Kernel-IO/Operational
Circular           20971520        2127 Security
Circular            1052672        2100 Microsoft-Windows-ServerManager-DeploymentProvider/Operational
Circular            1052672        2028 Microsoft-Windows-ServerManager-MultiMachine/Operational
Circular            1052672        1912 Microsoft-Windows-ServerManager-MgmtProvider/Operational
```

In *step 8*, you displayed the number of Windows updates that were discovered (and installed) on SRV1, which looks like this:

```
PS C:\Foo> $LN = 'Microsoft-Windows-WindowsUpdateClient/Operational'
PS C:\Foo> $Updates = Get-WinEvent -LogName $LN |
            Where-Object ID -EQ 41
PS C:\Foo> $Out = Foreach ($Update in $Updates) {
            $HT = @[]
            $HT.Time = [System.DateTime] $Update.TimeCreated
            $HT.Update = ($Update.Properties | Select-Object -First 1).Value
            }
PS C:\Foo> New-Object -TypeName PSObject -Property $HT
PS C:\Foo> $Out | Sort -Property Time
            Sort-Object -Property TimeCreated |
            Format-Table -Wrap

Time              Update
----              ------
28/11/2018 18:47:54 Definition Update for Windows Defender Antivirus - KB2267602 (Definition 1.281.1002.0)
02/12/2018 10:52:02 Definition Update for Windows Defender Antivirus - KB2267602 (Definition 1.281.1232.0)
03/12/2018 10:37:17 Definition Update for Windows Defender Antivirus - KB2267602 (Definition 1.281.1289.0)
03/12/2018 12:23:40 Definition Update for Windows Defender Antivirus - KB2267602 (Definition 1.281.1292.0)
04/12/2018 10:41:42 Definition Update for Windows Defender Antivirus - KB2267602 (Definition 1.281.1349.0)
04/12/2018 13:39:37 Definition Update for Windows Defender Antivirus - KB2267602 (Definition 1.281.1358.0)
05/12/2018 08:42:15 Definition Update for Windows Defender Antivirus - KB2267602 (Definition 1.281.1412.0)
05/12/2018 13:39:34 Definition Update for Windows Defender Antivirus - KB2267602 (Definition 1.281.1424.0)
06/12/2018 08:11:38 Definition Update for Windows Defender Antivirus - KB2267602 (Definition 1.281.1479.0)
06/12/2018 13:39:41 Definition Update for Windows Defender Antivirus - KB2267602 (Definition 1.281.1491.0)
07/12/2018 13:39:42 Definition Update for Windows Defender Antivirus - KB2267602 (Definition 1.283.59.0)
08/12/2018 05:20:14 Definition Update for Windows Defender Antivirus - KB2267602 (Definition 1.283.111.0)
08/12/2018 13:39:28 Definition Update for Windows Defender Antivirus - KB2267602 (Definition 1.283.135.0)
08/12/2018 20:41:54 Definition Update for Windows Defender Antivirus - KB2267602 (Definition 1.283.148.0)
08/12/2018 22:37:13 Update for Adobe Flash Player for Windows Server 2019 (1809) for x64-based Systems (KB4462930)
08/12/2018 22:37:13 2018-12 Security Update for Adobe Flash Player for Windows Server 2019 for x64-based Systems (KB4471331)
08/12/2018 22:37:36 2018-11 Cumulative Update for Windows Server 2019 (1809) for x64-based Systems (KB4467708)
09/12/2018 03:56:04 Definition Update for Windows Defender Antivirus - KB2267602 (Definition 1.283.179.0)
11/12/2018 20:42:27 Update for Windows Defender Antivirus antimalware platform - KB4052623 (Version 4.18.1812.3)
11/12/2018 20:42:27 Definition Update for Windows Defender Antivirus - KB2267602 (Definition 1.283.372.0)
11/12/2018 21:02:27 Definition Update for Windows Defender Antivirus - KB2267602 (Definition 1.283.372.0)
12/12/2018 20:02:23 Definition Update for Windows Defender Antivirus - KB2267602 (Definition 1.283.445.0)
12/12/2018 21:02:29 Definition Update for Windows Defender Antivirus - KB2267602 (Definition 1.283.449.0)
14/12/2018 09:01:52 Definition Update for Windows Defender Antivirus - KB2267602 (Definition 1.283.572.0)
```

There's more...

In *step 1* and *step 2*, you examined the Windows event logs that exist on two systems (SRV1 and DC1). As you can see, the logs that are available differ—on DC1, you can see the Active Directory Web Services log, which does not exist on SRV1.

In *step 3*, you cleared the application log on DC1. As a best practice for event logs, you should only clear a log once you have copied the log elsewhere for safe keeping. Naturally, mileage varies on this point, since the vast majority of event log entries are not of very much use in day-to-day operations.

In *step 4*, you saw the different classifications of events, including one with a name of 0. In this case, the property containing the event log entry type is based on an enum, and this enum was not updated, so PowerShell was unable to display the entry name for this event log entry type.

In *step 6* and *step 7*, you examined the service and application logs that exist on SRV1. These steps demonstrate how additional features or applications can result in additional event logs.

Step 8 showed you how to dive into a specific event in a specific event log. In this case, you examined the Software Update service's operational log to discover events with an event ID of 41. In general, when retrieving information from your event logs, you need to know which log and which event ID to look for.

Index

W